Life Course, Work, and Labour in Global History

Work in Global and Historical Perspective

Edited by
Andreas Eckert, Sidney Chalhoub, Mahua Sarkar,
Dmitri van den Bersselaar, Christian G. De Vito

Work in Global and Historical Perspective is an interdisciplinary series that welcomes scholarship on work/labour that engages a historical perspective in and from any part of the world. The series advocates a definition of work/labour that is broad, and especially encourages contributions that explore interconnections across political and geographic frontiers, time frames, disciplinary boundaries, as well as conceptual divisions among various forms of commodified work, and between work and 'non-work'.

Volume 18

Life Course, Work, and Labour in Global History

Edited by
Josef Ehmer and Carola Lentz

DE GRUYTER
OLDENBOURG

ISBN 978-3-11-114590-7
e-ISBN (PDF) 978-3-11-114752-9
e-ISBN (EPUB) 978-3-11-114796-3
ISSN 2509-8861
DOI https://doi.org/10.1515/9783111147529

Library of Congress Control Number: 2023937300

Bibliographic information published by the Deutsche Nationalbibliothek
The Deutsche Nationalbibliothek lists this publication in the Deutsche Nationalbibliografie;
detailed bibliographic data are available on the internet at http://dnb.dnb.de.

© 2023 with the author(s), editing © 2023 Josef Ehmer and Carola Lentz, published by Walter de
Gruyter GmbH, Berlin/Boston. This book is published with open access at www.degruyter.com.

Cover image: Seasonal labour: cane cutters from highland villages, working on the sugar plantation
San Carlos, Ecuador, 1983–1984. © Carola Lentz
Printing and binding: CPI books GmbH, Leck

www.degruyter.com

Remembering Josef (Sepp) Ehmer (1948–2023)

When Sepp Ehmer sent the last email he would address to me on May 8 – two days before his passing – he was already in hospital. But this had not stopped him from working on the final touches to this volume, in which he had invested so much time, energy, and care. Did he sense then that he would not be in Berlin for the book's release at re:work's final conference? We will never know.

Sepp's sudden departure has left us struggling with an immeasurable sadness and a void that is hard to fill. He was a remarkable intellectual, and, for many, a wonderful mentor, colleague, and friend. But as we think back with love and gratitude to all that he has meant for us, we must contend above all with the loss of an amazingly dignified, generative, warm, firm and yet gracious person. What follows are a few personal reminiscences of Sepp during his re:work years.[1]

Sepp Ehmer was one of the providers of ideas who helped pave the way to a successful application to the German Federal Ministry of Education and Research to fund re:work. In 2006–2007, Jürgen Kocka and I were contemplating the possibilities of a major project on "rethinking labour history", when Jürgen suggested consulting Sepp Ehmer, whom he respected immensely as a foremost exponent of (European) social and labour history with a strong interest in demography and questions of ageing. And it was Sepp who first suggested a focus on life course. Over the years, he also helped emphasize this thematic aspect in re:work's intellectual endeavours by initiating numerous debates through workshops and publications related to life course and work. To highlight just a few such efforts: in 2011, Sepp put together a special issue of the *Österreichische Zeitschrift für Geschichtswissenschaften* on "Retirement" that included contributions from a number of re:work fellows; in 2012, he organized, on behalf of re:work, a panel on life course and labour at the World Economic History Congress in Stellenbosch, challenging with some success the habitual scepticism of economic historians regarding the significance of this topic. On this and many other occasions, I was struck by Sepp's refusal to show off his broad knowledge, or be drawn into polemics, even as he quietly and firmly criticized some colleagues' intellectual apathy and inertia.

Sepp himself remained intellectually curious and open to the end. During the re:work years, he began engaging with the history of labour and work in world regions beyond the North Atlantic realm, and very soon, he became a much

---

1 For a comprehensive obituary (in German) see: https://wirtschaftsgeschichte.univie.ac.at/institut/aktuelles/einzelansicht/news/nachruf-auf-em-o-univ-prof-dr-josef-peter-ehmer-1948-2023/ (last access June 10, 2023).

sought-after discussion partner for scholars from Asia, Africa, and Latin America. In addition, he served as a mentor to younger fellows, always encouraging them, and sometimes helped sharpen the framing questions of their projects. Sepp's engagements as a discussion partner on such occasions might serve as an exemplar of what could be called non-sentimental solidarity. He was caring and always ready to provide constructive support, be it for scholarly arguments, political frustrations, or personal problems.

In 2010–2011, Sepp Ehmer was part of re:work's second fellow cohort. In 2011, we invited him to assume the position of Associate Fellow – a role he accepted with characteristic seriousness and grace. Every year he participated in the fellow selection process, reading hundreds of applications without complaint, assessing candidates fairly and with sound judgement. Once a fellow year started, Sepp gave talks introducing the theme of work and life course to nearly each cohort of fellows. As far as I can recall, he always participated in the final year conferences, often delivered the concluding remarks, and was a frequent and enthusiastic presence on the dance floor at the end-of-the-year parties. Indeed, one of my favourite photographs displayed along the corridors of re:work captures Sepp demonstrating his skills under a glitterball.

Two final recollections. During his fellow year, as was the case with all fellows and staff members, Sepp had to cook at least once for the entire team. In a fit of culinary patriotism, Sepp embarked on an ambitious project of preparing *Wiener Schnitzel* – not an easy task given the small kitchen (equipped with only one stove and oven) and 25 hungry people waiting in the seminar room. It was probably one of the more stressful moments for Sepp during his re:work years, and he needed three days to recover from the experience. And finally, I remember that the re:work staff went on an excursion to Vienna in the fall of 2013. Of course, one could not hope for a better guide than Sepp to discover Vienna with. His carefully planned walk through the city brought alive "Red Vienna", the antifascist resistance and the many transformations that have shaped the social history of the city. Perhaps not surprisingly, the tour included a stress-free (for Sepp) lunch at a restaurant specializing in *Wiener Schnitzel*, while the evening ended at his favourite *Heuriger*.

It was a great honour and a privilege to work and spend time with Sepp Ehmer over the last fifteen years. And while it seems unimaginable that he will never be back on the sixth floor of Georgenstraße 23 and that we will never again exchange views about current political developments over coffee, I take consolation in the certainty that our dialogue with him does not end here, and that Sepp will continue to inspire us all in our future endeavours.

Andreas Eckert, June 2023

Table of Contents

Remembering Josef (Sepp) Ehmer (1948–2023) —— V

Figures and Tables —— IX

Foreword —— XI

Josef Ehmer and Carola Lentz
Work and the Life Course in a Global and Multidisciplinary Perspective: An Introduction —— 1

Karl Ulrich Mayer, Rolf Becker, and Anette Fasang
The Puzzle of Flexibilization: Stability and Changes in Working Lives in (West) Germany, 1920s to 2015. Evidence from Quantitative Life-Course Research —— 41

Lutz Raphael
Life Courses, Career Paths, and the Search for Employment in Times of Change: Industrial Workers in Germany, France and Britain, 1970 to 2000 —— 71

Yoko Tanaka
Tumbling Down the Standard Life Course: The _Ice Age Generation_ of the Turn of the Twentieth Century and the Origins of Polarisation in Japan —— 95

Ju Li
When They Told Their Stories: Industrial Workers' Life Courses in the People's Republic of China —— 133

Therese Garstenauer
The Life Courses and Careers of Public Employees in Interwar Austria —— 153

Mary Jo Maynes and Ann Waltner
Textile Work, Gender, and the Female Life Course in Europe and China since the Beginning of the "Great Divergence," Eighteenth to Early Twentieth Centuries —— 179

Lamia Karim
Older Female Workers in the Global Apparel Industry in Bangladesh —— 203

Susan Zimmermann
The Changing Politics of Women's Work and the Making of Extended Childcare Leave in State-Socialist Hungary, Europe, and Internationally: Shifting the Scene —— 225

Carola Lentz
Family, Work, and Social Mobility: Perspectives from Ghana —— 259

Erdmute Alber
The Linking of Vital Conjunctures: Negotiations over Girls' Futures —— 281

Neda Deneva
Mobile People Versus Static Institutions: National School Policies in the EU and the Life Course of Transnational Grandparents —— 297

Heike Drotbohm
Contingent Return: Moral Assessments of the Life Course in Transnational Cape Verde —— 319

Chitra Joshi
Life and Labour on the Road: Mail Runners and Palanquin Bearers in Nineteenth-Century India —— 339

Josef Ehmer
Wage Labour as a Life Phase: Life-Cycle Service and Petty Commodity Production in Early Modern Europe —— 359

Notes on Contributors —— 389

Index —— 393

Figures and Tables

Mayer, Becker, Fasang
Figure 1:   Occupational mobility – expected and empirical survival curves (Mayer, Grunow, and Nitsche 2010) —— **50**
Figure 2:   Occupational mobility in West Germany – cohorts born between 1929 and 1971 (Mayer, Grunow, and Nitsche 2010) —— **51**
Figure 3:   Yearly job shifts within firms and employer changes between 1984 and 2008 (Giesecke and Heisig 2010) —— **52**
Figure 4:   Upward, downward, and lateral mobility during the first 20 years of employment – labour market entry cohorts 1932–1989 (Stawarz 2018) —— **54**
Figure 5:   Upward, downward, and lateral mobility rates of men between 1945 and 2005 – cohorts born between 1929 and 1976 (Becker and Blossfeld 2017) —— **55**
Figure 6:   Occupational prestige of men between 1945 and 2005 – cohorts born between 1929 and 1976 (Becker and Blossfeld 2017) —— **56**
Figure 7:   Occupational mobility in West Germany between 1958 and 1999 (Mayer, Grunow, and Nitsche 2010) —— **61**
Figure 8:   Modernisation trend and development of labour market situation (1918–2015) —— **61**
Table 1:   Overview of longitudinal cohort studies on employment stability —— **47**

Tanaka
Figure 1:   Unemployment rate and rate of job openings in Japan, 1989–2019 —— **97**
Figure 2:   Career trajectory patterns of 15 to 34 year-old individuals in 2007 —— **98**
Figure 3:   Employment forms among male workers by age (1987) —— **102**
Figure 4:   Wage development of Mr. A (assembly line worker, day and night shift, between 38–52 years old), 1982–1997 —— **107**
Figure 5:   Ratio of Toyota workers hired between 1956–1959 who reached 20 years of continuous service by gender and educational background —— **109**
Figure 6:   The life courses of toyotamen: New graduates simultaneously hired and married mid-career hires —— **111**
Figure 7:   Proportion of regular workers by age group, men and women, 1987–2017 —— **113**
Figure 8:   Changes in men's employment status by age, cohort, and first employment —— **115**
Figure 9:   Women's employment status by age, cohort, and first employment —— **116**
Figure 10:   Annual income by gender, cohort, and career trajectory —— **120**
Figure 11:   Changes in rates of unmarried individuals by gender and age, 1960–2015 —— **122**
Figure 12:   Proportion of men in their 20s and 30s who are married or in a relationship by annual income (in US Dollars) —— **123**
Figure 13:   Marriage and relationship status of the 20s and 30s by gender and employment form —— **123**
Figure 14:   Marriage rates by gender, age, and employment type (2017) —— **124**
Figure 15:   Rates of cohabitation with parents by employment and marriage status and gender (individuals, at age 40) —— **125**

Garstenauer

Figure 1:   Age distribution of government employees September 1923 —— **161**
Figure 2:   Distribution of measures based on the *Verordnung zur Neuordnung des Österreichischen Berufsbeamtentums* —— **172**
Table 1:   Marital status of government employees September 1923 —— **162**
Table 2:   Percentage of civil servants with children September 1923 —— **162**

Zimmermann

Table 1:   Involvement of women in paid work, around 1960 —— **228**
Table 2:   Percentage of economically active women by age group —— **229**

Joshi

Figure 1:   Kalipada Mura: treading through the forests —— **354**
Figure 2:   Moving through watery tracts —— **355**

Foreword

The editors of this volume have been privileged to spend time in Berlin as fellows of the International Research Centre "Work and Human Lifecycle in Global History." This centre, a *Käthe Hamburger Kolleg* situated at Humboldt University of Berlin, was for twelve years – from 2010 to 2022 – a vibrant and stimulating host for altogether about 150 invited fellows from all over the world who represented a wide range of disciplines within the humanities and social sciences, with a focus on history, anthropology, and sociology. The abbreviated title of the centre, "re:work," rapidly became renowned throughout international scholarly communities as an affectionate nickname.

Each fellow was invited to the centre on the basis of his or her individual project and enjoyed the freedom to pursue this project while in residence in Berlin. But everyone was also encouraged to refine this project within the programmatic framework of the centre, with its focus on the key concepts of work and the life course and their interrelationship in a global perspective from the early history of humans up to the present.

Fostering scholarly communication among fellows and joint reflection about these core themes was a central mission of re:work beyond its support for individual project development. The centre developed various strategies to create an intellectually stimulating and sociable atmosphere of communication. It organised – or helped organise – guest lectures and informal workshops as well as large conferences, and it provided space for continuous informal exchange, be it at the weekly luncheon meetings, during daily coffee breaks in the kitchen, or at various group leisure activities. Most of the contributors to this volume spent a full year in this attractive and productive environment, while others came for shorter stays or participated in conferences.

The name of the research centre signals the high programmatic appreciation for the life course approach, which distinguished it from other research institutions worldwide that study the global history of work and labour. In the actual research projects of fellows, however, the life course played different roles. For some scholars, the life course approach was very important, whereas for others, it stood more at the periphery of their analysis, and still others were interested in life course theory and methods but did not deploy them in their current projects. However, all scholars brought fresh ideas to and made thought-provoking insights into life course research. This variety mirrors, at least to some degree, the fellows' distinct disciplinary backgrounds. In sociology, the relationship between work and the life course has ranked high on the research agenda for several decades, but the focus has been predominantly the developed Western world. In anthropology, interest in age, the sequence of life phases, and the transitions between them, has been well established since the very beginning of the discipline; however, the connections between the life course and family, community, or generational relations have often figured more prominently than the connections between the life course and work. In the context of the "New Social History" that developed in the 1970s, the life course has been highly valued and regarded as crucial for the "rediscovery of complexity," as Tamara K. Hareven put it. Nevertheless, the impact of the life course approach on actual scholarship in the historiography of work and labour is still rather slight.

Such disciplinary gaps and shortcomings, but also the substantial conceptual and empirical achievements of the centre, which emerged from individual research and collective thought and discussion, served as strong motivations for us when we began to conceptualise this volume. We wanted to use the production of this book to intensify discussions about life course theory and methodology. We planned to organise a conference that would allow the authors to develop cross-thematic discussions on the basis of early chapter drafts. However, the manifold turbulences in the global academic world caused by the COVID pandemic – which began shortly after we sent out the first letter of invitation – curbed our ambitions, and much to our regret, we had to abandon plans for our conference. Furthermore, several authors had to withdraw from the book project, and others took longer than planned to finish their chapters. We are incredibly grateful and pleased that so many authors managed to overcome so many obstacles and enrich this volume with their significant contributions. As a rather modest substitute for a conference, we tried to intensify communication between the editors and authors to strengthen the coherence of the volume. We are much obliged to authors for their willingness to make – at times profound – revisions to their first drafts.

On the one hand, the rich thematic diversity of this book demonstrates that a life course approach is not only fruitful but indispensable for a thorough analysis of the global world of work and labour, its long-term history, and its recent dynamic transformation. On the other hand, the wide temporal, geographic, disciplinary, and methodological scope of the book provides a foundation for a convincing critique of any narrow or reductionist life course conceptualisation and demonstrates the fruitfulness of an open and flexible life course approach.

This volume has been initiated, encouraged, and extensively supported by the International Research Centre "Work and Human Lifecycle in Global History." Both editors are immensely grateful to its intellectual, social, and organisational centre – Andreas Eckert, Felicitas Hentschke, Jürgen Kocka – and to its whole staff. We would also like to thank Emily Gioielli for her great help with language and copy editing.

Josef Ehmer and Carola Lentz   Vienna and Mainz/Munich, November 2022

Josef Ehmer and Carola Lentz

Work and the Life Course in a Global and Multidisciplinary Perspective: An Introduction

This book is about the intimate entanglements between work and the life course. It examines how age and life course phase – alongside class and gender – shape the variety of work and nonwork activities individual people perform, as well as the ways they are combined and balanced. This book also asks how the life course – as an institution and as an individual experience – depends on the social organisation of work, particularly on the historically variable division of labour. Unlike most studies in this field, the volume approaches this entanglement from a global and historical perspective, looking at developments in different regions of the world and during diverse time horizons ranging from the early modern period up to the present. We also use the widest possible meaning of the term "work," including gainful work (*Erwerbsarbeit*) across a broad spectrum of social configurations (employer, self-employed, employee, wage labourer), as well as unpaid work, particularly work that takes place in the family and community, such as housework and care work or voluntary commitments.

In the pages that follow, we will first offer some conceptual reflections on the work–life course entanglement. We will then provide an overview of the chapters, with a focus on their specific contributions to the basic questions of the volume and the four thematic clusters into which they fit: stability and instability of work life courses; women's work and the gendered life course; social mobility, spatial mobility, and the family as work life course determinants; and pre-industrial work life course patterns. Finally, we will discuss some overarching research results that seem particularly relevant for scholarly and political debates on work and the life course: the theory of the institutionalisation of the life course; the question of standardisation versus de-standardisation of working lives; the gendered division of life courses as they relate to the interplay of productive and reproductive work; and the changing relations between housework, care work, and gainful employment in industrial and post-industrial societies.

Towards a Broader Understanding of the Work–Life Course Entanglement

What people do when they "work" and in which social constellation changes continuously during their lifetime, from childhood to old age. Further, change does not proceed in a linear manner but "as a sequence of age-linked transitions that is embedded in social institutions and history," as Bengtson, Elder, and Putney (2005: 493) define the life course. This change is a multidimensional phenomenon: It consists of individual bio-physiological and psychological processes of development and ageing, of growing up and growing old;[1] of socialisation in and acculturation to a given society; of changes in people's immediate social environment – consisting of, above all, family and kin; and of the transformation of societies on the whole. All of these dimensions have their own temporal dynamics, and all of them combine permanent change with long- or short-lasting structures that introduce elements of continuity into working lives. It is the interaction of all these dimensions that defines both the range of possibilities of what people do when they work and the set of roles they fulfil when they work. Individuals thus practice various forms of work and labour throughout their lives, and their experiences with work reflect not only current conditions but also layers of earlier circumstances. We think that this dynamic and developmental perspective on work and labour as a human activity and as a social relationship[2] has enormous potential to enrich our understanding of what work actually is and what it means for individual men and women. We are also convinced that this potential is still not yet sufficiently exploited in academic disciplines that deal with work and labour, particularly not in the field of labour history.

Conversely, life course research has put greater emphasis on work since its beginning as an academic field. Yet, work has been integrated into life course research in very different ways and with different levels of intensity. In anthropological life course research, work is certainly considered, but it stands in the shadow of *rites de passage*, family relations, and kinship. Since the 1960s, social and cultural history became interested in single life phases like childhood, youth, or old age;

---

1 In accordance with much of the recent literature, we understand "ageing" and human development as life-long processes, from birth to death.
2 In this volume, we make use of both terms "work" and "labour" without drawing a strict distinction between them. Nevertheless, we don't regard them as identical. In our understanding, work has a slightly stronger emphasis on the activity, and labour – generally – on the social relationship in which the activity is performed, and specifically on dependent work such as wage labour or forced labour. Both meanings are equally important for a life course approach.

relevant studies touch on work to a greater or lesser extent, but certainly not consistently.[3] Moreover, studies on the whole life course are still rare. An exception is the "New Social History," which since the 1970s has been an important promoter of life course research in history and is fully aware of the importance of work.[4] The same is true for some strands of women's and gender history. Work receives the most attention in life course sociology, which also contributes substantially to the methodological and theoretical conceptualisation of the work–life course nexus (see, for example, Heinz, Huinink, and Weymann 2006; Mayer 2009). The problem, however, is the field's almost-exclusive focus on the advanced industrialised or post-industrial societies of the Global North and, moreover, on the specific life course regimes and life course policies of welfare states.[5] In our view, this fosters narrow conceptualisations and obscures the view to both the manifold work–life course interactions that exist in the contemporary world and even more so in the past and to the co-existence and overlaps of various life course regimes. This volume is an attempt to bring the life course closer to historical and contemporary experiences of work and labour. Furthermore, it moves an epoch-transcending and global perspective on work closer to life course research.

The concept of life course itself has the potential to strengthen such an entanglement. It offers a "theoretical orientation" (Bengtson, Elder, and Putney 2005: 493) and analytical tools to conceptualise work–life course relations more flexibly. It is an open concept that has different usages in a wide range of disciplines in the humanities and social sciences, which is reflected in an equally broad terminology. The life course figures regularly as a concept, perspective, paradigm, approach, an "analytical construct" (Mayer), or as a theory or a "developmental theory" (Elder). This variety mirrors both the multiple layers of an almost hundred-year-old tradition of life course reasoning and the different disciplinary settings of actual research.[6] The chapters of this book follow different perspectives on the life course and demonstrate that precisely the vagueness of the concept makes it a useful analytical tool because it may be adapted to analyses of very different current and

---

3 Philippe Ariès's (1962) pathbreaking study on the history of childhood, for instance, refers several times to children's work, particularly to children sent into service, but work and labour do not play a conceptual role.

4 Frequently in this volume, references will be made to Tamara K. Hareven, who was the key figure in the promotion of the life course concept in social history.

5 Studies on work life courses in the Global South show up occasionally in foundational sociological scholarship but never in a consistent manner. See, for instance, Marshall, Heinz, Krüger, and Verma 2001; Heinz and Marshall 2003; Macmillan 2005.

6 Marshall and Mueller 2003; on the complex "archaeology" of life course sociology, see Mayer 2004: 167.

historical situations. At the same time, the different case studies in this volume share a core understanding of the life course concept, which comprises – following Glen Elder – an emphasis on "time and place," that is, the social and historical context of lives; the "interconnectedness of lives" or "linked lives" (on that see below); "human agency", that is: the idea that individuals have and make choices; a consideration of the whole "life-span"; and, finally, on "timing," which means the temporal and age-related placement of life course events and transitions and their synchronisation, for instance, between family life and work careers.[7] Many scholars regard time as "a core component of the life course paradigm" (Carr 2009: XIII). But time needs to be analysed in its multiple layers, as Tamara K. Hareven insisted when pointing to the necessary "re-discovery of complexity" and highlighting the relationship between individual and societal time:

> By focusing on the synchronization of various levels of timing, individual, familial, institutional and historical, the life course paradigm has provided a way of examining the interaction of individual lives with the forces of social history and an understanding of how external historical events impinge on individuals and families. The life course paradigm has offered a way of capturing the complexity in the impact of social change on people, and conversely, the contribution of people to facilitating or modifying social change. (Hareven 2001: 28)

In this volume, we approach this "complexity" through the lens of work by looking at the entanglement of work and the life course from two angles. First, we regard work as crucial for understanding individual development and family life, placing the focus on the sequence of work-induced and age-related transitions human beings perform and experience throughout their life. Second, we regard age and the life course as basic dimensions of the societal division of labour and as determinants of the position of individuals in the processes of production and reproduction, i.e., "work."

Following a broad understanding of "work," we are also interested in activities that may be regarded as "non-work" even though they are usually defined in relation to work, such as education and training or mandatory service, but also leisure activities and retirement. A special aim of the present volume is to foster our understanding of how people perform several of these work and non-work activities simultaneously or subsequently in the course of their lives, and how they combine them under very different historical and contemporary circumstances. How do

---

7 When Glen Elder, one of the preeminent pioneers in life course research, started to formulate these "basic principles" of life course research, his intention was not to create a normative system but to distil common themes from a wide range of actual research. Therefore, these principles are variable and have often been modified. See Elder 1994; Bengtson, Elder, and Putney 2005; or – for a very brief summary – elder.web.unc.edu/research-projects/.

these activities collide or how are they balanced? How are they embedded in familial and generational relations? How do they relate to upward or downward mobility as well as to migration and other forms of spatial mobility? How are they shaped by gender and class and, more generally, by their respective social, historical, and cultural contexts?

Throughout the chapters of this volume, four concepts proved useful to answer such questions and integrate individual life histories into the societal context: life course regime, cohort and generation, linked lives, and biography. The concept of *life course regime(s)* refers to the sets of norms, rules, and institutions that regulate people's journey through life, defining sequences of social roles and positions, thus constituting a framework for human agency. We advocate a flexible understanding of life course regimes, paying attention to social change and allowing for the identification of hegemonic patterns in societies at a particular historical moment, such as the "institutionalised" life course of modern Western societies (on that see below). This conceptual flexibility also allows for the recognition of the coexistence of various historical life course regimes. Work, however, is a basic dimension in all of them. *Cohort* and *generation* designate age groups who share, by virtue of the time of their birth, "a social and cultural history, experiencing events and cultural moods when they are in the same stage of life" (Bengtson, Elder, Putney 2005: 495). These events and moods include the dynamics of labour markets, business cycles, and economic upheavals. The common conditions and experiences of specific cohorts create distinctive lifestyles and perhaps even political orientations that distinguish them from other age groups within the same society. Moreover, generations in the Mannheimian sense (Mannheim 1928) might create a self-perception of forming a community, which also shapes the retrospective narration of life histories. *Linked lives*, one of the basic principles of Glen Elder's (1994) life course theory, addresses the interconnectedness of individual life courses with those of others, particularly persons within family and kin networks, but also with peers or work colleagues. (We will discuss this concept more broadly below in the context of family and the gendered life course). Last – but not least – *biography* comes into play. By biography we mean individual (or group) movements through life, including actual experiences as well as designs for life, plans and expectations, and the retrospective interpretation of experiences. The biographical perspective puts human agency at the forefront, but it also analyses the ways such agency is remembered, constructed, interpreted, and evaluated by individuals themselves, and how it is communicated to others in narratives such as those presented in autobiographies or interviews. As many chapters of this volume show, work experiences and occupational careers play a prominent role in biographical narratives.

The authors of the individual chapters use these four concepts to different de-grees and in various ways, but altogether, they create an informal conceptual framework for the volume. The chapters stem from different disciplinary contexts, follow different methodological approaches, and use different sources and data. The latter include quantitative evidence and statistical analysis as well as bio-graphical interviews and participant observation, classical archival sources, as well as critical re-readings of established literature. All the chapters, however, are empirically grounded and theoretically informed. Taken together, the volume makes a major contribution to research on work – foregrounding the dynamic di-mensions of age and life transitions – and enriches life course research, with a nod to the multitude of historical and global variations.

Individual Contributions and Thematic Clusters

Why is a life course perspective essential for a full understanding of the long-term history of and more recent changes to work and labour in a global perspective? The chapters in this book propose different answers to this question, underscoring the wide range and the complexity of our subject. Four thematic clusters became apparent and have inspired the order of the book: the stability and instability of work life courses; women's work and the gendered life course; social as well as spatial mobility and family as life course determinants; and, finally, work life courses in the early modern period.

The stability and instability of work life courses

The first thematic cluster concerns the stability and instability of work life courses in industrialised or industrialising economies during the twentieth century, and particularly the impact of de-industrialisation and the neoliberal restructuring of the economy. The assumption that a long-term process of de-standardisation of occupational life courses has taken place in Western industrial societies after the end of the post-war economic boom (around 1970) has become something of a truism widely accepted both in academia and in society at large. *Karl Ulrich Mayer, Rolf Becker,* and *Anette Fasang* begin their chapter by presenting the main arguments of the most influential advocates of the "great narrative of de-standardisation and increasing complexity of work lives." But are these arguments more than "strong beliefs"? A life course perspective and the use of longitudinal data are perfectly suited to test them empirically. *Mayer, Becker,* and *Fasang* ana-lyse data sets combined with research literature, which allows for the reconstruction of the life courses and occupational careers of the (West) German birth co-horts from the 1920s to the 1980s, who experienced gainful employment during the period between the 1930s and 2015. This long period covers very different his-torical situations: the economic turbulence of the interwar period; the Second World War; the post-war years; the "economic miracle" of the 1950s and 1960s; as well as the neoliberal restructuring and globalisation push from the 1970s on-wards. The result of this sophisticated quantitative analysis does not confirm the "great narrative" in the case of (West) Germany. Rather, it shows surprising con-tinuities throughout the entire period and across all generations and business cy-cles with respect to the scale of changes in occupations, jobs, and employers over the work life course; upward and downward mobility within the job; the complex-ity of working life courses; and other indications. *Mayer, Becker,* and *Fasang* reveal significant changes and fluctuations, but their general conclusion is that key fea-tures of work life courses show an "astonishing degree of stability."

Lutz Raphael's chapter focuses on industrial workers in Britain, France, and Germany. Since the late nineteenth century, this very specific group was regarded as the core of the economy, the working class, and the labour movement. They lost their prominent role during the dramatic de-industrialisation of western Europe during the last three decades of the twentieth century. What did that mean for the life courses and occupational trajectories of industrial workers? To answer this question, *Raphael* concentrates on the period from 1970 to 2000 and employs a multifaceted research strategy. First, he compares the three most important west-ern European industrial countries; then, he combines quantitative sources such as panel data with ego-documents, which reveal individual life narratives. Next, he looks at different cohorts and generations – older workers already in the job, some of them for many years, and younger workers who started factory work in the era of industrial decline. Finally, he includes differences with respect to qualification and ethnic background. *Raphael's* analysis reveals significant differ-ences between Britain, France, and Germany. The life courses of British industrial workers were most strongly affected by downsizing and closures. They suffered more often from forced occupational mobility, unemployment, and decreasing in-comes than their (West, *not* East) German counterparts, with France somewhere in the middle. All countries, however, displayed gaps between cohorts and genera-tions. The spread of early retirement regulations offered – sometimes provoked – emergency exits for older workers, while young people faced more difficult tran-sitions into other forms of employment and atypical labour relations during the early stages of their work lives. Nevertheless, after a turbulent start, a part of the young workers in industry could still expect and achieve long-term, stable em-ployment. *Raphael's* conclusion is that – not only, but particularly in Germany – changes in work life course patterns were slower than assumed. The widespread feeling of an uncertain future even strengthened loyalty to firms and discouraged mobility.

The example of Japan is particularly instructive for the history of "normalised work" (*Normalarbeitsverhältnis*) and the standardisation–de-standardisation debate from a global perspective. *Yoko Tanaka's* chapter describes the emergence of a comprehensive and rigid life course regime in Japan's industrial sector, which regulated not only the workplace but also the private lives of workers and their families. "Regular work" promised the direct transition from school to employment; a life-long commitment to a firm that offered in-house training, promotion, and increasing wages; and a secure retirement. This life course was closely related to an equally stable and regulated "standard household" and family life based on the male breadwinner model. The Toyota car company provides an ideal-typical example of this life course regime, but it became hegemonic for Japanese society as a whole from the 1960s onwards and reached its peak in the 1980s, when Europe and the United States had already experienced years of de-industrialisation. The collapse of the Japanese bubble economy in the late 1980s and the subsequent long-term recession led to a dramatic breakdown of this system, which disturbed both the stability of working lives and the "standard family." The "Ice Age Generation," which left school in the 1990s and early 2000s, faced serious problems finding "regular work" and, consequently, establishing their own household and family. *Tanaka* concludes that in recent years, the standardised life course regime remained or recovered for parts of the workforce, but its hegemonic and universal character was irreversibly replaced by a polarised structure.

Ju Li's chapter deals with the individual life histories of employees of a large steel enterprise established in a remote region of Sichuan province in the 1960s as one of the Chinese state's many industrialisation projects. The women and men she interviewed belonged to some of the first cohorts of employees. As such, they had spent their entire working life, until retirement, at this factory, and they lived their private lives in the surrounding "company town." Their life histories provide insight into the complex relationship between their own agency and the limits to it, which were determined by external forces. The life trajectories of the cohorts born in the 1940s and 1950s in particular were strongly shaped by state policies. State policies in China from the 1960s to the early 2000s underwent several dramatic turnarounds, such as the Cultural Revolution of the 1960s, the economic reforms beginning in the late 1970s, and the communist-style neoliberal transformation of China's economy and society from the 1990s onwards. The cohorts of steel workers born in the 1940s and 1950s neither experienced nor expected a stable life course regime. During all the state-induced turning points of their lives, they had to adapt to new requirements – or to take new opportunities to satisfy their own needs and interests. Sometimes they had more room to manoeuvre, sometimes less, sometimes hardly any at all. When narrating their life histories, all of them emphasised one specific historical period, namely the smooth and controlled economic liberalisation of the "long 1980s," from around 1978 to 1996. They remembered this period as a "glorious age" in which they could develop their talents and build a career as well as enjoy the securities offered by a planned economy. The following neoliberal period, in contrast, was a shock for *Ju Li's* interview partners – some of them by this point high-ranking employees. Because they were now in their fifties and sixties – which meant at or near retirement age – they were especially hard hit by the re-structuring of the steel enterprise. This included measures such as forced early retirement, pension cuts, and the cancellation of welfare programs, which had been, until then, the responsibility of the enterprise. *Ju Li* shows that the overlap of certain ages with economic upheaval or – in Hareven's words – the overlap of "individual time" and "historical time" was particularly damaging for her respondents.

Civil service has been rightly regarded as a forerunner of the standardisation of labour relations. Unified admission rules, predictable career trajectories, life-long employment, and pensions existed in some European countries already from the late eighteenth century onwards. *Therese Garstenauer* looks at the actual life courses of public employees in Austria in the first half of the twentieth century and reveals a much more nuanced pattern. The development of employment statutes was indeed oriented towards an ever-increasing stability of working life courses. In practice, however, this life course was shaped by two limitations. First, employment and income security were closely connected with the norm of the male-breadwinner family. The security offered by the state to its "servants" included their families, for instance in form of child allowances and widow and orphan pensions. In turn, it was accompanied by state interventions in family life. Until 1914, civil servants "had to ask for permission before getting married," and the marital status of women strongly affected their employability. The share of women in public service was small and by and large limited to unmarried women in menial positions. Second, male occupational careers were neither homogeneous nor fully predictable. There was a surprising variety of pathways into public service and historical events significantly influenced career trajectories. The period *Garstenauer* focuses on was characterised by a series of regime changes, political upheaval, and economic crisis, all of which affected public finances. Such historical events led to layoffs, dismissals, stunted careers, wage cuts, and quite often to forced early retirement. *Garstenauer* provides a detailed account of the waves of economic, political, ethnic, and "racial" re-structuring of the Austrian public service and their impact on the life courses of state employees. For many of them, civil service remained only one episode in their whole work life course. However, *Garstenauer* also shows that a majority of (male) state employees kept their jobs throughout all these upheavals. Work life courses in public service were more stable and secure than in other segments of the labour market but by no means were they uniform.

Women's work and the gendered life course

Women's work and the gendered life course is a second thematic cluster and one of the major threads that runs through the entire book. Three chapters, however, concentrate on this theme. *Mary Jo Maynes* and *Ann Waltner* start their chapter with the statement that the relation between work and the life course "is always gendered." The assignment of specific work activities to women and men, to life course stages, and to age groups, however, varies over historical time, differs between cultures, and is strongly related to the family and kinship systems in place. *Maynes* and *Waltner* approach this relationship in a multi-layered, comparative analysis focused on textile production and its technological transformation in the "long" nineteenth century. They compare a Chinese region with three western European regions, and they compare the distinctive labour associated with the production of different textiles, namely silk, cotton, and linen. Textile production is perfectly suited for such an analysis because it is carried out in several stages that differ with respect to the gendered division of labour. When textiles were produced in households, spinning was the task of women and – sometimes very young – girls in all the regions analysed. However, weaving was a female occupation in China, in contrast to Europe, where weavers were mainly men. *Maynes* and *Waltner* show that the transformation of textile production from household to factory production partly maintained and even strengthened and partly overthrew the traditional division of labour by gender and age. Mechanised spinning in factories remained a female domain, employing an even larger share of unmarried young women and girls both in China and Europe. Domestic weaving – when yarn was already factory-produced – was gradually taken over by women in Europe, and weaving in factories became a predominantly female job in both world regions. *Maynes* and *Waltner* conclude that the division of labour by gender and age was more similar in China and Europe around 1900 than it had been hundred years earlier. They consider this finding an indication that the "Great Divergence" between early modern and early industrial China and western Europe was partly replaced by a "re-convergence."

Lamia Karim draws our attention to a very specific type of industrial worker whose emergence was part of the global relocation of the textile and garment industries from the 1970s onwards. These workers disappeared almost completely from western Europe (see the chapter by *Lutz Raphael* in this volume) as a result of the parallel boom in East and Southeast Asia. The rise of the garment industry in Bangladesh – as in some other East Asian countries – since about 1980 enticed millions of single young women to leave their rural communities for factory work in cities. Their life courses reveal both the aspirations and the great difficulties faced by the first generation of factory workers in the region who had to cope with entirely new working and living conditions that were shaped by age and gender. *Karim* places particular emphasis on the spousal and family relations of these female industrial workers and on the interaction between housework, care work, and wage work. She tells the life histories of elderly (former) workers, using their own words taken from a series of interviews. Many of these women started in factory work, married, and gave birth to their children at a very young age, and they frequently became the main or sole breadwinners as husbands were unreliable or abandoned their wives. The hardships of work were accompanied by the instability of marital relations, which were only partially tempered by the support of the – distant– extended family. When these women were phased out of their factory jobs between the ages of approximately thirty-five and forty, the precarity of their lives increased further. Their employment in the garment industry was unstable and often interrupted, and they changed employers regularly, sometimes voluntarily and sometimes because they were forced to leave their jobs. But as long as they were employed, they earned a regular wage, however small. After being phased out, they had to rely on irregular income earned through self-employment, domestic work, or short-term stints in the sweatshops of subcontractors. Nevertheless, they do not paint their life stories only in dark colours. Even if most of their hopes – for a good life, for companionship and love, for their children's education and upward social mobility – were dashed, they achieved self-esteem and independence by earning their own money as wage workers.

Female and male work life courses differ in many ways depending on historically variable gendered divisions of labour, gender roles, and ideas of femininity and masculinity. In European history, however, historical variations have been shaped by a structure of *longue durée*, namely the allocation of care work to females. In domestic modes of production, care work and housework may have been performed by girls and women of different ages and household positions. In the nuclear family households of industrial societies, married women in particular were responsible for housework and care work. Caring for infants and children became regarded as a task to be carried out by their mothers. For women and mothers engaged in gainful employment outside their homes, this led to a "principal tension between women's paid and unpaid work," as *Susan Zimmermann* writes. Her focus is on the economic boom period of the 1960s, when this tension was a widely discussed social and labour policy issue throughout Europe, not least among policy makers involved in international organisations such as the International Labour Organisation (ILO). The common problem during this period of rapid economic growth was how to reconcile the growing demand for working women with their – unquestioned – "family responsibilities." Proposed solutions, however, differed between states and particularly between state-socialist and capitalist countries. *Zimmermann* uses the example of Hungary to highlight the emergence of a specific measure that has, to date, shaped women's work life courses, namely extended childcare leave. Hungary was the European "trendsetter," as it established the right to extended paid childcare leave for up to three years already in 1967. *Zimmermann* describes the early implementation of this measure as result of the interaction of various actors and the overlap of different policy goals. Extended childcare leave promised – and actually implemented – the increasing willingness of women to take up employment, and the demand for labour in a rapidly industrialising economy complied with the socialist vision of lifelong, full-time employment as a means of women's emancipation. Moreover, the reduction of the numerous and irregular absences of working mothers with small children allowed for more reliable production planning; paid childcare provided by mothers at home was considered better for children and cheaper than investing in nurseries; and, last but not least, extended paid leave was expected to increase birth rates and protect against population decline. This sustainable intervention into female work life courses by politicians and economists was enthusiastically welcomed by (potential) working women themselves and strongly promoted by their unions.

Social mobility, spatial mobility, and the family as life course determinants

The third cluster reveals how closely spatial mobility, social mobility, and family relations are interconnected. Hareven's notion of the interrelatedness of individual time, family time, and historical time, and Elder's concept of "linked lives" have inspired generations of life course researchers. Individual life courses are not only embedded in their broader historical context but are also interwoven with family life cycles and the life trajectories of other family members. A most interesting question is, in our view, how links between family members relate to their spatial mobility since work life courses are strongly influenced by migration and other forms of spatial moves. The strength of relations within family and kinship networks across geographical distances depends on various factors, not least on the family structures and cultural patterns that prevail in a given society. The two chapters by *Carola Lentz* and *Erdmute Alber* deal with "extended families" in the West African states of Ghana and Benin. Both states are presently experiencing a very specific historical constellation of social change characterised by social and cultural differentiation as well as the entanglement between the agricultural inland regions in the north of these states and southern urbanised coastal areas.

Carola Lentz studies "extended family and kinship networks" in the rural society of Northwestern Ghana, where "traditional" peasant modes of living and value systems interact with new opportunities offered by a modernising state and a globalising economy. An expression of these opportunities is the emergence of a growing urban middle class particularly in the south of Ghana, which is continuously fuelled by descendants of rural extended families. Most members of this class in-the-making, however, "remain bound to multi-local, large multigenerational families" from which they descend. The ancestor's farmstead and land are the symbolic and social centre of the whole family, for those who stay in the village as well as for those who move to cities or even abroad. Urban middle-class family members and their rural peasant relatives share a common sense of belonging and responsibility for each other despite vastly differing lifestyles and levels of wealth. *Lentz's* central question is how and for whom is the extended family a resource for social advancement or, on the contrary, a hinderance. She shows that the answer to this question is different depending on gender, age, and sibling rank; it is also increasingly related to occupational success and individual aspiration. Labour migration and aspirations for social advancement are generally valued and encouraged, but they need to be balanced against the farmstead's demand for labour and monetary income. Therefore, individual life course trajectories are the subject of negotiations – be they harmonious or conflict-ridden – within the extended family. One family member's freedom to move might mean another one's commitment to stay, and migrants might (have to) return when needed. "Linked lives" unfold in the tension between traditional values based on land, gerontocracy, age hierarchy, and status in the village community and new values based on meritocracy and social recognition in the wider world.

Erdmute Alber's study on family and kin networks in Benin looks at a comparable constellation from a different angle. Her focus is on the life course trajectories of girls and on the dimension of conflict in "linked lives" and intergenerational entanglements. *Alber* shows that the "circulation of children" is an important element of kin relations between Benin's rural north and urban south. This concerns particularly young girls from northern villages who are welcomed, for a certain period, by relatives in the urban south. Their position in the host family is usually that of a "helping girl" or – if the relation is closer and more durable – of a "foster child." "Helping" means that they participate in housework or take care of children. They do not receive any pay for their work, but their host or foster parent has an obligation to provide support for their charges' further careers, such as financing an apprenticeship or supplying a dowry. During their stay, girls become accustomed to urban or middle-class lifestyles, which also shape their "expectations, desires and imagined futures." These expectations, however, easily come into conflict with the life plans or decisions made by the girls' families of origin. Due to the customs and moral values of the rural society, it is a father's right and duty to decide on the marriage of his daughter. *Alber's* case studies reveal the bitter conflicts that emerge when girls are called back to the village for an arranged marriage or when they, nevertheless, try to impose their own will and return to the city. These conflicts involve parents, foster parents, distant relatives, the family of the pre-selected groom, and the whole village. "Linked lives" might easily become "battlefields of conflicts." In methodological terms, *Alber* favours the concept of "vital conjunctures" as an analytical tool to understand the divergent needs and attitudes of all involved parties and how they change over life courses.

Labour migration has an impact on the life courses of not only migrants themselves but also on the life courses of the younger and the older generations of their families – spread across continents. *Neda Deneva* shows how particularly close links emerged between individual and family life courses among "hyper-mobile" Bulgarian labour migrants, focusing on migrants coming from impoverished rural Roma communities. Living in extremely precarious conditions after the breakdown of state socialism, they try to earn their livelihood by searching for work in western European countries. Since they usually find only short-term employment in the unregulated and most unstable segments of the open EU labour market, most are unable to settle abroad permanently or at least for longer periods. Rather, they move between various western European countries regularly and travel back and forth between their Bulgarian homes and abroad. This system works for a certain period in the life courses of adult migrants, but it collapses when their children reach school age. *Deneva's* main concern is the profound contradiction between the EU's freedom of labour mobility and the national structures of educational systems, which are designed for sedentary populations. For permanent or perhaps perpetual migrants, it is rarely possible to enrol their children in schools in destination countries, where they reside and work for only a short time. Nevertheless, to provide their children with a proper education, these migrant parents usually try to return or send only their children back to the home country until the child completes school. But who cares for children when their parents are absent and most of their adult relatives are also pendular labour migrants? *Deneva* shows that a new norm and moral obligation has come into existence among Bulgarian Roma communities, namely that grandparents terminate their own labour migration prematurely and relocate permanently to care for their school-age grandchildren. That means, however, that these – mostly young – grandparents experience a painful break in their work life courses and life plans. They lose the opportunity to earn a living themselves, are forced into a much too early and highly precarious retirement, and become dependent on remittances from their migratory children.

Heike Drotbohm's case study investigates the life histories of labour migrants from the Cape Verdean Islands to the United States. She looks at the interaction between life course trajectories and transnational social and kin networks from the angle of return migration, and she is particularly interested in the negotiation of individual life plans in families. Migratory relations between the Cape Verde Islands to the United States have existed for about two centuries. Even if many migrants remain in the United States forever – and a robust Cape Verdean diaspora exists particularly in New England – many (former) migrants maintain a relationship to their (or their parents') place of origin. Therefore, return migration remains an option that can be chosen in response to contingent life events or retains the potential to shape future life phases such as school completion or retirement. *Drotbohm* reveals a broad spectrum of reasons for going back; these include voluntary individual desire, family decisions, or return compelled by immigration law or economic rupture. They range from the enjoyment of an admirable retirement after a successful career abroad to a precarious existence due to deportation after a prison sentence or impoverishment abroad. However, the forms and causes of return migration are also influenced by age, life course phase, and the historical context of immigration to the United States. The age of children strongly affects the return migrants' ability to adjust more or less successfully to the American school system and lifestyle; the security of residence status depends on the actual timing of immigration and the immigration and naturalisation regulations in force; and economic success or misfortune is affected by business cycles. Things become even more complicated when members of a migrant's family move at different times, ages, and life course phases. *Drotbohm* shows that the non-simultaneity of a family's migration is a potential source of trouble for which the return of one or two family members may serve as a solution.

Work life courses in the early modern period

The fourth and final thematic cluster deals with work life courses in colonial India and early modern Europe. In both modern and premodern societies, life course regimes have regulated what people do for work, in what type of labour relationship they perform this work and at which age, and how all this changes (or not) throughout the different phases of their lives. Life-long employment with one employer was not impossible in pre- and early industrial societies, although usually it was an option only in very specific occupations or economic roles. *Chitra Joshi's* chapter deals with mail runners and palanquin bearers in nineteenth-century

India. This purely male occupational group played a central role in the transport of goods, persons, and mail. Runners were the backbone of colonial communication networks before the expansion of roads and railways, and in remote areas even long after. *Joshi's* focus is on runners and bearers who worked for the British East India Company. Their job required extreme physical strength and resilience as well as a high level of skill and experience with respect to carrying heavy loads, finding the best routes through jungles and forests in changing weather conditions, and avoiding encounters with dangerous animals such as tigers. Learning these skills began very early, as *Joshi* shows, and often, these skills were passed down within the group or caste of "Kahars" – sometimes within a family – from one generation to the next. It implied "all-round training" for boys starting around the age of seven, and from the age of seventeen or eighteen, they were regarded as completely capable. Maintaining these skills and staying in shape, however, required continuous practice. This, along with the East India Company's high demand for the experienced and reliable bearers and runners promoted long-term employment relations; some runners and bearers worked for the company for over thirty years. Moreover, being completely exhausted after so many years of hard work, runners and bearers could apply for a pension based on old age or disability. Surprisingly, the East India Company applied to these workers the principles of social security, which were in-the-making for the civil service in the British imperial metropole. *Joshi* reveals that some elements of the work life courses of this now extinct and seemingly exotic occupational group mirrored expectations associated with Western welfare states in the twentieth century.

The early modern period and the period of transition to industrial capitalism is the focal point of *Josef Ehmer's* chapter. He argues that the institution of "life-cycle service" represented a hegemonic life course regime in many parts of early modern and early industrial Europe that has not yet received sufficient attention by historians of work and labour. The term denotes those children, adolescents, and young adults of both genders who lived for a certain period of their lives in the households of employers and worked for wages as farmhands, apprentices, or journeymen. In *Ehmer's* view, they formed an essential element of a specific mode of production that dominated early modern economies in western and central Europe and persisted into early industrial capitalism, namely "petty commodity production." Households and families were the basic units of production, but they were complemented by wage workers who shared characteristics of dependent family members: they were young and single and subordinated to the authority of their masters. In contrast to "real" family members, however, they were employed and integrated into households for a defined term only after which they were free to move to another workplace. Furthermore, this specific labour relation was not regarded as lifelong but was limited to a distinct phase in the life course.

The core of *Ehmer's* consideration is the assumption that a close "triangular relationship" existed between the life course regime, mode of production, and the historical expansion of wage labour. The awareness of this relationship offers a fresh
approach to the high prevalence and economic functionality of life-cycle service as
well as contributes to a full understanding of its social and cultural logic.

The diversity of the contributions to this volume undeniably transcend the limitations of previous scholarship on work and the life course. As outlined above, the
volume goes beyond "the West" by including chapters on state-socialist life course
regimes in China and eastern Europe; and it goes beyond Europe and the Global
North as the majority of chapters focus on East Asia and Africa. Most chapters relate to the twentieth century, but some offer a perspective on earlier periods in
European, Chinese, and Indian history. Finally, women's life courses and the gendered dimensions of life courses play a much stronger role in this volume than is
often the case in the fields of labour history and life course research.

The temporal and spatial range of the volume allows for a broader and more
differentiated understanding of the main actors, institutions, and social structures
that shape work life courses. The chapters show, first, the different impact of the
state, depending on its constitution – liberal, totalitarian, democratic – and the degree to which it penetrates society. In all these variants, the state also enters the
narrative as a very special employer. Second, the chapters invite reflection on
the impact of different family forms: from the nuclear family, single persons,
and single mothers and their children to multigenerational extended families living under one roof or dispersed across the country, continent, or world. Third, the
chapters in this volume refer to different socio-economic structures and modes of
production, including the agricultural family economy, household-bound petty
commodity production, and factory-based industry in capitalism and state socialism. Many chapters focus on periods of basic economic transformation such as
the onset of industrialisation – be it in early modern European history or in the
contemporary Global South – or de-industrialisation and the shift to a service
economy in economically advanced societies.

The volume shows how all these mediating institutions and structures continuously define and redefine the scope and limitations of individual agency in making one's way through life. The many life histories analysed in this volume make it
clear that individuals have to navigate very different types of state, family, and
economy configurations over their respective life courses. Moreover, they often
must navigate different institutional configurations at the same time when these
coexist simultaneously in a given society. The global perspective of this volume
clearly demonstrates that all the variations discussed above are not – or at least
not only – ideal-types belonging to specific historical periods but that they coexist

in the present. Therefore, the volume moves the idea of the "contemporaneousness of the uncontemporary" (*die Gleichzeitigkeit des Ungleichzeitigen*, according to Ernst Bloch) much closer to life course research and labour history.

Cross-cutting Issues

As varied as the chapters are, they not only form thematic clusters but are linked by cross-cutting interests and issues that enable them to intervene in scholarly debates as well as public discourses. In the discussion that follows, we present four cross-cutting issues: the theory of the institutionalisation of the life course; the question of standardisation versus de-standardisation of work life courses; the gendered division of life courses in the interplay between productive and reproductive work; and the changing relations between housework, care work, and gainful employment in industrial and post-industrial societies.

The institutionalisation of the life course

The "institutionalisation of the life course" has become an influential theory over the past four decades. Martin Kohli, one of its most important proponents, regards the life course as "one of the major institutions" of "fully modernized societies." It "has been structured around the new *system of work* based on wage labour" in the shape of a "'tripartition' into periods of preparation, 'activity', and retirement," organised in a "chronologically standardized, normative" manner (Kohli 2007: 255). Inherent in this "tripartition" is, therefore, a work/non-work dichotomy. The working life course is framed by a work-free period at an early age, which includes training and formal education, and a work-free period of retirement in one's later years, which offers room for a range of leisure activities.

The present volume does not principally question this ideal-typical "master narrative" (Kohli 2007: 255). However, the historical and geographic range of the case studies in this volume widens our understanding of the character of and relations between the three basic life phases of the institutionalisation theory. The chapters deal with historical preindustrial societies and, among contemporary societies, some that are indeed "fully modernized" and others that are not. Our approach is twofold: first, instead of "contrasting" (Kohli 2007: 255) fully modernised societies with others, we are looking for similarities, continuities, and overarching developmental processes. Second, our interest is not in contrasting the three life course periods but looking at processes of transition, overlaps, and combinations. The focus of the volume, then, is not the sharp contrast between ideal-types of work and non-work life phases but the fluid and ambiguous transitions in individual life courses and in societies.

The variety of children's transitions into the world of work is addressed in several chapters.[8] Joining the workforce was a gradual process when and where families and households were the predominant sites and units of production both in the past and in many contemporary societies of the Global South. Children in present-day African agricultural family economies, for instance, participate in work tasks performed by their families according to their bio-physiological and psycho-social development. Their work is learning by observing and doing; it leaves time for play; and it includes acculturation into the local community.[9] A gradual integration of children into their family's workforce also took place in proto-industrial textile production in early modern China and Europe, where very young girls were taught to spin (Maynes and Waltner). Because proto-industry meant production for markets and specialisation in a specific product, however, children were exposed to a much stricter form of work discipline than those in less market-oriented family economies, and work was much less intermingled with play and rest.

Similarly, Indian mail runners started to accompany adult family members who worked in the business at age seven or eight and became regarded as mature runners at seventeen or eighteen (Joshi). The most widespread form of children's and adolescent's wage labour in pre- and early industrial Europe was life-cycle service in agriculture, crafts, and trades. These boys and girls were often used for housework and care work at the beginning of their labour career, before approaching more complex agricultural or artisanal labour tasks (Ehmer). The abrupt transition of children into exploitative full-time wage labour in factories or mines accompanied the Industrial Revolution wherever it took place (Maynes and Waltner; see generally Humphries 2010), and it still exists in the Global South. But from a long-term historical perspective, it is rather an exception than the rule.

Several chapters of this volume deal with the spread of elementary schooling, which has had a profound effect on children's transition into working life, particularly where it has been compulsory, as in many European countries since the late eighteenth century. Compulsory schooling, however, cannot be equated with a work-free childhood. In European history well into the twentieth century, school-based education and work coexisted in various combinations (Ehmer; see generally Beattie 2010; Papathanassiou 1999). A work-free childhood is a late phe-

---

8 In the following paragraphs, author's names in parentheses without any further explanation refer to chapters in this volume.

9 See, for instance, Alber 2012; Polak 2012; and other chapters in Spittler/Bourdillon 2012.

nomenon in fully developed countries, and it still does not exist in large parts of the Global South. Chapters on West Africa in this volume show the combination of enrolment in school and daily work in the family economy before and after school (Lentz) or the performance of domestic chores as "helpers" in the urban households of relatives (Alber). A conflicting combination of school and work is to be found in the decisions of parents to send only some of their children to school and keep some of them at home to work in the family farmstead or household (Lentz).

The implementation of elementary schooling and the expansion of higher education, however, has a further and, quite likely, global meaning, as several chapters of this volume reveal. Formal education has become regarded worldwide as a precondition for and pathway to decent work and social advancement, preferably through white-collar jobs in administration. A positive attitude towards education is displayed by children themselves but perhaps even more so by their parents. Parents from a lower-class or peasant background long for better and more prestigious jobs for at least some of their children than they themselves have. This hope for advancement is shared by Bangladeshi factory workers (Karim), Bulgarian labour migrants (Deneva), peasants in Benin and Ghana (Alber; Lentz), and Cape Verdean labour migrants who express "high expectations for their children's career" (Drotbohm). Often, remittances are sent back to enable left-behind children to attend a good school, and sometimes the return migration of parents or grandparents is triggered for the same reason (Deneva; Drotbohm). The significant appreciation of formal education might indeed be a step toward work-free childhood on a global scale, even if the ambitious aspirations of lower-class parents quite often fail to materialise (Karim).

In fully modernised societies, a clear break between a work-free life phase devoted to education and full labour force participation has indeed come into existence. From the 1960s to the 1980s, Japan's large firms, for instance, used to hire graduates directly from school (Tanaka). This type of school-work transition, however, is only one among others, and it is presumably not a globally hegemonic one. Two forms of gradual transition have developed during the last four decades. First, the neoliberal transformation of industry made the entry of young workers into jobs much more difficult (Tanaka). In countries like France and Britain in the 1980s and 1990s, work careers of school graduates frequently began with a phase of unemployment, continued with poorly paid fixed-term jobs, and took many years to work up to a stable job (Raphael). Second, the global expansion of higher education since the 1960s had an ambiguous impact on young people's transition into employment. On the one hand, high school and university students are increasingly engaged in paid work during the term and even more so during breaks and vacations. The combination of study and paid work seems to have become a new lifestyle (de Vries 2008; Ehmer 2015). On the other hand, the expansion of higher education clearly postpones people's full-time entry into the labour force until the late teens or even twenties. This affects the occupational trajectories of young people, who start their careers with higher levels of qualification and, consequently, higher starting incomes. In turn, however, firms reduce in-house training, which has negative consequences for the career opportunities of young employees who have not earned post-secondary school qualifications (Raphael; Tanaka). Many chapters in the present volume stress the complex and dynamically changing character of entrance into the world of work.

Retirement is a second basic pillar of institutionalisation theory. In Western-style welfare states, retirement as a financially protected work-free life phase following paid work has indeed become universal as a social and cultural norm. It is seen as a reward for long-term employment or loyalty to a firm (Tanaka). In other parts of the world, retirement programs have long existed, although not as universal institutions but as a privilege for specific occupational groups. In colonial times, this concerned jobs in colonial administrations, which were treated like civil service positions in European metropoles. In India in the early nineteenth century, even native mail runners who served the East India Company could apply for an "extraordinary" old-age or widow's pension (Joshi). Throughout the twentieth century and particularly after decolonisation, retirement programs also spread to/in the Global South for – mostly urban-based – occupational groups such as civil servants, members of the armed forces, bank employees, white-collar employees of transnational corporations, and others (Conrad 2015). There is certainly a trend in developing countries towards retirement as a financially protected life phase. However, it has not yet reached a significant part of the population. The meaning of retirement in a global and cross-cultural perspective needs further conceptual reflection as well as more comparative empirical research (Luborsky and LeBlanc 2003).

The present volume contributes to a differentiated understanding of the character of retirement and the manifold work–retirement transitions from two angles. First, where public or occupational retirement systems exist, they are less chronologically standardised and less secure than institutionalisation theory assumes. Civil-service pensions have been heavily affected by political and economic upheavals and thereby exposed to the loss of entitlements, forced early retirements, or pension cuts (Garstenauer). The same has been true for state-owned industries, for instance in the People's Republic of China during the neoliberal turn of the late 1990s (Li). Western Europe experienced a massive spread of early retirement schemes in the context of de-industrialisation in the last decades of the twentieth century. Forced, semi-voluntary, or financially promoted early retirement (i.e., "buy-outs") became a highly useful tool to reduce significant parts of the workforce based on public consensus and negotiations by firms, state, and trade unions (Raphael). The timing of retirement and the pathways from work to retirement proved to be highly variable and flexible.

Second, retirement is not necessarily a work-free life phase. In western Europe, a growing number of pensioners take paid jobs due to financial need or their enjoyment of work (Ehmer 2021a). In Ghana, retired employees of the United Africa Company used to set up their own small businesses or engage in other economic activities. There is a range of "cultural factors that made the concept of leisurely retirement unattractive in the Ghanaian context" (van den Bersselaar 2011: 136). Retirement has a specific meaning for workers who have to withdraw from regular paid work for various reasons without any entitlement to financial support. This is the case, for instance, for Bangladeshi female factory workers who are usually phased out of their jobs relatively early, between the ages of 35 and 45. They try to make a living through the informal urban labour market, hope their children can support them, or return – without any means – to their villages of origin (Karim). Such experiences are shared by middle-aged Bulgarian labour migrants who are pressured by their – also labour migrant – children to withdraw from western European labour markets and return to their home village to take on the care and education of their grandchildren, whose parents remain working abroad (Deneva). From a global perspective, retirement is an ambiguous life phase with multifaceted meanings.

Standardisation versus de-standardisation of working life courses

A further cross-cutting issue of our volume concerns a topic that for many years has ranked high on the agenda of scholarly debates as well as in public and political discourse, namely the assumption of a radical "de-standardisation" of life course regimes and work biographies in contemporary advanced capitalism. We touched on this topic already in the thematic cluster on the stability and instability of work life courses, but it is so politically and ideologically charged that it deserves a more thorough discussion.

A pronounced trend towards "de-standardisation," many scholars argue, is due to globalisation, the neoliberal restructuring of the economy and the welfare state, and the fundamental transformation of information and communication technologies. This assumption is usually embedded in a narrative about the long-term history of labour relations, life course regimes, and work biographies, moving from "traditional" societies to the near future.[10] The focus of the standardisation/de-standardisation debate, however, concentrates on a shorter time frame: from the middle of the twentieth to the early twenty-first centuries, which is labelled as the era of the rise and decline of "normalised" work and standardised life courses (Wadauer 2021: esp. 13–16; Ehmer 2018). In this narrative, the era of the post-World War Two boom in the Western world, and particularly in Europe, appears as an era of economic growth, strong unions, mass production, and the expansion of the welfare state, which led to stable and homogeneous work careers, continuously increasing incomes, and socially protected life courses. The economic crisis of the mid-1970s, in contrast, is considered to have initiated a trend reversal towards unstable and insecure working and living conditions as well as to rising social inequality. In this period, the predominance of "normal work" and the "standardisation" of work lives – which was achieved slightly before – is seen as being endangered, if not replaced, by "de-standardisation" and precarity. In the last three decades of the twentieth century, life courses are said to have become volatile and turbulent. Specifically, the diagnosis of the rise and fall of standard working life courses has become a "standard narrative" and been broadened to apply to the whole society, not only the world of work. "Actually, the de-standardisation of life courses appears as a core element – perhaps the most important element – in the continuing transformation process of West European societies."[11]

This evolutionary narrative proposed by – for example – Andreas Wirsching, received broad approval from both academics and the general public. Prominent German sociologists such as Ulrich Beck (1999) predicted that the trend towards discontinuity and precarity of employment will bring about the convergence of European living conditions and work biographies with those already in existence in the Global South. He predicts a process of "Brazilianization" *(Brasilianisierung)* (Beck 1999: 7). This prognosis was taken up by sociologists and labour historians who work on global processes of "informalisation" such as Jan Breman and Marcel van der Linden (2014).

There is no question that the world of work has been undergoing dynamic changes across the globe during the past half-century, which affect labour relations, life course regimes, and work biographies. And it is beyond doubt that even in western Europe, some occupations and workplaces are exposed to excessive exploitation, insecurity, and precarity (Mayer-Ahuja 2003). But does the stand-

---

10 For a summary of – mainly sociological – concepts relating to the historical development of life course regimes, see Mayer 2004: 169–173.

11 "Tatsächlich erscheint die Entstandardisierung der Lebensläufe als ein Basiselement, vielleicht sogar das wichtigste Element in dem anhaltenden Wandlungsprozess der westeuropäischen Gesellschaften" (Wirsching 2009: 87).

ardisation/de-standardisation narrative actually capture long-term historical developments and contemporary social change? Several chapters of this volume plead for a more cautious approach and offer empirical evidence that does not support this "grand narrative."

Mayer, Becker, and *Fasang's* analysis reveals a surprising amount of continuity and stability in German working life courses throughout the twentieth century based on several key indicators, for which they provide highly convincing empirical evidence. Neither the assumed standardisation period from the 1950s to the early 1970s nor the subsequent period of assumed de-standardisation show significant deviations from longer-term trends. *Raphael* shows that the mass de-industrialisation of western European economies in the last three decades of the twentieth century had diverse effects on the labour biographies of industrial workers. Developments differed considerably in Britain, France, and Germany, as well as between cohorts, generations, and genders. Particularly – but not only – West German industrial workers maintained stable work careers to a remarkable extent during this era.

In the debate on Europe, the "oil crisis" of the mid-1970s figures most prominently as the great watershed between the *"trente glorieuses"* (Fourastié 1979) and the presumed era of increasing work life course destabilisation. The global perspective of this volume favours a more nuanced chronology. Economic upheaval accompanied the transformation from the industrial to the knowledge and service economy in all industrialised and industrialising countries, although to different degrees, at different times, and with different results. Moreover, the lasting effects of economic shocks on life histories often materialise only after some time or even in the next cohort, as Elder showed in his pathbreaking study on *Children of the Great Depression* (1974).

The most significant event in Japan was the collapse of the "bubble economy" in 1992, which led to a long-term recession and to the breakdown of a particularly rigid industrial life course regime. The recovery of the economy during the last few years, however, re-established the "standard life course . . . in most Japanese companies" for parts of the workforce, but there was no longer a universal life course regime (Tanaka). Chinese industrial workers remember the period of "reform consensus" from the late 1970s to the mid-1990s as a "golden era," while the successive years of radical neoliberal restructuring had profoundly negative effects on their actual working life courses as well as their biographical orientations (Li). A strategy broadly implemented by companies in industrialised countries was the relocation of capital to the Global South in search of cheap, flexible, and unregulated labour. Bangladesh, for example, experienced the rapid development of a garment industry since about 1980, which was founded with South Korean capital. This industry currently employs more than four million young female workers. The elderly women *Karim* interviewed remember their time in the factories as difficult and exhausting but also as a life phase in which they enjoyed regular income and experienced a degree of personal autonomy they never had as young girls in their rural villages or enjoyed since they were phased out of their jobs by management in their late thirties and early forties (Karim). The life phase of factory work appears as more stable and secure than the life phases before and after. A close look at life histories from both a national and global perspective demonstrates that the development of work life course regimes in the twentieth century is a puzzling and complex terrain and reveals that the "grand narrative" discussed above is hardly helpful for navigating it.

Gendered work life courses and the family: continuity, divergence, or convergence?

Human labour "has virtually always been marked by gender" (Frader 2021: 27). Throughout history, the place of women in the social organisation of work is shaped by the overlap of two dimensions: first, by cultural perceptions of gender differences which generally regard women as "naturally" destined or better suited than men for certain forms of work – even though the gendered division of labour in practice is much more flexible. Second, this general binary pattern varies over female life courses in ideology and practice. Gendered assignments are differentiated – to historically and culturally varying degrees and mitigated by issues of class – by age and, therefore, by social roles linked to life course phases. These roles, in turn, are closely tied to the respective organisation of social reproduction in families and households. The continuing allocation of the main responsibilities of social reproduction to women means that all forms of women's work are much more affected by family-related life course events and by the labour activities and aspirations of other family and household members than is men's work. A full understanding of the gendered division of labour and its inherent power relations is hardly possible without a life course perspective with a strong emphasis on the family. Gender is a fundamental category we have already discussed implicitly in the previous sections on the institutionalisation of the life course and the (de)standardisation of working lives. However, it must be explicitly addressed.

Two concepts have been used to analyse the interaction between individual life courses and the family. First, from the interwar period onwards, the concept of "family life cycle" or simply "family cycle" has been in use (Loomis 1936). The term denotes a sequence of social roles and "stages" beginning with a couple's marriage, moving to parenthood, children growing up and leaving home, and ending with widowhood and the death of the other spouse (Elder 1978: 42–55). The focus of this concept is on demographic family events and on the nuclear family as a co-residential group, with work playing only a minor role. Nevertheless, the concept has some merit for understanding women's work lives as it draws attention to the changing size, composition, and age structure of the family. These aspects matter because they refer to both the care needs and the labour capacity of the family as a whole and of its individual members. Thus, "the family cycle construct . . . introduced a developmental perspective into the historical study of the family" (Hareven 1978: 2).

However, the concept of the family life cycle also has serious limitations. It is modelled on the "normal," Western-type nuclear families of the first two-thirds of the twentieth century; it implies a "strong normative underpinning . . . [and] . . . a clear perception of the temporal order of family events"; and it excludes "deviant patterns" such as childless couples, single parents, divorced persons, or non-marital cohabitation (Konietzka and Kreyenfeld 2021: 75).[12] It is hardly a suitable concept for an analysis of the huge variety of historical European and non-Western forms of interaction between women's work and the family and for an exploration of the dynamics of recent change.

We prefer, therefore, Elder's concept of "linked or interdependent lives" (Elder 1998: 4), which is also particularly relevant for gendered perspectives on the work life course (Moen 2003). Elder, too, puts the emphasis on family relations, but his concept is open to diverse historical and cultural family forms and marriage patterns; to multiple sequences of family events; to the inclusion of wider kin networks, intergenerational relations beyond households, and non-related persons within households; and – going beyond family and kin – to the inclusion of "friends and coworkers" (Elder 1994: 6). "Linked lives" refers to the family as a kin group *and* as a work group and to the whole spectrum of social relations ranging from love and solidarity to bitter conflict.[13]

What does that mean for a long-term historical perspective on women's work over the life course? In the paragraphs that follow, we discuss major life course-related variations of the gendered division of labour from the early modern period to the present. For many years, historians of work and gender assumed that the social, economic, and cultural transformations of European societies throughout the early modern era (about 1500–1800, including merchant capitalism, state formation, religious reformation, etc.) led to the "growing gender division and the devaluation of women's labour," and that the emergence of industrial capitalism

---

12 On the fluidity and reversibility of family positions including motherhood, see Alber's chapter in this volume.

13 Several chapters of this volume conceptualise "linked lives" – not only, but also – as "battlefields of conflict" (Alber).

"sharpened" the gendered division of work and gender inequality further (Frader 2021: 31, 34). More recent research questions this view.[14]

Studies on the gendered division of labour in early modern Europe, for instance, reveal a complex pattern of similarity and difference between women's work and men's work. Both genders performed physically demanding labour, and men and women worked within and outside the home almost to the same extent. Household-based petty commodity production coexisted and merged with work and wage labour outside the household mainly due to a typical combination of agricultural, artisanal, proto-industrial, and trading activities. Among the lower classes and the middling sort, both genders were engaged in a variety of activities for basic sustenance and to earn a living. With increasing commercialisation and class differentiation, the scope of these activities widened, and the share of paid and income-generating work grew for both women and men. Research on early modern Sweden demonstrates that most activities (except military work) were carried out by both genders, but some were performed by men only whereas others were performed exclusively by women. A gendered division of labour certainly existed, but all in all, the "notions of gender specialisation and separate spheres are clearly inadequate" (Lindström et al. 2017: 237, 239–241).

Such regional findings are, presumably, not generalisable for either the whole of Europe or even just its northwest. On the one hand, strong guild regulations in southwestern Germany, for example, sought the exclusion of women from skilled work in the crafts and trades (Ogilvie 2003). In economically advanced regions such as England or the Netherlands, on the other hand, the options for women were probably even wider and more diverse than in Sweden (Ågren 2014: 398), and, consequently, the pressure on women to earn money was greater. The chapters on preindustrial work life courses in this volume confirm such ambiguous findings, providing examples of exclusively female work (Maynes and Waltner), exclusively male work (Joshi), and gender-independent work (Ehmer).

A life course perspective allows for further insights. The similarities and differences in men's and women's work were strongly influenced by age and life course phase. Children's work was characterised by strong similarities between sexes, and among (mainly adolescent) servants, the gendered division of labour was even less marked (Ogilvie 2003: 115, 121). For married women, the pattern is less clear. Sheilagh Ogilvie's study of southwestern Germany concludes that married women were

---

14 This includes a methodological turn that combines detailed micro-studies with large databases, which include both nominal, qualitative, and quantitative evidence. As paradigmatic examples, see several studies by Sheilagh Ogilvie (e.g. Ogilvie 2003) on early modern southwestern Germany and the scholarship of Maria Ågren (2014, 2018a, 2018b) on early modern Sweden – to mention just two particularly important scholars.

much more occupied with housework and care work than were daughters, maid-servants, and all categories of men although almost two-thirds of married women's workload was *not* domestic (Ogilvie 2003: 141). The Swedish research project on "Gender and Work," in contrast, points to the similarity of the labour of married men and women and to their shared position as heads of household (Ågren 2018a: 150). This supports the assumption that the division of labour between unmarried (mostly young) and married women (and widows) was stricter than the division of labour between genders (Ågren 2018b; Lindström et al. 2017: 243–248).

Several chapters of the present volume contribute to this debate. With respect to early modern Europe, *Ehmer's* article on life-cycle servants in husbandry, crafts, and trades strengthens – in a broad comparative view – the notion of a weak gendered division of labour among young people. In addition, *Ehmer* shows the impact of age and age-bound hierarchies among servants. Young apprentices in crafts and trades were used for various kinds of housework that would be refused by older apprentices or live-in journeymen. There is also an overlap of life course phase and social class. The labour relation between married and unmarried women was not only a relation between employer and wage worker but also a class relation in a wider sense as most servants came from lower-class families. That made it perhaps easier for a married women of the middling sort to rid herself of tasks she detested and "transfer the heaviest and most boring tasks to her own maid" (Lindström et al. 2017: 248).

Such "transfers" were not restricted to master–servant relations; they also structured the division of labour within the family and kinship networks. *Maynes* and *Waltner's* chapter in this volume shows that in textile production in early modern and early industrial Europe and China, spinning was one of the few jobs that was almost entirely women's work. Different marriage patterns and family systems, however, created a difference in the social status of spinners. In China, it was not servants or daughters but the daughters-in-law of the head of the household who carried the bulk of the workload. Such daughters-in-law were young girls, due to a family and kin system characterised by very early marriage and the cohabitation of fathers and married sons. In Europe, by contrast, unmarried girls and women formed the core of the labour force.

Household-based modes of production did not vanish from Europe with the Industrial Revolution but accompanied industrialisation and urbanisation throughout the nineteenth and – with decreasing importance – the twentieth centuries. Family economies in combination with extended family structures are still predominant in some rural regions of the Global South even if they are nowadays embedded in modernising societies with pluralistic ways of life. *Lentz's* chapter in this volume shows how age and generation hierarchies influence the division of labour in rural societies of present-day Ghana. Young married girls, for instance, are responsible for domestic and care work in the households of their parents-in-law. Elder sons and daughters have better chances than younger ones to leave the family economy and earn money elsewhere at least for a couple of years even if gerontocratic principles are increasingly undermined by meritocratic ones. Taken together, the contributions to the present volume strengthen the assumption that in very different historical settings, the division of labour by age and life course phase overlaid and sometimes even overruled the gendered division of labour.

The multiple relationships between housework, care work, and gainful employment in industrial and post-industrial societies

In pre-industrial modes of production as well as in contemporary family economies in some regions of the Global South, the household has been the very site where men's work and women's work overlap. The separation of the workplace from the household in the industrial age led to a substantial reconfiguration of the sexual division of labour, even more so because it has been accompanied by the spread of a bourgeois family ideal and gender ideology (Ehmer 2021b: 151–153). The principal assignment of housework and care work to women intensified, and its tension with gainful employment increased. Throughout the nineteenth and twentieth centuries, several patterns emerged to balance both sets of activities, which resulted in a variety of distinct female work life courses. Some of these patterns became hegemonic in certain historical periods and regions, but principally, all of them have coexisted as options to date, although with changing frequency and acceptance. In the following paragraphs, we discuss major patterns in an ideal-typical manner.

In the early stages of the Industrial Revolution, many women were fully employed in the industry or the service sector outside their homes continuously over their life course, from childhood to old age. Scholars agree on the labour force participation of working-class girls, single adult women, and widows; however, there is an ongoing discussion about the extent of married women's paid work. With respect to early nineteenth century Britain, some historians consider that "in a range of industries, especially textile manufacturing," many married women "remained in employment throughout much of their life cycle" (Rose 1986: 115). Others argue that in "mill towns" (i.e., towns dominated by textile factories), indeed "a significant minority of the female workforce was married," but that "the great majority of women left work shortly before marriage or soon after, and most never went back" (Seccombe 1993: 34).

The withdrawal of married women from employment outside their homes might have existed in England already in the early nineteenth century, but it was only at the turn of the century that it gradually became hegemonic across the entire industrialised world.[15] The socio-economic context of the breakthrough of the "male breadwinner/female housekeeper family" was the so-called "Second Industrial Revolution" from – roughly – the 1870s onwards: industrialisation began to encompass large parts of the economy; the factory became the predominant site of production; economic growth and technological diffusion accelerated; and mass production stimulated the mass consumption of an increasing variety of consumer goods. Trade unions gained influence and contributed to the reduction of work hours and the rise of real wages. Last but not least, these trends were accompanied by the final enforcement of compulsory schooling and, thus, the limitation of child labour. The cultural frame was the bourgeois family ideal, the ideology of "separate spheres" for women and men, and a redefinition of masculinity as an attribute of the sole breadwinner. Added to this frame was the growing importance of wives' proper household management for the well-being of working-class families. Married women had not "left work" but exchanged wage labour for intensified and increasingly sophisticated housework and parenting (Seccombe 1993: 45–49). An often overlooked precondition of the functioning of the breadwinner–housekeeper model, however, was stable marital relations. *Karim's* chapter in this volume reminds us of the many husbands who were unreliable or abandoned their families, thus turning their wives into sole breadwinners.

A life course perspective paints a more nuanced picture. One of the pioneering historical studies on shifts between unpaid work in the family and gainful employment over the life course was Louise A. Tilly and Joan W. Scott's *Women, Work, and the Family* (1978), which was to become a classic of feminist social history. Tilly and Scott were among the first historians who used the life course approach as a major methodological tool. They identified a relatively stable British work life course pattern from about 1850 to 1960, which was characterised by a very high labour force participation rate for girls and single women, a still high but lower rate for childless married women, an extremely low rate for married women with children under five years old, and an again rising rate of employment when children

---

15 There are ongoing discussions among historians on questions of when, how, and where this model became hegemonic – as an ideal and as an actual practice, and, particularly, why. Here is not the place to elaborate on such questions. What we can take for granted, however, is that monocausal explanations are not helpful (Janssens 1997: 22). For studies looking beyond the Western world, see Joshi 2002.

grew older and particularly when married women themselves aged. This pattern became famous as the "U-curve" of female employment and labour force participation over the life course, which seems to be typical for highly industrialised societies – such as Britain – between the mid-nineteenth and mid-twentieth centuries. The curve gives the impression that the withdrawal of women from paid work during a certain life course phase due to marriage and motherhood had indeed become hegemonic but also that only a minority of women practiced this pattern in its pure form. The "U" rather symbolises a gradual removal from and an equally gradual return into the labour force over the life course.

The "U-curve" certainly represents a clear break with pre- and early industrial female work life patterns, which have been characterised by a different metaphor, namely the "N-curve" as an expression of the "substantial fluctuations in women's time allocation between household and income earning work" (Ogilvie 2003: 337 f.). Micro-sociological and micro-historical studies, however, question such a juxtaposition. Already in 1901, Seebohm Rowntree's classical study on poverty in the English city of York around 1900 concludes that it was "unusual for the wife to go out to work if her husband is in employment" (71). But a married woman was expected to work outside home when her husband was ill or unemployed, or – as a widow – after his death. Hareven's (1982) study on "family time and industrial time" in the Amoskeag Manufacturing Company in Manchester, New Hampshire, from about 1900 to the 1930s, the period when it was the world's largest textile mill, reveals an even higher flexibility of labour force participation of married women. Married women principally stopped or reduced work in the factory after marriage and even more so when children began to earn (Hareven 1982: 182–214), but they were also ready to come back on a short-term basis when their family needed additional income; when the company needed additional workers for a limited time, as in case of big orders; when another family member – for instance because of illness – had to be replaced on the shop floor; or when the husband's earning capacity decreased due to old age. Married women dropped out and returned and "timed their jobs in relation to the rhythms of family life" (Hareven 1982: 130). Their flexibility was based on two conditions. First, as former full-time workers, they were familiar with work processes and machinery. Second, they were part of female networks that cared for children in the absence of mothers, including grandmothers, other kin, or neighbours who were just out of employment (Hareven 1982: 204 f.). Such evidence suggests that the long-lasting "N-curve" and the shorter-lived "U-curve" of female work life courses are not only ideal-types specific to particular historical periods but that, in practice, they also merge.

The present volume contributes to the discussion of the male breadwinner/female housekeeper model from two angles. First, full employment by women over substantial parts of their life course and family cycle, including marriage and motherhood, must not be neglected. Several chapters show that full employment of married women and mothers remained an option throughout the last two centuries and that it gained particular significance in historic constellations characterised by the high demand for industrial workers. Industrialisation projects and the establishment of factory industries created a particular desire of companies and states to mobilise a sufficient, cheap, and not necessarily skilled workforce composed of both genders, including married women. This becomes particularly apparent in the chapters by *Maynes* and *Waltner* (in connection with the transformation of textile production from the household to the factory in nineteenth-century China and France); by *Zimmermann* and by *Li* (in the context of the rapid industrialisation efforts of state-socialist regimes in Hungary and China after 1945); and by *Karim* (in the framework of the rapid expansion of the garment industry in south-east Asia starting in the 1980s). These chapters make a significant contribution to the history of married women's work as they address various strategies women used to reconcile factory work with family obligations. *Zimmermann* shows the extent to which the ILO in the 1960s was concerned about the difficulties mothers faced when trying "to combine home and work responsibilities." Extended child-care leave, for the first time introduced in Hungary in the 1960s, was one of the measures discussed. Already in the 1930s, Shanghai textile workers went on strike for paid maternity leave (Maynes and Waltner). Societies in which girls are regularly married off at early ages constitute a special case. In *Karim's* chapter on contemporary Bangladeshi female garment workers, marriage occurs around the age of fifteen – as was usual under Muslim law – and coincides with their leaving the village and starting factory work in a city. In China, the tradition of early marriage and extended-family households prevailed far into the industrial age. Around 1900, both single and married young women were sent to urban textile factories in cities like Shanghai, where they lived in dormitories set up by the enterprise (Maynes and Waltner). In both cases, children were left behind or sent back to be cared for by their rural extended families.

The actual duration of "full employment over the life course" depended, however, not only on decisions by women themselves or family strategies but also on the willingness of management to employ elderly workers. In the Bangladeshi garment industry, for example, women are usually phased out of their jobs in their mid-thirties, after having served their companies for about twenty years and often suffering from exhaustion and bad health (Karim). In nineteenth-century European industrial labour markets, elderly workers of both genders also were confronted with age discrimination. In Britain in the 1850s as well as in Germany about 1900, to be forty or fifty years old was considered a critical turning point beyond which it was hard to keep one's job in industry and almost impossible to get a new one after dismissal. In all these cases, elderly industrial workers had to go on with odd jobs or return to agricultural work in the regions from which they originated (Ehmer 1988; Ehmer 1990: 64–69).

Labour-migrating women and couples experience particular difficulties in caring for their children as they have to work hard to gain foothold abroad (such as the Cape Verde emigrants to the United States in *Drotbohm's* chapter) or to earn enough to have a livelihood back home in the off season (like Deneva's Bulgarian temporary migrants to western Europe). Kinship networks – or simply grandparents – in the (former) homelands of migrants are a vital resource for providing care for working mothers' children. Moreover, married women's work outside the home cannot be limited to factories or offices, particularly not in a global perspective. A widespread activity of married women in various African urban settings is, for instance, running a stall at local markets as vendor or monger of a wide range of products. In such a situation, young girls from different branches of rural families might be recruited to serve as "helpers" in urban households, as Alber shows in her chapter.

Second, two chapters in this volume demonstrate that the breadwinner–housekeeper model was not only a hegemonic and variable system but that in specific historical situations, it had the potential to be transformed into an enforced life course regime. During the period of Austro-Fascism (1933–1938), this particularly concerned civil servants. Married women were not allowed to enter work as public employees or were dismissed when already in employment if their husband was also employed in the civil service (Garstenauer). German National Socialists even tried to apply such principles to the whole workforce; they campaigned against "double earners" and designed the attractive offer of "marriage loans" (from 1933) as a means to keep married women away from paid work (Somcutean 2022). In Japan, it was during the post-war economic boom when the model of a "standard life course" was designed, and it was based on two pillars: the male "standard worker" and the "standard family" with a housewife at its centre. The Toyota Motor Corporation became an ideal-typical exemplification of this model. In the late 1950s, "labour and management agreed upon forcing married women out of employment" (Tanaka). In a range of political systems, not only totalitarian states, such norms might have been firmly established due to patriarchal traditions, which have been, for many centuries, "endemic to European [and not only European, J.E./C.L.] culture, a resource to be drawn upon and an ideal to be invoked as the occasion requires" (de Vries 2008: 214).

The third quarter of the twentieth century shows ambivalent attitudes towards married women's paid work. Kohli regards the 1960s as the culmination of the "'Fordist' model of social structure and the life course" in advanced capitalist economies, which "consisted in a 'normal work biography' of continuous full-time employment and long job tenure for most of the male population – with most women gravitating around a male breadwinner with various forms of limited engagement in paid work or none at all" (Kohli 2007: 257 f.). In some European countries, such as Sweden, "the highpoint of the breadwinner–homemaker household roughly occurred between 1930 and 1970, with a crescendo in the 1950s," particularly for the blue-collar working class (Edvinsson and Nordlund Edvinsson 2017: 172, 181).

At the same time, however, critical views gained momentum. The work of housewives became regarded as unproductive, unstimulating, and generally dissatisfactory, especially if a housewife was not caring for small children (as a paradigmatic example, see Myrdal and Klein 1956). Labour and women's movements stressed women's "right to work," and in the state-socialist regions of Europe, female gainful employment was propagated as major path towards gender equality (see, generally, Zimmermann; for the example of the German Democratic Republic, see also Trappe 1995; Trappe 2015: 232–233). And indeed, the labour force participation rate for married women began to rise from the 1960s onwards at increasing speed. In "recent decades the rise in female labour force participation has been driven primarily, often exclusively, by the growing participation of married women, especially married women with children" (de Vries 2008: 247). Marriage ceased to be a relevant factor for leaving the workforce,[16] and motherhood was no longer an automatic reason for withdrawal from the labour market – even if the birth of a child usually leads to interruptions of work careers in accordance with respective national maternity leave regulations. In the vastly different economic and political systems of the United States and the GDR, it was the generation born in the 1950s and 1960s for whom the U-curve of female labour force participation over the life course disappeared almost completely, and male and female work life courses converged (Huinink, Mayer, and Trappe 1995: 109; de Vries 2008: 247–251). A general trend throughout the Western world in the later decades of the twentieth century was the expansion of women's educational and occupational opportunities, which often manifested in a "seismic divide in the life choices" available to women of two generations, namely mothers and daughters (Carr 2009: XIII–XIV).[17]

---

16 This was certainly interrelated with the general decline of marriage as an institution or a precondition for cohabitation. See Edvinsson and Nordlund Edvinsson 2017: 185.

17 Convergence of work life courses, however, does not automatically mean gender equality. An important topic in sociological life course research concerns the current "gendered life course regimes" and "dual careers" of spouses. See, for instance, Krüger 2001, 2003; Moen 2003, Moen and Han 2001. Kohli observes that "with regard to the 'linked lives' of women and men . . ., there is . . . a persistent inequality. As a result, the mutual harmonization of the life course options of the two

Nevertheless, the developments in the GDR and the United States do not represent a general pattern but rather the extreme poles on a broad spectrum of variations. Continuous full-time female employment over the whole work life course is still an exception in many European countries, and parenthood continues to be an important factor for the reduction of gainful employment, which goes beyond short-term interruptions of paid work around birth and during the first years of a child's life. The most common longer-term strategy to reconcile wage work with care work and parenting is part-time work, and part-time work is in most countries an almost exclusively female affair.[18] Already in the 1960s, the ILO recommended part-time work as one of the strategies to reconcile paid work and "family responsibilities" (Zimmermann). The rising popularity of part-time work from the 1970s onwards, however, was strongly related to the restructuring of the European economy and particularly to de-industrialisation. Downsized industries became almost entirely male, while women moved to the expanding service sector, which offers – and partly enforces – higher flexibility in working hours (Raphael). For this reason, the gendered division of work was redefined but not eliminated.[19] Among German women born in the 1950s, there was hardly anyone who did not experience part-time episodes in their work biographies (Klammer and Tillmann 2001: 152, 153). However, permanent part-time work is an exception as well. Women's work biographies are rather characterised by the combination of different forms of work and non-work (Kohli 2007: 262). In Germany, a clear majority of women experience episodes of full-time employment, part-time work, unemployment, and non-work over their life course (Klammer 2006: 2675). The expectations on women and their readiness to increase or reduce their paid work and to harmonise it with the demands of household and family, husband and children, and with their own – often ambivalent and changing – expected roles or identities reproduces gender differences in life course patterns and work biographies. The long-term trend of male and female work biographies and career trajectories reveals processes of convergence as well as new forms of divergence and, in the back-

partners remains more important for women, and they more often adjust their options to those of their male partners than vice versa" (Kohli 2007: 262).

18 However, there are strong differences within Europe both with respect to the share of part-time work and its gender allocation (Möhring 2016).

19 A similar redefinition took place in South Asia, although in the reverse direction. The global perspective of the present volume reminds us that the female exodus from industry in Europe was part and parcel of the relocation of textile and garment industries to Southeast Asia and, therefore, of the emergence of a female industrial working class in countries like Bangladesh, India, and China. See Karim and, generally, Mezzadri 2019.

ground, the persistent continuity of gender differences "in the work-family nexus" (Kohli 2007: 265).

* * *

The name of the research centre where the editors of this volume were privileged to have been fellows, "Work and Human Lifecycle in Global History," promised a focus on the life course, which was intended to distinguish the centre from other research institutions that focused on the global history of work and labour. Nevertheless, our experience has been that there was a certain gap between the high-level programmatic emphasis on the life course and fellows' actual research agendas. With this in mind, the aim of our volume is twofold.

First, we want to highlight the importance of the concept of the life course for a deeper understanding of the wide variety of work activities people perform and experience over time. This variety is partly due to the impact of gender, class, and the societal division of labour, but also relates to age, social role, position in the family, and to the influence of earlier life events on subsequent ones. We are convinced this volume demonstrates that an interest in the life course is indispensable for a fuller and nuanced analysis of the dynamics of historical change in the world of work and its impact on working men's and women's identities.

Second, we consider an interdisciplinary approach essential for this endeavour, and we want to promote dialogue among scholars of sociology, anthropology, and history about the connections between work and the life course in various past and present social contexts. For this book, we have invited scholars from various disciplines to provide fresh empirical evidence and conceptual ideas to the analysis of the work–life course entanglement. Therefore, the geographic, historical, and methodological scope of the contributions is very wide. We believe that precisely this wide horizon and the unusual connections and comparisons that we have identified in this introduction, in the thematic clusters, and in the sections on cross-cutting issues, help unsettle premature certainties in life course research. They open up new perspectives on the theoretically and empirically productive relations between research on the life course and the study of work and labour.

References

Alber, Erdmute. 2012. "Schooling or Working? How Family Decision Processes, Children's Agencies and State Policy Influence the Life Paths of Children in Northern Benin." In *African Children at Work: Working and Learning in Growing Up for Life*, edited by Gerd Spittler and Michael Bourdillon, 169–194. Münster: LIT.

Ågren, Maria. 2014. "Emissaries, Allies, Accomplices and Enemies: Married Women's Work in Eighteenth-Century Urban Sweden." *Urban History* 41, no. 3: 394–414.

Ågren, Maria. 2018a. "Making Her Turn Around: The Verb-Oriented Method, the Two-Supporter Model, and the Focus on Practice." *Early Modern Women: An Interdisciplinary Journal* 13, no. 1: 144–152.

Ågren, Maria. 2018b. "The Complexities of Work: Analyzing Men's and Women's Work in the Early Modern World with the Verb-Oriented Method." In *What is Work? Gender at the Crossroads of Home, Family, and Business from the Early Modern Era to the Present*, edited by Raffaela Sarti, Anna Bellavitis, and Manuela Martini, 226–242. Oxford: Berghahn.

Ariès, Philippe. 1962. *Centuries of Childhood: A Social History of Family Life*. New York: Vintage.

Beattie, Cordelia. 2010. "Economy." In *A Cultural History of Childhood and Family*, edited by Sandro Cavallo and Sylvia Evangelisti, 49–67. Oxford: Berg.

Beck, Ulrich. 1999. *Schöne neue Arbeitswelt. Vision: Weltbürgergesellschaft*. Frankfurt am Main: Campus.

Bengtson, Vern L., Glen H. Elder Jr., and Norella M. Putney. 2005. "The Lifecourse Perspective on Ageing: Linked Lives, Timing, and History." In *The Cambridge Handbook on Age and Ageing*, edited by Malcolm L. Johnson, 493–509. Cambridge: Cambridge University Press.

Breman, Jan, and Marcel van der Linden. 2014. "Informalizing the Economy: The Return of the Social Question at a Global Level." *Development and Change* 45, no. 5: 920–940.

Carr, Deborah. 2009. "Preface." In *Encyclopedia of the Life Course and Human Development*. Vol. 1: *Childhood and Adolescence*, edited by Deborah Carr, XI–XVIII. Detroit, MI: Macmillan Reference USA, Gale eBooks.

Conrad, Christoph. 2015. "Work-Retirement Arrangements in an Aging World: Inter-Temporal and Transnational Perspectives." *Conference Volume, International Research Centre: Work and Human Lifecycle in Global History, Sixth Annual Conference*, Berlin, July 2015.

de Vries, Jan. 2008. *The Industrious Revolution: Consumer Behaviour and the Household Economy, 1650 to the Present*. Cambridge: Cambridge University Press.

Edvinsson, Rodbey, and Therese Nordlund Edvinsson. 2017. "Explaining the Swedish 'Housewife Era' of 1930–1970: Joint Utility Maximisation or Renewed Patriarchy?" *Scandinavian Economic History Review* 65, no. 2: 169–188.

Ehmer, Josef. 1988. "Lohnarbeit und Lebenszyklus im Kaiserreich." *Geschichte und Gesellschaft* 14, no. 4: 448–471.

Ehmer, Josef. 1990. *Sozialgeschichte des Alters*. Frankfurt am Main: Suhrkamp.

Ehmer, Josef. 2015. "Work Versus Leisure: Historical Roots of the Dissociation of Work and Later Life in Twentieth-Century Europe." In *Challenges of Aging: Pensions, Retirement and Generational Justice*, edited by Cornelius Torp, 135–164. Basingstoke: Palgrave Macmillan.

Ehmer, Josef. 2018. "Zur Geschichte des Normalarbeitsverhältnisses. Rekonstruktion und Kritik." In *Normalarbeit – Vergangenheit oder Zukunft?*, edited by Johanna Muckenhuber, Josef Hödl, and Martin Griesbacher, 21–39. Bielefeld: Transcript.

Ehmer, Josef. 2021a. "Alter, Altern, Arbeitswelt." In *Handbuch Alter und Altern. Anthropologie – Kultur – Ethik*, edited by Michael Fuchs, 232–241. Stuttgart: Metzler.

Ehmer, Josef. 2021b. "A Historical Perspective on Family Change in Europe." In *Handbook on the Sociology of the Family (Research Handbooks in Sociology)*, edited by Norbert F. Schneider and Michaela Kreyenfeld, 143–161. Cheltenham: Edward Elgar.

Elder, Glen H., Jr. 1974. *Children of the Great Depression: Social Change in Life Experience*. Chicago, IL: University of Chicago Press.

Elder, Glen H. Jr. 1978. "Family History and the Life Course." In *Transitions: The Family and the Life Course in Historical Perspective*, edited by Tamara K. Hareven, 17–64. New York: Academic Press.

Elder, Glen H. Jr. 1994. "Time, Human Agency, and Social Change: Perspectives on the Life Course." *Social Psychology Quarterly* 75, no. 1: 4–15.

Elder, Glen H. Jr. 1998. "The Life Course as Developmental Theory." *Child Development* 69, no. 1: 1–12.

Fourastié, Jean. 1979. *Les Trente Glorieuses, ou la révolution invisble de 1946 à 1975*. Paris: Fayard.

Frader, Laura Levine. 2021. "Gender and Labor in World History." In *A Companion to Global Gender History*, edited by Teresa A. Meade and Merry E. Wiesner-Hanks, 27–42. Hoboken, NJ: John Wiley & Sons.

Hareven, Tamara K. 1978. "Introduction: The Historical Study of the Life Course." In *Transitions: The Family and the Life Course in Historical Perspective*, edited by Tamara K. Hareven, 1–16. New York: Academic Press.

Hareven, Tamara K. 1982. *Family Time and Industrial Time: The Relationship between the Family and Work in a New England Industrial Community*. Cambridge: Cambridge University Press.

Hareven, Tamara K. 1991. "The History of the Family and the Complexity of Social Change." *The American Historical Review* 96, no. 1: 95–124.

Hareven, Tamara K. 2001. "The Impact of Family History and the Life Course on Social History." In *Family History Revisited: Comparative Perspectives*, edited by Richard Wall, Tamara K. Hareven, and Josef Ehmer, 21–39. Newark: University of Delaware Press.

Heinz, Walter R., and Victor M. Marshall, eds. 2003. *Social Dynamics of the Life Course: Transitions, Institutions, and Interrelations*. New York: Aldine de Gruyter.

Heinz, Walter R., Johannes Huinink, and Ansgar Weymann. 2006. "General Introduction." In *The Life Course Reader: Individuals and Societies Across Time*, edited by Walter R. Heinz, Johannes Huinink, and Ansgar Weymann, 15–22. Frankfurt am Main: Campus.

Huinink, Johannes, Karl Ulrich Mayer, and Heike Trappe. 2015. "Staatliche Lenkung und individuelle Karrierechancen. Bildungs- und Berufsverläufe." In *Kollektiv und Eigensinn. Lebensverläufe in der DDR und danach*, edited by Johannes Huinink, Karl Ulrich Mayer, Martin Diewald, Heike Solga, Annemette Sorensen, and Heike Trappe, 89–143. Berlin: Akademie Verlag.

Humphries, Jane. 2010. *Childhood and Child Labour in the British Industrial Revolution*. Cambridge: Cambridge University Press.

Janssens, Angélique. 1997. "The Rise and Decline of the Male Breadwinner Family? An Overview of the Debate." *International Review of Social History* 42: 1–23.

Joshi, Chitra. 2002. "Notes on the Breadwinner Debate: Gender and Household Strategies in Working-Class Families." *Studies in History* 18, no. 2: 261–274.

Klammer, Ute. 2006. "Flexicurity in der Lebenslaufperspektive." In *Soziale Ungleichheit, kulturelle Unterschiede. Verhandlungen des 32. Kongresses der Deutschen Gesellschaft für Soziologie in München*. Volumes 1 and 2, edited by Karl-Siegbert Rehberg, 2673–2684. Frankfurt am Main: Campus.

Klammer, Ute, and Katja Tillmann. 2001. *Flexicurity. Soziale Sicherung und Flexibilisierung der Arbeits- und Lebensverhältnisse. Forschungsbericht*. Düsseldorf: Wirtschafts- und Sozialwissenschaftliches Institut (WSI)/Hans-Boeckler-Stiftung.

Kohli, Martin. 2007. "The Institutionalization of the Life Course: Looking Back to Look Ahead." *Research in Human Development* 4, no. 3–4: 253–271.

Konietzka, Dirk, and Michaela Kreyenfeld. 2021. "Life Course Sociology: Key Concepts and Applications in Family Sociology." In *Research Handbook on the Sociology of the Family*, edited by Norbert F. Schneider and Michaela Kreyenfeld, 73–87. Cheltenham: Edward Elgar.

Krüger, Helga. 2001. "Social Change in Two Generations: Employment Patterns and Their Cost for Family Life." In *Restructuring Work and the Life Course,* edited by Victor W. Marshall, Walter R. Heinz, Helga Krüger, and Anil Verma, 401–423. Toronto: University of Toronto Press.

Krüger, Helga. 2003. "The Life-Course Regime: Ambiguities Between Interrelatedness and Individualization." In *Social Dynamics of the Life Course: Transitions, Institutions, and Interrelations,* edited by Walter R. Heinz and Victor M. Marshall, 237–258. New York: Aldine de Gruyter.

Lindström, Jonas, Karin Hassan Jansson, Rosemarie Fiebranz, Benny Jacobsson, and Maria Ågren. 2017. "Mistress or Maid: The Structure of Women's Work in Sweden, 1550–1800." *Continuity and Change* 32, no. 2: 225–252.

Loomis, Charles P. 1936. "The Study of the Life Cycle of Families." *Rural Sociology* 1, no. 2: 180–199.

Luborsky, Mark R., and Ian M. LeBlanc. 2003. "Cross-Cultural Perspectives on the Concept of Retirement: An Analytical Redefinition." *Journal of Cross-Cultural Gerontology* 18: 251–271.

Macmillan, Ross, ed. 2005. *The Structure of the Life Course: Standardized? Individualized? Differentiated?* Amsterdam: Elsevier.

Mannheim, Karl. 1928/1952. "The Problem of Generations." In *Essays on the Sociology of Knowledge,* 276–322. London: Routledge & Keagan Paul.

Marshall, Victor W., Walter R. Heinz, Helga Krüger, and Anil Verma, eds. 2001. *Restructuring Work and the Life Course.* Toronto: University of Toronto Press.

Marshall, Victor W., and Margaret M. Mueller. 2003. "Theoretical Roots of the Life-Course Perspective." In *The Social Dynamics of the Life Course: Transitions, Institutions, and Interrelations,* edited by Walter R. Heinz and Victor M. Marshall, 3–32. New York: Aldine de Gruyter.

Mayer, Karl Ulrich. 2004. "Whose Lives? How History, Societies, and Institutions Define and Shape Life Courses." *Research in Human Development* 1, no. 3: 161–187.

Mayer, Karl Ulrich. 2009 "New Directions on Life Course Research." *Annual Review of Sociology* 35: 413–433.

Mayer-Ahuja, Nicole. 2003. *Wieder dienen lernen? Vom westdeutschen "Normalarbeitsverhältnis" zu prekärer Beschäftigung seit 1973.* Berlin: edition sigma.

Mezzadri, Alessandra. 2019. "The Afterlife of Cheap Labour: Bangalore Garment Workers from Factories to the Informal Economy." *Working Paper CIVIDEP India & Female Employment & Dynamics of Inequality (FEDI) Network,* no. 12.1.8.1: 2–12.

Moen, Phyllis. 2003. "Linked Lives: Dual Careers, Gender, and the Contingent Life Course." In *Social Dynamics of the Life Course: Transitions, Institutions, and Interrelations,* edited by Walter R. Heinz and Victor M. Marshall, 237–258. New York: Aldine de Gruyter.

Moen, Phyllis, and Shin-Kap Han. 2001. "Reframing Careers: Work, Family, and Gender." In *Restructuring Work and the Life Course,* edited by Victor W. Marshall, Walter R. Heinz, Helga Krüger, and Anil Verma, 424–445. Toronto: University of Toronto Press.

Möhring, Katia. 2016. "Life Course Regimes in Europe: Individual Employment Histories in Comparative and Historical Perspective." *Journal of European Social Policy* 26, no. 2: 124–139.

Myrdal, Alva, and Viola Klein. 1956. *Women's Two Roles: Home and Work.* London: Routledge & Kegan Paul.

Nederveen-Meerkerk, Elise van. 2012. "The First 'Male Breadwinner Economy'? Dutch Married Women's and Children's Paid and Unpaid Work in Western Europe Perspective, c. 1600–1900." In *Working on Labour: Essays in Honor of Jan Lucassen,* edited by Marcel van der Linden and Leo Lucassen, 323–352. Leiden: Brill.

Ogilvie, Sheilagh. 2003. *A Bitter Living: Women, Markets, and Social Capital in Early Modern Germany.* Oxford: Oxford University Press.

Papathanassiou, Maria. 1999. *Zwischen Arbeit, Spiel und Schule. Die ökonomische Funktion der Kinder ärmerer Schichten in Österreich 1880-1939.* Wien: Verlag für Geschichte und Politik.

Polak, Barbara. 2012. "Peasants in the Making: Bamana Children at Work." In *African Children at Work: Working and Learning in Growing Up for Life,* edited by Gerd Spittler and Michael Bourdillon, 87–112. Münster: LIT.

Rose, Sonya O. 1986. "'Gender at Work': Sex, Class and Industrial Capitalism." *History Workshop* 21: 113–131.

Rowntree, B. Seebohm. 1901. *Poverty: A Study of Town Life.* London: Macmillan.

Seccombe, Wally. 1993. *Weathering the Storm: Working-Class Families from the Industrial Revolution to the Fertility Decline.* London: Verso.

Somcutean, Cristina. 2022. "Mass Weddings, Baby Boom and Full Employment? Nazi Germany's 1933 Marriage Loan and Its Efficacy in Theory and Practice." *Jahrbuch für Wirtschaftsgeschichte/ Economic History Yearbook* 63, no. 1: 267–301.

Spittler, Gerd, and Michael Bourdillon, eds. 2012. *African Children at Work: Working and Learning in Growing Up for Life.* Münster: LIT.

Tilly, Louise A., and Joan W. Scott. 1978. *Women, Work, and the Family.* London: Routledge.

Trappe, Heike. 1995. *Emanzipation oder Zwang. Frauen in der DDR zwischen Beruf, Familie und Sozialpolitik.* Berlin: Akademie Verlag.

Trappe, Heike, Matthias Pollmann-Schult, and Christian Schmitt, "The Rise and Decline of the Male Breadwinner Model: Institutional Underpinnings and Future Expectations." *European Sociological Review* 31: 230–242.

van den Bersselaar, Dmitri. 2011. "'Old Timers Who Still Keep Going': Retirement in Ghana?" *Österreichische Zeitschrift für Geschichtswissenschaften* 22, no. 3: 136–152.

Wadauer, Sigrid. 2021. *Der Arbeit nachgehen? Auseinandersetzungen um Lebensunterhalt und Mobilität (Österreich 1880-1938).* Wien/Köln/Weimar: Böhlau.

Wirsching, Andreas. 2009. "Erwerbsbiographien und Privatheitsformen. Die Entstandardisierung von Lebensläufen." *Auf dem Weg in eine neue Moderne? Die Bundesrepublik Deutschland in den siebziger und achtziger Jahren,* edited by Thomas Raithel, Andreas Rödder, and Andreas Wirsching, 83–87. München: Oldenbourg Verlag.

Karl Ulrich Mayer, Rolf Becker, and Anette Fasang
The Puzzle of Flexibilization: Stability and Changes in Working Lives in (West) Germany, 1920s to 2015. Evidence from Quantitative Life-Course Research

Introduction

"That lives have become less predictable, less collectively determined, less stable, less orderly, more flexible, and more individualized has become one of the most commonly accepted perceptions of advanced societies" (Brückner and Mayer 2005: 28). This core tenet of the self-understanding of contemporary societies applies especially to the sphere of work and the degree of continuity and discontinuity in the trajectories of working lives. There is a multitude of good reasons to assume massive changes: de-industrialisation and the rise of the service economy, globalisation, the decline of trade-union membership and power, the increasing share of the female labour force, automation, and occupational restructuring, as well as value changes in the direction of post-materialism and self-realisation.

While the general idea of major changes in working lives has been readily accepted, it is much less clear whether these changes are merely strong beliefs or actual facts. It has also been less clear which specific changes are being hypothesised, e. g., the increase of inter- or intra-firm job shifts, occupational mismatches and occupational changes, recurrent moves in and out of employment, or the increase of downward career mobility. Additionally, there is considerable confusion concerning when – that is, in which historical period – such changes occurred and what the shape of historical change looks like (e. g., continuous trends versus periodic shocks).

The empirical evidence is scattered and inconclusive. Many studies are cross-sectional or cover only short – and diverse – periods of time. Historians often rely more on actual discourses or selections of biographical material rather than on representative quantitative data. And data on the composition of the labour

Acknowledgments: We gratefully acknowledge exemplary research support by Antonino Polizzi and critical comments by Malte Reichelt. Anette Fasang gratefully acknowledges funding from the project EQUALLIVES, which is financially supported by the NORFACE Joint Research Programme on Dynamics of Inequality Across the Life-course, which is co-funded by the European Commission through Horizon 2020 under grant agreement No 724363.

force is generally used rather than longitudinal observations on working lives. Controversies about the stability and orderliness of working lives can only be resolved if we focus on longer-term observations across both lifetime and history, and if we carefully distinguish between specific aspects of work trajectories.

After a review of the debate on the transformation of working lives and some conceptual clarification, this chapter analyses the recently available empirical evidence on long-term changes in working lives in (West) Germany. It is based on various longitudinal sources for tracing the life courses of women and men born between the 1920s and the 1980s, whose working lives ran from roughly 1940 to 2015. Our conclusion is that – at least for (West-) Germany – we do not find much support for the alleged trends. We conclude with our reflections on why we do not observe what appears so believable.

The Debate about the Transformation of Work Lives

Beliefs about the loss of the stability in working lives have been at the core of a wider debate about changes in the sphere of work (Ehmer 2018; Mayer 2000). In this section we present those elements of this debate that have been particularly influential for and relevant to our topic.

In 1999, Richard Sennett published his book, *The Corrosion of Character*, which was based on observations he made about the children of (US) American individuals he had interviewed approximately twenty-five years earlier for his book *The Hidden Injuries of Class* (Sennett and Cobb 1972). In his later book, he observed a fundamental change in the structure and the meaning of work. In what he calls "flexible capitalism," workers no longer have "careers," i. e., lifelong economic pursuits; rather they are expected to be "flexible" and "open to change" at short notice.

Traditional jobs gave meaning to life as a linear narrative and contributed to self-respect. New "flexible" jobs do not necessarily imply lesser wages, but for many people, moving and changing jobs frequently are indicative of a loss of control:

> The most tangible sign of . . . change might be the motto "No long term." In work, the traditional career progressing step by step through the corridors of one or two institutions is withering; so is the deployment of a single set of skills through the course of a working life. Today, a young American with at least two years of college can expect to change jobs at least eleven times in the course of working, and change his or her skill base at least three times during those forty years of labor. (Sennett 1999: 22)

Sennett relegates the former, more stable jobs to a relatively short period, approximately the three decades following Second World War, which were characterised by an advanced economy that included strong unions, welfare state guarantees, and large-scale corporations. In contrast, long-term work experience has become rare. New flexible work also impacts other social relations like the family: "How can a human being develop a narrative of identity and life history in a society composed of episodes and fragments? The conditions of the new economy feed instead on experience which drifts in time, from place to place, from job to job" (Sennett 1999: 26–27).

One of the changes that has taken place is the loss of skill.[1] Sennett gives the example of bakers who monitor machines but no longer know how to bake bread. "Overqualification is a sign of the polarisation which marks the new regime" (Sennett 1999: 89). Occupational mobility becomes an unintelligible process, more often going sideways than upward: "Failure is no longer the normal prospect facing only the very poor or disadvantaged; it has become more familiar as a regular event in the lives of the middle classes. . . . Downsizings and reengineerings impose on middle-class people sudden disasters which were in an earlier capitalism much more confined to the working classes" (Sennett 1999: 118).

While Richard Sennett's essay has become the most compelling story intertwining new forms of work with the "corrosion of character" and the breakdown of collective trust, Arne L. Kalleberg's review article from 2000 has become a classic for its empirical evidence on "non-standard employment relations." Like Sennett, Kalleberg traces micro-level changes in work in the macro-changes to the economy since the 1970s: global economic changes, increased competitive pressure for profit, increasing unemployment, improvements in communication and information technology, outsourcing, just-in-time production, avoidance or circumvention of labour protections for core workers, and demographic changes in the composition of the labour force, whereby the increased presence of married women and older workers in the workforce has meant an increasing preference for flexibility through non-standard work arrangements (Kalleberg 2000: 342).

Kalleberg's review covered the following forms of non-standard work: part-time work, temporary and contract employment arranged through third parties (agencies), short-term employment, contingent work, and independent contracting. While the evidence Kalleberg marshals is mixed with regard to the types of non-standard work and the comparison between the United States and European countries, and while he calls for both better measures and better data, his overall con-

---

1 In contrast to this thesis of de-skilling, there have been claims and evidence for skill upgrading (Oesch and Piccitto 2019; Spitz-Oener 2006).

clusion is that there has been an increase in the incidence and forms of non-standard kinds of work.[2]

The most radical, or at any rate the most pronounced version of the new world of work has been developed by Ulrich Beck over nearly twenty years (1986, 1999, 2000). He calls it "Brazilianization," which is the idea that the labour markets of advanced societies have increasingly come to resemble the fragmented and precarious economies of Latin America. A minority of workers have permanent work contracts: "the impact of the precarious, discontinuous, relaxed, and informal into Western work" (Beck 1999: 8). This is postulated as taking many forms: the shrinking of wage labour, precarious and informal job arrangements, the increase of marginally self-employed and temporary workers, workers with fixed-term contracts, people working in the "shadow economy", unemployment and underemployment, and high-tech nomads. For Germany in the year 2000, Beck predicted that only half of all dependent workers would have "normal jobs": full-time, continuous employment cushioned by health, unemployment, and old-age insurance (Beck 1999: 86). He viewed the transformation of "normal biographies" into self-constructed biographies as one of the main consequences of the new flexibility of labour. Employment is 'segmented' (*zerhackt*) both in time and in contracts. Against this dismal picture, Beck then proposes an alternative, positive model: from a society based on wage labour to a society based on plural forms of labour and "civic work".[3]

In the first decade of the millennium, globalisation came into the debate as a new (and additional) mega-trend fostering even more discontinuous working lives and non-standard employment relationships. This topic was promoted by the large-scale project on "Life Courses in the Globalization Process" (GLOBALIFE) directed by Hans-Peter Blossfeld, Melinda Mills, and their group of international collaborators (Blossfeld et al. 2006a; Blossfeld et al. 2006b). GLOBALIFE characterised globalisation as a set of joint processes: the internationalisation of markets and the decline of national borders, the intensification of competition, the spread of global networks of people and practises linked by information technology, and the predominance of market coordination (Blossfeld et al. 2006b: 4–5). For countries with more open employment relationships, the researchers expect a decrease in economic security, more employment and labour flexibility, and a higher rate of job mobility. For countries with more closed employment relationships, they expect an increase in precarious work (fixed-term contracts and part-time work), difficult transitions into the labour market, and a comparatively lower rate of job mo-

---

2 See also Kalleberg and Vallas (2017).
3 For a critique of Beck, see also Mayer (2001).

bility (Blossfeld et al. 2006b: 7–8). The conclusion is that globalisation leads to more economic uncertainty and less stable working lives, but the outcomes differ between countries and institutional settings. Biemann, Fasang, and Grunow's (2011) findings for West Germany show that globalisation in industries measured as import–export volume is not correlated with employment complexity. Instead, their data showed that women's careers change the most across cohorts due to factors unrelated to globalisation.

As in other contributions to the debate even before globalisation took centre stage, changes in working lives are understood as varying between countries, men and women, workers from different age groups, as well as between core- and peripheral industries and their dual labour markets. Men are perceived as suffering more than women (Hollister 2011), younger and older workers more than core workers, and workers in liberal countries with fewer labour protections differently (more layoffs) than workers in more corporatist countries (labour market outsiders versus labour market insiders).[4]

The most recent and probably the most radical scenario for observing changes in working lives have been raised in reflections about the effects of the Covid pandemic. Lockdown measures massively strengthened the shift towards digitalisation and, due the necessity of establishing a "home office", also opened up a new era of collapse in the spatial and time divisions between the home and the workplace, between private and public life. The separation of family life and work was one of the major features of industrialisation that took place during the nineteenth and twentieth centuries, with significant implications for the workplace as a location of communication and social recognition. While the home office blurs the boundaries of daily working time, it can also be expected to have consequences for the continuity and stability of work lives far beyond work-related emailing from home: "gainful employment, partially removed from factories and service companies, administrations, schools and universities, [is subject to] a profound individualization and de-institutionalization. Work loses much of its socialising power, which can only be developed in communication with others . . . "[5]

---

4 There have been a number of attempts to trace changes in the stability of work in the aftermath of the financial crisis of 2008 and 2009 (Schoon and Bynner 2017). While the (partially temporary) rise in unemployment, especially of younger workers, is uncontested, most studies could not document massive changes due to the Great Recession in Germany (Blossfeld 2017). In regard to working lives and careers, this might be due to the fact that the distance from the financial crisis was still too short to assess such changes.
5 ". . . die Erwerbsarbeit, teilweise aus den Fabriken und Dienstleistungsbetrieben, den Verwaltungen, Schulen und Universitäten herausgelöst, [unterliegt] einer tiefgreifenden Individualisier-

(Kocka 2020: 5). Any positive effects of work-from-home options on autonomy and work–family (or work–life) balance that have been predicted especially for working mothers have to be evaluated within the context of home-schooling requirements that greatly limit flexibility.

What we can identify, then, is a highly persuasive narrative that also proves to be highly persistent across decades and is, in fact, constantly fuelled by external shocks and internal forces. But what is evident in this debate are references to a multitude of phenomena that tend to move in the same direction and are, in part, alternative responses to similar underlying factors.

Historical Changes in Working Lives in West Germany: The Evidence from Quantitative Longitudinal and Cohort Studies

In recent decades, a large number of both retrospective and prospective longitudinal data collections for representative national populations have been conducted, and these have become something of a "gold standard" for social science. For the purpose of assessing the validity of far-reaching claims concerning a "new world of work", they offer extraordinary analytical opportunities because many of them not only cover working lives in the sense of employment and occupational trajectories but also provide evidence for ever-longer periods of time (Mayer 2015a). Working lives in these studies are usually observed in terms of yearly or monthly employment episodes defined by being employed, permanent or fixed contracts, or occupational category or firm. Changes across historical time can be assessed by comparisons between birth cohorts or labour market entry cohorts.

Three such data collections have proven to be especially fruitful for our purpose:

i) The German Life History Study (GLHS) (Mayer 2015b)
ii) The Survey of Health and Retirement in Europe (SHARE) (Börsch-Supan, Brandt, Hunkler et al. 2013)
iii) The National Educational Panel (NEPS) (Blossfeld, Roßbach, and von Maurice 2011)

---

ung und De-Institutionalisierung. Arbeit verliert damit viel von ihrer vergesellschaftenden Kraft, die nur in der Kommunikation mit anderen . . . entfaltet werden kann."

In the following, we will review existing analyses of such data for Germany. In order to maximise observation periods, we will restrict ourselves to West Germany since the working lives of East Germans after reunification were subject to very specific disturbances (Diewald et al. 2006; Liao and Fasang 2021; Mayer and Schulze 2009). Our aim is to collect empirical evidence on the postulated longer-term trends and the postulated form of such trends, i.e., either as slowly emerging processes or as "period" shifts between labour market regimes. Note that we cannot include migrants, who are important to the story of flexibilization, especially in low-skill employment sectors. Most data sources used in the studies below do not cover migrants representatively and in sufficient case numbers.

Table 1: Overview of longitudinal cohort studies on employment stability (sorted by order of appearance in text).

No.	Author(s)	Data	Birth cohorts	Labour market entry cohorts	Period	Country and gender
Occupational stability (external & internal)						
1	Mayer et al. (2010)	GLHS	1930, 1940, 1950, 1955, 1960, 1964, 1971 (3 years each; 1964, 1971: 1 year each)		~ 1945– 2005	West Germany, men & women
2	Giesecke and Heisig (2010)	GSOEP			1984– 2008	West Germany, men & women
Trajectories of occupational prestige (upward & downward, variability)						
3	Manzoni et al. (2014)	GLHS	1920, 1930, 1940, 1950, 1955, 1960, 1964, 1971 (3 years each; 1964, 1971: 1 year each)		~ 1935– 2005	West Germany, men & women
4	Stawarz (2015)	GLHS/ NEPS	1920, 1930, 1940 (3 years each), 1944–75	1932–39, 1940–89 in 10-year intervals	1932– 2011	West Germany, men & women
5	Stawarz (2018)	GLHS/ NEPS	1920, 1930, 1940 (3 years each), 1944–75	1932–39, 1940–89 in 10-year intervals	1932– 2011	West Germany, men & women

Table 1: Overview of longitudinal cohort studies on employment stability (sorted by order of appearance in text). *(Continued)*

No.	Author(s)	Data	Birth cohorts	Labour market entry co- horts	Period	Country and gender
6	Hillmert (2011)	GLHS	1920, 1930, 1940, 1950, 1955, 1960, 1964, 1971 (3 years each; 1964, 1971: 1 year each)		~ 1935– 1999	West Germany, men & women
7	Becker and Blossfeld (2017)	GLHS/ NEPS	1930, 1940, 1950, 1955, 1960, 1965, 1970, 1975 (3 years each)		~ 1945– 2007	West Germany, men
9	Lersch et al. (2020)	GLHS/ NEPS	1919–21, 1929–31, 1939–41, 1944– 49, 1950–59, 1960–69, 1970–79			West Germany, men & women
Employment trajectories including non-employment						
10	Van Winkle and Fasang (2017)	SHARE	1918–63, mostly in 3-year intervals		1933– 2008	14 European countries, men & women
11	Van Winkle and Fasang (2021)	SHARE	1916–1966 in 3-year intervals		1934– 2016	30 European countries, men & women

Notes: GLHS: German Life History Study; GSOEP: German Socio-Economic Panel Study; NEPS: National Education Panel Study; SHARE: Survey of Health, Ageing and Retirement in Europe.

In contrast to the often rather sweeping claims of the narrative outlined above, such analyses require empirical precision. We, therefore, select studies on specific aspects of working lives that are partially related to different methods of statistical analysis (see overview of studies in Table 1). The first aspect relates to "events" in the employment history and the relative "duration" of work episodes and changes in the "rates" of such events, especially a) the shift between employment status; b) job changes, job stability, and job tenure; c) changes in employer and firm; and d) changes between occupational sectors. The second aspect relates to the social status of occupations, e) upward and downward (status) mobility and f) the status trajectories across careers. And the third aspect aims to detect in a holistic manner

g) whole sequences of positions for longer stretches of working lives and to provide measures of their overall "complexity" and their changes.

With regard to the above debate, what we should expect to see are increasing rates of job changes and shorter durations of job tenure, increasing rates of moves between employers and, thus, shorter tenures at firms, and ultimately less continuity and more change in employment histories. Regarding "work life complexity", we would expect to see a decline in "orderliness" and an increase in "complexity". One further consideration concerns the overall length of working lives observed in these studies: due to restrictions in sampling and study design, many studies tend to concentrate on the stages of life running from early adulthood to middle age. We, therefore, have less evidence on older workers and the transition to retirement (see Dingemans and Möhring 2019; Fasang 2012; Tophoven and Tisch 2016).

We first examine evidence concerning *occupational stability.* The "end of the lifelong occupation" is one of the claims made about historical changes in working lives. For Germany, occupational qualifications in the form of apprenticeships and occupationally segmented labour markets have been a distinguishing mark among advanced societies (Blossfeld and Mayer 1988; Hall and Soskice 2001). Mayer, Grunow, and Nitsche (2010) use data from the retrospective German Life History Study (Mayer 2015b) to analyse and evaluate occupational stability. They analyse the duration of the first occupation for women and men of the three-year birth cohorts born around 1930, 1940, 1950, 1955, 1960, and the single-year birth cohorts from 1964 and 1971. Their study covers the historical period between roughly 1945 and 2005, i.e., a span of sixty years. As it turns out, the perception of a "lifelong occupation" was always a myth: on average, 41 percent of men and 38 percent of women left their first occupation within the first eight years of the working life. Figure 1 shows expected survival curves of remaining in the first occupation organised by birth cohort, which are predicted by the flexibilization thesis on the top and the empirically estimated survival curves on the bottom. Empirically, the "survival curve" of staying in one's first occupation is not only fairly similar between cohorts at the bottom of figure 1; it also does not follow the clear historical trend pictured in the top panel of figure 1. The occupational mobility of men born around 1955 is partially higher than for the other cohorts, but it converges again. The occupational stability of the last observed cohort – born around 1971 – is somewhat average, i.e., clearly not extraordinary. Therefore, in these data, we see neither a trend nor a period change between two labour market equilibriums (Figure 2).

Mayer et al. (2010) do find, however, marked differences between earlier and more recent cohorts regarding direct (uninterrupted) occupational changes and changes following employment interruptions of at least two months (Figure 2). For both men and women, they find the exact opposite of what is suggested by the narrative outlined above: the cohorts born between approximately 1940 and

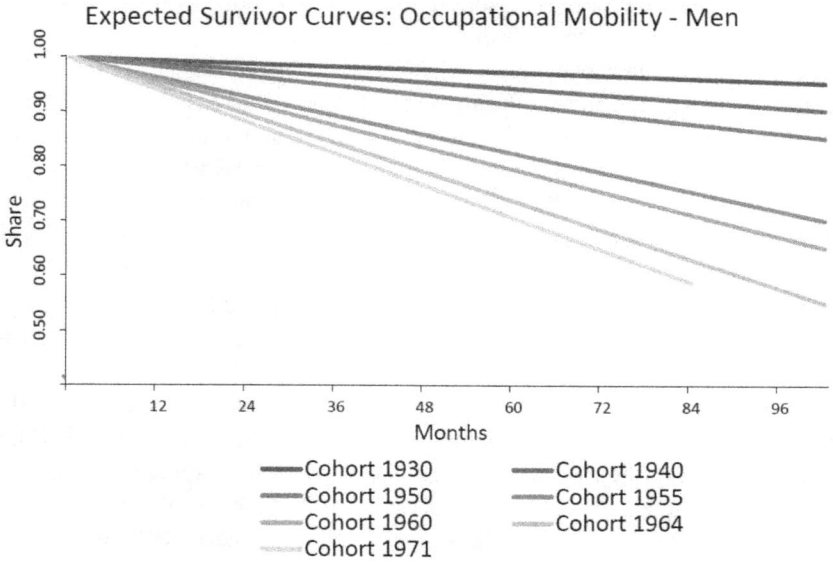

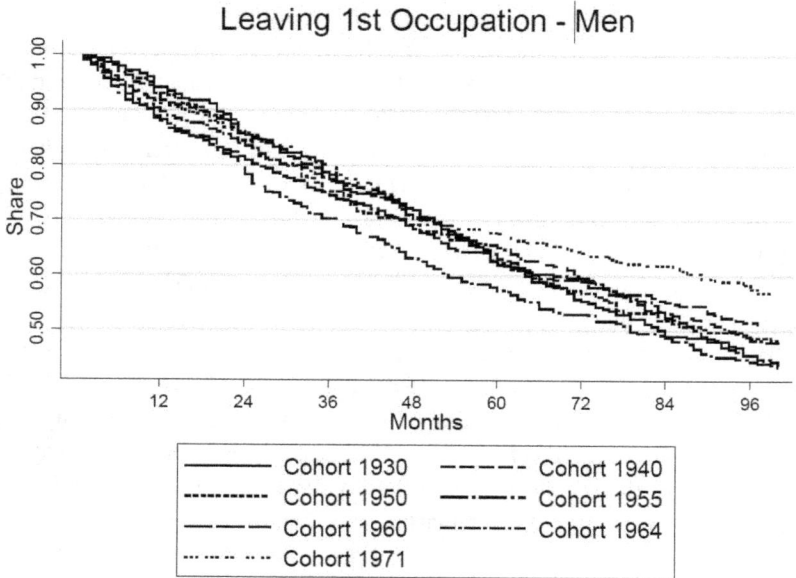

Figure 1: Occupational mobility – expected (top) and empirical (bottom) survival curves (Mayer, Grunow, and Nitsche 2010).

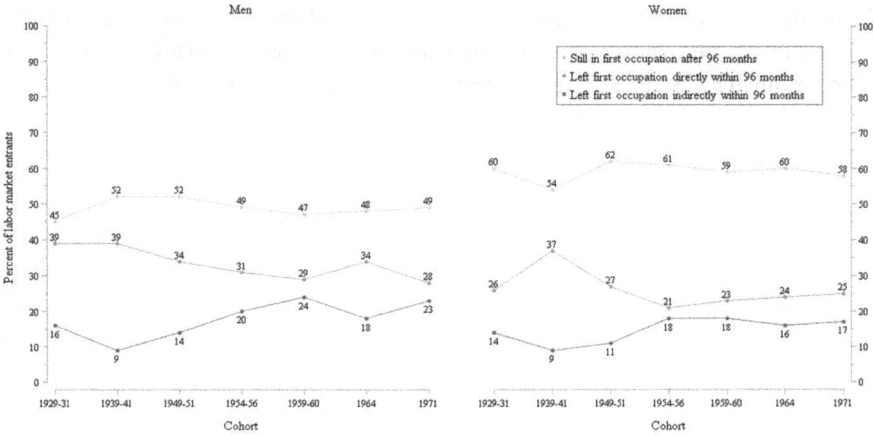

Figure 2: Occupational mobility in West Germany – cohorts born between 1929 and 1971 (Mayer, Grunow, and Nitsche 2010).

1955 changed occupations without interruptions in their work history more often than the cohorts born between 1960 and 1971. One of the potential reasons for this greater occupational stability is that the attainment of higher educational levels operates like an elevator that allows persons to start their careers in a higher position in comparison to earlier periods, when the overwhelming majority began with an apprenticeship and then experienced differential career opportunities. The case of "indirect" moves after employment interruption is just the reverse. More recent cohorts experienced occupational changes after interruptions more often than earlier cohorts. For instance, 10 percent of men and women born around 1940 reported an occupational change after an interruption within the first eight years of their working lives, and this percentage doubled for the 1971 cohort. This change is obviously not recent, but it occurred before the 1990s and not afterward. Brief periods of unemployment are (for men) the most important source of interruption, and these doubled between the two earliest and the two most recent cohorts (from around 20 to around 40 percent).[6]

The high levels of employer–worker loyalty and opportunities for career advancement within firms are another prominent feature of what is portrayed as the "glorious" German past. Thus, we next analyse the evidence concerning firm tenure. Giesecke and Heisig (2010) use work life data from the prospective German household panel SOEP to test claims about destabilisation and de-standardisation.

---

6 For findings on subjective perceptions of occupational mobility, see Nitsche and Mayer (2013).

In particular, they examine rates of year-to-year mobility between firms, mobility within firms, and more precisely, upward mobility within firms for men and women during a much shorter historical time period, 1984 to 2008 (Figure 3).

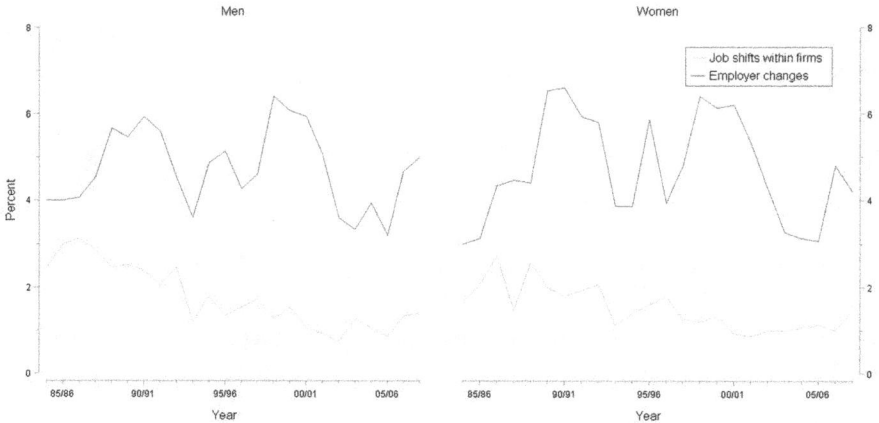

Figure 3: Yearly job shifts within firms & employer changes (Giesecke and Heisig 2010).

For mobility between firms, they find a trendless cyclical pattern for both men and women, whereas for shifts within firms, they find a moderate trend towards less internal job shifts, with a slight reversal for the latest periods of the analysis. For men, they also find a decline in upward moves connected to internal job changes from more than one-third to about a quarter of all internal employment shifts. For labour market entrants (comparable to the group described in the former section), they find decreasing rates of internal job shifts and internal promotions. Thus, there appear to be declining opportunities for long-term career growth in the same company. This can be interpreted either as a real decline of opportunities or, as above, a consequence of the "elevator" effects of educational expansion that place persons in higher-level positions at the start of their careers. This is corroborated by a trend-like upgrade of occupational status at the career entry point (Manzoni et al. 2014). Giesecke and Heisig identify a trend towards more company changes (and increasing periods of unemployment) only for low-skilled men and women, which is in line with the reinforced labour market dualization that took place after the Hartz reforms of 2003, which disproportionally increased employment instability among lower skilled workers.

Changes in working lives both in terms of decreased time spent with a single employer and occupational stability have often been perceived as something negative and threatening. But whether this is the case or not depends on the direction of career mobility – upward or downward – and can be evaluated based on the evidence on *trajectories of occupational prestige or status*. Measures of occupational prestige, i. e., occupational status, permit observations not only about the relative rank, for example at the labour market entry point, but also about the relative changes of status across working lives, careers, and the distribution of status within birth cohorts. Manzoni et al. (2014) and Stawarz (2015, 2018) rely on data from the German Life History Study and the National Educational Panel covering cohorts born between 1919 to 1971 and 1919 to 1975, respectively. First, they show that for all cohorts, occupational status is highly fixed already at the start of the working life and changes relatively little across the next fifteen to twenty years. Additionally, overall, occupational status at the beginning of the career improved consistently over the period roughly between 1940 and 2000. Together, these findings reject narratives of elevated and/or high levels of instability and increasing downward mobility across cohorts. Second, they demonstrate that the shape of the (average) status trajectory (strong initial growth then levelling off) accelerated across the historical periods covered by the comparison between birth cohorts, i. e., roughly 1948 and 1980. This suggests that initial upward mobility is increasingly concentrated in shorter periods of the life course, followed by longer periods of stability at one occupational status. Third, they observe that the shape of the status trajectories only differ in level but not in form between educational and social class categories – evidence against an increasing polarisation of occupational status between educational or social class categories over the life course.[7]

Stawarz (2018) raises further questions about whether the proportion of stable horizontal, upward, and downward trajectories has changed across historical time (Figure 4). Overall, stable career patterns are most frequent across all cohorts (around 80 percent), and upwardly mobile patterns are more likely than downwardly mobile ones. For men, he finds very similar levels of stable careers (except for those who began working between 1950 to 1959, who experienced even more stability) and no clear trend related to either upward or downward mobility. If anything, there appears to be a downturn trend in career mobility for men who began working between 1940 and 1959 and an upward trajectory for those who began working between 1980 and 1989 (Stawarz 2018: 7).

In "Occupational Mobility and Developments of Inequality Along the Life Course," Hillmert (2011) analyses the working life courses for the cohorts born between 1919 and 1971 based on data from the German Life History Study. Overall, Hillmert observes strong stability in mobility patterns and attributes this to the

---

7 For a comparison of status trajectories between West Germany and Sweden, see Härkönen, Manzoni, and Bihagen (2016).

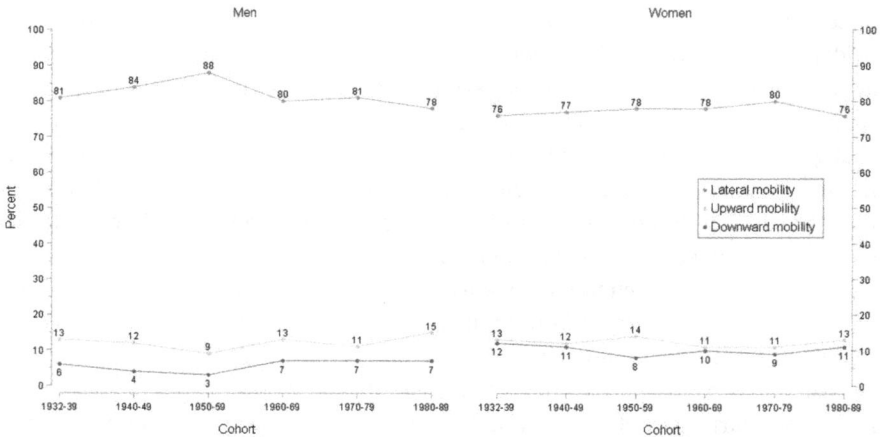

Figure 4: Upward, downward, and lateral mobility during first 20 years of employment – cohorts born between 1932 and 1989 (Stawarz 2018:7).

specific German institutional context, defined by a preference for strong educational qualifications combined with a differentiated system of education and training. "Occupational boundaries are strong, and occupational mobility tends to be much lower than job mobility" (Hillmert 2001: 408). Together with a sharp division of labour between men and women, these features have produced a high level of continuity in the working lives particularly of men in West Germany. [8]

Higher-level and lower-level positions are allocated early on in the career trajectory, and entry into the labour market occurs relatively late, after the completion of necessary training. After the first few years of employment, occupational mobility tends to level off, and careers tend to be highly stable. This means that there are only moderate changes in overall status inequality across the entire spectrum of careers. Stable and continuous career patterns lead to a continuous and proportional accumulation of advantage and disadvantage.

Like the other studies discussed above, Hillmert (2011) observes a long-term trend in occupational upgrading which seems to have come to an end with the baby boom cohort born around 1964. Status differences also tend to increase for the more recent cohorts. Regarding status mobility (defined by 10 percent increases or decreases in SIOPS prestige scores), increasing mobility emerges as a long-term trend: the cohorts born around 1930, 1940, and 1950 had the lowest levels of mobility, with increases for those born after 1950, but also an exceptionally

---

8 See also Kurz, Hillmert and Grunow (2006).

high level of mobility for the cohorts born around 1920 (see also Mayer 1988), which were greatly affected by the war and its aftermath.

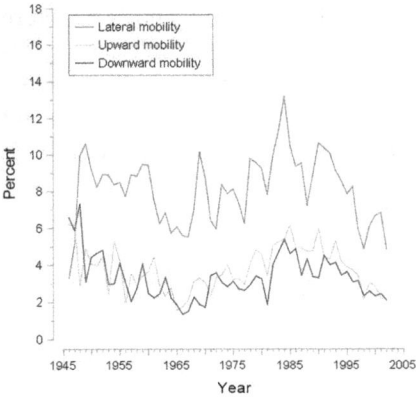

Figure 5: Mobility rates in percent for West German men (born between 1929 and 1976) across periods (Becker and Blossfeld 2017).

Similar analyses have been carried out by Becker and Blossfeld (2017), who observed cohorts of West German men born between 1929 and 1976 based on the German Life History Study and the "adult cohort" of the National Educational Panel. They likewise do not find any clear trends in upward or downward status mobility (indicated by a 10 percent increase or any decrease in magnitude prestige scores). Figure 5 presents the percentage of each cohort that was either upwardly, downwardly, or horizontally mobile across periods identified in their study. According to their measures – based on the change in occupational prestige scores across job changes as a measure of how "good" a job was, a metric that included not only material but also non-material rewards such as job responsibilities, job satisfaction, reputation, and/or authority – a somewhat cyclical pattern of upward mobility within a narrow range emerged. The authors found that this type of mobility was obviously affected by economic modernisation and the state of the labour market, though consecutive birth cohorts were affected differently depending on their career stage: mobility decreased from after World War Two up to about 1970, then it increased until the early 1990s; and then decreased again up to 2005, the last year of the study. An almost identical pattern emerges for downward mobility. For lateral mobility, defined by no change of prestige after a job change or an increase of less than 10 percent, an even more mixed pattern appears: an increase up to about 1960, a decrease in the 1960s, a rapid increase until the late 1970s, and a downturn in lateral mobility during the most recent period. In sum, taking into account entries into and departures from employment as well as company and industry changes, the mobility rates of West German men are rather low across the period of investigation, but differences between different co-horts are significant.

Becker and Blossfeld (2017) also provide robust evidence for status upgrading at the beginning of the career for the cohorts born between 1929 and 1976 (Figure 6). Each line in figure 6 shows the average entry status and status trajectory across job changes for each cohort. The development of this broader measurement of the returns on investment in education/training is the aggregated result of different mobility events across the working lives of West German men in different birth cohorts.

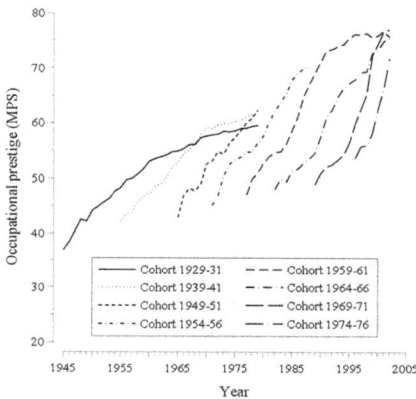

Figure 6: Occupational prestige of men across working lives – cohorts born between 1929 and 1976 (Becker and Blossfeld 2017).

In addition to the shape of status trajectories and the percentages of different kinds of mobility, discrete status measures also permit the calculation of the dispersion or variance of status across the working life. This aspect of the analysis at least indirectly demonstrates how homogeneous or divergent status trajectories are. Lersch, Schulz, and Leckie (2020) use data from the German Life History Study and the National Educational Panel to analyse the working lives of the cohorts born between 1919 and 1979, restricted to West Germany. They have observed the development of status inequality within cohorts and across the working life. In particular, they apply models that allowed them to distinguish between entry variability, variability in status growth, and fluctuation variability, whereby status growth relates to "smoothed" curves and fluctuation variability to shocks or heterogeneity. For both men and women, and for all three aspects of variability, Lersch and Schulz find similar differences between cohorts. Variability is highest for the cohort born between 1919 and 1921; it then declines for the next two decades until the cohort born between 1939 and 1941, and then rises again and remains about the same from the 1944–1949 cohort to the 1960–1969 cohort, with what appears to be an increase for the most recent cohort born in the 1970s (see also Van Winkle and Fasang 2021). The authors also conclude that the divergence in careers paths is mainly driven by the degree of divergence at the point of entry and changes very little afterwards, further substantiating conclusions about the crucial role career entry plays in the studies on occupational mobility and occupational status trajectories discussed above. Interestingly, entry and growth variability are negatively related. In other words, initial homogeneity leads to more divergence across careers and vice versa. Most likely, this has to do with the large pool of people qualified through apprenticeships in older cohorts.

One obvious objection to the research findings reported above is that they all focus on one specific aspect of "flexibilization" or "de-standardisation," whereas the claims in the narrative were more comprehensive and allowed for substitution effects. For instance, the higher unemployment rates of labour market "outsiders" is sometimes seen as a substitute when employment protections prevent companies from laying off workers. Also, many of the reported findings concentrate on early and smaller segments of the working life. Importantly, studies on occupational status and occupational mobility usually do not distinguish between different reasons for leaving or remaining out of the labour force and, overall, are limited in how they can account for recurring mobility in and out of the labour market (Fasang and Mayer 2020). Yet, recurrent moves in and out of the labour market for different durations and reasons are an integral part of the flexibilization and de-standardisation thesis, especially their gendered expressions. The application of "sequence models" as a holistic method by Van Winkle and Fasang (2017, 2021) and others (Biemann et al. 2011; Liao and Fasang 2021; Tophoven and Tisch 2016) addresses many of these problems.

Their contributions are also instructive because they cover not only a long historical time span but also a large number of (European) countries. Van Winkle and Fasang (2017) and a more recent 2020 update that includes younger cohorts and more countries use the SHARE study – a large comparative study on health and retirement – as their empirical basis. It has the great advantage of covering long stretches of the life course (ages 15 to 45 [2017] and ages 18 to 50 [Van Winkle and Fasang 2021]); indeed, for cohorts born between 1916 and 1966, it covers a span of almost half a century that the authors use to map work and family life in the historical period between 1933 and 2016.

Employment "states" are defined as 1) in education, 2) in full-time employment, 3) in part-time employment, 4) unemployed, 5) inactive, or 6) in retirement. These states also include a number assigned to each employment period to distinguish mobility between jobs from the first job, to the second, and so on. On this basis, they apply a measure of job "complexity," which takes into account both the number of different employment states as well as their relative duration (Gabadinho, Ritschard, and Müller et al. 2011).

On this basis, they conclude i) that differences between countries are much larger than differences across historical time; ii) that complexity only very moderately increases across birth cohorts; and iii) that (West) Germany occupies a fairly average position in the overall degree of complexity which ranges from low (Portugal) to high (Denmark).

One obvious objection to the original conclusions in Van Winkle and Fasang (2017) is that they do not cover cohorts born after 1963 and, therefore, might miss the opportunity to respond to the claims made in the "debate." Van Winkle and Fasang (2021) recently provided an update to their previous study and widened its scope considerably by increasing the lifespan (now ages eighteen to fifty), adding sixteen more countries (now totalling thirty countries), and, most importantly for us, adding new cohorts (born 1964 to 1966).

Although country differences are, again, larger than differences across birth cohorts, the trend towards increasing employment complexity is even more prominent when an additional decade of birth cohorts are included in the data analysed by Van Winkle and Fasang in their 2017 study. Also, the proportion of complexity variance attributable to change across time is more than twice as large as was previously found. Their results show that changes in the two decades between 1980 and 2000, when the 1960s cohorts were entering and establishing themselves on the labour market, led to an overall trend of increasing employment complexity that is substantively meaningful, albeit moderate. The average trend across the sample of European countries shows increases from below average levels typical of Southern Europe to above average levels typical of East Germany, Finland, the Netherlands, and Estonia. Moreover, the trend towards increasing complexity is approximately linear: there is no evidence that a certain birth cohort or cohorts were suddenly affected by an event that increased only their average complexity levels. Moreover, Van Winkle and Fasang find no statistically significant deviations from the overall cohort trend within countries.

Van Winkle and Fasang (2021) first corroborate previous findings that show that contrary to common assumptions, increases in employment complexity have been moderate in twentieth century Europe. This includes cohorts born after 1960 who experienced their employment and family lives in the 1980s, 1990s, and 2000s. These are precisely the cohorts whose employment lives were thought to be the most complex due to economic restructuring and recession, globalisation, and new human resource management schemes, technological changes, and occupational polarisation (Hollister 2011).

Second, by comparing changes in life course complexity across cohorts against stable differences across countries, Van Winkle and Fasang are able to contextualise the scope of effects and understand their social significance. Their results demonstrate that 15 percent of the variance in structure of employment complexity was ascribed to differences across countries, but only 5.5 percent was attributable to change across birth cohorts, even in the updated study that included the younger cohorts. This corroborates Van Winkle and Fasang's (2017) argument that cross-cohort differences are relatively small compared to much more substantial cross-national differences.

Overall findings support the conclusion that occupational mobility is moderate, has changed little across cohorts, and occupational success significantly depends on labour market entry. Taken together, there is evidence for moderately higher career instability (flexibilization) and internal cohort variation (de-standardisation) for the oldest cohorts whose employment was interrupted by World War Two, and for younger cohorts born after 1960, who built their careers in the 1980s, 1990s, and 2000s (Lersch et al. 2020; Van Winkle and Fasang 2021). This is precisely the period in which women entered the German labour market in greater numbers, a development accompanied by profound labour market and family policy reforms between 2000 and 2010. Moreover, the increase in employment complexity in Germany still pales in comparison to much larger and stable cross-national differences.

A major further objection to the findings presented so far is that they do not cover directly what was probably at the centre of the debate about changes of work – namely *precarious* work. Bachmann, Felder, and Tamm (2018) also use data from the adult cohort of the National Educational Panel and the method of sequence analysis to analyse cohort changes regarding various forms of atypical work. Atypical work is measured as fixed-term employment, part-time employment, marginal employment ("Mini-Jobs"), temporary agency work, and freelance work. Inversely, regular employment is understood as regular employment with a permanent contract, more than 31 hours of work per week, and social security contributions. For West Germany, Bachmann et.al. differentiate between the cohorts born 1944–1953, 1954–1963, 1964–1973, and 1974 to 1986. For East Germany, they include one cohort born between 1974 and 1986.

Observing the sixteen years of work life after the age of 16 for West Germany and for both women and men, they find hardly any differences between the two oldest cohort groups, but do observe a marked increase of atypical employment for the youngest cohort. As a next step, the researchers performed a cluster analysis and discover one cluster marked by long-term atypical employment. For men in West Germany, this atypical working life increases from 4 to 5 percent in the two oldest cohorts to 9 percent in the youngest cohort (13 percent in East Germany). For women, this share increases from 9–11 percent to 14 percent (in East Germany, 16 percent). So here we finally have clear evidence of an increase of atypical working lives, but on a very low level. Additionally, the employment situation of the youngest cohort fell within a period marked by an especially difficult labour market and, therefore, may be more a sign of a special period than of a larger trend.

Getting Closer to Social History: Macro-forces, Periods, and Cohorts

The bewildering variety of our empirical findings appears to defy the simplicity of the narrative of an overall trend of working lives' increasing flexibilization, de-standardisation, and complexity. But how can we unravel the puzzle of long-term changes in working lives? First, in terms of "causes", we need to distinguish between relatively persistent institutional contexts, global forces of macro-development, and specific periods that are especially visible in the business cycle. This reflects a logic that corresponds closely to A-P-C- (age-period-cohort) analysis in demography (Mayer and Huinink 1990). Regarding "outcomes", we need to distinguish between labour market entry (often a longer transition than a single event), the nature of working trajectories, and the various forms of career complexity. And we need to acknowledge that not all forms of continuity are good and not all forms of discontinuity are bad: consider, for example, interruptions for parental leave (of a moderate length) or changing occupations to align more closely with personal preferences and labour market opportunities.

First, we want to examine whether we can find some kind of support for the narrative elucidated above. As a partial test, we can also ask whether overall changes and trends can at least be found for one or more specific dimension of working lives. Second, we can search for particular periods during which there were high levels of either stability or turbulence. And third, we can focus on the circumstances of individual birth (or labour market entry) cohorts and ask whether "generation" might be a part of this more complex story. To support such interpretations, we have prepared an additional graph for crucial findings now tied to historical periods rather than to birth cohorts (Figure 7). Note that figures 3–6 are already arranged according to period.

Prior attempts to capture macro-development and cyclical conditions for Germany using a number of time series have resulted in two very robust historical paths: one captures overall socio-economic development and the more cyclical changes of the labour market (Becker and Mayer 2019). After fluctuations in the 1920s and 1930s, socio-economic development remained rather flat until a persistent take-off and upward trend began in the 1960s (Figure 8). The labour market

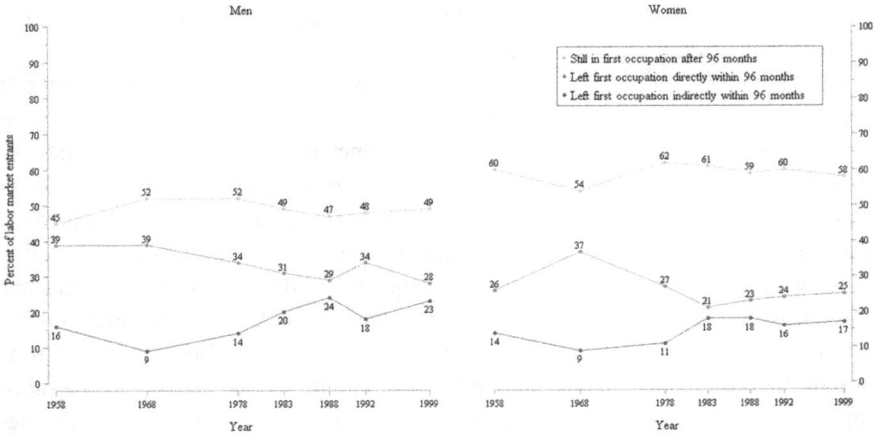

Figure 7: Occupational mobility in West Germany between 1958 and 1999 (Mayer, Grunow, and Nitsche 2010).

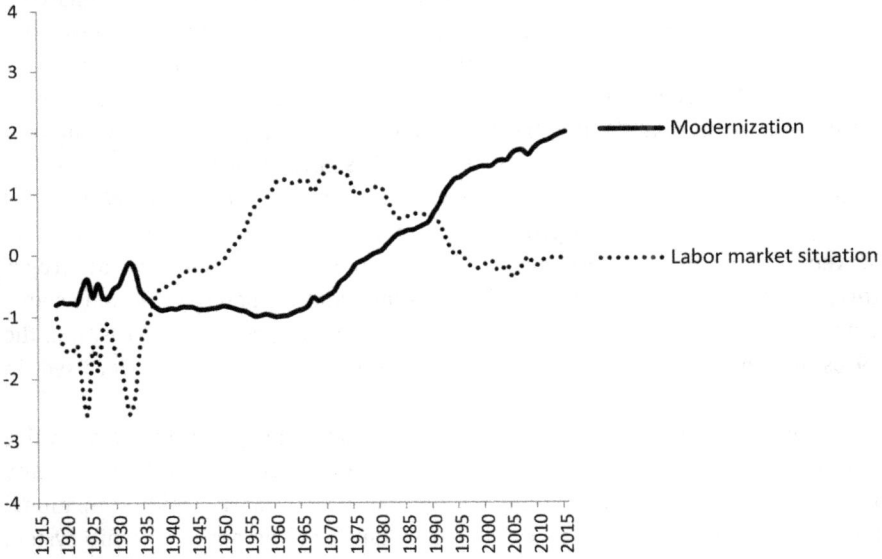

Source and explanation: Becker and Mayer (2019: 154)

Figure 8: Modernisation trend and development of labour market situation (1918–2015) (Becker and Mayer 2019).

situation improved after the Second World War until the late 1960s and then declined until it stabilised in the late 1990s and early 2000s.

If we map our cohort observations onto eras, we do not find changes in work life patterns that correspond to either of these two macro developments; quite the contrary. We find remarkable historical consistency in occupational tenure (Mayer et al. 2010) as well as a high level of stability in occupational status (Stawarz 2018) between about 1950 and 2000. But between the middle of the 1980s and about 2005, job changes between and within firms fluctuated (Giesecke and Heisig 2010). Likewise, we find no patterns in connection to upward or downward mobility (Becker and Blossfeld 2017; Stawarz 2018). We do, however, see a long-term upward trend in the relative status of labour market entry positions brought about by the renovation of the occupational structure, the delay of labour market entry, and the more rapid initial upward mobility resulting from educational expansion and the decreasing significance of apprenticeships as an initial qualification (see especially Figure 6).

We next ask whether there are trends relevant for a shorter segment of the longer historical period between roughly 1950 and 2000 covered in our analyses, for example, corresponding to the economic recovery in the 1950s or the neoliberal restructuring after the mid 1970s. It is the latter period that is the focal point of the grand narrative about the de-standardisation of work lives. And for men, we do observe an increase in the number of job changes after employment interruptions roughly during this period (Mayer et al. 2010). This development is also moderately reflected in the increase of occupational complexity detected by Van Winkle and Fasang (2017, 2021). The most pronounced patterns of historical change can be observed for changes in the occupational prestige of entry-level positions and trajectories. Given these criteria, careers for both men and women have become somewhat more similar – more standardised – for the two post-war cohorts, i.e., the 1950s and the 1960s, and have become less similar, that is less standardised, in the 1970s, plateauing thereafter.

In general, however, we do find very little empirical support for the narrative that asserts massive changes in the stability of working lives. This relative stability might well be the result of the distinct German labour market and occupational structure; entry conditions are still heavily shaped by the apprenticeship system and higher occupational qualifications that reward remaining with the same company and within the same occupation.

To better understand how the occupationally segmented German labour market works and to make more sense of our data, we can examine if and why this general structure broke down or became noticeably weaker for specific cohorts.

The cohort born around 1920 experienced high levels of employment interruption due to Word War Two and its aftermath. The cohorts born around 1930 had to enter apprenticeships at the end of World War Two or in the early post-war period. Many of them were not successful, and as a consequence, their entry level status and their status trajectory were below all prior and all later cohorts. Despite the "Economic Miracle" of the 1950s and 1960s, they could never make up the lost ground, e. g., the proportion of unskilled workers among these cohorts was the highest (Becker and Blossfeld 2017; Brückner and Mayer 1987; Manzoni et al. 2014; Mayer 1977, 1980, 1988).

The cohorts born around 1940 and 1950, who first entered the labour market during the Economic Miracle of the 1950s and 1960s, mark a return to "normality" in both status entry and occupational mobility. Another deviation emerges for the "Baby Boom" cohorts born around 1964. They began their careers at a lower status level, but – in contrast to the post-war cohort born around 1930 – they were able to compensate for this difficult start throughout the rest of their working lives (Becker and Blossfeld 2017; Hillmert and Mayer 2004). The men and women born around 1971 showed an extraordinary increase in occupational re-training. In West Germany, this second educational phase was an effort to reorient their occupational lives; in East Germany, re-training was an adaptation to the breakdown of the economic order following unification (Jacob 2004; Mayer and Schulze 2009).

But overall, we observe an astonishing degree of stability in (West) German working life patterns. One aspect of this is the extent to which trajectories are fixed when entering the labour market; the other is the shape of working life trajectories. This stability has a lot to do with the occupational qualification labour market typical of Germany. What seems to have changed, however, are two developments which, in the end, might look very similar. Initially, apprenticeships as the dominant labour market entry qualification opened up a wide array of initial individual trajectories. This pattern was historically displaced by increasing levels of educational attainment which functioned as an "elevator" and tracked people into their final working life trajectories relatively quickly. For the more recent birth cohorts, the labour market entry transition phase again became more extended and complex and was punctuated by periods of unemployment (Liao and Fasang 2021; Mayer et al. 2010).

Discussion

Why do we observe less change than can plausibly be expected? The impact of economic macro-forces on working lives can occur in two different ways. One way is by cohort replacement: older workers leave the labour force and are replaced by new, younger workers in different occupational categories. Changes have occurred but not so much in the structure of working lives as discussed here but, e. g., in the more difficult transition to first jobs, unemployment, longer periods in the transition system, and more fixed-term jobs. The second way is through changes during the working life which then result in job changes, employer changes, and occupational shifts. If employers cannot easily dismiss workers or change contractual conditions due to market regulations, adaptation is affected by changing the conditions of new labour market entrants. Several findings point in this direction for Germany. Van Winkle and Fasang (2017, 2021) show that cross-national differences in work life complexity highly correlate with the level of labour market regulation. Strong employment protections indeed reduce career complexity caused by involuntary moves substantially. Dütsch, Liebig, and Struck (2013) show an increase in occupational mismatches for labour market entrants, and Brady and Biegert (2017) document an increase in fixed-term contracts.

A second explanation might be that changes in working lives only apply to certain segments of the labour force. For instance, globalisation led to a restructuring of the manufacturing sector but not to a major loss of industrial jobs (Dauth et al. 2018; Reichelt et al. 2020). There is also evidence that technological changes in Germany led not to wage polarisation but rather to skill upgrading (Oesch and Piccitto 2019; Spitz-Oener 2006).

Changing gender relations and women's massive influx into the labour force have arguably been at least as relevant in the changing the world of work as globalisation and technological change (Brückner 2004; Goldscheider et al. 2015). Whereas female employment, predominantly in full-time jobs, was consistently above 80 to 90 percent in the German Democratic Republic, in West Germany, only about 48 percent of working-age women were employed in 1960. The female labour force participation rate increased, especially during the 1990s and 2000s, finally reaching 76 percent in 2018 (Statistisches Bundesamt 2020). Yet, 47 percent of employed women in 2018 were employed in part-time jobs, which are more likely to be lower paid and temporary. Women's increasing employment was driven and enabled by changing gender norms, the decline of male breadwinner wages, and, more recently, by a paradigm shift in German family policy (Geisler and Kreyenfeld 2019). Men and women, particularly those with higher education, have interrupted their employment for a few months (mostly fathers) and up to a year (mostly mothers) since introduction of the new parental leave scheme (*Elterngeld*) in 2007. The *Elterngeld* was coupled with the expansion of public childcare for children starting from the age of one. The new parental leave scheme, thus, introduced more career variability over the life course, especially for women, who now return to the labour market after giving birth sooner and more frequently readjust their labour from full time to part time over their working life course.

A final point relates to an aspect of work trajectories we did not systematically cover in our review of empirical findings. Since 2000, the number of employment interruptions and the proportion of part-time work has significantly increased both for women and men (from 33 to 38 percent up to 2014 for women, and from 3 to 7 percent for men) (Biewen et al. 2018; Fitzenberger and Seidlitz 2020). These changes contribute to less orderly careers, which have been identified as a "new" trend by us as well as by Van Winkle and Fasang (2021).

Overall, our findings point to remarkable stability in careers in Germany, offer little support for the flexibilization thesis, and highlight the crucial role of changing gender dynamics and work–family regulations for the moderate increase observed in the stability and variability of employment lives for cohorts born after 1960. Although we found little support for the grand narrative of more flexible, disorderly, and de-standardised working lives in Germany in general, we should not assume that this relative stability will continue. The Covid pandemic's disruption of the start of qualification, employment, and occupational trajectories and the massive, ongoing restructuring of the German manufacturing sector are just two major developments that point towards change rather than stability.

References

Bachmann, Ronald, Rahel Feder, and Marcus Tamm. 2018. "Labour Market Participation and Atypical Employment over the Life Cycle: A Cohort Analysis for Germany." *IZA Discussion Papers*, no. 12010 (December).

Beck, Ulrich. 1986. *Risikogesellschaft. Auf dem Weg in eine andere Moderne.* Frankfurt am Main: Suhrkamp.

Beck, Ulrich. 1999. *Schöne neue Arbeitswelt. Vision: Weltbürgergesellschaft.* Frankfurt am Main: Campus.

Beck, Ulrich. 2000. *The Brave New World of Work.* Cambridge: Polity Press.

Becker, Rolf, and Hans-Peter Blossfeld. 2017. "Entry of Men into the Labour Market in West Germany and Their Career Mobility (1945–2008)." *Journal for Labour Market Research* 50: 113–130.

Becker, Rolf, and Karl Ulrich Mayer. 2019. "Societal Change and Educational Trajectories of Women and Men Born between 1919 and 1986 in (West) Germany." *European Sociological Review* 35: 147–168.

Biemann, Torsten, Anette Eva Fasang, and Daniela Grunow. 2011. "Do Economic Globalization and Industry Growth Destabilize Careers? An Analysis of Career Complexity and Career Patterns over Time." *Organization Studies* 32: 1639–1663.

Biewen, Martin, Bernd Fitzenberger, and Jakob de Lazzer. 2018. "The Role of Employment Interruptions and Part-Time Work for the Rise in Wage Inequality." *IZA Journal of Labor Economics* 7: 10.

Blossfeld, Hans-Peter, Sandra Buchholz, and Dirk Hofäcker, eds. 2006a. *Globalization, Uncertainty and Late Careers in Society.* London: Routledge.

Blossfeld, Hans-Peter, and Karl Ulrich Mayer. 1988. "Arbeitsmarktsegmentation in der Bundesrepublik Deutschland: Eine empirische Überprüfung von Segmentationstheorien aus der Perspektive des Lebenslaufs." *Kölner Zeitschrift für Soziologie und Sozialpsychologie* 40: 262–283.

Blossfeld, Hans-Peter, Melinda Mills, and Fabrizio Bernardi, eds. 2006b. *Globalization, Uncertainty and Men's Careers. An International Comparison.* Cheltenham: Edward Elgar.

Blossfeld, Hans-Peter, Hans-Günther Roßbach, and Jutta von Maurice, eds. 2011. *Education as a Lifelong Process. The German National Educational Panel Study (NEPS) (Zeitschrift für Erziehungswissenschaft, Special Issue 14)*. Wiesbaden: VS Verlag für Sozialwissenschaften.

Blossfeld, Pia N. 2017. "Labor Market Entry in Germany before and after the Financial Crisis. An Analysis of Duration of Labor Market Entry, Quality of First Job, and Fixed-Term Employment." In *Young People's Development and the Great Recession. Uncertain Transitions and Precarious Futures*, edited by Ingrid Schoon and John Bynner, 208–232. Cambridge: Cambridge University Press.

Börsch-Supan, Axel, Martina Brandt, Christian Hunkler, Thorsten Kneip, Julie Korbmacher, Frederic Malter, Barbara Schaan, Stephanie Stuck, and Sabrina Zuber. 2013. "Data Resource Profile: The Survey of Health, Ageing and Retirement in Europe (SHARE)." *International Journal of Epidemiology* 42: 992–1001.

Brady, David, and Thomas Biegert. 2017. "The Rise of Precarious Employment in Germany." In *Precarious Work (Research in the Sociology of Work, Volume 31)*, edited by Arne L. Kalleberg and Steven P. Vallas, 245–271. Bingley: Emerald Publishing.

Brückner, Erika, and Karl Ulrich Mayer. 1987. "Life History and the Transition to Retirement: The Cohorts of 1919–21." *Zeitschrift für Sozialisationsforschung und Erziehungssoziologie* 7: 101–116.

Brückner, Hannah. 2004. *Gender Inequality in the Life Course.* New York: De Gruyter.

Brückner, Hannah, and Karl Ulrich Mayer. 2005. "De-Standardization of the Life Course: What It Might Mean? And If It Means Anything, Whether It Actually Took Place?" *Advances in Life Course Research* 9: 27–53.

Dauth, Wolfgang, Sebastian Findeisen, and Jens Suedekum. 2018. "Adjusting to Globalization in Germany." *IZA Discussion Paper* 11299. Bonn: Institute of Labor Economics (IZA).

Diewald, Martin, Anne Goedicke, and Karl Ulrich Mayer. eds. 2006. *After the Fall of the Wall. Life Courses in the Transformation of East Germany.* Stanford, CA: Stanford University Press.

Dingemans, Ellen, and Katja Möhring. 2019. "A Life Course Perspective on Working after Retirement: What Role Does the Work History Play?" *Advances in Life Course Research* 39: 23–33.

Dütsch, Matthias, Verena Liebig, and Olaf Struck. 2013. "Is the Significance of Occupational Qualifications Declining? An Analysis of the Development and Determinants of Occupational Mobility." *Kölner Zeitschrift für Soziologie und Sozialpsychologie* 65: 505–531.

Ehmer, Josef. 2018. "Zur Geschichte des Normalarbeitsverhältnisses. Rekonstruktion und Kritik." *Normalarbeit. Nur Vergangenheit oder auch Zukunft? (Gesellschaft der Unterschiede, Volume 37)*, edited by Johanna Muckenhuber, Josef Hödl and Martin Griesbacher, 21–39. Bielefeld: Transcript.

Fasang, Anette Eva. 2012. "Retirement Patterns and Income Inequality." *Social Forces* 90: 685–711.

Fasang, Anette Eva, and Karl Ulrich Mayer. 2020. "Lifecourse and Social Inequality." In *Handbook on Demographic Change and the Lifecourse*, edited by Jane Falkingham, Maria Evandrou, and Athina Vlachantoni, 22–39. Cheltenham: Elgar.

Fitzenberger, Bernd, and Arnim Seidlitz. 2020. "The 2011 Break in the Part-Time Indicator and the Evolution of Wage Inequality in Germany." *Journal for Labour Market Research* 54, no. 1: 1–14.

Gabadinho, Alexis, Gilbert Ritschard, Nicolas S. Müller, and Matthias Studer. 2011. "Analyzing and Visualizing State Sequences in R with TraMineR." *Journal of Statistical Software* 40: 1–37.

Geisler, Esther, and Michaela Kreyenfeld. 2019. "Policy Reform and Fathers' Use of Parental Leave in Germany: The Role of Education and Workplace Characteristics." *Journal of European Social Policy* 29: 273–291.

Giesecke, Johannes, and Jan Paul Heisig. 2010. "Destandardization and Destabilization: For Whom? Job-Shift Patterns in West Germany, 1984–2008." *Kölner Zeitschrift für Soziologie und Sozialpsychologie* 62: 403–435.

Goldscheider, Frances, Eva Bernhardt, and Trude Lappegård. 2015. "The Gender Revolution: A Framework for Understanding Changing Family and Demographic Behavior." *Population and Development Review* 41, no. 2: 207–239.

Hall, Peter A., and David Soskice, eds. 2001. *Varieties of Capitalism. The Institutional Foundations of Comparative Advantage.* Oxford: Oxford University Press.

Härkönen, Juho, Anna Manzoni, and Erik Bihagen. 2016. "Gender Inequalities in Occupational Prestige across the Working Life: An Analysis of the Careers of West Germans and Swedes Born from the 1920s to the 1970s." *Advances in Life Course Research* 29: 41–51.

Hillmert, Steffen. 2011. "Occupational Mobility and Developments of Inequality along the Life Course: The German Case." *European Societies* 13: 401–423.

Hillmert, Steffen, and Karl Ulrich Mayer, eds. 2004. *Geboren 1964 und 1971. Neuere Untersuchungen zu Ausbildungs- und Berufschancen in Westdeutschland.* Wiesbaden: VS Verlag für Sozialwissenschaften.

Hollister, Matissa. 2011. "Employment Stability in the U.S. Labor Market: Rhetoric versus Reality." *Annual Review of Sociology* 37: 305–324.

Jacob, Marita. 2004. *Mehrfachausbildungen in Deutschland. Karriere, Collage, Kompensation?* Wiesbaden: VS Verlag für Sozialwissenschaften.

Kalleberg, Arne L. 2000. "Nonstandard Employment Relations: Part-Time, Temporary and Contract Work." *Annual Review of Sociology* 26: 341–365.

Kalleberg, Arne L., and Steven P. Vallas, eds. 2017. *Precarious Work (Research in the Sociology of Work, Volume 31).* Bingley: Emerald Publishing.

Kocka, Jürgen. 2020. "Motor der Beschleunigung." *Tagesspiegel*, May 17, 2020, 5.

Kurz, Karin, Steffen Hillmert, and Daniela Grunow. 2006. "Increasing Instability in Employment Careers of West German Men? A Comparison of the Birth Cohorts 1940, 1955 and 1964." In *Globalization, Uncertainty and Men's Careers. An International Comparison*, edited by Hans-Peter Blossfeld, Melinda Mills, and Fabrizio Bernardi, 75–113. Cheltenham/Nort: Edward Elgar.

Lersch, Philipp M., Wiebke Schulz, and George Leckie. 2020. "The Variability of Occupational Attainment: How Prestige Trajectories Diversified within Birth Cohorts over the Twentieth Century." *American Sociological Review* 85: 1084–1116.

Liao, Tim Futing, and Anette Eva Fasang. 2021. "Comparing Groups of Life-Course Sequences Using the Bayesian Information Criterion and the Likelihood-Ratio Test." *Sociological Methodology* 51: 44–85.

Manzoni, Anna, Juho Härkönen, and Karl Ulrich Mayer. 2014. "Moving On? A Growth-Curve Analysis of Occupational Attainment and Career Progression Patterns in West Germany." *Social Forces* 92: 1285–1312.

Mayer, Karl Ulrich. 1977. "Recent Developments in the Opportunity Structure of (West-)German Society 1935–1971." *SPES-Arbeitspapier* 67. Frankfurt am Main: DFG Sozialpolitische Forschergruppe.

Mayer, Karl Ulrich. 1980. "Sozialhistorische Materialien zum Verhältnis von Bildungs- und Beschäftigungssystem bei Frauen." In *Bildungsexpansion und betriebliche Beschäftigungspolitik. Aktuelle Entwicklungstendenzen im Vermittlungszusammenhang von Bildung und Beschäftigung. Beiträge zum 19. Deutschen Soziologentag*, edited by Ulrich Beck, Karl H. Hörning, and Wilke Thomssen, 60–79. Frankfurt am Main: Campus.

Mayer, Karl Ulrich. 1988. "German Survivors of World War II. The Impact on the Life Course of the Collective Experience of Birth Cohorts." In *Social Structures and Human Lives (Social Change and the Life Course*, Volume 1), edited by Matilda White Riley, Bettina J. Huber, and Beth B. Hess, 229–246. Newbury Park, CA: Sage.

Mayer, Karl Ulrich. 2000. "Arbeit und Wissen: Die Zukunft von Bildung und Beruf." In *Geschichte und Zukunft der Arbeit*, edited by Jürgen Kocka and Claus Offe, 383–409. Frankfurt am Main: Campus.

Mayer, Karl Ulrich. 2001. *Discontinuities in Working Lives: How to (Mis-)Understand the Consequences of Global and Non-Global Changes. Also a Comment on Ulrich Beck, Wolfgang Bonß and Christoph Lau, The Theory of Reflexive Modernization: Problematic, Hypotheses and Research (2001).* (Unpublished Manuscript).

Mayer, Karl Ulrich. 2015a. "An Observatory for Life Courses: Populations, Countries, Institutions, and History." *Research in Human Development* 12: 196–201.

Mayer, Karl Ulrich. 2015b. "The German Life History Study: An Introduction." *European Sociological Review* 31: 137–143.

Mayer, Karl Ulrich, Daniela Grunow, and Natalie Nitsche. 2010. "Is Occupational Flexibilization a Myth? How Stable Have Working Lives Been and as How Stable Are They Being Perceived?" *Kölner Zeitschrift für Soziologie und Sozialpsychologie* 62: 369–402.

Mayer, Karl Ulrich and Johannes Huinink. 1990. "Age, Period, and Cohort in the Study of the Life Course. A Comparison of Classical A-P-C-Analysis with Event History Analysis, or Farewell to Lexis?" In *Data Quality in Longitudinal Research*, edited by David Magnusson and Lars R. Bergman, 211–232. Cambridge: Cambridge University Press.

Mayer, Karl Ulrich, and Eva Schulze. 2009. *Die Wendegeneration. Lebensverläufe des Jahrgangs 1971.* Frankfurt am Main: Campus.

Nitsche, Natalie, and Karl Ulrich Mayer. 2013. "Subjective Perceptions of Employment Mobility: A Comparison of East and West Germany." *Comparative Sociology* 12: 184–210.

Oesch, Daniel, and Giorgio Piccitto. 2019. "The Polarization Myth: Occupational Upgrading in Germany, Spain, Sweden, and the UK 1992–2015." *Work and Occupations* 46: 441–469.

Reichelt, Malte, Samreen Malik, and Marvin Suesse. 2020. "Trade and Wage Inequality: The Mediating Roles of Occupations in Germany." *Kölner Zeitschrift für Soziologie und Sozialpsychologie* 72: 535–560.

Schoon, Ingrid, and John Bynner, eds. 2017. *Young People's Development and the Great Recession. Uncertain Transitions and Precarious Futures.* Cambridge: Cambridge University Press.

Sennett, Richard. 1999. *The Corrosion of Character. The Personal Consequences of Work in the New Capitalism.* New York: W. W. Norton & Company.

Sennett, Richard and Jonathan Cobb. 1972. *The Hidden Injuries of Class.* Cambridge: Cambridge University Press.

Spitz-Oener, Alexandra. 2006. "Technical Change, Job Tasks, and Rising Educational Demands: Looking outside the Wage Structure." *Journal of Labor Economics* 24: 235–270.

Stawarz, Nico. 2015. "Social Mobility in Germany Revisited: The Development of Career Mobility over the Last 80 Years." *Kölner Zeitschrift für Soziologie und Sozialpsychologie* 67: 269–291.

Stawarz, Nico. 2018. "Patterns of Intragenerational Social Mobility: An Analysis of Heterogeneity of Occupational Careers." *Advances in Life Course Research* 38: 1–11.

Statistisches Bundesamt. 2020. "Pressemitteilung Nr. N 010 vom 6. März 2020." Accessed March 10, 2021. https://www.destatis.de/DE/Presse/Pressemitteilungen/2020/03/PD20_N010_132.html.

Tophoven, Silke, and Anita Tisch. 2016. "Employment Trajectories of German Baby Boomers and Their Effect on Statutory Pension Entitlements." *Advances in Life Course Research* 30: 90–110.

Van Winkle, Zachary, and Anette Fasang. 2017. "Complexity in Employment Life Courses in Europe in the Twentieth Century: Large Cross-National Differences but Little Change across Birth Cohorts." *Social Forces* 96: 1–30.

Van Winkle, Zachary, and Anette Eva Fasang. 2021. "The Complexity of Employment and Family Life Courses across 20th Century Europe: More Evidence for Larger Cross-National Differences but Little Change across 1916–1966 Birth Cohorts." *Demographic Research* 44: 775–810.

Lutz Raphael

Life Courses, Career Paths, and the Search for Employment in Times of Change: Industrial Workers in Germany, France and Britain, 1970 to 2000

De-Industrialisation, Social Inequality, and Life Course Research

Between 1970 and 2000, when West European countries entered a period characterised by rapid de-industrialisation and dramatic changes in the economy and society caused by the introduction of new information technologies, economic, social, and cultural inequality grew. This widened the gap between the "winners" and "losers" (as they were called contemporarily) of this economic turmoil (Reitmayer and Marx 2020). At the macro level, the dimensions of this transformation are well documented: the exclusion of a growing number of persons from employment or welfare services, the return of poverty, and increasing disparities between centres of economic growth and regions in decline; and the growing return rates of capital invested in business and real estate have deeply changed the social landscape in Western Europe.

The following chapter looks at the way this transformation affected the life courses of those people who were directly touched by de-industrialisation and who have been perceived as the "losers": members of the industrial working class. How did male and female workers of different age cohorts cope with the dramatic changes in their working lives: new workplaces, unemployment, the search for new jobs, or early retirement? By comparing the employment trajectories of British, French, and West German industrial workers, this study looks at national differences and general patterns in reaction to an international economic process. Britain, France, and West Germany were chosen as they were the largest national economies inside the European Union whose political elites followed rather different strategies of managing the crisis of de-industrialisation. The comparative perspective provides new insights into the variety of options available to workers both at the macro and the micro level (Raphael 2019: 35–91).

In all three countries, the ongoing social transformation was predominantly seen as a challenge for the individual whose opportunities were highlighted in public and whose chances of becoming a winner of social change were an integral part of the meritocratic legitimacy of all three democracies. "Human capital" was the buzz word behind all kinds of activities that centred on the individual and his or her self-optimisation in work and life in general. This meant that for many people, the "biographical illusion" took on greater significance than before (Bourdieu 1987). "Biographical illusion" is understood here as the need for individuals to construct a coherent narrative about themselves and their place in society.

This comparative study of the working lives of British, French, and West German industrial workers, both male and female, concentrates on transitions: first, from school or vocational training to working life, and second, from working life to retirement. It then examines their employment trajectories or working life. By tracing these events, it is possible to compare and analyse the social logic of individual life courses and the emergence of specific types of life courses and how they are linked to the career paths of industrial workers in these three countries.

To perform this analysis, social historians may choose from a range of different methods. One is quantitative social surveys which provide the statistical data through which the outcomes of "objective possibility" (Weber 1949) within individual life courses can be interpreted at each point of capture. The creation of panel data is another method that can provide information about actual career paths and life courses for samples of varying sizes over periods of varying length. This makes it possible to trace life course patterns more precisely, and these can then be used as a basis for establishing different life course types. A third method is to construct detailed individual life narratives based on different types of ego-documents. From these, the types of behaviour and the logic of decision-making that contributed to the formation of these patterns and types can be more accurately reconstructed. In this study, a conscious effort is made to combine different methods and approaches for the purpose of socio-historical analysis. As a strategy, it seems all the more advisable as the major data sources for the three countries investigated here differ so significantly that, at least for the period in question, there is no single ideal method that could be applied to this kind of comparative study.[1]

---

1 The following databases were used: The database "Arbeiterhaushalte in Westdeutschland 1984–2001" created on the basis of the Socio-economic Panel (SOEP); data from the Labour Force Survey: UK SDA:Study Number 1758 (LFS 1975), 5876 (LFS 1995), 5857 (LFS 2000).; Life-history interviews in the UK Social Data Archive (UK SDA SN 4938), the British Library Sounds (BLSC): interview series Lives in Steel and Food; Life-history Interviews from the Enquete Emploi salarié et conditions de vie (Centre Maurice Halbwachs: 1996–1999).

Starting Points: Paths into Industrial Employment in the 1950s and 1960s

It is difficult in this context to establish a clear-cut boundary between the period from 1948 to 1973, when economies were booming, and the years that followed. The post-war "boom" years appear at first glance to contrast with the later period as a time when life courses, social positions, and group structures became decidedly more straightforward, homogenous, and standardised. The development of labour and employment laws providing legal assurances for wage labour led to the establishment of minimum standards, which in turn led to a much higher general standard of living and level of income than in the period, for example, around 1955. This was also reflected in the life courses and career paths of industrial workers, particularly men. Most of them had either started work or become industrial apprentices immediately after finishing their compulsory education and were now experiencing the transition to a financially secure retirement. The early period of hard work at the start of their working life was typically rewarded by high earnings and opportunities for promotion, and this meant that during this early phase between the ages of twenty and thirty, a large majority of them had been able to find a partner and start a family.

However, while the growth rates experienced in most branches of industry in these decades generated an increase in career and class mobility, they also produced labour markets that offered opportunities for a great variety of life courses and career paths. This meant that despite legal social standardisation, there were vast differences within the industrial labour force (Raphael 2019: 301–310; Mooser 1984; Raphael 2017).

It is important to emphasise the differences that had developed between Britain on the one hand, and France and Germany on the other. First, due to a much slower rate of industrial growth and a lower influx of migrant and agricultural workers into industry, the range of career paths for British workers was far narrower than in France and Germany. The differences that did exist among workers stemmed from variations between the various branches of industry and the regions (Scotland, Northern England, and Wales versus the South East). Second, it was not unusual at that time for unskilled and semi-skilled workers in Britain, particularly in the traditional industrial regions of the North, to experience unemployment, whereas there was practically no unemployment on the other side of the Channel (Marwick 2009: 124–140). The economic crisis of 1973/74 marked the beginning of a longer period of slower economic growth and swifter changes in the structure of industrial production. The career paths of both male and female industrial workers in Britain were affected by unemployment, new technologies, and crises in specific industrial sectors.

The lack of similarities between the data and sources available in each of the three countries makes it necessary to present the results for each country individually first.

Continuity and Change: Career Paths and Working Life Stories in Post-"Boom" France

The social and economic conditions for workers' career paths in France changed significantly after the economic crisis of 1973/74. Around 1.5 million industrial sector jobs were lost between 1972 and 2002, and between 1975 and 1985, the annual increase in real wages for workers fell to around 1 percent, dropping to more or less zero by 2005 (Chauvel 2010: 66). The relationship between skilled workers (*ouvriers professionnels*) and unskilled or semi-skilled workers (*ouvriers spéciaux*) shifted in favour of skilled workers between 1975 and 1995, but more and more unskilled industrial jobs became available in the second half of the 1990s so that by 1999, the proportion of skilled workers stood at 42 percent of all workers, practically the same as in 1975 (Amossé and Chardon 2006: 209).

An additional statistic is of interest: the number of migrants in the French industrial workforce. This figure remained relatively stable, only shrinking marginally from 13 percent in 1968 to 11 percent in 1995, although in the subgroup of unskilled and semi-skilled workers, it was slightly higher at 17 percent (Cézard 1996: 2). Also striking is a further shift in the gender hierarchy of industrial labour. The proportion of qualified female workers, which was already low before the crisis, sank further, from 17 percent to 12 percent between 1962 and 1995, while the proportion of unskilled female workers rose from 26 percent to 30 percent during this same period. This shows that in times of mass unemployment and mass redundancies, the traditional gender hierarchy in the world of industrial labour intensified. One final point is that in France, high youth unemployment was a constant accompaniment to de-industrialisation. The rate of fifteen- to twenty-four-year-olds who were registered unemployed rose continuously from around 5 percent in the early 1970s until it reached a peak of 25 percent in 1984, stabilising at around 20 percent in 1990 (Raithel 2012: 16).

After the *baccalauréat* (university entry qualification) became the widespread general secondary school leaving qualification in the 1980s, the proportion of those who had earned a vocational qualification or the *baccalauréat* or even higher qualifications but were working in unskilled jobs rose to 44 percent (Chardon 2001: 3).

This means that at the end of the period of this study, nearly half of all those working in unskilled jobs had the kind of qualification that thirty years earlier would have enabled them to begin a career at least as a skilled worker if not a technician. Long-term economic decline eventually reduced the chances of upward social mobility for every age group. Whereas approximately 30 percent of industrial workers moved up into another professional group during the "boom" years, objectively speaking, the chances of moving up into a higher status group (skilled worker, master, foreman, technician) stood at 5.4 percent in the crisis year 1982 and at 7.7 percent in 1998, the latter of which was a period of growth. That meant that only one out of twelve workers moved up into the group of mid-level employees; one in twenty became self-employed (Dupays 2006: 343–349).

What significance do these shifts in the socio-economic framework have for workers' career paths? One initial finding concerns age. De-industrialisation in France meant most notably that the age structure of the industrial workforce underwent a massive change. Factory work began much later in life and ended earlier. Consequently, the average length of the working life for all those born after 1925 gradually decreased. During the 1980s and 1990s, the last of the workers who had been employed for more than forty years, generally from the age of fifteen to sixty years old, retired from working life completely. After the mid-1980s, the typical respective ages for beginning and ending industrial working lives were twenty or twenty-five and fifty or fifty-five. When the statutory retirement age was lowered to sixty at the beginning of the 1980s, the "third age" (*troisième age*) soon became popular and like youth became an integral part of workers' lives. This was undoubtedly the greatest change in the life courses of French workers and, especially in connection with increasing life expectancy, the most lasting change. This was also true for workers in Germany and, to a lesser extent, Britain. As a result, the age structure of the workforce shifted further in favour of thirty- to fifty-year-olds. In most French industries, drastic reductions in the workforce compelled younger workers to change to a different career or a different branch of industry. From 1975 to 1990, between five and seven out of every ten workers in any one branch of industry moved to a different sector, became unemployed, or retired, often prematurely (Molinié 2000: 8). The risk of unemployment varied considerably depending on age, qualifications, and industrial sector. In the same period, from 1975 to 1990, for example, between 55 percent and 59 percent of female textile workers in France lost their jobs. Only 6 percent found a new job in the textile industry while a third of them moved to a different branch of industry, and 20 percent became unemployed or withdrew from the world of gainful employment. It was clearly women's careers that suffered the most from the decline of the clothing and textile industries – a frequently recurring pattern.

The move away from industry to another economic sector was sometimes accompanied by a change of legal status to become *employé(e)s* or, less often, *techniciens*, but frequently the person was now employed as a manual, often unskilled worker in the health sector, public administration, or the transport sector. As a result, the number of those employed as unskilled workers in France rose after the middle of the 1990s, an increase that took place mainly in the service sector. In 1990, 37 percent of the total category of "workers" were already employed outside the industrial sector, and between 1982 and 2001, 1.27 million new jobs were created for unskilled workers in the areas of health, social services, schools, trade, transport, logistics, and security.

This trend towards enforced career mobility was at odds with the resilience of patterns of stable, uninterrupted career paths within a business or company that was particularly common among skilled workers. In 1995, more than 56 percent of skilled workers had been working in the same company for more than ten years. While opportunities for wage increases and promotion within a company were often disappearing, the main motivation for company loyalty now was that it would provide protection from the dangers of unemployment. Company loyalty and professional routine had become the safest strategy, especially for older skilled workers. The social logic of clinging to a job even when there were fewer opportunities for promotion and lower wages resulting from a lack of bonus payments or extra shifts, for example, also applied to semi-skilled workers in large companies. This was because the chances of their being employed by an outside company sank dramatically after 1975 since the specific competences they had acquired with their long-time employer, whether as production line workers or highly specialised steel workers, were no longer in demand.

The price of or the prize for their loyalty in these cases was early retirement. It also must be noted that a certain proportion of labour migrants returned to their home countries and tried to continue their working lives there, partly as small business owners. But they were often confronted with endemic mass unemployment and, thus, precarious career trajectories (Benattig 1989).

In addition to mobility and continuity, a third pattern developed in which younger workers began their working life through a much less clear-cut and direct route as a result of greater access to education and training. In particular, an increasing number of young men completed vocational training or advanced education courses and then spent time searching for work while enrolled in job creation schemes or retraining courses for the young unemployed until they finally began their careers as unqualified industrial workers on fixed-term contracts. Depending on the economic situation, this could develop into longer phases of temporary work interspersed with periods of unemployment. It was typical for France that there was a relatively high proportion of contract workers (*intérimaires*) in this group. By 2001, the end of the period covered by this study, they comprised up to 10 percent of unskilled French industrial workers, both male and female (Chardon 2001: 3).

The behaviour of older workers who clung to their jobs in a company, however low in status, contrasted therefore with the mobility and flexibility demanded from younger workers. This has been described and analysed for the French automobile industry in the authoritative studies of the Peugeot plant in Sochaux by Nicolas Hatzfeld, Stéphane Beaud, and Michel Pialoux (Hatzfeld 2004; Beaud and Pialoux 2002). These scholars show that, on the one hand, for the first time in a long time, younger workers started joining the company, initially by means of fixed-term contracts and contract agencies at the end of the 1980s. They had vocational or other general qualifications and were counting on the organisational and technological re-structuring of their company to fulfil their ambitions and hoping for swift internal promotion opportunities. On the other hand, the majority of older production workers who had started working for the company with few or no qualifications and had "sat out" the cuts in the workforce for several decades were simply waiting for early retirement. As a result, they greeted any technical or organisational innovations in the company with scepticism and fiercely defended its established production system. As the sociologists' interviews show, the attitude of these two generations of workers towards each other was reserved, estranged, sometimes even hostile and mutually contemptuous (Beaud and Pialoux 1999: 293–332).

As an illustration of the situation of industrial workers in France during this period of change, one working life story will be described here in more detail. It is based on an autobiographical account published in 2015 by Abdallah Jelidi, who worked in a Renault automobile plant from 1975 to 1991. In it he describes the various phases of working life that were typical for many migrant workers who came to France from the Maghreb states – Morocco, Algeria, and Tunisia – during the "boom" years. Jelidi was the son of a day labourer from Gabès in Tunisia. In 1973 or 1974 (his narrative is unclear about this), at the age of 20, he arrived in Belfort in eastern France following a recruitment campaign by French companies. His working life began in the local Peugeot automobile factory as an unskilled industrial worker in the aluminium smelter. After a stint as a temporary contract worker in Paris, he entered the Renault factory in Billancourt, where he finally found permanent employment. Before the factory was closed and he was made redundant in 1991, Jelidi was employed in the smelter again, but then after an industrial accident, he spent twelve years as a semi-skilled worker fitting rear-view mirrors in the upholstery workshop. As both a representative of a trade union (CGT) and an immigrant (*immigré*), he was unable to find a better job in another department. However, despite being a critical trade-union member, he still identified wholly with the world of Renault, with its reasonably-priced, spacious company housing and other social benefits.

In 1991 at the age of thirty-eight, Jelidi found himself unemployed for the first time in his life. A re-training programme allowed him to quickly find the job he was still doing when he wrote his autobiography in 2015, namely as a truck driver delivering goods from his company to supermarkets in and around Paris at night. Jelidi's full account of his working life shows clearly how limited the opportunities for promotion and professional advancement were for unskilled and semi-skilled migrants. It also shows how typical precarious transition phases could only be happily or successfully overcome by gaining or regaining stable employment. The price Jelidi was forced to pay for the loss of his job as an industrial worker was high: for the last twenty years of his working life, he worked night shifts.

The developments in France can be summarised in a few points. First, mass unemployment cast a shadow over the career paths of workers of all ages. Typical evidence for the effects of this threat can be found in life stories of industrial workers that describe a lack of job security, long periods searching for employment, circuitous paths into careers for young, first-time workers, and the incorporation of periods of unemployment into workers' career trajectories. Second, the pattern of early retirement soon became established as a response to high youth unemployment and mass redundancies, resulting in the retirements of many industrial workers, both male and female, before their sixtieth birthday. Third, as the industrial workforce grew older and the labour market became potentially more precarious, a widespread strategy to secure a livelihood that developed was to remain with a single company for many years or to demonstrate calculated loyalty to that company. Fourth, the discrepancy between qualifications attained and jobs on offer, especially for those born after 1965, grew and with it the gap between the expectations and the reality of career paths.

Britain: Working Lives Caught between Catastrophe and Radical Change

One of the most salient factors in the case of Britain is that in the three decades between 1970 and 2000, British industry lost even more jobs and even greater market shares than its French and West German competitors. Between 1972 and 1992, 2.3 million jobs were shed, amounting to one in four jobs in the construction, mining, and manufacturing industries. Following the data provided by the International Labour Organization (ILO), another 544,000 jobs were lost between 1992 and 2002, representing a reduction of 13 percent compared to the already dramatically low level in 1992. The risk of losing your job as an industrial worker in Britain was nearly twice as high as it was in France and West Germany. In the 1980s, mass unemployment spread throughout many industrial regions in Britain. British workers, both male and female, found themselves confronted with radical changes that were as unexpected as they were long lasting, and whose immediate consequences were experienced by some in the shape of a decrease in income, job loss, and unemployment. As a result of the huge regional differences in wages and income, national averages in Britain are not very helpful. Depending on the method of calculation, the gross hourly wage paid to British industrial workers between 1972 and 1992 can be said to have stagnated in real terms or to have risen annually by a moderate 1.3 percent (Reid 1998: 83). But the era of increasing prosperity was clearly over for British industrial workers too, and in most cases, their concern was to try and maintain the status quo.

The standard reaction to this, as can be seen from the data, was reorientation. Many industrial workers moved horizontally into the gradually expanding service industries. In Britain it was again young people at the beginning of their careers and from working-class households who suffered initially from the fact that so many jobs in industry were cut and rarely replaced. The rate of youth unemployment was correspondingly high, exacerbated by the fact that access to general education was more restricted than in France and opportunities for retraining and obtaining further qualifications opened much later. At the end of the 1980s, at the height of the employment crisis, half of sixteen- to eighteen-year-olds were either unemployed or enrolled in employment programmes for school leavers known as Youth Training Schemes (Reid 1998: 260).

In a pattern similar to France and, as we will see below, West Germany, company closures and redundancies brought the working lives of a large number of older steelworkers and miners to an end. For many of those over fifty, their lives of hard work culminated in long-term sick leave, unemployment, or early retirement. This path had been followed since 1977 by the British steel industry with its offer of redundancy packages. In the mining industry, more than 175,000 people lost their jobs between 1985 and 2000. Half of them remained jobless, became either chronically ill or disabled, or retired early; others found part-time jobs. Only a minority found full-time work in the first ten years after the wave of redundancies (McIvor 2013: 242). In a related interview, a former miner and supporter of the strikes in 1984/85 commented on the situation, saying; "But I will say this: Maggie Thatcher closed the pits, right enough, but I think she saved my life. I was fifty-one when I finished and I would have been another fifteen years underground if they'd stayed open. But what would I have been like with another fifteen years underground?" (Hall 2012: 460).

The situation of the British miners may have been exceptional, but Terry Sargeant's remark about the unexpected (and originally unwelcome), premature end to his career illustrates the ambivalence that was felt towards this situation in all three countries. Many of those born before 1940 never actually came into contact with the new industrial worlds that were developing with the advent of the computer age. This meant they soon seemed rather like wounded veterans from a past industrial culture. In some cases, they found a new role in their regions as protagonists and witnesses of a bygone proletarian age and its values, such as solidarity and comradeship.

At this point, it is possible to conclude that the speed of British de-industrialisation forced many industrial workers who were forty or younger at the beginning of the 1980s to change jobs at a time when conditions on the labour market were particularly difficult. For some there was no alternative to a change of course as far as their work and life plans were concerned since the chances of finding work in the ailing industrial sector were shrinking fast. This could lead to a 20 percent or greater reduction in income as shown, for example, by an analysis of the employment of former auto workers after the closure of the Rover factory in Birmingham at the beginning of the millennium (Jones 2012: 151). Figures from the Labour Force Survey (carried out regularly since 1975) provide further evidence of change. Although some members of the labour force were compelled to be more mobile and flexible regarding their employment, the majority were able to secure long-term jobs in the industrial enterprises that survived. Once again, we find older workers adopting the strategy of sitting tight and remaining loyal to the company. In 1975, 63.1 percent of fifty-five- to sixty-four-year-olds had been working for their current employer for more than twenty years. In 2000, this figure still stood at 58.2 percent.[2] The difference between generations is brought into sharp focus here, considering that there was a sharp drop in the length of time younger workers between the ages of twenty-five and thirty-four remained in any one company during the same period. In 1975, 50.5 percent of these younger workers had been with the same employer for longer than five years, but by 2000, this figure had sunk to 37.5 percent. In Britain, as in France, the gap widened between loyal core workers and those who, whether in the short or long term, had to look to the more mobile, less secure jobs in the service sector for their working future. In 1995 and 2005, the proportion of the total number of people employed who were so-called low-wage earners was over 20 percent (Solow 2008: 5). This figure was only slightly lower for skilled workers – 18 percent – but rose to more than 50 percent in the trade and service sectors. In the industrial sector, it was

---

2 UK SDA, SN 1758, SN 5876, SN 5857.

the food industry that developed into a distinctly low-wage sector. A good third of employees in this sector, especially women, earned low wages. According to the Labour Force Survey, the proportion of low-wage jobs for skilled workers in Britain was 7.9 percent and 22.8 percent for production workers and operators (Mason et al. 2008: 46). The equivalent figures for West Germany in 1995 are as follows: a total of 8.9 percent were low-paid workers in manufacturing and 13.2 percent were skilled workers (Bosch and Kalina 2008: 112).

In summary and in comparison, it can be said that the decline of the industrial sector hit British industrial workers much harder than their French or, as we will see, their West German counterparts. The extent of this dramatic change and its effect on the career paths of many industrial workers, male and female, is evident from the large-scale return of precarious living conditions to working-class households and the sharp rise in benefit claims in the industrial heartlands of Northern England, Wales, and Scotland in the 1980s. Second, British workers, especially older skilled workers, also developed the safeguarding strategy of remaining loyal to a company over a long period. Third, Britain was similar to France in that it was particularly difficult for young people entering the labour market to find a way into (industrial) working life, especially as traditional paths into skilled jobs such as apprenticeships became much less easily available (Sheldrake and Vickershall 2010; Steedman 2010). This meant that in this period, the career paths and living conditions for younger male and female workers in industry became increasingly insecure and notably more precarious than those faced by workers during the "boom" years. Fourth, the spread of the low-wage sector and the rapid decline of the industrial sector caused British working-class households to adopt the dual-income model much earlier than their French and German counterparts.

Industrial Labour in West Germany between Growth and Precarious Stability

Between 1972 and 2002, 1.9 million industrial jobs were lost in former West Germany, amounting to an average loss of 13 percent every ten years. This development was similar to that in France and meant that the need to change jobs or sectors was much less compelling than in Britain. The career patterns of industrial workers in the northern industrial areas of Britain were much closer in this respect to those of former East German workers after 1990, when in a comparatively short period of time and over a much greater area, an almost complete process of regional de-industrialisation took place. In former West Germany, the process of adaptation and transformation developed much more slowly and along partially different lines. Here, too, the rise in incomes was lower during the transition phase than in the "boom" years, but not dramatically so, as can be seen from the fact that from 1975 to 2000, the annual increase in net real income was 1.35 percent (Weischer 2011: 234). This figure applies to the former West Germany, where the average earnings of both male and female industrial workers were higher than those of their British and French counterparts.

Data collected by the German Socio-Economic Panel (SOEP) from more than 12,000 households, first in West and then also in East Germany, since 1984 allow for a closer analysis of working life courses. The same people or the same members of the household were questioned in detail every year about their social and economic circumstances. As a result, we have access to information about the lives of respondents over a period of more than twenty years,[3] sometimes even for their whole lives up to 1984, so that in some fortuitous cases, it is possible to reconstruct an individual's entire working life right up to their retirement. The following analysis is based on the biographical data of more than three thousand people who could be classified as members of the industrial labour force in West Germany. From this sample, working life stories from 630 households were selected which provided detailed information about career paths over a period of at least fifteen years. First, quantitative analysis was carried out on key data concerning job situation, professional qualifications, age, gender, and nationality. To this end, the respondents were divided into five different age cohorts to better observe generational effects.[4] Second, the biographies of men (636) and women (405) were evaluated separately. Many of the women in the 630 households surveyed either

---

3 For the SOEP and the database created from its figures, see Socio-economic Panel (SOEP). <https://www.diw.de/en/diw_02.c.221178.en/about_soep.html>, last accessed on September 24, 2018. Its collection of data on more than 12,000 households (first in West- then also in East Germany), which began in 1984, provides detailed information not only on the socio-economic situation but also on the life courses and attitudes of a representative cross-section of residents in Germany. My own database of working households in West Germany 1984–2001 was derived from this comprehensive information. It comprises data collected on all households (including partners and children) who were surveyed for at least ten working years, and which consisted of one or more workers who had been employed and paying social insurance contributions for at least half of their working life or had become unemployed either in the year before or the year after the interview. This database contains data on more than 3,000 West German individuals. In the following, it is cited as *"Arbeiterhaushalte in Westdeutschland 1984–2001."*

4 The following age cohorts were defined: year of birth 1945 and earlier [1], year of birth 1946 to 1955 [2], year of birth 1956 to 1965 [3], year of birth 1966 to 1969 [4], and year of birth 1970 to 1979 [5]. This differentiation allows for changes in the labour market for different age groups to be more clearly detected and situations specific to the generations to be identified. All the following calculations are my own based on the SOEP 1984–2001. *Lebensläufe aus (Industrie)arbeiterhaushalten.*

did not work outside the home at all or worked in other non-industrial economic sectors. Those who were employed in the industrial sector like their husbands and partners were in the minority, and it is only their career paths that are analysed in detail here.[5] Third, a distinction was made between German and non-German workers, and since there were only very few cases of people of other nationalities, only the largest group of foreign workers, those from Turkey, were incorporated into the analysis.[6] Fourth, continuity of employment was included as a category. The criterion taken here was one included as a variable in the SOEP, namely, how often the respondent changed jobs and/or industrial sector.[7] In the sample selected, workers' career paths were taken from all the major industrial sectors[8] in order to reconstruct different patterns of working life courses. Their social logic could then be analysed more closely with reference to individual careers and with a view to discovering possible patterns.

The first example comes from the oldest cohort, i. e., those who born before 1946 could look back on at least ten years of work and were in the middle of their working lives when their companies were hit by structural and economic turbulence after 1975. What is initially striking is how many of the workers in this middle age group continued to be employed in the same factory or company. A typical example is the working life of A., a trained carpenter born in 1939 – so part of this first age cohort [1] – and living in a village not far from Bremen. After finishing his apprenticeship, he began work in 1957 and was employed as a skilled worker from then on without a break, and from 1965 on even in the same branch of the automobile industry. In the 1980s, he became a foreman or head of a team but was made redundant in 1996 at the age of fifty-seven, presumably under a severance scheme. He was unemployed for twenty months until he went into early retirement. During the 1980s, his real wages rose more or less steadily, but after 1989, so after his fiftieth birthday, they began to fall, and by 1996, they had reached a level 17 percent below that of 1990.[9] His wife, who was born in 1948 (age cohort [2]), had also been employed since she left school, at first as an unskilled worker

---

5 94 women, 62 with a German family background and 32 of Turkish origin.

6 473 und 163 men. They make up 74 and 26 percent respectively of all the male life stories evaluated. This means the life stories of migrants are overrepresented in my sample, since they comprise "only" 17.2 percent of the 3,565 cases documented in my database, "*Arbeiterhaushalte in Westdeutschland 1984–2001*," itself based on the SOEP.

7 In very few cases was there a change of job and this category was used to analyse particular preconditions of precarious jobs and job insecurity.

8 Construction (10.2%), metalworking (9.6%), chemicals (5.1%), automobile (4.3%) machine engineering (4.3%), electrics (2.4%), wood and furniture manufacturing (2.6%).

9 SOEP PID 85201, 85202.

on the shop floor of a plastics company, and then as a semi-skilled worker in a large company canteen. During the 1990s, her wage increases were able to compensate for the losses suffered by her husband, who was nine years her senior. Neither of these working life courses were seriously affected by the post-"boom" upheavals, adhering to older patterns of working lives.

An analysis of the figures from the samples here shows that of older workers in West German households (age cohort [1], born before 1946), 68 percent ended their working lives before they were sixty years old, and for Turkish workers in this cohort, this figure was 81 percent. The path leading from the end of work to the point at which they could draw a pension varied considerably and could entail longer periods of unemployment or collecting disability benefits. Whereas most German workers managed to continue working until they were between fifty-seven and fifty-eight years old, 37 percent of Turkish workers left work when they were between fifty and fifty-five. For this age cohort, a working life of often more than thirty years, generally begun at the age of fourteen or fifteen, ended in early retirement as a rule. The same is as true here as it was for British workers, namely that this premature end to their working life constituted a break in their lives that they viewed with ambivalence. On the one hand, it prevented further damage to their health and opened up new opportunities in their private lives; but on the other hand, it usually brought an abrupt end to their integration into social networks and other kinds of social contacts at work and could put a strain on their marriage and family life. When they had arrived in Germany, decisions about where to start a family, whether to buy a suitable flat or house, and where the focal point of their lives still had to be made. By 1973 at the latest, however, the majority of first-generation Turkish migrant workers had decided more or less of their own accord to stay in West Germany for good and bring their families to join them, thus committing themselves to a long-term career in industry (Hunn 2005). At this point, they also experienced a dramatic change in their job prospects. A premature end to their working life often brought with it the end of social contacts within the region to which they had migrated and meant that they had to fall back on their families or other migrants from their home country.

The working life courses depicted above are examples of two different variants of a pattern that can be ascribed to the so-called "core workforce" of West German industrial workers. When they were between thirty-five and forty years old, this age group survived the first wave of redundancies and subsequently profited from the economic growth of the 1980s. However, when they reached their fifties, they began to be affected by the imminent threat of early retirement or an interim period of long-term unemployment. It is important to realise that this was a pattern that had been established in industry in West Germany – as it had in France and Britain – since the late 1970s, and it had been welcomed and promoted not only by industry itself but also by trade unions and the state. The introduction of new manufacturing techniques and the constant re-organisation of production had the same effect as the closure of older plants and the "death" of certain branches of manufacturing: it brought about the end of traditional industrial employment, and this was often implemented by sending long-serving workers into early retirement. But it was also part of a general trend in former West Germany: the employment rate of sixty- to sixty-four-year-olds sank from 70 percent to 40 percent between 1970 and 1983 and remained more or less stable at around 33 percent between the late 1980s and the late 1990s (Torp 2015: 269).

We turn now to the career paths of younger workers, that is those who first started working after 1975, when there were already signs of restructuring and upheaval. Their careers differed from those of their older colleagues in that they were much more varied, and this variation was on a much wider scale (Mutz et al. 1995). In the sample period between 1980 and 2000, workers in the age cohorts [2],[3], and [4], i.e., those born between 1946 and 1969, frequently changed jobs across the boundaries of companies and industrial sectors, and these changes were much more frequently accompanied by periods of unemployment than in the case of their older colleagues. This initially appears to suggest a pattern similar to that found in France and also in Britain. However, closer analysis shows that in spite of some delay and uncertainty, many workers managed to secure stable employment usually linked to long-term service and loyalty to one company. These working life stories are a clear indication of the opportunities available to young industrial workers as a result of the expansion and reform of the dual vocational training system in Germany at the time. It explains the fact that the career paths of younger skilled workers in Germany in this study were frequently characterised by in-company promotion and/or further professional qualifications (Lappe 1993; Henninges 1991).

B, who was born in 1958 and lived in Duisburg in the 1980s and 1990s, began his working life there in 1975, after nine years at school and a three-year apprenticeship as an electrician. He was taken on by the company that trained him, presumably the Thyssen steelworks in Duisburg, just fifteen minutes away from his home, and worked his way up within the company. After training as an industrial supervisor from 1990 to 1993, he became the head of a team in 1993 at the age of thirty-five. In 1996, he moved up into the category of higher-status employee (*Angestellter*) and became a supervisor. Throughout this period, his real wages rose steadily, and by 2002, when he was forty-five, the amount he was earning was three-and-a-half times his earnings in 1985 after being adjusted for inflation.[10] In the SOEP interviews, he was regularly asked to rate his job satisfaction. In 1985, 1990, and 1992 (when he was studying for further professional qualifications), it was very high, but between 1992 and 1995, it fell dramatically from ten to only three points on the scale. The young man may well have been frustrated by the threat of a thwarted career until 1996, when he finally gained the promotion he had hoped for within the company.[11] In-company promotion continued to be an essential element in the careers of skilled workers, especially when the chances of moving to another company diminished either because there were no local alternatives or because it would have meant moving to a different area.

However, even in these prosperous and stable zones, there were changes. Young industrial workers now went to school for ten or eleven years (much more frequently attending the middle school – Realschule) before they started an apprenticeship, meaning they began their careers much later. Whether their careers will end as early as those of their older colleagues remains to be seen since those who were born in 1960 or later are only now reaching retirement age. The working life of a young man of Turkish origin may serve as an illustration. He was born in 1966, came to Germany as a school-age adolescent, and lived first in Wuppertal and then Duesseldorf. He was unable to gain any German school-leaving qualifications or complete any vocational training, and his working life was initially very erratic. Over more than twelve years, he was evidently in search of a decent job, was made redundant four times, was unemployed, and worked in various branches of industry. This phase of short-term solutions and experimentation came to an end in 1995 when at the age of twenty-nine, he got a job in a steelworks, first as a forklift driver and later in the foundry. According to the most recent information available in 2001, when he was thirty-five years old, he was still working in the same job and had been with the same partner since 1992.[12]

The pattern so clearly described in this life story is different though not totally new and began to spread in 1975. It included a clear initial phase of working life defined by precarious and short-term jobs, particularly in the case of unskilled workers. It was evidently not a pattern restricted to British and French workers. It was frequently encountered among younger migrants who had moved to West Germany while they were still at school or shortly afterwards. Compared to the lives of their fathers, older brothers, and cousins who had arrived between 1965

---

10 These figures are based on the monthly net wage (converted into euros) provided by the respective surveys carried out by the SOEP. They were then adjusted to inflation to exclude depreciation. See. SOEP PID 110101, my figures for 1984, 1998 and 2006.

11 SOEP PID 110101.

12 SOEP PID 563701.

and 1970, their careers clearly demonstrate the effects of de-industrialisation and technological change. In the core industrial production areas, jobs for unskilled workers in Germany were being progressively cut, making it increasingly difficult to find a way into highly paid industrial jobs, especially without the added social capital of family contacts. Most of their working lives began in the construction industry or in trades like auto repair, and by no means all of them ended up in a stable industrial job. As a result, the period of unstable, precarious work for this cohort of unskilled workers in West Germany extended, as it did in France, until they were about thirty years old. Evidence for the frequency of this kind of career path is provided by the quantitative evaluation of the sample of working life stories. The results show that in the age cohorts [3] and [4] born between 1956 and 1969, 16.5 percent of men entering the labour market were registered unemployed in more than two calendar years. On the other side, the career paths of 72 percent of this age cohort were fairly steady, which was demonstrated in the interviews by the fact that a change of job or industrial branch or a period of unemployment occurred no more than three times in fifteen years.

With regard to the women in these working-class households, it would appear initially that very little had changed for them compared to the "boom" period. Now, as in the period before 1975, only a minority (22 percent) were engaged in full-time work, and of this group, the majority were employed in unskilled or semi-skilled posts for five or at the most seven years. Their careers generally ended between the ages of twenty and twenty-five when they married or had their first child. Most of the cases analysed here can be defined as "domestic" careers rather than professional careers. In other words, the type and extent of these women's employment was determined primarily by the needs and requirements of the household in which they were living as wives, mothers, or daughters. Their working life courses were evidently dictated by their age and number of children and their partner's job situation to a much greater extent than by any career options available in their workplaces. The model of part-time employment to bring in extra income that was so successful in the 1960s had developed to an even greater extent in Germany in subsequent decades. In the households studied here, this kind of life course was widespread among migrant women and German-born women alike.[13] Although new, specifically female career patterns developed during this period, they were typically found either in the service sector or in the education and health sectors, and mainly among highly qualified women, particularly those working in academia. These options are demonstrated by one distinct group in the sam-

---

13 A third of the women in this sample belonged to this category: 94 out of 275 women of German origin and 39 out of 130 women of Turkish origin.

ple: those who returned to working life as widows or single mothers after a family crisis. This path was followed by around a quarter of women, but only a small minority (thirteen out of ninety-nine) had a career in industry.

Looking Backwards and Forwards

Influenced not least by empirical data from the "boom" years, life course research in the social sciences has tended to emphasise the significance of institutional frames (schooling, employment status, qualifications/vocational training, retirement age) for the formation of stable, long-term careers. These frames were then used to create standards based on gender and age, which provided the foundation for so-called "standard" or "normal" life courses regarding employment and the household. Other much less stable life course patterns had existed before the recession in 1973/74, but they had for the most part been typical of groups excluded from mainstream society, most notably migrants. However, as shown above, the change in these life course patterns in what was formerly the core sector of industrial labour was much slower in the three decades after the "boom" than was initially allowed for by contemporary perceptions and preoccupations with long-term unemployment, youth unemployment, and non-standard or atypical employment (part-time, temporary, or contract work). The technological and organisational restructuring of industrial production also suggested more far-reaching and immediate consequences to contemporary observers than those that were actually detectable in retrospect.

How can this be explained? Precisely because the labour market was becoming more volatile and most people felt confronted with an overall more uncertain future there was a growing desire in society for security and, more precisely, for stability in the field of employment. This may have been a coping strategy on the part of industrial workers, but it also suited the strategy of businesses. Complex technological advances, the pressure of increased competition, and rapidly rising quality standards meant that businesses became more reliant on the competence and cooperation of their workforce. The extent to which this applied varied in the three countries in question as well as in various branches of industry. Other strategies were also implemented such as stricter performance-related checks on fluctuating workforces, reductions in labour costs, and the "Taylorisation" of production. The number of different patterns of working life courses was, therefore, largely determined by the strategies adopted in reaction to the globalisation and Europeanisation of the industrial production process, but it was also determined by the negotiating power of the workers' councils and trade unions when it came to job cuts and the design of redundancy and severance schemes. A key factor here was the recognition and exploitation of specialist knowledge and the competence of skilled industrial workers.

These differences, as well as the fact that fewer industrial jobs in total were shed in former West Germany than in France and Britain, were the main reason why, even in the years of transformation after the "boom," the working careers of most young skilled industrial workers in Germany followed the same pattern of internal promotion and continuous employment, but they started working later than their older colleagues. This career pattern may also be encountered in some sectors in France and Britain, where it survived the rifts of the 1980s and 1990s caused by rationalisation, ownership changes, and plant closures. In France, it was found primarily in the public sector and in nationalised industries. In both Britain and France, certain large-scale businesses used their human resources and training policies to encourage their core workforce to follow this kind of in-house career. These were, however, no more than small pockets of stable employment in a world of industrial work that was characterised to a much greater extent by precarity and the encroachment of far less stable employment patterns typical of the rapidly growing basic service sector. It is clear, therefore, that the extent to which this first element of stability was sustainable depended largely on the conditions in each of the individual nation states.

Changes in the general economic climate and in competitive conditions brought the working lives of many older workers in former key industries to an abrupt end. In response to the increasing demands of globalised competition, they were sent into early retirement. Within a surprisingly short space of time, the demise of industrial labour forced many steelworkers, miners, shipbuilders, and other major groups of male industrial workers to end their working lives while still in their fifties.

In Britain, France, and Germany, a kind of general social consensus seemed to emerge that held that at this late stage of their careers, the older generation of industrial workers could not be expected to endure the job losses and permanent unemployment they would have faced as a result of de-industrialisation and rationalisation. Consequently, businesses, trade unions, and the state united to establish conditions under which it was possible to adhere to working life patterns that avoided the demands of flexibility and the risks of a more precarious existence. Working life stories show the significance of social citizenship, for the older generation in concrete terms by providing them with security in old age but also for their households and families. Part-time work and more extended and repeated phases of unemployment indicate that the incidence of precarious work began to spread and threaten the standards of social citizenship.

It is also evident that remaining loyal to the same company and in the same kind of job were also strategies frequently adopted by workers in an attempt to secure their livelihoods. They were increasingly openly referred to as "possessing" a job and had very few opportunities to change jobs or risk re-training. The social cost of this safeguarding strategy was borne on the one hand by women, whose careers in the industrial sector remained virtually non-existent with very few exceptions, and on the other, by young workers at the start of their careers, especially in Britain and France. They often had to put up with unemployment, precarious (fixed-term), and poorly paid jobs in order to get their foot in the door of relatively stable industrial employment. As a result, the initial phase leading up to a career path as an industrial worker was extended by a good ten years, meaning that the careers of an increasing number of young people did not start until they were between twenty-five and thirty years old. This, in turn, shrank the actual active phase of employment in the lives of male industrial workers from forty years to between twenty-five and thirty years.

Labour-related migration was a particularly significant factor. In Germany and France, labour migrants played an important role as unskilled and semi-skilled workers in mass production when this sector was booming in the period up to 1975. The same was true for Britain although the numbers there were far lower. Older migrant workers were often part of the group of those who took early retirement, whereas for those who had migrated later and/or were younger or second-generation migrants, the consequences of belonging to an ethnic subgroup were far more apparent. It was much more difficult for this group to gain access to further qualifications and higher-status jobs. In all three countries, they made up a disproportionately high share of the unskilled and semi-skilled workers, and as such, their working life patterns frequently reveal erratic and/or interrupted career paths. This lack of security was a part of the class-specific and generation-specific context of the social protests staged by young people in the suburbs and *banlieues* of Britain and France that have received increasing attention from the media since the 1980s. However, it would be incorrect to speak of a systematic exclusion of specific groups from better-paid and more secure industrial jobs.

In the industrial world of all three countries, the gender-specific division of labour remained unchanged. The declining number of women working in industry were "stuck" in unskilled and semi-skilled jobs, and the option of a career in industry for women was unrealistic except for a small minority of skilled workers. The proportion of part-time workers increased, and with it the proportion of those who could be considered to have (unpaid) "domestic" careers. However, the working lives of women began to play an ever-increasing role in the social and economic lives of the predominantly male industrial labour force. The short-lived bourgeois dream of the male "paterfamilias" and single breadwinner was soon brought to an abrupt end by the change in socio-economic conditions. Whether the men in question were skilled or unskilled workers, they were often in a relationship or married to women who themselves were employed in jobs in education, social work, or administration, or in the health sector, retail, or any of the other numerous jobs available in the rapidly growing service sector. As the threat of unemployment increased and wages stagnated or even fell, the strategic importance of women's contribution to the household income increased. There is an urgent need for more research into the working lives of these women, particularly those employed in low and mid-level jobs in the service industry, to discover more about the social realities of the working classes in Britain, France, and Germany after the "boom" (Mayer-Ahuja 2003).

Many important aspects have had to be neglected in this analysis. The sociocultural contexts of these working life stories have only occasionally surfaced, for example, as have the very different ways they were embedded in the life plans and career expectations of their families and neighbours. It was also not possible to take into consideration any of the ideas and concepts related to the particular period, nation, or social class in question, which may have influenced different phases of life like youth, partnership, young family, and retirement. Nevertheless, the life course patterns that have emerged here should be able to help researchers see beyond trends specific to individual countries and better recognise and interpret transnational similarities and differences in the world of industrial labour during a period of globalising production systems. For example, they allow us to propose a working hypothesis that the patterns of working lives in East Germany post-1989 were more similar to British career paths, where the relevant developments began ten years earlier, than to their West German counterparts. It is also true that the proportion of precarious or "flexible" career paths in "atypical" forms of employment in the industrial sector in Germany increased steadily after the turn of the century. As Philip Ther recently pointed out, in Europe, a trend towards a clear polarisation of industrial working life courses according to qualifications and/or social or ethnic background emerged (Ther 2014: 277–305).

Finally, it is also important to clarify whether the discovery of early retirement as the least controversial and most socially acceptable means of softening the effects of job loss was as widespread in other European countries as it was in France, Britain, and West Germany. In the face of swiftly rising pension costs, it soon became one of the areas of tension in social relations between generations. This was particularly the case in France, where the reduction of the retirement age was perceived as the ideal way to bring about a socially acceptable transformation of the economy and society.

We see that the impact of the general institutional frames like schooling, public retirement, or social insurance systems on the standardisation of working lives and career patterns was much more limited than has often been assumed. The transformation of industrial production in Western Europe in the last three decades of the twentieth century generated more differences among the contemporary largest social group, workers, than before, and their households had to cope with ongoing economic uncertainties. Flexibility was the common denominator among the very different types of reactions and strategies people developed to bring stability back into their working lives. The comparative perspective on working lives in three countries makes clear that workers' search for stability strongly depended on political and economic preconditions that prevailed on the national and the international level much more than the contemporary ideology of individuality and subjectivity presumed.

References

Amossé, Thomas, and Olivier Chardon. 2006. "Les travailleurs non qualifiés: une nouvelle classe sociale?" *Economie et statistique* 393–394: 203–227.

Beaud, Stéphane, and Michel Pialoux. 1999. *Retour sur la condition ouvrière: Enquête aux usines Peugeot de Sochaux-Montbéliard.* Paris: Fayard.

Beaud, Stéphane, and Michel Pialoux. 2002. "Jeunes ouvrier(e)s à l'usine." *Travail, genre et sociétés* 8: 73–103.

Benattig, Rachid. 1989. "Les retours assistés dans les pays d'origine: une enquête en Algérie." *Revue européenne des migrations internationales* 5: 79–102.

Bosch, Gerhard, and Thorsten Kalina. 2008. "Low Wage Work in Germany: An Overview." In *Low Wage Work in Germany*, edited by Gerhard Bosch and Claudia Weinkopf, 19–112. New York: Russell Sage Foundation.

Bourdieu, Pierre. 1987. "The Biographical Illusion." In *Working Papers and Proceedings of the Center of Psychosocial Studies 14*, edited by Richard J. Parmentier and Greg Urban, 1–7. Chicago, IL: The Center.

Cézard, Michel. 1996. "Les ouvriers." *INSEE première* 455: 1–3.

Chardon, Olivier. 2001. "Les transformations de l'emploi non qualifié depuis vingt ans." *INSEE première* 796: 1–4.

Chauvel, Louis. 2010. *Le destin des générations: Structure sociale et cohortes en France du XXe siècle aux années 2010.* Paris: Presses universitaires de France.

Dupays, Stéphanie. 2006. "En un quart du siècle, la mobilité a peu évolué." *Données sociales: La société francaise*: 343–349.

Hall, David. 2012. *Working Lives: The Forgotten Voices of Britain's Post-War Working Class.* London: Corgi Books.

Hatzfeld, Nicolas. 2004. "L'individualisation des carrières à l'épreuve." *Sociétés contemporaines* 54, no. 2: 15–33.

Henninges, Hasso von. 1991. *Ausbildung und Verbleib von Facharbeitern: eine empirische Analyse für die Zeit von 1980 bis 1989.* Nürnberg: Bundesanstalt für Arbeit.

Hunn, Karin. 2005. *"Nächstes Jahr kehren wir zurück": Die Geschichte der türkischen "Gastarbeiter" in der Bundesrepublik.* Göttingen: Wallstein.

Jelidi, Abdallah. 2015. "Abdallah Jelidi." In *Ceux de Billancourt*, edited by Laurence Bagot, 99–112. Ivry-sur-Seine: Les Editions de l'Atelier/ Editions Ouvrières.

Jones, Owen. 2012. *Chavs: The Demonization of the Working Class*. London, New York: Verso.

Lappe, Lothar. 1993. *Berufsperspektiven junger Facharbeiter: eine qualitative Längsschnittanalyse zum Kernbereich westdeutscher Industriearbeit*. Frankfurt am Main: Campus.

Lloyd, Caroline, and Geoff M. K. Mason, eds. 2008. *Low-Wage Work in the United Kingdom*. New York: Russell. Sage Foundation.

Marwick, Arthur. 2009. *British Society Since 1945*, 4th ed. London: Penguin Books.

Mason, Geoff, Ken Mayhew, Matthew Osborne, and Philip Stevens. 2008. "Low Pay, Labour Market Institutions, and Job Quality in the United Kingdom." In *Low Wage Work in the United Kingdom*, edited by Caroline Lloyd, Geoff Mason, and Ken Mayhew, 41–95. New York: Russell Sage Foundation.

Mayer-Ahuja, Nicole. 2003. *Wieder dienen lernen? Vom westdeutschen "Normalarbeitsverhältnis" zu prekärer Beschäftigung seit 1973*. Berlin: Ed. Sigma-Verlag.

McIvor, Arthur. 2013. *Working Lives: Work in Britain since 1945*. Basingstoke: Routledge, 2013.

Molinié, Anne-Francoise. 2000. "Industrial Workforce Decline and Renewal." *INSEE Studies* 43: 1–17.

Mooser, Josef. 1984. *Arbeiterleben in Deutschland 1900–1970: Klassenlagen, Kultur und Politik*. Frankfurt am Main: Suhrkamp.

Mutz, Gerd, Wolfgang Ludwig-Mayerhofer, Elmar J. Koenen, Klaus Eder, Wolfgang Bonß. 1995. *Diskontinuierliche Erwerbsverläufe: Analysen zur postindustriellen Arbeitslosigkeit*. Opladen: Westdeutscher Verlag.

Raithel, Thomas. 2012. *Jugendarbeitslosigkeit in der Bundesrepublik: Entwicklung und Auseinandersetzung während der 1970er und 1980er Jahre*. München: Oldenbourg Verlag.

Raphael, Lutz. 2017. "Arbeitsbiografien und Strukturwandel 'nach dem Boom': Lebensläufe und Berufserfahrungen britischer, französischer und westdeutscher Industriearbeiter und -arbeiterinnen von 1970 bis 2000." *Geschichte und Gesellschaft* 43: 32–67.

Raphael, Lutz. 2019. *Jenseits von Kohle und Stahl: Eine Gesellschaftsgeschichte Westeuropas nach dem Boom*. Berlin: Suhrkamp.

Reid, Ivan. 1998. *Class in Britain*. Cambridge, UK, Malden, MA: Polity Press.

Reitmayer, Morten, and Christian Marx, eds. 2020. *Gewinner und Verlierer nach dem Boom: Perspektiven auf die westeuropäische Zeitgeschichte*. Göttingen: Vandenhoek & Ruprecht.

Sheldrake, John, and Sarah Vickerstaff. 1987. *The History of Industrial Training in Britain*. Aldershot: Avebury.

Solow, Robert. 2008. "The German Story." In *Low Wage Work in Germany*, edited by Gerhard Bosch and Claudia Weinkopf, 1–14. New York: Russell Sage Foundation.

Steedman, Hilary. 2010. *The State of Apprenticeship in 2010: International Comparisons*. London: LSE.

Ther, Philipp. 2014. *Die neue Ordnung auf dem alten Kontinent: Eine Geschichte des neoliberalen Europa*. 3rd ed. Berlin: Suhrkamp.

Torp, Cornelius. 2015. *Gerechtigkeit im Wohlfahrtsstaat: Alter und Alterssicherung in Deutschland und Großbritannien von 1945 bis heute*. Göttingen: Vandenhoeck & Ruprecht.

Weber, Max. 1949. "The Logic of Cultural Sciences." In *The Methodology of the Social Sciences*, edited by Alan Sica, 169–188. New York: The Free Press.

Weischer, Christoph. 2011. *Sozialstrukturanalyse: Grundlagen und Modelle*. Wiesbaden: VS Verlag für Sozialwissenschaften.

Yoko Tanaka

Tumbling Down the Standard Life Course: The *Ice Age Generation* of the Turn of the Twentieth Century and the Origins of Polarisation in Japan

Transformation of the Life Course Regime in Japan

This chapter analyses the transformation of the Japanese life course regime through a comparison of the life course of the so-called Ice Age Generation who came of age in the early 1990s with the standardised life course of prior generations. In Japan, the standardisation of the life course, the processes by and order in which certain life events becoming increasingly universal among a specific population, was significantly shaped by the employment practices of Japanese firms from the 1950s through the 1970s and remained hegemonic until the Ice Age Generation, which triggered a life course regime change.

Until the early 1990s, the working style of post-war Japan was discussed around the globe as a defining aspect of the Japanese employment system. Characteristics of the Japanese corporate system such as "lifetime commitment" (Abegglen 1958) and long-term relationships based on consideration (Vogel 1979; Ouchi 1981) were viewed as aspects of an "organization-oriented" organic corporate community culture (Dore 1973) and were connected to Japan's economic and social success. The high level of commitment of workers engaged in the lean production system of the automobile industry (Womack and Roos 1990; Liker 2004) was lauded widely, and Japan, like Germany, was celebrated as having achieved a long-term community system that had realised "the connection between efficiency and solidarity" (Albert 1991). The World Bank judged that Japan's "sustained economic growth," along with other factors such as "creating human capital" and "rapid productivity growth," had brought about "declining income inequality and reduced poverty" (World Bank 1993: 28–32, 46–59). This perception was reflected in public consciousness as well. From the 1970s onwards, the percentage of Japanese persons who considered themselves "middle class" reached 90 percent, and the notion that Japan was a "middle class society" became widespread (Cabinet Office 1979).

Circumstances changed substantially when the so-called "Ice Age Generation"[1] came of age after the collapse of the overheated Bubble Economy in the early 1990s.[2] The Japanese government defines the Ice Age Generation as "the generation who graduated from schooling around 1993–2004, when the hiring of new graduates sharply contracted after the collapse of the "Bubble economy." Some seventeen million individuals born between the early 1970s and the mid-1980s fall into this category (Council on Economic and Fiscal Policy 2019). From 1993 to 2003, the unemployment rate rose sharply, and the ratio of job openings to job applications dropped far below 1:1 (Figure 1). During this period, many emerging adults failed to secure regular employment after finishing their schooling and were unable to embark on the standard life course that Japanese firms provided to their regular workers.[3]

Further, Japan experienced a "Super Ice Age" after the 2008 Global Financial Crisis, recovery from which was delayed by the 2011 Great East Japan Earthquake and the Fukushima nuclear accident. Young people who entered the workforce during the "lost twenty years" between approximately 1993 and 2013, a large proportion of whom failed to secure regular employment, have been called the "lost generation."[4]

Researchers of education and youth employment were among the first to notice this decline in regular youth employment.[5] Since the early 1990s, high school students have failed to find regular work and have also lost their "social locations"

---

1 "Employment Ice Age" and "Ice Age Generation" was coined in the November 1992 issue of *Job Journal* published by Recruit Co. In 1994, the term received the grand prize in the 11th annual "New and Most Popular Japanese Words of the Year" and has since become a common term widely used throughout Japan.

2 The "Bubble Economy" in Japan, which was triggered by the appreciation of the yen and the reduction of the official discount rate as a result of the Plaza Accord in 1985, led to soaring land and stock prices and a dramatic increase in lending and investment. This overheated economy collapsed in the early 1990s, causing asset values to plummet, companies to go bankrupt, and massive amounts of non-performing loans, leading to a prolonged recession and deflation in the Japanese economy.

3 Full-time, direct employment with an indefinite contract. Regular workers are, in general, guaranteed a monthly salary, regular pay raises, two annual bonuses, health and pension insurance, and a retirement allowance. Long working hours, overtime, and relocation are often required, but dismissal is rare, and employment is stable and secure.

4 "Lost Generation" was first used in Asahi Shimbun's January 2007 serialised article, "The Lost Generation—Wandering 20 Million Youth," and "Lost 20 Years" also came into common usage through the book *"The Lost 20 Years"* (Asahi Shimbun 2009).

5 In postwar Japan, young people graduating from junior high school (13–15 years old) and high school (16–18 years old) either entered the workforce or continued their education through vocational school (2 years), junior college (mainly women, 2 years), or university (4 years).

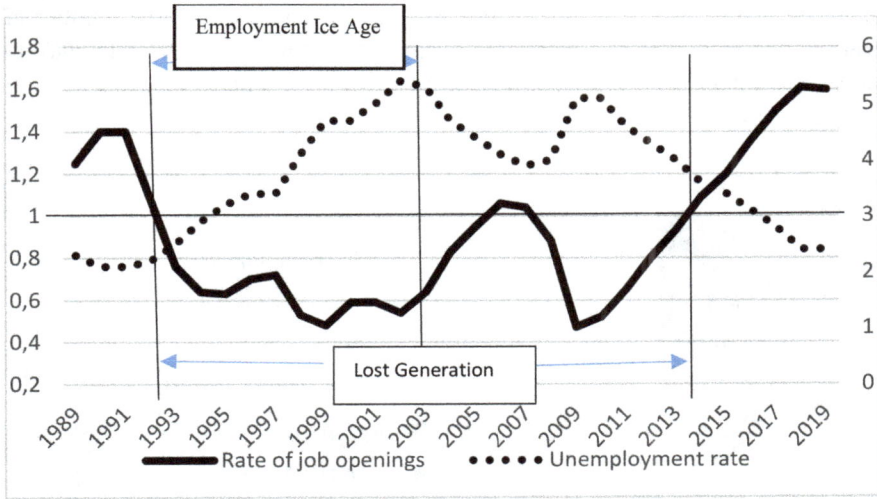

Figure 1: Unemployment rate and rate of job openings in Japan, 1989–2019.
Source: Ministry of Health, Labour and Welfare, Job Placement Security Statistics; Statistics Bureau of Japan, Labour Force Survey.

as the trust-based relationships between schools and firms have narrowed. Particularly students from lower-ranking high schools were obliged to engage in non-regular labour (Yajima and Mimizuka 2001; Miyamoto 2002; Brinton 2008).

At the same time, the term "freeter" also became a buzzword. The Japanese government defines a "freeter" as "a person between the ages of 15 and 34 who is not in school, and, if a female is unmarried, is engaged in employment deemed part-time or *arubaito*,[6] or [a person] who is unemployed and desires to engage in part-time employment or *arubaito*" (Labor Force Survey). Early discourse around freeters was divided between a positive appraisal of young people seeking the freedom to not be tied to firms and condemnation by older generations who saw these young people as idle, unmotivated, and lazy. According to Kosugi, because the freeter discourse was grafted into a "youth discourse" that emphasised "free choice," recognition that freeters were actually a manifestation of the growth of precarious employment came extremely late (Kosugi 2002, 2008). The freeter phenomenon was initially observed among junior high and high school graduates, but it expanded to include graduates of vocational schools and junior colleges, and eventually

---

6 *Arubaito* (derived from the German word "Arbeit") is short-term temporary low-paid employment taken on mainly by high school and university students concurrent with their studies.

even university graduates and advanced degree holders. By 1997, the number of freeters had increased to 1.73 million, swelling to 2.51 million in 2002. In 2007, 40 percent of all 15 to 34-year-olds had failed to secure regular employment after schooling (Hori 2019).

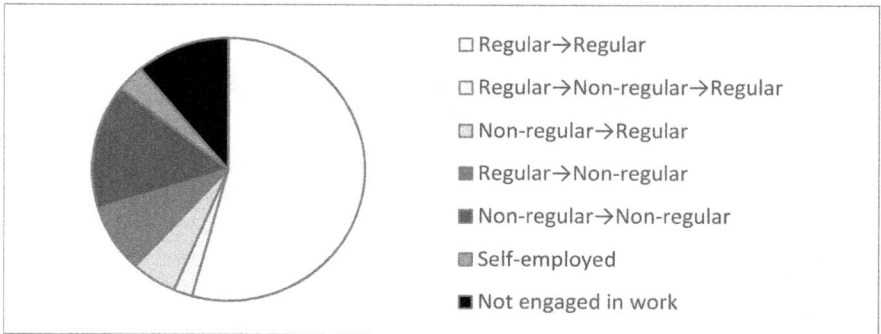

Figure 2: Career trajectory patterns of 15 to 34 year-old individuals in 2007.
Created from the data of JILPT 2019: 23, based on the individual form of employment structure basic survey 2017, excluding housewives.

The term "NEET," defined as "unemployed individuals who have given up on finding jobs," also came to be regarded as a conspicuous phenomenon among young people during the 2000s (MHLW 2007). Honda has diagnosed NEET as victims of structural problems: deteriorating social circumstances blocked these individuals from working even if they wanted to take up employment (Honda 2006). NEET include *hikikomori*, social shut-ins who withdraw from all contact with the outside world. Genda has argued that economic factors are behind the NEET and *hikikomori* phenomena because companies reduced job openings for new graduates in order to protect the jobs of middle-aged workers during the recession (Genda 2001).

As the lost generation aged, "youth problems" grew into "middle-aged problems." As members of the first Ice Age Generation entered their forties in the latter half of the 2010s, poverty among the "Around Forty Generation" attracted social attention (NHK 2019; Amamiya 2016). Because freeters were statistically defined as "15 to 34 years old," a new classification of "over-aged freeters" for freeters over the age of thirty-five was created in response (JILPT 2019: 54–55), just as society grappled with the formation of a new social class unable to be subsumed into the conventional conceptualisation of the standardised Japanese life course regime.

The de-standardisation of the life course can be seen in many Western countries as well. Karl Ulrich Mayer has argued that the "industrial, Fordist life course regime" formed in Europe and the United States between 1955 and 1973 was trending towards de-standardisation. Mayer describes the standardised linear and homogeneous life course as characterised by stable employment contracts, long working lives in the same occupation and firm, age-graded living wages, social insurance for the male breadwinner that allowed women to stay at home and children to receive more education, well-defined and stable social identities, and homogenised stratification. However, this social structure shifted after 1973 into the post-industrial, post-Fordist life course regime characterised by increasing de-standardisation across the lifetime. More workers enter the labour force under temporary contracts, employment is frequently interrupted by unemployment, job shifts are common, and careers are highly contingent (Mayer 2004: 170–173).

The de-standardisation of the life course in Japan differs from the Western case in two respects. First, in Japan, the hegemony of the standard homogeneous life course provided by Japanese firms peaked *after* the 1973 oil shock (ISS 1991–1992), as evident in discourse around the Japanese employment system globally from the 1970s to the early 1990s. Second, the meaning of the non-standard life course differed between the West and Japan. The only option available to Japanese young people who were excluded from the standard life course was poorly compensated, insecure non-regular labour. Significant extensions of personal autonomy or any of the positive qualities of this transformation in the West were non-existent in Japan (Allison 2013; Fujita 2020).

In this chapter, I compare the pre- and post-Ice Age Generation life course in order to clarify the historical transformation of Japan's life course regime. First, I examine how the state envisioned the standard life course through social institutions and their constituent requirements. I then conduct an in-depth analysis of the Toyota Motor Company using multiple worker surveys conducted in the 1970s and 2000s to demonstrate how conditions for the standard life course under the auspices of firms were realised before 1990. This is followed by a contrasting analysis of the Ice Age Generation life course based on government statistics and recent panel data and survey studies; this analysis sheds light on the work and family trajectories of members of this generation. Finally, I discuss whether the Ice Age Generation commits to the cohort problem or to the life course regime change.

Definitions of Japan's Standard Life Course

As a starting point, it is important to understand the conditions of Japan's standard life course. Such an assessment is possible through an examination of how the Japanese state has defined "standard" within social systems, which appears in its statistics. First, a "standard worker" was defined in the Basic Survey on Wage Structure by the Ministry of Health, Labor and Welfare: they "are employed upon graduating from educational institutions and continue to work under the same employer." The clause "employed upon graduating from educational institutions" refers to the simultaneous recruitment system, or the continual transition from school to work. Firms secure their necessary personnel while young people are still in school, and the new employees all begin work on April 1, immediately after they graduate. Any other hiring practice is considered a deviation from this norm.

This system emerged during the nineteenth century among firms recruiting graduates from elite educational institutions into white-collar positions. It became the primary recruiting system for administrative and technical positions during the 1920s and 1930s (Sugayama 2011; Wakabayashi 2018). In the 1960s, this simultaneous recruiting system was systematised in high schools and was based on direct relationships between firms and schools. High school teachers recommended students suitable for firm positions. This practice saved the firm the trouble of candidate selection while providing the student with employment at a firm where he could expect to receive support from his school's alumni. This system of simultaneously recruiting new graduates for both white-collar and blue-collar regular labour became the standard human resource allocation practice in Japan (Brinton 2008; Sugayama 2011).

The second characteristic of a "standard worker" is "continuous work under the same employer," described as "lifetime commitment" in the discourse on the Japanese employment system (Abegglen 1958; Koike 1991, 1996). This "lifetime commitment" is connected to career development based on the premise of stable employment and long-term human relationships. A worker acquires firm-specific skills developed in-house and receives regular salary increases and promotions. Conversely, "lifetime commitment" precludes employment interruptions and job shifts. Changes in one's place of work are considered deviations from the "standard"; thus, "standard workers" were employed as regular workers just after school graduation and have worked at that firm for a long time. Employment forms among men in 1987 indicate that the percentage of working men aged 25 to 50 employed as regular workers exceeded 95 percent (Figure 3). Although a certain number of men aged 15 to 24 were employed in *arubaito*, and a segment of men aged 55 to 59 years were employed as *shokutaku*,[7] almost all men aged 20 to 54 were regular workers.

The "standard family" was established on the basis of men securing employment as regular workers. The definition of "standard household" in Household Surveys by the Statistics Bureau of Japan has been "a household consisting of a married couple and two children, with only one household head." In other words, a nuclear family in which only the husband worked and the wife and two children did not work was considered "standard."[8]

Under the Employees' Pension Insurance system, model pensions were calculated according to the "standard household" defined by the Ministry of Health, Labor, and Welfare as "A single-income household, namely, a couple with an employed husband earning the average standard monthly remuneration of actively working men, who is enrolled in an employee pension for the standard period, and a wife who has never enrolled in an employee pension" (Pension Model). The standard pension enrolment period, that is, the number of years the husband was expected to work, was modelled at twenty years in 1965; this period was repeatedly extended until 1985, when it reached forty years. The "standard" employee was expected to work continuously as regular worker for forty years.

To help enforce this model, a "third category" for dependent wives of employed men was established within the social insurance system in 1985. This system entitled a dependent wife to receive a basic pension from her husband's employee pension even if she had not paid premiums herself. A wife's pension was covered by her husband. The wife and children's health issues were covered by the husband's health insurance. In addition, men with dependent wives and children received family allowances from their firms and tax deductions from the state. This system also treated wives with an annual income of 1 million yen or less in non-regular employment the same way it treated housewives: as "dependents" of their husbands. In other words, it was "standard" for a wife either to not work or to only work part time for a very short period.

The social systems designed were based on these definitions of the "standard worker" and the "standard household." As a result, the "standard" life course in Japan consists of a male worker securing regular employment as a new graduate, his long-term and continuous employment at the same firm, and his responsibility for the livelihoods and social security of the entire family.

---

7 *Shokutaku* refers to a form of often fixed-term employment taken up mainly by retired regular workers.

8 The number of farming families with multi-generation households fell sharply from the 1950s to the 1960s as more young people moved to the cities and the nuclearisation of the family progressed among urban workers (National Census).

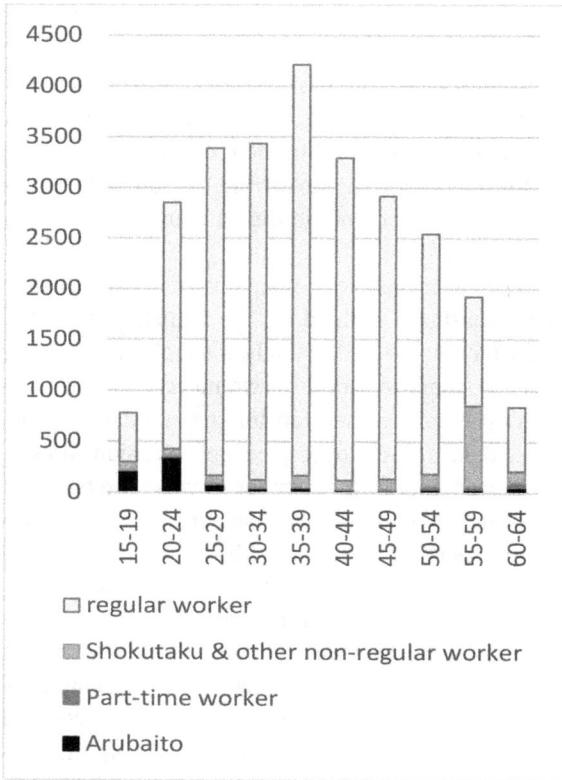

Figure 3: Employment forms among male workers by age (1987).
Source: Statistics Bureau of Japan, Employment Structure Basic Survey, 1987.

The Toyota Life Course

Surveying the lives of workers at the Toyota Motor Corporation demonstrates how these conditions of the "standard" life course were realised in practice.[9] In this section, I will trace the trajectory of the "Toyota Man" using data from multiple Toyota worker interview surveys conducted between the 1970s and the 2000s, official

---

9 Toyota became a popular topic of interest from the 1980s to the 2000s, when considerable research was conducted on its competitiveness, success, the corporate culture of the Toyota System, and its lean production (Monden 1983; Cusumano 1985; Womack, Jones, and Roos 1990; HBS/IG Metall 1992; Kochan et al. 1997; Fujimoto 1999; Liker 2004; Liker and Hoseus 2009).

corporate histories, and the Toyota Worker's Career Data (TWCD), a massive personnel records database created by Katsuji Tsuji.[10]

The simultaneous hiring of new graduates

Since the company's establishment in 1937, Toyota has maintained the simultaneous hiring of new graduates for positions requiring a degree. Starting on April 1, junior high school graduates begin their training at an in-house training school for three years before being deployed to their factory assignments. New high school graduates were positioned to take up clerical and technical positions and, starting in 1962, jobs as technicians. The company-wide system of simultaneously hiring new graduates with the first day of work set as April 1 was formally regulated in 1953 (Tanaka 1982: 64; Koyama 1985: 373–375; Toyota 1987a: 236).

During the 1950s and 1960s, Toyota experienced serious labour shortages due to the rapid expansion of its production. In addition to the recruitment of new graduates, it expanded its hiring of temporary workers, including former personnel from the Japanese Self Defense Forces. Initially, most of these temporary workers were seasonal workers from surrounding rural areas employed only during the agricultural off-season. The later expansion of this non-regular labour force included the sons of farmers and self-employed people from all over Japan who left their hometowns to join Toyota. The ratio of temporary workers soared to 20 to 40 percent of all Toyota employees until the mid-1960s. While a system for promoting these temporary workers to regular workers was established in 1959, and the number of temporary workers soared in the 1960s, the number of such workers significantly decreased to below 10 percent from the 1970s onwards because of the internal system of promotion. Instead of reducing the temporary workforce, all the regular factory workers were expected to have a wider range of skills and were responsible for multiple tasks including process maintenance and daily improvement, which lead to the creation of the Toyota Production System (Komatsu 2007: 141–145; ORI 1994: 32–330, 343; Tanaka 1982–2: 67–68; Tsuji 2011: 39–42).

As for female employees, in 1957 both labour and management agreed that married women should be forced out of employment. Except for certain circumstances such as a husband's death or illness, women "quitting or being forced to

---

10 Research on labour at Toyota made great strides in the 1970s and 1980s through multiple questionnaires and interview surveys mainly conducted by the Nagoya-based group of Yoichi Koyama et al. and the Kansai-based group of Hikari Nohara et al. (Nomura 1993). Since the turn of the twenty-first century, this research has been advanced by research groups led by Masaki Saruta and Katsuji Tsuji, respectively.

quit upon marriage" became a firmly established norm. Female factory workers during the war and the immediate post-war period transformed into junior high and high school graduates with an average age of 20, who were then placed in clerical positions as "workplace flowers." Of these women workers, 70 to 80 percent married Toyota employees (Nohara 1988: 151–153; Tanaka 1982; Saruta 1995).

All regular workers were officially urged to join in-house "voluntary" associations according to their educational backgrounds and gender: former apprentices joined the "Hoyo club," university graduates the "Hoshin club," temporary workers promoted to regular workers joined the "Horyu club," and so on.[11] These "voluntary" associations were intentionally designed by the company to promote long-term relationships between group members after the Great Strike at Toyota in 1950 (ORI 1980: 330–331; Tanaka 1982–1: 39–41).

In-house training and integration within the firm

Male regular employees hired as new graduates received systematic on-the-job training under the direction of senior colleagues (*senpai*) and managers who integrated them into the corporate culture. Training in Toyota factories was conducted according to the Toyota Job Instruction method that was systematised during the 1960s: The trainer explains the importance of the product and the whole process to completion many times, then shows how to do steps 1–3 of 1–10, emphasising the key points. Then he lets the trainee try it, corrects their mistakes, and has the trainee explain what he was doing while doing it, having him recite the key points out loud. If the trainee can do it, the trainer has him do it repeatedly, then more quickly. The trainee determines a person he can ask for help (Liker and Meier 2007; Koyama 1985: 203–204, 287–289).

At the same time, Toyota expanded its development of the quality control (QC) circle and worker-generated problem-solving activities. The "Personal Touch" (PT) activity or, since 1976, "Personal Training" was also systemised, with one *senpai* assigned to be a mentor to each new high school graduate employee. PT leaders invited new workers to participate in recreational activities including social gatherings and drinking, hiking trips, and exercise and sport programs. For half a year, new workers took turns writing in a diary with their *senpai* and foremen. The "Toyota Man" mindset was thus cultivated and conveyed as corporate culture (Toyota 1967: 806; Toyota 1987: 7; Nohara and Fujita 1988: 258–260, 455).

---

11 *Ho* is another pronunciation of *Toyo* of Toyota.

All new workers were not only organised into in-house associations and PT recreational groups; they were also integrated into a multi-layered social network of organisations according to the year of recruitment, prefecture of origin, the gathering and drinking unit in each department, section, division, and group, and Toyota's official thirty-six sports clubs and forty-three cultural circles (Toyota 1978: 369; Toyota 1987: 228–231; Nohara and Fujita 1988: 256–257). "The workers are tied up both vertically and horizontally by countless informal groups" (Tanaka 1982: 42), and workers commented that "there are too many associations; if one is active in all of them, he will have no time off" (Koyama 1985: 391). Yet, being perceived as a "motivated Toyota Man" through group participation was thought to pave the way to promotion and lead to a "happy life within the corporation" (Koyama 1985: 332; Nohara and Fujita 1988: 460–462).

Advancement opportunities and wages increases

The majority of regular workers who built their careers at Toyota advanced within the company and enjoyed regular wage increases although work at Toyota was arduous. In 1981, the total annual working hours exceeded 2,200, and the average amount of leave taken annually was 8.9 days, used mostly for illnesses and ceremonial occasions such as weddings and funerals. The workday on the production line, including commuting time, was eleven to fourteen hours. Many workers suffered from sleep disorders and physical maladies due the weekly rotation between day and night shifts. If one was promoted to line leader, or *Kumi-cho*, he was able to get out of high-intensity direct work (Koyama 1985: 359, 367, 569; ORI 1994: 365).

The evaluation criteria for promotion was not one's skill because of standardisation; rather, emphasis was placed on his ideas for job process improvement or *kaizen*, leadership in managing workers, and record of participation in in-house associations. The enthusiasm for QC activities, sports activities, and in-house association participation was highly competitive and was evaluated as such. It was said that "you'll advance three years faster if you've worked as a leader there"; half of workers and 80 percent of managers actively participated in the various events held by in-house organisations (ORI 1980: 325–326; Koyama 1985: 361–364, 382–384, 392; Nohara and Fujita 1988: 448–450).

In general, a factory worker was promoted to *Han-cho* or 'group leader' after approximately ten years, with three out of four group leaders promoted to *Kumi-cho* ('line leader') after approximately fifteen years, and two out of five line leaders promoted to *Ko-cho* or 'foreman' after twenty-five years (ORI 1980: 324–325; Tsuji 2011: 128–132). Wages rose steeply with promotion to managerial positions (Nohara and Fujita 1988: 241–253; Liker and Meier 2007: chap. 11). Although workers who were married and had previous experience when they joined the company "could not be promoted any higher than group leader," promotion was possible for young workers who had joined as unmarried, fixed-term contract workers (Koyama 1985: 379, 381).

For example, Mr. A, a factory worker, was born in 1944. He became a regular worker at Toyota in 1966 at the age of twenty-two, after his promotion from temporary worker. He was an average blue-collar worker, working day-to-night double shifts on the assembly line for over thirty-five years and advancing from group leader to team leader. During his career, he had a "standard" family of four with his wife working part time. Excluding a period when illness resulted his absence from work, Mr. A's base salary rose every year (Figure 3). His annual income of $46,000[12] at the age of thirty-eight had doubled to $91,000 by the age of fifty-two. His base salary accounted for approximately 60 percent of his monthly salary, which rose progressively year after year. Mr. A also received a family allowance of $180 for the wife and children he supported, as well as $1,360 as a premium for extra work such as overtime, late-night work, and shift work (Tsuji 2011: 391–397).

Working conditions for university graduates were also strict; "7 am to 7 pm were basically regular working hours, though [workers] usually worked until after 10 pm" (Tanaka 1982: 1–50). University graduates endured these harsh conditions with the dream of advancing to section chief. Three out of four workers who entered the company in the same cohort (organised by year) were promoted to division chief with an average time to promotion of thirteen years. Of these division chiefs, 70 percent were promoted to section chiefs after approximately four years. One in six section chiefs were promoted to deputy general managers, and 2 percent of the same cohort became directors thirty-two to thirty-eight years after joining the company (ORI 1980: 324–325; Tsuji 2011: 94–100, 132–134, 440).

Another example, Mr. B, was hired as a clerical worker upon his graduation from university in 1959. At the age of thirty, Mr. B was promoted to division manager in human resources, and at thirty-seven, he advanced to the position of section manager of the legal office in corporate headquarters. After gaining experience as section chief of a computing department, he was promoted to deputy general manager at forty-four years old. At fifty, he was loaned to an affiliated company as deputy director. He left Toyota at age fifty-two to become the director of the same affiliated company. Although Mr. B was an elite employee in the preeminent computing department, he was unable to advance to director within Toyota. For such workers, the company offered opportunities for secondments and

---

12 Calculated as US$1 = 110 yen (April 2021).

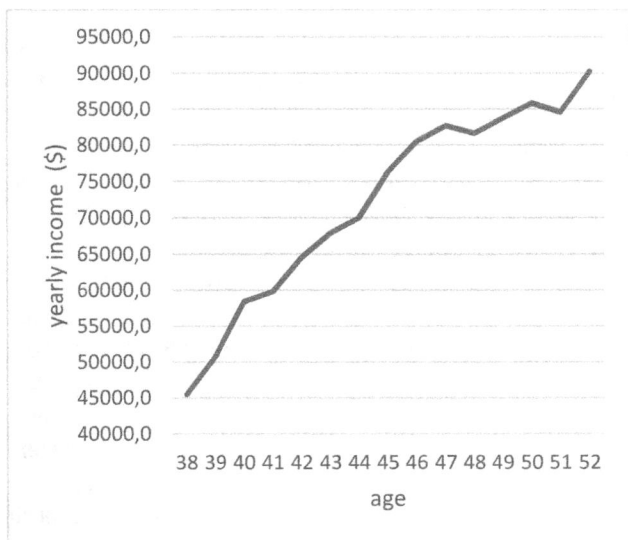

Figure 4: Wage development of Mr. A (assembly line worker, day and night shift, between 38–52 years old), 1982–1997.
Source: Pay slips of Mr. A in Tsuji 2011:392.

transfers in a quasi-internal labour market with affiliated companies domestically and abroad. Mr. B's career trajectory, during which he transferred to an affiliated company as an officer or director, was fairly typical (Tsuji 2011: 57–59; Toyota 1987: 240–241; Komatsu 2007: 154–155).

Family and home ownership

Toyota workers were heavily dependent on the company in other aspects of their lives as well. Daily life consisted of living in company housing near the factory, shopping for daily necessities at the Toyota Coop founded by the company in 1946, using the Toyota Hospital, driving a Toyota car purchased with a company loan, and participating in company-sponsored recreation and sports events. The company and the Toyota Coop held athletic competitions, summer festivals, an *eki-den* road relay race, bowling tournaments, bazaars, and community clean-ups in which workers could participate with their entire families on weekends and holidays. Around 60 percent of workers participated in these types of company-sponsored activities at least once a month, and more than 10 percent participated at least three times a month (Nohara and Fujita 1988: 397, 426–428; Toyota 1978b).

In 1976, the company described the "Toyota Man's Average Life" as follows: "He buys a car shortly after gaining employment. He gets married around the age of 25 and acquires a house around the birth of his second child in his late 20s to early 30s." In fact, for male workers who joined the company in 1964, the average age of marriage was twenty-seven, to a woman of twenty-three, who subsequently gave birth to their first child when her husband was twenty-nine and their second child when he was thirty-one (Koyama 1985: 547; Tsuji 2011: 451).

Upon joining the company as a new graduate, male workers generally lived in dormitories for single men that were constructed *en masse* between the 1950s and 1970s. Upon marriage, workers moved into company family housing and eventually acquired their own homes. The rate of home ownership among Toyota workers was particularly high, and the average age of purchase was particularly young – only thirty-one years old. This was because starting in the 1960s, the company promoted homeownership among workers through the low-interest mortgage system of the Human Resources Department and home sales of the Toyota Housing Company. For Toyota workers, building savings through an in-house savings deposit system and purchasing a home with a twenty-five-year company-sponsored mortgage was a commitment to be bound to the company in return for lifetime stability. Another reason was the small size of company housing units, which prevented night-shift workers from sleeping undisturbed during the day because of their children (Toyota 1978a: 366–367; ORI 1980: 322, 366; Yamashita 1981: 34; Nohara and Fujita 1988: 255, 421–422; Tsuji 2011: 449).

Since many workers had left their hometowns to join Toyota, over 90 percent of families were nuclear. Approximately 80 percent of white-collar clerical workers and technicians' wives were full-time housewives, while 70 percent of blue-collar factory workers' wives worked part time after their children had matured (Nohara and Fujita 1988: 404). These wives had no relatives living nearby, and their husbands returned home late. "My husband leaves home around 6 o'clock [in the morning] and returns home at 9:30 [at night] at the earliest," lamented an employee's wife. "When he gets home, he eats and hurries off to bed at 11 o'clock. He even goes to work on two of his days off a month. When I am worried about something, I have no choice but to solve it myself. I have stopped expecting things of my husband" (ORI 1980: 366–367). Husbands acknowledged the toll that their working conditions had on their families: "The reason I was able to work hard at Toyota would have to be my wife. I am a 'company man' (*kaisha ningen*), and my wife supported me in all sorts of ways. She also raised our children, and she did all the work around the house because I don't do it. I was able to dedicate myself to the company with peace of mind because she took care of the family so well" (Tsuji 2011: 490). These statements illustrate the reality of the "standard" Japanese family.

Long-term continuous employment and post-retirement

Toyota defines lifetime employment as the company's will not to dismiss workers (Yamamoto, Former Human Resource Management Director) (Tanaka 1982: 2–73). The corporation values long-term employment, celebrating workers who have reached milestone years of long-term service since 1952. Although "some workers had the courage to change jobs, and others' met with failure after changing jobs," remembered one Toyota worker, labour turnover at Toyota was limited, with the percentage of workers who voluntarily chose to leave Toyota 4.3 percent in 1980 and 3.7 percent in 1981. A high proportion of Toyota workers desired "life stability," and many "did not consider leaving the company" (Tanaka 1982: 2–71; Tsuji 2011: 45, 486–491).

Figure 5 shows the ratio of workers who joined the company between 1956 and 1959 and reached twenty years of continuous service. It reveals that "lifetime employment" was realised by 80 to 90 percent of male university graduates, 70 to 80 percent of male junior high and high school graduates, and almost no women.

	# of individuals hired	%
Male university graduate, clerical and technical worker	50	80.0
Male university graduate, clerical worker	27	88.9
Male university graduate, technical worker	48	87.5
Male high school graduate, clerical and technical worker	33	81.8
Male high school graduate, clerical worker	9	77.8
Male high school graduate, technical worker	20	70.0
Junior high school graduate trainee	194	73.7
Female university graduate, clerical worker	7	0.0
Female high school graduate, clerical worker	104	3.8
Female junior high school graduate, clerical worker	80	0.0
Total	572	52.6

Figure 5: Ratio of Toyota workers hired between 1956–1959 who reached 20 years of continuous service by gender and educational background.
Source: Toyota Worker's Career Data (TWCD) and *Toyota Newspaper*, cross-checked by Tsuji (2011:291–292). The names for each hiring category are listed only between 1956–1960. "Clerical and technical" is the category descriptor in *Toyota Newspaper.*

Upon their retirement at age of fifty-five (or sixty since the 1970s), workers were paid company retirement allowances. Line leaders and foremen with forty years of service received about $180,000, with clerical workers and technicians receiving an additional $100,000 or more depending on rank (Koyama 1985: 495). Regular workers received a pension equivalent to 68 to 69 percent of their previous remuneration (for those who reached retirement age between 1980 to 1994) through the public employee pension system. In addition, workers also received generous pensions from the Toyota Corporate Pension depending on their length of service and position at the company. For this reason, Toyota employees were able to lead comfortable lives even in old age.

After retirement, former workers maintained the social connections they had built through the company, participating in their local organisation for Toyota retirees, the "Hoju Club," returning to work as *shokutaku* for three to five years, and going on trips with people with whom they worked (Toyota 1978: 368; Koyama 1985: 409, 406, 579; Tsuji 2011: 489–490). The life courses of Toyotamen are summarised as follows (Figure 6).

In interviews, workers of retirement age looked back on their lives and reminisced: "I've been at Toyota since I was 15 years old, so it's like native soil to me. I feel so much gratitude; Toyota looks out for me. It did when I needed to borrow money or bought a house" (junior high school graduate, apprentice). Others stated, "I'm glad I came to Toyota. I was even able to send my kids to school and build a house" (worker who had been promoted from temporary to regular employment); and "I felt great satisfaction in my work. I received proper appreciation for my work. I was able to get to where I am without many restraints" (university graduate technician) (Koyama 1985: 357, 488–493, 522).

The above analysis demonstrates that at Toyota, a worker's life course constituted the following: (1) the simultaneous hiring of new graduates into regular work; (2) in-house training and the commitment to and integration in the corporate organisation culture; (3) advancement opportunities, wage increases, career development, and long-term continuous employment; (4) family formation and home ownership; and (5) a stable post-retirement period supported by a pension, retirement allowance, and firm-based social relationships.

Toyota met all the conditions necessary for the Japanese standard life course by hiring their employees as new graduates, promoting long-term service, and providing family support for full-time male employees. It provided long-term stability under its corporate auspices in return for the hard work of the husband and the shadow labour of the wife. Although the case of the Toyota Motor Company is distinct, it nevertheless served as a leading model for many firms and served as the basis for the standardised life course regime in Japan.

New graduates simultaneously hired

	15-19	20-25	26-30	31-35	36-40	41-45	46-50	51-55	56-60	(61-65)
Work	graduate/ simultaneously hired 17.8	worker	group trainer 26.1, Team leader (Hancho) 30.4	line leader (Kumicho) 35.2		(Foreman (Ko-cho))			retirement	pension life, shokutaku worker
Family		marriage 25.7	first child 26.5	second child 31		high school graduation of the first child 44.5				
Residence	Company single dormitory	Company housing	Home ownership 29.2	Repaying mortgage				Loan repayment completed		

Married, mid-career hires

	15-19	20-25	26-30	31-35	36-40	41-45	46-50	51-55	56-60	(61-65)
Work				mid-career hire 33.2	worker	group trainer, group leader (Hancho)	(line leader(Kumi-cho))		retirement	pension life, shokutaku worker
Family			marriage 26.5, first child 29.2				high school graduation of the first child 47.2			
Residence				Company housing, home ownership 35.9	Repaying mortgage				Loan repayment completed	

Figure 6: The life courses of Toyotamen: New graduates simultaneously hired and married mid-career hires.
Sources: Average age of persons in the new graduates group (54 cases) and married, mid-career hiring group (11 cases). The single, mid-career hire group (49 cases) with an average age of employment of 22 is located in the middle of the two groups. Koyama 1985:545–547.

The Formation of the Non-standard Life Course

This Japanese standardised life course regime was severely damaged around the time the so-called Ice Age Generation was born. Drawing on data from government statistics, newly established long-term panel data, and multiple interview surveys concerning the Ice Age Generation, this section will examine the condition of the non-standard life course of members of this generation in contrast to the life course of the Toyotamen described above.

The failure to transition to regular worker after graduation

The most striking change in this generation was the steep decline in the number of individuals making the uninterrupted transition from school to work. One of the three key conditions for the standard life course, the simultaneous hiring of new graduates, went unfulfilled. Figure 7 reveals a sharp increase in the number of young people entering the labour market who were unable to secure regular employment starting in the 1990s.

Compared to 1987 and 1992, the proportion of regular workers among both men and women significantly declined after 1997, and especially after 2000. The drop in the proportion of regular workers among the 15 to 24 age group was rapid, with the ratio of male regular workers aged 20 to 24 shrinking from 85 percent to 60 percent. The trend for women was similarly bleak; while 72 percent of female high school graduates had secured regular work in 1987, this ratio plummeted to 18 percent by 2012. For women in the 20 to 24 age group, the ratio fell from 84 percent to 56 percent. The condition of being hired as a new graduate, which was necessary for living the standardised life course, was seriously undermined after the mid-1990s.

Differences in employment trajectories

Could individuals who were unable to secure regular employment as new graduates gain regular employment later on? Figure 8, based on the "Longitudinal Survey on Employment and Fertility: LOSEF," [13] shows changes in the employment status of men born between 1961 and 1966 and that of the Ice Age cohort born between 1976 and 1981, separated by whether they entered the workforce in regular employment or not.

For the 1961 to 1966 cohort, those who began their careers in regular employment (A) represent the standard life course in which nearly all men remained in regular, long-term employment. Among the men in this cohort who started out in

---

13 The longitudinal tracking people's work and life trajectories did not exist in Japan for many years. However, in 2011, Prof. Takayama of Hitotsubashi University and his team constructed Japan's first long-term panel data, the "Longitudinal Survey on Employment and Fertility: LOSEF," from pension records.

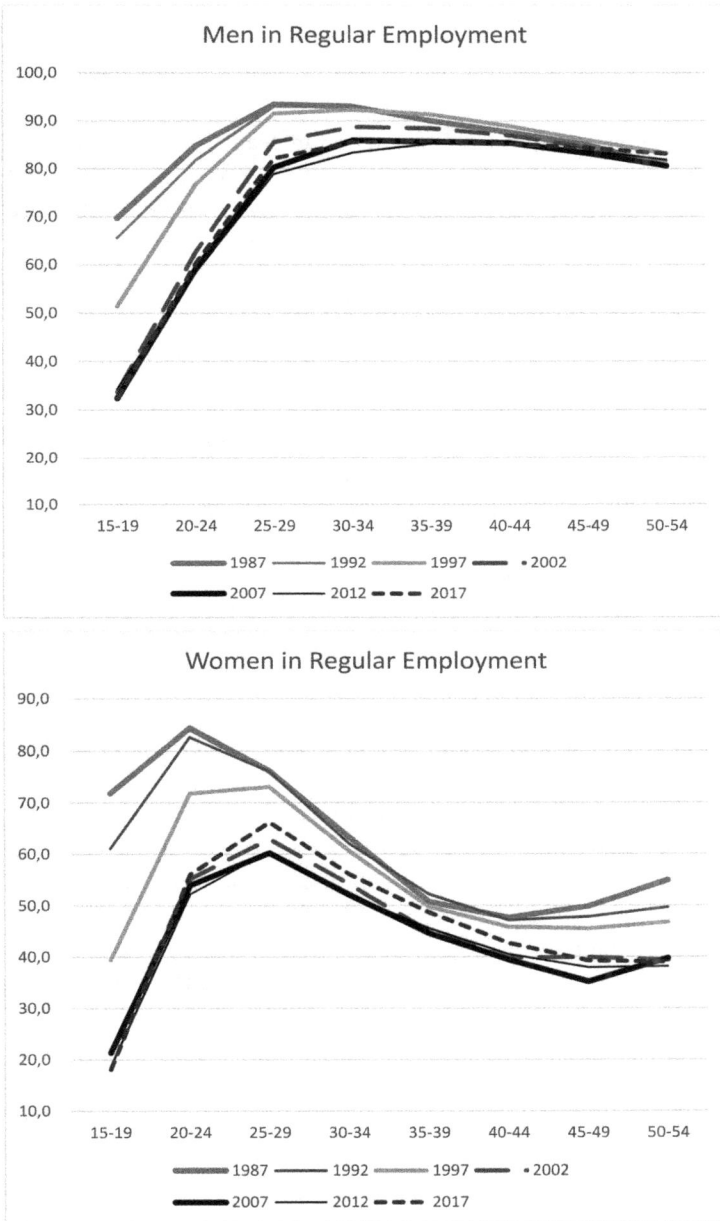

Figure 7: Proportion of regular workers by age group, men and women, 1987–2017.
Source: Created with data from the Employment Structure Basic Survey, 1987–2017.

non-regular employment (B), 80 percent became regular employees in their late twenties to late thirties. These two employment paths match those of Toyota's newly graduated regular workers and temporary workers who were converted to regular employment.

In contrast, the proportion of men starting out in regular employment is 10 percent lower among men of the 1976 to 1981 Ice Age cohort (C). Very few men from this cohort (D) engaged in non-regular employment were able to become regular workers. When this cohort reached their mid-thirties, nearly 40 percent of men were still engaged in non-regular employment. This large proportion of non-regularly employed men formed a social class beyond the scope of the assumptions of the standard life course.

In the standard life course, women usually worked in regular employment until their mid-twenties, married a regular male worker, and either spent the rest of their lives as full-time housewives or worked part time as their children grew up. The 1961 to 1966 cohort of women who started off in regular employment in Figure 9 (A) closely reflects this life course. As they aged, the proportion of female regular workers declined, with half of them becoming housewives in their thirties. The increase in the proportion of non-regular workers after the age of forty represents women working part-time to supplement the household income after their children reached school age. Because the ratio of unmarried women during this period was 4.5 percent for women aged forty to forty-four years old, and the average age at which they gave birth to their first child was twenty-six years old, the increase in women engaging in non-regular labour appears when their children were between ten and fifteen years old. Even among women who started working in non-regular (B) employment, the number of full-time housewives peaked at 40 percent during their thirties, with the ratio of women working part time increasing thereafter.

For the 1976 to 1981 cohort, the trajectories of women who started their careers as regular workers (C) were similar to those of the 1961 to 1966 cohort. However, like men, nearly 70 percent of women who started out as non-regular workers (D) were stuck in non-regular labour through their twenties, and many remained in such employment for much longer. While more than 40 percent of these women became full-time homemakers after the age of thirty-two, another 40 percent remained in non-regular labour into their thirties. Because the percentage of unmarried women in the 1976 to 1981 cohort was 35 percent among those in their thirties, many female non-regular workers of the Ice Age Generation were supporting themselves.

This situation stands in stark contrast to the previous generation of women who had worked part time primarily to supplement household income as part of the framework of the standard life course. While more than a few male non-reg-

Men, Regular,1961–1966 cohort (A)

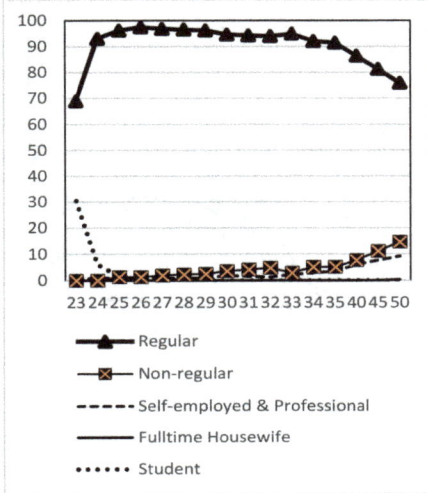

Men, Non-regular, 1961–1966 cohort (B)

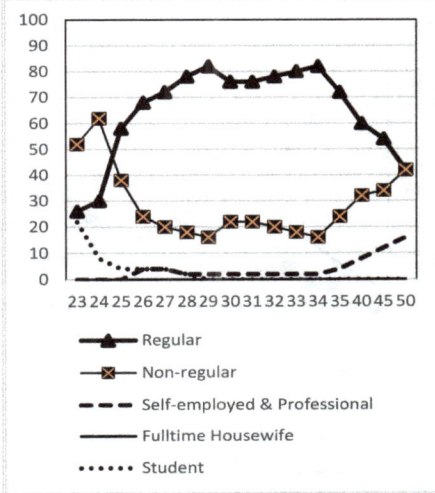

Men, Regular, 1976–1981 cohort (C)

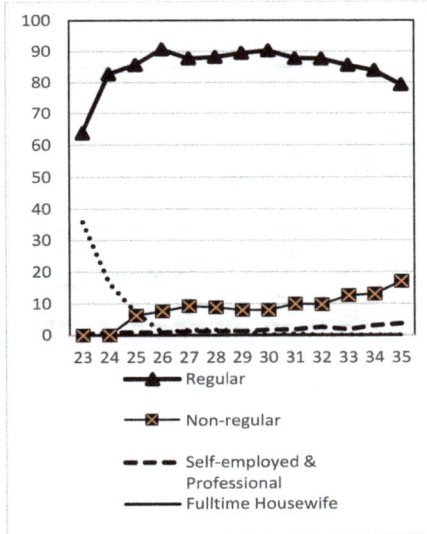

Men, Non-regular, 1976–1981 cohort (D)

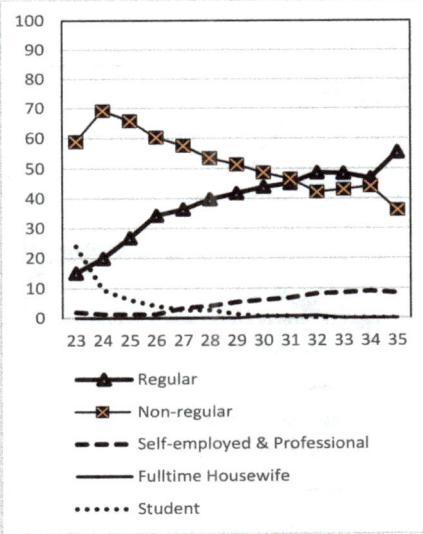

Figure 8: Changes in men's employment status by age, cohort, and first employment.

Men, Regular, 1961–1966 cohort (A) Men, Non-regular, 1961–1966 cohort (B)
Men, Regular, 1976–1981 cohort (C) Men, Non-regular, 1976–1981 cohort (D)
LOSEF Data provided by Prof. Kohsuke Shiraishi.

Women, Regular, 1961–1966 cohort (A)

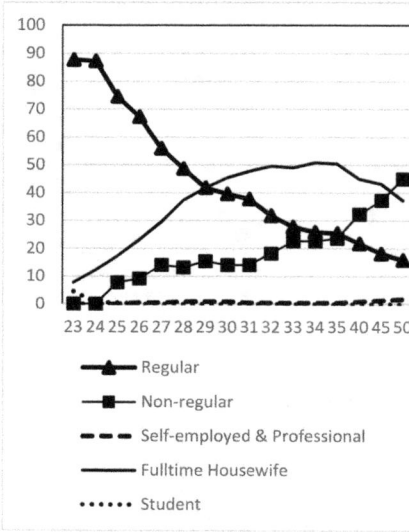

Women, Non-regular, 1961–1966 cohort (B)

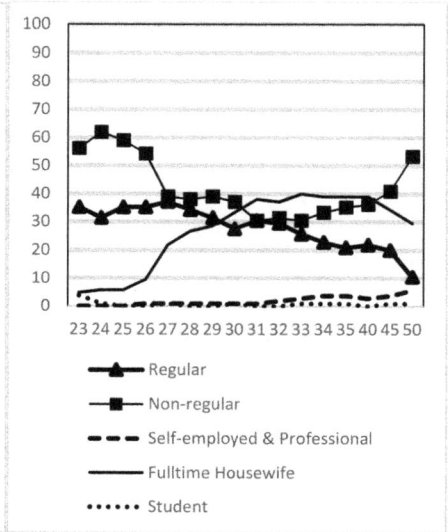

Women, Regular, 1976–1981 cohort (C)

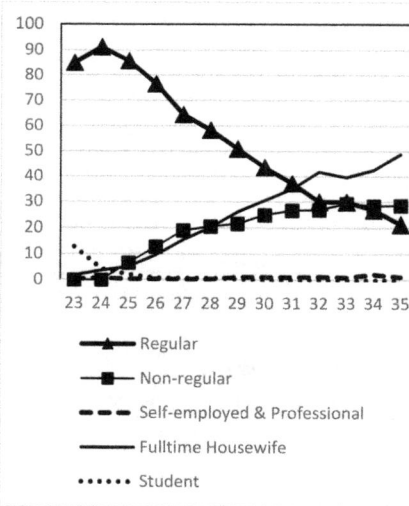

Women, Non-regular, 1976–1981 cohort (D)

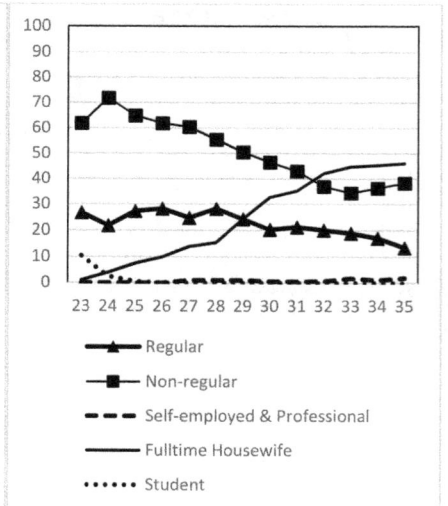

Figure 9: Women's employment status by age, cohort, and first employment.

Women, Regular, 1961–1966 cohort (A)
Women, Regular, 1976–1981 cohort (C)
LOSEF Data provided by Prof. Kohsuke Shiraishi.

Women, Non-regular, 1961–1966 cohort (B)
Women, Non-regular, 1976–1981 cohort (D)

ular workers were able to move into regular labour by their thirties, women did not experience this kind of mobility as a gendered disadvantage (Bukodi and Dex 2010).

In-house training and the career divide

The second condition of the standard life course, in-house training and career advancement, was rarely possible for new graduates unable to secure regular employment.

For example, Mr. C, a man in his twenties, graduated from high school during the Employment Ice Age. After graduation, he attended a vocational school, aspiring to become a systems engineer. But due to the prolonged recession, he was unable to find a regular position and took work arranged through a human resource outsourcing company for the manufacturing industry. He worked at more than thirty factories in eight years – including Toyota, Mitsubishi, Canon, YKK, Isuzu, and Fuji Xerox – as a dispatch employee, attaching automobile differential gears in fifty-eight seconds, inspecting fasteners, and pasting film on liquid crystal displays. His work at each factory lasted for a maximum of a few months and at minimum, a few days. Just when he became accustomed to the work and the people, he moved on to the next placement. Because he lived in an apartment procured by his employer, he risked homelessness if he refused a new job assignment. As a consequence, he continued to move all over Japan, failed to develop skills, build a career, or form human relationships, and he lived solely for the joy of watching his favourite anime (Asahi Shimbun 2007: 39–42).

Another example, Mr. D, a man in his forties, graduated from a well-known university during the Employment Ice Age. He was unable to secure regular employment despite applying to more than one hundred firms. Mr. D had no choice but to register with a temporary worker dispatch agency and accept a job at the call centre of an electronics manufacturer. The contract was for one year, the take-home pay was $1,300 to $1,400 per month, and there were no salary increases or bonuses. Mr. D's income was about 40 percent of a regular employee's salary. He was told that dispatch workers cannot participate in in-house training. Even so, he continued to work with the expectation that he would be hired as regular employee mid-career if he gained experience as a dispatch worker. However, his hopes were dashed as expanded hiring targeted new graduates, and mid-career positions went to regular workers changing employers. After Mr. D turned forty, outside job opportunities often required "management experience," making changing jobs even more difficult for him since he had never overseen a subordinate. Mr. D gave up on becoming a regular worker and became a temporary city employee, earning $1,500 a month (NHK 31–43).

In the last case recounted here, Ms. E, a woman in her late thirties, graduated from a women's junior college in 2000 hoping to work in publishing and joined a small firm as a regular worker. However, because she received very poor compensation and no social insurance there, she quit after two years. She became a dispatch worker at an advertising agency, which turned out to be a so-called "black company."[14] Ms. E's workload was so heavy that she would not return home for as long as a week, spending the night at the office in a sleeping bag. As those she worked with left, Ms. E's physical condition deteriorated, and she also wound up quitting. After this ordeal, she worked in several different jobs in publishing as a dispatch and contract worker but quit because of the discrimination, bullying, and harassment directed at non-regular workers. She then found work at yet another publishing company as a fixed-term contract worker. Ms. E is single, and her parents and unmarried older brother live in the countryside. Since her father was a regular worker at a major company, he has a sufficient pension and owns a condominium. However, he recently became physically disabled, and with Ms. E's mother caring for him, Ms. E is worried about her future and aging (Amamiya 2016: 27–43).

These experiences demonstrate that even with long years of continuous service in non-regular employment, it is extremely difficulty to develop a career, form human connections, receive in-house skill development and training, or secure any of the benefits that were part-and-parcel of the standard life course in Japan. Repeating simple tasks for several days or several months does not allow one to acquire firm-specific skills, and no matter how many years one continues to work in a call centre, he or she cannot gain the skills that will make them employable if they want to change employers. In the above cases and in many others, significant experience in non-regular employment does not lead to upward mobility through regular employment or wage increases.

According to a 2016 survey by the JTUC Research Institute, although 89 percent of men in the 45 to 49 age group reported receiving "sufficient" or "some degree" of guidance in the workplace, this percentage was only 66 percent among the 35 to 39 age group of the Ice Age Generation. This gap was far more pronounced among non-regular workers, 66 percent of whom reported "hardly receiving" or "not re-

---

14 *Burakku kigyō* ('black company') is a term used to describe firms whose working conditions are exploitative and the management abusive. The Ministry of Health, Labour, and Welfare called these "firms which exploit the youth as disposable" and launched an investigation in the 2010s.

ceiving any" education or training. This proportion was also high among those who had changed employers.

Annual income and continuous employment

Denied opportunities for in-house training and promotion, non-regular workers are stuck in low-wage positions. Figure 10 provides LOSEF data on annual income (in US dollars) by gender, cohort, and employment type. We can see that among men, regular workers have the highest income, with workers who have transitioned from non-regular to regular workers earning 20 percent less but still enjoying the expectation of increasing income. In contrast, the annual income of non-regular workers is as low as $17,000 per year regardless of how they entered the labour market, and this changes little with generation or age. This is because the average hourly wage of part-time and *arubaito* workers is $7.50, with virtually no wage increases (JILPT 2009: 105). The annual income of women is significantly lower than that of men, with even regular workers earning only 50 to 70 percent of the pay of men and receiving only small salary increases. The annual income of women engaged in non-regular labour is even lower than that of men – around $11,400 regardless of generation, age, and career trajectory pattern.

According to the JTUC research, the average annual income of university graduates who continued in their first regular employment after being hired as new graduates was $62,000. Those who were hired into regular employment as new graduates but changed employers earned $48,800 on average, or 79 percent of that of continuously employed regular workers; and the average annual income for those who started off in non-regular labour and later were converted to regular workers was $47,000, or 76 percent that of continuously employed regular workers. Those who started in non-regular labour and remained in non-regular labour earned $33,500, only 54 percent of that of continuously employed regular workers (NHK 2019: 25). This comparison puts into perspective the great advantage of being hired into continuous regular labour as a new graduate. Those who change employers or become regular workers mid-career see a 20 to 30 percent decline in their annual income compared to their regularly employed peers who have continued working for the same employer. This disparity increases to 50 percent for non-regular workers.

The proportion of workers who continued to work for the same company also decreased. At pre-Ice Age Toyota, the proportion of employees who were university graduates and continued to work until the age of 50 was 80 to 90 percent. In contrast, among the university graduates of the Ice Age Generation, this ratio was 38.2 percent in the 40 to 44 age group and 43 percent in the 35 to 39 age group. JTUC

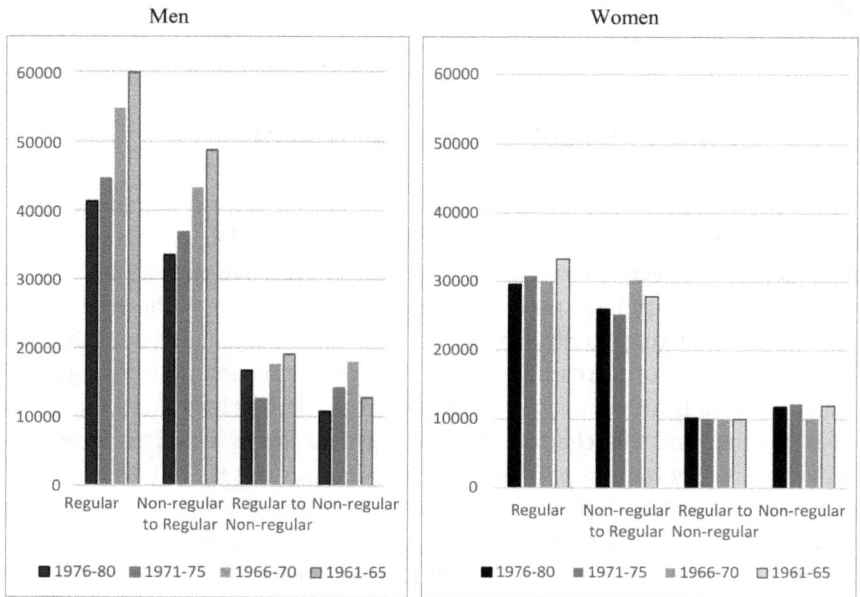

Figure 10: Annual income by gender, cohort, and career trajectory.
Source: Created from LOSEF data; Takayama and Shiraishi 2012:32.

concluded, "Japanese firms' competence development systems based on the premise of long-term employment came to an end with the Employment Ice Age" (JTUC 2016: 41–42, 46–47).

Increasing numbers of unmarried individuals

This increase in non-regular labour has also had a major impact on family formation, with the inability to marry, particularly among young men, becoming a widespread social issue in Japan. The trend towards delaying marriage until later in life began around the 1980s and was accompanied by rising rates of educational achievement; the rate of unmarried individuals in their thirties and forties rose sharply from the 2000s to the 2010s (Figure 11).

For men aged 40 to 44, rates of unmarried individuals increased from 12 percent in 1990 to 29 percent in 2015, and for women, the rate increased from 5.8 percent to 19 percent. According to the 2014 Cabinet Office's "Awareness of Marriage and Family Formation Survey," the rate of men who are married or in a relationship with a specific partner increases as their annual income increases up to $90,000 (Figure 12). At the bottom of this spectrum, fewer than half of men earning less than $27,000 per year are married or in a relationship, and many have no relationship history at all.

Looking at the same data by employment category (Figure 13), the proportion of men who are married or in a relationship is highest among regular workers, lower among non-regular workers, and lowest among the unemployed. More than 60 percent of men with an annual income of less than 4 million yen (approximately $32,000) report believing that they are unable to marry because of "insufficient funds for living expenses" and "unstable employment".

According to an examination of family formation among 35- to 44-year-old men, the marriage rate among men who continued to work for the same employer was 70.6 percent, whereas the rate among those who had changed employers was 57.6 percent. The ratio for having children was 57.8 percent for continuous regular workers and 45 percent for workers who had changed employers (JTUC 2016: 40).

Figure 14 uses data from the Employment Structure Basic Survey to show the marriage rate by employment type, gender, and age. On the one hand, the highest rates of marriage for men are among regular workers, and for women among part-time workers – a pattern aligned with the standardised family life course of male regular worker plus housewife with part-time employment. On the other hand, 60 to 70 percent of female regular, *arubaito*, dispatch, and contract workers under the age of forty are unmarried. The rate of unmarried individuals among male non-regular workers is even higher. Among male part-time, *arubaito*, and dispatch or contract workers, only one in four is married by the age of forty.

Non-regular workers of the Ice Age Generation can be said to have created a new non-standard family in which many individuals in their thirties and forties do not form relationships or marry because of their precarity (Miyamoto 2011; Kosugi and Miyamoto 2015; Amamiya 2016; Fujita 2020).

Co-habitation with Parents and the 70/40 Problem

Members of the Ice Age Generation who remain unmarried and work in non-regular labour often avoid falling into poverty by living with their parents. Figure 15 shows rates of co-habitation with parents of individuals of the Ice Age Generation at the age of forty by marriage and employment status; 93 percent of married men are employed, 35 percent of married women are full-time housewives, and 65 percent of married women work. The majority of these individuals can be considered part of standard families. In contrast, nearly 80 percent of unmarried men, even if they are working, live with their parents, and a full 24 percent are unemployed.

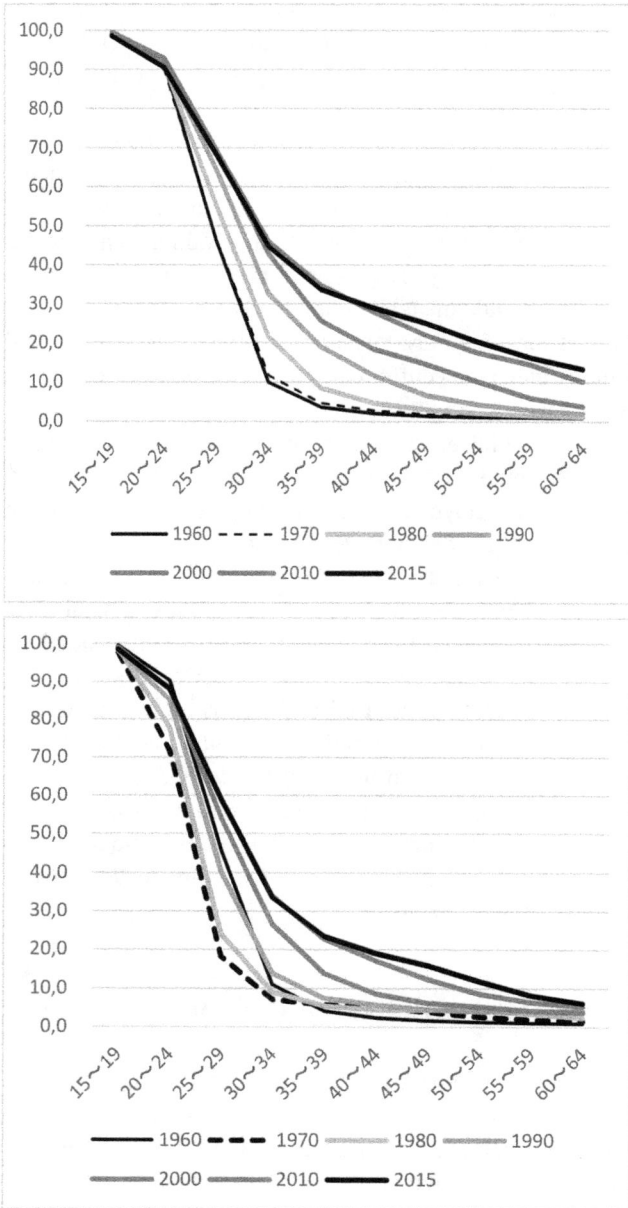

Figure 11: Changes in rates of unmarried individuals by gender and age, 1960–2015.
Source: National Census data.

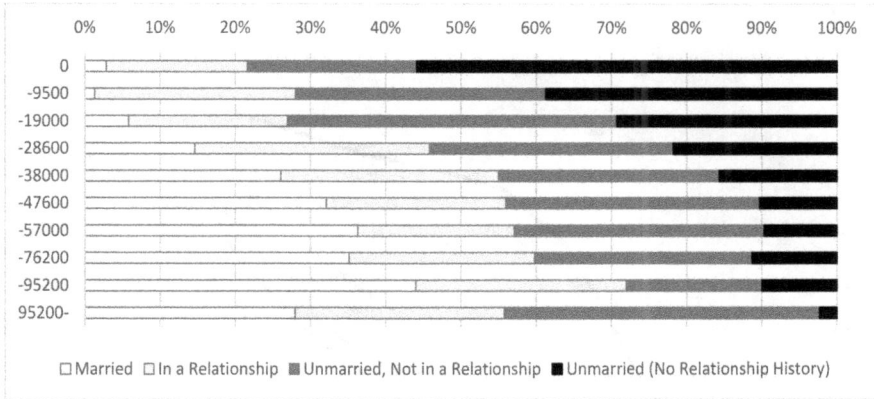

Figure 12: Proportion of men in their 20s and 30s who are married or in a relationship by annual income (in US Dollars).
Source: Cabinet Office 2011:15.

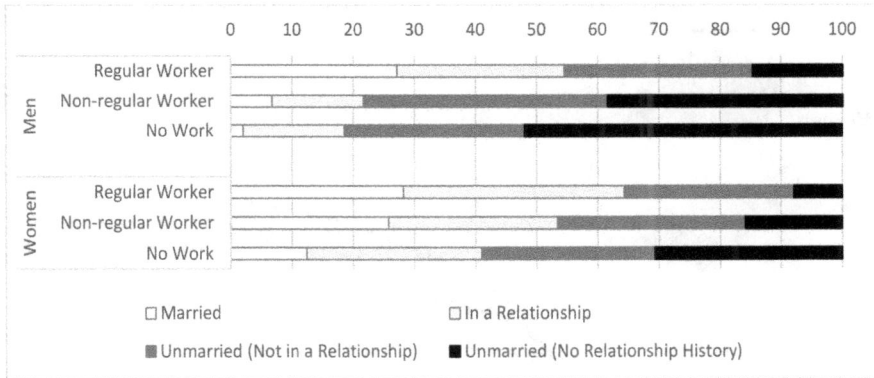

Figure 13: Marriage and relationship status of people in their 20s and 30s by gender and employment form.
Source: Cabinet Office 2011:30.

This figure includes a large number of non-regular workers whose annual incomes are insufficient for them to live independently as well as *hikikomori*. Among unmarried women as well, nearly 80 percent live with their parents, and more than two-thirds of them are supported financially by their parents. Only 17 percent of working unmarried women live independently from their parents (NHK 2019: 125–126).

Men

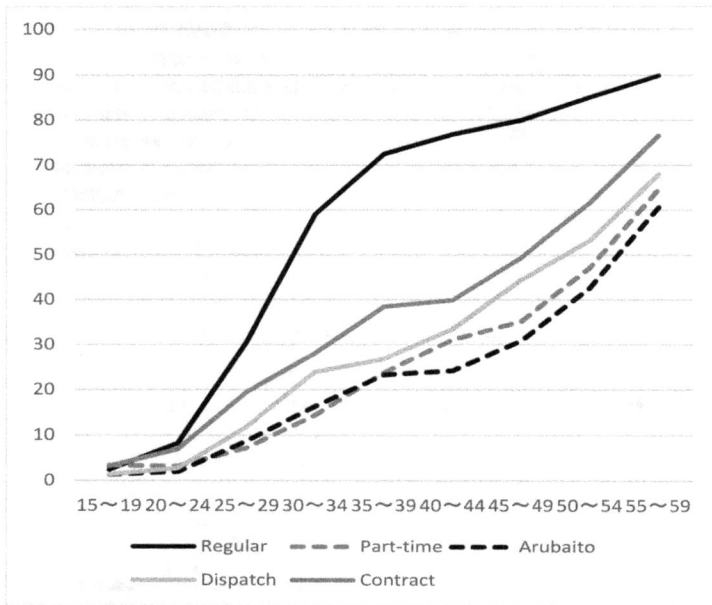

Women

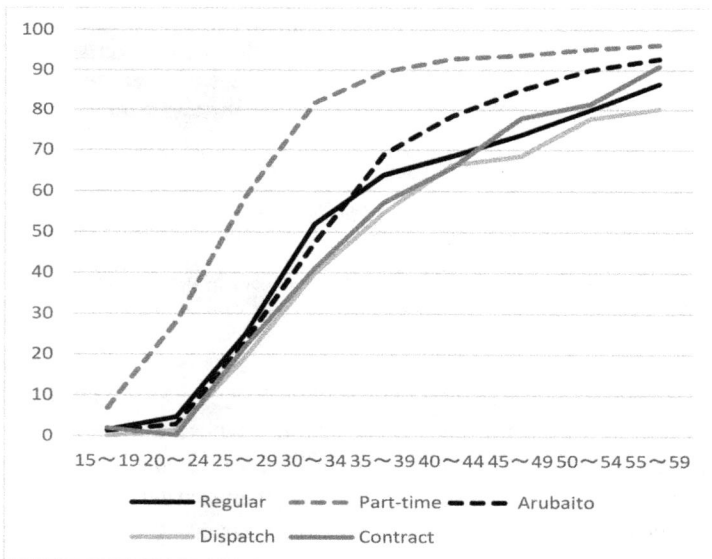

Figure 14: Marriage rates by gender, age, and employment type (2017).
Source: Created from Employment Structure Basic Survey, 2017.

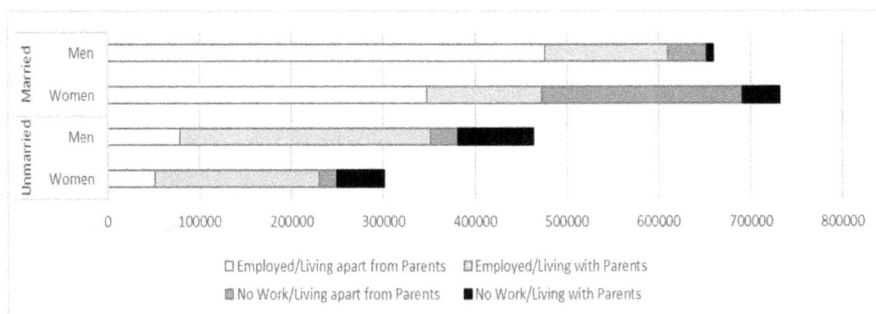

Figure 15: Rates of cohabitation with parents by employment and marriage status and gender (individuals, at age 40).
Source: Created with 2015 National Census data.

According to the 2017 Employment Structure Basic Survey, 930,000 men and 1.1 million women in their thirties and forties – a total of more than two million people – are unmarried and engaged in non-regular labour. The Ice Age Generation marked the birth of a class of unmarried, non-regular workers who do not belong to the standard life course regime. Still, until recently, the precarity of this new class had not yet been recognised as a social problem as many were supported by their regularly employed, relatively affluent parents (JILPT 2009: 18–19).

However, new problems concerning illness, long-term care, and the death of the parents are appearing as members of the Ice Age Generation enter their forties and fifties and their parents enter their seventies and eighties. Genda has called this the "70/40" problem – the mutual, simultaneous decline of parents in their seventies and their non-regularly employed, unemployed, or *hikikomori* children in their forties. As both parties continue to age, this issue is evolving into the "80/50 problem," with further crises looming as aging and long-term care issues compound with those of unstable, low-wage labour and unemployment.

Members of the Ice Age Generation rarely organise themselves or take collective action to protest their precarity. But statements from the perpetrator of a series of intimidation and threatening incidents in 2012–2013 could be said to represent the self-perception of this generation. A 42-year-old (as of 2020) man named Hirofumi Watanabe, who went to prison for making repeated death threats triggered by his jealous obsession with a famous manga creator, was an unmarried non-regular worker from the Ice Age Generation.[15] Watanabe had no friends

---

15 "'Kuroko's Basketball' Threat Incident" refers to an episode in 2012–2013, when a series of

and a troubled relationship with his parents, and he had worked for many years as a dispatch worker with an annual income that never exceeded $18,000. He had been working as a day labourer in the days before his arrest. In his post-prison memoirs, Watanabe wrote:

> I felt that my life was dirty, ugly, and miserable. I also recognised that there was no chance it would ever improve. I was the lowest of all the losers, and without the prospect of ever escaping the suffering of a wasted life. I think the best explanation is that I was trying to commit suicide because I wanted release from the suffering. I should have quietly committed suicide on my own, but at that time, I became obsessed with that manga creator who had everything, who got all the "things that I wanted but couldn't get," and I was aghast at how different our lives were, and I thought that I wanted to take at least one slash at this enormous rival. I named this type of crime "a life course disparity crime" (Watanabe, 2014).

Structural Changes in Japan's Standardised Life Course Regime

In closing, I would like to consider how the Ice Age Generation relates to changes in Japan's standardised life course regime. The standardised life course regime in Japan formed within an integrative social system. The regular employment systems of companies, the standard household, and non-regular employment all developed as complementary linkages in a single framework of life course regime based on the core premises of this system: a husband as male-breadwinner engages in regular employment for many years, financially supporting the entire family, and a wife provides care for her husband and children at home, enabling her husband's complete dedication to his employer. Non-regular labour, which acted as a buffer to protect regular core workers, was performed mainly by wives employed in part-time work, children as students in *arubaito*, and retired pensioners in *shokutaku*. Such non-regular labour was premised on the security of the family's living standard, which was itself guaranteed by a regularly employed husband. For this reason, it was not considered socially problematic that women were stressed by their work in unstable, dead-end, low-wage jobs that made it difficult to achieve financial independence. The standardised life course regime can be conceptualised as a construct defined by a reciprocal relationship among hardworking men as regular workers, their wives as care providers, and wives, children, and retirees as

threatening letters were sent to the alma mater of manga author Tadatoshi Fujimaki, event venues, a university, and other establishments linked to Fujimaki's manga series.

non-regular workers who function as buffers to protect regular employment from economic fluctuations.

The Employment Ice Age after the collapse of the Bubble economy in the 1990s upset this delicate balance. Because of the failure of many young people to transition to regular labour as new graduates and their inability to extract themselves from the quagmire of non-regular labour, single persons and *hikikomori* formed a new generation that included numerous individuals unable to meet the conditions of the standard life course. In other words, the Employment Ice Age created a new population for whom the standardised life course never materialised. In this sense, the Ice Age Generation definitively damaged the standardised life course regime in Japan, which persisted until the beginning of 1990s.

On the one hand, the Ice Age Generation is considered a special birth cohort that was dealt a bad hand because of historical timing. Homing in on this particular cohort, the Japanese government has repeatedly implemented measures to promote their "re-challenge" since 2003.[16] On the other hand, the Ice Age Generation was not a cohort confronting a transitory problem. The Generation is the result not only of the prolonged recession of the Japanese economy and an extension of the so-called "lost generation"; more importantly, the Ice Age Generation was the first generation whose historical timing overlapped with globalisation, IT innovation, and neoliberalism. Facing tough competition, Japanese companies have consistently increased the share of non-regular workers to reduce fixed labour costs, which is combined with the Japanese government's deregulation of the labour market. The ratio of non-regular workers reached 38 percent among all workers, and 55 percent of women workers in 2019 despite improvements in the ratio of job openings (Labor Force Survey). Consequently, the Ice Age Generation ushered in fundamental changes in Japan's employment structure that emerged from the structural transition of the world economy and were compounded by historical timing. The non-standardised life course was not, therefore, a temporary phenomenon but rather one that became deeply rooted in Japanese society.

The potential for the standard life course still exists in most Japanese companies, and many young people enter the work force as new graduates in practice. However, it no longer constitutes a life course regime. The presence of a vast population of non-regular workers with precarious livelihoods, particularly middle-aged singles, is creating a deep social divide. In this sense, Japan's Ice Age Generation transformed the standardised life course regime, characterised by long-lasting stability and equality, into a polarised life course regime. The fortunate gener-

---

16 "Youth Independence/Challenge Plan" (2003); "Re-challenge Support Plan" (2006); Youth Employment Promotion Act (2015); "Employment Ice Age Generation Support Plan" (2020).

ation who believed that hard work and persistence would lead to success and stability are now followed by younger generations deeply sceptical of these older values and conscious of the risks before them. Japanese society will be seriously tested in terms of its ability to overcome this polarisation in the years to come.

References

Abegglen, James C. 1958. *The Japanese Factory: Aspects of Its Social Organization*. Glencoe, IL: Free Press.

Albert, Michel. 1991. *Capitalisme contre capitalisme*. Paris: Éditions du Seuil.

Allison, Ann. 2013. *Precarious Japan*. Durham, NC: Duke University Press.

Amamiya, Karin. 2016. *Women Who are Non-regularly Employed, Single, and Around 40 Years Old: Despair and Hope of the "The Lost Generation" [Hi seiki tanshin arafō josei. 'Ushinawareta sedai' no zetsubō to kibō]*. Tokyo: Heibonsha.

Asahi Shimbun. 2007. *The Lost Generation. Wandering 20 million Youth [Samayou 2000 man nin]*. Tokyo: Asahi Shimbun-sha.

Asahi Shimbun. 2009. *The Lost "20 Years" [Ushinawareta <20 nen>]*. Tokyo: Iwanami.

Brinton, Mary C. 2008. *Lost in Transition: Youth, Education, and Work in Post-industrial Japan [Ushinawareta-ba o sagashite. Rosutojenerēshon no shakai-gaku]*. Tokyo: NTT Publishing.

Bukodi, E., and S. Dex. 2010. "Bad Start: Is There a Way Up? Gender Differences in the Effect of Initial Occupation on Early Career Mobility in Britain." *European Sociological Review* 26, no. 4: 431–446.

Cabinet Office, Government of Japan. 1979. *Public Opinion Survey on the Life of the People [Kokumin seikatsu ni kansuru seronchōsa]*.

Cabinet Office. 2011. *Survey Report on Marriage and Family Formation 2010 [kekkon kazoku keisei ni kansuru chōsa hokokusho]*.

Council on Economic and Fiscal Policy. 2019. *Toward Redesigning the Life of the Employment Ice Age Generation [Shūshoku hyōgaki sedai no jinsei sai sekkei ni mukete]*. April 10, 2019.

Cusumano, Michael A. 1985. *The Japanese Automobile Industry: Technology and Management at Nissan and Toyota*. Cambridge, MA: Harvard University Asia Center.

Dore, Ronald. 1973. *British Factory, Japanese Factory: The Origins of National Diversity in Industrial Relations*. London: Allen & Unwin.

Elder, Glen H. Jr. 1994. "Time, Human Agency, and Social Change: Perspectives on the Life Course." *Social Psychology Quarterly* 57, no. 1: 4–15.

Fujimoto, Takahiro. 1999. *The Evolution of a Manufacturing System at Toyota*. New York: Oxford University Press.

Fujita, Takanori. 2020. *Abandoned Generation: The Ice Age Generation, Abandoned by the Government, Will Destroy Japan*. Tokyo: SB Creative.

Genda, Yuji. 2001. *A Nagging Sense of Job Insecurity: The New Reality Facing Japanese Youth [Shigoto no naka no aimaina fuan — yureru jakunen no ima]*. Tokyo: Chuokoron-Shinsha.

Genda, Yuji. 2005. *A Nagging Sense of Job Insecurity: New Reality Facing Japanese Youth*. Translated by Jean Connell Hoff. Tokyo: LTCB International Library Trust/International House of Japan.

Hans-Böckler-Stiftung, IG Metal, ed. 1992. *Lean Production: Core of a New Corporate Culture and an Innovative Social Work Organization? [Lean Production: Kern einer neuen Unternehmenskultur und einer innovativen und sozialen Arbeitsorganisation?].* Baden-Baden: Nomos.

Honda, Yuki. 2006. *Don't call them NEET! [Nitotte Iuna].* Tokyo: Kobunsha.

Hori, Yukie. 2019. "The Current 'Employment Ice-Age' Situation: Perspective on the Transition from School to Work" ['Shūshoku hyōgaki sedai' no ima: ikō kenkyū kara no kentō]. *Japan Institute for Labor Policy and Training* 706, 17–27.

Institute of Social Science (ISS), University of Tokyo, ed. 1991–1992. *Modern Japanese Society.* Tokyo: University of Tokyo Press.

Japan Institute for Labor Policy and Training (JILPT). 2009, 2014, 2019. *Work, Careers and Vocational Development [Jakunensha no shugyo jokyo, kyaria, shokugyo noryoku kaihatsu no genjo]* 1–3.

Japanese Trade Union Confederation (JTUC) Research Institute for Advancement of Living Standards. 2016. *Preventing the Creation of a New Employment Ice Age Generation [Aratana shūshoku hyōgaki sedai o umanai tame ni].* Tokyo.

Kochan, Thomas A., Russell D. Lansbury, and John Paul Macduffie, eds. 1997. *After Lean Production: Evolving Employment Practices in the World Auto Industry.* Ithaca, NY: Cornell University Press.

Koike, Kazuo. 1991/1996. *The Economics of Work in Japan.* Tokyo: LTCB International Library Foundation.

Komatsu, Fumiaki. 2007. "The Toyota Production System and the Increase in Atypical Employment" [Toyota seisan hōshiki to hi-tenkei koyō-ka]. In *The Sociology of Careers: An Approach from Vocational Ability and Career Tracks [Kyaria no shakai-gaku: Shokugyō nōryoku to shokugyō keireki kara no apurōchi],* edited by Katsuji Tsuji. Kyoto: Minerva Shobo.

Kosugi, Reiko. 2002/2008. *Escape from Work: Freelancing Youth and the Challenge to Corporate Japan [Jiyū no daishō/furītā: Gendai wakamono no shūgyō ishiki to kōdō],* translated by Ross Mouer. Melbourne: Trans Pacific Press.

Kosugi, Reiko, and Michiko Miyamoto, eds. 2015. *Women becoming a Lower Class: Labour, Exclusion from the Family, and Poverty [Kasō-ka suru josei-tachi: Rōdō to katei kara no haijo to hinkon].* Tokyo: Keiso Shobo.

Koyama, Yoichi. 1985. *Megacorporate Systems and Workers: A Case Study of Toyota [Kyodaikigyoutaisei to Roudousha].* Tokyo: Ochanomizu Shobo.

Liker, Jeffrey K. 2004. *The Toyota Way: 14 Management Principles from the World's Greatest Manufacturer.* New York; London: McGraw-Hill.

Liker, Jeffrey K., and D. Meier. 2007. *Toyota Talent: Developing Your People the Toyota Way.* New York/London: McGraw-Hill.

Liker, J. K., and M. Hoseus. 2007. *Toyota Culture: The Heart and Soul of the Toyota Way.* New York, McGraw-Hill.

Mayer, Karl Ulrich. 2004. "Whose Lives? How History, Societies, and Institutions Define and Shape Life Courses." *Research in Human Development* 1, no. 3, 161–187.

Ministry of Health, Labor, and Welfare (MHLW). 2007. *Research on the Situation and Measure for the Youth as NEET.* Tokyo.

Miyamoto, Michiko. 2002. *Youth Falling into "the Socially Disadvantaged" [Wakamono ga 'Shakaitekijakusha' ni tenrakusuru].* Tokyo: Yosensha.

Miyamoto, Michiko. 2011. *The Polarization of Youth and Self-Reliance Support: Approaching the "Youth Problem" [ni kyoku-ka suru wakamono to shiritsushien: 'Wakamono mondai' e no sekkin].* Tokyo: Akashi Shoten.

Monden, Yasuhiro. 1983. *New Developments in Toyota Production Method [Toyota seisan hōshiki no shin tenkai]*. Tokyo: Japan Management Association.

NHK. 2019. *The "Around 40" Crisis: The Looming Crisis Facing the "Unfortunate Generation" [Fugū no sedai' ni semaru kiki]*. Tokyo: Shinchosha.

Nohara, Hikari, and Eishi Fujita. 1988. *The Automotive Industry and Workers: Structure of Worker Management and the Worker Image [Jidōsha sangyō to rōdō-sha: Rōdō-sha kanri no kōzō to rōdō-sha-zō]*. Kyoto: Horitsu Bunka Sha.

Nomura, Masami. 1993. *Toyotism: The Maturation and Transformation of the Japanese Production System [Toyotism: nihon teki seisan sisutemu no seijuku to hen'yō]*. Kyoto: Minerva.

Occupation and Lifestyle Research Group (OLR), ed. 1994. *Corporate Society and Humans: The Labour, Life, and Geographical Region of Toyota [kigyō shakai to ningen: Toyota no rōdō, seikatsu, chiiki]*. Kyoto: Horitsu Bunka Sha.

Ouchi, William G. 1981. *Theory Z: How American Business Can Meet the Japanese Challenge.* Boston: Addison-Wesley.

Saruta, Masaki. 1995. *Toyota System and Labor Management [Toyota sisutemu to Romu Kanri]*. Tokyo: Zeimukeiri Kyokai.

Sugayama, Shinji. 2011. *Birth of Shusha Society: From White Collar to Blue Collar [Shusha shakai no Tanjo]*. Nagoya: Nagoya University Press.

Takayama, Noriyuki, and Kousuke Shiraishi. 2012. "'Bad Start, Bad Finish' Issues in Japan" [Nihon no 'Bad Start, Bad Finish' mondai]. Discussion paper 567, Center for Intergenerational Studies, Institute of Economic Research, Hitotsubashi University.

Tanaka, Hirohide. 1982. "The People Who Have Established Japanese Employment Practices: A Conversation with ex-Toyota Director Mr. Yoshiaki Yamamoto (1)–(2)," *Japan Labour Association Magazine*, no. 280: 38–556; no. 281: 64–81.

The Toyota Motor Corporation. 1967. *A 30-year History of Toyota Motors [Toyota jidōsha 30-nen-shi]*. Toyota: Toyota Motors Co.

The Toyota Motor Corporation. 1978. *Toyota's Progress: Toyota Motor Corporation's 40th Anniversary [Toyota no ayumi: Toyota jidōsha kōgyō kabushikigaisha sōritsu 40 shūnenkinen]*. Toyota: Toyota Motors Co.

The Toyota Motor Corporation. 1978b. *Wheel/Harmony, Technology, Wheel Track [Wa, Waza, Wadachi]*. Toyota: Toyota Motors Co.

Toyota Motors. 1987. *Infinite Creations: A 50-year History of Toyota Motors [Sōzō kagirinaku. Toyota jidōsha 50-nen-shi]*. Toyota: Toyota Motors Co.

Tsuji, Katsuji. 2011. *The Postwar History of Toyota Human Management System [Toyota Jinji Houshiki no Sengo-shi]*. Kyoto: Minerva.

Vogel, Ezra F. 1979. *Japan as Number One: Lessons for America.* Cambridge, MA: Harvard University Press.

Wakabayashi, Yukio, ed. 2018. *Business History on Educational Background and Disparity [Gakureki to Kakusa no Keieishi]*. Tokyo: Nihon Keizai Hyoronsha.

Watanabe, Hirofumi. 2014. *The End of the Living Corpse: The Whole Truth of "Kuroko's Basketball Threat Incident" [Ikeru shikabane no ketsumatsu—'kurokonobasuke' kyōhaku jiken no zen shinsō]*. Tokyo: Tsukuru Shuppan.

Womack, James P., Daniel T. Jones, and Daniel Roos. 1990. *The Machine that Changed the World*. New York: Rawson Associates.

World Bank. 1993. *The East Asian Miracle: Economic Growth and Public Policy*. Washington, DC: World Bank.

Yajima, Masami, and Hiroaki Mimizuka, eds. 2001. *Youth and Vocational World. Sociology of Transition [Kawaru Wakamono to Shokugyo Sekai]*. Tokyo: Gakubunsha.

Ju Li

When They Told Their Stories: Industrial Workers' Life Courses in the People's Republic of China

It is not that something different is seen, but that one sees differently. It is as though the spatial act of seeing were changed by a new dimension.
—Carl Jung

The relationship between structure and agency has persistently been debated among social scientists, including scholars of life course (Elder 1994; Mayer 2009; George 2003; Kohli 2007; MacMillan 2005). While the power of structure to shape individuals' life courses cannot be denied, scholars strive to identify the ways and measure the degree to which individuals can exert agency and control their lives within ineluctable structural limits (Mayer 2003, 2004; Elder 1994; Marshall 2000). An individual's unique life trajectory or biography is nevertheless the result of ongoing interactions between the micro level of individuals and the macro level of social structure, and between individual time and historical time. So-called agency, therefore, embodies itself in these concrete and interacting processes when individuals try to actively interpret and manipulate the environment, even within highly constrained and volatile historical structures. This chapter, which records and analyses life trajectories as narrated by four former Chinese state workers as they lived through major social upheavals and transitions in contemporary Chinese history from the socialist period to the reform era, aims to provide another in-depth case study of agency in the field of life course research.

In addition to illustrating how these workers exerted their agency through their particular responses and adjustments to and navigation of each social change that occurred during their working life, I highlight the importance of agency in these workers' active memories of their working life stories: how they interpret, reflect on, grant meaning to, find purpose in, and draw conclusions about their past experiences. Memory is a story that people tell for a purpose. Narrating their life trajectories gave my narrators the opportunity to reprocess their past in a highly coherent and reflective manner; thus, it empowered them in a particular way. The feeling of having control over their own life stories in the midst of seemingly insurmountable obstacles and upheaval that eventually receded must be the major reason all my narrators were eager to talk to me, and we established mutual trust. This subjective dimension of the life course, I argue, constitutes an important but largely unrecognised aspect of agency in life course research.

The four protagonists featured in this article, two females and two males, belong to the same cohort; they were born around the same time (1940s/1950s) and, consequently, experienced various historical events concurrently. Before retirement, they all worked at the same state-owned factory, which I refer to here by its anonymised name NS, from the 1960s to the early 2000s. They were endowed with different resources (some were more educated than others, for example); came from different social backgrounds; and performed different kinds of jobs. Yet, it is hard to categorise them not just because class divisions had been intentionally blurred for ideological reasons during the socialist period but also because their own employment and class status constantly changed due to shifting state policies and turbulent socio-political transformations. Nevertheless, as we will see below, the different social backgrounds of my protagonists came to signify their distinct though discontinued life trajectories.

A huge state-owned enterprise (SOE), NS had been developed as one of thousands of "third-front enterprises" during the Third Front Construction (TFC) era in the 1960s – the largest defensive industrialisation project during the socialist period directed against the potential military threats coming from the United States and the Soviet Union. From its inception, the TFC was hailed as a "revolution" and praised for "building a new world" and "buying time against the imperialists" (Li 2019). My protagonists joined NS around this time. During its heyday in the 1980s and early 1990s, when cautious and embedded market reform was introduced, NS was one of the largest taxpayers in Sichuan province and employed around 30,000 workers. From the mid-1990s to the early 2000s, a variety of radical, market-oriented reforms – mergers, partial privatisation, downsizing for efficiency, burden reductions, large-scale lay-offs, and so on – were imposed on NS. These programs were destructive and introduced tremendous chaos into the factory, drove common workers into poverty and the community into a period steady decline, turning it into a post-industrial slum. All these uneven social changes, largely induced by shifting state policies, constantly restructured institutional resources, constraints, risks, and opportunities for my protagonists and other NS workers and, consequently, greatly shaped their life courses. As scholars have argued for other contexts, the state may have played a central role in shaping the structure of the life course (Mayer and Müller 1986; Mayer and Schoepflin 1989). While the life courses I trace here do exemplify the determining power of structure, they also display distinct details of individuals.

As we will see below, all the narrated life stories of my protagonists unfold around the most crucial turning points in their working lives. Turning points, according to Tamara Hareven, denote a substantial change in the direction of one's life and can be determined either subjectively or objectively (Hareven 2018: 153). They not only involve specific events at particular moments but also point to radical changes in the direction of the life trajectory over the long term. For my protagonists, these turning points included being hired at NS, career development/change, and the waning of the career/retirement. Rather than signalling stops on a continuous and cumulative pathway, all these turning points were triggered and determined by the abrupt larger historical upheavals caused by shifting state policies that significantly changed political and economic structures, working and living conditions and opportunities, and the prevailing hegemonic value systems of the country. It was these turning points that my protagonists constantly returned to, ruminated on, scrutinised, evaluated, and analysed – in other words, reflected on – in order to make sense of their lives. That is the nature of agency I emphasise in this article.

The interviews in this chapter are part of a larger project that investigates the labour and social history of NS over five decades (Li 2019). They were conducted and recorded with the interviewees' consent during my visits to NS for fieldwork between 2007 to 2014.

Coming to NS: "We Were So Young Then"

The decision to come to NS was the first turning point in people's working lives. Given the TFC's defensive aims, almost all TF projects had to be located in the most remote areas of inner China as outlined in the official guidelines: "near the mountains, easy to hide, and geographically decentralised." Most of the enterprises were built from nothing. Confronted with shortages of technology, equipment, and experienced labour for most TF enterprises, the central state had to mobilise and, when necessary, force massive migration to TF labour sites. "Good people and good horses go to the Third Front" and "Going to the places where our motherland needs us most" were the slogans used during this migration process. By appealing to people's patriotic feelings and highlighting the highly selective standards used to recruit participants, these slogans emphasised the importance and singularity of the project – only people who were "progressive," "revolutionary," and "patriotic" enough could be selected by the Party as honourable participants in the TFC. Such slogans also implied the free will of participants eager to serve their country. People's retrospective recounting of this crucial turning point in their lives, however, paints a much more complicated picture. All my protagonists came to NS in the mid-1960s to early 1970s, the most radical and turbulent period of socialism, characterised by a harsh political environment, a highly idealist/revolutionary value system, and a chaotic social reality. They did not really have much choice: the overall rigid structure strictly defined and highly delimited their available options. Yet, at the same time, even under such tight constraints, each of them interpreted and responded to the situation in ways that reflected her/his own distinct situation, background, calculations, beliefs, and personality. Concrete and dynamic life experiences full of struggle, frustrations, survival instincts and calculations, pain, as well as passion and courage, as I will record below, not only diminished and even ridiculed the upbeat and empty political slogans; they also unmoored the monolithic image of the overarching structure.

Before coming to NS, Zhang Guirong had worked in a state-owned construction company in Shanghai. When the Third Front Construction era started, he and his colleagues were ordered to move to NS to construct the factory in 1965:

> I didn't have other choices, you know. Our whole company was transferred to Sichuan. Everybody had to go . . . Who wanted to leave a big city like Shanghai and come to a poor place hidden in the mountains? But you had to go; otherwise, you would be fired immediately. At that time, your job was assigned by the state, so if you got fired, you were doomed.

Under the state policy called "Three Ways for Veterans to Help Beginners" – based on the idea that old industrial bases should help new industrial bases; that old enterprises should help new enterprises; and that senior workers should help junior workers – the strong hand of the state created, mobilised, and/or forced a continuous flow of managers, workers, equipment, and technologies from "mother" enterprises located in other parts of China to newly built Third Front enterprises. Zhang was one of these workers. For him, his arrival at NS, a turning point in his life course, was imposed upon him by the state. Individuals' total dependence on the state for a formal job made acquiescence the only rational choice at that time. However, in the following memory, Zhang meaningfully reflected of his initial decision:

> Several of my colleagues had refused to go and, so, had gotten fired. But that decision later turned out to be a good thing for them. Without formal jobs, they had to start some small underground businesses surreptitiously in order to make a living. So, when reform started in the 1980s, they quickly grasped the opportunities with their previously accumulated savings and experiences and became rich . . . I wish I had chosen to do that too, but anyway, who could have known about that change beforehand?

Such reflective remarks, on the one hand, indicate the unpredictability of state policy and how it could reverse a common people's fate by making their once-rational choice seem stupid and a once-irrational choice smart. On the other hand, they also helped convince Zhang that precisely because of hardship and the unpredictability of external larger forces, more daring and defiant choices might be more optimal in the long run. Realising that empowered and benefited him later.

Not everybody who came to NS did so by force and with regrets. Despite all the destruction and chaos the radical political shifts wrought on Chinese society, a highly inspirational and idealist value system characterised by revolutionary romanticism, patriotism, and collectivism was produced and widely embraced by most common people, especially young and passionate college students. Ma Ruixing was one of them.

> In 1967, the year I was graduating from Tsinghua University, I saw a job on the job-assignment list in Fulaerji, my hometown. Meanwhile, there was another job in Chengdu, where my boyfriend worked. I wrote to my father asking for his advice. I wrote, "My teacher has told me about available jobs. If I choose Fulaerji, I can live close to you and mother. If I choose Chengdu, I can be with my boyfriend. What's your suggestion?" Do you know what my father wrote back to me? He wrote, "I got your letter. It seems that you are struggling a lot. But your struggles have not sprung out of their small, individualist circle." These were the exact words of my father. You know, he had never criticised me like that before. Now he was criticising me in a very serious way. That's why I can still recite every word he wrote in the letter: "I have told you before that we raised you not to support us in our old age but to do your duty for our country. Haven't you considered the fact that it was our country that educated you all these years? You can say all those beautiful and loyal words in the classroom of Tsinghua University. That's easy. But now is the time for the Party to test you. Why don't you consider the place where our country needs you the most? Right now is a great moment for our country, constructing the Third Front. Many capable people are needed. The circumstances might be arduous, very different from the comfortable environment you enjoy in Tsinghua University. You have to build it from nothing. Be prepared for it. It will be just like how the Soviet Union built Komsomolsk!" I felt so ashamed and angry when I read the letter. It was as if my father was denying all I had said and done before. It seemed that he was accusing me of forgetting the needs of our country and only thinking about my parents and boyfriend in the face of a real test! So, I quickly decided that I would go neither to my hometown nor to Chengdu with my boyfriend. In 1967, after I graduated from Tsinghua, I came here.

Ma was 23 when she came to NS. Her then-boyfriend, later husband, joined her shortly afterwards. As we can see from the narrative, it was an involuntary choice. Yet, it was not one person's choice – she was strongly influenced by her father. But while she ultimately followed his advice, it was not merely out of daughterly submission but also from a sense of patriotism shared between two generations of Chinese intellectuals during the period. Her father's letter, which Ma could still recite, reads very much like a propagandistic cliché today. But for many Chinese intellectuals who had experienced China's chaotic and humiliating pre-1949 history and, thus, passionately embraced the hope and promise of the new PRC promised by the Party, such "clichés" could be very authentic. Ma's life course was reoriented towards NS by her desire to move beyond the individualistic calculation based on mere economic or pragmatic self-interest and to connect individual lives in a more meaningful way for a greater purpose within the range of life possibilities made available by the state and social structure of the day. And she has always been proud of her choice.

For Du Zhang – a so-called "educated youth" sent into rural areas under the policy and banner of "educated urban youth going to the countryside" during the Cultural Revolution – coming to NS was a blessed escape from the impoverished countryside, and his arrival renewed his hope for a better future. He describes his two-year-stay in the countryside as follows:

> Before I came to Nanfang Steel, I was an educated youth who had been sent to the countryside. Before that I had been a student, a high-school student. To put it more accurately, I had been a student Red Guard. When the Cultural Revolution began in 1967, I was in the second grade of high school. Soon the school closed, and the Revolution began . . . Then, Mao had to deal with these millions upon millions of student Red Guards, who, because of the Revolution, had no schools to go to and no jobs to do. Having been formed under the banner "Rebellion Is Justified," these former students-cum-Red Guards didn't know what they could do . . . Then Chairman Mao adopted the policy of "educated urban youth going to the countryside." We went to the countryside against this background. We knew that we had already seen the dead end of the Cultural Revolution; we were also fully aware that we had lost our direction, whether in our studies or in our contributions to the country. We didn't know what we could do, and the country didn't know how to handle us . . . I went to the countryside in 1969 . . . I felt desperate there. It was not because of hardships but because of the unknown or even dark future. What should and could I do? Will I be a peasant forever? It was ok to be a peasant, but our education always told us to be scientists! Besides, the status of peasants in China was very low, even though politically it was extolled so highly . . .

Those are highly reflective and critical remarks towards state policies and political movements from an individual who was, at the time, buffeted by these external waves. As Du rightly pointed out, the movement of "educated urban youth (zhishi qingnian, 知识青年) going to the countryside" after 1968 was launched largely as a response to the millions of increasingly uncontrollable student Red Guards organised under the banner of "Rebellion against Bureaucracy" during the Cultural Revolution in 1967. With schools still closed due to these rebellions, the government sought to remove these numerous, roaming, and potentially militant urban youths to rural areas. From 1968 to 1975, approximately twelve million urban youths, including secondary school graduates and university students were mobilised and sent "up to the mountains and down to the villages" (上山下乡, shang shan xia xiang) under the slogan, "going to the sweeping countryside to fully realize our potential" (Yang 2016; Gu 1997). These glorified ideals and slogans soon ran headfirst into the harsh and disheartening realities of the countryside. The original passion that students had harboured soon receded and was replaced with outright fear, as Du expressed in our discussions. People like him began to grasp desperately at any opportunity that might change their fate. Third Front Construction offered such a chance, as Du recalled:

> It wasn't until 1971 that the policy regarding the sent-down educated youth began to loosen. Since Third Front Construction had already started, recruitment began . . . We were all so happy. Everybody wanted to go. But the quota was very small in the beginning, and the competition was fierce . . . We had to pass the communal evaluation, the health examination, and then the political records examination . . . It would take two months for the decision to be finally made. During these two months, we were so anxious that we almost couldn't work . . . Every step was risky . . . The whole family had to exhaust its material and financial resources (to bribe the communal Party Committee members) to guarantee success [of their child's application]; otherwise, their son or daughter would stay in the countryside forever . . . I finally went to Nanfang in 1971 . . . I didn't care what kind of enterprise it was as long as I could leave the countryside.

Different from Zhang and Ma, "coming to Nanfang" for Du was a turning point that allowed him to escape the uncertainty and chaos brought about by radical political shifts and rural poverty. While many urban youths who had been "sent down" finally managed to leave the countryside through various means, labour recruitment for the Third Front Construction provided the first ray of hope for these despairing students. Out of desperation, people such as Du managed to take hold of the opportunities the TFC offered and changed their destiny.

For Gong Yapin, coming to NS was not a lifeline but an unanticipated crucial event that turned her life upside down. Her father, a former high-status cadre working at a privileged industrial base in the northeast, had been transferred to NS by the state to become the First Party Secretary of the factory in 1966. One year later, the other family members joined him. This reunion, which Gong envisioned would be an exciting event, turned out to be a shocking nightmare:

> It was the winter of 1967. I was twelve. We got off the train, and I saw my father waiting for us at the station. I will never forget that image my whole life. My father wore a tattered cotton coat, obviously had not shaved for a long time, and didn't smile or hug us. I could hardly recognise him: he used to be such a handsome guy, always neat and well-dressed; now he looked like a beggar. And this place! It looked so dirty and poor . . . When we arrived at my father's almost empty flat, father and mother went directly to their bedroom and talked for a long time, and I heard mother crying. I then realised that something bad happened to my father and our family . . . My life was suddenly changed. I stopped going to school: there were no schools to go anyway . . . I grew up almost immediately. I learned every chore: not just cooking, washing cloth, cleaning, but also drawing water from the well and cutting wood . . . I did these all by myself without any complaints . . . I even became famous: everybody knew that the second daughter of Gong's family worked like a real man . . . All of these [chores] were nothing for me, but the hardest thing was how they treated my father. Every evening at 7:00 P.M., the loud horn in the factory would repeatedly announce the place and time of the meeting to denounce my father. That was the moment I felt humiliated the most . . . Posters were

everywhere with my father's name on it . . . They also beat him . . . Can you imagine how a twelve-year-old girl just endured all these sudden misfortunes by herself?

Under the banner "Rebellion Is Justified," which was popularised at the high point of the Cultural Revolution which sought to disrupt the old bureaucratic order, high-status officials such as Gong's father were targeted: they were dragged down from their formerly high statuses and openly criticised, humiliated, and sometimes physically attacked by "rebellious" workers, not necessarily out of "revolutionary passion" but instead due to various hidden resentments and individual interests. The cruelty and frenzy of the movement destroyed the privileged and protected life Gong enjoyed prior to her arrival at NS; it dragged her into a hostile and strange world and forced her to become an adult immediately in order to shoulder family responsibilities. Recounting and reflecting on that part of her life aroused bitterness, but it also gave her pride: being able to bear all these sudden misfortunes at such a young age shows courage and perseverance, qualities Gong prized and highlighted from time to time.

The four life stories recorded here provide us with a rich and subjective illustration of one of the most important turning points in my protagonists' respective life courses: how and why they came to NS, the place where they would spend the rest of their working lives and, consequently, come to regard as their second hometown. Larger structural forces including international geopolitics, turbulent domestic political movements, and harsh state policies highly constrained people's life choices as they were seemingly pushed toward NS by historical events out of their control. Yet, they arrived at NS under various circumstances that were shaped by different calculations and beliefs. Maybe even more important, at least in retrospect, was that this turning point in the life course had a distinct meaning for each individual: for Zhang Guirong, it was an acquiescent but slightly regrettable decision from which he learnt a valuable life lesson; for Du Zhang, NS was a lifeline out of rural poverty; for Gong Yaping, it was a nightmare; and for Ma Ruixin, it represented the possibility of a more meaningful life. It is here that a turning point, even while shaped by the strong hand of external forces and common to all my protagonists, still reflects individual agency: both in the ways they manoeuvred through the constraints of the socialist era and, more importantly, in their retrospective interpretations of the event in the present. And that is the power of the subjective dimension of life course – it gives meaning and coherence to our lives.

Working Through Golden Time: "The Most Glorious Years of My Life"

My era / Suddenly struck its drum / Behind my back

When Beidao, a famous Chinese poet, wrote the above poem in 1979, the Third Plenary Session of the 11th Central Committee had just declared that the major role of the Party would shift away from political and ideological struggle towards economic development and modernisation. The general policy of Reform and Openness was, thus, established. The drumbeat of the era, sudden and thunderous, announced the significant turn of the country. It was a final farewell to a harsh and radical revolutionary era and signified the dawning of a new age. Such structural changes greatly altered the opportunity structures and, not surprisingly, reshaped individuals' life trajectories (Zhou and Moen 2001). The end of austerity and political chaos, the normalisation of production, and the burgeoning non-state market all provided new challenges and opportunities for my narrators, creating another turning point in their lives.

Most likely inspired by his bolder former colleagues – who had refused to leave Shanghai for NS and accordingly had been fired in the 1960s but later became more prosperous as the precursors of the market reforms – Zhang Guirong sensed the larger changes taking place and took advantage of new opportunities created by the policy shift as early as possible:

> I started moonlighting outside of NS very early, earlier than most people. It was in the early 1980s. There were opportunities outside [the factory] already . . . I worked for those private construction contractors, making project budgets for them . . . It was hard work: sometimes I didn't have time to sleep all night. But I made some money . . . Then, some people got jealous of me and reported my moonlighting to the factory administration, but the factory declared that it would neither encourage these behaviours nor object to them, so I was able to keep on doing that . . .

Since the 1980s, the slow dissolution of the rigorously planned economy opened up some space for non-state sectors to grow. This development broke up the monopolistic role of the state as the only job provider and created new potential sources of income for more risk-tolerant people like Zhang. Not everybody dared to take risks at the beginning of the reform era. The uncertainty of market-based opportunities and the unpredictability of state policy implied benefits as well as risks. Yet, Zhang thought it over and jumped in with both feet. This decision turned out to be crucial for him and his family. Thanks to the extra money he made and saved from his second job, he could afford his daughter's college education in the 1990s, when higher education was no longer free and became expensive for common workers. And he was very proud of it: by being shrewder and bolder than many others and working hard, he could finally take control of his life to a certain extent and tried to give his daughter a better future.

New opportunities not only emerged from the development of alternative economic entities and the expansion of the market; the normalisation and stabilisation of production, the heightened role of technology and science, and the recovery and rapid growth of state enterprises also provided people with unprecedented opportunities. For Ma Ruixin, the turning point of her working life came when she was transferred from the construction team to the newly established technology group in NS:

> Then the Cultural Revolution ended, and the Spring of Science came! Deng Xiaoping said intellectuals were now also part of the working class. We were no longer the "stinky number nine" who had to be reformed through labour. Science was also a productive force, even the primary productive force! That was really something! On January 13, 1978, the technology group was established in NS, and we college graduates all moved into it . . . Now everything was good because I could finally apply what I had learned at university to my work . . . We were now living in a peaceful environment; what couldn't we do? . . .

Upon her arrival to NS in 1967, Ma had been assigned to the construction team, working side by side with construction workers. "'Learning from the working class' was all right," Ma told me, "but I had always wished I could use all the knowledge I had learnt from Tsinghua." The normalisation of production in NS and the elevated role of science and technology finally granted her wish. After her move to the technology group, she wholeheartedly dedicated herself to this opportunity:

> I was very good at my job. As long as I knew the technical requirements for the steel, I could always figure out what the whole process should be in my head and what the sample should look like under the microscope after it was complete. Accordingly, I would design the whole production process . . . After the steel was produced, I looked at the final samples through the microscope and saw that the result was exactly as I had predicted! I can tell you that that was a great feeling. That sense of accomplishment and happiness was incomparable . . . I always worked overtime voluntarily. Once, I worked ten days and nights continuously, with only three hours of sleep every day. Now, if you wrote all these things down, the Americans would think that there were no human rights in China. How could people work like that? But for our generation, this was natural. This was how we got educated: by dedicating yourself to your work, your factory, and your country. I never minded. During the several decades I worked in the factory, I always had a feeling of happiness and achievement: staying with the workers and seeing my designs succeed. For me, the whole process was a blessing, just like you plant a tree: you sow the seeds, you nurture them, and you see them grow. Those whose only concerns are money or fame could never understand me . . .

Before retirement, Ma was the most respected engineer at NS; she was famous for her expertise, dedication, and integrity. After the "lost ten years" of the Cultural Revolution, she could finally use her knowledge and education, work to her full potential, and realise her value. For her, working at NS in the technology group was a blessing. Looking back at her career gave her a deep sense of satisfaction and made her life meaningful.

Du Zhang's turning point came when he was appointed the principal of the factory-sponsored school in 1986. NS had established its own school in 1971 to educate the children of its workforce. When Du came to NS from the countryside that same year, he was assigned to the school. He remembered that he was very unhappy with the assignment: "everybody wanted to be a worker then: the working class was the biggest brother; besides, workers' wages and benefits were much better than those of schoolteachers." He stayed, nevertheless. But when dramatic social changes occurred, his life also took a turn:

> The National College Entrance Examination was resumed in 1977. This event was crucial since it made visible all the problems of our school: from 1978 to 1985 there were only one or two students who could pass the exam and be admitted to universities . . . The informality and low quality of our school system, though not a problem before, now started to cause panic among parents who wanted their kids to receive higher education and have a better future. So, the school system had to be improved. I became the school principal in 1986 in this context. I knew I had to be responsible for our children and their parents, so I was determined to change the situation . . . and I did. Our school later became one of the top three schools with the highest college acceptance rate among more than three hundred in the district . . . These ten years of being the school principal, from 1986 to 1996, were the most glorious years of my life . . . The school's glory made me glorious.

The shifting meaning, status, and necessity of education, which resulted from the changing logic of development and modernisation, created a turning point in Du's life course. Once a negligent schoolteacher with a social status much lower than that of factory workers, the new reform era granted him a golden opportunity to build a "glorious" career with meaning and significance. He concluded: "Whenever I think of those days, I feel peaceful because I know that I did something real and useful during this period."

Shifting state policy combined with the changing regime altered the life trajectory of Gong Yaping even more drastically. With the end of the Cultural Revolution, her father stepped back into his prominent post in 1979 and retired three years later in 1982. Gong's life finally returned to normal. Moreover, largely due to her intelligence, perseverance, and hard work, her career quickly took off:

> I started working in the accounting office of NS in 1979. I worked very hard, so I was promoted in 1988, and then again and again. In 1993, I became the director of the auditing office and the

vice secretary of the discipline inspection commission . . . At the time, there were many problems in these offices that had accumulated from the previous period . . . I started investigating
immediately, talked to people day and night, and began restructuring . . . Soon, things began
improving . . . I also started to investigate corruption in NS . . . I exposed several cases involving high-status cadres . . . There were obstacles for sure, but I was not afraid: I had experienced the Cultural Revolution; I had guts.

From the daughter of a counterrevolutionary cadre to one of the highest-ranking
administrators in NS, Gong experienced a major ascent in her working life course.
Without the dramatic policy changes in the reform era, such a trajectory would
have been unimaginable. The rules of the game changed and created new opportunities and opened new doors for Gong, and she made the most of them. In retrospect, even the hardship she experienced during the Cultural Revolution became
an asset: it gave her "guts" and helped her accomplish something of which she was
proud.

All of my four narrators' life courses took a major leap forward starting in the
late 1970s up until the mid-1990s; this was not a coincidence. Many Chinese scholars have referred to the long 1980s as "the decade of reform consensus," implying
that the legitimacy of reform, based as it was on the general improvement of people's standard of living, was accepted by the majority of people (Gan 2007; Wu and
Yu 2014). Even though the so-called "reform consensus" is highly debatable, there is
no doubt that increased ideological flexibility, the normalisation and orderly implementation of production reforms, and the development of a market economy
together produced a relatively secure, predictable, and stable political and work
environment and opened up more life choices for my narrators. The "reform consensus" also gave them the opportunity to have a different life and to realise their
dreams, pursue their careers, and achieve something meaningful and praisewor-
thy. In retrospect, this era was so important, indeed revered, by all four narrators,
they called it the "golden era."

Displacement and Turbulence: "It Was Another Movement"

The "golden era" ended abruptly when the state decided to make another sharp
policy turn in the mid-1990s. More cautious and embedded market reform policies
were determinedly pushed aside, while a whole package of radical marketisation,
including the so-called "SOE restructuring," which the state had been reluctant to
launch earlier on, was decisively launched. The privatisation and bankruptcy of
state-owned enterprises became widespread starting in 1995 (Lin, Cai, and Li

2001). In NS, a series of radical restructuring measures – massive layoffs, forced early retirements, burden reductions, and mergers – were imposed on the company by the government. These measures were incredibly destructive and chaotic, and they turned workers into paupers and industrial communities into slums. The sudden rupture of the system again upended people's lives.

Ma Ruixin's career came to a sudden end in 1996. Despite her excellent performance and devotion to her work, she was forced into early retirement according to the one-cut policy:

> The one-cut early retirement policy came in 1996. All female engineers suddenly had to retire at the age of fifty-five. I wasn't prepared for that. You know, when that day came, I had just returned to my office from the workshop, exhausted. Then the Party secretary of our department came to me and said that I didn't need to come back the next day since I had to retire earlier according to the new policy . . . I was so shocked and angry that I couldn't respond at all. After so many years of dedication and hard work, it was suddenly over in such a cruel way. I had dreamed about a more honourable retirement, you know, with flowers and warm celebrations . . . The cut-off age for female engineers was fifty-five, but it was sixty for male engineers. Wasn't that gender discrimination, discrimination against women? It doesn't matter if this person is useful for the factory or not; as long as he is a man, he could stay! I worked so hard, but I was sent home at such a young age! It was a loss for the factory, wasn't it? I was so good at my job; I felt all my talents and knowledge hadn't been used up. I could still contribute; I was still useful. What could I do with all this knowledge if I had to retire? Bring it to the crematorium when I die?

Tears still filled Ma's eyes when she recounted that crucial moment more than ten years later. It still cut deeply. Work had been the most important dimension of her life: it brought her the deepest sense of satisfaction, the purest happiness, gave her life meaning, and made her feel valuable. The sudden deprivation of her job produced a strong sense of betrayal and pain. Her life had suddenly lost its direction and purpose. Additionally, together with the broader decline of the factory, it also made her feel very vulnerable as she reached old age:

> I lived a hard life, but now I have nothing left. The older I become, the sadder I feel . . . I also feel more vulnerable . . . Since the factory has cancelled all of its welfare programs, there is no support for older people here. If the government could organise something for us, at least there would be some support. Governments in big cities like Chengdu would do such a thing, but in small places like here, the government does nothing. The factory stopped all its support a long time ago . . . I had always been so confident about my work, but now I feel like a loser . . .

The radical shift in state policies not only deprived her of her beloved job; it also destroyed the social safety net she had planned to rely on when she retired. Together, these blows forced Ma to face a new and harsh reality and re-evaluate her former idealist life choices with both indignation and dignity:

> People might think that my story was straight out of *Arabian Nights* and could not really happen. Or they might think that I am a fool. How could there exist such a fool in the world! . . . But to tell you the truth, I have no regrets, even today! They could not understand me? I could not understand them either! Especially those corrupt officials! Why did they need so much money? You just have one mouth to eat and one body to dress. Even if you have nine luxury houses, you only need one bed to sleep in at night, right? I just could not understand them. Maybe I was a fool. Or was I insane? I don't think so.

Those are highly reflective and defiant remarks. In a society and culture that now cannot envision any other reason for working hard other than money or some other form of wealth or fame, Ma could be regarded as nothing more than a dupe; all her previous efforts – her passion and the beliefs she had cherished and from which she derived so much pride – have been mocked as "outdated" or "brainwashing." Yet, despite the changes to her life course forced upon her by blunt external forces, and despite the mockery, rejection, and indeed oblivion she has experienced from the contemporary money-oriented society in China, Ma stands firm on all of her life choices: "I have no regrets, even today!" This is an honourable, powerful, but also desperate reflection.

The neoliberal transformation of NS also dramatically changed Du Zhang's career trajectory when the school system was forcibly transferred to the local municipal government in 1998 as part of the restructuring package called "burden alleviation." Together with layoffs, burden alleviation was considered a convenient measure to reconstruct and streamline poorly performing SOEs. In principle, it aimed to peel off unproductive, ancillary entities from SOEs including hospitals, schools, and utility supplies, the costs of which had long been shouldered by the enterprises, and transfer them to local municipal governments. In practice, the transfer of the NS's school system, which took place between 1998 and 1999, was an unpleasant battle that ended the glory days of Du's career rather ignominiously:

> The reformers never considered the concrete process nor the costs of transferring . . . The whole process was so difficult for us. The factory was eager to get rid of the school, but the local government didn't want it because public schools wouldn't bring them money but instead required money . . . They just kept on bargaining on the budget . . . What they really wanted was to maximise their own interests . . . So we had to keep on begging the local bureaucrats, "please, please take over our school." I was so angry deep in my heart. Such a good school had developed from nothing! The best school in the area! How much effort had our teachers put into it over all these years! Who wanted to hand it over?! But we didn't have any choice . . . I constantly wanted to cry.

Once again, we can see Du's assertive judgements and criticisms of state policies, which were also on display in his narrative about his earlier life. Being aware of what was really going on at the macro level and how that affected his own individual life empowered Du in certain ways in that at least he was not being pushed around by invisible forces. Nevertheless, when the transfer was finally completed in 1999, many teachers, including Du, chose to leave the school. With the departure of so many good teachers and the chaos produced in the transfer process, the school quickly deteriorated into a low-quality institution. Du was later transferred to the administrative office of the factory. He earned more money at his new job, but he did not value the position, describing it as "merely making a living." It never gave him the same feeling of satisfaction and achievement that his former job had.

At first glance, the radical neoliberal restructuring movement seemingly had a lesser effect on Zhang Guirong. This was largely because he had already partially cut ties with the factory when he became involved in the burgeoning market economy in the late 1970s; the economic restructuring of the late 1990s accelerated his complete break with NS:

> When I reached the age of early retirement in 1999, I was only too happy to leave. The factory had been performing poorly since 1997: delayed and reduced wages and no bonuses at all . . . So, I had wanted to leave NS a long time ago, but I couldn't since I had to wait to reach a certain age in order to qualify for the pension. Now I could retire early, nothing could be better. . . Afterwards, I worked full time for private bosses . . . My wife also retired early a little later. She is now working in a private dental clinic in Chengdu . . . You know, I always told these young college graduates who had just come to work at my former place: "leave NS as soon as you can find jobs somewhere else; there is no hope and future here at all."

Always pragmatic, with a talent for sensing policy changes and an eagerness to take risks, Zhang also managed to transfer his family members' household registrations back to Shanghai, where the welfare package is much better than that offered by NS. But he was not satisfied:

> Yes, it is good that we could finally go back to Shanghai. But now we have to buy a flat in Shanghai in order to have a place to live. But it's so expensive! Even for a very small flat, it would cost us our entire savings plus debt. So, you see, all the money we made working hard day and night in the end flew to the pockets of the real estate developers; after that, we had nothing left . . . I am too old to work anymore.

Though an apparent beneficiary of the market reforms of the "long 1980s," Zhang's account was, nevertheless, full of frustration. The market had given him a new source of income he had used to support his daughter's expensive education – which had been free in the socialist era – but when the market became more predatory and vulturous later on, especially in the real estate sector, his life-long savings were completely wiped out, and he even had to go into debt. Although he admitted that his life was much better than those who were still stuck working at NS, the rampant and unscrupulous development of capitalism made Zhang feel vulnerable:

> I have had a good-for-nothing life; I achieved nothing . . . I miss the planned economy. At that time, as long as you worked, life was stable and secure; you worried about nothing: neither your children's education nor your medical expenses . . . Now I am constantly anxious . . . Sure, compared to my old pals stuck in NS, my life is better . . . Some of my old friends, their lives are so hard it makes me feel sad . . . To tell the truth, I have no interest in market reform at all. I think we should go back to the planned economy so we could have a guaranteed and more secure retirement.

Zhang's account was filled with such a sense of futility and vulnerability, despite his hard work and boldness, it made him conclude his life was "good-for-nothing." On the one hand, when facing omnipotent and uneven external forces, individual efforts could be so easily overridden, even when one attempted to adapt to the changed circumstances. Yet, on the other hand, Zhang's powerful and definitive statements such as "I have no interest in market reform at all" or "I think we should go back to the planned economy" unequivocally challenged the state policies and structural forces that negated his lifelong efforts.

Compared to Zhang Guirong, the change to Gong Yapin's life trajectory was much more dramatic. The turning point imposed on her was a militant protest organised by NS pensioners. The protest was triggered by a decision made by the factory in 2002 to stop subsidising pension payments, which was a part of the larger restructuring package. This decision triggered the largest, longest, and most militant and desperate protest organised by pensioners in NS's history. All the grievances and anger that had accumulated through the years of radical reform, along with the sense of having been betrayed and abandoned, finally erupted. The same day they were officially informed of the decision, the pensioners immediately besieged and partially occupied the factory's administration building. Since Gong was the chairperson of the factory union at the time, the factory pushed her to the frontlines to face down the protesting pensioners:

> After the document was dispatched, I dared not go to my office for two days since these pensioners were everywhere. Then, on the third day, the factory asked me to talk to the workers because I was the union chairwoman at the time. From that day on, I spent five months standing in the hall of the administration building, trying to calm down these angry pensioners by talking through a megaphone. There were so many of them in the building, these elderly people. They sat or stood everywhere, with their hair as white as snow . . . Once, two old gentlemen forcibly grabbed my arms and another old lady took hold of my lower body, and together they tried to pull me down the stairs. Fortunately, there were several plainclothes policemen

around me, and they seized me from these angry old people. Our policy at the time was to take all the beatings and rebukes and never escalate or fight back. A lot of these old workers used to be so nice to me, and they also knew me very well—I had always called them "aunt" or "uncle." But now they hated me, they hated me so much I thought they might kill me . . . But I could never blame these pensioners. Everybody needs to survive. I just wished I could do more for them, but I didn't have such powers. What kind of cadres we were in these loss-generating SOEs!

Unsurprisingly, pensioners' indignation was directed at managers, not the system. The former were condemned as "betrayers of the enterprise," thus becoming scapegoats for the failed market-oriented reforms and all the destruction, pauperisation, and chaos they caused in NS. Pensioners' resentments and even hatred towards managers produced an uneasy and painful situation for those among the management who saw themselves as mediators for and allies of the workers. The feeling of being scapegoated and wronged became so unbearable for Gong that she finally resigned from her post in 2003:

You know why I wanted to leave this place forever? Because I felt so sad deep down in my heart. It seems that the bigger context distorted everything. I had always thought of myself as a good and honest person; I tried so hard to do something good and to achieve something . . . But in the end, none of this was recognised, and so many people hated me . . . Once, when I was buying food in the market, an old gentleman approached me and said loudly, "Bastard!" I was so upset: my image in their eyes should not have been so evil . . . I wanted to leave because I felt that I had already become a clown in this environment: people didn't trust you anymore; they thought everything you said and did was simply a lie; they regarded you as a monster . . . Whenever I thought about all this, I couldn't sleep night after night; my blood pressure would rise; and I just wanted to scream and cry . . .

Gong's voice was still trembling when she recounted this final period of her working life, which ended in despair, grievance, and humiliation. Actually, the strong feeling of being wronged and scapegoated became so suffocating she finally left NS forever and moved to another city to live with her adult daughter. Gong had been very formal and reserved the first time I talked to her. But after a few times, when she finally decided to trust me, words just kept pouring out of her as if the floodgates opened. Talking to me, a scholar who would record and potentially publicise her story, did not just allow her to vent her anger; maybe more importantly, it allowed her to respond to being scapegoated and wronged and to make sense of her working life and find meaning in it.

The radical neoliberal restructuring that has taken place in China since the second half of the 1990s – described by one of my interviewees as "another movement" – significantly changed my four narrators' lives in different ways. It either abruptly ended or significantly altered their working lives; it also disrupted their anticipated life narratives, uprooted their working identities, nullified their cumulative achievements, mocked their deeply held values, and, to a varying degree, flung them into a state of purposelessness, insecurity, and instability. For individuals, sudden life changes throw light on the seemingly inescapable power of structural forces. If the earlier mild and highly embedded market reforms had increased the number of life choices for my protagonists by providing them with a relatively stable and predictable environment and an alternative labour market, the later reckless and draconian neoliberal reforms imposed by the state and the unscrupulous ascendant power of capital in cahoots with the state narrowed their choices and disempowered them. Yet, all the anger, regret, grievance, and frustration expressed in their subjective narratives about this turning point in their lives could also be read as their active intervention in these decisive events since their emotions tell us what they think made everything go wrong and how they think their lives should have turned out, but didn't. I consider that a crucial form of agency.

Conclusion

The life stories I have recorded here were highly constrained and volatile, shaped by turbulent social transformation largely caused by shifting state policies. Yet, they are also diverse, unique, vibrant, and dynamic, exemplifying the distinct and concrete interactions between each individual and her/his environment, thus contrasting sharply with the seemingly monolithic structure. These details and this distinctiveness illustrate the possibilities within the established limits, that is, the agency within the structure. Moreover, the meaning of agency goes beyond the actual processes interacting at a particular moment; it also expresses itself through active remembering and reflection on those processes when looking back.

As I have shown in this chapter, my protagonists did not merely narrate their life trajectories. Most of the time, they contemplated, interpreted, evaluated, and criticised both the concrete events that happened in their life courses as well as the external forces that shaped them. When talking about the crucial turning points in their working lives, they always embedded them within the larger context. It seems that only when they looked back, the uncontrollable and sometimes incomprehensible external forces became much clearer to them as they correlated their life trajectories with the larger historical processes unfolding at the time. It is through these introspections that they began to ruminate on what/how/why everything had happened, to connect each dot, to find logic, purpose, and meaning in their lives. Thus, despite external forces outside their control, and despite the fact that most of the time they were merely buffeted by the tides of history, by re-processing the past, they could finally gain control of their own life course narra-tives.

Robert Penn Warren once wrote, "you live through . . . that little piece of time that is yours, but that piece of time is not only your own life, it is the summing-up of all the other lives that are simultaneous with yours. It is, in other words, History, and what you are is an expression of History" (Warren 1994: 134). This rings true: history is composed of individuals' lives, and it shapes our individual life trajecto-ries. But let me add something: by trying to grasp the meaning of history and its connections to their lives, people finally have a say in what and who they are. That is the power of agency in the subjective dimension of the life course.

References

Elder Jr., Glen H. 1994. "Time, Human Agency, and Social Change: Perspectives on the Life Course." *Social Psychology Quarterly* 57, no. 1: 4–15.

Gan, Yang. 2007. "The Chinese Road: Three Decades and Six Decades." *Du Shu* 6 (2007): 3–13. (甘阳. "中国道路: 三十年与六十年." 读书).

George, Linda. K. 2003. "Life Course Research: Achievements and Potential." In *Handbook of the Life Course*, edited by T. J. Mortimer and M. J. Shanahan, 671–680. New York: Kluwer Academic Publishers.

Gu, Hongzhang. 1997. *The History of 'Up the Mountain Down to the Countryside.* Beijing: China Procuratorate Press.

Hareven, Tamara K. 2018. *Families, History and Social Change. Life Course and Cross-cultural Perspectives.* London: Routledge.

Kohli, Martin. 2007. "The Institutionalization of the Life Course: Looking Back to Looking Ahead." *Research in Human Development* 4: 253–271.

Li, Ju. 2019. *Enduring Change. The Labor and Social History of One Third-front Industrial Complex in China from the 1960s to the Present.* Berlin: De Gruyter GmbH & Co KG.

Lin, Justin Yifu, Fang Cai, and Zhou Li. 2001. *State-owned Enterprise Reform in China.* Hong Kong: Chinese University Press.

MacMillan, Ross. 2005. "The Structure of the Life Course: Classic Issues and Current Controversies." In *Advances in Life Course Research*, special vol. 9: *The Structure of the Life Course: Standardized? Individualized? Differentiated?*, edited by Ross MacMillan, 3–26. Oxford: JAI/Elsevier.

Marshall, Victor. 2000. "Agency, Structure, and the Life Course in the Era of Reflexive Modernization." American Sociological Association Annual Meeting, Washington, DC, August 2000.

Mayer, Karl Ulrich, and W. Müller. 1986. "The State and the Structure of the Life Course." In *Human Development and the Life Course: Multidisciplinary Perspectives*, edited by Franz Emanuel Weinert, 217–245. United Kingdom: L. Erlbaum Associates.

Mayer, Karl Ulrich. 2003. "The Sociology of the Life Course and Lifespan Psychology: Diverging or Converging Pathways?" In *Understanding Human Development: Dialogues with Lifespan*

Psychology, edited by Ursula M. Staudinger and Ulman E. R. Lindenberger, 463–481. Boston: Springer Science & Business Media.

Mayer, Karl Ulrich. 2004. "Whose Lives? How History, Societies and Institutions Define and Shape Life Courses." *Research in Human Development* 1: 161–187.

Mayer, Karl Ulrich. 2009. "New Directions in Life Course Research." *Annual Review of Sociology* 35: 413–433.

Mayer, Karl Ulrich, and Urs Schoepflin. 1989. "The State and the Life Course." *Annual Review of Sociology* 15: 187–209.

Warren, Robert Penn. 1994. *Band of Angels.* Baton Rouge: Louisiana State University Press.

Wu, Jinglian, and Keping Yu. 2014. *Reform Consensus and China's Future.* Beijing: Central Translation Publisher. (吴敬链,俞可平. "改革共识与中国未来." 北京:中央编译局).

Yang, Guobin. 2016. *The Red Guard Generation and Political Activism in China.* New York: Columbia University Press.

Zhou, Xueguang, and Phyllis Moen. 2001. "Explaining Life Chances in China's Economic Transformation: A Life Course Approach." *Social Science Research* 30, no. 4: 552–577.

Therese Garstenauer

The Life Courses and Careers of Public Employees in Interwar Austria

Introduction

> I was born on February 6, 1896 and served in World War One from April 1915 until the col-
> lapse of Artillery Regiment No. 104. After the war ended, I was employed at the Austrian Rail-
> ways for a short time but was dismissed in the wake of reductions due to a surplus of person-
> nel; I then worked at the Krupp factory for fifteen years. On November 20, 1941, I was
> conscripted as a police reservist, and after two months of training, I was . . . assigned to serv-
> ice and am still working there (Personnel file Hinterweger).[1]

Josef Hinterweger's employment application from October 1945 explaining his
transfer into the municipal civil service of the city of Amstetten is not what one
expects from a description of a Weberian ideal-type career in civil service. He
had not been trained for the job nor had he dedicated his entire professional
life to state service. We see no indication of a career in the sense of a predictable
employment track. Instead, he was employed with the state railways, in a private
factory, and as a reserve policeman, the last of which he started at the age of forty-
five. Still, his particular career trajectory was not necessarily exceptional given the
circumstances of interwar Austria. Even high officials in the central administration could face gaps in their careers, for example Egbert Mannlicher (1882–1973),
who entered the civil service as a trainee in 1905 and worked in central state ministries starting in 1910. In the 1920s, he became a member of a commission charged
with downsizing the state apparatus (*Ersparungskommission*), and later he took a
position as the senator-president of the Supreme Administrative Court. Forcibly retired the civil service in 1934 on political grounds, he continued to serve as a
member of a legal committee (*Kodifikationskommission*) in the Federal Chancellery. After the 1938 *Anschluss*, he was reactivated and served in the Ministry of
the Interior in Berlin and in other influential positions despite never joining the

---

Note: The term "public employee" includes civil servants proper ("*Beamte*") and employees and workers employed at the federal, provincial, and municipal level of administration as well as the employees
of railways, nationalised enterprises, and teachers, judicial personnel, and police and gendarmerie
forces.

1 The source does not reveal whether Hinterweger's application was successful. All translations of
sources are mine.

National Socialist German Workers' Party (NSDAP, Nazi Party). Removed from service in 1945 and having been interned in the Glasenbach prison camp, he spent years in litigation to receive a pension as an Austrian government official; that lawsuit eventually succeeded.[2] From 1949 to 1971, he earned his living as a lawyer (Deak 2009: 418–425).

The professional careers of modern European government employees are traditionally considered to be stable and predictable, especially in comparison to those employed in other sectors of the economy,[3] and largely based on the male breadwinner model.[4] Consequently, the connection of the civil service with the concept of life course – understood as "a sequence of socially defined events and roles that the individual enacts over time" (Giele and Elder 1998: 22) – is rather obvious. As the service law for government employees takes into account events in the family life course[5] such as marriage and childbirth, the interaction between "individual time," "family time," and "historical time" (Hareven 2013: 1) becomes a central research focus.

For an Austrian civil servant in the early twentieth century, such a life course would typically imply a longer or shorter period of education depending on the position to which they aspired. Entry into civil service was normally confined to those between the ages of eighteen and forty. After a probationary period, one was appointed a civil servant and could expect to be promoted on a regular basis every few years. At the age of sixty (sixty-five for railway employees) and/ or after thirty-five years of service, a civil servant could retire. Thus, it comes as no surprise to read the following in the memoirs of the civil servant Erich Kneußl (1884–1968), written after he passed the last practical exam in 1912 at the age of twenty-eight:

> Now I was a full-fledged, permanently appointed civil servant. I had achieved my goal. It was only a matter of time until I advanced further up the ladder, which for middle-class civil servants would usually lead to a position as *Statthaltereirat* [a high provincial official, TG], assuming that performance was normal. (37)

---

2 As a holder of high office under the National Socialist regime, he was not entitled to a pension. But because he received a pension before March 1938, he was in fact eligible.

3 This applies to most European countries. See Horton 2011: 31–53.

4 "[T]he occupational form of the civil servant was gendered, because it was based on differentiation between work and family, the concomitant sexual division of labour, and the fact that its career and pay system was tied to the role of the male breadwinner" (di Luzio 2001, 164).

5 For sociological theories of family life course, see White and Klein 2002: 88–116.

Ten years later, there would be no more *Statthalterei*, and, as we will see below, Kneußl's individual biography would also differ from an ideal-typical civil servant.[6]

In this chapter, I will scrutinise Austrian government employment in the interwar period, which is characterised by seemingly opposing trends: just when a comprehensive employment law for the public sector, the *Dienstpragmatik*,[7] came into effect following the decades-long struggles of government employees' organisations, a number of events – World War One chief among them – took place, which impacted the stability of civil service careers. The chief aspects of this analysis are (1) employment security – could a public employee keep their job?; (2) income security – could a public employee support themselves and their dependents; and (3) did a public employee have opportunities for upward social mobility over the period of active service.

To begin answering these questions, I will first discuss the *Dienstpragmatik*, its predecessors, and subsequent adaptations, to show how it regulated the life courses and careers of civil servants in terms of the preconditions of service, entry into and exit from service, and salary increases tied to years spent in civil service, as well as how the civil service legislation addressed the needs of employees as they advanced through different stages and events in the family life course such as marriage and parenthood. A brief statistical portrait of the Austrian civil service in terms of age distribution, marital status, and number of children based on statistical data from 1923 will be presented. Then, I will elaborate on subsequent developments which had important consequences for careers in public service. These included: (1) economic crises leading to massive layoffs and the devaluation of salaries; (2) political restrictions for government employees, often, but not always related to regime changes; and, finally, (3) racist measures that affected persons employed in public service. Whereas there has been structural antisemitism that prevented persons of the Jewish faith from attaining higher positions all along (Pauley 1990; Melichar 2005), it was not until the *Anschluss* in 1938 that specific legislation banned from state service persons who were defined as "Jewish" according to the Nuremberg Laws of the National Socialists. Due to these three developments, careers in government employment were, in many cases, discontinuous and unstable, notwithstanding the traditional acquired rights (*wohlerworbene*

---

6 I am grateful to Katharina Haller-Seeber who has kindly given me a copy of Erich Kneußl's unedited memoirs, excerpts of which will be quoted throughout this article. For more information on this source, see Seeber 2015.

7 *RGBl 15 betreffend das Dienstverhältnis der Staatsbeamten und der Staatsdienerschaft (Dienstpragmatik) vom 25. Jänner 1914.*

Rechte) of civil servants.[8] But for all this precarity, was civil service as a lifelong career path ever called into question?

Gender as a structural category will be taken into account in my discussion of the aforementioned developments because it was a crucial factor in the careers of government employees in interwar Austria. The process of the "dissociation of work and family life" as described by Karin Hausen (1976) was most notably observed in households of the educated middle class, including those of civil servants. As Gaia de Luzio puts it, "the notion of holding a public office as an occupation was set off against the idea that occupational work and housekeeping are intertwined. It thereby corresponded to a new form of the family that had spread since the end of the eighteenth century in the middle class" (di Luzio 2001: 163).[9] Yet, since the late 1860s, women began to enter government employment, at first in subaltern positions and, as a rule, on private-law contracts, but not as civil servants (Nawiasky 1902; Heindl 2013b: 147–154). Already in the late Habsburg era, female activists such as postal employee Luise Greipl campaigned for equal rights for women and men in public employment: "At work, no distinction is made whether it is done by a man or a woman, and there should be, thus, equal remuneration. The times in which the man was considered the sole breadwinner of the family are in the past. In our circles, only a few families are so well-off that they can do without the additional earnings of the woman" (*Postmeisterinnen* 1913: 1). The question here is to what extent the economic and political developments outlined above affect women's careers in civil service and confirm the male breadwinner model (challenged to some extent already during the Dualist period, as Luise Greipl's statement suggests).

The *Dienstpragmatik* and Its Predecessors

The evolution of the modern civil service from the personal servants of a ruler to today's providers of professional public services unfolded over several centuries (Raadschelders and Rutgers 1996). In the Habsburg Monarchy, Empress Maria Theresia and particularly Emperor Joseph II are known for building the foundations of the modern Austrian civil service. Under their reigns, the number of gov-

---

8 This term figures in the constitution of the Weimar Republic ("*Die wohlerworbenen Rechte der Beamten sind unverletzlich,*" Art. 129/1), but not in the legal documents of the Austrian First Republic. However, it was used in newspaper articles in interwar Austria, especially concerning pension cuts for civil servants.

9 What she observes about German civil service is applicable to the Habsburg/Austrian case as well.

ernment employees increased, and their remuneration became more regulated than before. Most importantly, they introduced old-age pensions and pensions for dependent spouses and children as stipulated in the *Pensionsnormale* of 1781 (Heindl 2013a: 37). Far from providing sufficient means in all cases, the introduction of old-age pensions nevertheless contributed significantly to the constitution of old age as a specific stage in human life that took place after the end of professional activity (Ehmer 1990: 39). The introduction of objective criteria for admission – legal studies for some higher positions, examinations for others – was another important innovation (Kucsko-Stadelmayer 1986: 41) that contributed to the creation of modern civil service careers. Further regulations on public service careers were introduced in subsequent decades. In 1807, a system was decreed that consisted of twelve classes defined by the amount of travel allowances associated with the various ranks of civil servants (Heindl 2013a: 192). Lifetime employment was not officially introduced but rather "smuggled in," as Waltraud Heindl has put it, via a decree on disciplinary measures in 1815.[10] The next big step towards systematising wages and career steps for government employees was the *Gehaltsgesetz* of 1873,[11] which established eleven ranks and quinquennial promotions within one rank. Although it resulted in higher wages and more predictable careers, and thus more favourable conditions of life (Heindl 2013b: 136 f), there were still a number of shortcomings in the law.

The *Dienstpragmatik* (hereafter: DP)[12] of 1914 was truly a milestone for civil servants. Although not all of its elements were new, it proved innovative in its systematic compilation. It is also remarkable that (excluding the years 1938–1945) this law remained effective in Austria until 1979, when a new civil service law was introduced.[13] In the following paragraphs, I will discuss the parts of the DP that are most pertinent to questions of civil servants' careers as they relate to the life course and which set the course for a normal career trajectory. The existing eleven classes established in 1873 were retained with an additional five-part classification according to the education required for certain positions (*Verwendungsgruppen*)[14]

---

10 Although this decree and the following (*Hofkanzleidekrete* of March 9, 1815, June 3, 1816, and October 24, 1834) cannot be considered a modern and just disciplinary code, they prevented civil servants from arbitrary dismissals (Heindl 2013a: 48).

11 *Gesetz vom 15. April 1873 betreffend die Regelung der Bezüge der activen Staatsbeamten*, RGBL, 47/1873.

12 RGBl, 15/1914, as in footnote 8.

13 *Bundesgesetz vom 27. Juni 1979 über das Dienstrecht der Beamten (Beamten-Dienstrechtsgesetz 1979 – BDG 1979)*, BGBl, 333/1979. The new law still contains elements of the DP (Wojta 2012: 48).

14 For further changes in the system of ranks until 1924, see Megner 2020.

ranging from E (primary school) to A (full secondary school and a university degree).

Persons between the ages of eighteen and forty[15] who possessed Austrian citizenship, an honourable record (*ehrenhaftes Vorleben*), and the required mental and physical abilities qualified for entrance into the civil service. Service usually began with a provisional employment stage called preparatory service (*Vorbereitungsdienst*). Whereas the DP did not specify the duration of this initial stage during which the employment could be terminated if the candidate fell short of the authorities' expectations, the *Gehaltsgesetz* of 1924 stipulated a duration of two years.[16]

The employer (*Dienstbehörde*) had to maintain specific documentation on every civil servant and their career development: first, the *Standesausweis* in which all personal data had to be registered, including that which was relevant for promotion and pension calculation; and, second, a yearly assessment of the performance of a civil servant (*Qualifikationstabelle*). The civil servant had the right to see this document and could object to an assessment if he found it unjustified. Advancement from one salary level to the next could be achieved in three years for the three classes at the lowest rank and in four years for those in the higher ranks, depending on the *Verwendungsgruppe* (Gruber and Pfaundler 1934: 122).

In a commentary about the DP in November 1913, jurist Hans Nawiasky remarked that the salary for civil servants was similar in part to wages paid as compensation for non-state service, but it also catered to the specific economic and social needs befitting civil servants' status (*standesgemäßer Unterhalt*):

> It [. . .] varies according to life stage. I will touch on only the main points that are of central influence here: marriage, children, maturation of children, children becoming independent, and the increase in needs in advanced age. As interesting as it would be to expand on the design that would ensue if all these circumstances were considered when devising an appropriate salary structure – I will simply mention that it would not have to be a straight line but a curve – I will confine myself to the statement that salary needs generally call for a gradual increase until the time of retirement. (Nawiasky 1914: 12)

In the early years of the First Republic, there existed various laws organising the hierarchies according to the rank and income of civil servants. Whereas the ear-

---

15 RGBl, 15/1914, § 2. Exemptions from this rule were possible, but they required special authorisation from the respective ministry.
16 *Bundesgesetz vom 18. Juli 1924 über das Diensteinkommen und die Ruhe- und Versorgungsgenüsse der Bundesangestellten (Gehaltsgesetz)*, BGBl, 54/245, § 4 Abs.4.

liest regulation[17] put more emphasis on the so-called principle of alimentation, the laws of 1921[18] and 1924[19] focused more on achievement and seniority.[20] In his memoirs, Erich Kneußl was rather critical of the earlier system:

> Due to the favourable treatment of the lower ranks of public employees in terms of salaries in the first years after the war, the salaries of higher ranks were out of proportion with those of the lower. The number of children and years spent in service were the decisive factors. This is why for some time I [as acting district commissioner, TG] received a lower salary than my clerk (*Amtsdiener*), who was older and had three children [Kneußl had two at the time, TG]. For these shortcomings, which were apt to inhibit any zeal and willingness to accept responsibility, one could thank the demagoguery that was prevalent not only among Social Democrats after the war. Soon it became obvious how impossible this situation was, and a new law based on the principle of achievement was passed. Thus, it was hoped that the civil service corps could be returned to the high standard it held before the war, thanks to which the construction of a new state became possible in such a short time. (Kneußl: 109)

Before the DP was enacted, government employees had to ask for permission before getting married. It sufficed to inform the employer about the marriage within fourteen days.[21] A civil service appointment was for one's entire lifetime. Once appointed, an official was either in active service or retired, but they remained a civil servant. Retirement could be temporary if the civil servant was only unfit for service temporarily, or it could be permanent due to illness, accident, or old age. Forced retirement – and in severe cases a reduced pension – were among the most rigorous sanctions for disciplinary offences. The relationship between a civil servant and the state could be terminated either at the request of the civil servant, thereby forgoing all rights and claims vested in the appointment, or by the employer, albeit only under special conditions related to disciplinary offences. Dismissal was the most severe sanction in disciplinary law. Civil servants who were convicted in

---

17 *Gesetz vom 18. Dezember 1919 zur vorläufigen Regelung der Besoldung der Zivilstaatsbeamten, Unterbeamten und Diener und der Volksbeauftragten (Besoldungsübergangsgesetz).*

18 *Bundesgesetz vom 13. Juli 1921 zur Regelung der Besoldungsverhältnisse der Bundesangestellten (Besoldungsgesetz).*

19 *Gehaltsgesetz*, as in Footnote 18.

20 The salary system enacted in the Weimar Republic in 1920, as Jane Caplan reports, also attempted to balance the traditional alimentation principle and newer principles of merit and social justice (Caplan 1988: 79).

21 In the early nineteenth century, civil servants would even have to prove a certain income level before they were permitted to marry (Megner 1986: 165). Marriage restrictions remained in place for security personnel and female teachers employed by the federal provinces well into the 1930s. However, marriage restrictions related to income (*politischer Ehekonsens*) applied virtually to the entire population of the Habsburg monarchy. It was abolished in most regions in 1869, but was valid in others, e.g., Tyrol, up to 1921 (Lanzinger 2015: 189).

the criminal courts were always dismissed. In cases of hardship, however, the dismissed individual or his dependents could apply for a subsistence allowance.

The DP pertained to civil servants and servants *(Diener)*,[22] whereas the legal rules for clerical personnel whose employment was based on a private-law contract with the state were laid down in a separate decree issued on the same day.[23] Among other things, the latter stipulated that only unmarried, divorced, or widowed women without children were admitted to service (§ 2). Only the children of male employees were entitled to orphan pensions (§59). This was not changed until 1919, when the clerical personnel were made part of the lower ranks of the civil service proper based on the *Pragmatisierungsgesetz*.[24] Although this was a major improvement for many female government employees, they continued to be largely confined to the lower ranks of the civil service and clerical work.[25]

In 1898, railway personnel had already succeeded in obtaining a service law that guaranteed regular increases in salary and rank (Gruber and Pfaundler 1934: 121; Megner 1986: 75). Federal teachers received a DP of their own in 1917. It was similar to the one enacted for administrative personnel in 1914.[26]

A Socio-demographic Portrait of Austrian Government Employees in the Early First Republic

Having now established that service law and the traditions of government employees beyond matters of the office also accounted for events in their family life course, I will provide a brief statistical portrait of what the personnel of the Austrian state apparatus looked like in terms of family status and number of children. Detailed information on civil servants was rarely publicised in the interwar peri-

---

22 *"Diener"* was the lowest rank of civil servants; they performed mainly menial tasks. Their rights and obligations were laid down in a specific subchapter of the DP. See Megner 1986: 291–296.
23 *Verordnung des Gesamtministeriums vom 25. Jänner 1914 betreffend das Kanzleihilfspersonal bei den staatlichen Behörden, Ämtern und Anstalten*, RGBl, 21/1914.
24 StGBl 100/1919, *Gesetz betreffend die teilweise Änderung des DV der Kanzleioffizianten und Kanzleioffiziantinnen, der Kanzleigehilfen und Kanzleigehilfinnen, ständigen Aushilfsdiener und Landpostdiener.*
25 Women were admitted to legal studies at Austrian universities – the prerequisite for a career in the higher ranks of civil service – only in 1919 (Heindl 1990: 24).
26 *Gesetz vom 28. Juli 1917 betreffend das Dienstverhältnis der Lehrerschaft an staatlichen mittleren und niederen Unterrichtsanstalten (Lehrerdienstpragmatik)*, RGBl, 319/1917.

od, with the exception of the *Beamtenstatistik* of September 1923 (*Statistische Nachrichten,* 64–74).

The age distribution displays a strong representation of persons in their twenties and a notable decline beginning with those over forty years of age. This tendency is even more visible for the personnel of the general administration and the railways, and less so with employees of the post and telegraph and the Südbahn railways (nationalised only in 1923). To some extent, these figures reflect the initial effects of the mass layoffs of government employees that took place between 1922 and 1925, particularly with regard to the older cohorts. The high proportion of young personnel may be due to the fact that while limits on the number of new entries into the civil service were put in place starting in 1918, employment was still possible.[27]

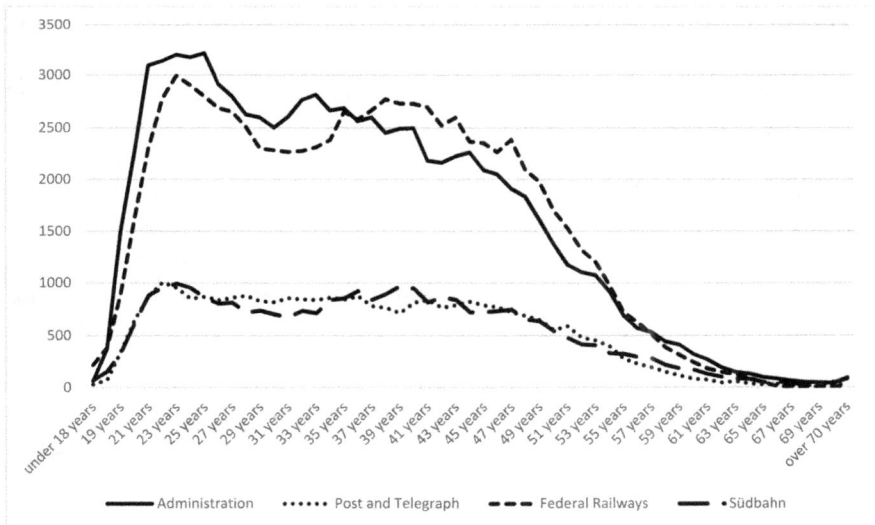

Figure 1: Age distribution of government employees September 1923, n = 249,269 (Statistische Nachrichten 1924:70).
Source: Statistische Nachrichten 1924:70.

In terms of the gender ratio, the statistics show that the percentage of women in public employment amounted to 10 percent of the workforce. As for marital status, there was a clearly gendered pattern in the distribution of married and unmarried

---

27 See the following sub-chapter for information regarding certain age groups' likeliness to lose their jobs during the personnel cutbacks of the 1920s.

public employees. More than three-quarters of female employees were unmarried, and only 13.6 percent of women were married, while among their male counterparts, the pattern was reversed: 28 percent of male employees in the civil service were unmarried, and nearly 70 percent were married.

Table 1: Marital status of government employees September 1923, n = 231,879.

	Unmarried	Married	Widowed	Divorced/separated	Total
Women	76.0%	13.6%	8.7%	1.7%	100%
Men	28.0%	69.8%	1.1%	1.1%	100%

Source: Statistische Nachrichten 1924:67.

Although married women were no longer *de jure* excluded from service starting in 1919, the 1923 numbers still reflect this social and legal norm. For public employees who were not working under collective bargaining agreements,[28] the number of children under the age of twenty-one for whom they could receive allowances was specified. Of all these employees, 44.1 percent received such allowances; that is to say, less than half had children under twenty-one living in their household. If we exclude unmarried employees, that percentage rises to 64.6 (Statistik 1924: 68). Of those who had children, almost half had one child and nearly a third had two. It was rather uncommon for government employees to have three (or more) children in the early 1920s.

Table 2: Percentage of civil servants with children September 1923, n = 102,383.

	1 child	2 children	3 children	4 children	5 children	6 children	More than 6 children
% of employees receiving allowances for...	46.7%	29.0%	13.4%	6.0%	2.7%	1.3%	0.9%

Source: Statistische Nachrichten 1924:68.

Several contemporary newspaper articles expressed worries about the declining number of children in Austrian families in general and particularly in civil serv-

---

28 It was mostly the workers and employees of public enterprises who were working under collective bargaining agreements. They are not included in this statistic.

ants' families. These numbers also point to the fact that the higher the position of a government employee, the fewer children they tended to have. In Upper Austria in the 1920s, for example, the average number of children in a road mender's family was 4.04, whereas grammar schoolteachers had 1.84 children on average. The author of the article states that these numbers were fairly similar to those before World War One (without naming sources for the numbers quoted [*Linzer Volksblatt* 1925: 1]). A small 1936 survey in an office of the Vienna city administration showed that of its eighty employees, eight were unmarried, forty were married without children, twenty-three were married with one child, seven were married with two children, and only one had three children (*Reichspost* 1936: 3). These numbers are in line with the observation that members of the educated middle classes, including civil servants, were among the first to use birth control (Ehmer 2013: 106 f). The prospect of a plannable career may have furthered the idea and practice of planning the number of one's children.

Economic Crises

The DP became effective in January 1914, only half a year before the outbreak of World War One. The initial inflation caused by the conflict devalued the fixed incomes of government employees, and the ensuing hyperinflation lasted until 1922. "German-Austria will be a poor state, and it will not be able to afford a large bureaucratic apparatus" (*Wiener Zeitung* 1918: 5), declared Chancellor Karl Renner in his speech to the civil servants of the state chancellery on November 14, 1918. A document composed by a committee of senior officials from various ministries dealing with matters related to government employees in the new Austrian Republic[29] proclaimed that there should be "fewer but better paid" civil servants (Megner and Steiner 2020: 58). The first attempts to downsize the bureaucratic apparatus consisted of excluding civil servants who did not possess German nationality on the basis of certain criteria such as their parents' nationality, their native language, or their spoken language (*Umgangssprache*) as indicated in the census of 1910 (Garstenauer 2021). Furthermore, civil servants who had reached the age of sixty and served enough years to claim at least 75 percent of their pension were encouraged to retire. Those who had already achieved their full pension entitlement regardless of age were to be retired *ex lege*. These measures, based on a law enacted in July

---

29 *Richtlinien für die vorläufige Behandlung einiger Staatsbedienstetenfragen*, published in *Wiener Zeitung*, November 24, 1918, 1.

1919,[30] did not have visible effects on the number of civil servants. Those who took advantage of the opportunity to retire experienced financial losses or even pauperisation in the years to come because the allowances to offset the consequences of inflation were lower for pensioners than for active civil servants (Megner and Steiner 2020: 74).

The economically fragile Austrian Republic had to rely on a loan from the League of Nations to stabilise its currency. One of the conditions for granting this loan was a massive reduction in the number of civil servants (Deak 2010: 136). That reduction affected almost 100,000 civil servants, i.e., slightly less than 30 percent of all public employees.[31] In the central administration, 19 percent were made redundant. The percentages were even higher in the postal service (21.9 percent), state-owned enterprises (32.2 percent), and the railways (33.7 percent).[32] As a comparison, the Weimar Republic, which was also grappling with hyperinflation, reduced the number of its public employees by about 20 percent between 1923 and 1924. The groups most strongly affected were young employees, older employees, and women; mid-career male civil service employees in Germany were the least affected by the reductions (Fattmann 2001: 43).

In a newspaper article from April 1924, a speaker of the Provincial Conference of Austrian Railway Workers is quoted as saying that those made redundant were mainly younger persons – such as Josef Hinterweger, mentioned at the beginning of this chapter – or older persons close to pension age. "[. . .] those middle-aged railway employees for whom it is more difficult to find new subsistence have been spared wherever possible. Yet, the younger ones, largely unmarried persons who could switch to something else more easily, as well as older persons already receiving a corresponding pension were impacted more negatively" (Landeskonferenz 1924: 15). The statistical data on age presented in the previous subchapter, which depicts the situation about a half year before the conference, support this observation, at least with regard to the situation of older employees. It must be pointed out, however, that long before this crisis, railway personnel already retired before the age of sixty-five: the average pension age between 1900 and 1902 was 52.77 years (Pospíšil 1915: 46); clerical personnel remained in service longer compared to station employees, engine drivers, and conductors (Pospíšil 1915: 55).

---

30 *Gesetz, womit Maßnahmen zur Erleichterung des Übertrittes von Zivilstaatsangestellten in den dauernden Ruhestand getroffen werden. (Pensionsbegünstigungsgesetz.),* StGBl. Nr. 411/1919, *vom 30. Juli 1919.*
31 Peter Melichar has collected and compared the figures given in various contemporary sources, which are often incompatible with one another because of different classifications (Melichar 2013: 45 f).
32 Numbers as of August 1924, *Statistische Nachrichten* II/1924: 224.

The large representation of young railway personnel in the statistics from 1923 implies that either the statement at the conference referring to them was not representative or that measures affecting younger staff were not yet effective in the first years of the mass layoffs.

The law on which these cutbacks were based contained one article that impacted widowed women. It stipulated that the widow of a civil servant who was receiving a widow's pension *and* was an active civil servant herself would have to forego her pension; otherwise, she was not allowed to remain employed.[33] In a commemorative publication on the occasion of its twenty-fifth anniversary, an association of women civil servants in administrative and clerical positions lamented that the percentage of women among those made redundant in the first half of the 1920s had been particularly high (Zentralverein 1933: 32).[34] In the archive of the Agency of the Mail and Telegraph for Vienna, Lower Austria, and the Burgenland, the personnel files of fourteen women who entered this service can still be found. These demonstrate that those women entered service between the ages of nineteen and thirty-three (an average age of twenty-four) and retired between the ages of thirty-six and fifty-nine (an average age of forty-eight), and therefore served between seventeen and thirty-one years (an average of twenty-four years). Nine of these fourteen women were retired in the wake of cutbacks in the early 1920s (Steiner 1994: 137f.).

Interestingly, in individual memoirs, the massive personnel reductions were not necessarily mentioned. Erich Kneußl, who dedicated forty-eight of the 365 pages of his memoirs to the 1920s, does not refer to cutbacks at all. He recalls family events such as the death of his younger sister (100) and the birth of his third child (119). Furthermore, he proudly noted that he was appointed to the position of district commissioner *(Bezirkshauptmann)* of Lienz in Osttirol, having reached this career step only twelve years after entering the civil service (even his father had taken fifteen years to achieve this [100]). Despite the extent of the cutbacks, the majority of government employees experienced continuity in their careers.

Following the collapse of the *Creditanstalt* bank, which led to financial crises in many European countries and beyond, the early 1930s saw another contraction of the state apparatus, although this time it involved fewer civil servants. The pertinent law implied that a onetime reduction of allowances *(Zulagen)*, which constituted 30 percent of civil servants' income, would be introduced in the same year to

---

33 *Bundesgesetz vom 24. Juli 1922, betreffend Maßnahmen zur Verringerung der Zahl der Bundes(Bundesverkehrs)angestellten (Angestellten-Abbaugesetz)*, BGBl, 499/1922, § 11.

34 The available data on the reduction of the number of public employees from the 1920s and 1930s are not itemised by gender, so the overall impact on women government employees cannot be explained.

ease the burden on the national budget. The reductions were two-thirds for childless persons, one-half for those with one or two children, and one-third for those with three or more children – marking another time that the principle of alimentation became operative.[35]

One of the measures for downsizing the state apparatus touched specifically on gender relations: the *Doppelverdienerverordnung* of 1933.[36] It required female civil servants whose husbands were also employed in the civil service *and* who had an income exceeding a certain limit to be retired on short notice. Furthermore, no married women were allowed to be hired as civil servants or public employees if their spouse was already a civil servant. And if two civil servants opted for cohabitation instead of marriage, it amounted to a disciplinary offence. It is difficult to assess how many women and men were affected by the *Doppelverdienerverordnung*, for beyond its numerical effects it was a measure with a high symbolic impact (Bei 2012, 197). Social scientist and activist Käthe Leichter stated that the Austrian regulation went even further than the German one insofar as it prohibited cohabitation (quoted in Bei 2012: 201). Female civil servants faced restrictions in many European countries at the time, with the exception of France:

> Single women, divorcees, and widows were grateful for steady employment, and married women administrators could count themselves lucky when they compared their situation to that of other European and even American counterparts. Unlike England and many other European countries, France had no "marriage bar," nor did it have American-style state or local nepotism rules preventing both husband and wife from holding public jobs. Unlike Nazi Germany and Fascist Italy, Republican France did not fire women whose political views displeased those in power. (Clark 2004: 205)

Owing to the economic crises of the first half of the twentieth century, there were not only considerable reductions in the number of government employees. The loss in income due to the devaluation was also felt by many civil servants as reflected in the activities of civil servants' organisations throughout the 1920s (Naderer 1931). A 1950 study has shown that the real income of government employees in 1949 amounted to about one-third of that in 1914, meaning that in the long run, they fared worse than other workers (Kosian 1950: 103). However, this is not to say that government employees suffered more than other professional groups during

---

35 *Bundesgesetz vom 16. Juli 1931 über die Verminderung der Personallasten im Jahr 1931*, BGBl, 212/1931, § 1.

36 *Verordnung der Bundesregierung vom 15. Dezember 1933 über den Abbau verheirateter weiblicher Personen und andere dienstrechtliche Maßnahmen*, BGBl, 545/1933.

the economic crises of the interwar period, as high unemployment affected considerable portions of the working population.[37]

Effects of Political Restrictions on the Careers of Civil Servants Prior to the *Anschluss*

Some scholars have observed that the regime change from monarchy to republic did not imply a substantial caesura for government employees (e. g., Melichar 2013: 41). Most civil servants did not find it problematic to pledge loyalty to the republic instead of the emperor. Unlike Weimar Germany, there were no noteworthy public debates on the altered oath of service (Conze 2013; Enderle-Burcel and Follner 1996: 10). As long as civil servants met the criteria for German nationality, they were initially absorbed into the service of the First Republic.[38] The constitution of the new republic entitled everyone, including government employees, to the freedom of association and the right of assembly. Unlike German government employees, their Austrian counterparts were entitled to go on strike, although this was frowned upon by conservative politicians (Naderer 1932: 31).

In November 1931, though, the political activities of government employees were restricted by a decree issued by Chancellor Karl Buresch[39] after an attempted *coup d'état* by the Styrian *Heimwehr*[40] leader Walter Pfrimer. As a result, it became illegal to belong to any political organisation or to display political emblems during service hours; even carrying political leaflets on one's person was forbidden (Enderle-Burcel and Jeřabek 2011: 27). An even stricter decree issued by Chancellor Engelbert Dollfuß in April 1933, following his establishment of an authoritarian if not fascist regime (Kirk 2003): civil servants not only had to refrain from any political activities they also had to inform on colleagues who defied such rules (Sedlak 2006: 6). The disciplinary rules laid down in the *Dienstpragmatik* were complemented and intensified by a decree in May 1933 *(Verordnung der Bundesregierung vom*

---

37 For accounts of unemployment in interwar Austria, see Stiefel 1979 and Vana 2015. For an international perspective, see Eichengreen and Hatton 1988.

38 The ensuing measures to pension off all civil servants who had reached the age at which they could claim a full pension (*Pensionsbegünstigungsgesetz* of July 1919) had rather little effect on the number of active civil servants, unlike those between 1922–1925. See the above sub-chapter on economic crises in Austria.

39 "Die politische Betätigung der Beamten. Ein Erlaß des Bundeskanzlers," in *Kleine Volkszeitung*, December 3, 1931, 2.

40 The *Heimwehr* (i.e. home defence force) was a paramilitary force closely associated with the Christian Social Party.

10. Mai 1933 über besondere Maßnahmen, betreffend die öffentlich-rechtlichen Bundesangestellten), which stipulated that public employees could be dismissed altogether for forbidden political activities and lose their income in the process. In cases of unusual hardship, they could apply for a subsistence allowance. A special commission *(Besondere Disziplinarkommission)* consisting of senior officials was installed to deal with such cases more rapidly than the normal disciplinary commissions. Additionally, Josef Arbogast Fleisch, a high-ranking civil servant from the Ministry of Agriculture and Forestry, became the Federal Commissioner for Personnel Matters, and it became his task to keep the political ambitions of civil servants under control. After the February Uprising of 1934,[41] a decree[42] made it possible to suspend politically suspicious civil servants from service and reduce their income by a third (Sedlak 2006: 11).

Such measures taken against politically active civil servants after 1931 implied a significant change in disciplinary regulations: whereas the *Dienstpragmatik* remained vague as to what exactly amounted to a disciplinary offence, the new decrees explicitly referred to political activities in a broad sense (barring obligatory membership in the Fatherland Front).[43] Yet these measures affected only a small number of civil servants. Hence, the February 1938 minutes of the Council of Ministers report a total of 2,273 civil servants who had been sanctioned between 1931 and 1938 – among them, Egbert Mannlicher mentioned earlier in the chapter. Of this number, 1,389 had been dismissed or retired. Most who were subject to sanctions sympathised with National Socialism; only a small portion were Social Democrats or Communists (Sedlak 2006: 19).

Immediately after the *Anschluss,* i. e., the annexation of Austria into Nazi Germany, civil servants considered ineligible for service to the new regime were *de facto* removed from their posts. At the end of May 1938, a decree came into effect which, among other things, intended to restructure the state apparatus by retiring or dismissing civil servants who were unacceptable to the National Socialist administration for political or racial reasons. I will discuss the consequences of that decree in the following section.

---

41 Between February 12 and 15, 1934, there was an armed uprising by Social Democratic forces in several Austrian cities, which was brutally crushed by the Dollfuß government. This was followed by a ban of the Social Democratic Party.

42 *Verordnung vom 23. Februar 1934.*

43 The Fatherland Front *(Vaterländische Front)* was the unitary organisation of the Federal State of Austria, which claimed to be non-partisan and aimed to unite people across social and political boundaries. Civil servants were pressured to join the organisation.

Racial and Political Purges under National Socialism

It is safe to say that Jews – persons of the Jewish faith as well as converts – were underrepresented in the early twentieth-century Habsburg civil service, especially in the higher ranks (Rozenblit 1983; Bavouzet 2019: 184). Marsha Rozenblit's analyses of the professions of taxpaying members of the Jewish Community *(Israelitische Kultusgemeinde)* in Vienna and Lower Austria shows a percentage of 6.4 percent of Jews working in civil service in the early 1900s (Rozenblit 1983: 59), a rather low number when compared to the total Viennese workforce of 1900, 24.3 percent of which were public employees (Ibid. 1983: 67). During the First Republic, the number of Jewish members of the civil service corps declined even further. Bruce Pauley has pointed out that whereas before World War One, there were thirteen Jewish judges in Vienna, not one had been appointed after 1918 (Pauley 1992: 217). In 1935, only 682 of nearly 160,700 government employees were Jewish. In his analysis of Otto Ender's[44] estate, Peter Melichar (2018: 140–143) found letters from January 1934 indicating that under Engelbert Dollfuss, Jews were *de facto* never admitted to civil service. Had there been any such official regulation, it would have violated the constitution of the First Republic.[45]

Anti-Semitism was common and widespread in interwar Austria and led to an underrepresentation of Jews in civil service. The National Socialist takeover, however, was a turning point. First, it established a legal definition of who was a Jew; second, it interfered with the ongoing careers of civil servants. Regarding the first point, the Nuremberg Laws specified that a person was Jewish when at least three of their grandparents belonged to the Jewish religion according to the confession indicated in their baptismal certificate. Persons with one or two Jewish grandparents were classified as 'half- or quarter-Jews' *(jüdische Mischlinge ersten bzw. zweiten Grades)*.[46] As for the second point, it was only few months after the *Anschluss*, on May 31, 1938, that a decree to restructure Austrian officialdom was issued;[47] it

---

44 Otto Ender (1875–1960): politician (Christian-Social Party), lawyer, governor of Vorarlberg (1918–1930, 1931–1934), state chancellor (1930–1931).

45 In these letters, the rumour of a Jewish person being appointed by the Ministry of Social Affairs is discussed, with the result that no person with the name implied in the rumour could be found among the staff of the ministry.

46 *Erste Verordnung zum Reichsbürgergesetz vom 14. November 1935*, Deutsches Reichsgesetzblatt, 125/1935.

47 *Verordnung zur Neuordnung des österreichischen Berufsbeamtentums*, Deutsches Reichsgesetzblatt, 87/1938.

was modelled after a German law from 1933.[48] According to that decree, civil servants who were either politically unreliable or unsuitable on racial grounds – the latter on account of being "Jewish" or "half-Jewish" or being married to such a person – were not entitled to serve the National Socialist state. They were pensioned off, sometimes with their allowances reduced by a quarter or half, and in some cases, they were even dismissed. In other cases, based on other sections of the decree, civil servants were either pensioned off due to the administrative restructuring or they were transferred to a different position. Soon after the *Anschluss*, every government employee had to complete a questionnaire about their affiliations with political parties and organisations as well as the confessional identities of their parents and grandparents. Based on these questionnaires, review procedures were set in motion.

Erich Kneußl, who had been politically active as a member of the National Council for the Christian Social Party in the 1920s and 1930s, was fifty-four years old in 1938. He was urged by the provincial government to file an application to retire. The examination by a public health officer, which was required for retirements before the age of sixty yielded no specific results; thus, the reason for Kneußl's retirement from further service was explained by his "advanced age" (Kneußl: 249). He received his notice of retirement on January 4, 1939 (a "New Year's gift," as Kneußl sarcastically remarks), with a reduced pension (75 percent) based on his political unreliability.

> Thus, my career as a civil servant, which had started on April 9th, 1909, seemed to have ended ingloriously. On the one hand, my retirement was a severe blow for me; I was condemned to inactivity and suffered a considerable reduction of my income, and at a point where the education of Kurt and Ditha was not finished yet [. . .] On the other hand, I was not forced to serve a cause and a system that I rejected or where I risked being transferred to the north of Germany or even to the East, as was the case with many Austrian civil servants who had remained in service. But I considered my retirement as an undeserved injustice. (Kneußl: 249)[49]

He attempted to receive a concession to work as a legal advisor or tax consultant, but to no avail. In 1944, he was imprisoned for several months. Incidentally, it was during these years of professional inactivity that Erich Kneußl began writing his memoirs (Seeber 2015: 13).

---

48 *Gesetz zur Wiederherstellung des Berufsbeamtentum vom 7. April 1933*, Deutsches Reichsgesetzblatt, 34/1933.
49 Erich Kneußl's memoirs end in the year 1945, when he was reactivated and appointed first a state commissioner; he was elevated to the position of *Landesamtsdirektor*, the highest possible position in the civil service of an Austrian province, a year later. He retired in 1950 and lived for eighteen more years.

To assess the scope of these measures, I have analysed 14,582 administrative notices related to the aforementioned decree sent to former Austrian civil servants between June 1938 and April 1940. The articles of the decree on which these notices were based allow us to distinguish, to some extent, whether the evaluation was based on political, racial, administrative, or other grounds. The most striking result is that more than one-quarter of those screened by the authorities faced no sanctions. The second largest group, a little less than one-quarter, were those dismissed or pensioned off for political reasons. A little more than one-fifth (21 percent) were demoted or transferred to another position with the same or a lower status; in these cases, it is unclear on which grounds these actions were taken.[50] Some 15 percent of the notices analysed imply retirement due to racial criteria. Displacement from employment was but one aspect of racial persecution as many Austrian Jews faced forced emigration or even extermination. Only 1 percent of those included in the sample managed to remain in service despite being Jewish, at least up to early 1940. Another article of the decree implied forced retirement due to administrative reasons (*zur Vereinfachung der Verwaltung* or *im Interesse des Dienstes*), which was the case listed on 11 percent of the dismissal notices. 1 percent of the cases were taken back into service after being dismissed or retired based on the decree of May 1938. In another 1 percent of cases of retirements and dismissals, it was impossible to specify the grounds. Of all the measures taken, there were about 5,500 (39 percent) forced retirements.[51] Additionally, about 315 persons who had already retired suffered reductions or the total loss of their pension based on the "political" reasons listed in section four of the decree.

This tentative analysis does not give the whole picture of the National Socialist purges. It instead focuses on the situation between June 1938 and April 1940, covering only those cases processed immediately following the decree of May 1938. Although this analysis does not include all persons who retired of their own accord (certainly not voluntarily) before implementation,[52] went into exile, or committed suicide soon after March 1938, it can be viewed as a valid contribution to the discussion of how many government employees were affected by the National Socialist purges and precisely how they were affected. In academic publications thus far, only one particular statistic has been mentioned: the so-called *Rot-Weiß-Rot-Buch*

---

50 There is evidence that in some cases, the transfers or demotions served as a milder sanction for persons who were considered politically unreliable.

51 This measure cannot, however, be used as an indicator of age, or only to some extent, since persons with at least ten years of service could be pensioned according to the decree of May 1938 (Schneider et al. 1938: 44).

52 Some of them figure under "no measures" because they were already retired, and some of them received reduced pensions retroactively.

compiled by the Austrian Ministry of Foreign Affairs in 1946 – a publication whose main objective was to prove that Austria had been a victim of Nazi Germany – estimates there were 16,237 cases of civil servants who were dismissed or otherwise disciplined (*Rot-Weiss-Rot-Buch* 1946: 77).[53]

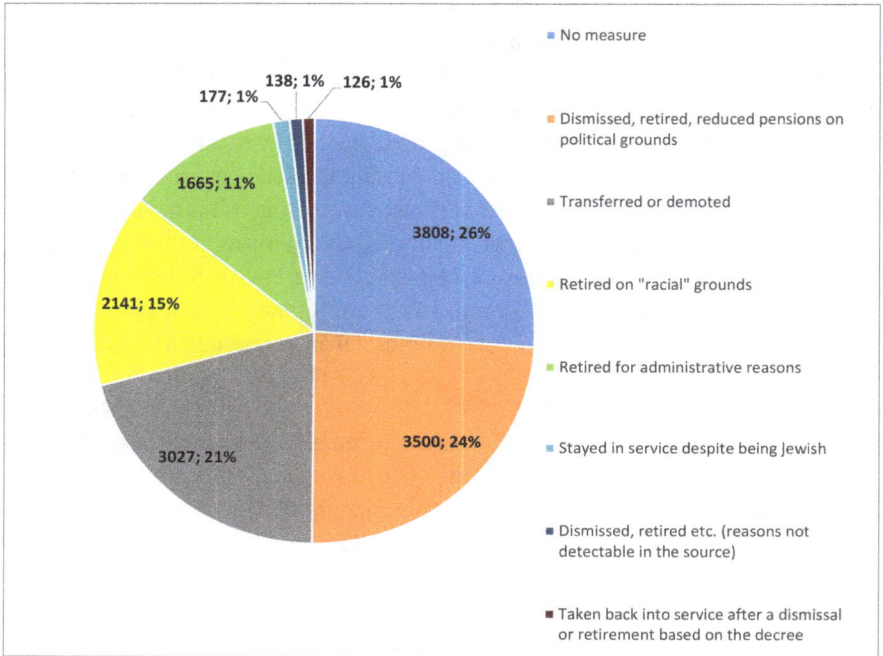

Figure 2: Distribution of measures based on the Verordnung zur Neuordnung des Österreichischen Berufsbeamtentums (n=14,582).

The bottom line here is that the nature of National Socialist interventions into the former Austrian civil service was new even though they did not affect a huge portion of the entire civil service corps. If we look at the number of government employees in 1935 (excluding those in the armed forces, which were not subject to the decree) as based on statistical handbooks (Bruckmüller 1983: 407), we arrive at a total of 140,811 employees. Assuming that there had not been massive changes in these numbers in the following years, we find that slightly more than 10 percent of the civil service corps had been subject to inquiry based on the decree of

---

53 This publication, which was allegedly based on official sources, does not specify where this figure comes from. There is evidence that local authorities reported to the Ministry (Nachbaur 2009).

May 1938. If we then exclude those who were scrutinised but not disciplined in any way, a little more than 7 percent remain who were either transferred, demoted, retired (sometimes with reduced pensions), or dismissed. There were, of course, considerable differences depending on the rank of civil servants. Michael Dippelreiter (2011: 10), whose research has focused on elite bureaucrats, claims that purges affected 60 to 70 percent of these circles. This appears to be similar to the situation in Germany in 1933. In that case, Hans Mommsen (1966: 14) has warned historians not to overestimate the effects of the purges, despite changes in those holding leadership positions.

After the decline of the Nazi regime, Austria was occupied by the Allied powers, who insisted on the denazification of the civil service. The regulations and more lenient rules subsequently decreed by the Austrian government did not result in major changes (Stiefel 1981: 125–142). In the Second Republic established in 1955, public employment became a stable livelihood unaffected by political or economic crises.

Conclusion

The discussion of aggregated numbers as well as individual cases above shows that the traditional relationship between the state and its employees became unsettled during the interwar period. Just after it had been comprehensively laid down in law in the DP of 1914, the idea and practice of building a career in civil service was called into question. Layoffs and the devaluation of fixed salaries made it difficult or impossible for a considerable number of people to earn their livelihood in public employment following a certain sequence of life events such as education, training, promotions, marriage and parenthood (optional), and retirement. The sequence was either interrupted or the earnings did not cover the required costs of each life stage. As a result, both the traditional ideal of lifelong employment and employees' ability to fully concentrate on their public employment were difficult to achieve. Further, changes in the 1920s impacted more public employees than did modifications in subsequent years. By contrast, the interventions of the 1930s, which were made on political and racial grounds, disrupted fewer careers but amounted to a noticeable qualitative change regarding service law and disciplinary regulations.

Despite these developments, a majority of government employees, even in the first half of the 1920s, were still able to maintain stable careers and take advantage of the traditional acquired rights of civil service. Whereas individual persons and sometimes a considerable number of public sector employees suffered losses regarding their economic and social status, the civil service as an institution was not jeopardised. Not even a totalitarian system such as National Socialism, which was against the idea of a civil service that functioned independently from party influence, was able to eliminate it. In terms of service law, the regulations in post-World War Two Austria were strongly linked to the legislation of the First Republic (Wojta 2012: 86), not least in the form of the DP, which remained in force until 1979 (ibid.: 48).

Public opinion as well as some of the legal regulations of the interwar period suggest that women were rather marginalised in the public sector. Yet some women could reach higher positions in the civil service in the 1930s (Melichar 2013: 51 ff), and statistical data suggests a rising proportion of women in terms of numbers and percentages in the public sector between 1910 and 1934 (Rigler 1976: 145). This is not to say that the breadwinner model had lost its popularity. Quite the contrary. After the turbulence of war and the post-war years, it gained popularity and prevalence far beyond the families of civil servants in most Western European countries (Crompton et al. 2007: 3).

References

Archival Sources

Personnel file Josef Hinterweger, City Archive Amstetten.
Memoirs of Erich Kneußl (private property, family archive Kneußl [Mühlau]).

Newspaper Articles

"Angelobung." 1918. *Wiener Zeitung.* November 15, 1918, 5.
"Die Familienbeihilfe für die Bundesangestellten." 1925. *Linzer Volksblatt* 149/57, July 3, 1925: 1.
"Die politische Betätigung der Beamten. Ein Erlaß des Bundeskanzlers." 1931. *Kleine Volkszeitung*, December 3, 1931: 2.
"Landeskonferenz der Eisenbahner." 1924. *Tagblatt*, April 6, 1924: 15.
"Postmeisterinnen und Postexpedientinnen. Referat, erstattet von Postmeisterin Luise Greipl, in der Generalversammlung des Zentralvereins am 5. Juni l. J.." 1913. *Die Postanstaltsbeamtin* 7: 1.
"Um die Ausgleichskassen." 1936. *Reichspost*, January 15, 1936: 3.

Secondary Sources

Bavouzet, Julia. 2019. "A Prosopographical Survey of the High Civil Service Corps of the Ministries in the Hungarian Part of the Dual Monarchy." In *The Habsburg Civil Service and Beyond.*

Bureaucracy and Civil Servants from the Vormärz to the Inter-war Years, edited by Franz Adlgasser and Fredrik Lindström, 167–186. Wien: Austrian Academy of Sciences Press.

Bei, Neda. 2012. "Austrofaschistische Geschlechterpolitik durch Recht. Die Doppelverdienerordnung." In *Österreich 1933–1938: Interdisziplinäre Bestandsaufnahmen und Perspektiven: Interdisziplinäre Annäherungen an das Dollfuß-/Schuschnigg-Regime*, edited by Ilse Reiter-Zatloukal, Christiane Rothländer, and Pia Schölnberger, 197–206. Wien/Köln/Weimar: Böhlau.

Bruckmüller, Ernst. 1983. "Sozialstruktur und Sozialpolitik." In *Österreich 1918–1938. Geschichte der Ersten Republik*. Vol. 1, edited by Erika Weinzierl and Kurt Skalnik, 381–436. Graz/Wien/Köln: Styria.

Clark, Linda. 2004. *The Rise of Professional Women in France. Gender and Public Administration since 1830*. Cambridge: Cambridge University Press.

Conze, Vanessa. 2013. "Treue schwören. Der Konflikt um den Verfassungseid in der Weimarer Republik." Historische Zeitschrift 297, no. 2: 354–389.

Crompton, Rosemarie, Suzan Lewis, and Clare Lyonette. 2007. "Introduction: The Unravelling of the 'Male Breadwinner' Model—and Some of its Consequences." In *Women, Men, Work and Family in Europe*, edited by Rosmarie Crompton, Suzan Lewis, and Clare Lyonette, 1–16. Houndmills, Basingstoke: Palgrave Macmillan: 1–16.

Deak, John. 2009. *The Austrian Civil Service in an Age of Crisis: Power and the Politics of Reform, 1848–1925*. Ph.D. thesis, University of Chicago.

Deak, John. 2010. "Dismantling Empire: Ignaz Seipel and Austria's Financial Crisis." In *From Empire to Republic: Post World War I Austria*, edited by Günter Bischof, Fritz Plasser, and Peter Berger, 123–141. Innsbruck/New Orleans: uno Press.

Dippelreiter, Michael. 2011. "Beamtenentlassungen in den höchsten Dienstklassen nach der nationalsozialistischen Machtübernahme 1938/39. Paper given at the conference "Österreich 1933–1938," Vienna, November 20–26, 2011. Accessed July 30, 2020. https://www.univie.ac.at/zeitgeschichte/cms/uploads/Paper-Dippelreiter.pdf.

Ehmer, Josef. 1990. *Sozialgeschichte des Alters*. Frankfurt/Main: Suhrkamp.

Ehmer, Josef. 2013. *Bevölkerungsgeschichte und Historische Demographie 1800–2010*, München: Oldenbourg.

Eichengreen, Barry, and Timothy J. Hatton, eds. 1988. *Interwar Unemployment in International Perspective*. Dordrecht, Boston, London: Kluwer Academic Publishing.

Enderle-Burcel, Gertrude, and Michaela Follner. 1996. "Biographien der Spitzenbeamten der Ersten Republik – ein Beitrag zur Elitenforschung." In *Diener vieler Herren. Biographisches Handbuch der Sektionschefs der Ersten Republik und des Jahres 1945*, edited by Gertrude Enderle-Burcel and Michaela Follner, 5–20. Wien: DÖW/ÖGQ.

Enderle-Burcel, Gertrude, and Jeřabek, Rudolf. 2011. "Verwaltungseliten in Umbruchzeiten. Spitzenbeamte des Bundes 1918 / 1933 / 1938 / 1945." In *Biographien und Zäsuren. Österreich und seine Länder 1918–1933–1938*, edited by Wolfgang Weber and Walter Schuster, 17–54. Linz: Archiv der Stadt Linz.

Fattmann, Rainer. 2001. *Bildungsbürger in der Defensive. Die akademische Beamtenschaft und der "Reichsbund der höheren Beamten" in der Weimarer Republik*. Göttingen: Vandenhoeck & Ruprecht.

Garstenauer, Therese. 2021. "Unraveling Multinational Legacies: National Affiliation as an Admission Criterion for Government Employees in Post-Habsburg Successor States." In *Narratives of Multinationalism in the Late Habsburg and Ottoman Empires – Alternatives to Nationalism, 1848–1918*, edited by Johanna Chovanec and Olof Heilo, 213–236. London: Palgrave Macmillan.

Giele, Janet Z., and Glen H. Elder Jr. 1998. *Methods of Life Course Research: Qualitative and Quantitative Approaches.* Thousand Oaks, CA: SAGE.

Gruber, Erich and Richard Pfaundler. 1934. "Die Besoldungsverhältnisse der Beamtenschaft und die neue Entwicklung der Besoldungspolitik in Österreich." In *Die Beamtenbesoldung im modernen Staat*, 2. Teil, edited by Wilhelm Gerloff, 107–183. München/Leipzig: Duncker & Humblot.

Hareven, Tamara K. 2013. "Introduction: *The Historical Study of the Life Course.*" In *Transitions: The Family and the Life Course in Historical Perspective*, edited by Tamara K. Hareven, 1–16. New York, San Francisco, London: Academic Press.

Hausen, Karin. 1976. "Die Polarisierung der 'Geschlechtscharaktere' – eine Spiegelung der Dissoziation von Erwerbs- und Familienleben, –." In *Sozialgeschichte der Familie in der Neuzeit Europas*, edited by Werner Conze, 363–393. Stuttgart: Klett-Cotta.

Heindl, Waltraud. 1990. "Die Entwicklung des Frauenstudiums in Österreich." In *"Durch Erkenntnis zu Freiheit und Glück . . ." Frauen an der Universität Wien (ab 1897)*, edited by Waltraud Heindl and Martina Tichy, 17–26. Wien: WUV-Universitätsverlag.

Heindl, Waltraud. 2013. *Gehorsame Rebellen, Bürokratie und Beamte in Österreich.* Vol. 1, 1780–1848. Wien: Böhlau.

Heindl, Waltraud. 2013. *Josephinische Mandarine. Bürokratie und Beamte in Österreich.* Vol. 2, 1848–1914. Wien/Köln/Weimar: Böhlau.

Horton, Sylvia. 2011. "Contrasting Anglo-American and Continental European Civil Service Systems." In *International Handbook on Civil Service Systems*, edited by Andrew Massey, 31–53. Cheltenham: Edward Elgar Publishing.

Kirk, Tim. 2003. "Fascism and Austrofascism." In *The Dollfuss/Schuschnigg Era in Austria: A Reassessment*, edited by Günter Bischof, Anton Pelinka, and Alexander Lassner, 10–31. New Brunswick, NJ: Transaction Publishers.

Kosian, Wilhelm. 1950. *Das Realeinkommen verschiedener Berufsgruppen des Arbeiterstandes und das der öffentlichen Beamten in Österreich in der Epoche von 1910–1949.* Ph.D. thesis, University of Vienna.

Kucsko-Stadelmayer, Gabriele. 1985. "Die Entwicklung des österreichischen Beamtenrechts." *Österreichische Zeitschrift für Öffentliches Recht und Völkerrecht* 36: 33–76.

Lanzinger, Margareth. 2015. *Verwaltete Verwandtschaft. Eheverbote, kirchliche und staatliche Dispenspraxis im 18./19. Jahrhundert.* Köln/Weimar/Wien: Böhlau.

di Luzio, Gaia. 2001. "Reorganising Gender Relations in the German Civil Service: Administrative Reform, The Decline of the Male Breadwinner Model, and Female Employment." *German Politics* 10, no. 3: 159–190.

Megner, Karl. 1986. *Beamte. Wirtschafts- und sozialgeschichtliche Aspekte des k.k. Beamtentums.* Wien: Austrian Academy of Sciences Press.

Megner, Karl. 2020. "Rang- und Besoldungssysteme der österreichischen Bundesbeamten." In *Hofratsdämmerung. Verwaltung und ihr Personal in den Nachfolgestaaten der Habsburgermonarchie 1918 bis 1920*, edited by Peter Becker, Therese Garstenauer, Veronika Helfert, Karl Megner, Guenther Steiner, Thomas Stockinger, 31–43. Wien/Köln/Weimar: Böhlau.

Megner, Karl, and Günther Steiner. 2020. "Transformation des öffentlichen Dienstes 1918–1920 anhand von gesamtstaatlichen Normen und Einzelfallbeispielen." In *Hofratsdämmerung. Verwaltung und ihr Personal in den Nachfolgestaaten der Habsburgermonarchie 1918 bis 1920*, edited by Peter Becker, Therese Garstenauer, Veronika Helfert, Karl Megner, Guenther Steiner, Thomas Stockinger, 53–82. Wien/Köln/Weimar: Böhlau.

Melichar, Peter. 2005. "Who is a Jew? Antisemitic Defining, Identifying and Counting in Pre-1938 Austria." *The Leo Baeck Institute Yearbook* 50, no. 1: 149–174.

Melichar, Peter. 2013. "Objekt der Begierden? Staatliche Verwaltung und Bürgertum in der Ersten Republik." In *Brüche und Kontinuitäten 1933–1938–1945. Fallstudien zu Verwaltung und Bibliotheken*, edited by Gertrude Enderle-Burcel, Alexandra Neubauer-Czettl, and Edith Stumpf-Fischer, 39–80. Innsbruck: Studienverlag.

Melichar, Peter. 2018. Otto Ender 1875–1960. *Landeshauptmann, Bundeskanzler, Minister. Untersuchungen zum Innenleben eines Politikers.* Wien/Köln/Weimar: Böhlau.

Mommsen, Hans. 1966. *Beamtentum im Dritten Reich.* Stuttgart: Deutsche Verlags-Anstalt.

Nachbaur, Ulrich. 2009. *Österreich als Opfer Hitlerdeutschlands. Das Rot-Weiß-Rot-Buch 1946 und die unveröffentlichten Vorarlberger Beiträge.* Regensburg: Roderer.

Naderer, Hans. 1931. "Geschichte der österreichischen Beamtenbewegung unter besonderer Berücksichtigung der Entwicklung der Besoldungsverhältnisse von der Schaffung des Gehaltsgesetzes im Juli 1924 bis Ende 1926." *Jahrbuch der Österreichischen Beamtenschaft:* 13–56.

Naderer, Hans. 1932. "Geschichte der österreichischen Beamtenbewegung unter besonderer Berücksichtigung der Entwicklung der Besoldungsverhältnisse von Ende 1926 bis Ende 1928." *Jahrbuch der Österreichischen Beamtenschaft:* 13–52.

Nawiasky, Hans. 1902. *Die Frauen im österreichischen Staatsdienst.* Vienna: Deuticke.

Nawiasky, Hans. 1914. *Die Dienstpragmatik. Vorlesung gehalten in der freien Vereinigung für staatswissenschaftliche Fortbildung in Wien im November 1913 von Dr. Hans Nawiasky, Privatdozent an der Universität Wien.* Wien: Tempsky.

Pauley, Bruce. 1990. "Politischer Antisemitismus im Wien der Zwischenkriegszeit." In *Eine zerstörte Kultur. Jüdisches Leben und Antisemitismus in Wien seit dem 19. Jahrhundert*, edited by Gerhard Botz, Ivar Oxaal, Michael Pollak, and Nina Scholz, 221–246. Buchloe: Obermayer.

Pauley, Bruce. 1992. *From Prejudice to Persecution: A History of Austrian Anti-Semitism.* Chapel Hill: University of North Carolina Press.

Pospíšil, J. 1915. "Das durchschnittliche Aktivätsalter der Bediensteten der Österreichischen Staatsbahnen." *Statistische Monatsschrift* 20: 46–65.

Raadschelders, Jos C. N., and Mark R. Rutgers. 1996. "The Evolution of Civil Service Systems." In *Civil Service Systems in Comparative Perspective*, edited by Hans A. G. M. Bekke and Frits M. Van Der Meer, 67–99. Bloomington: Indiana University Press.

Rot-Weiss-Rot-Buch: Gerechtigkeit für Österreich. Darstellungen, Dokumente und Nachweise zur Vorgeschichte und Geschichte der Okkupation Österreichs. Band 1. Nach amtlichen Quellen. 1946. Wien: Österreichische Staatsdruckerei.

Rozenblit, Marsha. 1983. *The Jews of Vienna, 1867–1914: Assimilation and Identity.* Albany, NY: SUNY Press.

Schneider, Richard et al. 1938. *Neuordnung des österreichischen Berufsbeamtentums. Verordnung vom 31. Mai 1938.* Berlin: Verlag Beamtenpresse GmbH.

Sedlak, Eva Maria. 2006. "Politische Sanktionen im öffentlichen Dienst in der Ära des österreichischen 'Ständestaates'." *Zeitgeschichte* 33, no. 1: 3–24.

Seeber, Katharina. 2015. *Lebenserinnerungen des Tiroler Beamten Erich Kneußl in Mezzolombardo 1914–1917.* Master thesis, University of Vienna.

"Statistik der Bundesangestellten." 1924. *Statistische Nachrichten* 2/3 (March 1924): 64–74.

Steiner, Christiane. 1994. *Die Anfänge der Frauenarbeit im Staatsdienst am Beispiel der Österreichischen Post- und Telegrafenanstalt 1869–1919.* Masters thesis, University of Vienna.

Stiefel, Dieter. 1979. *Arbeitslosigkeit: soziale, politische und wirtschaftliche Auswirkungen – am Beispiel Österreichs 1918–1938.* Berlin: Duncker & Humblot.

Stiefel, Dieter. 1981. *Entnazifizierung in Österreich.* Wien, München, Zürich: Europaverlag.

Vana, Irina. 2015. "The Use of Public Labour Offices by Job Seekers in Interwar Austria." In *History of Labour Intermediation. Institutions and Individual Ways of Finding Employment,* edited by Sigrid Wadauer, Thomas Buchner, and Alexander Mejstrik, 194–235. New York/ Oxford: Berghahn.

White, James M., and David M. Klein. 2002. "The Family Life Course Development Framework." In *Family Theories,* edited by James M. White and David M. Klein, 88–116. Thousand Oaks, CA: SAGE.

Wojta, Edgar. 2012. *Zäsuren in der Entwicklung des Dienstrechts des österreichischen öffentlichen Dienstes in der II. Republik am Beispiel der Gebietskörperschaft Bund.* Masters thesis, University of Vienna.

Zentralverein der Bundesbeamtinnen im Verwaltungs- und Kanzleidienst. 1933. *Zur Feier des 25jährigen Bestandes 1908–1933.* Wien: self-published.

Mary Jo Maynes and Ann Waltner

Textile Work, Gender, and the Female Life Course in Europe and China since the Beginning of the "Great Divergence," Eighteenth to Early Twentieth Centuries

Introduction

The relationship between work and life course has varied enormously across time and space, and it is always gendered. In this chapter, we will focus on textile labour, using a comparative historical approach to examine the gender and life course dimensions of the transition from household to factory production in Europe and China. Our comparative approach stems from our longstanding interest in European and Chinese family, household, and gender systems. We see certain aspects of these systems – including ideologies and practices around lineage, generational relations, the household organisation of labour, gendered life course transitions, and marriage and kinship practices – as having had wide social, economic, and cultural ramifications. Here we examine the ramifications for labour systems and their response to changing historical conditions of textile production between the late-eighteenth and the early-twentieth centuries. The time frame, thus, encompasses periods of important commercial and technological development in the textile industries of both Europe and China. We draw our evidence very broadly, but we concentrate on several regions of proto-industrial and industrial textile production: the Jiangnan region in east-central China, which was heavily involved in market-oriented production of both silk and cotton beginning around 1800; southern Germany, especially Württemberg, where primarily linen

Acknowledgements: The authors would like to thank several colleagues and supportive institutions that allowed us the time and space to develop our comparative ideas. First, we want to thank "re: work – Work and Human Life Cycle in Global History," and in particular Andreas Eckert, Jürgen Kocka, and Felicitas Hentschke for their support during our stay there and ever since. The re:work center provided the intellectual space where we were able to work through and do research on the comparative ideas that were before then only a glimmer. Since our time in Berlin, we have presented several papers based on this research, including one at the 2015 meeting of the International Committee of Historical Sciences in Jinan, China. That paper was revised and published in a collection edited by Mary O'Dowd and June Purvis (2018), whose comments were immensely helpful. That work focused on girls' work in the period around 1800 and served as the starting point for further development of the comparison across other phases of the female life course and into the twentieth century.

and woollen goods were produced; south-eastern France, a centre of silk production; and Ireland, where linen and later cotton were produced. By way of conceptual framing, we begin with a brief introduction of the main elements of our comparison: textile production systems and their relationship to household and marriage systems. We then examine the effects of factory industrialisation on age- and gender-based divisions of labour.

A Comparative History of Gendered Life Courses, Textile Production, and the "Great Divergence"

When, why, and how the economies of China and Europe diverged have been topics of much debate since the phrase "Great Divergence" was first coined by Samuel Huntington in the 1990s. Much recent discussion centres on arguments made by, among others, Kenneth Pomeranz in *The Great Divergence: China, Europe, and the Making of the Modern World Economy* (Pomeranz 2000). Many of these arguments have revolved around the construction from scattered evidence of wage and price series, which scholars use to make arguments about comparative trends in standards of living and labour productivity in Europe and China around 1800. Ongoing debates suggest that there is as yet no agreement about how to interpret this sort of evidence, or even about how to define the relative well-being of the populations in question.[1] Our interest in comparing Europe and China around 1800 takes up different, if related, questions: we centre our analysis on similarities and differences stemming from the nature of family and household organisation in Europe and China. Since, as feminist historical analysis has made clear, family and gender relations, household, and economy have long been intricately interlinked, we focus our attention on aspects of European and Chinese family and household economies as they figure into long-term economic development patterns.[2]

One of the striking regional particularities that had emerged in many regions of Europe by the seventeenth century was a pattern of relatively late marriage – that is, relative to other regions of the world at the same time, where some form of mar-

---

[1] For a thoughtful and provocative engagement with recent contributions to the debate, see the review essay by Shami Ghosh (2015). See also the essay by Prasannan Parthasarathi and Kenneth Pomeranz (2019).

[2] See Louise Tilly and Joan Scott (1978); Olwen Hufton (1998); Jack Goldstone (1996); Marion W. Gray (2000); Mary Jo Maynes and Ann Waltner (2011); Mary S. Hartman (2004); Susan Mann (1991); Susan Mann (1997); Francesca Bray (1997).

riage, at least for women, usually occurred shortly after puberty. In addition, a substantial minority of early modern European men and women never married, in contrast with nearly universal marriage elsewhere. These European marriage practices have been closely connected with particular family–economic links; in brief, customs of betrothal and property transfer discouraged marriage before the couple commanded the resources required for at least limited economic independence, meaning a shop and tools in the case of the artisan, or, for peasants, a house, land, and the basic equipment required to farm. Late marriage was also rooted in the widespread practice of *neo-locality* – the expectation that a bride and groom would set up their own household at or soon after marriage – common in much of Northern, Central, and Western Europe, though by no means universal.[3]

The traditional Chinese family system was characterised by early age at marriage, nearly universal marriage for women, and *virilocal* residence – that is, a newly married couple typically resided with the groom's parents. From the sixteenth through the twentieth century, Chinese couples married much younger on average than did their European counterparts. According to Chinese demographic historians, "in China, females have always married universally and early . . . in contrast to female marriage in Western Europe, which occurred late or not at all" (Lee and Wang 2001: 65–68). Roughly speaking, whereas around 1800 all but 20 percent of Chinese women were married by the age of twenty, among European populations, between 60 and 80 percent of women were still unmarried at this age, depending on the region.

These general contrasts between early modern Europe and other world regions, including China, meant that in Europe, a labour pool of unmarried girls was available to a degree uncommon elsewhere. Unmarried girls had the potential to engage full-time in tasks like spinning, uninterrupted by the increased domestic responsibilities brought on by marriage and childbearing. Moreover, while many unmarried European youth worked at home, a period of service away from home in a farm household, as an apprentice, or as a domestic servant in an urban household, was characteristic of both male and female youth in many regions of Europe as a phase of the life course preceding marriage. This contrasts with the situation in China. Because the new couple in China would ordinarily reside in the household of the groom's family, it was not necessary for a male artisan to become established or for a peasant couple to acquire a farm before marrying. The newly married

---

3 The classic article pointing out the Western European marriage pattern is John Hajnal (1965); this article generated a debate among Europeanists that is still ongoing. More recently, Kenneth Pomeranz has argued that despite this difference, in terms of several key demographic variables, the European pattern does not differ markedly from China, Japan, or Southeast Asia. See Pomeranz (2000). See also James Lee and Feng Wang (2001); and Th. Engelen and A.P. Wolf, eds. (2005).

couple participated in the ongoing economic enterprise in the groom's father's household. Therefore, the category of female "youth," which was so significant for European social and economic history, has no precise counterpart for most of Chinese history. Young Chinese women laboured, to be sure, but the location of their work typically moved from the household of their father to that of their husband. There were, of course, female domestic servants in China; but domestic service was not a prelude to marriage for girls in China as it was in Europe.[4] Knowledge about the nature of their servitude is fragmentary; however, generally, sending daughters into domestic service appears to have been far less normative in China than in Europe, and going into service may have been an employment of longer duration than the temporary servitude so common in Europe. The nature of young women's marriage and labour patterns in the Chinese and European contexts held implications for the particular ways in which early modern economic development occurred in the two regions. In a comparative history of domestic production, the fact that the young female labour force in China was, to an extent far greater than that of Europe, both married and "domesticated" within a male-kin-headed household needs to be part of the story.

The relatively high number of European women who never married also had implications for economic development patterns. In contrast with most regions of China, where typically only 1 or 2 percent of women remained unmarried at age thirty, between 15 and 25 percent of thirty-year-old Western European women would still have been single. For men, the differences, though in the same direction, are far less stark (Lee and Wang 2001: 65). In the early twentieth century, these differences in the proportions of women who remained single were actually increasing: the percentage of women in China who never married dropped to and remained around one percent, whereas the proportions of never-married women in Europe increased in many regions. Although there was wide regional variance within Europe by the end of the twentieth century, as many as 25 percent of women remained unmarried at age forty-five in Northern Europe; and, except for Eastern Europe, the percentage across Europe was typically between 10 and 20 percent (Lee and Wang 2001: 68; Lundqvist et al. 2014: 293).

We will now turn to an examination of historical patterns of female life-course labour. Despite the challenges of making general comparisons based on

---

4 For a discussion of servants in eighteenth-century China, see Mann (1997: 38–44). See also Maria Jaschok (1994). Johanna Ransmeier (2017), writing about the late nineteenth and early twentieth centuries, shows ways in which domestic servitude was part of a larger pattern of trafficking in women. According to Lu Hanchao (1999: 47–48), a 1922 local gazetteer from Fahua, in the hinterland of Shanghai, reports that women worked as domestic servants as well as produced handicrafts.

very different sources and historiographic traditions, a large number of regional and local studies of textile history offer a possible grounds for comparisons of specific cases.[5] For our purposes, evidence about the gender and life course divisions of labour in household and early factory production of textiles, and about relationships between household production and changing global markets is most relevant. Labour organisation in textile production in China and Europe varied depending on the fabric produced; here we most often discuss the silk industry, but we have also drawn on historical evidence about the production of other textiles – linen, cotton, and wool – to highlight the particularity of life course and labour connections. Moreover, specific attention to different phases of the textile production process – especially spinning and weaving – highlights comparative similarities and differences.

Women's Work in Household Production Systems around 1800

Europe's "proto-industrial" textile industries in regional and global markets

Europe's textile industries underwent dramatic growth and change long before the earliest textile factories appeared in the second half of the eighteenth century. By the seventeenth century, artisans and peasants in many regions of Western and Central Europe were producing wool, linen, or silk thread or cloth for transregional and even transcontinental markets in a system historians call "proto-industry" as well as under more traditional guild systems of production. Merchant entrepreneurs involved in proto-industry organised the production of cloth in both urban handicraft shops and rural peasant homes. Some markets were regional or continental; by the eighteenth century, products of European proto-industry increasingly found their way into global markets. Some of these textiles even served as a form of currency in the market for slaves in West Africa, and they also clothed the residents of New World settler colonies and slave plantations.[6]

In this context of rising global exchange, European merchant entrepreneurs had an incentive to move from merely buying and selling fabric to reorganising

---

5 See, for example, Giorgio Riello and Prasannan Parthasarathi, eds. (2009); Bozhong Li (1998); and Kenneth Pomeranz (2005).
6 For recent work making these connections, see Jonathan Eacott (2016); Anka Steffen (2016), and Xiaolin Duan (2017).

production. In many regions, merchant entrepreneurs introduced a "putting-out" system to organise labour, whereby these merchants advanced raw materials to spinners or weavers, who then were required to sell back their finished products to these merchants to repay the advances. Even before the factory, then, proto-industry brought increasing numbers of rural and urban household members of varying ages and genders into mass market textile production.[7]

A range of entrepreneurial and state strategies for increasing profits or encouraging economic development emerged by the eighteenth century. Southern German weavers produced linen and wool in a proto-industrial system. The rulers of Württemberg chose to encourage local textile industries by negotiating state-licensed monopolies or concessions; the right to trade in wool or linen was sold to a group of merchants or weaver-merchants who in turn organised textile production in towns and peasant villages (Ogilvie 1997 and 2003; Medick 1996). In southern France, the textile growth sector was silk. State interest intensified at the beginning of the seventeenth century. Initial state intervention focused on encouraging mulberry tree plantations since mulberry leaves were the basis of the silkworms' diet. By the end of the eighteenth century, silk production in France had grown into an industry worth 130 million *livres* a year, or roughly 15 percent of the kingdom's total industrial production (de la Farelle 1852: 4–5). Weaving was largely controlled by urban guilds, but the production of silk thread was done in the countryside. In Ireland, the British state followed a logic of empire that favoured metropolitan interests; the production of woollen cloth was prohibited because it competed with the British wool trade; instead, the state laid the groundwork for preindustrial linen production in the colony.

Despite their impressive growth, by the mid-eighteenth century, all these proto-industrial textile industries were feeling the impact of the "cotton craze." Cotton textiles, which had been produced in India, China, Africa, and the New World for centuries, entered European markets in appreciable amounts only in the late 1600s, mainly through British ports. Despite import bans pushed by British textile interests, continued European growth in the demand for cotton focused attention on establishing domestic cotton production in England, thus contributing to the mechanisation of production in cotton that launched the "Industrial Revolution" as it is usually understood – that is, the gradual switch to large-scale, factory-centred production. At the same time, the search for raw cotton, which unlike

---

7 Works on European proto-industrial labour include Karl Ditt and Sidney Pollard, eds. (1992); Sheilagh C. Ogilvie (1997); Hans Medick (1996); and Maynes (2004).

wool, flax, or silk could not be grown in Europe, fuelled the colonial plantation economy in the Americas and elsewhere.[8]

The gendering of labour processes in artisanal and proto-industrial textile production in Europe around 1800 varied by fabric and region. Weaving was rarely done by women in Europe. Generally, weaving was organised either by urban guilds of male artisans or by rural state-chartered corporations of male merchants or merchants-weavers who regulated the linen trade. In both situations, women were excluded from weaving, though some women apparently assisted at home looms formally operated by their husbands (Ogilvie 2003). However, in some regions such as the proto-industrial linen-producing Oberlausitz region of Saxony, because weaving was a cottage industry rather than a guild industry, it was not considered an "honourable" trade, and women wove alongside men (Quataert 1985; Steffen 2016).

Spinning was gendered very differently from weaving in Europe. In southern French silk-producing areas, most contemporary descriptions used language that revealed the presumption that spinning raw silk involved a series of female occupations. François-Félix de la Farelle, in his history of proto-industrial raw silk production in southern France focusing on the 1820s, explicitly identified the critical workers as female: "The first female worker (*ouvrière*), called a *fileuse*, would detach this [silk] strand [from the worm] with a marvellous dexterity, and still does so today. A second female worker turned the wheel and bore the title of *tourneuse*" (de la Farelle 1852: 2). As illustrated by this passage, the French words employed for the occupations involved in silk thread production took the feminine form – *fileuse, tourneuse, devideuse*.[9] This gendered occupational pattern was also apparent in demographic records from around 1800. Early censuses for southern France are uneven in their recording of occupations beyond that of the household head. Very few enumerators in silk-producing regions listed occupations for women or children. However, trends in the occupations reported by women themselves at the time of their marriage help to correct for the silences of the census. For example, in the city of Avignon, one of the older silk centres of southern France, during the 1820s, over forty percent of brides reported themselves in the marriage registers to

---

8 For important analysis of these arguments, see Beverly Lemire (1991); Giorgio Riello and Prasannan Parthasarathi, eds. (2009); and Maxine Berg (2014). See also Eacott (2016); and Robert S. DuPlessis (2016).

9 The labour processes in the production of silk thread and its preparation for weaving, and hence the name of associated occupations, are somewhat different than for preparing thread or yarn from other fibres. De la Farelle here calls the three main jobs *"fileuse, tourneuse, devideuse,"* which best translate as "spinner, reeler, bobbin winder." However, some of these jobs changed with mechanisation.

be silkworkers (*ouvrières en soie* or *devideuses*), a proportion that would continue to rise in the following decades (Archives Départementales de Vaucluse).[10]

Spinning other fibres for proto-industrial production was also generally women's work. In southern Germany, where the most commonly produced textiles were linens, wools, and blends, spinning was almost exclusively women's work, although it is rarely named as a formal occupation in most historical records. Reliable information about the female workforce is, thus, scarce before the second half of the nineteenth century. However, Sheilagh Ogilvie has tracked gendered and life course patterns of work as depicted in court records from the wool-producing town of Wildberg in Württemberg between 1674 and 1800. From crime reports, she documents the activities in which witnesses to crimes were engaged at the time they observed the crime. The two most commonly mentioned work activities of women witnesses were agricultural labour and spinning. In the witness accounts of women who mention what they were doing when they happened to witness a crime, spinning was specifically mentioned as the activity of 12 percent of unmarried daughters, 5 percent of married women, 4 percent of widows, and 13 percent of unmarried women living on their own (Ogilvie 2003: 116, 142, 208, 274). Women apparently engaged in spinning across their life course, but they were more likely to be spinning when they were unmarried.

In all these cases where we have detailed evidence, the proto-industrial spinning labour force, based mainly in households, relied heavily on female workers. Unmarried women, who were a relatively large sector of the female population compared to other world regions, were especially crucial to the spinning of the silk, flax, wool, or cotton yarn that eventually made its way onto weavers' looms. Most of these were young women not yet married, but they were joined by older women who had never married and some widows. Married women did some spinning as well, but, where the records allow us to differentiate, they were less likely to be working at spinning than were unmarried women and widows.

Gender and generational division of labour in artisanal and household textile production in China

The Chinese historical record as it pertains to women and work, though rich, is not without its problems, especially regarding young women and girls. The imperially

---

10 The *devideuses* were most likely employed in winding bobbins of silk thread for use by male weavers.

commissioned eighteenth-century encyclopaedia *Qinding Gujin tushu jicheng* [Imperially approved synthesis of books and illustrations past and present] is one example of a valuable yet problematic source. It contains biographies of 27,141 exemplary women culled from local histories from the Ming dynasty (1368–1644). Occupations are given for about a tenth of the women: for 2,286 of them, the occupation is given as "spinning and weaving" (*fangzhi*), and for 399, the occupation is listed as "women's work" (*nühong*), which always refers to textile work. There are virtually no other occupations given for women. Housework and childrearing are not marked as occupations (Liang 2001: 41).[11] These biographies make clear the importance of textile work in the lives of Chinese women, and their inclusion in the encyclopaedia also demonstrates that the importance of their labour was recognised. But the biographies (which are in general only three or four lines long) do not distinguish between spinning and weaving, nor do they tell us whether the woman is working in cotton, silk, or some other fabric. But they do tell us that women in dire straits were often able to use their skill in working in textiles to support themselves and their families. They further suggest that these women, who were often widows when their biographies were composed, engaged in textile work throughout their lives.

Chinese textile production flourished during the early Qing Dynasty (1644–1911). Chinese silks were in high demand and were exported to Europe, Mexico, and Japan. During the eighteenth century, production of both cotton and silk cloth increased rapidly. Although it is difficult to arrive at reliable figures, Bozhong Li estimates that cotton production in Jiangnan doubled between 1700 and the mid-nineteenth century. Chinese cotton began to replace Indian cotton in Southeast Asia, and silk exports to Europe and the Americas were also on the rise in the eighteenth century.[12] Li estimates that silk production for Chinese domestic markets tripled from the early-seventeenth century to the mid-nineteenth century (Li 1998: 107–109).

Both cotton thread and cotton cloth were produced primarily in rural households. Households that did spinning did not necessarily grow the cotton they spun; indeed, as the cotton industry in Songjiang in Jiangnan grew, large amounts of raw cotton were imported from outside the area (Zurndorfer 2011: 710). Local histories show that spinners might obtain raw cotton from the market. For example, a local history from Songjiang in the sixteenth century tells us that "village women go in the morning to the market with cotton yarn, which they exchange for raw cotton

---

11 For a discussion of *nügong*, see, among others, Bray (1997: 237–272). For a description of the *Qinding Gujin tushu jicheng*, see Wilkinson (2015: 605–607).
12 For a discussion of Chinese silk exports to Mexico, see Duan (2017: 18–27).

and then they go home" (Tanaka 1994: 27–28). Sources on cotton production suggest the omnipresence of brokers – middlemen who were key to organising links between various de-centralised production processes such as growing, ginning, spinning, and weaving.

Weaving cotton cloth for local use was nearly always seen as women's work. To maximise the efficiency of cotton weavers (who in home production were often adult married women), other members of the household (often younger girls or older women) would spin the needed yarn, especially in areas where yarn was not available on the market (Bossen and Gates 2017). Kenneth Pomeranz has estimated that in Jiangnan, it would take four hours of spinning cotton to produce enough yarn to occupy a weaver for an hour and that there was very little yarn on the market (2005: 247–249). Even very young girls in China seem to have worked at spinning along with older girls and women to produce the needed thread. Bozhong Li cites two Qing dynasty texts which talk about the process of teaching young girls to become expert textile workers: "a girl who is five or six *sui* can be taught to spin cotton; at 10 *sui* she can weave cloth," and another, which is slightly less ambitious in its expectations regarding girl workers: "A girl at seven or eight *sui* can spin; at twelve or thirteen she can weave" (Li 2000: 68).[13] Li further argues that in textile producing regions, women left agricultural work completely by the late eighteenth century and: "only the better skilled and stronger women were occupied in weaving. Younger, older, and less dexterous females were employed instead in spinning, using single-spindle wheels or, more rarely, three-spindle machines" (Li 2009: 309).

Nearly all simple cottons were woven by women and girls in rural households; these cottons were mainly for local consumption, although there were certainly women "cottage" weavers who wove cotton goods for more distant markets, including "kerchiefs" and socks, which were the specialties of Songjiang. Fancier cottons were produced in urban workshops in which looms were operated by men (Zurndorfer 2009; Tanaka 1995: 42). The final finishing processes of fancy cotton fabric (dyeing and calendering) were also done in workshops, which were often urban, and the workers were also generally male (Santangelo 1993: 108).

The processes of silk production were quite different from cotton. The care of silkworms was done mainly by peasant women assisted by children, both boys and girls. Households that raised silkworms sometimes had their own mulberry trees, or they might purchase mulberry leaves in the market. Both men and women har-

---

13 A child in Qing China was one *sui* at birth; at the next New Year, the child would become two *sui*. Thus, a child born right before the New Year would be two *sui* after the New Year, but only weeks or months old by Western calculations.

vested mulberry leaves, and women and children fed the worms.[14] Once the worms had spun their cocoons, women and girls worked over the vats of hot water, to unreel and twist the strands of silk fibre from the cocoons and turn them into thread (Kuhn 1988: 301–307). Some silk cloth was woven in the household, although this was increasingly rare by the eighteenth century (Bray 1997: 235); around 1800, domestic weaving of silk cloth was the exception rather than the rule. Silk cloth was woven in urban workshops or on rural estates, and the weavers were men. Bozhong Li concludes that "in Ming-Qing Jiangnan the last good [produced by the rural household] was reeled silk and twisted or untwisted floss (Li 1997: 92).

One big comparative observation is that, although spinning was "women's work" – and disproportionately young women's work – in both regions, women also commonly wove in China – in the case of cotton, at least, if not silk – whereas, as we have seen, artisanal and proto-industrial weaving in Europe was mostly done by men. Women were weaving in China, and around 1800, an increasing proportion of the cloth they wove was destined for markets – regional, national, and international – as opposed to household use. With rising production for markets during the eighteenth century, and especially export markets, women in rural households in some cotton-producing regions began to focus their work efforts more and more on the production of cotton cloth while their husbands increasingly specialised in farming. Age and gender divisions of labour were implicated in specific ways in regional economies, and they changed as those economies became more embedded in local and distant markets and as new technologies and spaces of production developed.

Age, Gender, and Labour in Textile Industries in the Era of Mechanisation

Women's textile work in Europe in the factory era

As textile production mechanised and moved unevenly into factories, the logic of age and gender labour patterns played a key role in the transition. Younger unmarried women arguably comprised the majority of Europe's earliest modern factory

---

14 See the illustrations in Kuhn 1988: 294–300. Kuhn does not discuss the gender of the harvesters, but it is clear from the illustrations in agricultural handbooks that both men and women were collecting the leaves. See also Bray (1997: 248).

labour force. Their significance in early factory workforces grew out of proto-industrial divisions of labour, along with the presumed mobility of youthful labourers. Recruiting a workforce for larger and more concentrated workplaces required worker mobility, from home or shed to factory, and often from rural to urban areas. The availability of a relatively cheap, skilled, and mobile labour force provided a competitive advantage in the global struggle for domination of various textile markets.

Some specific new technologies that revolutionised European textile production beginning in the eighteenth century were developed with an eye towards a workforce that was imagined as young and female. According to Maxine Berg writing about textile technologies in Britain, "new techniques in calico printing and spinning provide classic examples of experimentation on a child and female workforce" (Berg 1998: 61). This workforce was imaginable by textile entrepreneurs because it already existed. Until the eighteenth century, women workers had mostly worked in households and small shops: however, many young women who were not yet married had also routinely travelled in search of work on farms or as domestic servants in cities. Others had found paid employment as spinners in proto-industrial households other than their own. It was not a dramatically different pattern, then, for young, unmarried women to seek work in handicraft manufactories or larger silk reeling sheds for a few months, a year, or longer. Eventually, they moved into jobs in factories whose spinning and weaving machines were powered by water or steam.

This pattern of labour force participation by mobile, young, unmarried women remained a key distinction between Central and Western Europe and much of the rest of the world until the end of the nineteenth century. As Deborah Simonton has documented, early European textile industrial centres were filled with young women:

> The image of factory and workshop labour is the 'mill girl' . . . Of the 260 employees at Heilman Freres at Ribeauvillé, 39.2 percent were females between sixteen and twenty-five years of age. In Manchester and Salford in 1852, 76 percent of fourteen-year-old girls were in the mills, and 82 percent of the female textile workers of Roubaix were under thirty. (Simonton 1998: 139)

But as in proto-industrial textile production, the new labour patterns also varied by fabric and region.

In the Irish linen industry, proto-industrial production was not immediately displaced by factory production but rather persisted alongside of it.[15] First, me-

---

15 Research by Jane Gray, Betty Messenger, and Brenda Collins demonstrates the interplay of skill,

chanical spinneries displaced hand spinning. Hand spinning of flax virtually disappeared from Ulster in the 1840s because machine-produced yarn was easier to weave and cheaper, although it was not suitable for the highest-quality linens (Collins 1997: 24). This shift caused economic contraction in many proto-industrial yarn regions where handloom weavers could not pay cash for factory-produced yarns nor compete with weavers who could. Women, especially young women, still predominated in spinning work, but that work moved out of homes and into mechanised spinneries. By the late nineteenth century, in jobs in the spinning mills, "females outnumbered males approximately three to one at the general operative level, holding most of the jobs in the preparing, spinning and reeling rooms" (Messenger 1978: 20–23).

The factory system then brought dramatic changes to the weaving workforce. As the demand for hand-spun yarn disappeared, some girls and women in linen villages began to weave. The new factory-produced yarns, which were easier to weave, along with changes in the looms meant that "even little slips of girls" could weave, according to one 1840 observation. In 1851, 34 percent of handloom linen weavers in the region of Northern Ireland that Brenda Collins investigated were already female workers (Collins 1997: 238). Even as weaving factories were introduced, household handloom production continued in some regions of Northern Ireland even into the early twentieth century, but with an even larger predominance of female weavers.[16] Collins found that in 1901, in Lagan Valley Townlands, 61 percent of linen handloom weavers were women (Collins 1997: 123). In one particularly detailed source for a district, Collins tracked the precise relationship of the weaver (in single-weaver households) to the household head. There were: six female heads of household; twelve wives; nine daughters or nieces; two sons, and seven male heads who wove. And not all these weavers were fulltime. In the new logic of household division of labour, men and boys typically combined agricultural work with weaving. Housewives combined housework and weaving. The primary weaving workforce were the young people – "more girls than boys" – who spent the highest proportion of their time weaving (Collins 1997: 240–241).[17] The particular age, gender, and life course patterns of textile labour

---

gender-specific work and wages, and geopolitics in the process of the mechanisation of Irish linen production. See especially Gray (2005); Messenger (1978); and Collins (1997).

16 According to Collins (1997: 229–252), whereas prior to 1800, most weavers were male, after the Famine years (1845–1847), more women and girls began weaving at home.

17 These household labour patterns in both Irish linen and French silk production follow the contours first outlined by Tilly and Scott (1978) in their conceptualisation of the transition in Europe from a "family economy" to a "family wage economy."

had shifted, but the overall logic of life course labour patterns stemming from adaptative household survival strategies was still apparent.

Mechanisation affected French silk production somewhat later than Irish linen, but in this industry as well, changes in technologies and sites of production – along with an added factor of silkworm disease – also forced households to adopt new age, gender, and life-course labour strategies. In early-nineteenth-century France, the delicate task of unwinding silk cocoons was still done by hand; the worms were still raised on peasant farms. But the invention of steam taps to help the *fileuse* adjust the water temperature encouraged the concentration of spinning into larger steam-powered filatures. The *tourneuse* was displaced by a machine. But according to de la Farelle, instead of being thrown out of work, the *tourneuse* could retrain herself in three or four years of apprenticeship to take on the better-paid job of *fileuse*, for which there was now more demand than ever. In fact, because mill owners were always looking for skilled *fileuses*, "a large number of families, whether from the countryside, the bourgs or the small cities, who up until then had never been involved with silk filature were lured by the possibility of considerable earnings to have their women and daughters take part in it" (de la Farelle 1852: 2–3). In 1840, the labour force in some 400 silk reeling filatures and spinning mills of the Midi totalled more than 20,000 workers, of whom over 90 percent were women or children (de la Farelle 1852: 15–18).

However, even as de la Farelle was documenting the silk industry's prosperity, a major disruptive force was in motion. A virulent silkworm disease, first noted in the 1820s, intensified in the 1850s. French cocoon production peaked in 1853 at 26,000 tons. By 1856, production dropped to 7,500 tons (*Musée de la Soie*). Raw silk production elsewhere – most notably Italy – nearly recovered to pre-disease levels by the 1880s, but French raw silk production stagnated at around a quarter of its pre-disease level throughout the rest of the century (Ma 1996: 332). French silk weavers were increasingly supplied with raw silk from Asia, first from China and then Japan. In addition, after 1905, factory-produced rayon was increasingly substituted for silk thread.

In a development that paralleled what we have seen in Irish linen production, the disappearance of female employment in raw silk production was followed by shifts in the age and gender composition of the silk weaving labour force. Although silk weaving had long centred in Lyon as an urban male craft, silk merchants began to employ rural weavers in the 1830s in the wake of revolts of urban male weavers. In the early 1850s, about two-thirds of the region's 60,000 silk looms were still urban. By the 1870s, the number of looms had risen to 120,000, but only around 25,000 of these were in Lyon. Thereafter, a protracted economic crisis that began in the 1870s threw the majority of weavers out of work; according to Keith Mann, silk production did not reach 1875 levels again until 1914 (Mann

2010: 83). At the same time, an increasing number of urban and rural looms were mechanised, and mechanised-loom weaving was feminised. In the 1870s, 115,000 of the 120,000 silk looms were still hand powered. But by 1914, two-thirds of the region's 60,000 silk looms were mechanised; 80 percent of Lyon's mechanical loom weavers worked in large factories. The shrinking number of urban handloom weavers were typically male, but 75 to 80 percent of mechanised loom weavers, whether in rural cottages or urban factories, were women and girls. As was the case in the linen industry, households in rural weaving villages survived by adapting their gendered life course labour patterns to the new conditions. In rural areas, they combined male agricultural work with female weaving. In urban areas, men moved into new occupations as women and girls took over weaving. Some factories increasingly relied on family teams. For example, in the artificial silk factory in Décines in 1926, just under 20 percent of women workers had daughters working alongside them. By 1929, this figure had risen to nearly 70 percent (Mann 2010: 172).

The changes that had occurred in the French silk industry between the early nineteenth and the early twentieth century were startling. Cocoon raising and silk reeling, once the employer of hundreds of thousands of women, especially young women, had disappeared. Silk weaving, once the domain of highly skilled adult men working handlooms in the city of Lyon, was now done on mechanised looms operated by women and girls in rural and urban areas across France. Households still relied on survival strategies that entailed gendered and life course patterns of work, but which family members did which specific jobs, had changed completely. Moreover, in factory cities at least, there is evidence that married women continued to work in factories – that is, outside the home – at least intermittently across their life course. This contrasted with household-based textile production in rural areas, where households had more control over the working hours and tasks performed by various family members, and married housewives could devote more time to reproductive labour while unmarried daughters spent more time at the loom.

Women's textile work in the move to factories in China

Household-based textile production for market distribution as well as for domestic use persisted in China as well, even as mechanisation was introduced. And even as household production processes differed significantly between cotton and silk, so too did the move, towards the end of the nineteenth century, of some of these processes into factories.

In the late nineteenth century, most of the cotton cloth used for domestic consumption was still produced in rural households. Xinwu Xu has estimated that in

1860, 99.5 percent of the cotton worn in China was still produced in rural households; as late as 1920, 65 percent of the cotton consumed in China was what Xu calls "rural native cotton" (Xu and Min 1988: 43). Moreover, well into the twentieth century, peasant households were still producing textiles for their own use, a phenomenon that Xu labels "a distinctive phenomenon in world history" (Xu and Min 1988: 39). Indeed, it was not uncommon for women in rural households in some areas of China to weave cloth for household use as late as the 1970s (Eyferth 2015: 145).

Still, despite this notable persistence, factory production of cotton did make its entry into the Chinese textile production system. By 1920, there were over 30,000 cotton workers in mills in Shanghai, about half of whom were women. The workers, often girls recruited as contract labour from the countryside while still in their early teens (or even as young as eight years old or so), were often housed in dormitories supervised by female company employees or recruiters (Cliver 2014: 120). According to data compiled by Christian Henriot, by 1925, there were 63,730 Shanghai residents in what he calls "western plant dormitories" in Shanghai. Henriot's data does not distinguish between workers in cotton and silk industries; and which enterprises would have been included in the category of "western plant" is also complex in the semi-colonial context of Shanghai. Nonetheless, the figures show that a substantial number of textile factory workers had likely been recruited from the countryside and lived apart from their families (2019: 99). Moreover, as in the Irish linen industry, factory production of cotton yarn in China also affected domestic cotton weaving. By the end of World War One, China had moved from being a net importer to a net exporter of factory-produced cotton yarn; and home weavers of cotton also began to switch to weaving factory-produced yarns, some domestically produced and some imported.

The contracts for girl cotton factory workers in Shanghai would often have been made with their fathers; some of the contemporary documents even refer to the girls as being "bought" and "sold," using language similar to that used for acquiring concubines or servants (Honig 1983: 23–24). But older women also worked in cotton factories. A study of 230 households of cotton textile workers done in western Shanghai in 1927/28 shows that women brought in 34.6 percent of the household income. Wives brought in 19.8 percent; daughters brought in 10.2 percent. The remaining 8.9 percent was brought in by women categorised as "other" – other female kin or non-kin residents in the household (Yang and Tao 1931: 36–37).

Silk industrialisation presents a somewhat different story. Even in its household forms, although it relied mainly on family labour, the production of silk thread did sometimes employ girls who were either servants or wage labourers or who worked in a putting-out capacity in silk production. Even after filatures were introduced to produce silk thread, cocoons were still raised in peasant households.

There were two major areas of industrial silk production in late nineteenth and early twentieth-century China – the regions around Shanghai and Canton. The silk filature workforce in both places was overwhelmingly female. Elizabeth Perry estimates that the filature workforce in Shanghai in the early twentieth century was 90 percent women and children. The weaving of silk cloth had long been done in urban workshops by men; men continued to dominate weaving and constituted a kind of labour aristocracy (Perry 1993: 167–168).

Labour recruitment into the new style of filatures looked similar in some instances in the two regions, but there were also regional particularities based in local kinship practices. One of the earliest mechanised silk filatures was established in Canton province by the entrepreneur Chen Qiyuan in 1874. Chen had studied French filatures in Vietnam and modelled his filature on what he had learned about French processes there (Cliver 2020: 35). According to Ma, Chen established a system of female labour recruitment: "Mobilizing the lineage and village organization, he successfully recruited female workers in neighbouring areas . . . female workers of a particular factory were usually recruited from the same lineage-based village community sharing a common family name, whereas hiring from outside the lineage was discouraged" (Ma 2005: 204–205). This resembles recruitment practices seen elsewhere in China. However, a specific kinship practice in Canton province, namely a practice called "delayed transfer marriage," had implications for labour recruitment. In this form of marriage, brides would not take up residence with their husbands but instead would move from their natal households to a "girls' house," where they would live, often for a number of years, before joining their husbands. These women were prized as workers in the filatures because they did not have the normal household responsibilities of young married women (Eng 1990: 80). There is evidence that younger women went to work in the filatures while older women stayed at home and raised the cocoons (Eng 1986: 62). It needs to be noted here that the success of this recruitment of young women through delayed transfer marriage was perhaps related to increasing overseas emigration at this historical moment, which took young men from this region to Southeast Asia and also across the Pacific to the Americas. This gender-specific emigration would have disrupted pre-existing age and gender patterns of labour. There is clear evidence of delayed transfer marriage as early as the late eighteenth century – that is, long before mechanised filatures were introduced to Canton and before the most massive male emigration from China (Siu 2016: 224). Nonetheless, the conjunction in later periods between the practice of delayed transfer marriage and male emigration created a pool of young women available to work in filatures in Canton.

Shanghai, in contrast to communities in the Canton area, was a rapidly growing city of immigrants, which meant that it was one of the first Chinese cities to develop a new and distinctly urban household labour pattern. From the late nineteenth century on, the overwhelming majority of city residents were immigrants from the surrounding countryside (Lu 1999: 43). Lillian Li offers insights about what drove some of this migration by documenting the implications of Shanghai's mechanised filatures for the surrounding countryside. First, with the introduction of large-scale filatures in the late-nineteenth century, the household system was altered in that peasants increasingly sold cocoons to filatures, rather than selling reeled silk to weavers. Therefore, as in the Irish linen industry, reeling was no longer a largely rural and domestic enterprise. The household reelers were, thus, displaced and either had to change the work they did or move to the filatures. According to Li, in Shanghai filatures, girls from eight to twelve years old were assigned the most unpleasant tasks– tending the basins and finding the cocoons' threads – while older women did the actual reeling (Li 1981: 29). The workforce in filatures in Shanghai was approximately 90 percent female, and before 1930, about 20 percent of the workforce was children (Cliver 2020: 81).

In a new pattern, women at various phases of the life course worked in Shanghai filatures. Robert Eng cites several contemporary sources which describe young girls learning how to reel silk in filatures in Shanghai from their mothers or older sisters, suggesting a multigenerational workforce (Eng 1990: 81). Workers were often asked to refer to their supervisors as "venerable grandmother," suggesting at the very least a metaphorical age-based hierarchy (Smith 2002: 25). Strikes were frequent in Shanghai filatures; one of the demands that female workers made during a strike in 1926 was that a woman who had worked for at least two years receive a month of paid maternity leave. That demand was granted (Cliver 2020: 99). Many of the women who worked in the filatures were wives of stevedores, coolies, and rickshaw pullers. A newspaper in 1924 published a poem in which a woman textile worker, married to a rickshaw puller, lamented her fatigue at the end of a hard day's work. The poem ends "I hurried back home and heard my child crying/Oh sweetheart don't ask mama to hold you – /Mama's whole body aches unbearably./Is Daddy back from rickshaw pulling?/Mama can cook if he brings rice home" (Eng 1990: 80). In Shanghai and other industrial cities, some women bore the burden of supporting the entire family (Lang 1946: 156).

Re-convergences?

The evidence suggests that it had become possible to move women workers at various phases in their life course into urban factory settings in China by the early twentieth century even though the terms of their mobility and the nature of their occupations still reflected the persistence of a household organisation of labour processes and household control over labour. Interestingly, however, the gendered logic of household labour deployment around 1900 looked more similar to that in several European textile industries than it had around 1800. In some respects, we are seeing a re-convergence that ran counter to the divergence postulated for the late proto-industrial era, although with fabric-specific particularities and regional variations within both Europe and China.

Certainly, around 1900, the production of cotton cloth looked very different in China, where weaving was still largely domestic (even if increasingly using factory-produced yarn), than it did in Europe, where cotton spinning and weaving were the pioneering products of mechanisation and factory production. But in the case of silk production, many more similarities appear. Women were the main workforce in factory weaving and had taken over that role from men. Younger women dominated many factory jobs, but in both China and Europe, women worked at various points in the life course, sometimes even in family teams.

Furthermore, as Ma has noted, there were intensifying global interconnections between European and Chinese textile industries that were becoming crucial to production in both regions by around 1900. French silk cloth production relied on thread produced in Chinese (and Japanese) filatures (Ma 1996). Chinese cotton cloth production in households and factories, as we have seen, depended on yarn produced in factories, both European and domestic. It would be an exaggeration to argue that family and life-course labour patterns were converging overall. Key differences remained, especially the marriage patterns so significant for household formation and the allocation of household labour. Nevertheless, we see evidence in both Europe and China of the strategic re-working of age and gender patterns of labour to accommodate new technologies and new places of work that produced some surprising similarities between Europe and China around 1900 as well as reversals in both world regions of what had been gender-normative work around 1800.

References

Unpublished Archival Material

Archives Départementales de Vaucluse, Série E, Etat Civil.
Landesarchiv Baden-Württemberg, Hauptstaatsarchiv Stuttgart, Series E 14/Bü 1170.
"Le Musée de la Soie de Saint Hippolyte du Fort." Accessed August 15, 2020. https://www.museedela soie-cevennes.com/savoiruk.html.

Contemporary Printed Material

de la Farelle, François-Félix. 1852. Études Économiques sur L'industrie de la Soie dans le Midi de la France. Paris: Guillaumin.

Secondary Sources

Berg, Maxine. 1996. "What Difference Did Women's Work Make to the Industrial Revolution?" In Women's Work: The English Experience, 1650–1914, edited by Pamela Sharpe, 149–172. London: Arnold.

Berg, Maxine. 2004. "In Pursuit of Luxury: Global History and British Consumer Goods in the Eighteenth Century." Past & Present 182: 85–142.

Bossen, Laurel, and Hill Gates. 2017. Bound Feet and Small Hands: Tracking the Demise of Footbinding in Village China. Stanford, CA: Stanford University Press.

Bray, Francesca. 1997.Technology and Gender Fabrics of Power in Late Imperial China. Berkeley: University of California Press.

Cliver, Robert. 2014. "China." In The Ashgate Companion to the History of Textile Workers, 1650–2000, edited by Lex Heerma van Voss, Els Hiemstra-Kuperus, and Elise van Nederveen Meerkerk, 103–139. Burlington, VT: Ashgate.

Cliver, Robert. 2020. Red Silk: Class, Gender and Revolution in China's Yangzi Delta Silk Industry. Cambridge, MA: Harvard University Asia Center.

Collins, Brenda. 1997. "The Loom, the Land, and the Marketplace: Women Weavers and the Family Economy in Late Nineteenth- and Early Twentieth-century Ireland." In The Warp of Ulster's Past, edited by Marilyn Cohen, 229–252. New York: St. Martin's Press.

Ditt, Karl, and Sidney Pollard, eds. 1992. Von der Heimarbeit in die Fabrik. Industrialisierung und Arbeiterschaft in Leinen- und Baumwollregionen Westeuropas während des 18. und 19. Jahrhunderts. Paderborn: Ferdinand Schöningh.

Duan, Xiaolin. 2017. "Fashion, State, and Social Change: Chinese and Mexican Silk in Early Modern Manila Trade." Paper presented at the meeting of the American Society for Eighteenth-Century Studies, Minneapolis, Minnesota, March 30, 2017.

DuPlessis, Robert S. 2016. The Material Atlantic: Clothing, Commerce, and Colonization in the Atlantic World, 1650–1800. Cambridge: Cambridge University Press.

Eacott, Jonathan. 2016. Selling Empire: India in the Making of Britain and America, 1600–1830. Chapel Hill, NC: University of North Carolina Press.

Eng, Robert Y. 1986. Economic Imperialism in China: Silk Productions and Exports, 1861–1932. Berkeley, CA: Institute for East Asian Studies.

Eng, Robert Y. 1990. "Luddism and Labor Protest Among Silk Artisans and Workers in Jiangnan and Guangdong, 1860–1930." Late Imperial China 11, no. 2: 63–101.

Engelen, Th., and A.P. Wolf, eds. 2005. Marriage and the Family in Eurasia. Perspectives on the Hajnal Hypothesis. Piscataway NJ: Aksant Academic Publishers.

Eyferth, Jacob. 2015. "Liberation from the Loom? Rural Women, Textile Work, and Revolution in North China." In Maoism at the Grassroots: Everyday Life in China's Era of High Socialism, edited by Jeremy Brown and Matthew D. Johnson, 131–153. Cambridge, MA: Harvard University Press.

Ghosh, Shami. 2015. "The 'Great Divergence', Politics, and Capitalism." Journal of Early Modern History 19: 1–43.

Goldstone, Jack. 1996. "Gender, Work, and Culture: Why the Industrial Revolution Came Early to England but Late to China." *Sociological Perspectives* 39, no. 1: 1–21.

Gray, Jane. 2005. *Spinning the Threads of Uneven Development. Gender and Industrialization in Ireland During the Long Eighteenth Century.* Lanham, MD: Lexington Books.

Gray, Marion W. 2000. *Productive Men, Reproductive Women: The Agrarian Household and the Emergence of Separate Spheres During the German Enlightenment.* New York, Oxford: Berghahn Books.

Hajnal, John. 1965. "European Marriage Patterns in Perspective." In *Population in History: Essays in Historical Demography,* edited by David Victor Glass and David Edward Charles Eversley, 101–146. London: Edward Arnold.

Hartman, Mary S. 2004. *The Household and the Making of History, A Subversive View of the Western Past.* Cambridge: Cambridge University Press.

Henriot, Christian, Lu Shi, and Charlotte Aubrun. 2019. *The Population of Shanghai, (1865-1953): A Sourcebook.* Leiden: Brill.

Honig, Emily. 1983. "The Contract Labor System and Women Workers: Pre-Liberation Cotton Mills of Shanghai." *Modern China* 9, no. 4: 421–454.

Hufton, Olwen. 1998. *The Prospect Before Her: A History of Women in Western Europe 1500-1800.* New York: Vintage.

Jaschok, Maria. 1994. *Women and Chinese Patriarchy: Submission, Servitude and Escape.* Hong Kong: Hong Kong University Press.

Kuhn, Dieter. 1998. *Textile Technology: Spinning and Reeling.* Vol. 5, pt. 9 of *Science and Civilization in China.* New York: Cambridge University Press.

Lang, Olga. 1946. *Chinese Family and Society.* New Haven: Yale University Press.

Lee, James, and Wang Feng. 2001. *One Quarter of Humanity: Malthusian Mythology and Chinese Realities, 1700–2000.* Cambridge, MA: Harvard University Press.

Lemire, Beverly. 1991. *Fashion's Favourite: The Cotton Trade and the Consumer in Britain, 1660-1800.* New York: Oxford University Press.

Li, Bozhong. 1998. *Agricultural Development in Jiangnan.* New York: St. Martin's Press.

Li, Bozhong. 2000. *Jiangnan de zaoqi gongye hua 1550-1850* [Early Industrialization in Jiangnan 1550–1850]. Beijing: Renmin University Press.

Li, Bozhong. 2009. "Involution and Chinese Cotton Textile Production: Songjiang in the Late-Eighteenth and Early-Nineteenth Centuries." In *The Spinning World: A Global History of Cotton Textiles, 1200-1850,* edited by Georgio Riello and Prasannan Parthasarathi, 387–397. Oxford and New York: Oxford University Press.

Li, Lillian. 1981. *China's Silk Trade, Traditional Industry in the Modern World, 1842-1937.* Cambridge, MA: Harvard University Press.

Liang, Chu-bin. 2001. "Mingdai nügong yi beifang funu wei zhongxin zhi tantao" [An exploration of women's work in the Ming dynasty, focusing on the north]. Ph.D. thesis: National Central University.

Lu, Hanchao. 1999. *Beyond the Neon Lights: Everyday Shanghai in the Early Twentieth Century.* Berkeley, CA: University of California Press.

Lundquist, Jennifer Hickes, Douglas L. Anderton, and David Yaukey. 2014. *Demography: The Study of Human Population.* Grove, IL: Waveland Press.

Ma, Debin. 1996. "The Modern Silk Road: The Global Raw-Silk Market, 1850-1930." *The Journal of Economic History* 56, no. 2: 330–355.

Ma, Debin. 2005. "Between Cottage and Factory: The Evolution of Chinese and Japanese Silk-Reeling Industries in the Latter Half of the Nineteenth Century." *Journal of the Asia Pacific Economy* 10, no. 2: 195–213.

Mann, Keith. 2010. *Forging Political Identity: Silk and Metal Workers in Lyon, France 1900–1939*. New York and Oxford: Berghahn Books.

Mann, Susan. 1991. "Grooming a Daughter for Marriage." In *Marriage and Inequality in Chinese Society*, edited by Patricia Ebrey and Rubie Watson, 203–230. Berkeley: University of California Press.

Mann, Susan. 1997. *Precious Records: Women in China's Long Eighteenth Century*. Berkeley: University of California Press.

Maynes, Mary Jo. 2004. "Arachne's Daughters: European Girls' Labor in the International Textile Industry, 1750–1880." In *Secret Gardens, Satanic Mills: Placing Girls in European History*, edited by Mary Jo Maynes, Birgitte Soland, and Christina Benninghaus, 38–53. Bloomington, IN: Indiana University Press.

Maynes, Mary Jo, and Ann Waltner. 2001. "Women's Life-Cycle Transitions in World-Historical Perspective: Comparing Marriage in China and Europe." *Journal of Women's History* 12, no. 4: 11–21.

Medick, Hans. 1996. *Weben und Überleben in Laichingen. Lokalgeschichte als allgemeine Geschichte*. Göttingen: Vandenhoeck & Ruprecht.

Messenger, Betty. 1978. *Picking Up the Linen Threads: A Study in Industrial Folklore*. Austin, TX: University of Texas Press.

O'Dowd, Mary, and June Purvis, eds. 2018. *A History of the Girl: Formation, Education and Identity*. Basingstoke: Palgrave Macmillan.

Ogilvie, Sheilagh. 1997. *State Corporatism and Proto-industry: The Württemberg Black Forest, 1580–1797*. Cambridge and New York: Cambridge University Press.

Ogilvie, Sheilagh C. 2003. *A Bitter Living: Women, Markets, and Social Capital in Early Modern Germany*. Oxford: Oxford University Press.

Parthasarathi, Prasannan, and Kenneth Pomeranz. 2009. "The Great Divergence." In *Global Economic History, 1500–2000*, edited by Giorgio Riello and Tirthankar Roy, 19–37. London: Bloomsbury.

Perry, Elizabeth. 1993. *Shanghai on Strike: The Politics of Chinese Labor*. Stanford, CA: Stanford University Press.

Pomeranz, Kenneth. 2000. *The Great Divergence: China, Europe, and the Making of the Modern World Economy*. Princeton, NJ: Princeton University Press.

Pomeranz, Kenneth. 2005. "Women's Work and the Politics of Respectability." In *Gender in Motion: Divisions of Labor and Cultural Change in Late Imperial and Modern China*, edited by Bryna Goodman and Wendy Larson, 239–264. Lanham, MD: Rowman and Littlefield.

Quataert, Jean H. 1985. "The Shaping of Women's Work in Manufacturing: Guilds, Households, and the State in Central Europe, 1648–1870." *American Historical Review* 90, no. 5: 1122–1148.

Ransmeier, Johanna. 2017. *Sold People: Traffickers and Family Life in North China*. Cambridge, MA: Harvard University Press.

Riello, Giorgio, and Prasannan Parthasarathi, eds. 2009. *The Spinning World: A Global History of Cotton Textiles, 1200–1850*. Oxford and New York: Oxford University Press.

Riello, Giorgio, and Tirthankar Roy, eds. 2019. *Global Economic History, 1500–2000*. London: Bloomsbury.

Santangelo, Paulo. 1993. "Urban Society in Late Imperial Suzhou." In *Cities of Jiangnan in Late Imperial China*, edited by Linda Cooke Johnson, 81–116. Albany: State University of New York Press.

Simonton, Deborah. 1998. *A History of European Women's Work,* London: Routledge.

Siu, Helen. 2016. "Where Were the Women? Rethinking Marriage Resistance and Regional Culture in South China." In *Tracing China: A Forty-year Ethnographic Journey*, edited by Deborah Simonton, 221–243. Hong Kong: Hong Kong University Press.

Smith, S.A. 2002. *Like Cattle and Horses: Nationalism and Labor in Shanghai, 1895–1927*. Durham, NC: Duke University Press.

Steffen, Anka. 2016. "Silesians and Slaves: How Linen Textiles Connected East-Central Europe, Africa and the Americas." Paper presented at the conference "Dressing Global Bodies," Alberta, Canada.

Stockard, Janice. 1989. *Daughters of the Canton Delta: Marriage Patterns and Economic Strategies in South China 1860–1930*. Stanford, CA: Stanford University Press.

Tanaka, Masatoshi. 1994. "The Putting-out System of Production in the Ming and Qing Periods: With a Focus on Clothing Production, part 1," *Memoirs of the Research Department of the Toyo Bunko* 52: 21–43.

Tilly, Louise, and Joan Scott. 1978. *Women, Work and Family.* New York: Holt, Rinehart and Winston.

Wilkinson, Endymion. 2015. *Chinese History: A New Manual, Fourth Edition.* Cambridge, MA: Harvard University Asia Center.

Xu Xinwu, and Byun-Kim Min. 1988. "The Struggle of the Handicraft Industry against Machine Textiles in China," *Modern China* 14:1: 32–49.

Yang Ximeng, and Tao Menghe. 1931. *A Study of the Standard of Living of Working Families in Shanghai.* Beijing: Institute of Social Research.

Zurndorfer, Harriet. 2009. "The Resistant Fibre: Cotton Textiles in Imperial China." In *The Spinning World: A Global History of Cotton Textiles, 1200–1845*, edited by Georgio Riello and Prasannan Parthasarathi, 43–62. Oxford: Oxford University Press.

Zurndorfer, Harriet. 2011. "Cotton Textile Manufacture and Marketing in Late Imperial China and the 'Great Divergence.'" *Journal of the Economic and Social History of the Orient* 54: 702–738.

Lamia Karim

Older Female Workers in the Global Apparel Industry in Bangladesh

The global garment industry in Bangladesh is forty years old and has a workforce of approximately four million persons, 80 percent of which is female.[1] It should be borne in mind that this female-dominated industrial labour force is in a formative period, and its incubation in historical time is relatively short. These female garment workers join factory work around the age of fifteen years on average and are phased out of work by factory management when they reach thirty-five to forty years old, when they are deemed to be no longer productive. Once they age out of the industry, these women disappear either into the urban informal economy or return to their villages due to the lack of work. There is very little research on this group of women's life circumstances after they leave factory work.

Between 2014 and 2018, I worked in staggered phases for three and a half years studying workers in the global garment industry in Bangladesh. During my research, I noticed that there were very few women over the age of thirty-five working in the factories. I found that no institution – the Bangladeshi state, the leading organisation of factory owners known as the Bangladesh Garment Manufacturers and Exporters Association (BGMEA), the Bangladesh Institute for Labour Studies (BILS), the International Labour Organization (ILO), and labour rights NGOs – was concerned with tracking these women once they exited the work force. It was the absence of studies on older women workers pushed out of factory work that guided me to this research.[2] This research is shaped by the following questions: In addition to much-needed wages, what were the aspirations that structured the lives of older female workers in the garment industry in Bangladesh, and what were they able to achieve at the end of their working lives?

These older women's lives are intermingled with the life course regime and life history as defined by Tamara K. Hareven, but in the specific context of rural society in Bangladesh. "The life course paradigm has offered a way of capturing the complexity in the impact of social change on people, and conversely, the contribution of people to facilitating or modifying social change" (Hareven 2001:

---

1 This number does not include the workers in the informal subcontracting sector of the garment industry.

2 These workers are not old; they still have another fifteen to twenty years of their working life left. Factory management deems them as less productive and replaces them with a younger cohort of workers.

28). Hareven goes on to add that "Another important contribution of the life course paradigm has been the recognition of life stage as an important determinant for specifying the impact of historical events on individual lives" (Hareven 2001: 29). The life course regime in my analysis refers to the patriarchal construction of the rural family, women's gender roles, kin obligations, factory work, and marriage in Bangladesh.

Starting in British colonial times, Bangladesh was an impoverished state due to extractive capitalism that destroyed the indigenous textile industry. Later, under Pakistani rule (1947–1971), rural poverty was not adequately addressed in former East Pakistan (now Bangladesh). After gaining independence from Pakistan in 1971, the newly formed government of Bangladesh left the management of rural society largely to non-governmental organisations (NGOs). Funded with Western development assistance, NGOs provided much-needed essential services to rural communities, from credit, to primary education, to women's training programs under the rubric of "empowerment" (Karim 2011).[3] While feminist scholars have critically debated this term, in this context, it is the World Bank's definition of empowerment that shapes the discourse. "In its broadest sense empowerment is the freedom of choice and action. It means increasing one's authority and empower control over resources and decisions that affect one's life" (Darrow 2003: 155). The social structure that impacted rural women's lives and life course was the growth of industrial capitalism in the global ready-made garment industry. In the 1980s, when garment factory work became available, large numbers of poor women began to migrate to the city to enter factory work. It was access to factory work that led to several significant changes in these women's lives including delayed marriages for young women as well as delayed childbirth. Prior to the advent of factory work, the average rural birth rate was between five to six children. At present, the birth rate among garment workers has gone down to an average of two children. In this chapter, I show how the twin processes of factory work and wages have shaped women's lives and given them forms of freedom and the ability to fulfil some of their aspirations.

Writing about private life is a messy and difficult process. In writing garment women's lived experiences, I found many gaps and absences rather than a linear narrative. In telling their stories, these older women would forget dates, confuse chronology and events, and contradict themselves. They were not accustomed to narrating their personal life histories; this was a new mode of discourse for

---

3 Bangladesh is world famous for its innovative NGO structure, including BRAC, the world's largest NGO, and Grameen Bank, which won the 2006 Nobel Peace Prize. Since 2011, the power of NGOs in Bangladesh has declined, and the state is now more active in rural society.

them that should be kept in mind. Similarly, the idea of time is structured differently for these older women who grew up before globalisation penetrated rural society. Important dates are remembered in terms of major events (war, cyclone, floods, etc.) and not in the European sense of chronological time. The older women could not remember the date they were born because birthdays are not major social events in rural society. They remembered their birth or marriage dates by referring to a major historical event such as, "I was born before or after the big war" (this refers to 1971, when Bangladesh separated from Pakistan). In Bangladesh, when you ask a rural person about their age, they usually give an approximation and not an exact figure, "my age is probably between 45–47 years." Therefore, a European understanding of the life course structured around precise dates does not fit these women's lives. Many of these gaps remained unbridgeable, but following the ethnographic method, I have contextualised their comments within the discursive field they inhabited.

Our knowledge of the women who make our clothes extends primarily to notions around wages, workers' rights, work conditions, and trade unions – practices that are extremely important for creating a decent work environment; nonetheless, these categories fail to capture the full human dimensions of these women's lives. This chapter goes beyond these stereotypical notions of the worker primarily as a labourer who seeks decent work conditions and trade union membership. Instead, it examines the worker as a human subject with aspirations and desires that help us understand these women not only as workers trapped in the global supply chain of commodity production but also as agents who strive to create a good life (*shundor jibon*).[4]

Workers seek a good life through improvements in the material conditions of their lives and a better diet, housing, and education for their children, which would lead to class mobility. They also seek the good life in terms of affect – their desire to be seen as women who love and can be loved. As one woman said to me, "For more than eight hours a day, I stitch clothes. My body embraces the sewing machine. At night, an emptiness enters my life. There is no embrace waiting for me." It is this striving for a good life of material comfort and loving companionship that undergirds their humanity as full human subjects with rights, dignity, and desire.

---

4 I have refrained from framing these women's aspirations in Aristotelian terms of the individual's capacity to reason as the signature of a good life. Bangladeshi rural women should be analysed through native terms that shape their ideas of the good life. Their moral compass is formed in the village society, through folk views regarding Islam. In Islam, the good life means following the commands of Allah as laid out in the Quran.

The Bangladeshi garment industry began in 1978. In less than forty years, it has grown into the second largest garment industry in the world after China's. Its emergence under the condition of globalisation has created work conditions that are culturally specific and significantly different from those experienced by the industrial workforce in Europe in the nineteenth century. I have outlined a couple of these divergences below. There are two important aspects concerning industrial workers in a global comparative context that merit some comment. First, in the Euro-American context, industrialisation made men and women leave the rural economy for industrial towns where workers created new lives tied to manufacturing. In contrast, Bangladeshi workers maintain a circular tie to their rural roots and return to their village multiple times during their lives for marriages, births, deaths, and religious holidays. Part of this is due to the strong kinship structure that defines life in Bangladesh. Almost 98 percent of Bangladeshis maintain close bonds to their ancestral village and extended family ties, and industrialisation has not broken the rural–urban distinction in Bangladesh. Instead, it has integrated these two locations through a network of improved telecommunications, and through bridges and highways linking the periphery to the metropolitan centre, which have dramatically reduced travel time for commuters.

Second, European and American female workers left work to raise children and re-entered the workforce after their children were older. That is, social reproduction interrupted the work life of female workers, which also reduced their income compared to men due to childcare. In Bangladesh, we find that garment workers live in extended families, and most women do not exit the labour force for social reproduction. In the extended-family structure, parenting is not the sole responsibility of the birth mother. Grandparents, aunts, uncles, and older siblings all participate in the raising of children as surrogate parents. This is a relationship of reciprocity that ties several generations together in the reproduction of the family. While this economy of care has stretched and weakened with the migration of family members, it is still available to migrant workers as a viable option. These garment workers have a circular relationship with rural society that is renewed through kin relations, remittances, telecommunications, and travel between the migrant worker and her family.

Methods

Industrial work, wages, and urban living have touched every aspect of these working women's lives from rural-urban connections, to who they marry/how they raise their children (do they keep them in the city or send them to the village), their relationship with their absent husbands and families, urban living arrangements, workers' protests and demonstrations, factory work routines, and, finally, in creating new social identities that were previously absent in their rural lives. My research indicates that there is no clear demarcation between the work life and life after work. Workers' life stories disrupt this distinction between the (private) and the public (factory), creating a tapestry of aspirations where the public/ private distinctions collapse and merge (Bhattacharya 2006). Most of these workers enter factory work around the age of fifteen on average. Many of them come to the city as unmarried young girls who were sent to work in factories by their poverty-stricken families. The majority of workers are recruited for factory work by relatives who already live in the city. Once in the city, they live in the slums that have grown up around factories. Then the normative cycle of life begins. They fall in love with someone they met at work or in the city, get married, have children, get separated, remarry, and are abandoned again or widowed until they age out of work.

In my research plan, I adopted what George Marcus termed "follow the story" (Marcus 1995). The story is the map that takes the researcher to new sites and ideas of exploration. The story is not only in the spoken words but is contained in physical movements: pitch, eye movement, bodily gestures, and silences. The speaker adopts a range of tactics to tell their story, and the craft of the ethnographer is to search for hidden maps within the spoken words. "It is often in gaps and silences, as well as the triangulation of accounts and reading against the grain of informants' testimonies and our own analyses, that the most enlightening observations and theory can be advanced" (Freeman 2020: 73). The ethnographer also locates the ethnography within the broader cultural landscape and identifies other relevant issues to frame and analyse the conversation. I follow a particular formula in conducting my ethnographic research. I develop a network of insiders and trusted people who come from the community I am engaged in researching. I enter private spaces and conversations with the help of a trusted member from the community.

My research assistants and I interviewed over one hundred currently employed factory women and sixteen older workers who were forced out of factory work.[5] I also interviewed the men in these women's lives, their adult children, factory managers, trade union leaders, and labour rights activists. We had one-on-one

---

5 This research is coming out as a book entitled *Castoffs of Capital: Work and Love Among Garment Workers in Bangladesh* (University of Minnesota Press, 2022). Over the course of my research, I was assisted by four researchers, two women and two men. Three of these researchers were provided by a local labour rights organisation, and they had long-term immersion with garment workers. The fourth researcher was a university student. The research assistants helped me with recording and transcribing the interviews and in contextualising and interpreting the ethnographic data.

and focus-group interviews. I met each of the women whose life histories I recorded on three separate occasions. At the beginning of my research in 2014, I conducted a survey of one hundred women workers who were currently employed to get some baseline data such as the age at which each worker entered the factory, the number of years worked at factories, work disruptions, marital status, the number of children, and what these women liked about their new urban factory lives, what benefits they saw from factory work, and so on. A majority of these workers were all below the age of thirty-five, with only a few over that age. This was a randomised survey, and the only requirement for participation was that the workers had to be currently employed at a garment factory.

According to the last census taken in 2011, 90 percent of the population of Bangladesh is Muslim. All the workers in my study group were Muslims. Although I do not have precise statistics, I was informed by labour activists working with garment workers in my area that only 5 percent of the garment labour force is Hindu. The majority of the Hindu women employed come from the lowest caste known as Dalits. Unlike most of the Muslim women workers who come to the city as young, unmarried girls, most of the Hindu women workers tend to be married, and many of them come to the city with their husbands. Factory work has offered both Hindu and Muslim women some limited forms of practical freedom that I discuss later in the chapter. Here I have selectively extracted some aspects in the lifecycle changes of older women in a landscape where work, family, marriage, gender, sexuality, and aspirations intersect, often in devastating ways.

Situating the Study

In Bangladesh, women work primarily in the agricultural sector as non-paid workers, and they conduct "80% [of] pre-and post-harvest activities in addition to their daily household chores" (BILS 1995: 6). Prior to the emergence of the garment industry, poor rural women worked primarily as domestic workers, cooks, cleaners, mud-cutters for rural road construction, and brick-breakers in real estate development.[6] These are all low-paid, non-unionised jobs, and compared to men, women are paid less in all these sectors. In the formal sector, women's labour participation is the largest in the ready-to-wear garment sector. While a small number of Muslim women may have worked in the jute industry in Bangladesh, the first jute mill was opened in former East Pakistan only in 1954, and there are no studies on Muslim

---

6 In real estate development, women are used for breaking pieces of brick into smaller fragments that are mixed with cement to build houses.

women workers in the jute mills. Suffice it to say that the incorporation of millions of Muslim women into the industrial labour force as garment factory workers is a profound sociological transformation in terms of women's work, agency, marriage, family, and sexuality.

I situate my research within two broad categories of writing on female factory labour – (a) feminists and anthropologists writing on female factory labour; and (b) scholars writing on female factory labour in Bangladesh. In the first category, studies show women's exploitation due to their positional vulnerability, the browning of low-skilled industrial work, and the singular absence of women and social production in labour studies (Fuentes and Ehrenreich 1983; Nash and Fernandez-Kelly 1983; Wolf 1992). These studies reveal how poor women as "nimble fingers" bear the costs of the feminisation of industrial work caused by low wages, stigma, gender disparity in income, and exposure to occupational hazards (Elson and Pearson 1981). Within this category, a set of scholars have analysed forms of resistance adopted by female workers against factory-level oppression (Ong 2010; Kabeer 2002). Hewamanne analysed how Sri Lankan garment workers cultivated "an overarching identity for themselves as a gendered group of migrant workers who are different from other women and from male industrial workers" (Hewamanne 2008: 4).

The most comprehensive study on the Bangladesh garment industry is the edited volume by Sanchita B. Saxena, *Labor, Global Supply Chains, and the Garment Industry in South Asia: Bangladesh after Rana Plaza.* Each of the articles in this volume argue for improving workers' labour conditions. To solve the problems of low wages and worker oppression, Saxena argues for a multi-stakeholder and multi-pronged approach (Saxena and Baumann-Pauly 2019: 14); Kabeer identifies global buyers and their lust for extreme profits as the key reason for keeping workers continuously at risk (Kabeer 2019: 31–260); Feldman and Hossain advocate for stronger government participation in regulating the garment industry (Feldman and Hossain 2019: 21–44); and Huq argues that factory upgrades have failed to meet workers' demands (Huq 2019: 65–83). Siddiqi explores the complicity of the state with global capital that endangers progressive workers' politics (Siddiqi 2019: 100–114). Although they make a significant contribution to the scholarship, these studies are constrained by the construction of the woman as primarily a worker. The study that comes closest to my research questions is the 2019 study on older garment workers in Bangalore, India (Mezzadri and Majumdar 2019).

The Bangladeshi Garment Industry

Under the Multi-Fiber Arrangement (MFA, 1974–1994 [Phase 1], 1995–2004 [Phase 2]), the United States and European countries regulated textile production. In the mid-1970s, the MFA restricted the importation of manufactured clothing from middle-income countries (Hong Kong, Taiwan, and South Korea), which were the main exporters of textiles to the United States and European markets. Instead, the MFA gave unrestricted market access to garments produced in the least developed countries (LDCs) like Bangladesh, Sri Lanka, and Vietnam to help build their economies. South Korean exports were severely curtailed by MFA quota restrictions. To circumvent these restrictions, the South Korean company Daewoo, a major apparel producer, partnered with Desh Company in Bangladesh in 1978. Within a relatively short time, many male Bangladeshis trained in factory management by Daewoo went on to open their own factories with lucrative government incentives.

By the late 1980s, the industry had begun to slowly take off, and Bangladeshi policy makers left the industry open to market forces to enable capital to develop. Both the United States and European Union were particularly influential in the growth of the garment industry by giving apparel exports from Bangladesh preferential access to their markets, and they eventually "brought Bangladeshi garments to doorsteps all over the world" (Caleca 2014: 284). In 2018, 60 percent of apparel produced in Bangladesh went to the United States, although it makes up only 6 percent of the apparel market there, and 40 percent went to the EU, with Germany as the largest buyer. By the 1990s, Korean, Chinese, and Indian factory owners were operating alongside Bangladeshi owners, taking advantage of the country's quota-free status, extremely low wages, no oversight of factories, and the benefits of a non-unionised labour force. All these conditions helped keep production costs depressed in the garment industry. The key factor behind the spectacular growth of this industry was its extremely low wages. Between 1994 to 2006, wages for workers remained flat at $12 per month. Wages only rose after thousands of workers demonstrated for higher monthly wages and better working conditions in 2006, when the monthly wage was raised to $22, in 2010 to $30, and in 2013 to $67. After the 2013 Rana Plaza factory collapse that killed over 1,100 workers and injured another 2,500, global outcry about the precarious work conditions and lack of trade union representation in Bangladesh was finally addressed. Yet, changes in the wake of this disaster have been minimal compared to the needs of workers, and the growth of monthly wages fall far below the rate of inflation. The beneficiaries of these changes have been younger workers who will be in the work force much longer than their older colleagues. Trade union representation is more available now although genuine trade unions remain small compared to the fake unions that factory owners have created to circumvent workers' rights.[7]

The growth of the garment industry was also enabled by the availability of a large labour force of female migrants which resulted from the World Bank's structural adjustment policies and the Bangladeshi government's disinvestment in the rural economy. Factory owners targeted these young women, who could be coerced into working long hours at very low wages in substandard factories and hazardous conditions. By the early 2000s, Bangladesh had become a significant producer of ready-made garments for the global market, but the MFA under which it received tariff-free market access expired in 2004. Instead of losing its market share, the Bangladeshi garment industry began to surge post-MFA, and it did remarkably well during the global economic recession of 2007–2008. In 2005, ready-made garment exports totalled six billion dollars. By 2008, exports rose to ten billion dollars; that is, exports nearly doubled during the global recession, and this became known as the Walmart effect.[8] During the recession, consumers bought low-priced clothes, and Bangladesh's garment industry is the production site for cheap apparel. While the garment industry grew exponentially, the cost of production was transferred to workers through low wages and poorly maintained factories, which has resulted in multiple work-related injuries and deaths.[9]

Older Women Workers

The older women I met came to the city to flee poverty and, in many instances, spousal abuse. Once in the city, the fortunate ones found factory employment; the less fortunate found temporary employment. Many of them returned to the village once they were fired from their factory jobs and could no longer afford to live in the city. I found that not only do their lives weave in and out of the rural and urban economies and from non-paid to paid work; they also weave in and out of failed marriages and romantic relationships. The women run away from abusive relationships, their husbands abandon them and take a second wife, but after some time, their husbands take them back, their parents' force them to return to their husbands, or the women themselves accept their husbands back into their lives. Some women were able to exit these toxic relationships, but they

---

7 The data on fake unions is not available but it is a widely known fact about trade unions in garment factories.

8 https://www.bgmea.com/bd.

9 For an expanded study of the economic history of the Bangladeshi garment industry, see Rahman 2015.

were again thrown into the precarity of industrial work without any stable social anchor.

All sixteen older workers interviewed were born in the village. These women were between forty-five and fifty-five years old. They had all faced intense poverty and deprivation during their childhoods. A couple of them moved to the city as children with their parents due to debt and the loss of arable land. Nine of these women were illiterate, five had between a third- and fifth-grade education, and only one had studied up to tenth grade. Fourteen of them came to the city between the ages of eleven and eighteen. For this reason, at a very young age they had to adapt to urban rules without the support of parents who could guide them through difficult social situations they confronted daily. For example, Marjina, a forty-five-year-old worker in a factory, came to Dhaka after the 1998 floods washed away her home. She said, "If I didn't have this factory job, we would not have any place to stay, money for food; we would have all died." Another fifty-two-year-old worker described her village life as a time when they ate a gruel of broken wheat and rice for two weeks of the month. For them, life was divided into rural life without work, wages, or food, and urban life with factory work, wages, and food. But life in the city remained equally tenuous. Most of these workers entered factory work at very low wages that neither allowed them to have a good life nor to save for old age.

In the individual life histories of the older women, the following pattern emerged – workplace harassment and defrauding workers' of their rightful wages and retirement funds, marital abandonment, cohabitation with the husband's second wife, remarriage, the failure to provide their children with education and gainful employment, and severe spousal abuse. Their husbands often confiscated their wages and severely beat them if they refused to hand over the money. One aspiration that structured these older women's lives was their desire to educate their children, move them into the middle-class, and provide them with better employment options. All the women I met said that they did not want their daughters to join the garment industry as assembly-line workers. They wanted their daughters to work in factory management, government employment, or in the service sector, the burgeoning retail industry that is mushrooming in Bangladesh. Most of the women went into debt to put their children through school. However, in most instances, their daughters entered the garment industry as assembly-line workers. Their lives were caught between the exhilarating expectation that good things would happen now that they earned wages and the destruction of that sentiment, which profoundly shattered these women's hopes.

Among the sixteen women, nine were abandoned, two of the nine later remarried, one was a widow, and six remained married at the time of my interviews. There were rare instances when a woman left her husband because of spousal abuse and neglect. In most cases, the husband disappeared after the woman became pregnant or gave birth to a child, transforming the woman into the primary caregiver and breadwinner. Husbands abandoned their wives instead of divorcing them because abandonment did not require them to pay alimony. The older women did not have officially registered marriages and, therefore, could not seek redress through the courts. These marital abandonments were in violation of Muslim family law because most husbands did not seek their first wife's permission before taking a second wife.[10] Most of the younger women registered their marriages, giving them access to divorce settlement money. Unlike the older women, the younger women had higher levels of education and were more accustomed to appealing their cases in front of judges in family courts with the help of NGOs.

Once laid off from factory work, these older women first tried to re-enter another factory on a short-term basis or joined the unregulated subcontracting operations as part-timers. Their work options were few since most of them did not have the financial capital to start a small business. A few women operated creches for garment workers' children or provided cooked meals for single workers in the slums. But most of them worked as day labourers or as domestic workers. Some of them had adult children who assisted them financially, but this support fell short of what the women had anticipated in their old age. When all opportunities dried up, the women returned to their village to live out the remainder of their lives.

Changing Norms of Factory Work, Agency, Family, and Marriage

Factory work

With their inclusion into factory work regimes, the modern clock regulated and routinised these women's lives. Clocking into work, clocking out of work, and finishing their quota on time gave these women a new perspective on how time structured their lives. Their day began between 5:00 and 5:30 a.m. In the slums, workers must make lines for a ten-minute shower in a shared bath. Again, they wait half an

---

10 According to the Hanafi school of *sharia* law followed by Bangladeshi Sunni Muslims, a husband can take a second wife if the first wife is unable to fulfil marital relations or if she cannot conceive a child. But the husband must treat both wives equally and seek the permission of his first wife before taking a second wife.

hour to cook their meals in a shared kitchen. The workers set out for work between 6:30 a.m. and 7 a.m. to reach the factory gates by 8 a.m., after which factory gates are locked. Being late for work results in reprimands by managers and a potential loss of income for tardiness. Several late arrivals would get them fired. In their new work life, punctuality equalled job security.

Many workers said that physical assaults such as slaps or hair pulling used to be common practice in the past, but this type of abuse has declined with the onset of regularised production operations. Management has realised that workplace disruptions cause delays in manufacturing that hurt the bottom line. In recent years, they have operationalised stricter disciplinary surveillance of workers instead of using physical assault to make them work faster. Supervisors walked up and down the assembly lines to let workers know that their activities were being closely monitored. Workers noted another form of punishment that they found demeaning: Workers who arrived late or were negligent at work were publicly humiliated by being made to stand outside the factory gates. For women workers, standing outside factory gates exposed them to mockery and the gaze of male passers-by.

Both young and old workers complained about two issues: the high pressure on them to meet their quota, which doubled from 60 to 120 pieces after the wage increase in 2013 from $30 to $67 per month. If they could not meet their daily quota, workers had to remain behind on their own time without overtime pay to finish the work, and they were accused of being "slow" by management. They also complained about their supervisors' verbal abuse at work, which they found deeply offensive. It was commonplace for supervisors to call female workers "daughter of a whore" and "hag," to berate them with comments such as, "why are you so slow, who were you sleeping with last night?" and to use similar slurs to shame the women workers in front of their peers.

Agency

Work and wages offered the women a sense of agency that they had previously lacked in their rural communities. Many of the women told me that the happiest day of their life was when they received their monthly wages. Touching the money and counting the currency gave them a sense of accomplishment. It indicated that they could work, earn money, and be a worthy person. While the women recognised that their labour had to be compensated, they were pawns in the hands of the factory management, who used various nefarious methods to trick them out of their rightful wages. For example, hours worked were often changed in logbooks. Without proper trade union representation in the factories, workers had few options for recompense.[11]

The self as a semi-autonomous subject – this is who I am, this is what I can do – remained an important structure in their lives, linking them to familial obligations, especially older workers. City life and factory work have enabled women to move about in limited ways that were previously denied to them. A woman could now walk around, sit at a restaurant with a friend, and talk to a non-kin man without her intentions being scrutinised by family. This new freedom of mobility was enjoyed by all the women I met. Overnight, their lives changed from living within the four walls of their rural homestead to an urban jungle without boundaries. Women's agency intersected with other domains such as marriage and sexuality. Women married for love but also for sexual security because a single woman faced many risks in the city. But many women, young and old, also expressed bold sexuality. For example, a young woman said, "I have sexual needs, so my boyfriend and I live together. But we do not tell anyone that we are not married. I hope to go to Mauritius and make more money. Once I have seen the world, I may settle down." What was remarkable about this statement was her candid expression of her sexual desires, a topic that most Bangladeshi women would not speak about openly to an outsider.

Traditionally, women are expected to make their bodies and voices invisible because a woman who is loud and visible is considered a shameless person. In Bangladesh, it is common to hear people say that one knows a garment worker by how fast she strides. These garment women walk fast and with purpose and confidence. They speak loudly when necessary. These are significant changes in women's attitudes and comportment in public spaces. An older woman said that one day, while she was returning from work, a man touched her on the back. She said that she spun around and slapped him. She added, "Had I lived in the village, I would not have developed this courage." Had these women lived in the village, their fathers, husbands, or a male member of their extended kin would be responsible for their physical security and the protection of family honour. Now the responsibility of personal safety was on the shoulders of these women, and they had to learn how to navigate the city and its many dangers on their own, without familial support.

---

11 Trade unions were restricted in the garment industry through bureaucratic barriers. After the 2013 Rana Plaza industrial accident that killed over 1,100 workers, Western governments, the ILO, and labour rights organisations have insisted that trade unions be allowed to operate without intimidation. However, only 2 percent of the garment labour force is unionised.

Family

What I outline next are the prevailing norms of family life in Bangladesh. It should be noted that they are transforming under the pressures of globalisation and migration. The women and men I studied are heterosexual and reproduce the heteronormative patriarchal family in which the lines between feminine and masculine duties and roles are clearly demarcated. In rural society, the man is the head of household, and the family is organised as an extended family, with rules of reciprocity regulating the behaviour of its members. In families, older members have higher status than younger members, and within that classification, men have higher status than women. With status comes responsibilities: the man as the head of household is the provider, and the woman is the nurturer. All members of the family are expected to respect the eldest living male and accept his word on marriage, inheritance, work, education, and so on.

Women's new roles as industrial wage earners and de facto heads of households have radically challenged the normative family order. Women now make critical decisions pertaining to work-related issues, children's education, marriage, and so on. While migration has stretched workers' physical proximity to their extended families, family life has not completely dissolved into a nuclear structure. Instead, the nuclearisation of the family has gradually encroached into their urban lives, disturbing prevailing kin relations. Sarah White has noted how the "cultural norm of a joint family household . . . is being gradually eroded, as more separate ('nuclear') households become the norm" (White 2012: 1443). In rural society, these separations are visible in the spatial arrangement of the living quarters – there are usually three to four small units (based on the number of sons) that all face the family courtyard. Decisions pertaining to the family, marriage, divorce, the sale of land, education, and migration are all discussed among the extended family, although individual sons live with their families in separate households. The nuclearisation of the family in urban slums is more radical because there is no shared space and family members do not encounter each other on a regular basis, limiting familial support for these women.

In the survey I took in 2014, 59 percent of the women in the city lived in nuclear family units, but they maintained close ties with their parents and in-laws in the village. They spoke to family members on the phone and visited them during the Muslim high holidays. However, this was not the nuclear family of Western industrialisation, which is less attached to close kinship ties. In examining this new urban nuclear household in the making, I was interested in mapping the gender dynamics around housework. In that survey, 59 percent of women also mentioned that their husbands and children helped with housework. Most of the women surveyed were young (under the age of thirty-five), and many had met their spouses through romantic alliances formed in the city. Within the younger generation, especially among those couples where both husband and wife worked in the factory, there was a shared household mechanism at play. In one interview a young woman said: "I cook the evening meal before I leave for work in the morning; my husband warms the food and feeds our children in the evening." Her husband, who was sitting next to her, said that the income she made from working overtime at the factory helped the family have some additional comforts, so he was happy to do the chores when she could not manage. While the gendered expectations around women's work (she is expected to cook the meal) had not changed, the man's expected role had shifted. He now participated in housework by taking care of the children and feeding them.

Among the older women workers, most of their husbands did not do household chores. An older male worker explained the situation to me in the following terms: "Only 5 percent of my male co-workers help their garment-worker wives. Helping one's spouse is a result of education and social awareness. Many of the older men do not possess that attitude. For them, a wife must do double duty, earn wages as well as keep them well fed and sexually satisfied." He added that men who were socialised in the city and saw their mothers work in the factory tend to be more supportive versus young men who grew up in the village, where they did not see their fathers help their mothers with housework.

Marriage, divorce and sexuality

One area of increased autonomy for the women was in their ability to choose their husbands, a choice they lacked in the villages. Many of the women now meet their husbands at work, and they contract love marriages as opposed to arranged marriages. But these romantic alliances have not increased marital security for women. In many instances, most of these marriages break down after the birth of a child, usually a daughter due to the lower social value placed on a female child. In Muslim families, first-cousin marriage is common, and rural marriages usually occur among close kin to reduce property disputes and the fragmentation of the family unit. So, the families are familiar with the prospective groom and bride. With increased migration, however, that relationship is being challenged. Factory women now meet men from different regions of the country. While their choice of potential partners has widened, these spousal choices decrease a family's ability to scrutinise the character of prospective grooms prior to marriage. The consequences of these marriages can be devastating. After marriage, many women find out that the man they married misrepresented himself. She discovers that he already has a wife in the village, is a gambler, does not have a job, is physically abusive, and/or demands that she hand over her money to him. In such cases, the younger women tend to initiate divorce. Due to their education and higher income potential as compared to that of older women, the younger women I met more often refuse to accept husbands whose behaviour they do not condone. Had they remained in the village, these women would be subordinated to the wishes of their family, and older male relatives would mediate marital disputes on their behalf.

Divorces and separations are considered family affairs in which older members of the family determine the outcome. If the two parties cannot come to an amicable resolution, a village *shalish* (public adjudication) is held, and the community participates in the process. Nowadays with the advent of courts in small towns, families often seek adjudication by a presiding judge instead of the village *shalish*. During the peak of micro-credit in the 1990s and early 2000s, NGOs, especially BRAC, taught rural women how to properly register marriages and divorces in order to educate them about their marital rights. These NGOs taught women and men that verbal divorce, the customary practice of a man saying "I divorce you" three times, was not legal according to the Muslim Family Law Ordinance of 1961.[12] I found that many families supported their daughters when they wanted a divorce or separation. What I discovered was that the families saw their garment-factory daughters as conduits to income. By supporting their daughter's marital break-up, the family could make full claims on her income for their financial needs – medical expenses, a new roof, a sibling's education, etc. That these marital breakdowns are a recent phenomenon becomes obvious when we compare an older generation tied to agricultural production against a new generation of workers connected to migration and industrial work. All the parents of the older women I interviewed had remained married despite poverty, whereas their factory daughters faced marital dissolution soon after marriage. Consequently, poverty, while a critical factor, was not the sole cause of the rise in marital separations among the younger generation.

While there are several reasons as to why men abandoned their wives, one key factor that emerged from my study was these women's new sense of self as wage-earning factory workers who exercised control over their income. When their husbands demanded the money, the women would talk back to their husbands and say, "It is my money, I will spend it as I please." These are forms of speech that are new and threatening to male authority. The men felt that they should not have to ask their wives for money. For them, it was easy to blame women and not the factory management for their loss of income or their inability

---

12 Muslim Family Laws 1961, http://bdlaws.minlaw.gov.bd/act-305/section-13539.html.

to find jobs, and this led to an increase in violence perpetrated against their spouses. This is not to suggest that all Bangladeshi rural men abandoned their wives and families or abused their wives. Rather, this is an indication that we need to seriously engage with the dynamic of spousal abandonment that is on the upswing among this demographic.

As mentioned earlier, it was uncommon to find Hindu women workers in the garment industry, and even less common to find inter-religious marriages among Hindu women and Muslim men; they do occur although those statistics are not available. Below is the story of Shikha, a Hindu woman who married a Muslim man against her family's wishes.

Shikha, a twenty-two-year-old Hindu garment worker, had married a Muslim man she met at work against her family's wishes. Soon after their marriage, she found out that he had been married twice before, a fact he hid from her. After she had a child with him, her husband abandoned her for another woman. With a seven-month-old baby to care for, she could not return to work. It was at this time that her mother began to help her. Finally, her mother convinced her father to take her back. Shikha now lives with her parents and has returned to work at the factory. However, she has remained Muslim.

Her marriage to a Muslim man had social consequences for her parents. They could no longer visit their village because their daughter was now an outcast of their Hindu community. Shikha could return to her Hindu faith through a process known as purification (*prayeshchitra*), but she said that she would not do that. When asked to explain her decision, she replied:

> For a Muslim woman, the social sanctions against marriage are not as severe as those for Hindu women. As a divorced woman, it would be difficult for me to marry a Hindu man, whereas that is not the case in Islam. Remarriage of divorced women and widows is allowed in Islam. Also, my Muslim daughter will not be accepted within my former Hindu community. So, why should I convert back to Hinduism since it will not offer me social protection?

Shikha's life did not turn out the way she hoped it would. In her case, her parents stepped in to help. Regardless of age and religion, women as wage-earning factory workers are able to exercise some autonomy over their private lives that they previously lacked. As most of my case studies document, these choices do not always work out, but this indicates that the sphere of choices is broadening for Bangladeshi women.

Summarising Older Worker's Lives

In comparing the life courses of a generation of older workers (those over forty-five years old) and a younger generation of workers (those under thirty-five) from my ethnographic data, the following key differences emerge.

First, the difference in the earning capacity of the older versus younger workers was a major issue. Between 1994 and 2006, workers' wages remained stagnant at $12 per month. After widespread protests, workers' monthly wages were raised thrice: to $22 in 2006, $30 in 2010, and $63 in 2013 (Hasan 2019: 60). The last wage increase was to $90 per month in 2018. These later wage increases did not benefit older workers because they had entered factory work in the 1980s, when wages were unregulated, abysmally low, and there was no national wage board. In comparison, younger women who entered factory work after 2006 earned more and could save and spend money on themselves.

Second, the older workers had low levels of education, most between a third- or fifth-grade education, and many were illiterate. As a result, most of them could not read the documents that factory owners made them sign when they hired and fired them. The younger workers had between an eighth- and twelfth-grade education and could read their hiring and firing documents. This was a result of the 1994 government policy that made primary education universal and offered free stipends to girls to remain in school. While the older women recognised the manifold indignities of factory work, they had fewer resources with which to resist factory-level oppression compared to younger cohorts of workers who were better informed about their labour rights.

This landscape of change in the lives of older and younger workers brings us to the last observation. Where both older and younger women's lives converged was in their private lives and their search for the good life of love and care. For the most part, both categories of women failed to attain the loving companionship they sought from their husbands and marriages. There were women who found a sustainable life, as Hena's story below shows, but it came at a personal cost.

Hena's story

I first met Hena on September 28, 2017. She had retired as a senior sewing operator in 2017, and her wages totalled taka 7,700. She said that her age was approximately fifty. That would make her birth year 1967. Her mother died when Hena was a child, and her father remarried. Hena said she could not live with her stepmother; they constantly argued. Finally, when she was around eight years old, she went to live with her paternal uncle and aunt. In 1982, when she was fifteen years old, her uncle and aunt married Hena off to a vegetable vendor who was ten years older than her. For the first five years of her marriage, she lived with her parents-in-laws. Hena said that her husband loved her. But within a few years, his business began to lose money. By 1988 they had come to Dhaka to look for work. Initially they lived with a cousin who worked at a garment factory, and he helped secure a job for Hena at his factory. The garment industry was only a decade old at that time, and workers' wages were very low. She was twenty-one years old when she became a garment factory worker. She joined as a helper (a sewing operator's assistant) and made taka 150 ($5) per month. Her husband began to drive a three-wheeled taxi, which is a popular mode of passenger transport in Dhaka.

They lived in a slum close to the factory where Hena worked, and she soon gave birth to her first child. She and her husband were doing relatively well, and they bought a TV for entertainment. A young girl who lived next door would come and watch TV in their house. It was at this time that her husband developed a romantic relationship with this girl. Then one day, he married her and left; this was in 1992. He lived with this woman for twelve years.

After he left, Hena's life completely changed. She took her daughter to live with her mother-in-law in the village. Although her husband had left her, her parents-in-law fulfilled their kin obligations and looked after their grandchild. Hena continued to work in the garment industry to raise enough money for her and her daughter's upkeep. In the first fifteen years of her work life, she suffered a lot of instability and changed factories several times. For the last fifteen years – between 2003 until 2017 – she worked at the same factory, and she was able to save for retirement. However, due to long-term work and a poor diet, her health began to suffer. During her factory life, she often worked late-night shifts. When I met her, she said she suffered from severe insomnia and constantly felt exhausted. In addition, she developed arthritis in her hands, and has frequent headaches and overall poor health. She said she once fainted from weakness in the factory. She has also developed a serious lung infection from working in poorly ventilated factories where the air is full of cotton dust from the manufacture of clothing.

Almost after seven years, her husband contacted her again in 1999. They renewed their conjugal relations although he still lived with his second wife. During this time, she had another daughter with him. Then, in 2003, her husband got into a road accident and was sentenced to five years in jail. During his incarceration, she visited him regularly and brought him home-cooked meals. His second wife no longer maintained any contact. After her husband was released from jail, they began their life together again. Although her husband betrayed her, she believes he really loves her. She said that she never has to ask him for housekeeping money; he always gives it to her voluntarily. He also buys her new clothes. Her husband said that when he was in jail, neither his second wife nor his brother helped him; only Hena was there. According to Hena, she now means everything to him. When I asked Hena why she wanted to live with a man who abandoned her, she said very plainly, "Because I love him, and I knew that he would come back to me."

When she retired in 2017, Hena was supposed to get taka 90,000 (around $1,125) from her retirement fund. She only received taka 63,000 ($787). She said that she did not fight for this additional money because she felt beaten down by the system. "I would never win against factory management. They are powerful and devious." She invested taka 50,000 from her retirement funds in a savings account. Hena said that even though she worked very hard all her life, she was able to achieve two of her goals: she was able to educate her younger daughter and prepare her to attend college. Her older daughter joined the garment factory at a young age. Together Hena and her elder daughter bought a small piece of land in the village. In summing up her life, Hena said, "Am I happy? I cannot answer that question. I am quite sick from long-term factory work, and my health expenses are draining our finances. But garment work gave me confidence and a lifeline. Now I can voice my opinions. My husband listens to me. I could buy a small piece of land in the village. As for my future, one day I will build a house and return to the village to spend the rest of my life." In a later communication during COVID in 2020, I found out that Hena's health had deteriorated further, and she had to mortgage the piece of land to pay medical bills. Her younger daughter had withdrawn from school and joined the garment factory to help support the family.

Hena's life replicates the life course of most older workers in Bangladesh's garment industry that I have met. She was born into a poor family in the village. As a child, she did not receive any education. She was married off at a young age. She came to the city and engaged in garment factory work. Her husband left her and did not support her financially. She had two children she raised on her own. Then her husband returned to her. After thirty years of hard work, Hena's life was a zero-sum game. She failed to educate her younger daughter and lost the small plot of land she had purchased. What Hena did achieve, though, was the support of her family in her old age, which was missing in the lives of most of the older women interviewed.

Through factory work, these older women earned a limited form of sovereignty over their lives. But their circumstances also forced them to take their lives into their own hands. They left abusive spouses, stood up to factory management when they faced work-place injustice, and tried to build better lives for their children. The goal of these older factory women was to help their children reach the new middle class emerging through industrial capitalism in Bangladesh. But many of them recognised the limits of upward mobility in a deeply hierarchical society. As one older woman said to me, "My son has received his bachelor's degree. He wants to work in a government office (become a civil servant), but I do not have the social contacts to help him. He now works at a store." Ultimately, these older women's lives remained trapped in globalisation's false promises.

References

Bhattacharjee, Anannya. 2006. "The Public/Private Mirage: Mapping Homes and Undomesticating Violence Work in the South Asian Immigrant Community." In *The Anthropology of the State*, edited by Aradhana Sharma and Akhil Gupta, 308–329. Malden, MA: Wiley Blackwell.

Feldman, Shelley, and Jakir Hossain. 2019. "The Long durée and the Promise of Export-led Development." In *Labor, Global Supply Chains, and the Garment Industry in South Asia: Bangladesh after Rana Plaza*, edited by Sanchita Banerjee Saxena, 21–44. London: Routledge.

Caleca, Alexandra Rose. 2014. "The Effect of Globalization on Bangladesh's Ready-Made Garment Industry: The High Cost of Cheap Clothing." *Brookline Journal of International Law* 40, no. 1: 279–320.

Elson, Diane, and Ruth Pearson. 1981."'Nimble Fingers Make Cheap Workers': An Analysis of Women's Employment in Third World Export Manufacturing." *Feminist Review* 7: 87–107.

Freeman, Carla. 2020. "Feeling Neoliberal." *Feminist Anthropology* 1: 71–88. Accessed January 3, 2022. www.feministanthropology.org.

Fuentes, Annette, and Barbara Ehrenreich. 1983. *Women in the Global Factory.* Boston: South End Press.

Hareven, Tamara K. 2001. "The Impact of Family History and the Life Course on Social History. In *Family History Revisited: Comparative Perspectives*, edited by Richard Wall, Tamara K. Hareven, and Josef Ehmer, 21–39. Newark: University of Delaware Press.

Hasan. Mohammad. 2019. "Minimum Wage in Readymade Garment Industry in Bangladesh." *Asian Business Consortium:* 57–66.

Hewamanne, Sandya. 2008. *Stitching Identities in Free Trade Zone.* Philadelphia: University of Pennsylvania Press.

Huq, Chaumtoli. 2019. "Opportunities and Limitations of the Accord: Need for a Worker Organizing Model." In *Labor, Global Supply Chains, and the Garment Industry in South Asia: Bangladesh after Rana Plaza*, edited by Sanchita Banerjee Saxena, 65–83. London: Routledge.

Kabeer, Naila. 2002. *The Power to Choose: Bangladesh Garment Workers in London and Dhaka.* London: Verso.

Kabeer, Naila. 2019. "The Evolving Politics of Labor Standards in Bangladesh: Taking Stock and Looking Forward." In *Labor, Global Supply Chains, and the Garment Industry in South Asia: Bangladesh after Rana Plaza*, edited by Sanchita Banerjee Saxena, 231–260. London: Routledge.

Karim, Lamia. 2011. *Microfinance and Its Discontents: Women in Debt in Bangladesh.* Minneapolis: University of Minnesota Press.

Khan, Emran, and Abdullah Karim. 2017. "The Prevention of Women and Child Repression Act 2000: A Study of Implementation Process from 2003 to 2017." *Journal of Humanities and Social Science* 22, no. 7: 34–42.

Kibria, Nazli. 1998. "Becoming a Garments Worker: The Mobilization of Women into the Garments Factories of Bangladesh." *United Nations Institute for Social Development*, no. 9: UNRISD Occasional Paper: 1–23.

Darrow, Mac. 2003. *Between Light and Shadow: The World Bank, International Monetary Fund and International Human Rights Law.* London: Bloomsbury Academic Publishing.

Marcus, George. 1995. "Ethnography In/Of the World System: The Emergence of Multi-sited Ethnography." *Annual Review of Anthropology* 24: 95–117.

Mezzadri, Alessandra, and Sanjita Majumdar. 2019. "The Afterlife of Cheap Labor: Bangalore Garment Workers from the Factory to the Informal Economy." *FEDI Network,* Working Paper No. 12.18.1.

Muhammad, Anu. 2013. "Bangladesh RMG: Global Chain of Profit and Deprivation." *bdnews24.com,* May 17, 2013. https://opinion.bdnews24.com/2013/05/17/bangladesh-rmg-global-chain-of-profit-and-deprivation/.

Nash, June, and Maria Fernandez-Kelly. 1983. *Women, Men and the International Division of Labor.* Albany, NY: SUNY Press.

Ong, Aihwa. 2010. *Spirits of Resistance and Capitalist Discipline: Factory Women in Malaysia.* 2nd ed. Albany, NY: SUNY.

Rahman, Shahidur. 2015. *Broken Promises of Globalization: The Case of the Bangladesh Garment Industry.* Lanham, MD: Rowman & Littlefield.

Saxena, Sanchita Banerjee. 2014. *Made in Bangladesh, Cambodia and Sri Lanka: The Labor Behind the Global Garments and Textiles Industries.* Amherst, MA: Cambria Press.

Saxena, Sanchita Banerjee, ed. 2019. *Labor, Global Supply Chains, and the Garment Industry in South Asia: Bangladesh after Rana Plaza.* London: Routledge.

Saxena, Sanchita Banerjee, and Dorothy Baumann-Pauly. 2019. "Off the Radar: Sub-contracting in Bangladesh's RMG Sector." In *Labor, Global Supply Chains, and the Garment Industry in South Asia: Bangladesh After Rana Plaza,* edited by Sanchita Banerjee Saxena, 45–62. London: Routledge.

Siddiqi, Dina. 2019. "Spaces of Exception: National Interest and the Labor of Sedition." In *Labor, Global Supply Chains, and the Garment Industry in South Asia: Bangladesh after Rana Plaza,* edited by Sanchita Banerjee Saxena, 100–114. London: Routledge.

Van Klaveren, Maarten. 2016. "Rise of the Garment Industry." In *Wages in Context in the Garment Industry in Asia,* 18. Amsterdam: Wageindicator Foundation.

White, Sara C. 2012. "Beyond the Paradox: Religion, Family and Modernity in Contemporary Bangladesh." *Modern Asian Studies* 46, no. 5: 1429–1458.

Wolf, Diane. 1992. *Factory Daughters: Gender, Household Dynamics, and Rural Industrialization in Java.* Berkeley: University of California Press.

Susan Zimmermann

The Changing Politics of Women's Work and the Making of Extended Childcare Leave in State-Socialist Hungary, Europe, and Internationally: Shifting the Scene

On October 4, 1966, the politburo of the Hungarian Socialist Workers' Party (*Politikai Bizottság* of the *Magyar Szocialista Munkáspárt* MSZMP) made a landmark decision that was to substantively alter the labour and life course regime in this Eastern European state-socialist country. Working mothers of children born starting from January 1, 1967 could, after the expiration of mandatory maternity leave, choose to stay home until the child turned two and a half (soon it would be three) and receive a substantial childcare leave benefit during this prolonged period ("MSZMP PB October 1966:" esp. 5–6). With the introduction of extended childcare leave under the name Childcare Benefit (*gyermekgondozási segély*), soon widely known as *gyes* (expressions such as "she's on *gyes*" have been ever present in the everyday life of the country since the introduction of the benefit), Hungary became a trendsetter for an altered life course regime among many countries in both state-socialist and capitalist Europe. At the time, Austria alone had a regulation, introduced in 1960, that allowed qualifying mothers to choose to stay home until the first birthday of the child and receive, depending on other family income, a benefit covered by funds from the unemployment benefit scheme (Bundesgesetzblatt 1960, Laws 240, 242; Manetsgruber 2016: 4–6).[1]

Extended childcare leave was a policy instrument that touched upon but also departed from an inherited policy vision and practice that addressed maternity and women's responsibility for the care of infants and small children. Adjacent instruments included: maternity protection and benefits before and after childbirth

Acknowledgements: I would like to thank Josef Ehmer for his inspiring comments on the original version of this chapter (which looked very different compared to this final text), and the ZARAH Team (https://zarah-ceu.org/team-members/) for their comments, which helped me sharpen the argument pursued in the final version.

Funding note: This chapter belongs to the research project ZARAH, which has received funding from the European Research Council (ERC) under the European Union's Horizon 2020 research and innovation programme (Grant Agreement No. 833691).

1 As a rule, single mothers could receive the full benefit equaling the unemployment benefit, whereas mothers in partnerships tended to receive 50 percent less.

typically granted for (certain groups of) working women and also envisioned as a measure inclusive of all women; "mothers' pensions," often imagined as a benefit enabling single mothers of infants and small children to stay home; and family allowances aimed at supporting child rearing. Like the newly emerging politics of extended childcare leave, all these policies addressed the principal tension between women's paid and unpaid work. Yet extended childcare leave was also, as we shall see, a historically new response to a historical change in the world of paid work, namely women's growing involvement in and, in particular, the changing forms of their involvement in paid work. Extended childcare leave, while reifying and redescribing women's responsibility for the care of infants and small children, was aimed at enabling women's more consistent and sustained involvement in more regular forms of employment.

In the decades after 1945, European state-socialist countries made progress in terms of bringing about a refashioning of women's paid work in international comparison, and from the late 1960s/early 1970s onwards, state-socialist Europe led the way in bringing about policy changes which, in the end, produced a new politics of extended childcare leave. The coupling of these two developments happened against a particular socio-economic background. Beginning in the 1940s, the countries now belonging to the Soviet sphere of influence pursued a large-scale program of state-led catch-up development characterised by rapid economic growth and industrialisation, an expanding service sector, a steadily expanding labour market, and rapid social transformation. Work, including women's emancipation through paid work, was at the core of the societal vision to which state socialism aspired. Unsurprisingly, then, in the scholarship, the "Eastern bloc" has been described as a society of full-time workers, implying a more-or-less uniform labour and life course regime imposed on both women and men, barely changing over time, and characterised by long-term and full-time involvement in the world of paid work.

In this chapter, against the backdrop of developments in other state-socialist as well as Western European countries, I discuss the emergence and expansion of extended childcare leave for working mothers in Hungary and parallel innovations in the international policy-making of the International Labour Organization (ILO). I argue that such a focus on the history of gender, work, and the life course helps us move beyond the amorphous vision of state socialism as a society of full-time workers and allows us to place the history of gender and labour in state-socialist Europe in a broader framework, thereby overcoming the implicit Western European bias in European labour history. The history of state-socialist Europe as a trend-setter for a changing international and European labour and life course regime brings to the fore an array of motivations and trajectories of – in the end – converging social policy reform in East and West as well as internationally which evolved around issues of work and labour. "Thinking together" Western European, Eastern European, and international arguments and actions that informed the introduction of extended childcare leave and related measures makes visible both differences and similarities. The integrative perspective suggested in this chapter points to the limited representation, both on the international stage at the time and in scholarship up to the present day, of Eastern European developments and actors, among them state-socialist trade unions and women trade unionists who, in their own way, aimed to present and represent women workers' experiences and viewpoints.

Working Women with Small Children in Europe after 1945: Actors and Interests in East and West, and Internationally

The introduction of extended paid childcare leave in Hungary in 1967 and analogous schemes in other countries was a response to a particular historical conjuncture. From the 1960s onwards, policy-makers within countries and internationally began to address an overarching, shared policy challenge. This challenge resulted from dissimilar trajectories of women's involvement in the labour markets of European state-socialist and capitalist countries and the common tension between paid and unpaid work faced by working women with small children.

When European countries west and east of the "Iron Curtain" entered an era of labour-intensive economic growth after the post-1945 reconstruction years, the strategies employed to meet the growing demand for labour differed markedly. Not least based in the doctrine of women's emancipation through paid work, state-socialist countries pursued a politics of involving ever larger segments of the female population, including women with small children, in full-time, paid employment. This politics was facilitated by the payment of low (though highly unequal) wages to both women and men, and it left intact traditionalist ideas and practices of women's responsibility for childcare and family work. The politics of labour under state socialism in this sense can be characterised as a dual-earner/one-wage/one-caregiver economy (Zimmermann 2010). By contrast, from the later 1950s onwards, many Western European countries embarked on a politics of meeting the growing demand for labour by importing migrant labour from the southern European periphery and beyond, as well as from (formerly) colonised territories. By 1970, the proportion of the foreign population in leading industrial countries such as France and the Federal Republic of Germany reached approximately 5 percent, and it would increase further (Tomka 2013: 40–41).[2] Women's labour force participation ratios in general remained visibly behind the figures produced by state socialism, and many more women with small children stayed home. The resulting differences in terms of women's overall involvement in paid work are summarised in Table 1, while Table 2 shows that in Eastern Europe, indeed, many more women of the age groups in which family responsibilities tended to peak stayed in the workforce as compared to women in Western Europe.

Table 1: Involvement of women in paid work, around 1960.

Region	Economically active women, % of total female population	Women workers, % of total economically active population
Eastern Europe (incl. YU, without SU)	40	42
Soviet Union	41	48
Western Europe	29	33
Southern Europe (ES, PT, EL, IT)	20	25

Source: ILO Estimate based on ILO Statistics, given in International Labour Office 1963:25.

Because of the growing need for workers, by the 1960s, policy-makers in the Western industrial countries and internationally felt the need for reforms and regulations that would enable and entice women to stay in or return (faster) to the labour market once they had given birth to one or more children. Such measures could also help make young women conceive of paid employment as a long-term prospect and contribute to the emergence of a reliable, dedicated, and productive female labour force.

State-socialist Eastern Europe had begun to push young women onto the labour market earlier with the goal of turning them into lifelong full-time workers. In Hungary, women's share in the active workforce rose from 29 percent in 1949 to 36 percent in 1960, and it would reach 41 percent in 1970. In the industrial sector, women's share was even higher, reaching 33 percent in 1960 and 42 percent in 1970. Women's labour-force participation ratio (i.e. the number of active working women in the female population of working age) rose dynamically from 35 percent in 1949 to 50 percent in 1960. By 1970, the ratio would be 64 percent, to which, at this point, another 6 percent of inactive female earners had been added; the latter

---

2 The state-socialist countries imported very few foreign workers in comparison.

figure had risen sharply after the introduction of *gyes* in 1967, from less than 1 percent in 1960 (Központi Statisztikai Hivatal 1977: Tables 1.1., 1.3.). Table 2 demonstrates that these developments were driven in particular by the increase of the percentage of economically active women between twenty-four- and forty-four years old.

Table 2: Percentage of economically active women by age group.

Country	15–19 years	20–24 years	25–34 years	35–44 years	45–54 years	55–64 years	65 and over
Bulgaria (1956)	48	69	71	77	69	49	23
Poland (1950)	57	68	61	64	62	51	29
Austria (1951)	73	74	50	46	44	31	13
France (1954)	43	57	41	42	47	39	13
Sweden (1950)	54	57	32	27	30	23	8
Hungary (1950)	56	45	*age 25–29* 36 *age 30–34* 33	*age 35–39* 30 *age 40–44* 29	*age 45–49* 28 *age 50–54* 27	*age 55–59* 29 *age 60–64* 27	20
Hungary (1960)	54	55	*age 25–29* 49 *age 30–34* 49	*age 35–39* 51 *age 40–44* 52	*age 45–49* 50 *age 50–54* 46	*age 55–59* 31 *age 60–64* 26	20

Source: International Labour Office 1963: 33 (all data except Hungary); International Labour Office 2000:83 (Hungary).

Throughout the 1960s, Hungarian policy-makers were confronted with mounting societal and economic tension related to the presence of ever more women in the labour force. Among other things, the "unreliability" of working women with small children who failed to juggle the demands of paid labour and unpaid family work caused problems for the economy at large, and the industrial sector in particular. Women's problems were exacerbated by the fact – as a report submitted to the politburo as late as 1973 put it – that "[t]he division of labour in the family is ossified and mirrors the impact of conservative views" ("MSZMP PB February 1973:" report on population matters, esp. 15). In the policy reform process that eventually would lead up to the introduction of *gyes*, high-ranking women trade unionists responsible for women's affairs within the National Federation of Trade Unions (*Szakszervezetek Országos Szövetsége*, SZOT) played, as we shall see, an important role; they did so with reference to ongoing and expected developments on the international plane, and within the ILO in particular. SZOT was one of the key actors involved in the preparations for any relevant decision-making involving the labour force. In August 1965, Erzsébet Déri,[3] the SZOT officer responsible for women's issues, reported to her superior on the preparations for *gyes*. Déri in her "strictly confidential" internal memo put her finger on the tensions surrounding the employment *en masse* of women with small children. The memo captured both working mothers' escapism from and the intrusion of the consequences of the burden of unpaid care work on the world of paid work in general and demanding factory work in particular in an exemplary manner:

> There is no sufficient supply of nurseries for working women with children. The establishment of nurseries is expensive . . . 70 percent [of the existing nurseries] are not up-to-date and adequate . . . At present, we speak about the general overburdening of women, in particular where there is a small child. The households are not adequately equipped with machinery, and existing apparatuses are expensive . . . Another factor impacting the [potential childcare] benefit is the fact that in our day, one could count on grandmothers as child educators within the family only to a very limited extent. Elderly women today receive a retirement benefit and, indeed, do not depend on their children's support . . . [They] want to live autonomously, independently. Another issue is that the elderly women are not suited to bring up children, especially if we think of grandmothers from villages in relation to urban youngsters (religiosity, anachronistic diet, and so on) . . . A woman who has an infant cannot meet her workplace's expectations because she must care for the family and the infant, or, more precisely, she is not a full-value member of the workforce. Until the child reaches the age of one . . . they miss 160 out of 290 working days. Their irregular absences negatively influence production . . . In factories with two and three shifts, twenty-five percent of the mothers of infants leave their jobs for good, using childrearing [as justification] . . . The present state is an impediment from the perspective of the mother and the infant, too. ("Déri, *Feljegyzés gyes javaslat* 1965")

Erzsébet Déri crafted her memo in response to a meeting with a representative of the Ministry of Labour who had informed her about plans related to *gyes*. A few days later, Déri – in a separate memo ("Déri, *Feljegyzés beszélgetés* 1965") – recounted conversations she pursued at that earlier meeting with seven women workers at one of the sites of the Hungarian Cloth Factory (*Magyar Posztógyár*) located in the outskirts of Budapest. Déri proactively sought to convey the voices

---

3 In Hungarian, her name would invariably be given as Mrs. Ernő Déri since the name of married women at the time was given as "Mrs." and then the given and family names of their husband. Many women officials and other women in everyday parlance used to give their husband's family name and their own given name. Whenever I know the given name of a woman, I use this version.

of those "who are the most competent (*a legilletékesebbek*)" – i. e. the women concerned – to the trade union leadership as a point of reference for SZOT's decision-
making. Déri recounted what the workers had said "as close to their original words
as possible (*lehetőség szerint szó szerint*)" in her memo.[4] She had asked her interviewees about their views, concerns, reflections, and suggestions as working
women with small children. The narratives generated shed light on the real-life
conditions under which women with small children, working in a three-shift factory, struggled to combine paid and unpaid work to ensure a livelihood for their
families. After giving birth, women workers had the opportunity to bundle together various benefits and legal and de facto avenues to acquire a few months of paid
leave from factory work. After this period was over, some women took additional
unpaid leave; others placed their child in the factory or neighbourhood nursery, or
they hired a private nanny for around 500 forints per month. In terms of reconciling conflicting time commitments, the women faced two key problems: what to do
with the child if it had to be withdrawn from the nursery because of illness or an
outbreak of an infectious disease – a constant occurrence, according to the interviews; and how to juggle three-shift work and childcare? The latter issue directly
combined with the material question: some women were offered the option to
switch to permanent morning shifts, but this would come with a considerable
loss of earnings (e. g., "300–400 Forint"). The complete loss of earnings was, of
course, the key driving force to return to the factory for women who had taken
unpaid leave. As to their standing in the factory, the women testified to solidarity
and assistance, including offers to switch to one-shift work, as well as conflicts. One
woman explained: "My main shift foreman is a woman, and she still doesn't understand my trouble. She criticises me a lot, telling me she can't count on me because I am absent a lot; but it's not my fault, it hurts me the most when my child is
sick, and on top of that, I don't make any money. I do understand her as well, because for her, the [production] plan, and not my personal problems, is the most
important."

Déri recorded that she had avoided telling the women the reasons for her inquiries. Still, several interviewees declared that if they just received monthly support of 600 or 800 forint they would be willing to stay at home, some happily so;
gyes, which was only disbursed after the expiration of the generously funded regular maternity leave, would be set at 600 forints, which at the time was approximately half the wages earned by the women interviewed by Déri, or around 40
percent of a women's average income [Haney 2002: 104; Göndör 2012: 71]). The

---

4 The report does not give the names of the women and notes what the women said in the first
person singular.

women came up with other options too, all of which were intended to ease the tension between paid and unpaid work, including part-time labour and housework.

Hungary embarked on preparations for *gyes* during a period when the politics of women's work had attracted renewed attention in the international arena. The question of wage-earning mothers in industrial and rapidly industrialising countries constituted one focal point of the related activities. In the ILO, the initiatives that eventually culminated in the adoption of Recommendation 123 on "Employment (Women with Family Responsibilities)" in 1965 reached back into the 1950s (International Labour Office 1964: 71–72).[5] In the early period, the subject to be addressed was often phrased using terms such as "married women" or "working mothers" engaged in regular, non-home-based employment rather than talking about working women "with family responsibilities," terminology that was introduced somewhat later. There was consensus early on that additional social measures "were needed in order to enable" this growing group of women engaged in employment "to be good mothers and to combine home and work responsibilities harmoniously" (ILO Governing Body June 1962: 46).

In October 1959, the newly installed tripartite ILO Panel of Consultants on the Problems of Women Workers (replacing the earlier Correspondence Committee on Women's Work) discussed the problems of women with family responsibilities at its first meeting. The Soviet government was represented by Antonina Vistavkina, the Senior Inspector of the State Labour and Wages Committee, and Ines Cerlesi was present as an observer on behalf of the communist-leaning World Federation of Trade Unions (WFTU) ("ILO Meeting Panel of Consultants 1959"; ILO Governing Body March 1959: 24–26, 100–101; ILO Governing Body May/June 1959: 46). For panel members, it "was evident that concepts influencing the employment and governing the approaches to the problems of married women of all categories varied considerably according to the country, its philosophy, its economic position and its experience and needs as it developed as a nation" ("ILO Meeting Panel of Consultants 1959," Appendix: 14). The panel deliberated on various support options targeting married women at work, including part-time work, "measures for the lightening of household tasks," institutional childcare, and the option for mothers to stay at home with their children. Already at this point, the idea of employment guarantees for mothers who wished to remain home beyond the regular period of maternity leave was advocated for by one panel member.[6] This measure was also dis-

---

5 The 1955 session of the ILC had adopted Resolutions on part-time employment and in relation to the employment of women with dependent young children, expressing the hope that future sessions and the ILO Regional Conferences would come back to the question.

6 Neither the report summarising the discussion and recommendations of the meeting laid before the Governing Body of the ILO nor the related archival material identify the panel member.

cussed as a possible option in the extensive preparatory report the International Labour Office laid before the Panel of Consultants. The report highlighted the difficulties working women faced trying "to make the ends of time meet" as they combined their work and home lives. Describing this problem as possibly "the crux of the next phase of social policy relating to women workers," the report discussed various solutions, problems, and contradictions at length and pointed to the open-endedness of developments to come ("ILO Working Paper 1959").

The Panel of Consultants also recognised the urgency of the problem of the "employment of married women," advising the ILO to expand and intensify its activities in this policy area, among others. Yet, for the time being, the Panel's sole recommendation was the collection of various data including information on the existing "arrangements for . . . part-time employment," and it summarised:

> It was apparent . . . that national concepts regarding [childcare] . . . were extremely varied. They ranged from a belief in the total responsibility of the parent alone to advocacy of a full-fledged system of state care for children. The latter system was advocated by one consultant [i. e. Panel member, SZ], while others stressed . . . the need for flexibility in plans and measures for the care of children. There was complete agreement on the need to prevent children of all ages from suffering neglect or harm as a result of the mother's absence from the home. . . . General emphasis was placed on the desirability of implementing social policies which would enable married women with young children to stay at home if they so wished. . . . [O]ther suggestions made by individual consultants . . . included . . . that . . . the period of authorized maternity leave without forfeiture of job rights should be studied. ("First Meeting" 1960, incl. all preceding quotes)

A few years later, employment guarantees during a prolonged period of absence from work after the expiration of maternity leave would form the core of ILO Recommendation 123 adopted in 1965, and these guarantees formed one of the two pillars of the Hungarian *gyes* scheme introduced in 1967. The other pillar of *gyes* was a material benefit attached to leave, a key provision that was *not* part of Recommendation 123. When in early 1964 Hungarian women trade unionists and manpower planners developed and promoted the vision of *gyes* with the second pillar included, they did so with a focus on both the tensions around women's work in Hungary and international developments, including the upcoming first discussion of a "Recommendation concerning the employment of women with family responsibilities" by the ILO's International Labour Conference in June and July 1964. In spring 1963, the International Labour Office received detailed material from Hungary. A. Béguin, an officer in the Manpower Planning and Organisation Section, considered the report from Hungary on "*Women in Employment and at Home . . .* very useful in our work, particularly in conjunction with preparations for the 1964" session of the International Labour Conference (ILC). János Timár, head of the Department for Manpower Planning of the Hungarian National Planning Office (*Országos Terv-*

hivatal), told Béguin "about the work going on in Hungary on questions relating to the employment of women," and Béguin had informed him "of our special interest in the question" ("Letter Béguin to Bényi April 1963"). In February 1964, Timár, who in Hungary would soon play a key role in realising the plans for *gyes*,[7] publicised the vision for *gyes* in the *International Labour Review*, the ILO's globally esteemed flagship publication. He explained:

> For economic reasons also, we have set ourselves the aim of further increasing as far as possible the number (and consequently the ratio) of active women in the economy. This will raise the level of employment of the population and, together with the increase in productivity, will result in a rising standard of living . . . [A]n estimate can be made of the ratio and the number of women in employment in 1980. But before this figure can be adopted for planning purposes, the question of household work must also be considered. When a significantly increasing number of women have been drawn into organised social labour they must . . . be relieved of a major part of the work connected with raising children and with the household . . . [I]nfant care is best undertaken, both from the medical and the educational points of view, by mothers. In the long-term plan, therefore, we reckon that the capacity of infant nurseries need not be very greatly enlarged but that *the present fully paid maternity leave of five months for working women must gradually be raised to one year.* For children over one year of age we intend to develop a broad system of kindergartens and day nurseries to enable working mothers to place their children in them, if they wish to, for the whole time they are working. (Timár 1964a: 109–110, emphasis added)

In a detailed analysis published in Hungary – which went to press in May 1964 – Timár discussed the varieties of such a future scheme of extended childcare leave. The description carries the traits of the as yet unknown, a measure whose contours were still in the making; but the goal was clear: "In the longer term, and precisely in view of the much higher employment of women than at present, it will be advisable to further increase maternity leave or to enable working mothers to stay at home at least until the baby is one year old through other means, for example by providing a special family allowance of a higher amount" (Timár 1964b: 48). SZOT's committee in charge of issues related to the "special situation of working women" in March 1964 translated the idea into a concrete demand for a scheme closely resembling what would become *gyes* only a few years later. Referring to the imminent decision-making of "several world organisations," including the ILO and the WFTU, on how to enable working women "to fulfil their duties as family mothers," the committee advocated that children be raised at home until their first birthday; "working mothers" should be enabled to do so via the introduction

---

7 Sociologist Zsuzsa Ferge remembers János Timár and Ervin Frigyes of the National Planning Office as the "inventors *(találták ki)*" of *gyes*. Author's email correspondence with Zsuzsa Ferge, March 3, 2017. Inglot, Szikra, and Rat 2011: 28, similarly talk about Timár as the "father" of *gyes*.

of a new benefit, a "special family allowance" to be paid out for seven months after the expiration of maternity leave (Jelentés a dolgozó nők helyzetéről 1964a). The committee called on SZOT to "study, and then draw up" the relevant scheme (Jelentés a dolgozó nők helyzetéről 1964b),[8] and the leadership of SZOT followed the decision-making proposal of the committee (A SZOT Elnökségének állásfoglalása 1964).

These events in Hungary formed part of multiple international developments and exchanges that responded to challenges related to the increased employment of women of child-bearing age. After careful preparation within and by the International Labour Office, the Governing Body of the ILO decided in two meetings in June and November 1962 that the 1964 session of the ILC would deliberate on the question of "women workers in a changing world." Among the three components singled out for discussion under this overarching heading, the only question suggested for deliberation with a view to its adoption as an ILO-Instrument was "the employment of women with family responsibilities" (ILO Governing Body June 1962: 14–19, 72–73). This meant that in all likelihood, this topic would come up for a vote at the 1965 session of the ILC.

Women from both sides of the "Iron Curtain" played a vital role in exerting pressure on the ILO decision-making process in 1962. In April, ILO Director-General David A. Morse received a delegation of WFTU leaders that included WFTU Secretary Elena Teodorescu, who was head of the federation's department of economic and social affairs and, as such, was responsible for women's issues ("Record of interview April 1962"[9]). Teodorescu emphasised that the ILO's Equal Pay Convention C100, and the issue of women's salaries more generally, were "important, but there were other questions of greater importance. The social problems of women were manifold, and they were of the opinion that now was the time to take the initiative in order to treat this subject on an international basis". In response, the ILO's Director-General reassured the WFTU delegation of the importance he ascribed to the subject – yet, he added that "he was unable to indicate as to when he would be able to deal with the matter as it raised the difficult problem of preparation . . . He also had in mind other problems which were of very great significance, so for him, it was a question of priorities. He assured Mme Teodorescu, however, that he had definitely made up his mind to present a report on this subject at some future date." Upon receiving such a response, WFTU General

---

8 The initial version of the Report by the SZOT committee, likely by mistake, referred to the second and the third Five Year Plans (1961–1970) as period within which to introduce (what would become) *gyes*. The second version, which alone included the demand quoted here, talked about the third and the fourth Five Year Plan.

9 The following quotes come from this same source; typo corrected.

Secretary Louis Saillant pointed to the upcoming WFTU women's conference, high-lighting that the WFTU wished to deal with the problem of women workers, which was "an over-all question . . . on the basis of greater collaboration" with the ILO. "They did not want to do this through the back door but wanted to come through the main entrance."

The meeting between the WFTU leadership and David A. Morse was preceded by a personal conversation between Elizabeth Johnstone, the responsible officer in the International Labour Office for the women's, young workers,' and older work-ers' question, and Elena Teodorescu. Johnstone's report on the meeting demon-strates her willingness to collaborate with the WFTU women[10] on common con-cerns:

> Mrs. Teodorescu explained their preoccupations and plans and told about the Conference on Women Workers' Problems which the [WFTU] plans to hold next year – a Conference which promises to be of some importance, since they plan to build it around some broad but out-standing needs and problems of working women. ... Mrs. Teodorescu said that she hoped that the Director-General would . . . consider including the question of the employment of women in the agenda of an early session of the [ILC]. In this connection, please see my report on the last (16th) session of the [UN] Commission on the Status of Women, in which I men-tioned a similar plea from the [USSR] delegate . . . I told her what we are doing on women workers' problems: the follow-up on equal pay and discrimination in employment; the study on the vocational preparation of girls and women for work life; the study on part-time employment; the study on maternity protection; . . . and the hopes that the Panel of Con-sultants of Women Workers might meet in 1964 after an interval of five years; etc. . . . It seems to me the [WFTU] has no basic preoccupations with women's and youth questions which we do not share . . . and that there are no controversial points as regards programme content and emphasis in these fields, though naturally approaches and solutions differ. ("Note Johnstone April 1962")

Historian Dorothy Sue Cobble has shown that in the months between October 1961 and September 1962, Esther Peterson, Director of the United States' Women's Bu-reau similarly aimed to push the ILO, in "a lonely campaign," towards a "revival of a woman's program," likewise advocating for a focus on employment. Both Pe-terson and Teodorescu had participated in the 1961 session of the ILC; in a letter dated October 1961, Peterson remarked that "delegates from other countries, in-cluding from newly-developed countries, brought home to me the urgency" of the situation (Cobble 2021: 354–359).[11]

---

10 Indeed, she would participate in the WFTU Bucharest conference in 1964.
11 "Lonely campaign" is Cobble' wording, the other two quotes are Peterson's. The US government representative George Weaver, to whom Peterson had turned, indeed urged the Governing Body to include the item on the conference agenda (ILO Governing Body November 1962, 16).

Soon after the Governing Body of the ILO finally made the decision in November 1962 to indeed put the question of women's employment on the agenda of the 1964 session of the ILC, Elena Teodorescu, participating in another meeting between the WFTU leadership and the ILO Director-General, noted "that she was very happy to learn of the decision . . . which corresponded exactly to their wishes" ("Record of interview November 1962").

On the large public stage of the ILC, representatives of the state-socialist world repeatedly emphasised the "absolute equality of rights" women enjoyed in their countries. There, women's increasing involvement in the "industrial process" did *not* generate the un-"fortuitous situation" characteristic in "Western countries," where women were "torn between their work and their family." This had been implied, claimed the Bulgarian government delegate at the 1961 session of the ILC, in the ILO Director-General's response to the findings of the Panel of Consultants on the Problems of Women Workers[12] (*ILC Proceedings 1961:* 71, 134). Speaking from their own international platforms, communist-leaning trade unionists similarly tended to foreground the pressure on working women with small children in Western countries alone. At its 5th World Congress in December 1961, when the WFTU decided to convene its second World Conference of Women Workers, WFTU General Secretary Louis Saillant once again pointed to the "great difficulty" working women faced in capitalist countries alone when they needed to place their children in kindergartens and creches (Weltgewerkschaftsbund [1961]: 73–74, 1011). In June 1962, the WFTU Executive decided that the women's conference should take place in Bucharest in 1963. At the ILO in November 1962, the observer representing the WFTU at the Governing Body supported the inclusion of the item "women workers in a changing world" in the agenda of the ILC that would convene in 1964[13] (ILO Governing Body November 1962).

At the same time, women trade unionists from state-socialist countries began to address more openly in their international networks those problems faced by so many women workers in state-socialist countries which were somewhat similar to the problems of women in Western industrial countries. We have seen that back in Hungary, Erzsébet Déri, early on and with reference to her personal encounters with women workers, worked hard to convey to her superiors the urgency and seriousness of women workers' problem of combining full-time employment and care for small children and families. At the International Trade Union Conference on the Problems of Working Women organised by the WFTU in Bucharest held just

---

12 Mr. Tonchev noted that the Report tended "to reduce the role of women in labour."
13 The representative of the government of the Soviet Union on the Governing Body, while supporting the workers' groups' desire to see this item discussed in 1964 had not included it in his own, primary proposal.

before the 1964 session of the ILC, the Hungarian delegation brought this openness to the international platform of the trade union women. The speech given by the leader of the delegation, which was characterised by its "realist tone" and did not shy away from addressing "our problems as well, . . . met with great success." Mrs. Oszkár Barinkai pointed to, among other things, the fact that women often had difficulties "reconciling their work with their calling as a mother (*anyai hivatás*)" (*Békés Megyei Népújság* July 16, 1964[14]). The Bucharest conference adopted a foundational "Charter on the Economic and Social Rights of Working Women" and a "Preliminary Memorandum to the Director General of the ILO." The memorandum urged the ILO to "step up its activities in favour of working women"; approved of the proposal for a new instrument concerning the employment of women with family obligations before the ILC; and pressed for the establishment "of a representative tripartite commission [on women's work, SZ] made up of delegates of countries from all the regions of the world and with different economic and social systems – a commission on which the International Trade Union Organisations should be represented with full rights"[15] (*WFTU Women's Conference 1964:* 99, 105–115).

At the ILO, the process leading up to the adoption of ILO Recommendation 123 on the employment of women with family responsibilities exposed how, in the Cold War context, the state-socialist politics of women's work were simultaneously influential and severely marginalised on the international stage.

In connection with some of the issues discussed, the advanced or innovative character of some elements of the politics of women's work in the state-socialist world became highly visible and were seriously considered. This was the case regarding the vision, advocated by the International Labour Office, that centralised policy agencies responsible for the ever more important and complex "special problems of women workers" should be set up in all countries. The ILO considered such agencies a key instrument for designing and coordinating the politics of women's work. It suggested the adoption of an ILO Resolution regarding "the desirability *(a)* of establishing a central administrative office or unit for co-ordinating re-

---

14 The local daily paraphrased a report on the Conference given by Júlia Turgonyi, a member of the Hungarian delegation; see below for more on Turgonyi.

15 The documents did refer to discrimination against married working women but not to childcare leave after compulsory maternity leave. The Memorandum to the ILO also reminded the ILO of a past initiative of the WFTU, referring to 1956, when "a WFTU delegation submitted a first Memorandum to the ILO together with the documents adopted by the First Conference of Working Women" calling for a general debate on working women's issues at the ILO. The Report of the 1964 Conference also mentions the WFTU's 1947 initiative "set[ting] in motion procedure which . . . resulted" in the adoption of the ILO's Equal Pay Convention C100.

search, planning, programming and action on women workers' opportunities, needs and problems, and *(b)* of developing systematic arrangements for consulting the organisations primarily concerned, including in the first instance the employers' and workers' organisations." The Office acknowledged the pre-existing, advanced institutional arrangements in the state-socialist world as well as the special role trade unions played in this regard, and it placed the relevant institutions in the Soviet Union on par with developments on the other side of the "Iron Curtain." In "the U.S.S.R. and the other socialist countries of Eastern Europe, the trade unions have a special responsibility for promoting the welfare and advancement of women workers." The central USSR trade union federation operated a commission that brought together "leaders in production, science, education, government service and the trade union movement" for this express purpose, and it was complemented by similar commissions at the lower levels of the organisation. Acknowledging the wide variety of possible institutional arrangements facilitating the central coordination of the politics of women's work, the Office also noted that "[s]uch arrangements are particularly prevalent" in Latin America, and it did not waste the opportunity to introduce the United States' well-known Women's Bureau[16] (International Labour Office 1963: 115–119).

Regarding the issue of working women with small children – the sole question singled out for regulation through an ILO-instrument – the position, policy needs, and initiatives of the state-socialist countries were, by contrast, marginalised in ILO discourse and decision-making in 1964 and 1965, even though information on measures already in place in Eastern Europe was made available. The initial report circulated by the International Labour Office in preparation for the 1964 session of the ILC highlighted the following as part of, but also accentuating, a global trend: "[i]n the U.S.S.R. and the Eastern European countries the participation rate [in employment] of married women with dependent children is very high." The "substantial increase in the employment of younger married women, very many of whom may be presumed to have dependent children" in many parts of the world demanded the development of childcare facilities, the reduction of household tasks, special arrangements concerning working hours, the guarantee of labour and social rights in part-time employment,[17] and measures to facilitate and guarantee "re-entry into employment." Measures to achieve the latter were framed as a new invention justified by foundational historical reasoning. They included "maintaining [women's] employment rights in their previous jobs or in a

---

16 The ILC 1964 indeed adopted a resolution addressing this subject. *ILC Proceedings 1964*, 820–821.

17 Part-time employment was described as a feature characteristic for several highly developed Western countries and Japan alone.

comparable job for a stipulated period of absence on prolonged maternity leave, in much the same manner as men's rights are guaranteed to them during periods of absence on compulsory military service." The Office suggested a period of up to one year for such guarantees (International Labour Office 1963: 14–18, 71–103, 125). The initial report contained a questionnaire asking governments to contribute to the preparation of the planned ILO-instrument on women workers with family responsibilities. The answers provided by the governments and subsequently summarised by the International Labour Office in its second report published in preparation for the 1964 session of the ILC brought to light that state-socialist countries, including the Soviet Union as the leading power, in an effort to address the problems that resulted from the large-scale involvement of women with small children in the labour force, had already instituted employment guarantees for working mothers during periods of prolonged absence, prefiguring Recommendation 123. In Albania, unpaid leave could be granted for one year or more based on agreements negotiated between employers and trade unions, and in Hungary, a provision allowed for (but did not grant an unqualified right to) unpaid leave until the child reached the age of three. Ukraine and the USSR reported somewhat similar but more limited regulations. State-socialist Eastern European countries expressed strong support for inscribing related measures into the planned international instrument. This enthusiasm contrasted with the hesitation and (initial) rejection that characterised the responses of other governments in Western and "developing" countries, and later contributions to this discussion made by some employers' and governments' representatives from these world regions in Geneva. The statements by these actors were characterised by cautiousness, in particular with regard to concerns about granting women workers both excessive rights to return to work, and far-reaching employment rights for women workers with young children given the right to choose prolonged childcare leave (International Labour Office 1964). Neither Eastern European procedures guaranteeing mothers' employment rights, nor the regulations found here and there in less important Western countries with a "conservative" gender regime would be invoked, as we shall see, as the inspiration for Recommendation 123 on the broader international stage at Geneva.

In addition to the question of employment guarantees, the International Labour Office invited governments to also consider whether the proposed international instrument should refer to "fiscal and social policies" enabling women "with young children, to stay home if they so choose," i. e., a material benefit attached to the right to prolonged childcare leave. The information obtained from governments regarding this question revealed a complex political constellation between East and West. The Eastern European governments tended to emphasise, not unexpectedly, the classical "old left" dogma of women's emancipation through paid employment, emphasising that the right to work for all women had been universally implemented in the state-socialist world and advocating measures beyond financial support for the prolonged leave of young mothers, e.g., the expansion of childcare services to enable these women to reduce the "double burden." However, against the background of women's fully realised right to work, Poland as well as Hungary declared themselves in favour of both fiscal and social measures which formed – as Hungary put it – "a suitable starting point" for "ensuring freedom of choice." They considered, in other words, the material benefit attached to the stay-at-home option for mothers as key for ensuring that women would have a real choice. Poland wanted to see women of older disabled children included in such a scheme. By contrast, representatives of highly developed Western countries stressed their reservations about benefits attached to the stay-at-home option for mothers. The US government was most explicit in rejecting stay-at-home benefits, invoking the "inequities that still exist in many countries" with regard to married women's freedom of employment. In keeping with its particular mandate concerning "labour and manpower functions," the ILO was advised to focus on helping women who chose employment over extended childcare leave; promoting part-time work was one of the options advocated in this context.[18] Among European countries, only those known for their "conservative" gender regimes such as Spain and Austria made a case for financial supports for a prolonged period of parental leave. Israel alone explicitly referred to pronatalist aims as an important justification for such benefits (International Labour Office 1964). There was, thus, a de-facto coalition of governments nurturing "conservative" family values and two state-socialist governments that promoted material benefits for working mothers of young children with the goal of temporarily easing the "double burden" experienced by the large and constantly growing numbers of working mothers. Recommendation 123 would not include references to material benefits attached to prolonged childcare leave.

Building on these preliminary discussions, the ILO embarked on negotiations for what would become Recommendation 123 during the 1964 and 1965 sessions of the ILC. That some Eastern European countries (and Austria and Spain) already had legal arrangements that guaranteed employment rights during childcare leave and for leaves of absence longer than one year did not come into play and

---

18 In parallel, among the state-socialist countries, Hungary, Czechoslovakia, Ukraine, Yugoslavia, and the USSR advocated for the international regulation of part-time work, while Yugoslavia alone mentioned women's and men's shared responsibility for family work. Cobble (2021: 359–364) provides an excellent analysis of the debate over part-time work and Esther Peterson's advocacy of this tool to be included in the Recommendation. Peterson was present as Advisor to the US government's representative.

would not have any effect on the framing of debates and decision-making during the conference sessions. In 1965, when the adoption of Recommendation 123 was on the agenda, the delegates from state-socialist Europe did, in fact, address what they experienced as their marginalisation in terms of reduced representation. In the Conference Committee on women's work, which constituted the key intra-ILC body responsible for negotiating all relevant interests and preparing for final decision making, the members from Hungary, Poland, and the Soviet Union abstained from voting when committee officers were elected. From their point of view, "there had not been adequate regard to the principle of equitable geographical distribution" (*ILC Proceedings 1965:* 638).

The ILC's discussion of the agenda item "women workers in a changing world" in both 1964 and 1965 was characterised by a spirit that effectively masked the realities of (women's) working lives and the politics of women's work in state-socialist Europe in the contributions of many speakers. First, emphasis was placed on the need to bring "outmoded thinking" about women's mass employment "into line with real life" – such thinking that continued to shape the perception of women's work, and married women's work in particular, in many countries in the West and the Global South. Second, the focus was "the mobilisation of our human resources" as opposed to the present "underemployment of women workers." This state of affairs was to be remedied by "making it possible for women with family responsibilities to become or to remain integrated in the labour force as well as to re-enter the labour force." This argumentation strategy was repeatedly connected to the insistence that women with family responsibilities should be able to freely choose between employment and family work rather than being forced into employment by economic necessity. As such, this discourse was fully oblivious to the realities of the world of work in state-socialist countries. By contrast, delegates from state-socialist countries, represented by the Hungarian government delegate Mrs. Konrád for example, asked to enshrine women's "full" right to work in the ILO instrument in progress[19] and stressed "the need to coordinate women's employment policy with economic and social policy as a whole" (*ILC Proceedings 1964:* 457–474, 739–746 and *1965:* 372–388, 638–649).

---

[19] The right to work was not questioned in the debate. Opponents of insertion pointed to the fact that the ILO's position on this was unequivocal anyway. To the delight of the Polish Government Advisor Mrs. Jakubowicz, a related reference was indeed included in the section on the General Principles of Recommendation 123 after "long discussion"; this was primarily in reference to the continuing legal restrictions on married women's right to work in some "countries in Europe." For Jakubowicz's statement, see *ILC Proceedings 1965:* 378; for the initial wording of the recommendation suggested by the International Labour Office, which did not contain such a reference, see International Labour Office 1964: 18.

In short, special employment guarantees for women with family responsibilities were construed in Geneva as a means of enticing women into and keeping them in the labour force rather than as a solution for the problems of mothers of small children regularly employed *en masse* in state-socialist countries. As was so vividly illustrated in Erzsébet Déri's memos to her trade union superiors quoted above, these women inevitably found themselves fully engaged in the labour market and thus needed to juggle the "double burden" as full-time workers; exiting the labour force for good was not a genuine option.

Working Women with Small Children in Hungary: The Creation and Development of *gyes* in Context

By the time the ILO voted for Recommendation 123 on the employment of women with family responsibilities in June 1965, Hungarian policy-makers had, as highlighted above, "already worked on the plan for the introduction of the childcare benefit" *gyes* (Horváth 1986: 109). The interactions within SZOT in 1964 and Erzsébet Déri's description of the tensions mounting in Hungary around the issue of mothers of small children regularly employed *en masse*, which she laid before her trade union superiors in August 1965, reflected women trade unionists' proactive role in the ongoing preparations for *gyes*. As these preparations reached the implementation stage in late summer 1965, SZOT was approached by a representative of the Ministry of Labour, and Déri's first memo produced on the occasion summarised and discussed information received from this official regarding these practicalities.[20] Besides the Ministry of Labour and SZOT, the National Planning Office – here János Timár took the lead – and the Ministry of Finance were involved in the process ("Déri, Feljegyzés gyes javaslat 1965").

Among the broader Hungarian public and expert circles at the time, and in scholarship up to the present day, the introduction of extended childcare leave – initially discussed as a temporary measure ("Déri, Feljegyzés gyes javaslat 1965") – came to be considered a policy response to multiple concerns. In one non-public expert discussion in 1968, the rationale for introducing *gyes* was summarised as "kill[ing] three birds with one stone," namely: demographic decline, i. e., counteracting the low birth rate; labour-market planning, or, in concrete terms, managing a short-term over supply in the labour market predicted as a result of a peak number of youths entering the labour market; and as a response to the extreme scar-

---

20 The exact origins of the range of statements and arguments contained in Déri's memo cannot be determined.

city of institutional pre-kindergarten infant care, with reference to the fact that the cost of institutional care for one infant was much higher than the planned benefit for mothers staying at home with their child ("A dolgozó nők helyzetével foglalkozó tanulmány 1968").

In terms of immediate causes, first and foremost, *gyes* came into being as a "labour force-management instrument" (Bódy 2016: 282). It was introduced one year before the New Economic Mechanism *(Új gazdasági mechanizmus* or *Új gazdaságirányítás,* NEM) came into effect in 1968. NEM was a major attempt at economic reform aimed at, among other things, more effective economic performance through the increased autonomy of enterprises. At a time when high-birth-rate age groups born in the early 1950s were set to enter the labour market, the reform was expected to reduce the need for unskilled workers, among whom women were represented in large numbers. *Gyes* could counterbalance the anticipated labour market tensions (Bódy 2016: 282–283; Inglot, Szikra, and Rat 2011: 27[21]).

It would soon turn out that NEM did not bring about the hoped-for better, i. e., greater "economical manpower-management." The 1970s were characterised by the constant demand for additional labour (Horváth 1986: 47–48),[22] a fact that made the tensions caused by the large-scale presence of women of child-bearing age or women with small children in regular employment a constant concern of policy-makers and trade unionists throughout the decade. Furthermore, within this context, the connection between women's "double burden" on the one hand, and anxieties about the low birth rate and pronatalist rhetoric and practices on the other – which were present both well before the advent of *gyes* and in the policy process leading up to its introduction – remained a constant feature of the Hungarian politics of women's work.

From the very start, top-level policy-makers considered the low birth rate, among other things, to be a consequence of the unresolved tensions around childcare, as masses of young women took up paid employment. As early as 1962, the politburo discussed a report on the "demographic situation" or, more precisely, the declining birth rate, proposing countermeasures that focused on improving the material circumstances of families with children and easing the "double burden" experienced by working women with small children ("MSZMP PB June 1962:"

---

21 Bódy discusses primary material documenting high-level decision makers' pondering over the pros and cons of introducing either *gyes* or a short-term benefit aimed at redirecting the dismissed surplus workforce into employment; Inglot, Szikra, and Rat refer to their interview with András Klinger.

22 NEM was curtailed early in the 1970s. Horváth also points to the lower birth-rate age groups entering the labour market in the 1970s as an explanation for the steady hunger for additional labourers in the workforce.

esp. 4, 23–25, and attached report; see also Bódy 2016: 271–272). Alongside the expansion of the creche system and increasing family allowances, the report promoted measures to help keep women out of factories and offices after childbirth. This included the extension of paid maternity leave to six months; the option that might allow mothers to remain on paid sick leave until the first birthday of the child; and the opportunity for the mother to take "unpaid leave" until the third birthday of the child, whereby she would retain "all the rights connected to the employment relationship" with the exception of the entitlement to sick leave benefits. Only a few months later, János Kádár, General Secretary of the MSZMP, announced the introduction of the last measure – extended unpaid leave – as well as the forthcoming extension of paid maternity leave in a speech at the 1962 MSZMP Congress (Inglot, Szikra, and Rat 2011: 25). During the discussion of the report submitted to the politburo, Kádár pointed to a possible connection between the low birth rate and the liberal abortion regulation dating from summer 1956 which de facto granted abortion on demand (though one had to receive permission from a committee). Bringing into play a possible complementary and repressive line of pronatalist policies, Kádár thus made sure to stress that "not for anything in the world should we resort to state measures in this matter."

In hindsight, with this interjection into policy discussions, Kádár laid the foundation for the bifurcation of pronatalist policies based on social policy incentives as opposed to repressive measures. This bifurcation would remain in place, numerous challenges notwithstanding, until well into the 1970s. In the run-up to the introduction of *gyes* in the 1960s, the planned reform was repeatedly discussed as a pronatalist measure and connected to the abortion question. In the spring of 1966, *Népszabadság*, the most important nationwide daily, published the records of a roundtable discussion on "population growth and abortion." It was within this framework that the idea of *gyes* – as potentially financed by a new tax for childless individuals and combined with abortion restrictions – was introduced to the larger public[23] (March 13, 1966 and April 30, 1966).

In 1966, the politburo, by contrast, again shied away from linking *gyes* as a pronatalist incentive to the introduction of abortion restrictions. When it decided on the introduction of *gyes* at its meeting on October 4, 1966, the politburo also discussed at length a new report on the "demographic situation." The latter issue had been hived off from the list of other measures in the area of social welfare

---

23 In contrast to the men participating in the discussion, the General Secretary of MNOT Zsuzsa Ortutay advocated for a shorter period of extended childcare leave; for the "pill" to be made universally available in due course; and for systematic family planning counselling. MNOT at this point explicitly rejected changes to abortion regulations, as mentioned in "MSZMP PB October 1966" but not in the information about the Roundtable published in *Népszabadság*.

and standard-of-living politics of which it had been part in the original preparations for the October 1966 meeting. Discussing the "demographic situation," speakers rejected the idea of introducing part-time work for mothers, considering it a measure "nearly impossible to carry out in practice"; instead, they favoured the option that mothers would be able to stay home "for two years or four years," which was considered a practicable idea. Discussing abortion, the question Kádár considered to be the "key issue" at stake, many politburo members, including at this point Kádár himself, tended towards restriction. While Imre Párdi, the primary person responsible for economic politics in the MSZMP Central Committee, considered it not advisable "for political reasons in the first place" to "now" introduce abortion restrictions, Deputy Prime Minister Jenő Fock and others advocated the abolition of abortion for those who could afford children (i. e., those who lived in an appropriate flat, earned an appropriate income, and did not have children yet). Kádár considered the existing abortion regulations dating from June 1956 as "not right" and right-wing liberal. He felt that abortion should not be possible whenever a woman who did not yet have children became pregnant. Yet again, the politburo took no action. Rather, the propositions contained in the report and the remarks made during the discussion would form the basis for "further work" on the population question to be carried out by the party and the Minister of Health. The report supporting the introduction of *gyes* discussed by the politburo at the same meeting, in turn, stated that *gyes* "in all likelihood would have an advantageous impact on population growth." Additionally, it referred to the high cost of operating a large system of creches, the low performance of mothers with small children at work, the advantages of family over creche care, and the work opportunities *gyes* would generate for housewives and "girls" who could not be employed without the opening of jobs that would result from the introduction of *gyes* ("MSZMP PB October 1966:" report on living standard etc., esp. 2–3).

The larger policy process and public debate surrounding the introduction of *gyes*, thus, clearly framed the new benefit as a measure enabling motherhood for women employed in full-time jobs. The pronatalist thrust inscribed into *gyes* was a differentiated one. From the start, the new benefit de facto prioritised regular, low-income workers. For women with higher incomes, the lump-sum assistance was less attractive. Women not engaged in employment or only irregularly involved in paid labour, among them many Romnja, were not entitled to the benefit (Varsa 2005: 213–215); over time, however, additional groups qualified.

Once operational, *gyes* was instantly fully embraced by the population concerned. Many more women went "on *gyes*" than policy-makers had expected. Among working women who gave birth, a far higher percentage of those with low or medium levels of education made use of the benefit as compared to women with higher education and/or university degrees. In 1979, nearly 120,000 working women, 83 percent of working women who gave birth, claimed the benefit; altogether, more than 260,000 women were "on *gyes*" at the end of this year, equalling 10.2 percent of all women in Hungary between the ages of fifteen and forty-nine. Of those women "on *gyes*," 12 percent were recorded as giving birth to another child before the extended childcare period expired, while 43 percent returned to work before the benefit expired. Of the latter group, more than half of these women did so out of material need; the real value of the lump-sum benefit decreased over the years and reached no more than a quarter to a third of women's average wages at the time. All in all, *gyes* tempered but did not resolve the pressure experienced by working women with small children. The creche system expanded in parallel with the introduction of *gyes*, with the percentage of creche-aged children enrolled increasing from 9.5 percent in 1970 to 14.8 percent in 1980; over-enrolment also rose, reaching 127 percent in 1979. In the 1980s, the activity rate of women of working age was more than 80 percent if those "on *gyes*" are included, only a few percentage points behind the male activity rate. Starting in 1982, fathers could also claim the benefit once the child reached its first birthday, but the numbers of those who actually did remained extremely low. In 1985, a second tier was added to the system with a wage-related benefit available that was restricted to the period before the child reached two years old. The percentage of working women among all women who gave birth rose steeply, from 51 percent in 1965 to nearly 90 percent in the 1980s. This suggests that in effect, *gyes* worked not only to ease the "double burden" of working mothers with small children but also might have generated a pull-effect in terms of enticing women to enter the labour force in the first place and give birth afterward (Központi Statisztikai Hivatal 1981: 9, 19, 27; Horváth 1986: 34–37, 47, 66–67; Adamik 1991: 122–123; Göndör 2012: 77). *Gyes*, in other words, might likewise have fulfilled the main function the ILO and important Western industrial nations ascribed to the ILO's 1965 Recommendation 123 on women with family responsibilities, namely, to bring additional women into the labour market. Overall, *gyes* constituted an important gendered change of the life course regime in Hungary.

In 1973, the Hungarian government finally combined a social policy reform designed to ease women's "double burden" and serve as a pronatalist incentive with abortion restrictions, which constituted a key instrument of repressive pronatalist policy. Politburo decision making in February 1973 triggered both the restrictions and the additional incentives. An increase of the lump-sum available in the *gyes* scheme for the first child, as well as a higher sum attached to a second child and a still higher but stable lump-sum for a third and all additional children served as one of these incentives. Other improvements including additional material support for raising children and the accelerated development of institutional childcare were added. Both the SZOT Secretariat and the National Council of Hungarian Women (*Magyar Nők Országos Szövetsége*, MNOT) opposed the "tightening" of abortion regulations facilitated through the instalment of a committee with real decision-making power and bound by strict guidelines for decision making ("MSZMP PB February 1973"; *MK* 1973; "MNOT Tájékoztató 1973"; Göndör 2012: 72). Initially, SZOT declared in no uncertain terms that "it must remain a women's exclusive right to decide: does she or doesn't she want to give birth (*kíván-e gyermeket a világra hozni vagy sem*)?" After the decision to enact abortion restrictions was made, SZOT tried hard to water them down and postpone their enforcement ("[SZOT], Feljegyzés 1973"; "A SZOT Titkárságának véleménye 1972"). SZOT's central Women's Committee, installed in 1970, claimed to have been instrumental in bringing about SZOT's suggestion that both *gyes* and the family allowance should be raised in a "differentiated" manner, which was subsequently "accepted" by the government (*Népszava* December 24, 1973).

Extended Childcare Leave in Perspective

Against the background of extensive economic growth and expanding labour markets, the employment of women with young children became a fact and political desire in Europe and internationally in the 1960s. Yet, the employment of these women remained a political issue fraught with tension. When during the 1964 session of the International Labour Conference, the committee discussing the larger theme of "women workers in a changing world" endorsed the plan that the ILO prepare an international instrument on the employment of women with family responsibilities, it chose "the most controversial topic" among the various subjects considered (Cobble 2021: 359–364).[24] Diverse as they were, at their core, the tensions were centred on issues related to women's infamous "double burden," which resulted from the combination of unpaid family work, performed predominantly by women alone, and employment. The problems generated by the "double burden" included both the lack of reliability and the reduced performance of women with small children at the workplace and the difficulty of enticing women into the labour market and keeping them there. The former problem worried policy-makers in the state-socialist countries more than the second, whereas for the time being, their peers in developed industrial countries were more preoccupied with the latter. Behind both concerns lurked anxiety over the "stability of the family" or, to put it more bluntly, the defence of the inherited, "ossified" domes-

---

24 Cobble provides an eloquent discussion of the conflict surrounding the issue of part-time work in particular.

tic non/division of labour that freed men from most of the burdens of family work and the desire to ensure the quality of childcare and family work. Policy-makers in both the East and West were united in their related concerns, notwithstanding the fact that in the East, the desired "help" of fathers with family work and praise of the younger generation of men for their increasing involvement in this sphere of life formed an inevitable element of party and public discourse.

Policy-makers in East and West as well as at the ILO incessantly emphasised the primary or even exclusive responsibility of mothers as opposed to fathers to care for infants and small children. Institutional care for the youngest age group, i.e., the creche system, as one policy response aimed at easing working women's "double burden," was more widely accepted and more advanced in the East versus the West. Hesitancy to expand the creche system was nourished by two factors. First, the high financial cost of the creche system, conceived of as a partial alternative to extended childcare leave, was a major problem in both East and West. This was, in fact, one of the factors triggering the introduction of *gyes* in Hungary. Second, the anxieties around the preservation of the family and the male prerogative in the domestic sphere and the high-quality care delivered by mothers themselves played an important role. While in official party communications in Hungary the second set of issues was barely addressed directly, the motherly vocation of women became a hotly discussed topic in public discourse facilitated by or involving high-ranking dailies, journals, intellectuals, and professionals. Women politicians tried hard to keep the related "retrograde" tendencies in check. Women trade unionists in particular never failed to emphasise that they endorsed *gyes* "only" if it was linked to the accelerated expansion of the capacity of creches ("[SZOT], Feljegyzés 1973"), the latter constituting the second vital pillar of the doctrine of real choice they had voiced at the ILO when demanding that a material benefit be attached to any stay-at-home option for mothers. Reference to men's role and responsibility in sharing the burden of unpaid care work was also present in the women trade unionists' discourse, but much less widespread. It was exceptional when in 1973 – the period when the debate was at its height and abortion restrictions were coming into effect – trade unionist researcher and employee of the Social Science Institute of the Central Committee of the MSZMP (MSZMP KB *Társadalomtudományi Intézete*, TTI) Júlia Turgonyi voiced a radical critique of male insolence rather than focusing on the lack of creches as root-cause of women's unbearable "double burden." She argued that the "parasitic" attitude of husbands, who often made their wives into their "servers, or should I say 'lawful servants,'" must cease to exist:

> [Today], equal rights still means substantially more rights for men, or, if you like, they constitute a "right" which can be asserted via damaging the other sex, given the fact that in

most families, the woman, in addition to her job, takes care of the children and the husband ...
[W]omen are increasingly less inclined to reconcile themselves to this situation. It becomes
clearer and clearer that in order to validate women's equal rights, *male prerogatives* must
be *curtailed*, and finally abolished. ... [W]omen and men alike have a double vocation." (Turgonyi 1973: esp. 28–30, 35–36, emphasis in the original).[25]

Male and mainstream policy-makers in East and West thoroughly failed to pay attention to this dimension of the problem. At the same time, while they advocated
for extended childcare leave for women as a cheaper alternative to creches, they
implicitly acknowledged the hidden and yet very real material value of care work.
The question of to what extent the hidden value of care would be transformed into
a visible (financial) cost constituted an even more urgent problem, though one that
was somewhat less convoluted, and in any case more evident in the East than the
West. This was the case for a number of reasons: more young women with children were employed; there was a pressing need to address the problem of care
due to the overall context of material scarcity and fewer private funds that
could be used to fund childcare; and the high general macroeconomic cost of transforming unpaid labour into paid care work could be directly addressed, as did
János Timár in his 1964 article published in the *International Labour Review*:

> A specific problem of economic efficiency arises in connection with the increasing employ-
> ment of women – namely whether the organisation by society of the care of children and
> of a large part of household work will not involve a greater labour input or social cost
> than the rise in the national income to be expected from that increased employment. It is
> therefore necessary to examine how much labour can be saved by socially organising the
> care of children and household work and what is the relation between the national income
> generated by the women to be drawn into the labour force and the costs of establishing (and
> maintaining) the institutions that must be provided before they can be employed – costs
> which come out of national income. (Timár 1964b: 113)

As a result, and because extended childcare leave was prioritised over the more
expensive creche system in the larger context of state-socialist welfare expansion
set in motion starting in the 1960s, Eastern European countries took the lead in the
all-European turn towards extended childcare leave. The ILO, when taking stock of
the position of women workers around the world in the run-up to the United Nations' International Women's Year (1975), duly documented this state of affairs:

> One of the more interesting recent developments ... has been the extension of the period of
> authorized maternity leave beyond the normal statutory or prescribed period, without loss of

---

25 The best scholarly analysis of the debates mentioned here is contained in Mária Adamik's unpublished dissertation. For a glimpse into her perspective, see Adamik 2001.

employment rights, as recommended by [R 123]. This extension of leave is now common practice in the Socialist countries in Eastern Europe. . . . Certain other European countries have also introduced somewhat similar arrangements. (International Labour Office 1973: 6–7, 38)

In fact, the regulations in place in Eastern Europe at the time, and their further expansion in the years to come, went well beyond the propositions contained in Recommendation 123. Within a few years after the introduction of *gyes* in Hungary, state-socialist Europe experienced a wave of childcare leave innovations. The schemes introduced in Poland in 1968, Czechoslovakia and the Soviet Union in 1970, and Bulgaria in 1973 granted childcare leave well beyond a child's first birthday, and sooner or later (Bulgaria and the USSR, respectively), extended the leave option for even longer periods. In most cases, the schemes came with a degree of material compensation (in Poland and the USSR only beginning in the early 1980s). With the exception of Czechoslovakia, they were conditional on an existing or previous employment relationship. In some cases, such reforms were combined with extensions of the often fully paid compulsory maternity leave and the enhancement of other maternity-related fringe benefits, such as paid leave to care for an ill child. In the German Democratic Republic, a "baby year" with some compensation was introduced in 1976. In Yugoslavia starting in 1981, women could work part time until the first birthday of the child, receiving full compensation for the loss of income from the health care fund. Some of the schemes providing for extended childcare leave were designed as such in a visibly pronatalist manner, e. g., adding extra time or money for additional children (Hungary starting in 1973, Bulgaria, and Czechoslovakia, where migrant workers from Vietnam were severely discriminated against in terms of motherhood-related benefits), and in some countries, these schemes were combined with restrictive abortion regulations as in Hungary starting in 1974 (International Labour Office 1973: 38–39; Bodrova and Anker 1985 [contributions by Anker, Pavlik, Holzer/Halina Wasilewska-Trenkner]; Horváth 1986: 109–121; Alamgir 2014: 141–146; Zajkowska 2020: 124).

In Western Europe, compensated leave beyond the child's first birthday would be granted only starting in the middle of the 1980s onward, and only in a few countries, among them Belgium in 1984 and Austria in 1990. Leave and compensation up to the first birthday was available earlier in Austria (1960) and Italy (1981), whereas France and Spain granted a longer period of unpaid leave already in the 1970s[26] (International Labour Office 1973: 39; Horváth 1986: 112–113, 119; Morgan and Zippel 2003). A European Union directive on parental leave was first proposed in 1983; the vision at this point was to grant leave up to the third birthday of

---

26 I have not been able to determine whether leave in Spain had already been offered earlier.

the child. A much more flexible European Council Directive was finally enacted in 1996 (Council Directive 1996).

By that time, the vision of extended childcare leave promoted and placed into policy directives by the ILO and many Eastern and Western European countries beginning in the 1960s was in decline. With a bird's-eye view, this leave can be described as a key element of a dual-earner/one-paid-caregiver economy. Complementing the Western European one-earner/one-carer economy (in place for some strata of the population) and the Eastern European dual-earner/one-wage/one-unpaid-caregiver economy, the new policy instrument became relevant for a considerable portion of the population only during the comparatively affluent decades following the post-1945 reconstruction period and preceding the period commonly referred to as neoliberalism which swept across Western Europe starting in the 1980s and Eastern Europe in the 1990s. In this altered context, the transformation of this policy measure into a gender-neutral benefit available to both women and men in many places came with or was followed by the erosion of its material value, limited eligibility, and other problems.

Although designed and showcased internationally in a top-down manner as a labour force planning instrument, the invention of *gyes* in Hungary in the 1960s involved dedicated women trade unionists, functionaries, and researchers as key actors. These women seized the opportunity to direct the attention of Hungarian policy-makers to the plight of working women, pressuring them towards the introduction of *gyes*. The women trade union functionaries and their allies did so, of course, within the confines of their own positioning within the stratified Hungarian state. This included both the fact that their position in relation to other Hungarian policy-makers was one of negotiation and soft power at best, and their own dedication to the state-socialist project. Within the latter historical setting, cheap women's labour was put to use *en masse* for the project of economic development under materially constrained conditions. Women trade unionists, as they interviewed women workers in many factories, sought not simply to legitimise ongoing policy changes but to generate space within the political process and the wider public for both their own vision of women's emancipation and that of women workers themselves, insofar as it was shared or conveyed by the interviewers.

The Hungarian developments formed part of an international conjuncture focused on the ILO in Geneva, which involved trade unions, women's networks dedicated to improving the lot of working women, and other international actors from both sides of the "Iron Curtain." In the early 1960s, women trade unionists and other responsible actors steering the course of development of the state-socialist world of work were pivotal for the consideration of innovative social policy instruments that could ease the tension between women's full-time employment and childcare duties. This was because women with small children working full-time were a mass phenomenon in state-socialist countries, and their importance within the labour force was expected to expand even further. The introduction of extended childcare leave was a means to simultaneously keep these women in (and, just as in many Western countries, entice more of them into) the labour force and ease the related economic and social tensions generated as a result. The realities of state socialism and the related international engagement of Eastern European actors unmistakably left their imprint on the ILO's Recommendation 123 on "Employment (Women with Family Responsibilities)" in 1965 as it foregrounded extended childcare leave over the many alternatives discussed in Geneva since the late 1950s. At the same time, while employment guarantees alone formed the core of Recommendation 123, many Eastern European countries additionally attached a substantial material benefit to the employment guarantees, accentuating a specificity of the state-socialist politics of women's work. Both this expanding and ongoing specificity and the role of Eastern Europe in the making of Recommendation 123 were and remained relegated to the margins of dominant international social policy discourse for a long time to come.

In Hungary, less than a year after the introduction of *gyes* in 1967, another round of interviews with 260 workers was conducted in six factories as part of a large-scale research project on the "work and life circumstances of female industrial workers" carried out by the TTI under the leadership of Júlia Turgonyi. These workers, or rather their voices as conveyed by Turgonyi, explained with striking clarity what extended childcare leave meant to them and how measures such as *gyes*, which sought to ease the "double burden," might improve the position of women. One skilled spinner employed in a textile factory in the southern outskirts of Buda in Budapest for fourteen years declared that in her opinion, *gyes* "is the most human measure of the past decade" ("[Turgonyi], Feljegyzés Textilkombinát 1967"). Similarly, an unskilled worker from a pharmaceutical factory in the eastern Hungarian city of Debrecen explained: "A woman's ability to rest to overcome exhaustion would be a very important precondition for women's emancipation" ("[Turgonyi], Feljegyzés BIOGAL 1967").

References

"A dolgozó nők helyzetével foglalkozó tanulmány vitája a Társadalomtudományi Intézetben" [The discussion of the study on the condition of the working women in the Social Science Institute]. June 4, 1968, 904f. 67 ő.e. TTI, Magyar Nemzeti Levéltár Országos Levéltára [Nationwide Archives of the Hungarian National Archives, MNL-MOL].
"A SZOT Elnökségének állásfoglalása, a dolgozó nők családellátásának és munkakörülményeinek javításával kapcsolatos távlati megoldására" [Position taken by the SZOT Leadership on the long-term solution of the improvement of the family provision and the labour conditions of

working women]. July 3, 1964, 288 f. 22–1964–10 ő.e. MSZMP KB Agitációs és Propaganda Osztály [Campaigning and Propaganda Division of the Central Committee of the MSZMP (MSZMP KB APO], MNL-MOL.

Adamik, Mária. 1991. "Supporting Parenting and Child Rearing: Policy Innovation in Eastern Europe." In *Child Care, Parental Leave and the Under 3s. Policy Innovation in Europe*, edited by Sheila B. Kamerman and Alfred Kahn, 115–144. New York, Westport, London: Auburn House.

Adamik, Mária. 2001. "The Greatest Promise, the Greatest Humiliation." In *Gender in Transition in Eastern and Central Europe. Proceedings*, edited by Gabrielle Jähnert, Jan Gorisch, Daphne Hahn, Hildegard Maria Nickel, Iris Peinl, Katrin Schäfgen, and Zentrum für interdisziplinäre Frauenforschung (ZiF) der HU Berlin, 190–199. Berlin: trafo verlag.

Alamgir, Alena K. 2014. "Recalcitrant Women: Internationalism and the Redefinition of Welfare Limits in the Czechoslovak-Vietnamese Labor Exchange Program." *Slavic Review* 73, no. 1: 133–155.

Békés Megyei Népújság. Available in database: *Arcanum Digitális Tudománytár*. Accessible online at: https://adt.arcanum.com/hu/.

Bodrova, Valentina, and Richard Anker, eds. 1985. *Working Women in Socialist Countries: The Fertility Connection*. Geneva: International Labour Office.

Bódy, Zsombor. 2016. "A Népességtudományi Kutatóintézet története és a népesedéspolitika a Kádár-rendszerben" [The history of the Research Institute for Population Science and population policy in the Kádár system]. *Demográfia* 59, no. 4: 265–300.

Bundesgesetzblatt für die Republik Österreich, 69. Stück. 1960. Accessed November 11, 2020. https://www.ris.bka.gv.at/Dokumente/BgblPdf/1960_239_0/1960_239_0.pdf.

Cobble, Dorothy Sue. 2021. *For the Many: A Global Story of American Feminism*. Princeton, NJ: Princeton University Press.

"Council Directive 96/34/EC of 3 June 1996 on the Framework Agreement on Parental Leave Concluded by UNICE, CEEP and the ETUC." Accessed July 12, 2020. https://eur-lex.europa.eu/legal-content/EN/ALL/?uri=CELEX%3A31996L0034.

"Déri, Erzébet. Gyermeknevelési segély és hitel bevezetésének javaslata. Feljegyzés" [Proposition for the introduction of a childcare benefit and credit. Memo]. August 26, 1965, 2. f. 19 / 1965–1966 / 1 doboz / 2 ő.e., Szakszervezetek Központi Levéltára [Central Trade Unions' Archive, SZKL], Politikatörténeti Intézet Levéltára [Institute of Political History, Archives, PIL].

"Déri, Erzsébet. Feljegyzés munkásasszonyokkal folytatott beszélgetésről" [Memo on the talk with [married] women workers]. September 4, 1965, 2. f. 19 / 1965–1966 / 1 doboz / 2 ő.e., SZKL, PIL [according to a handwritten note likely transmitted to Zoltán Fabok; the signature mistakenly gives the year 1964 while the text gives 1965].

Ferge, Zsuzsa. 2017. Email to author. March 3, 2017.

"First Meeting of the I.L.O. Panel of Consultants on Problems of Women Workers." 1960. *Industry and Labour* 23, no. 3: 76–82.

Göndör, Éva. 2012. "A gyermekgondozási támogatások az államszocializmus időszakában, különös tekintettel a Gyermekgondozási Segélyre" [Childcare support in the period of state socialism with a focus on the childcare benefit]. *Jog, állam, politika* 4, no. 4: 69–90.

Haney, Lynne. 2002. *Inventing the Needy. Gender and the Politics of Welfare in Hungary*. Berkeley, Los Angeles, London: University of California Press.

Horváth, Erika (Mrs. Sándor). 1986. *A gyestől a gyedig* [From gyes to gyed]. Budapest: A Magyar Nők Országos Tanácsa and Kossuth Könyvkiadó.

ILC. 1962. *Forty-Fifth Session, Geneva, 1961, Record of Proceedings*. Geneva: International Labour Office.

ILC. 1964. *Forty-Eighth Session, Geneva, 1964, Record of Proceedings.* Geneva: International Labour Office.

ILC. 1965. *Forty-Ninth Session, Geneva, 1965, Record of Proceedings.* Geneva: International Labour Office.

Inglot, Tomasz, Dorottya Szikra, and Cristina Rat. 2011. *Continuity and Change in Family Policies of the New European Democracies: A Comparison of Poland, Hungary, and Romania. Part I: Institutional Legacies and Path Dependence in Family Practice 1945 to 2000.* A NCEEER Working Paper. University of Washington.

International Labour Office. 1963. *International Labour Conference. Forty-Eighth Session Geneva, 1964. Sixth Item on the Agenda. Women Workers in a Changing World. Report VI (1).* Geneva: ILO.

International Labour Office. 1964. *International Labour Conference. Forty-Eighth Session Geneva, 1964. Sixth Item on the Agenda. Women Workers in a Changing World (Employment of Women with Family Responsibilities). Report VI (2).* Geneva: ILO.

International Labour Office. 1973. *Women Workers in a Changing World. Preliminary Report.* Geneva: ILO.

International Labour Office. 2000. *Estimates and Projections of the Economically Active Population 1950–2010.* Geneva: ILO.

"International Labour Office. Governing Body. 143rd Session. Seventh Item on the Agenda. Report of the Meeting of the Panel of Consultants on the Problems of Women Workers (Geneva, 12–16 October 1959)." November 17, 1959. GB 143–100–7, International Labour Office Archives (ILOA).

"International Labour Office. Minutes of the 141st Session of The Governing Body, Geneva, March 1959."

"International Labour Office. Minutes of the 142d Session of The Governing Body, Geneva, May–June 1959."

"International Labour Office. Minutes of the 152d Session of The Governing Body, Geneva, June 1962."

"International Labour Office. Minutes of the 153d Session of The Governing Body, Geneva, November 1962."

"International Labour Office. Working Paper on Item No. 1: Recent Trends in Women Workers' Opportunities and Needs". 1959. WN 2–1003–1–400 (A) (J.1), ILOA.

"Jelentés a szakszervezetek nők körében végzett munkájáról, a dolgozó nők helyzetéről. SZOT-nak a dolgozó nők sajátos helyzetével foglalkozó bizottsága" [Report on the work of the trade unions carried out among women and about the position of working women. SZOT-Committee considering the special situation of working women]. March 27, 1964(a), 288f. 22–1964–10 ő.e. MSZMP KB APO, MNL-MOL.

"Jelentés a szakszervezetek nők körében végzett munkájáról, a dolgozó nők helyzetéről. SZOT-nak a dolgozó nők sajátos helyzetével foglalkozó bizottsága" [Report on the work of the trade unions carried out among women and about the position of working women. SZOT-Committee considering the special situation of working women]. April 20, 1964(b), 288f. 22–1964–10 ő.e. MSZMP KB APO, MNL-MOL.

Központi Statisztikai Hivatal. 1977. *Adatgyüjtemény a kereső nőkről* [Collection of data on working women]. Budapest.

Központi Statisztikai Hivatal. 1981. *A gyermekgodozási segely igénybevétele és hatásai (1967–1980)* [Utilisation and effects of the Childcare Benefit (1967–1980)]. Budapest.

"Letter A. Béguin to Dr. József Bényi". April 22, 1963, WN 1–1–31, International Labour Office Archives (ILOA)

Manetsgruber, Sabrina. 2016. *Die Entwicklung vom Karenzgeld zum Kinderbetreuungsgeld unter besonderer Berücksichtigung gleichstellungsrechtlicher Aspekte.* Diploma thesis, Johannes Kepler Universität Linz. Accessible online at: https://epub.jku.at/obvulihs/content/titleinfo/1009622.

MK = *Magyar Közlöny. A Magyar Népköztársaság Hivatalos Lapja* [Hungarian Gazette. The Official Journal of the Hungarian People's Republic] (71): 1973: 1040/1973 (18 October) Mt. h., (1973) 80, 4/1973 (1 December) EüM. r.

"MNOT. Tájékoztató népesedési helyzetünkről" [Information on our demographic situation]. October 10, 1973, 2. f. 19 / 1973 / 2 doboz / 8 ő.e., SZKL, PIL.

"MSZMP PB June 1962" = Jegyzőkönyv a Politikai Bizottság 1962. junius 12-én megtartott üléséről [Minutes of the meeting of the politburo convened on 12 June 1962]." Accessible online at: https://adatbazisokonline.hu/adatbazis/mszmp-jegyzokonyvek/hierarchia.

"MSZMP PB October 1966" = Jegyzőkönyv a Politikai Bizottság 1966. október 4-én megtartott üléséről [Minutes of the meeting of the politburo convened on 4 October 1966]." Accessible online at: https://adatbazisokonline.hu/adatbazis/mszmp-jegyzokonyvek/hierarchia.

"MSZMP PB February 1973" = Jegyzőkönyv a Politikai Bizottság 1973. február 13-án megtartott üléséről [Minutes of the meeting of the politburo convened on 12 June 1962]." Accessible online at: https://adatbazisokonline.hu/adatbazis/mszmp-jegyzokonyvek/hierarchia.

Morgan, Kimberly J., and Kathrin Zippel. 2003. "Paid to Care: The Origins and Effects of Care Leave Policies in Western Europe." *Social Politics* 10, no. 1: 49–85.

Népszabadság. Available in database: *Arcanum Digitális Tudománytár.* Accessible online at: https://adt.arcanum.com/hu/.

Népszava. Available in database: *Arcanum Digitális Tudománytár.* Accessible online at: https://adt.arcanum.com/hu/.

"Note on Conversation with Mrs. Teodorescu by Elizabeth Johnstone". April 18, 1962, Z 1/1/1/22 (J.2), ILOA.

"Record of interview between representatives of the [WFTU] and the Director-General". April 18, 1962, Z 1/1/1/22 (J.2), ILOA.

"Record of interview between representatives of the [WFTU] and the Director-General". November 14, 1962, Z 1/1/1/22 (J.2), ILOA.

"[SZOT]. Feljegyzés a népesedéspolitikai határozathoz" [Memo on the population policy decision]. July 13, 1973, 2. f. 19 / 1973 / 3 doboz / 17 ő.e., SZKL, PIL.

"SZOT Titkárság. A SZOT Titkárságának véleménye a népesedéspolitikai feladatok c. előterjesztéshez" [Opinion of the SZOT Secretariat on the proposal on the population policy tasks]. November 10, 1972, 2. f. 19 / 1973 / 3 doboz / 17 ő.e., SZKL, PIL.

Timár, János. 1964a. "Long-Term Planning of Employment in the Hungarian People's Republic." *International Labour Review* 89, no. 2: 103–120.

Timár, János. 1964b. *Munkaerőhelyzetünk jelene és távlatai* [Present and perspectives of the position of our labourforce]. Budapest: Közgazdasági és Jogi Könyvkiadó.

Tomka, Béla. 2013. *A Social History of Twentieth-Century Europe.* London, New York: Routledge.

"[Turgonyi, Júlia] *Feljegyzés a debreceni BIOGAL Gyógyszergyár munkásnőivel folytatott beszélgetésről*" [Memo on the conversation with the female workers of the BIOGAL Pharmaceutical Factory in Debrecen, misspelling corrected]. November 27–28, 1967, 904 f. 64 ő.e., TTI, MNL-MOL.

"[Turgonyi, Júlia] *Feljegyzés a Kelenföldi Textilkombinát munkásnőivel folytatott beszélgetésekről*" [Memo on the group discussions with the women workers of the Kelenföld Textile Combine]. December 13, 1967, 904 f. 64 ő.e., TTI, MNL-MOL.

Turgonyi, Julia. 1973. "'Főhivatású anyaság' vagy teljes emberi élet? A nők társadalmi helyzetéről és hivatásáról" [Motherhood as chief-vocation' or full human life? The societal position and vocation of women]. *Társadalomtudományi Közlemények* 3: 25–47.

Varsa, Eszter. 2005. "Class, Ethnicity and Gender. Structures of Differentiation in State Socialist Employment and Welfare Politics, 1960–1980. The Issue of Women's Employment and the Introduction of the First Maternity Leave Regulation in Hungary." In *Need and Care. Glimpses into the Beginnings of Eastern Europe's Professional Welfare*, edited by Kurt Schilde and Dagmar Schulte, 197–217. Opladen and Bloomfield Hills, MI: Barbara Budrich Publishers.

Weltgewerkschaftsbund, ed. 1961. *V. Weltgewerkschaftskongreß. Protokoll. Moskau, 4. bis 15. Dezember 1961.*

WFTU, ed. *Working Women Shape Their Future. 2nd International Trade Union Conference on the Problems of Working Women. Bucharest, May 11 to 16, 1964.* Database: Women and Social Movements International, eds. Kathryn Kish Sklar and Thomas Dublin. https://search.alexanderstreet.com/wasi.

Zajkowska, Olga. 2020. "Parental Leaves in Poland: Goals, Challenges, Perspectives." *Problemy Polityki Społecznej Studia i Dyskusje* 46, no. 3: 121–136.

Zimmermann, Susan. 2010. "Gender Regime and Gender Struggle in Hungarian State Socialism." *Aspasia. The International Yearbook of Central, Eastern and Southeastern European Women's and Gender History* 8: 1–24.

(N.B. All printed ILO material is available online, including the titles enlisted here.)

Carola Lentz
Family, Work, and Social Mobility: Perspectives from Ghana

At the end of December 2016, I was invited to take part in the first "Yob Homecoming Festival," a celebration organised by a large Dagara family of which I had become part during my first field research trip to Ghana back in 1987.[1] Over five hundred family members from four generations gathered for several days at the family farmstead in Hamile, a village in Northwestern Ghana on the border with Burkina Faso. They came from cities in Ghana and Burkina Faso as well as from overseas. For some time already, this extended family comprised a geographically dispersed set of individual households, with only a minority still living on and from the land. Around 1950, the majority had still been peasants. Today, most family members work in non-agricultural professions, from craftsmen, primary school teachers, financial managers, accountants, and bank clerks to university professors. One has even become a bishop. Their social classes and income, lifestyles, and perspectives on the future have become increasingly heterogeneous. Paradoxically, however, geographic and professional diversification has reinforced the quest for family cohesion. Celebrations and the memory of family history are important factors in this regard. Particularly the migrant family members, or the "diaspora" as they like to call themselves, wish to be firmly rooted in an extended family with a clear genealogy. They are interested in defining foundational ancestors who can connect everybody and in keeping their place of origin intact, i. e., the old farmstead and the family cemetery. And they tend to tell the family history as a story of progress.[2]

Around Christmas and the new year, many extended families in Ghana organise similar large family celebrations. During the last ten years, many families founded associations of mutual support that aim to maintain the good name of the family (Noll 2016). This is, in fact, not dissimilar to Germany, where in the context of massive social transformations towards the end of the nineteenth and the

---

1 This paper has been published in German as "Familie, Arbeit und soziale Mobilität. Ghanaische Perspektiven." Berlin: De Gruyter, 2020 (Re:Work. Arbeit global – historische Rundgänge, 4). The English translation is by Tim Jack.
2 For further details concerning this family celebration, my acceptance into the family, and the work on family remembering that I undertook jointly with Isidore Lobnibe, an anthropologist and family member, see Lentz, Lobnibe, and Meda (2018a, 2018b); Lobnibe (2019); and Lentz and Lobnibe (2022).

early twentieth century, bourgeois families began to found associations directed towards establishing intrafamily solidarity and passing on the family history, following a model established by aristocratic houses much earlier (Sabean 2010).

Let us go back to the time around 1900, when the Dagara were colonised. Remarks in reports from colonial officials as well as oral history tell us that across the region, large family and patriclan meetings used to take place following the millet harvest in November and December. Offerings were made to the ancestors; young men and women were initiated into the bagre cult, the most important Dagara secret society; and everybody enjoyed exuberant celebrations with their neighbours as well as relatives living in far-off villages (Goody 1972).

These snapshots reveal the significance of the extended family as an economic and social network and as a symbolic resource to create a sense of identity and belonging. Then, as now, these gatherings were aimed at strengthening dispersed family networks. They served to exchange information, were instances of mutual support, and helped organise labour in addition to the inter- and intra-generational transfer of resources. However, just as salient are the profound changes that have taken place in the past decades: the increasing loss of the function of the family as an agricultural unit of production; the growing separation between work and the family sphere, between the public and private domains; new inter- and intra-generational decision-making hierarchies, gender relations, and authority roles; changing definitions of family membership, and many other issues.

The story of the Yob family, to which I repeatedly refer in this text, is tied into the radical socioeconomic transformation that many societies of the Global South such as Ghana went through during the last one hundred years.[3] Colonies with an economy based on agriculture and enclaves dedicated to agricultural production for export and mining became heterogeneous, partially urbanised economies with a commercial agricultural sector, some industrial centres, and a rapidly growing state apparatus and service sector. Subsistence farming, however, never completely disappeared. A central axis of this transformation is work – the shifts in work processes and labour relations, the development of new fields of economic activity with new education requirements and qualification profiles, the spatial reorganisation of production and reproduction, alongside many other aspects. These upheavals provided new frameworks and challenges for individual life courses and created opportunities for social mobility. However, they also involved risks: marginalisation and social relegation. Individual education and employment trajectories are closely linked with family relations; demonstrating these ties is the central concern of this chapter. As scholarship on the role of families in industri-

---

3 On the political transformation of Northern Ghana during the twentieth century, see Lentz 2006.

alisation processes in the Global North has shown (see below), families can be both a resource and promoter of as well as an impediment to individual social advancement and the transformation of the world of work.

In Ghana, like many countries of the Global South, a rapidly growing middle class has developed over recent decades, with white-collar jobs, new consumption patterns, and lifestyles accompanied by ambitious plans for their own and, in particular, their children's future.[4] There is, however, no consistent trend towards a dissolution of extended families to the benefit of small or nuclear families.[5] Members of the middle classes tend to live in smaller urban households, and even among subsistence farmers in rural areas, the size of households has decreased. Nonetheless, they remain bound into multi-local, large, multigenerational families, and prognoses, such as that by Ulrich Beck (1986), of a consistent individualisation and autonomisation of biographies and a significant pluralisation of lifestyles have not materialised. There are, however, discussions over whether the extended family blocks social advancement or is instead an indispensable resource for social mobility. Such discussions are not limited to academic circles but are also led by politicians and are taking place within families that are becoming increasingly heterogeneous regarding their members' social class and lifestyle.

Families play an important role in the profound processes of socioeconomic transformation that many societies of the Global South have experienced since the Second World War. From my point of view, taking a closer look at their role would effectively complement the questions sketched out recently by James Ferguson and Tania Murray Li (2018). They wish to oppose the no-longer-coherent modernisation-theoretical transformation narrative from "farm-based and 'traditional' livelihoods" towards "'proper jobs' of a modern industrial society" (2018: iii) with a more nuanced vision. However, they do not consider the embeddedness of individual life courses within family structures. With my examples from Northern Ghana, I wish to explore the dynamics of social mobility and labour in the context of the co-ordinates of individual time – family time – historical time (Hareven 1977). How

---

4 Lentz (2015, 2016) and Neubert (2019) provide an overview on research into the middle classes in the Global South.

5 Family is an ambiguous, flexible phenomenon that is hard to pinpoint. Co-residence, reproduction, and descent are elements that make up the family to varying degrees, but the diversity of family forms is significant. Hill and Kopp (2013: 11–13) propose the following working definition: a nuclear family consists of members of two generations; an extended family generally consists of three generations of related nuclear families (such as those of brothers) who cohabitate. I use the term "family" quite loosely, similar to my Ghanaian interlocutors, who also use the term "family" or "extended family" to describe networks of relatives who do not necessarily co-reside.

have the concepts of family and the sharing of resources between the generations changed as the importance of agriculture has dwindled? How does the diminished importance of farmsteads as the economic basis of livelihoods, accompanied by their increasing significance as a symbolic resource of social belonging, affect authority roles? How are individual education and employment biographies coordinated between siblings and cousins? Which kinds of intra-generational support enable social advancement that can cushion the threat of social decline, and which instances of sanction exist to ensure cooperation? How do families interact with the larger social framework of educational institutions, the labour market, and social security systems? In my view, quite "obstinate" and "stubborn" family dynamics mediate between individual life courses and larger social developments.

The history of the Yob family is a good example that encourages us to sharpen our theoretical understanding of the relationship between family, work, and social mobility. In what follows, I will first review some relevant theoretical approaches that address the continued existence of seemingly traditional extended families in societies that are modernising. Taking the Yob family as an example, I will then examine the changing inter- and intra-generational relations and their role in social mobility. Finally, I will return to the question of the role of the family in processes of social transformation that have also profoundly modified the world of work.[6]

Theoretical Inspirations

Discussions on the role of the family in the context of socioeconomic transformations, social mobility, and changing patterns of the life course frequently build on ideal-typical, normatively charged constructs. It is essential to debunk them if we wish to progress theoretically and empirically. I am referring here to the evolutionist narrative that ties the rise of modern industrial societies to the development and dominance of the institution of the modern nuclear family. This narrative alleges that extended, multi-generational families are typical of and functional to traditional agrarian societies and that in the modern context, they would be a moribund remnant of these earlier social formations. The assumed dichotomy between the nuclear family in modern industrial versus multi-generational extended families in pre-modern agrarian societies has multiple ramifications that I will not discuss in detail here. Modernisation is, for example, seen as a process that in-

---

6 For a more extensive discussion of the history of this family and the ways in which it is being remembered, see Lentz and Lobnibe (2022).

creasingly separates the public sphere of work from the private sphere of reproduction or one that de-politicises family relationships and relocates their pre-modern political role exclusively to the modern state.[7]

Already in the early 1980s, the French anthropologist and family sociologist Martine Segalen has argued that the issue of the family was complicated because, from the onset of industrialisation in the nineteenth century, the academic analyses of family structures became fused with practical-political discourses of reform and counter-reform. Many authors, Segalen explains, perceived the family in modernising societies as unstable, in crisis, caught in a process of dissolution, and threatened by state regulation; others saw in the family a powerful stronghold to resist the impositions of modernity and a "cold" bureaucracy. Both perspectives, she asserts, were grounded on normatively underpinned concepts of an almost mythical, ideal-typical, supportive, multi-generational family that had supposedly once been the dominant form in traditional societies – an assumption that actually lacks historical basis.[8] This modernist dichotomy is just as problematic and even harder to overcome when instead of opposing a "then" and "now" in one's own society, it is instead employed in spatial constructs as a difference between Europe and the rest of the world. There are attempts to oppose the supposedly harmonic and mutualistic African extended family with the egoist-individualistic European nuclear family. In numerous articles of the recent anthology *Extended Families in Africa and the African Diaspora* (Aborampah and Sudarkasa 2011), for example, we can observe how the idea that it is necessary to defend the African extended family vis-à-vis Western modernity can fuel identity politics.[9]

Empirical analyses and alternative theoretical concepts that challenge these concepts surfaced as early as the 1980s. They were, however, unable to establish themselves in broader public discourse and received little to no mention even in academic discourse beyond the small group of family historians and anthropolo-

---

7 See Goode (1963) for a classical modernisation model regarding family structures. For a typical application of his assumptions – the increasing dominance of the nuclear family over the course of urbanisation and industrialisation – for Ghana, see Caldwell (1969). In a critical review of Goode's works, Cherlin (2012) observed that family forms even in the West had become far more complex than Goode had predicted. The problematic "bifurcation in the study of kinship and politics" that results from the evolutionist idea that family relations are depoliticised when modern states develop is criticised by Thelen and Alber (2017).

8 See Segalen (1986: 1–12) (the original French edition was published in 1981); see also the overview in Hill and Kopp (2013: 39–49).

9 Alber and Bochow (2006) provide a useful overview of the research on African families.

gists.[10] I will now examine two examples of such research approaches that I have found inspiring.

The first is related to my own academic biography as a long-term junior colleague of Georg Elwert at the Free University Berlin: the "articulation of modes of production" approaches developed by the Bielefeld development sociologists Georg Elwert, Georg Stauth, Tilman Schiel, and – in a feminist version – Claudia von Werlhof and Veronika Bennholdt-Thomsen in the 1980s. They are based on the idea of a systematic link between subsistence production and capitalism.[11] The German discussion in Bielefeld, and later in Berlin, was inspired by the works of French Marxist economic anthropologists and Africa historians such as Claude Meillassoux (1976) and by Immanuel Wallerstein's global-systems approach (1974). The researchers in Bielefeld started from the observation that what appeared to be traditional kin groups and subsistence agriculture was rather resilient even in processes of modernisation. Only the feminist-inspired studies explicitly analysed family structures; implicitly, however, all Bielefeld scholars were convinced that the continuity of peasant subsistence production was premised on the continued existence of multi-generational families. Despite the massive socioeconomic transformation in peripheral societies towards capitalist forms of export-oriented production and the monetarisation of all social relations, the residues of traditional social forms appeared not to wither. To explain this fact, the Bielefeld sociologists looked at the functions that subsistence production fulfils in the capitalist mode of production. Following Meillassoux, they argued that migrant workers created close ties between the different sectors and that subsistence farming continuously subsidises the salaries and costs of reproduction of the capitalist sector. The feminist scholars expanded this argument, asserting that the division of labour within households effectively put housewives in the capitalist urban centres on the same level with peasant families in the periphery; they coined the somewhat unwieldy concept of the global "housewifisation" of labour. These were indeed inspiring approaches to theorise the role kinship and family play in processes of social transformation, yet in their extremity, they worked like a conspiracy theory. "Capital" was awarded a logic and power to act, while

---

10 In this paper I cannot discuss the history of the anthropology of family and kinship in detail; there are some excellent overviews such as the compact article by La Fontaine (2001), and the more detailed analyses of Parkin and Stone (2003: 1–23, 241–56).

11 See the programmatic anthology by the Bielefeld development sociologists working group (1979); see Bennholdt-Thomsen (1981) and Werlhof (1985) on its feminist variant. Bierschenk (2014) provides an overview of the Bielefeld School.

the agency and decision making of families, migrants, and subsistence farmers was hardly taken into consideration.[12]

The second stream of research I draw on are the Europe- and North America-focused family history studies by Martine Segalen (1986), David Sabean (2007, 2010), Simon Teuscher (2007), and others. A key finding of these works was that in the Middle Ages and during early modernity, large multi-generational families did not dominate, at least not everywhere. Conversely, the increasing capitalist penetration of domestic production and later industrialisation and urbanisation was by no means necessarily accompanied by a reduction in household size and the increasing dominance of the nuclear family. As some research shows, large family groups certainly were functional, e. g., for early capitalist workshops, and studies on industrial production such as Tamara Hareven's focused on "the family's contribution in facilitating the process of industrialization as well as adapting to it" (Hareven 2001: 23).[13] More recent family sociology studies argue in a similar vein. The typical two-generation family model allegedly related to modernisation was in fact the usual middle-class family form during the 1950s and 1960s. Theoretical and functional modernisation theories had then wrongly declared this exception to be the general model of development (Cherlin 2012).

Provisionally, then, we can conclude that family is a flexible institution, and its different forms are not tied to any specific larger socioeconomic formations. Even the noted "functionalist" scholar on family sociology, William Goode, who had initially near-to apodictically predicted the global dominance of the nuclear family in the course of industrialisation (Goode 1963: 6), took a more nuanced approach in later life. Regarding the role different family forms play in social mobility, he postulated, for example, that extended family networks can also be an important resource for social advancement in modern societies (Goode 1974 [1966]), and that it is the lower social classes that are more likely to live in nuclear families. Details, therefore, matter – or, to put it in the words of Martine Segalen (1986: 2): "As an institution, the family can both resist and adapt. [. . .] [it] has powers of flexibility and resistance." Instead of overarching evolutionist or functionalist theories, we need a fresh perspective capable of producing medium-range theories based on empirical findings.

---

12 See Braig and Lentz (1983) for an early critique of the conspiracy-theoretical dimension and de-historisation of the Marxist theory of value by authors of the Bielefeld School.
13 See Wall, Hareven, and Ehmer (2001), who also provide a good overview of family historiography. Further overviews can be found in Mitterauer and Sieder (1982), Sabean and Teuscher (2007) and, considering more recent debates, in Albera, Lorenzetti and Mathieu (2016).

Intergenerational Resource Transfers

Now I would like to return to Northern Ghana. First, I will analyse the intra-family division of labour and the intergenerational transfer of resources and how they facilitate or prevent social mobility.[14] I am particularly interested in the transition from a system where the family was the most important production unit to a situation in which most family members are no longer peasants but remain bound, through multiple ties, to the extended family and the farmstead. Family members who migrated relied (and still do to a certain degree) on their farming relatives and the access to land in their villages as a kind of emergency insurance. Yet, over time, the direction of support has been reversed: family members who found employment outside of the village started providing indispensable economic support for the peasant economy. But even then, the rural family of origin remained, and remains, a symbolic resource and an important element of identity politics. My understanding of "resources" is comprehensive here: they include material goods such as land, a farmhouse, and livestock but also knowledge, education, and skills. Furthermore, the family name, belonging to a patriclan, and ethnic identity as the foundation of local, regional, and even global networks are also crucial resources that decide social advancement or decline. Finally, attitudes such as habitus, work ethics, world views, and values play an important role.

Which changes can we observe in the Yob family and neighbouring Dagara kin groups? Until the 1940s and 1950s – and for some lineages, until today – the fundamental resources in the peasant economy were land and labour. Land was passed on from father to son. Generally, adult sons would work the land together until a decision was reached to divide it between them. However, until the late twentieth century, labour, not land, was the scarce resource. In the case of tensions within a family, the eldest sons could always leave with their wives and children and search for new land nearby or move close to a maternal uncle.[15] The younger sons then stayed with their father and later took over his land, which they usually divided between them only after his death. Generally, however, the eldest son inherited the farmhouse.

Subsistence agriculture rarely generated any significant surplus, let alone products that could be sold in exchange for money. However, such financial means were needed to purchase hoes and other agricultural implements, house-

---

14 See Jack Goody's (1962) classical study on inheritance among the Dagara; more generally on the question of the intergenerational transfer of resources with regard to social advancement or decline, see Bertaux and Thompson (1993) and (1997).
15 On agrarian expansion among the Dagara and its changing modalities, see Lentz (2013).

hold utensils, bicycles, and clothes. Since the 1920s, therefore, the heads of households allowed their sons to temporarily work in the gold mines or on export-oriented farms in the South of the colony. Yet, this migration was aimed at supplementing the family's own agriculture-based economy, and the labour requirements of local agriculture remained the imperative that took priority over all other activities. Occasionally this led to conflicts, and the Yob family history includes tales of "lost" sons who did not return as expected. However, those who wanted to be seen as respectable men in society locally needed to accept the inner-family division of labour and its related authority structures.

Since the 1950s, new opportunities outside agriculture developed for which new resources became important – particularly formal education, which opened the door to new occupations. The colonial regime and the Catholic mission, established among the Dagara in 1929, soon began to establish schools in the region. Since the mid-1930s, the sons of village chiefs and the children of Catholic catechists could attend school, granting them access to new professions. But only in the 1960s, when the post-independence government of Ghana invested heavily in expanding the school system, did an opportunity initially open only to a minority become an institution all children were expected to attend. The gradually improving infrastructure of roads and means of transport allowed for greater geographic mobility, facilitating seasonal and sometimes even several-years-long labour migration. For migrants, too, it became easier to maintain contact with their families if they so wished. New professions were initially tied closely to the church, the education system, and the colonial administration: opportunities as road builders, catechists, police officers, teachers, nurses, translators, court assistants, forestry workers, etc., began to open up, mainly for school-educated Dagara. Access to secondary school in the 1950s and university education since the 1960s further expanded the range of employment opportunities. Being able to work outside the region and take up professions such as lawyer, doctor, university professor, financial expert, or senior government official were ideas that young Dagara men and women only slowly began to grasp in the 1970s and 1980s.

How then did different families react, and who within extended families seized the new opportunities? What were the micro-dynamics of innovation at work regarding education and new professions? One important lever was the unequal position of sons within the gerontocratic order. Not all sons had the same opportunities in agriculture; as mentioned above, generally the eldest son enjoyed the greatest privileges. Yet, the youngest could also later gain access to important land resources if he continuously supported the head of the family. Consequently, the "middle sons" in particular had to find new ways of supporting their families. In the Yob family, all sons migrated seasonally. The eldest left when he was still young, and only for two years, after which he became the official heir and began to work the land with his father. Two of the middle sons migrated and "disappeared"; the family in Hamile lost contact with them. A third son became a tradesman, travelled a lot, and his sons only worked small patches of land at home.

It was the second youngest son, Anselmy, disadvantaged by the traditional hierarchy and order of succession, who seized an opportunity offered by the Catholic missionaries. He was offered the chance to undergo catechist training, was baptised in 1938 – like, for that matter, his father and other family members – and went on to work as a catechist. He was sent not to Hamile but other Dagara villages and later established his own large farm away from his father's property, on land that his father used to work in Upper Volta. Most importantly, he sent all his children to school. Working as a catechist outside the paternal farmstead meant he was outside of the direct control of his father and elder brothers. Exposure to information from the missionaries and the church's extended network revealed new employment opportunities to him. For Anselmy himself, catechist and later migrant labour in Accra were still combined with working as a farmer, which dictated the temporal framework of his mobility. Furthermore, his household remained tied into the extended family's economy to a certain extent. But his willingness to take risks and innovate was much greater than that of his brothers.

What we observe here is paradoxical to a certain degree. Undoubtedly, there are parallels with European transformation processes that took place during early modernity: a disadvantageous distribution of resources in the traditional family economy forced a re-orientation, which altered conditions in the larger socioeconomic framework then made possible. In the long term, what had at first appeared risky turned out to be the right choice. In particular, early access to the new but, over time, increasingly important resource of education provided a head start. Anselmy and other catechists could not know this when they decided to send their children to school. A certain habitus or rebellious personality were certainly influential here. Anselmy, for example, told me how as an adolescent he had been sent by his father with itinerant traders to their hometowns in Upper Volta to provide assistance, and how he had been outraged by their unfair treatment to the point that he had made his way back to his father's village on his own. When he talked about these stories, he was clearly disappointed by the fact that his father had seen him as rebellious and apparently wanted him out of the house. Yet, he was also visibly proud that his unwavering ambition had made him relatively wealthy and that his children were successful in this new professional world. His decision to take the risk of investing in new career paths was probably partly enabled by the Catholic Church: faith in God and a new, mutually supportive community of converts as well as support from the white missionaries helped him take an unknown path that seemed to offer no safety net in case of failure.

What form did the intergenerational transfer of educational resources and access to new occupations take? Whereas fathers like Anselmy were open to new employment opportunities – and had themselves worked in new occupations, even without formal education – their children had better chances in education and, therefore, access to new forms of employment. On the one hand, this was pragmatically related to information about the new opportunities provided by schools and novel employment options; the necessary contacts, for example, teachers or hosts at the education centres where schoolchildren had to stay, far away from their home villages; monetary income to pay for school fees, etc. On the other hand, the transmission of certain attitudes and values was also relevant, for example, a new perspective on the future; the willingness to be mobile; and patience regarding the delayed rewards for investments in education. In another research project, I analysed the lives of over sixty men with a university education from Northwestern Ghana regarding their family backgrounds. Many of them were the first university graduates in their extended families, and all of them had a father who had worked as a catechist, a policeman, an agricultural engineer, or in a similar profession during colonial times. In many interviews, I encountered an instructive transfer of an agriculture-based concept of "hard work" from physical to non-physical labour, centred on the idea that a career as an employee also requires hard work and discipline (Lentz 2008; Behrends and Lentz 2012).

For the intergenerational transfer of resources, the values held by mothers were at least as important as those held by fathers. Anselmy's wife Catherine, for example, told me that she had strongly supported her husband's decision to send all their children – eight sons and one daughter born between 1938 and 1963 – to school. However, she had expected all those who were not (yet) in boarding school to help with household chores and work in the fields before going to school in the morning. Catherine also mentioned her initial resistance to sending their only daughter to school. The girl grew up on Catherine's father-in-law's farm, the place Catherine had returned to after living away from home with her husband during his missions as a catechist. Her sisters-in-law and mother-in-law clearly told her that if she sent her only daughter to school, they would no longer offer to help around the house. Because this was considered her daughter's job, nobody would be willing to lend a hand. The question regarding which younger women in rural households can actively support their older female relatives poses a significant problem for all peasant families. In Catherine's case, a partial solution was found because one of the elder sons returned to support Anselmy on the farm, and he was already married to a woman who had not gone to school. She now took over much of the work at her parents-in-law's home; her daughters also had to help, which jeopardised their education. More generally, until the late 1970s, people considered it unnecessary and unproductive to send girls to school.

It took a long time before women – who were successful in their jobs and, therefore, capable of at least financially offering substantial support to their mothers back in the village – could demonstrate that education for girls was not necessarily a wasted investment.

As soon as the first secondary school and university graduates successfully found jobs, the intergenerational transfer of knowledge, attitudes, expectations, as well as material support for education grew. This process was not limited to an exchange between parents and their children but was embraced by the extended family; nephews and nieces and relatives even further away could also benefit. This remains the case today. The initiative for such transfers can come from both sides: members of the younger generation seek advice and support for their education and career paths, or the professionally successful family member seeks an "heir" for his or her expertise, contacts, etc. In particular, this occurs when this person remains childless or if, in spite of considerable efforts – and this happens quite frequently – their children underachieve at school. This phenomenon can also be observed in the Yob family. The household of a childless son of Anselmy, a man who worked as a university lecturer in Accra and went on to become the director of the Ghanaian Institute of Languages, became a magnet for several more or less closely related nieces and nephews. These relatives wanted to study and seek employment in Accra; in exchange for housing and support, they took over important tasks in their host's household.[16]

Extended family networks can, thus, play a crucial role in the intergenerational transfer of resources essential for educational advancement and access to new employment opportunities. Equally, however, in the case of the Yob and other Dagara families with a peasant background, the traditional resources of land and farmstead continue to be inherited following the classical patrilineal rules. However, the significance of these traditional transfers changes with the loss of the family's function as an agricultural unit of production. Sanctions that served to ensure intergenerational solidarity beyond the individual household no longer have the same disciplinary effect for families that no longer depend, or at least not fully, on agriculture to make a living. For non-peasant relatives, sanctions are more or less limited to refusing urban migrants social recognition and acceptance, which in Ghana is still very much observed among other members of the urban middle class. Large public funerals are the most important stage on which these struggles for recognition play out (Lentz 2009).

---

16 See Alber (2016) for examples from Benin on maids in educated households with a heterogeneous class composition.

A revealing study on family histories in Southern Ghana, where people have had access to higher education since the nineteenth century, shows that the patterns I have sketched out, i. e., of a widely spread transfer of resources relevant for new employment fields, continued for two or three generations (Noll 2019). Not until the third generation did branches of the original family develop that were, for example, mainly lawyers or doctors and transferred these resources within their smaller familial circles. Long-term studies on the professional and business traditions of European families have also revealed that relevant resources could often not be transferred within the closer family and therefore included distant relatives.[17] And intergenerational continuity has not always been successful, as Barbara Ehrenreich describes in her classical text *Fear of Falling* (1989).

The Intra-Generational Division of Labour

I have already touched briefly on the issue of the intra-generational negotiations on rights and duties and the co-ordination of life courses between siblings. This question is closely tied to intergenerational exchange and has greater implications both as a facilitator of and obstacle to social mobility than one might first expect. In peasant households, but also in families that are transitioning to new fields of employment, the social advancement of one sibling usually requires consensus, if not the active support of all others. The relationship between siblings – or also to cousins in the case of a multi-generational family with several neighbouring lineages – provides grounds for conflict. The nexus between life courses, the negotiation of divisions of labour and roles, time spent in occupational training, professional activity and starting a family, as well as the expectation of mutual (or unilateral) support, are complex.[18]

In the Yob family, significant changes took place in the relations between siblings. In the generation of Anselmy, the catechist, the division of labour between the brothers was ultimately decided by the father Yob together with his brothers and cousins, and it was guided by agricultural labour requirements. The rule was

---

17 See, for example, the work by Davidoff and Hall (1987).

18 The anthology by Alber, Coe, and Thelen (2013) explores diverse facets of the relations between siblings and highlights their often-neglected importance. In particular, the case study by Obendiek (2013) on Chinese education careers achieved through support between siblings offers many parallels with the example from Ghana discussed in this article. Glen Elder (1994) coined the term "linked lives" as a concept to capture how, in the context of extended families, individual educational and professional biographies and the founding of new families and households are interdependent.

that the eldest son was to return first from what was in any case only temporary labour migration as soon as the father required more support. After the father's death, the eldest son would take over the farm and could ask for the support of his brothers or give them their share of the father's land to start their own farm. As mentioned above, the younger brothers had more limited access to land resources but greater opportunities for mobility. In conversations, Anselmy's eldest son and one of his younger brothers recounted to me the dreams they had had, and which had not materialised, of a life beyond this rural existence. They expressed a certain degree of regret about having to return to the North, revealing that there had been conflicts when family roles were negotiated between the brothers. Differences in character and personality obviously also played a role. Anselmy, for example, as mentioned before, was particularly strong-willed and escaped pressure from his brothers by temporarily settling on family land far from his brothers' farm. Yet for all brothers, access to the family land – and with it the status of belonging to the lineage and clan – remained the ultimate sanction that secured the coordination of life courses under the primacy of agricultural production.

For Anselmy's children, who all went to school and most to university, gerontocratic rules of decision making and authority roles still play a part. As a matter of principle, before deciding on their career or whether to accept an employment opportunity, the younger siblings had to seek consent from the father and also from the eldest brother. In the specific case of Anselmy's family, it is difficult to say whether this would also have been the case if the eldest son had not decided to become a priest and then was elected head of the seminary and ultimately bishop. It is possible that a professionally more successful younger brother could have also become the decision maker, as I observed in numerous other families. Nevertheless, even when this occurs, decisions are still made with reference to the age hierarchy.

What is new, however, is that the decision of who returns North to help the ageing father and mother on the farm after finishing school and holding down their first jobs is no longer defined by the age of the sons. Rather, it is the son with the least success in his life outside of agriculture who is selected. At these junctures, decisions concerning the siblings' life courses were, and still are, interwoven with constellations that lay outside the family: education opportunities, the labour market, and the economic cycle. In the case of Anselmy's children, the second-eldest son, Bartholomew (Barth), was ordered back to his father's farm. He had worked as an agricultural advisor for the German NGO GIZ (*Deutsche Gesellschaft für Internationale Zusammenarbeit*) in Ghana and was already posted in the North of the country, where he became slightly ill and could not expect to advance further in his job. The eldest son, on the other hand, successfully directed the seminary, and behind the scenes, the father and eldest son probably jointly decided to not obstruct the futures of the younger sons, who were still studying.

The issue was not only about coordinating the professional careers of the brothers. Just as important was the coordination of marriages and starting a family. The decision that Barth would return home to Hamile was also motivated by the fact that he had married some time back, and that among his brothers, he was the only one whose wife had not attended school and did not have employment outside of agriculture. The farm back home not only needed a male labourer; equally important was a woman who could help work the land and look after the older generation in the house. Barth's brothers and his sister understood well that his return to their parent's farm was a sacrifice by the couple to the benefit of the entire family. They, therefore, generously supported him with money and gifts and ensured the education of Barth's children.

Seniority between siblings plays an important role regarding authority, decision making, and roles within the family, but it is crosscut by aspects related to social position outside the world of the rural family. This also reflects the fact that, with the dissolution of the family as an agricultural production unit, traditional criteria of status allocation change, and respectability is awarded by a different community than that of the village. Members of the village community are acquainted with this other world, but the different orders of status and hierarchies of authority still exist in parallel and may, at times, collide, leading to conflict. Between siblings as well as between generations, this potential conflict manifests itself especially when rank needs to be performed – for example, when determining in which order family members are greeted and speak, and who is given which place to sit, whether at the homestead or in the car.

Even without being bound in the agricultural economy, the relationship between siblings remains important for mutual support and can be a resource for social advancement as well as a safety net for those threatened by social decline. Among Anselmy's children, I observed that they viewed their own professional success as an opportunity to increase the family's prestige in the community – and thus an opportunity to enhance the possibilities for other family members' social advancement. Family is also an important symbolic resource that does not disappear with the loss of its function as a unit of production. But in spite of the potential for mutual support, negotiations over how individual life courses should adapt to family constellations and who has how much power in these discussions provide grounds for conflict. And this is not only the case for the Yob and Anselmy's family, but also generally among many other families where members rise to become middle class. They complain about parents and siblings restricting their individual plans as much as they bemoan the burdens of the material and social commitments towards their family of origin, which prevent them from investing in their own children (Lentz 1994).

The micro dynamics within and between family generations discussed here cannot be analysed in isolation. I have already mentioned the significance of the dynamics of the labour market and economic cycles in general for education and professional trajectories outside of the agricultural sphere. Here it is important to examine how individual time, family time – i. e., how life courses are coordinated – and historic time are interwoven, to once again refer to Hareven (1977). Moreover, the question concerning what types of social support the family continues to provide, and which kinds of assistance can be and are effectively outsourced to other institutions, is also important. In a large-scale comparative research project, Patrick Heady and his colleagues have explored how state welfare and social institutions and corresponding political framework conditions affect family and kinship; their work has shown that there are many different possible constellations in different European countries (Heady 2010). As far as I am aware, such a systematic analysis does not yet exist for Ghana. There are, however, a number of case studies that consider family relations within the context of transnational migration.[19] In particular, in transnational multigenerational families, legal concerns such as citizenship regulations, border regimes, and the interlocking of different systems of social security play an important role. In the case of the Yob family, transnational migration has remained the exception, but it is gaining importance in some lineages of the extended family.

To co-ordinate individual life courses within the family, the available communication technologies are also important. In Northern Ghana, the situation in this regard has changed dramatically since the 1950s, and especially in the last ten years. It has become far easier to reach the farmstead in Hamile from the cities in the South of the country and vice versa. Everybody in Hamile now has a mobile phone and regularly sends his or her relatives in the "diaspora" messages. Especially among younger family members, WhatsApp groups and Facebook have become important media to remain in contact but also to cope with emergencies and crises. The networks, i. e., who informs whom and who shares news, have broadened; second- and third-degree relatives often belong to such groups even if this does not necessarily translate into concrete support. In certain ways,

---

19 See, for example, Coe (2014) on transnational care for children and relations with grandparents in Ghana. For examples of efforts to create transnational family cohesion, see also Noll (2019). See Drotbohm (2010) on transnational liabilities (and the related conflicts), using the example of Cape Verdean migrants; on migrants from Cameroon in Germany, see Feldman-Savelsberg (2016) – to name just a few examples of Africa-related case studies concerning these questions.

those with access to these fast modes of communication also reinforce forms of mutual social control. The exchange of messages sets new inner-family standards of prestige and recognition that are not easy to sidestep. Gerontocratic norms have not been completely overridden, but the eldest family members do tend to remain excluded from these new forms of communication.

Let me return to the initial question: does the embeddedness of individual life courses within the dynamics of the extended family block or provide a resource for social advancement? There is no clear answer to this question. But we do observe that at least in the first generation of social climbers who no longer depend on subsistence farming to make a living, extended family networks remained important. Yet, these networks are defined flexibly. As the temporal axis from the Yob family, to Anselmy, to Anselmy's children reveals, authority roles and patterns of decision making have shifted. Both the definition of who is a member and the question of duties and rights connected to different types of membership have changed. I cannot discuss the recent debates surrounding family membership in the Yob family and among neighbouring kin groups in detail. However, a central issue is the extent to which the patrilineal definitions should be modified to include married daughters and their children. Here, too, we see flexible answers, with daughters and their children continuing to be seen as family members if they have climbed the social ladder and can potentially help provide access to resources outside of the family.

Martine Segalen's definition of the family as holding "powers of flexibility and resistance" (1986: 2) that I quoted at the outset describes the Yob family well. Any analysis of how "linked lives" (Elder 1994) facilitate or obstruct social advancement must consider demographic coincidences and numerous other uncertainties that, although I did not explicitly refer to them, linger in the background. Regarding vicissitudes such as unexpected childlessness, marriage failure, premature death, unexpected illnesses, and the like, extended family networks are an efficient institution. "Family" and "relatives" are concepts that, at least in principle, guarantee the necessary degree of responsibility and sense of commitment to ensure that family members receive the support they need to bypass, repair, and compensate for adverse situations.

In any case, when we want to understand the dramatic social transformation from a pre-colonial and colonial agricultural society to a post-colonial, semi-industrialised, urban, and highly globalised society, it is worthwhile studying how education and professional biographies are mediated through the changing institution of the family. As Ferguson and Li (2018) rightly highlight, this great political-economic transformation globally has not been a straight line of progress from an agriculture-based society to a modern urbanised industrial society with formal wage labour as the dominant sector. Neither can the complex patterns of formal and informal labour, combinations of agriculture and other sources of income, urbanisation without industrialisation, and diverse links between networks of social reciprocity and dependency be summarised in an undifferentiated narrative of a "dystopian failure" (Ferguson and Li 2018: 3). An ethnographic micro-analysis of how the generational upheavals in the Yob family – and more generally an analysis of how families process social change – can provide an important foundation to develop a more nuanced picture.

References

Aborampah, Osei-Mensah, and Niara Sudarkasa, eds. 2011. *Extended Families in Africa and the African Diaspora*. Trenton, NJ: Africa World Press.

Alber, Erdmute. 2016. "Heterogenität als gelebte Praxis, Norm und Zukunftsgestaltung. Mittelschichtshaushalte in Benin." In *Mittelklassen, Mittelschichte oder Milieus in Afrika? Gesellschaften im Wandel*, edited by Antje Daniel, Sebastian Müller, Rainer Öhlschläger, Florian Stoll, 177–194. Baden-Baden: Nomos.

Alber, Erdmute, and Astrid Bochow. 2006. "Familienwandel in Afrika. Ein Forschungsüberblick." *Paideuma* 52: 227–250.

Alber, Erdmute, Cati Coe, and Tatjana Thelen, eds. 2013. *The Anthropology of Sibling Relations: Shared Parentage, Experience and Exchange*. New York: Palgrave Macmillan.

Albera, Dionigi, Luigi Lorenzetti, and Jon Mathieu. 2016. "Introduction." In *Reframing the History of Family and Kinship: From the Alps toward Europe*, edited by Dionigi Albera, Luigi Lorenzetti, and Jon Mathieu, 7–18. Bern: Peter Lang.

Arbeitsgruppe Bielefelder Entwicklungssoziologen, eds. 1979. *Subsistenzproduktion und Akkumulation*. Saarbrücken: Breitenbach.

Beck, Ulrich. 1986. *Risikogesellschaft. Auf dem Weg zu einer anderen Moderne*. Frankfurt am Main: Suhrkamp.

Behrends, Andrea, and Carola Lentz. 2012. "Education, Careers and Home Ties: The Ethnography of an Emerging Middle Class from Northern Ghana." *Zeitschrift für Ethnologie* 137, no. 2: 139–164.

Bennholdt-Thomsen, Veronika. 1981. "Subsistenzproduktion und erweitere Reproduktion. Ein Beitrag zur Produktionsweisendiskussion." *Gesellschaft. Beiträge zur Marxschen Theorie* 14: 30–51.

Bertaux, Daniel, and Paul Thompson. 1993. *Between Generations: Family Models, Myths, and Memories*. London: Transaction Publishers.

Bertaux, Daniel, and Paul Thompson, eds. 1997. *Pathways to Social Class: A Qualitative Approach to Social Mobility*. Oxford: Clarendon.

Bierschenk, Thomas. 2014. "From the Anthropology of Development to the Anthropology of Global Engineering." *Zeitschrift für Ethnologie* 139, no. 1: 73–98.

Braig, Marianne, and Carola Lentz. 1983. "Wider die Enthistorisierung der Marxschen Werttheorie. Kritische Anmerkungen zur Kategorie 'Subsistenzproduktion.'" *Probleme des Klassenkampfs* 50: 5–21.

Caldwell, John. 1969. *African Rural-Urban Migration: The Movement to Ghana's Towns*. New York: Columbia University Press.

Cherlin, Andrew J. 2012. "Goode's World Revolution and Family Patterns: A Reconsideration at Fifty Years." *Population and Development Review* 38, no. 4: 577–607.

Coe, Cati. 2014. *The Scattered Family: Parenting, African Migrants, and Global Inequality.* Chicago: Chicago University Press.

Davidoff, Leonore, and Catherine Hall. 1987. *Family Fortunes: Men and Women of the English Middle Class, 1780–1850.* Chicago and London: University of Chicago Press.

Drotbohm, Heike. 2010. "Begrenzte Verbindlichkeiten. Zur Bedeutung von Reziprozität und Kontribution in transnationalen Familien." In *Verwandtschaft heute. Positionen, Ergebnisse und Forschungsperspektiven*, edited by Erdmute Alber, Bettina Beer, Julia Pauli, and Michael Schnegg, 175–201. Berlin: Reimer.

Ehrenreich, Barbara. 1989. *Fear of Falling: The Inner Life of the Middle Class.* New York: Pantheon.

Elder, Glen H., Jr. 1994. "Time, Human Agency, and Social Change: Perspectives on the Life Course." *Social Psychology Quarterly* 57, no. 1: 4–15.

Feldman-Savelsberg, Pamela. 2016. *Migranten, Recht und Identität. Afrikanische Mütter und das Ringen um Zugehörigkeit in Berlin.* Bielefeld: Transcript.

Ferguson, James, and Tania Murray Li. 2018. "Beyond the 'Proper Job': Political-economic Analysis after the Century of Labouring Man." Working Paper 51. Institute for Poverty, Land and Agrarian Studies (PLAAS). Cape Town: University of the Western Cape.

Goode, William J. 1963. *World Revolution and Family Patterns.* New York: Free Press.

Goode, William J. 1974. "Family and Mobility." In *Class, Status and Power*, edited by Reinhart Bendix and S. M. Lipset, 582–601. London: Routledge.

Goody, Jack. 1962. *Death, Property and the Ancestors: A Study of the Mortuary Customs of the LoDagaa of West Africa.* Stanford, CA: Stanford University Press.

Goody, Jack. 1972. *The Myth of the Bagre.* Oxford: Clarendon Press.

Hareven, Tamara K. 1977. "Family Time and Historical Time." *Daedalus* 106, no. 2: 57–70.

Hareven, Tamara K. 2001. "The Impact of Family History and the Life Course on Social History." In *Family History Revisited: Comparative Perspectives*, edited by Richard Wall, Tamara K. Hareveen, Joseph Ehmer, and Markus Cerman, 21–39. Newark: University of Delaware Press.

Hareven, Tamara K. 1999. *Families, History, and Social Change: Life Course and Cross-Cultural Perspectives.* Boulder, CO: Westview.

Heady, Patrick, ed. 2010. *Family, Kinship and State in Contemporary Europe.* Vol. 3. Frankfurt am Main: Campus.

Hill, Paul B., and Johannes Kopp. 2013. *Familiensoziologie. Grundlagen und theoretische Perspektiven.* Wiesbaden: Springer VS.

La Fontaine, Jean S. 2001. "Family, Anthropology of." In *International Encyclopedia of the Social and Behavioral Sciences*, edited by Neil Smelser and Paul B. Baltes, 5307–5311. Amsterdam: Elsevier.

Lentz, Carola. 1994. "Home, Death and Leadership: Discourses of an Educated Elite from Northwestern Ghana." *Social Anthropology* 2: 149–169.

Lentz, Carola. 2006. *Ethnicity and the Making of History in Northern Ghana.* Edinburgh: Edinburgh University Press.

Lentz, Carola. 2008. "Hard Work, Luck and Determination: Biographical Narratives of a Northern Ghanaian Elite." *Ghana Studies* 11: 47–76.

Lentz, Carola. 2009. "Constructing Ethnicity: Elite Biographies and Funerals in Ghana." In *Ethnicity, Belonging and Biography: Ethnographical and Biographical Perspectives*, edited by Gabriele Rosenthal and Artur Bogner, 181–202. Berlin: Lit.

Lentz, Carola. 2013. *Land, Mobility, and Belonging in West Africa.* Bloomington, IN: Indiana University Press.

Lentz, Carola. 2015. "Elites or Middle Classes? Lessons from Transnational Research for the Study of Social Stratification in Africa." Working Papers of the Department of Anthropology and African Studies, Johannes Gutenberg University Mainz 161.

Lentz, Carola. 2016. "African Middle Classes: Lessons from Transnational Studies and a Research Agenda." In *The Rise of Africa's Middle Class: Myths, Realities and Critical Engagements*, edited by Henning Melber, 17–53. London: Zed Books.

Lentz, Carola, and Isidore Lobnibe. 2022. *Imagining Futures: Memory and Belonging in an African Family.* Bloomington: Indiana University Press.

Lentz, Carola, Isidore Lobnibe, and Stanislas Meda. 2018a. "Family History as Family Enterprise? A Wissenschaftskolleg Focus Group's Views of a West African Family." *TRAFO – Blog for Transregional Research.* Accessed January 14, 2021. https://trafo.hypotheses.org/11214.

Lentz, Carola, Isidore Lobnibe, and Stanislas Meda. 2018b. "From History to Memory: A Wissenschaftskolleg Focus Group's Views of a West African Family – After Six Months Work." *TRAFO – Blog for Transregional Research.* Accessed January 14, 2021. https://trafo.hypotheses.org/11377.

Lobnibe, Isidore. 2019. "From the Narrow Pathways of the Black Volta Region to Wissenschaftskolleg zu Berlin: Navigating a Web of Kinship and Ways of Belonging with Carola Lentz." In *Zugehörigkeiten. Erforschen, Verhandeln, Aufführen im Sinne von Carola Lentz*, edited by Jan Beek, Konstanze N'Guessan, and Mareike Späth, 23–36. Köln: Köppe.

Meillassoux, Claude. 1976. *Die wilden Früchte der Frau. Über häusliche Produktion und kapitalistische Wirtschaft.* Frankfurt am Main: Syndikat.

Mitterauer, Michael, and Reinhard Sieder, eds. 1982. *Historische Familienforschung.* Frankfurt am Main: Suhrkamp.

Neubert, Dieter. 2019. *Inequality, Socio-cultural Differentiation and Social Structures in Africa.* Cham: Palgrave Macmillan.

Noll, Andrea. 2016. "Family Foundations for Solidarity and Social Mobility: Mitigating Class Boundaries in Ghanaian Families." *Sociologus* 66, no. 2: 137–157.

Noll, Andrea. 2019. *Verwandtschaft und Mittelklasse in Ghana: Soziale Differenzierung und familiärer Zusammenhalt.* Köln: Köppe.

Obendiek, Helena. 2013. "When Siblings Determine Your 'Fate': Sibling Support and Educational Mobility in Rural Northwest China." In *The Anthropology of Sibling Relations: Shared Parentage, Experience and Exchange*, edited by Erdmute Alber, Cati Coe, and Tatjana Thelen, 97–121. New York: Palgrave Macmillan.

Parkin, Robert, and Linda Stone, eds. 2003. *Kinship and Family: An Anthropological Reader.* London: Wiley Blackwell.

Sabean, David W. 2010. "Constructing Lineages in Imperial Germany. Eingetragene Familienvereine." In *Alltag als Politik – Politik im Alltag. Dimensionen des Politischen in Vergangenheit und Gegenwart. Ein Lesebuch für Carola Lipp*, edited by Michaele Fenske, 143–157. Berlin: Lit.

Sabean, David W., and Simon Teuscher. 2007. "Kinship in Europe: A New Approach to Long-term Development." In *Kinship in Europe: Approaches to Long-Term Development (1300–1900)*, edited by David W. Sabean, Simon Teuscher, and Jon Mathieu, 1–21. Oxford: Berghahn.

Segalen, Martine. 1986. *Historical Anthropology of the Family.* Cambridge: Cambridge University Press.

Thelen, Tatjana, and Erdmute Alber, eds. 2017. *Reconnecting State and Kinship.* Philadelphia: University of Pennsylvania Press.

Von Werlhof, Claudia. 1985. *Wenn die Bauern wiederkommen. Frauen, Arbeit und Agrobusiness in Venezuela.* Bremen: Edition Con.

Wall, Richard, Tamara K. Hareven, and Josef Ehmer, eds. 2001. *Family History Revisited: Comparative Perspectives.* Newark: University of Delaware Press.

Wallerstein, Immanuel. 1974. *The Modern World System: Capitalist Agriculture and the Origins of the European World Economy in the Sixteenth Century.* New York: Academic Press (and subsequent editions).

Erdmute Alber

The Linking of Vital Conjunctures: Negotiations over Girls' Futures

Introduction

> We are living in a transitional phase of a changing society, since for a rural girl, once you are in town, they do not want to return to the village. So, this is always creating family conflict" (*Dans la mutation de societe, nous vivons dans une etappe transitoire, parce-que une fille de village, si vous etez en ville une fois, elles ne veulent pas retourner au village. Alors il se cre toujours un mal entent dans la famille* [February 3, 2016]).

This lament was made by Woru Salifou[1], a retired banker, when we talked about how he and his wife Nuria were living as a childless, social climbing urban couple in Cotonou, the economic centre of the Republic of Benin. Living an urban upper-middle-class lifestyle, both husband and wife were at the same time connected to their rural kin. This connection manifested in, among other things, the fact that they were hosting several relatives born in the same rural area in northern Benin in their large three-story house. One of these relatives was Nuria's niece Salimatou, a young woman of about twenty-six years old, and her young son. As is usual in Benin, and even more so for childless couples, Woru and Nuria had taken Salimatou into their household at a young age to have a helping girl.[2] Unsuccessful in school, Salimatou was doing an apprenticeship when her birth father asked Woru to send her back to the village to get married. The girl refused, as did the foster parents, but the girl's father put so much pressure on them that they felt forced to accept the young woman's marriage. However, after one year of an unhappy marriage in the countryside, Salimatou ran away with her newborn son. Woru and his wife accepted her back into their household and provided her with space in their house. When I visited, this is where she was living together with her eight-year-old son, earning a living as a hairdresser.

---

1 All names in this text are anonymised.
2 The expression "help" is a translation of a local expression in Benin used to describe an arrangement in which rural girls who are not enrolled in schools are sent to urban households to do domestic labour. Talking about help instead of work circumscribes the fact that no salary is paid, but the household in which the girl is working is expected to "do something for her," as people call it. In fact, this means paying for an apprenticeship or contributing substantially to the dowry. Thus, in this context, "helping" could be translated as non-salaried work.

Woru's lament about inevitable family conflicts between urban and rural households resulting from negotiations over girls' life trajectories summarise the key empirical arguments in this chapter. First, Woru argues that the life course regimes of young women in Benin are changing, as are their life expectations, desires, and imagined futures. Second, these life course changes are due to broader societal change. The "transitional phase" Woru mentions is, I would argue, characterised by processes of class construction and the emerging differentiation of lifestyles and life expectancies. This becomes especially manifest in changing notions about the "right" life course for young women and in negotiations over who has the right to decide. In these processes, those in the urban middle classes are drawing new and different boundaries in their lifestyles than those of their rural (and almost always poorer) kin. At the same time, they accept some of their rural relatives' children into their households. This leads to changing and often conflicting norms concerning girls' education as well as to negotiations over girls' labour capacity and marriage arrangements. Third, the inevitable conflicts within extended kin networks are due to the fact that changes in the life courses of girls also affect the life courses as well as the expectations, moralities, and future-making processes of others. From a life course perspective, one could therefore argue that in moments of societal transformations that affect life course regimes, the entanglements of life trajectories – what Glen Elder has called "linked lives" (Elder 1994, 1998, Elder et al. 2003) – are becoming sources of personal and familial conflict.

The basic arguments of this chapter outlined above have already been raised in Salifou Woru's reflections. His argument of a transitional phase in Beninese society could be concretised as a process of ongoing urbanisation and the professionalisation of the urban labour sectors in Benin. This is related to the emergence of larger urban middle classes and accompanied by an increasing demand for formal education certificates as the starting point for social mobility. At the same time, large segments of the population are unable to attain this professional status, which results in an increasingly wide cleavage between urban and rural populations and also serves to diminish the economic expectations of those parts of the population excluded from access to social mobility. In the republic of Benin, as in many African countries, the rapid and ongoing process of differentiation is mitigated through deep interconnections, most often through kinship relationships. These connections are made manifest by, among other things, the circulation of children from poorer families to richer households, which leads to the building of "multi-class households" (Lentz and Noll 2021; Alber 2019). As a result, processes of unequal social mobility and related modes of exclusion lead not only to increasing social inequality in the nation-state of Benin but also to a high degree of inequality within kin groups.[3]

In this chapter, I question how these processes of increasing differentiation within kin groups are negotiated during conflicts over young women's life trajectories. Salimatou's case of involuntary return to the village, later followed by an escape back to the city, is one example among many I have followed during my research in Benin.[4] I have mainly described this case from her perspective and that of her foster parents, who jointly believed that her future was best served in the capital, where she could earn a living from her profession and ensure that her son had an urban future. Her foster parents did not regard her possible life trajectory as a married woman in the countryside – the future her father wished for her – as an appropriate path. At first glance, and in order not to contest to Salimatou's father's decision, they gave in to his demand that his daughter return to the village and marry. However, later on, they both diverged from her father's wishes and made different decisions: Salimatou made the decision to flee, and her foster parents accepted her back into their household. This gentler form of managing the situation – first accepting the father's decision and only later rejecting the marriage – nevertheless caused a family conflict, which was the reason Woru claimed that such conflicts among kin groups are practically inevitable today.

The case of Salimatou shows a confrontation between different visions of her future; the conflict between her father and her foster parents can also be understood as a clash over who has the right to decide her life trajectory. In an older and rural understanding of child fostering, as I have shown elsewhere (Alber 2003), foster parents have the right to make decisions concerning their foster children's future life path because they are the caregivers of the child. However, Salimatou's sojourn in Woru and Nuria's household could be interpreted in two different ways: it could be understood as either a foster arrangement or as an employment contract, which is also quite frequently used to structure rural girls' time in urban households. In the latter case, there is an agreement between birth parents and foster parents that the domestic labour of a rural girl living in an urban middle-

---

3 One important reason for these inter-familial processes of differentiation is the fact that during almost the entire twentieth century, especially rural parents generally sent only some of their children to school. Concerning schooling in Benin, see Fichtner (2012) and Tama (2014).

4 This chapter is a result of long-term field research in the Republic of Benin that was partially realised in the context of the BMBF-funded research project "Middle Classes on the Rise" (2012–2019) at the Bayreuth Academy of Advanced African Studies in Bayreuth. An initial version of parts of this chapter was published in the form of a working paper (Alber 2016) but has been further developed for this collection. I thank the editors of this volume for their critical reading.

class household for some years is compensated by paying for an apprenticeship or financing the expenses of the young woman's trousseau when she marries. But it is the birth parents who retain the right to decide their child's future by arranging a marriage of their behalf.

Today, both types of placing and accepting a rural girl into the urban household of kin are commonly practised by families from northern Benin who send their children to live in middle class households in the urban south. While in conversations these types of placements are distinguishable, the persons involved do not always make a sharp distinction between them at the start of such arrangements. This ambiguity may be because in Baatonum, the local language, clearcut distinctions between different child fostering arrangements for educational purposes or for labour are difficult to express. Additionally, norms of politeness and indirect speech as well as possible divergent expectations that are not articulated complicate such negotiations. As a result, conflicts frequently arise years later, when the future of the teenager who had been placed in an urban household as a child is discussed. Finally, sometimes interpretations of the initial agreement also change.

To theoretically position Woru's argument concerning inevitable family conflict resulting from the transitional historical moment, I will first take into consideration Glen Elder's (1994: 6) argument concerning the interdependency of lives, what he called "linked lives" (Elder 1994, 1998, Elder et al. 2003). Second, I combine this concept with Jennifer Johnson-Hanks's (2002, 2005) and others' explorations of vital conjunctures and turning points that shed light on the processual conflict dimensions of changing life trajectories and the fluidity of life stages. I will then apply my concept of interdependent vital conjunctures to a second case, the story of a rural girl named Gloria, who was, like Salimatou, first placed in an urban household but then was brought back to the village for an arranged marriage against her will. In my conclusion, I explain how these further layers of analysis relate to the dimension of time.

Linking Vital Conjunctures

Summarising different theoretical perspectives on the life course, psychologist and sociologist Glen Elder elaborated the concept of linked lives. He argued that "no principle of the life course is more central than the notion of interdependent lives" and explained the significance of the embeddedness of humans in social relationships with kin and friends across the life span. To elucidate its importance, he explained that "social regulation and support occur in part through these relationships" and ended with the important argument that the effects of linking lives endure not only over the individual life span but in the process of generational succession. Thus, he regards the linking of lives as important for the reproduction of class positionality.

Elder's understanding of linked lives is based on his reconstruction of the importance of family ties in determining the later life trajectories of children in impoverished families during the Great Depression. In his study *Children of the Great Depression* (Elder 1974), Elder proved that despite the fact that all the children were similarly poor, a large majority managed to successfully earn a living later on. However, there were remarkable differences between those whose impoverished parents had a middle-class background and children from working-class families. Whereas working-class children suffered the consequences of the Depression for the rest of their lives, middle-class children often became successful, sometimes even more successful than other middle-class children whose families were not affected by the Depression. The findings of this path-breaking study resulted in Elder's awareness of the interplay between life trajectories and historical eras as well as the effects of early life constellations for later periods in the life course.

Interestingly, when elaborating the importance of linked lives, Elder mentions "social regulation and support" (1994: 6), principally positively attributed activities summarised as care or education typically associated with the domestic sphere and often with kinship.[5] Conflicts, disparities, or tensions are, in his conceptual notes on the life course, not associated with linked lives but with what he calls the "timing of lives," i. e., with the ways individual life trajectories and related decisions refer to "the incidence, duration, and sequence of roles, and to relevant expectations and beliefs based on age" (Elder 1994: 6). Here, he mentions "ill-timed" events such as early pregnancy and the resultant tasks of scheduling trajectories and the work of decision making for all persons conceptualised as agents in decision making at any given moment of the life course (Elder 1994: 5).

Another field and cause of tension and conflict is the interference of historical time and events and the individual life course. For example, Elder mentions that the loss of income in the Depression led to changing family economies that resulted in more productive work for children and greater burdens for mothers (1994: 11). Arguing that relationships within families were "altered" (1994: 11) and families were "demoralized," Elder nevertheless does not question how these conflicts might affect the linking of lives.

---

5 A critical analysis of the association of "positive" or "warm" care with kinship, often set in contrast to the "cold" activities of the state can be found in Thelen, Thiemann, and Roth (2018). See also Thelen and Alber (2022).

Elder's important model of the life course was characterised by four important themes: (a) the linking of lives and historical time; (b) the interplay of human lives and historical period; (c) the timing of lives, linked or interdependent; and (d) human agency in decision-making, and it was a conceptual milestone in the scholarship on life course. The fact that he did not associate conflict with linked lives might be partially due to the methodology of his research, which largely relied on survey and panel studies, thus requiring him to retrospectively reconstruct the effects of changing historical formations on life trajectories.

In contrast, ethnographic methods of participant observation provided the methodological background of Jennifer Johnson-Hanks's (2002, 2005) study on young middle-class Beti women in Cameroon navigating[6] childhood and youth in the context of complex normative expectations concerning the honour of young women. Johnson-Hanks does not retrospectively reconstruct the life courses of her subjects but analyses her research interlocutors' present struggles and future aspirations and doubts by following ongoing conflicts. Here, she introduces the concept of *vital conjuncture* as an alternative to the older and widely criticised, but nevertheless still frequently used, concept of *life stage*.[7] In Johnson-Hanks's study, the young women's main goal is to become honourable adults by fulfilling the normative expectations of their society, which is to successfully finish their proper schooling. Due to their society's expectations, this decision often leads them to postpone motherhood since early motherhood is widely seen as shameful for educated girls. Johnson-Hanks argues convincingly that this postponement of mothering and, consequently, the full achievement of adult status does not require the women to abstain from sexuality but rather to make decisions in case of pregnancy. Girls have the option to carry the pregnancy to term and give up the child to foster parents after delivery so they may "return" to the status of schoolgirl. Or they might decide to terminate the pregnancy by seeking an abortion. A third option is to raise the baby and, thus, to become a mother and possibly a wife. Following this conflict-filled navigation of different options for the future, she argues for a more fluid conceptualisation of specific positions in the life course, such as motherhood:

> Rather than a clear threshold into female adulthood, here motherhood is a loosely bounded, fluid status. . . . Beti women who have borne children are not necessarily mothers, at least not

---

6 Concerning the terminology and concept of navigation, see Christiansen et al. 2006.

7 Elder, for instance, uses the concept of life stages to illustrate his argument about the timing of lives, explaining that life course events such as marriage or childbirth do not always fit well with professional trajectories, and that children were differently affected by the Great Depression than were persons in later stages of the life course (1994: 6).

all the time. Motherhood, instead, constitutes a temporary social status, an agent position that can be inhabited in specific forms of social action. . . . "Life stages" emerge only as the result of institutional projects; their coherence should be an object, rather than an assumption, of ethnographic inquiry. (Johnson-Hanks 2002: 866)

Johnson-Hanks' rejection of clear-cut life stages is that these might be the "result of institutional projects" – here I would add that they often serve as normative ideas about the correct life course – but they are not a lived reality. Rather, they are shaped by constant struggles and processes of decision-making which then might endorse or reject motherhood. In the process of struggling over and navigating towards a future, seemingly well-defined and stable stages of the life course such as motherhood become fluid. Whereas Johnson-Hanks referred to some anthropological literature (Goody 1982; Bledsoe 1980) that had already challenged the idea of motherhood as unambiguous, feminist scholarship had also argued in favour of the fluidity and negotiability of motherhood, reconceptualising it as "mothering" in order to express the constant work of motherhood (Ruddick 1989). Similar to Ruddick's processual approach but different with regard to the normative orientation of the study, Johnson-Hanks's conceptual approach not only focuses on constant struggle but also considers intense conflicts that might lead to mothering as well as processes of *undoing motherhood* (my terminology).

Further work on the fluidity of motherhood is Mette Line Ringstedt's (2007) article on the collision of the life courses of female teenagers in Tanzania with those of their children's grandmothers (maternal and paternal). She describes a variety of strategies the young women use to include grandmothers in childcare. Some of these older women reject these demands, arguing that they are still too young to become grandmothers. Some of the teenagers also argue that they are still too young to take responsibility for their children, which indicates the normative expectations concerning the timing of life courses. Other teenage mothers succeed in getting their mothers to become the mothers of their children. And finally, some simply neglect their children by leaving them at home when they go out to bars and clubs at night. As a result, these teenagers cross back over the imaginary boundary between adulthood and youth and become, once again, childless youths. With this ethnographic example, Ringstedt demonstrates that by negotiating responsibility for children and, thus, mothering, not only are teenagers traversing fluid boundaries in their life course but so too are their mothers, who also traverse the fluid border between adulthood and eldership by accepting their status as grandmothers. Altogether, mothering appears as fluid and processual as well as reversible and intensively entangled with other processes such as grandmothering or spousing. This conclusion resonates with the work of Notermans (2004), who argued that the decision to accept responsibility for caring for a grandchild could be understood as a negotiation over the fluid border between adult and elder.

By taking up Johnson-Hanks's argument about the fluidity of achieved positions in the life course, Ringstedt as well as Notermans have adopted Elder's argument for linked lives without citing him. Not limiting themselves to the issues of support and education as modalities for linking lives, they present negotiations over linked lives as arenas for conflict and negotiation over life trajectories and imagined futures. Among other things, they radicalise the argument for fluidity in life course positions by claiming the reversibility of achieved positions. This argument not only holds for mothering but also for other phases in the life course, for example, old age, as Tabea Häberlein (2015) convincingly demonstrated with respect to the fluidity of old age in northern Togo. Therefore, somewhat different from Johnson-Hanks's focus on the struggles of individuals to manage their life trajectories, conceptual work is required to grasp the interpersonal and often intergenerational entanglements of life trajectories. Anthropological scholarship thus confirms Elder's claim that a life course perspective should not focus solely on the life trajectories of individuals and their relationship to historical and societal change but also on the entanglements of an individual's life course with those of others. At the same time, the question of conflict in the linking of lives is raised.

An important dimension of Johnson-Hank's concept of *vital conjunctures* is that it covers not a single moment but a longer, open-ended time span. It bears a resemblance to the concept of *turning points* (Hareven and Masaoka 1988: 274 ff; Abbott 2001) as it grasps moments of transitions or "radical shifts" (Abbott 2001: 343) in the life course by stressing that these take time. While some scholarship (Voigt 2021: 103) argues that turning points or vital conjunctures always accompany a change in status (for instance, from childhood to adulthood), Johnson-Hanks defines it as "a socially structured zone of possibility that emerges around specific periods of potential transformation in a life or lives. It is a temporary configuration of possible change, a duration of uncertainty and potential" (2002: 871). Therefore, by stressing the uncertainty and potential of an unknown future, vital conjunctures might just as likely lead to a change in status as to a confirmation of the prior status. In any case, emphasis on timing in the life course highlights a relatively simple, albeit often neglected aspect, namely that decision-making is done on the basis of knowledge and experience related to the past and in relation to an envisaged but contingent future. In the case of Salimatou, this involved both the question of how she imagined her own future and her hopes for her son.

To sum up, Elder's concept of linked lives could be enlarged – with view to the cited literature – to a concept of linked vital conjunctures in which diverging imaginations of life trajectories are negotiated, quite often through conflict. Societal change and related shifting notions and expectations of an appropriate life course are not the only reasons conflict emerges in these processes; another important reason is the entanglement of individuals in webs of kinship, inter-generational relations, and even the different but related vital conjunctures of entwined lifetimes. A single person cannot make herself a married woman or a mother. Rather, she is related to others such as parents, siblings, or in-laws, whose life trajectories are also affected by these transitions and whose behaviour contributes to the making of a mother or wife, the return to adolescence, or, as in the case of Salimatou, the ability to live as a single mother in the city. I will now explain this entanglement further through a second case study: the story of Gloria and the linked lives of others concerned with her life course.

Negotiating Gloria's Future

Having broadly contextualised the story of Salimatou from her perspective and that of her urban-based supporters, I will now trace the interdependencies of turning points or vital conjunctures in greater depth by including the perspectives of rural relatives involved in a family conflict over the future of Gloria. When I firstly heard somebody talking about Gloria, she was still a young, unmarried woman. It was Kora, a peasant in the village of Tebo in northern Benin, who eagerly told me in 2010 that he had, some years before, engaged a girl from a neighbouring village for his foster son MamMam.[8] Although his son reached marriage age, and because Kora felt obliged to fulfil the parental duty of arranging a wife for his son, he was told by the future in-laws that the girl had been sent to live in an urban household in Cotonou to "help" there. He should, thus, wait a little longer. But Kora was worried about whether the wedding would still take place. Since he had already invested in the engagement by paying the bride price and sending regular gifts to the in-laws, and due to the pressure he felt to give his foster son a wife, he was extremely concerned that the marriage would fall through. The issue was even more serious from Kora's perspective because MamMam – with the financial help of his birth mother – had already taken another wife on his own, with whom he had already been living for several months. It would be a source of shame for Kora and would endanger his relationship with his foster son if, after the long period of time Mam-

---

8 Child fostering is a very widespread pattern in rural northern Benin (Alber 2003, 2018). Among other obligations, foster parents have the obligation to organise their foster children's marriages because they are regarded as the proper parents of the child.

Mam had lived in Kora's household and daily worked with him in agriculture, Kora would not be able to give MamMam a wife more quickly.

For his part, MamMam made similar arguments, telling me that he had already been impatiently waiting for the wife his (foster) father had promised him to arrive to the household. A year later, in 2011, I managed to get into contact with Gunu, the man who had taken the girl into his household in Cotonou. Once he understood that I had not been sent by the rural relatives to take the girl back to the village, he invited me into the house where he was living with his wife, two small children, and Gloria.

Gunu was a professional soldier who had left the village – and with it, a lifestyle, as he candidly told us. He had relatively little formal education but did have strong resolve to become an urban citizen, a member of the middle class. Therefore, he had envisaged climbing the social ladder in the army.[9] He never regretted this choice. When I met him in Cotonou, he was just back from an engagement in the UN peace-keeping forces in Ivory Coast. He immediately started talking about Gloria because this matter upset him, as he told me. For weeks he was regularly called by the villagers who demanded he send her back, but he did not plan to do so. He had taken her to Cotonou to pay for her apprenticeship after she worked some years in his household and did not want to let enter a marriage with a villager. I asked him to explain how and why he took her to Cotonou. Gunu answered that because he was often absent and his wife was also employed, he had been looking for somebody who could take care of the couple's children. First, he had wanted to bring his youngest sister, who was still living with their peasant parents, to live in his household in the city. His idea was to enrol her in school together with his child. However, his parents refused and so he began to look for another girl who had never attended school. He wanted the girl to care for the children and then planned to pay for an apprenticeship for her.[10] He asked his brother to send him such a girl, and his sibling suggested Gloria. She was a relative from Gunu's own village, the daughter of divorced parents who had grown up with an aunt who had previously sent Gloria to work for a family. The aunt had agreed to Gloria living in Gunu's household, but now his and Gloria's relatives repeatedly called Gunu to ask that he send the girl back to the village for an arranged marriage. He thought this was a stupid idea. Gloria did not want to return to the village, and she had already learned French. Why should he send her back to live

---

9 In contemporary Benin, the army as well as the police create the potential for social mobility among those persons lacking significant schooling.

10 Such an arrangement is frequently used to compensate for a girl's labour. In these cases, either the girls are hosted in the household of their master or remain with their foster family, which covers the costs for the apprenticeship. See Houngbedji 2021.

with backward peasants? When he told the girl he wanted to send her home, she began to cry.

Our next conversation took place in his home. Gunu was in the sitting room together with one of his children and Gloria, a girl around fifteen years old. I asked him if I could talk with her alone, and he agreed. Our conversation was difficult since she was very shy. She told me that she left the village three years ago without knowing a word of French but had now learned it in Cotonou. Gunu's family was good to her; the work was not too hard; and her future plan was to do an apprenticeship. However, that plan did not depend on her wishes alone, she told me. In any case, she did not want to return to the village. The conversation was short, and then Gunu came back and asked her to buy drinks for all of us. When she returned and we (including Gloria) were having drinks together – a fact that made clear that her status in the household was more the position of kin than of a domestic worker – she lost a bit of her timidity. Together with the son of the family, we looked at a family photo album in which there were some pictures of Gloria in the very same clothes as Gunu's birth children. This, again, demonstrates that she was seen at least partly as a member of the family and not an outsider brought in to perform labour.

One week later, I talked with Kora back in northern Benin. He again expressed that he was impatiently waiting for her return from Cotonou because he wanted to organize the marriage.[11] Then I went to Gloria's village where I first met Gunu's brother, who told me, to my astonishment, that Gloria had already been sent back from Cotonou. Indeed, he told us that Gunu had wanted to keep her in Cotonou, but because Gloria's family had insisted he send her back, he had to comply. After that, I went to the household where she was living. The brother of Gloria's aunt was the head of the compound. He told me he had sent Gloria to Cotonou, and now that she was back, he was very satisfied because the dowry she had taken from Cotonou was much larger than the normal dowries of village girls when they were sent into marriage by their families. He frankly told me that even if somebody had wanted to keep Gloria in Cotonou, this was never the plan her family had for her future life course. Finally, I had another short meeting with a very shy (again) Gloria. It was difficult to get her uncle's permission to talk with her. She only stated that she did not know why Gunu sent her back. Maybe,

---

11 Marriage is seen as the end of childhood, which often means the end of the fostering relation. The parents of both the bride and the groom are obliged to organise the wedding for their child, which includes a big party with several ceremonial elements. At the centre of these ceremonies is the transfer of the bride and her belongings from her household to that of her husband. On changing notions of marriage in the region, see Alber 2019.

she said, he was not satisfied with her work? I asked if she would now marry in the village. "What could I do?" she answered.

That same evening, I met Kora again. I was astonished to find some visitors in his compound: Gloria's household head together with some other men from her village. Immediately after my visit, they departed the village and walked the direct footpath to Tebo and arrived before me since my journey took longer because I had travelled the bad road by car. They were shouting and arguing. I understood from their many accusations that my arrival in their compound was interpreted as part of a plan to disrupt the wedding of MamMam and Gloria. Kora tried to explain that I was just an anthropologist studying kinship and assured them that the wedding would take place. In fact, the marriage was solemnised within a few days, and only a year later, I met Gloria, who was married, pregnant, and living in MamMam's newly built house together with him and his other wife. However, some years later, like Salimatou, Gloria had left her husband, though she left her small child in his household. She returned to the city, where she began an apprenticeship as a hairdresser with Gunu's help.

I understand the conflict and its specific dynamics as an entanglement of vital conjunctures in linked lives. First, it was a vital conjuncture in the life of Gloria, during which a central decision about her future was made. Should she continue to live in town, take up an apprenticeship, hopefully marry an urban young man, and become a mother relatively late? In Benin, similar to the case of Cameroonian girls described by Johnson-Hanks, remaining in school or receiving another form of formal education means the prolongation of childhood and youth and relatively late motherhood. Or should Gloria return to the village to marry a peasant and have children relatively early? Unlike the case studies presented by Johnson-Hanks, in Gloria's case, the decision was not made by her but by others: her foster mother, her uncle, and by Gunu, the cousin who hosted her in his household in Cotonou. In other similar cases, the decision about the life trajectory of a girl – even if she has her own hopes and plans and expresses them – are also commonly made by relatives.

However, the inclusion of others' decisions alone would not fully explain the dynamics in this particular conflict. A central driving force in the clash was Kora and his foster son MamMam, who reclaimed the girl and the marriage based on having already paid the bride price. And here comes my second point: the conflict over Gloria's future could be interpreted as a turning point in MamMam's life trajectory as well as that of his father Kora. Finally, the conflict emerged at a critical moment in the life trajectory of Gloria's uncle, who had accepted her engagement by taking the bride price from Kora. For him, too, allowing her to continue to live in Cotonou would have disturbed his position in the web of relations in his village. The intensity of the conflict is only explicable if these different perspectives are considered. To fully understand the meaning of this struggle, one has to examine the life course expectations for a rural youngster like MamMam.

As mentioned above, I am using life stage as a normative concept that explains how a society sees and values different stages in the lives of men and women. According to local norms, MamMam was at the right age to become an adult, and in the local context, this meant that it was time for him to take a wife that his father had selected or accepted on his behalf by paying the necessary bride price and exchanging gifts with his future in-laws. Since MamMam had spent his entire childhood as Kora's foster son, he had the right to a proper marriage arranged by Kora. Not providing his foster son with this rite of passage would be a source of shame for Kora. There was even more social pressure related to this matter because MamMam had already taken the initiative to become an adult with the help of his birth mother: he married a girl of his own choosing and, thus, began to transition into full adulthood. With this act, MamMam's birth mother challenged Kora's fostering or, at least, challenged his reputation as a good father. And there was another pressure on his foster father: as MamMam had been one of the few children of Kora who was never sent to school, and, therewith, not a single cent had been spent on his formal education, the pressure for a proper marriage was even higher.

Consequently, Kora felt even more pressure to give his foster son the wife in whom he had already invested. Both had no idea that their plan could go awry and that there was a chance that the girl would stay in Cotonou. But when I talked to them the first time, I noticed that both were nervous because they knew very well that societal change, evidenced by the new pattern that some girls working in cities would remain there, could upset the arrangement.

The entanglement of multiple vital conjunctures created the dynamics of the conflict described above. On the one hand, MamMam entered adulthood in accordance with local norms, which was related to his foster father's obligation to provide his foster son with the requisite rites of passage. On the other hand, there was the vital conjuncture of Gloria' entry into adulthood and the question of whether that should happen according to new urban norms of late marriage after having first learned a profession or to the rural norms of early marriage and motherhood. Additionally, Kora's recognition as a good father was challenged, as was the reputation of Gloria's uncle as a reliable in-law. Furthermore, the conflict became a confrontation because of different, competing conceptualisations of the future: for Gloria and MamMam, but also for Gunu and Kora. If Gunu had refused his rural relatives' calls to send the girl back, he would have risked ruining his relationship with them, something that almost all urban Baatombu I know try to avoid.

Conclusion

In light of the case studies of Gloria and Salimatou, I have shown that a combination of Elder's linking of lives with the concept of vital conjunctures that negotiate futures – often in the modality of family conflicts – is useful for gaining a better understanding of the multiple ways people become involved in these conflicts. The concept of linked vital conjunctures may help us understand how societal change not only influences individual life trajectories but also affects the linking of lives by often generating family conflicts in which new normative understandings of life stages are negotiated.

Methodologically, my analysis has shown that these processes of social change may be analysed by looking more closely at kinship conflicts. However, as my case studies have also demonstrated, analysing kinship is always a bit messy as people are simultaneously husbands, fathers, uncles, and maybe grandfathers or sons, and are entangled in the life trajectories of their wives, daughters, siblings, and parents. Therefore, looking at these relationships through the lens of entangled vital conjunctures, I fear, would not minimise the degree of messiness in kinship research; rather, scholarship would become as messy as real life.

References

Alber, Erdmute. 2001. "Child Trafficking in West Africa?" In *Frontiers of Globalization: Kinship and Family Structures in West Africa*, edited by Ana Marta Gonzales, Laurie de Rose, and Florence Oloo, 71–92. Trenton, NJ: Africa World Press.

Alber, Erdmute. 2003. "Denying Biological Parenthood – Child Fosterage in Northern Benin." *Ethnos* 68, no. 4: 487–506.

Alber, Erdmute. 2004. "Ethnologische Perspektiven zum Kinderhandel in Benin." In *Arbeit – Konsum – Globalisierung. Festschrift für Gerd Spittler zum 65. Geburtstag*, edited by Kurt Beck Till Förster, and Hans Peter Hahn, 145–158. Cologne: Rüdiger Köppe Verlag.

Alber, Erdmute. 2016. "Vital Conjunctures and the Negotiation of Future: Rural Girls between Urban Middle Class Households and Early Marriage." In *Vital Conjunctures: Gender in Times of Uncertainty*, edited by Nadine Sieveking, DFG SPP 1448 Working Paper Series, No. 18. Leipzig and Halle.

Alber, Erdmute. 2018. *Transfers of Belonging. Child Fostering in West Africa in the 20th Century.* Leiden: Brill.

Alber, Erdmute. 2019. "Heterogeneity and Heterarchy: Middle-Class Households in Benin." In *The Multiplicity of Orders and Practices: A Tribute to Georg Klute*, edited by Thomas Hüsken, Alexander Solyga, and Dida Badi, 29–50. Cologne: Rüdiger Köppe Verlag.

Bledsoe, Caroline. 1980. "The Manipulation of Kpelle Social Fatherhood." *Ethnology* 19, no. 1: 29–45.

Bledsoe, Caroline, and Uche Isingo-Abanike. 1989. "Strategies of Child-fosterage among Mende Grannies in Sierra Leone. In *Reproduction and Social Organisation in Sub-Saharan Africa*, edited by Ron J. Lesthaeghe, 442–474. Berkeley: University of California Press.

Bledsoe, Caroline, and Anastasia Brandon. 1992. "Child Fosterage and Child Mortality in Sub-Saharan Africa: Some Preliminary Questions and Answers." In *Mortality and Society in Sub-Saharan Africa*, edited by Étienne van den Walle, Gilles Pison, and Mpembele Sala-Diakanda, 279–302. Oxford: Clarendon Press.

Christiansen, Catrine, Mats Utas, and Henrik E. Vigh. 2006. "Introduction." In *Navigating Youth Generating Adulthood. Social Becoming in an African Context*, edited by Catrine Christiansen, M. Utas, and Henrik E. Vigh, 9–28. Stockholm: Nordiska Afrikainstitutet.

Elder, Glen. 1974. *Children of the Great Depression*. Chicago, IL: University of Chicago Press.

Elder Jr., Glen H. (1994): Time, Human Agency, and Social Change: Perspectives on the Life Course. In: *Social Psychology Quarterly* 57,1, S. 4–15.

Elder, Glen H. Jr. 1998. "The Life Course as Developmental Theory." Child Development 69, no. 1: 1–12.

Elder, Glen H. Jr., Monica Kirkpatrick Johnson, and Robert Crosnoe. 2003. "The Emergence and Development of Life Course Theory." In Handbook of the Life Course, edited by Jeylan Mortimer and Michael J. Shanahan, 3–22. New York: Kluwer Academic Publishers.

Fichtner, Sarah. 2002. *The NGOisation of Education: Case Studies from Benin*. Cologne: Köppe.

Goody, Esther. 1982. *Parenthood and Social Reproduction: Fostering and Occupational Roles in West Africa*. Cambridge: Cambridge University Press.

Häberlein, Tabea. 2015. "Intergenerational Entanglements – Insights into Perceptions of Care for the Elderly and Life Courses in Northern Togo." In *Anthropological Perspectives on Care: Work, Kinship and the Life Course*, edited by Erdmute Alber and Heike Drotbohm, 159–179. New York: Palgrave MacMillan.

Hareven, Tamara. 1995. "Changing Images of Aging and the Social Construction of the Life Course." In *Images of Aging. Cultural Representations of Later Life*, edited by Mike Featherstone and Andrew Wernick, 119–134. New York: Routledge.

Hareven, Tamara. 1997. "Familie, Lebenslauf und Sozialgeschichte." In *Historische Familienforschung. Ergebnisse und Kontroversen*, edited by Josef Ehmer, Tamara Hareven, and Richard Wall, 17–37. Frankfurt am Main: Campus.

Houngbedji, Gbeognin Mickael. 2021. "Narrative from an Old Photograph: How Absences Make the Story and Inspire Research on Craft Apprenticeship in Benin." *Ethnoscripts* 23, no. 1.

Howard, Neil, 2008. "Independent Child Migration in Southern Benin. An Ethnographic Challenge to the 'Pathological' Paradigm." Paper presented at the Research Workshop on Independent Child and Youth Migrants, Migration DRC, University of Sussex, May 6–8, 2008.

Johnson-Hanks, Jennifer. 2002. "On the Limits of Life Stages in Ethnography: Toward a Theory of Vital Conjunctures." *American Anthropologist* 104, no. 3: 865–880.

Johnson-Hanks, Jennifer. 2005. *Uncertain Honor: Modern Motherhood in an African Crisis*. Chicago, IL: University of Chicago Press.

Notermans, Catrien. 2003. "Sharing Home, Food, and Bed: Paths of Grandmotherhood in East Cameroon." *Africa Vol. 74/1: Grandparents and Grandchildren*: 6–27.

Ringstedt, Mette Line. 2007. "Collision in Life-Courses: Teenage Motherhood and Generational Relations in North-East Tanzania." In *Generations in African Connections and Conflicts*, edited by Erdmute Alber and S. Van Der Geest, 357–380. Berlin: Lit Verlag.

Ruddick, Sara. 1989. *Maternal Thinking: Toward a Politics of Peace*. Boston: Beacon Press.

Tama, Clarisse. 2014. *Etre enseignant au Bénin. Les mutations dún groupe professionnel.* Cologne: Rüdiger Köppe Verlag.

Thelen, Tatjana, André Thiemann, and Duška Roth. 2018. "State Kinning and Kinning the State in Serbian Elder Care Programs." In *Stategraphy: Toward a Relational Anthropology of the State*, edited by Tatjana Thelen, Larissa Vetters, and Keebet von Benda-Beckmann, 107–123. New York: Berghahn.

Thelen, Tatjana, and Erdmute Alber. 2022. "Introduction: Politics and Kinship." In *Politics and Kinship: A Reader*, edited by Erdmute Alber and Tatjana Thelen, 1–34. Abingdon: Routledge.

Neda Deneva

Mobile People Versus Static Institutions: National School Policies in the EU and the Life Course of Transnational Grandparents

I met Violeta in the Roma neighbourhood of a small town in Bulgaria. She was just sending her grandchildren to catch the school bus. Violeta was in her late forties, a young grandmother and the primary caretaker for her grandkids. Her daughter was a labour migrant somewhere in Europe as was Violeta before she returned to Bulgaria so her grandchildren could attend school and eventually graduate. While Violeta and her daughter were fairly successful in finding work in other EU countries, they could not settle permanently in any of the localities in which they found jobs, and so they alternated between periods in migration and periods back in Bulgaria to patch up their finances while waiting for new short-term employment opportunities. When the grandchildren reached school age, a family decision was made: Violeta would settle permanently in Bulgaria and take care of them while her daughter and son-in-law would continue their pendular labour migration and financially support the whole family.

The short-term jobs and hyper-mobile migration patterns that this community of Roma migrants engaged in led to persistently precarious living conditions and the impossibility of a consistent education for the children. Even if able to settle as migrants for the length of an entire school year, an unclear future and job insecurity meant that eventually, children might have to go back to Bulgaria and continue their education there. Moreover, other members of the community had negative experiences enrolling their children in Bulgarian schools after a period in migration. By the time Violeta's daughter had to decide where to enrol her eldest child, it had become the norm for migrants to send their children back to Bulgaria to start school there. Therefore, a family decision was taken that the children would relocate to Bulgaria for schooling, and Violeta would remain with them

Note: The work on this chapter was generously supported by IGK Work and Human Lifecycle in Global History, Humboldt-Universität zu Berlin, re: work, during my 2015/2016 postdoctoral fellowship there.
Acknowledgements: The work on this chapter benefited from the lively discussions of my colleagues at re:work during our 2015/2016 fellowships. I am particularly grateful to Josef Ehmer for his kind support and valuable feedback. I am also grateful to my colleague, Mila Mineva, with whom we collaborated during the research phase. The chapter has further benefited from the valuable comments of Anca Simionca, as always, and of Florin Faje, who also kindly took over the reproductive labour while I was writing.

as their primary carer. This move was done with the purpose of securing a better future for the next generation through an envisaged social mobility through education. Yet, it also meant endangering Violeta's present and future security by making her dependent on her daughter for financial support both in the present and in the future.

The case of return migration of the generation of young grandparents represents a pattern in many Bulgarian Roma migrant communities. It signifies the conflict between two regimes – temporary labour migration and a nationally regulated educational system. For most impoverished Roma communities, labour migration within the European Union is their only source of income. But their mobility is often pendular and temporary, involving precarious working and living conditions that do not allow them to stay permanently in one place. At the same time, educational systems are regulated at the level of the nation state, and consistent education requires permanently settled schoolchildren. Transfers between educational systems are difficult and often compromise learning progress and impede successful graduation. Consequently, we see a clash between labour and education, between freedom of mobility and free access to EU labour markets and non-transferable primary and secondary educational systems.

What we are witnessing here is an emerging paradox of two types of policies. On one hand, intensified mobility within the EU is growing, and the freedom of labour mobility is encouraged and enabled by EU-level migration and labour regimes. However, these regimes are centred on the individual worker. On the other hand, educational policies are nation based and focused on a static, permanently settled population. The reintegration of mobile children into the educational system has proven to be extremely difficult and is not keeping pace with the intensity of workers' mobility. What is more, individually centred policies fail to embrace the relational aspect of migrants' lives. Children in mobile families are hindered in their educational progress because of their mobility, i. e., following their parents. Ultimately, this clash between policies creates a conflict between the EU principle of freedom of movement and the obligation to obtain mandatory primary and secondary education for one's children.

This is a distinctly EU paradox in that mobility is encouraged and enabled only in certain aspects of EU citizens' lives. On one hand, there is a need for cheap labour from Eastern Europe to take up jobs that are precarious, uncertain, often informal, temporary, and poorly paid; this need combines with extreme poverty and the lack of labour opportunities back home. This generates particular migration patterns in which people engage in hyper-mobility between various localities, and this constant mobility is a survival strategy (Apostolova 2021). On the other hand, the idea of education as a key to social mobility and, hence, a better future for the next generation is not only deeply engrained in public policies towards the

Roma framed as integration measures, but also in the beliefs and attitudes of Roma parents themselves. Therefore, we see that to sustain their families financially, parents engage in pendular labour migration. But in order to ensure a better future for their children, they must provide stable, settled – that is immobile – lives for their children, which also involves finding alternative carers who can remain in one place. Dividing families and households and spreading care arrangements over generations and across borders has become a new coping technology for hyper-mobile migrants as a response to nationally based policies focused on static populations.

The chapter traces this paradox and the ways people struggle to adjust to it. Drawing on the case of Roma migrants and their extended families, I argue that these contradictory regimes reconfigure family composition, redistribute care roles, and condition new reciprocities and dependencies. I focus on the link between school-age children and their young grandparents. I trace how the grandparents make decisions that shape their life course in unexpected ways. Moreover, I show how the life course pattern of the elderly is linked with the structure and definition of the life courses of the two younger generations. It is impossible to understand the transitions and transformations that happen to the life courses of young grandparents without understanding the complicated links and relations between the three generations. These three generations operate according to three sets of needs – the need for education, the need for paid labour, and the need for unpaid care work. These sets of needs unfold in the distinct labour and mobility regimes of the European Union, and they frame the life trajectories and life decisions that three generations make in their linked lives. What we see in this case is how the life course of one generation, that of young grandparents, is shaped by the trajectories and hopes of the other two generations within the structural conditions of both EU and national-level policies and regimes.

Methodology

This chapter draws on empirical materials collected within the framework of two research projects on Roma migration from Bulgaria in the period between 2013 and 2015 which focused on mobile lives, access to social citizenship, and the education of "children in mobility."[1] The experience of transnational grandparents is

---

[1] Empirical data collection was conducted during a postdoctoral fellowship in 2014/2015 at the Centre for Liberal Strategies, Sofia in the framework of two research projects: "The (Im)Mobility Catch: Mobile People versus Static Institutions" and "Poverty, Ethnicity and Welfare: a Case Study of Bulgarian Roma Migrants."

analysed by drawing on the case of low-skilled migration from a rural region in northern Bulgaria, whereby Roma from the region intensively engage in short-term, recurring labour migration to the Netherlands, Belgium, and Germany. A mixed-method approach was used, combining policy and normative framework analysis on migration policies, educational regulations, employment and social benefits legislation on the one hand, and qualitative interviews with a variety of stakeholders on the other. Interviews were conducted with local stakeholders and experts including mayors and local government officials, education mediators, social workers, school directors, and teachers. The other pool of respondents were migrants and their families in several locations. I conducted interviews in the re-gional centre and in three villages with members of twenty-one families involved in pendular migration patterns and cross-border childcare. My focus are the daily manifestations of childcare arrangements, the everyday ruptures that these new arrangements trigger, and the ways people make sense of their practices and re-po-sitioning. Combining research on discourses and practices, my methods included life stories, extended semi-structured interviews, and informal conversations.

In what follows, I first look at how the concept of the life course intertwines with labour and care decisions and has readjusted life trajectories in the context of intensive migration. I then proceed to describe the specific character of Roma mo-bility as an emerging new pattern of hyper-mobility. The third section is devoted to educational policies and the distinct challenges mobile families face when reinte-grating their children into the Bulgarian educational system. I show the bias of the policy framework towards a static population and the national government's defi-ciencies in addressing the needs of mobile citizens. In the final section, I discuss how the practice of sending children back to the home country and into the care of grandparents entails reconfigurations of family relations, financial ar-rangements, employment, and future plans, and triggers new dependencies and insecurities. I pay special attention to the tensions and challenges that grandpar-ents in these transnational families are facing in both the paid labour and unpaid care work they are expected to perform. I conclude with a call for recognising care and its relational character in policy making at all levels.

Children in Mobility, Ageing Carers, and the Life Course

Transnational families and children sent back

Transnational families have been well researched. The effects of the spatial scattering of family members can be traced in reconfigurations of care arrangements, the intergenerational redistribution of responsibilities, and the transformations of kin hierarchies and moral obligations (see among others Baldassar 2007; Bryson and Vuorela 2002; Evergeti and Zontini 2006; Olwig 1999; Parennas 2001). But the social reproduction of individuals, families, and communities is challenged by mobility and the transnationalisation of the family. Care trajectories are embedded in different patterns of mobility, labour regimes, and policy contexts (Kofman 2012). In this chapter, I focus on the relations between different categories of family members and the shifts between different statuses made by transnational migrants. In this context, the category of transnational children has to be expanded to include children that have been mobile along with their parents for shorter or longer periods of time and might have been sent to the parents' home country at a certain point. I will refer to them as "children in mobility" to emphasise the effects that family mobility has on their own lives. Recently, attention has been paid to immigrant children and their transnational childhoods to show the challenges they face and their participation in the reconfiguration of transnational social fields and transnational practices (Coe et al. 2011; Gardner 2012; Orellana et al. 2001; Zeitlyn and Mand 2012; Punch 2012). Their particular connection with education has also been addressed either through the lens of immigrant children and their integration into the educational system of the host country broadly (see Adams and Kirova 2006; Panait and Zuniga 2016; Ryan and Sales 2013; Sarcinelli 2015), or the challenges that children left behind face in terms of educational success (Cortes 2015; Sarma and Rasyad 2016).

The children I discuss here, however, do not fit in either category. They have experienced the mobility of their parents both by accompanying them and, thus, becoming migrants themselves; but they become children left behind when they reach school age and are sent back to their country of origin and into their grandparents' care. They, therefore, maintain a peculiar position within the category of persons "in mobility" that has received little analytical or policy attention.[2] "Chil-

---

2 The challenges that children in mobility face with regard to static national educational systems are described in more detail in a research report by Grekova et al. 2015.

dren in mobility" have distinct needs that are different from children in other types of transnational families. They need carers that can adjust to their (children's) new mobility status. This means changes for the carers as well, who experience life transformations due to the relocation of the children. The type of hyper-mobility parents engage in affects children unfavourably, resulting in the ultimate decision to "leave" children behind, which in turn requires that grandparents also move back to the home country. In this sense, the mobility of different family members and kin relations is interconnected and dynamic.

Young transnational grandparents – between paid labour and unpaid care work

The type of care arrangements addressed here are intergenerational, between grandparents and grandchildren. The main carers are "young" grandparents, generally grandmothers but also grandfathers. From a relational perspective, these grandparents fall in the category of the "young old" as defined in the scholarship on generations (Neugarten 1974) due to their position in the care network. They might also be considered a "sandwich generation" that is still at an active working age but already has care obligations: towards their own elderly parents and their young grandchildren. But, they are too young to be considered elderly, and they are not the parents but the grandparents of the children they care for, which excludes them from the traditional meaning of the "sandwich generation" concept as it appears in the scholarship.[3] More recent literature on the life course offers a more accurate conceptualisation of these intergenerational relations by defining people's position through their embeddedness in institutional contexts, their social age, and their relational position in family and kin networks rather than by their biological age (Bengtson and Settersten 2016).

The practice of sending children back to the home country requires stretching and reconfiguring transnational family networks. Grandparents in these families have been mobile themselves both as workers and as carers and are still of an active working age, but they are simultaneously expected to engage in reproductive labour and care for their grandchildren. As my empirical material demonstrates, many of the grandparents of children sent back have had to relocate themselves and, thus, adjust to new circumstances. For most of those assuming full-time

---

[3] The term "sandwich generation" usually denotes middle-aged women who simultaneously work and provide care for both their still-dependent children and their aging parents. The case here differs since the in-between generation provides care for grandchildren.

care for their grandchildren in Bulgaria, their new care work responsibilities required that they give up their own labour-motivated migration, thereby diminishing, and in some cases fully eradicating, their own independent sources of income. For others like Violeta, care-motivated relocation has taken several steps between different countries and triggered new responsibilities and new dependencies, reconfiguring relations in their kin networks.

Transnational grandparents or transnational ageing carers have been a focus of migration studies for over a decade and have been examined from different perspectives (Brennan et al. 2013; Dossa and Coe 2017; Nedelcu and Wyss 2020; Tezcan 2019). What is clear from these diverse cases and analytical discussions is that care work is rarely taken seriously in policies that are informed by economic and political factors at the expense of other concerns (Zhou 2013). Even analyses of precarious working and living tend to focus on productive labour and neglect the importance of care as central to social reproduction (Ivancheva and Keating 2020). The cases of the care-oriented mobility of grandparents presented in this chapter emphasise the importance of thinking of migration as a family and relational project embedded in multiple policy contexts rather than an individual endeavour. Family members are entangled in paid labour and unpaid care work as a way to reproduce a family spread across borders, ultimately forcing some kin members into return migration. I have argued elsewhere that migration of individual workers is not an individual enterprise. It is made possible and sustained by the reproductive labour of a number of other agents in the migration process (both mobile and immobile). In the process of the transnationalisation of kin relations and the kin structure in which kin members live across borders, care arrangements are accordingly readjusted to extend between distant geographical locations (Wyss and Nedelcu 2018; Deneva 2012, 2017). This chapter takes this argument further, showing how structural conditions transform the life course of multiple interlinked generations.

Transnational families are forced to handle this situation by moving carers across borders while at the same time hampering carers' individual mobility and financial security. The tensions between paid labour and unpaid care work take on an additional meaning here by introducing distance, spatial separation, and the division of families into the equation. Intense mobility and the local specificities of the labour market (i. e., limited opportunities for formal full-time work) put these two obligations in conflict with each other. What is at stake is the autonomy of ageing carers who in taking over the care of their grandchildren and migrating back to Bulgaria also must relinquish their financial independence and shift to new reciprocities within the kin network. I have previously called this shift *a move to kinfare* (Deneva 2012). Here, I expand the analysis to include the effects of national policies on mobile populations. I argue that when policies do not acknowledge the reality of interconnected family and kin members, individuals in these family networks experience ruptures in their lives that force them to assume positions in their life course earlier than planned; ultimately this changes the ways in which they become interdependent on their kin. Consequently, to understand the transformations that returning grandparents are experiencing, scholars and policy makers need to keep in mind the relational context of migration and care.

The life course: linked lives, institutional context, and change

The life course perspective allows us to better grasp the importance of the relational aspect and social context on conceptualisations of age and generations, along with the expectations and responsibilities that go with them. A life course approach to multigenerational family research takes into account how family relations and the stages through which family members pass might change for each individual and family and how these processes are defined by their institutional and historical context. As Neugarten and Datan (1973) have argued, the life course is conceptualised as a sequence of age-linked transitions embedded in individual, social, and historical time. An individual's life is composed of a series of transitions embedded in trajectories and stages that give them a distinct meaning and involve specific roles and statuses (Elder, Jr. 1994; Marshall and Mueller 2003). By using the life course approach, I examine how the life trajectories of several generations and their movements between roles are transformed through a particular institutional and social context and through the linkages between individuals.

The institutional structuring of lives through the family, school, work, religious systems, the state, and policy regimes define the normative trajectories of social roles and key transitions, but also the individual pathways of people as they go through them (Shanahan et al. 2016). Thus, the social context defines the roles and responsibilities that people are expected to take when they transition from one stage to the next. Yet, the points of transition during the life course and the social roles assumed in each stage are variable and fluid to a certain extent. Transnational migration, translocal families, incorporation in multiple institutional regimes, and labour hyper-mobility generate transformations of individual trajectories and points of transition that result in tensions and overlapping or competing roles for some members of the multigenerational family, in this case, primarily grandparents. At the same time, lives are embedded in relationships with people; they do not evolve individually within structures. The interconnectedness of lives, particularly those linked across generations by bonds of kinship, is well described through the concept of "linked lives," which is the core of life course analysis (Bengtson et al. 2005). This formulation allows a better understanding of how transformations that affect one generation come to affect members of other generations as well. This interdependence of lives (Settersten 2003) is often concentrated on care and social reproduction, where the spatial and temporal dimensions are extended and produce new difficulties and changed relations (Coe 2015; Iossifova 2020). Along with the importance of the structural context for the life course, this understanding of interdependence allows us to grasp more clearly how educational policies and migration regimes end up affecting not one or two, but three generations of mobile people – children, their parents, and their grandparents.

Hyper-Mobility and Hyper-Precarity: Bulgarian Roma as Labour Migrants

Violeta's story from the beginning of the chapter describes the intensive mobility and shifting roles between paid labour and unpaid care work. It is an example of a widespread practice in the Roma community with whom I completed my research. Hers is a transnational family whose members are in constant flux, navigating precarious employment and care responsibilities across borders while at the same time facing static national institutions. The lack of stable employment opportunities paired with relaxed mobility and citizenship regimes within the European Union compel people like them to travel back and forth in search of a living and constantly readjust to new opportunities while facing new responsibilities. Violeta is part of the generation of young grandparents stretched between the dual expectations of financial independence – and even support for children – and increasing care responsibilities for other family members such as aging parents and grandchildren. At the same time, she is also one of the many hyper-mobile Eastern European workers who combine various sources of employment across borders over short periods of time. Her mobility, employment decisions, and care responsibilities depend on a complex matrix of factors that include the labour market, migration and citizenship regimes, and moral codes within her kin network.

Violeta and her family live in Shumen, in the northeast of Bulgaria. The region ranks among the poorest in the country. At the time of my research in 2013, the officially registered level of unemployment in the region was the highest in the country at 26 percent (double the national average). The rural share of the population was also higher than the average for the country. The structure of the economy there differs from the rest of the country, with agriculture playing a considerably greater role in the economy of Shumen at the expense of the service and industrial sectors. Agriculture is mainly specialised in cereal and industrial crops, which are highly mechanised and require very little manpower. During the state-socialist period, and particularly the late 1970s and 1980s, the Roma from the region were engaged in regular state employment either as low-skilled workers in heavy industrial factories or in state-run agricultural cooperatives. After 1989, deindustrialisation, restructuring, and privatisation resulted in developments similar to the rest of the country (Kofti 2018) and other post-industrial areas (Dunn 2004) such as mass layoffs and the general deregulation and flexibilisation of labour. This led to the long-term unemployment and impoverishment of the population. By 1992, most of the heavy and mining industries collapsed while the agricultural cooperatives were dissolved and privatised. Those most affected were agricultural workers and low-skilled workers. The Roma across the country suffered the most severe drop in employment – between 37 and 66 percent fewer persons were employed after 1989 (Tomova 2009). In the period between 1990 and 2001, there was a permanent increase in the number of unemployed Roma and the duration of unemployment (Tomova 2011). What made the Roma situation even worse in comparison to the low-skilled rural ethnic Bulgarian or Turkish population was that they did not own land or animal stock before collectivisation in 1945–1958 and could not become members of the new agricultural cooperatives. Moreover, due to their recent impoverishment and unemployment, they could not benefit from the land renting schemes that the state was offering. Consequently, with the dissolution of the old cooperatives and land restitution, the rural Roma population became the ultimate losers (Tomova 2009).[4]

As a response to the widespread unemployment and poverty in Shumen and in the country as a whole, the Roma from this region have been migrating to Germany, Belgium, and the Netherlands since 2001. The liberalisation of the mobility regime after 2001, the year Bulgaria was removed from the EU's negative Schengen visa list, allowed Bulgarian citizens to travel freely without visa restrictions across the EU for up to three months. After Bulgaria became an EU member in 2007, Roma migration intensified (Preoteasa et al. 2012). Fully lifting the restrictions for mobility resulted in the emergence of new patterns of migration – intensive, short-term, frequent, and cyclical. While before 2007 Bulgarian migrants had to observe the frequency and length of their stay unless they had a work and residence permit, after EU accession, sojourn became unrestricted, and those who engaged in tempo-

---

4 According to the last census in 2011, the share of people who identify themselves as ethnically Roma in the country is 4.9 percent. In the rural areas, this share is 8 percent (Census 2011). According to expert estimates, the share is even higher with an average of 9–10 percent across the country (Tomova 2011). For the region of Shumen, the ethnic distribution in 2011 shows 8.24 percent Roma and 30.3 percent Turks (with an 8.8 percent average for the country). The majority of Roma in the region master Turkish along with the Romani and Bulgarian languages, and many of them identify as Turks in statistical surveys, trying to avoid more extreme ethnic discrimination.

rary migration became much more diverse and numerous (Preoteasa et al. 2012). This conditioned the figure of the "restless bodies . . . caught in a contradiction between fixity and motion in the context of capital accumulation and fading welfare state" (Apostolova 2021: 1).

Among the Bulgarian Roma from poor regions like Shumen, the intensity and frequency of migrant trips – both for work and for care – increased. Over the last decade, a new pattern has emerged – low-skilled workers spent shorter periods of time (less than six months, but in some cases every few weeks) in migration, alternating with periods at home. Sometimes migrants travel between several countries within the same year. Some work irregularly in short-term jobs ranging from domestic service, construction work, road repair, and factory work, arrangements that border on illegality. Others find a source of income in regularised forms of begging, selling street newspapers, or playing music in designated street spots. Additionally, most rely heavily on various forms of social benefits. Back in Bulgaria, they live in a region where the few available activities are extremely precarious, flexible, and in most cases irregular: gathering and selling herbs, seasonal agricultural work, logging, and other short-term seasonal jobs, all paid per piece, without contracts or even day wages. For these Roma, making a living is a transnational endeavour combining short-term, irregular labour migration, small, irregular jobs in Bulgaria, and social assistance from various sources both in Bulgaria and abroad.

These precarious working lives and the intensity of their mobility creates uncertain living conditions for their children. Many of the migrants attempted to settle for longer periods in destination countries and took their children with them. This proved difficult for many of them due to the unstable character of their employment, insufficient financial means, and unreliable accommodation. Moreover, many people worked irregular hours and shifts. In terms of childcare, this meant that even when some form of institutional childcare like kindergarten or school was available, children still needed an extra adult to care for them when their parents worked after school hours. This required other kin members – usually grandmothers – to take up care work. Children followed their parents in their trips between countries several times a year. When the child was in kindergarten or in the care of a relative, this was not a problem. However, the migration calendar does not easily overlap with the academic year. Many of the migrant children were unable to attend school continuously because they travelled between countries in the middle of the academic year. The continuity of their education was compromised. Moreover, re-integration in the home country's educational system proved to be extremely difficult for migrant children who attended school abroad for a certain length of time. As the next section shows, Bulgaria's national education system is not designed to address the needs of highly mobile children; moreover, there are particular barriers that do not allow families to re-integrate children into the system if they have withdrawn from it for a certain length of time or if they have been educated in institutions outside the system. Consequently, a growing number of migrants have decided to send their school-age children back to Bulgaria permanently, leaving them in the care of grandparents so they can attend school continuously.

Education and Mobility

The European Union is an open space of movement, trade, labour, and interaction. This original vision of a united Europe emphasises mobility as *the* European mode of being and aims to turn mobility into the norm rather than the exception. Yet, national policies like welfare policies, education, and health services are designed to serve settled populations and are rooted in static nation-state institutions. While some policies have been adjusted to serve mobile populations, others have severely lagged in the creation of public institutions for mobile citizens. These institutional deficiencies appear both in sending countries like Bulgaria, which has no capacity to meet the needs of its own mobile citizens, as well as in receiving countries, whose institutions lag behind in equally incorporating mobile workers and citizens (Grekova et al. 2015). What national policies in countries like Bulgaria lack the most, however, is an appreciation for the mobility of their own citizens, especially new patterns of mobility that are short-term, highly intensive, and often circular or pendular.

Irrespective of whether they are facilitating or impeding migrant students' integration, national educational policies and isolated school systems share one common trait – they are designed for a static population and, thus, they are a source of rupture for transnational children (Hamann and Zuniga 2011). The rate of school-age children who have never attended school due to international migration and those who have dropped out of the educational system before finishing primary school is increasing (Kabakchieva et al. 2014). Once the continuity of education is disrupted and a child faces repeating a grade (or several grades), the risk of a major interruption or their dropping out of the educational system altogether grows exponentially.

In the case of Roma migrants from Shumen, there are two types of educational solutions for their children in mobility. One strategy has been for families to enrol school-age children in educational institutions in the country of current residence. This means that some children start their education in their parents' country of destination. Later, when parents decide to return to their home country or to interrupt their sojourn, children continue their education in Bulgaria for a certain period. Interviews with both parents and representatives of the educational institutions have demonstrated that this re-integration in the Bulgarian educational system proves to be very difficult and results in high drop-out rates.

The educational system in Bulgaria, like most educational systems, is nation-state bound and is a source of rupture for transnational children (Hamann and Zuniga 2011). The regulatory framework for enrolling children after a period of being abroad presents insurmountable challenges for migrant families wishing to enrol their children in the age-appropriate grade. Once a child misses a year or more in the system, re-enrolment turns out to be extremely difficult, and many children in such situations have to re-enrol in a lower grade. This means they lose up to two years of progress due to the rigid bureaucratic procedures of the formal educational system, falling behind their peers, which leads some to feel embarrassed and bored at school (Grekova et al. 2015). This discourages children from going to school, increasing the drop-out rates drastically. This tendency has become a wide-spread problem in the community.

As a result, many families have decided to send their children back to Bulgaria when they reach school age so as to start their education in the place they are most likely able to complete it. As the case of Violeta illustrates, the trend is grandparents accompanying school-age children back to the home country and assuming the role of primary caretaker. Dividing families and households in new ways, re-shuffling care arrangements, and spreading them over generations and across borders has become a coping technology for hyper-mobile migrants as a response to nationally based policies designed for static populations.

Children are not the only ones affected by this strategy. Those who replace parents as the primary caretaker face new challenges and are made to assume different roles. The return of young grandparents back to Bulgaria affects their life goals and trajectories as well as their relations within the larger kin network given their new dependence and the expectations placed on them. In what follows, I focus on the practice of sending or leaving children behind in the care of grandparents and the effects it has on grandparents.

Life Course Reconfigured: Transnational Grandparents from Labour Migrants to Carers

Families' decisions to leave children behind or to send them back to their home country after a period of migration seem very reasonable in view of the importance placed on education as a tool for social integration and mobility. Not taking education seriously and failing to complete school have been the subjects of persistent attacks against Roma by people on the far-right, nationalistic side of the political spectrum. Integration through education has also been at the centre of most Roma-focused public policies and NGO interventions.

Contrary to the popular belief that Roma do not value education or treat their children's education carelessly, Roma migrants are very concerned with the continuity of their children's education. By using a life course perspective, we can see that ensuring the first step, that is education, is central to how children's entire future is imagined. Securing their education, however, requires reconfiguring the lives of the other generations of the family. Parents have to live separately from their children and must work hard to support both themselves and their children and their children's carers through remittances. While this practice of "scattering families" is quite common in transnational families and is well documented in the scholarship, for the Roma families included in this study, the practice emerged as a secondary decision, after parents had migrated together with their children and were not responsible for financially supporting their parents – i.e., young grandparents. The decision to "send children back" brings about both prolonged spatial separation and additional financial burden. "Sending children back" because of static educational policies that cannot address the needs of hyper-mobile children is a novel practice that points to a belated realisation of precarity at all levels. For the grandparents, however, return means putting their lives as labour migrants on hold prematurely and becoming carers in their home country, financially dependent on their absent children. Withdrawing from paid labour and from financial independence is a stage and a role that the grandparents would not usually take on so early. Consequently, under these structural conditions, the future of the grandchildren directly transforms the present of the grandparents.

The phenomenon of children left or sent back to Bulgaria to start school triggers a number of changes in family and kin relations, creating new transnational dependencies and new ruptures in the lives of caretakers. Similarly, it transforms ageing carers' life trajectories and generates new intergenerational dependencies and inequalities.

> I don't know where I'll be in two months. And I have seen how other children have difficulties in school here and there, and here again. So, we wanted to have them in Bulgaria, with my parents, to make sure they really manage to graduate properly. I only have 6 years of school, and I can't find a proper job. So, I don't want this for my kids. I want them to have respectable jobs and not to have to travel all the time like us. Now my parents had to stop working, and we have to work even more to support everyone. But what else to do? We have no choice! (M., 27, migrant)

This is a quote from a woman in her late twenties who has been selling newspapers on the street in the Netherlands while her husband worked as a day labourer in construction. He used to work with his father-in-law who now is back to Bulgaria and cannot find a job to support himself there. As in so many other cases, the parents' generation remains working in migration but takes on the additional burden of supporting their parents – young grandparents – who lose access to income abroad while taking care of their grandchildren at home.

The link between the three generations and the orientation towards the future is very prominent in the village community I studied. Children do go to the village school and have good attendance rates. However, the material conditions in which they live together with their grandparents are below the bare minimum – no running water, over-crowded houses, and poor sanitary conditions, with outside toilets, no sewers, etc. The material conditions are limited because migrant parents are responsible for supporting three generations: themselves, their children, and their parents who perform unpaid care work.

Grandparents lose their own source of income and become dependent on remittances sent by their children. Becoming full-time carers, especially for younger children (six to seven years old), also means fewer opportunities to find any form of employment in Bulgaria for at least one of the caretakers (usually the grandmother). In this way, the decision to send children back creates new transnational relations among kin networks and disrupts the economic autonomy of carers, creating new forms of kin reciprocity.

Maria, one of the grandmothers who returned to care for her grandchildren, discussed the change in her life as follows:

> I wasn't planning to stop working so soon. I was happy I can make money in Holland, and it was tough work, very tiring. But I am not old yet; I thought I can do it for at least ten more years like this, if not more. But the grandchildren are the most important. So, when their parents said they have to study here in Bulgaria, we had no choice but to come back too. We are not that old, but we are the older generation. So, we left it to the young ones to work, and we are living here now, relying on them and what they send us. I don't like it, but for my husband it is even worse. To feel dependent, to not be free to go and earn his bread the way he can. Not easy. We'll see what happens when the grandkids grow older. Who will continue supporting us?

Maria continued, explaining how frustrating it is not to know what will happen in the future. She was not sure when she and her husband would be able to work full time again, let alone when, if ever, they would be able to resume travelling for work. And this created many uncertainties about the future since family roles were no longer clear. For Maria and others like her, dependence on children happened much earlier than it would have if the family lived in the same place. This is a common issue when migration separates generations and the activities and responsibilities that used to be easily combined are now spread across space. In a context where children reside in the same country as their parents and grandparents – whether as migrants or at home – care responsibilities are divided in a way that does not interfere with labour. Usually, young grandparents are still financially responsible for themselves and sometimes even support their children as they establish themselves. By the time they enter the next stage of their lives in which they need support because of advanced age, their grandchildren are already young adults making a living. But the division of families we see in this case requires re-arranging these stages of the life course.

Not being able to earn a living through work in Bulgaria is a source of moral tension for ageing carers. As persons in their mid-forties or early fifties, they consider themselves to be at a stage in their lives where they are still capable of working full time and supporting themselves financially. Migration enables this independence. The migration rates in Roma communities across the country are higher than the average. In rural areas like Shumen, there were hardly any families without at least one member working abroad. While the type of mobility they engage in is intensive and the work highly precarious, this kind of labour provides them with a higher income compared to what they could earn in Bulgaria, and they can support themselves. In this sense, when grandparents transition into the role of carer in Bulgaria, it means losing their role as a worker abroad. For many of the carers I talked to, this was a dramatic shift.

Shifting to a dependent carer creates a rupture not only in the present but also in the future. The imagined personal biography of these young-old grandparents included self-reliance for a longer period and even providing financially for the next generation. This scenario places them in a much different position in the future as they age and are no longer able to work at the same pace. Return migration to Bulgaria also transforms their position in the future, which now entails full reliance on the next generation in a relationship of reciprocity: financial support in exchange for childcare in the present and the future. Another respondent explained this as "being properly old" prematurely. In this sense, this is a reconfiguration of the way people imagined their life course.

> Now, when we came back for the grandchildren, we rely on the children to send us money. This was not the plan when we first left for Holland. We planned to stay there as along as we can, to work for many years, arrange the house here, even maybe make some savings. Now, all of this had to change. We are like the proper old people around, waiting for someone to send us money . . . And who knows what will happen in ten years, when the grandchildren don't need us anymore. Who will support us then? I am so worried about it. (K., 51)

Kalina, quoted above, is the fifty-one-year-old grandmother of four school-aged children. She used to work together with her husband in the Netherlands, but she initially returned to Bulgaria to care for the two children of one of her daughters, and then continued caring for her other daughter's two children. She express-es a worry shared among many of the return migrants: becoming dependent too early in her life. A transformation in the timing of when people move from one stage in their life course into the next is taking place, and this creates uncertainties in the present and for the future. At the same time, this development shows also how tightly connected different generations are in terms of their support schemes and their responsibilities.

These transformations are happening not just at an individual level; they are becoming a common pattern for the whole community. Individual families set a pattern that has begun to repeat itself as a new generation of children reach school age. Initially, the decision to send children back to Bulgaria together with their grandparents was made after failing to ensure their transnational education and being frustrated by the barriers to school enrolment back in Bulgaria. But by the time I was doing my research, many families were making the decision pre-emptively after having heard about the negative experiences of other families in their local community. In this way, the shift in roles and positions in the life course of young grandparents became a new norm rather than exceptional. The changes in personal biographies eventually formed a new moral expectation that they would become return migrants and the carers of their school-aged grand-children. For this type of migrant family – engaged in hyper-mobility labour pat-terns and kin networks that closely rely on each other for social reproduction – the clash between mobility patterns and national educational policies resulted in the transformation of the life course of and the moral expectations placed on the gen-eration of young grandparents.

While there were other relatives from the extended kin that could assume care responsibilities for the children, my research shows that this is seldom the case. Only on rare occasions has there been an uncle or aunt who might host the child who has returned to their home country, and this has lasted only until the grandmother or both grandparents could relocate permanently. This was ex-plained by the reciprocity arrangements between generations. In this community, care for grandchildren is seen as the responsibility of the older generation rather than distributed among other extended family members. Additionally, to be immo-bile is a decision that one must take. In most families, adults engage in some form of mobility at least once a year. Even though not everyone is constantly moving be-tween localities, there was hardly anyone who did not migrate at least once a year for an extended period. Therefore, children could not just be sent back to relatives who live in Bulgaria because there are rarely such relatives. The decision to take responsibility for caring for school-aged children means also to become immobile in contrast to almost everyone else in the community. In this way, the compromise that grandparents are making becomes even more apparent.

Conclusion

Labour-driven mobility regimes and national policies create various types of tensions for the people living their lives across borders. In this chapter, I examined how seemingly unrelated policies affect the lives of multiple generations of mobile people. I focused on the ageing carers in a community of highly mobile Roma persons to show how their life courses have been reconfigured. By using a relational perspective that includes different generations, I showed how the moral obligation towards the future of children transforms the ways grandparents position themselves on the spectrum of paid labour—care work. While previously they would have expected to remain in the active labour force as migrants for a longer period, they are now faced with a newly emerging norm: because of the importance of their grandchildren's education, they assume the role of carers and give up their financial independence prematurely. Beyond an individual fractured biography, a new communal norm has emerged in which the young-old become carers rather than remain workers.

This argument is deeply rooted in an analysis of policies that affect people's lives across generations even when they seem directed only at children. These policies are on a collision course with the precarious working lives that are part of the hyper-intensive mobility pattern in which these Roma communities engage. As a result, one generation remains without income, another generation must provide financially for themselves and send remittances to support their children and their children's carers, and a third generation lives separately from their parents in divided families. Migration ruptures these various relationships and transforms people's life trajectories. But this clash between migration and educational regimes also results in new insecurities about the future of the young-old generation. By providing opportunities for their grandchildren to have a better future, they end up compromising their own futures. The case of hyper-mobile migrants pushes us to further consider policy effects that spread beyond the nation-state and the settled population within it – be they citizens or settled migrants – taking into account the intersections between complex spatial scattering and the movement of family members, social reproduction responsibilities, and reconfigurations of generational relations.

References

Adams, Leah D., and Anna Kirova, eds. 2006. *Global Migration and Education: School, Children, and Families.* Mahwah, NJ: Erlbaum.

Alber, Erdmute, and Heike Drotbohm, eds. 2015. *Anthropological Perspectives on Care: Work, Kinship, and the Life-Course.* New York: Palgrave Macmillan.

Apostolova, Raia. 2021. "The Re(Production) of Restless Bodies: Freedom of Movement and Social Reproduction." *International Migration* 59, no. 1: 1–14. https://doi.org/10.1111/imig.12811.

Baldassar, Loretta. 2007. "Transnational Families and Aged Care: The Mobility of Care and the Migrancy of Ageing." *Journal of Ethnic and Migration Studies* 33, no. 2: 275–297.

Bengtson, Vern L., Glen H. Elder, Jr., and Norella M. Putney. 2005. "The Life Course Perspective on Ageing: Linked Lives, Timing, and History." In *The Cambridge Handbook of Age and Ageing*, edited by Malcolm L. Johnson, Vern L. Bengtson, Peter G. Coleman, and Thomas BL Kirkwood, 493–501. Cambridge: Cambridge University Press.

Bengtson, Vern L., and Richard Settersten, Jr. 2016. "Theories of Aging: Development Within and Across Disciplinary Boundaries." In *Handbook of Theories of Aging*, edited by Vern L. Bengtson and Richard Settersten, Jr., 1–7. New York: Springer Publishing Company.

Brennan, Deborah, Bettina Cass, Saul Flaxman, Trish Hill, Bridget Jenkins, Marilyn McHugh, Christiane Purcal, and Kylie Valentine. 2013. *Grandparents Raising Grandchildren: Towards Recognition, Respect and Reward.* Sydney: Social Policy Research Centre (UNSW).

Bryceson, Deborah Fahy, and Ulla Vuorela, eds. 2002. *The Transnational Family: New European Frontiers and Global Networks.* New York: Routledge.

Coe, Cati. 2015. "The Temporality of Care: Gender, Migration, and the Entrainment of Life-Courses." In *Anthropological Perspectives on Care: Work, Kinship, and the Life-Course*, edited by Erdmute Alber and Heike Drotbohm, 181–205. New York: Palgrave Macmillan US.

Coe, Cati, Rachel R. Reynolds, Deborah A. Boehm, Julia Meredith Hess, and Heather Rae-Espinoza, eds. 2011. *Everyday Ruptures: Children, Youth, and Migration in Global Perspective.* Nashville, TN: Vanderbilt University Press.

Cortes, Patricia. 2015. "The Feminization of International Migration and Its Effects on the Children Left Behind: Evidence from the Philippines." *World Development* 65: 62–78.

Deneva, Neda. 2012. "Transnational Aging Carers: On Transformation of Kinship and Citizenship in the Context of Migration among Bulgarian Muslims in Spain." *Social Politics* 19, no. 1: 105–128.

Deneva, Neda. 2017. "Flexible Kin Work, Flexible Migration: Aging Migrants Between Productive and Reproductive Labour in the European Union." In *Transnational Aging and Reconfigurations of Kin Work*, edited by Parin Dossa and Cati Coe, 25–42. New Brunswick, NJ: Rutgers University Press.

Dossa, Parin, and Cati Coe, eds. 2017. *Transnational Aging and Reconfigurations of Kin Work.* New Brunswick, NJ: Rutgers University Press.

Dunn, Elizabeth C. 2004. *Privatizing Poland: Baby Food, Big Business, and the Remaking of Labor.* Ithaca, NY: Cornell University Press.

Elder, Jr., Glen H. 1994. "Time, Human Agency, and Social Change: Perspectives on the Life Course." *Social Psychology Quarterly* 57, no. 1: 4–15.

Evergeti, Venetia, and Elisabetta Zontini. 2006. "Introduction: Some Critical Reflections on Social Capital, Migration and Transnational Families." *Ethnic and Racial Studies* 29, no. 6: 1025–1039.

Gardner, Katy. 2012. "Transnational Migration and the Study of Children: An Introduction." *Journal of Ethnic and Migration Studies* 38, no. 6: 889–912.

Grekova, Maya, Mila Mineva, Neda Deneva, and Petya Kabakchieva. 2015. *Mobile People versus Static Institutions*. Sofia, Bulgaria: CLS, RiskMonitor.

Grekova, Maya, Mila Mineva, Neda Deneva, and Petya Kabakchieva. 2015. "Мобилни хора срещу статични институции" [Mobile people versus static institutions]. Sofia: Centre for Liberal Strategies and Risk Monitor Foundation.

Hamann, Edmund T., and Victor Zúñiga. 2011. "Schooling and the Everyday Ruptures. Transnational Children Encounter in the United States and Mexico." In *Everyday Ruptures: Children, Youth, and Migration in Global Perspective*, edited by Cati Coe, Rachel R. Reynolds, Deborah A. Boehm, Julia Meredith Hess, and Heather Rae-Espinoza, 141–161. Nashville, TN: Vanderbilt University Press.

Hareven, Tamara K. 1996. *Aging and Generational Relations over the Life Course: A Historical and Cross-Cultural Perspective*. Berlin/New York: De Gruyter.

Iossifova, Deljana. 2020. *Translocal Ageing in the Global East: Bulgaria's Abandoned Elderly*. Palgrave Macmillan. https://doi.org/10.1007/978-3-030-60823-1.

Ivancheva, Mariya, and Kathryn Keating. 2020. "Revisiting Precarity, with Care: Productive and Reproductive Labour in the Era of Flexible Capitalism." *Ephemera: Theory & Politics in Organization* 20 (4).

Kabakchieva, Petya, K. Haralampiev, A. Stambolova, E. Stoykova, T. Tomova, S.Popova, V. Garnizova, G. Angelov, R. Smedovska, N. Bozakova. 2014. *Ефекти Върху Децата, Оставени От Роди Тели, Които Работят и Живеят в Чужбина* [Effects on the children left behind by their parents, working and living abroad]. Bulgaria: UNICEF.

Kley, Stefanie. 2011. "Explaining the Stages of Migration within a Life-Course Framework." *European Sociological Review* 27, no. 4: 469–486.

Kofman, Eleonore. 2012. "Rethinking Care through Social Reproduction: Articulating Circuits of Migration." *Social Politics: International Studies in Gender, State and Society* 19, no. 1: 142–162.

Kofti, Dimitra. 2018. "Regular Work in Decline, Precarious Households and Changing Solidarities in Bulgaria." In *Industrial Labor on the Margins of Capitalism: Precarity, Class, and the Neoliberal Subject*, edited by Chris Hann and Jonathan Parry, 111–133. Oxford, New York: Berghahn Books.

Marshall, Victor W., and Margaret M. Mueller. 2003. "Theoretical Roots of the Lifecourse Perspective." In *Social Dynamics of the Life Course: Transitions, Institutions, and Interrelations*, edited by Walter R. Heinz and Victor W. Marshall, 3–32. New York: De Gruyter.

Nedelcu, Mihaela, and Malika Wyss. 2020. "Transnational Grandparenting: An Introduction." *Global Networks* 20, no. 2: 292–307.

Neugarten, Bernice L. 1974. "Age Groups in American Society and the Rise of the Young-Old." *The ANNALS of the American Academy of Political and Social Science* 415, no. 1: 187–198.

Neugarten, Bernice L., and Nancy Datan. 1973. "Sociological Perspectives on the Life Cycle." In *Life-Span Developmental Psychology*, edited by Paul B. Baltes and K. Warner Schaie, 53–69. Amsterdam: Elsevier.

Olwig, Karen Fog. 1999. "Narratives of the Children Left behind: Home and Identity in Globalised Caribbean Families." *Journal of Ethnic and Migration Studies* 25, no. 2: 267–284.

Orellana, Marjorie Faulstich, Barrie Thorne, Anna Chee, and Wan Shun Eva Lam. 2001. "Transnational Childhoods: The Participation of Children in Processes of Family Migration." *Social Problems* 48, no. 4: 572–591.

Panait, Catalina, and Víctor Zúñiga. 2016. "Children Circulating between the US and Mexico: Fractured Schooling and Linguistic Ruptures." *Mexican Studies/Estudios Mexicanos* 32, no. 2: 226–251.

Parrenas, Rhacel. 2001. *Servants of Globalization: Women, Migration and Domestic Work.* Stanford, CA: Stanford University Press.

Preoteasa, A. M., Vlase, I., and A. Pamporov. 2012. *Roma from Romania, Bulgaria, Italy and Spain between Social Inclusion and Migration Comparative Study.* Edited by Daniela Tarnovschi. Bucharest: Soros Foundation Romania.
http://comunidadgitana.org/upload/19/58/Roma_in_Romania__Bulgaria__Italy_and_Spain_between_Social_Inclusion_and_Migration._Comparative_St.pdf.

Punch, Samantha. 2012. "Studying Transnational Children: A Multi-Sited, Longitudinal, Ethnographic Approach." *Journal of Ethnic and Migration Studies* 38, no. 6: 1007–1023.

Ryan, Louise, and Rosemary Sales. 2013. "Family Migration: The Role of Children and Education in Family Decision-Making Strategies of Polish Migrants in London." *International Migration* 51, no. 2: 90–103.

Sarcinelli, Alice Sophie. 2015. "Who Are Transnational Roma 'Attached' to? Parental and Children's Social Bonds, and the Implications for Social Work." *Transnational Social Review* 5, no. 2: 118–130.

Sarma, Vengadeshvaran J., and Rasyad A. Parinduri. 2016. "What Happens to Children's Education When Their Parents Emigrate? Evidence from Sri Lanka." *International Journal of Educational Development* 46: 94–102.

Settersten, Richard A. 2003. "Age Structuring and the Rhythm of the Life Course." In *Handbook of the Life Course,* edited by Jeylan T. Mortimer and Michael J. Shanahan, 81–98. Boston: Springer.

Shanahan, Michael J., Jeylan T. Mortimer, and Monica Kirkpatrick Johnson. 2016. "Introduction: Life Course Studies – Trends, Challenges, and Future Directions." In *Handbook of the Life Course: Volume II,* edited by Michael J. Shanahan, Jeylan T. Mortimer, and Monica Kirkpatrick Johnson, 1–23. Cham: Springer International Publishing.

Tezcan, Tolga. 2019. "First-Generation Circular Migrants Involved in the Upbringing of Their Grandchildren: The Case of Turkish Immigrants in Germany." *Ageing and Society* 41, no. 1: 1–24.

Tomova, Ilona. 2009. "The Roma in Bulgaria: Education and Employment." *Suedosteuropa Mitteilungen* 2: 66–87.

Tomova, Ilona. 2011. "Transnational Migration of Bulgarian Roma." In *Global Connections and Emerging Inequalities in Europe: Perspectives on Poverty and Transnational Migration,* edited by Deema Kaneff and Frances Pine, 103–124. London, New York: Anthem Press.

Wyss, Malika, and Mihaela Nedelcu. 2018. "Zero Generation Grandparents Caring for Their Grandchildren in Switzerland. The Diversity of Transnational Care Arrangements among EU and Non-EU Migrant Families." In *Childhood and Parenting in Transnational Settings,* edited by Viorela Ducu, Mihaela Nedelcu and Aron Telegdi-Csetri, 175–190. Cham: Springer.

Zeitlyn, Benjamin, and Kanwal Mand. 2012. "Researching Transnational Childhoods." *Journal of Ethnic and Migration Studies* 38, no. 6: 987–1006.

Zhou, Yanqiu Rachel. 2013. "Toward Transnational Care Interdependence: Rethinking the Relationships between Care, Immigration and Social Policy." *Global Social Policy* 13, no. 3: 280–298.

Heike Drotbohm

Contingent Return: Moral Assessments of the Life Course in Transnational Cape Verde

Introduction. Or: When the Life Course Moves out of the National Container

Anthropological and sociological approaches to the relationship between work and the life course differ primarily with regard to the question of what type of collective they consider. While anthropology focuses primarily on the changing position of the individual within family and ethnic networks, sociologists concentrate more on the institutional structuring of the life course, for example, through its intersection with phases of education, employment, or retirement. The following chapter brings both perspectives together and deals with a dimension of life course research that has been overlooked by both disciplines until the 1990s: a transnational perspective that understands that the ways the life course is framed, experienced, and judged is not necessarily confined to the limits of the nation-state but can extend beyond national borders.

In the following chapter, I will address the fact that this transnational momentum is often accompanied by uncertainties and contingencies which become particularly clear when we look at the phenomenon of return migration. As I intend to show, especially unintended, unexpected, and often involuntary forms of migrant return constitute an increasingly frequent element of transnational modes of life. In fact, some scholars locate re-migration in the context of radical global transformations taking place around the end of the twentieth century that have produced "expulsions from life projects and livelihoods, from membership, from the social contract at the center of liberal democracy" (Sassen 2014: 29). I will refer to this pessimistic diagnosis because several aspects certainly apply to the current configurations of transnational family life. However, I want to go beyond this conceptualisation to show that the non-functioning of the once-assumed meritocratic logics of transnational labour migration today already constitutes a "new normal." Therefore, return migration, although often taking place in unstable, improvised, and involuntary circumstances, does not necessarily imply resignation and failure.

Acknowledgments: I want to express my gratitude to all the islanders from Fogo and Brava who were involved in my research, as well as to Josef Ehmer and Konstanze N'Guessan who provided me with a critical reading of an earlier version of this text.

In general, whether an imagined or lived experience, whether for a short period or forever, whether self-determined or involuntary, the return of migrants to their country of origin tells us a great deal about the negotiation of social roles in transnational social fields including social status, aspirations, and self-esteem. Especially in societies in which everyday lives heavily rely on transnational connectedness, regular return migration is understood as a sign of success and as an expression of loyalty by those who went abroad and are willing, but also able, to remain in touch – with their kin and friends as well as with their community and networks and their nation of origin. The following chapter concentrates on those migrants who returned due to unforeseen circumstances. I will use their case studies to demonstrate that not only the individual but, above all, the respective social environment is significantly involved in establishing the normalisation of – and in this way removing the stigma of – irregular return.

To make this argument, first, I present my regional example, the Cape Verdean islands, and explain the historically changing meanings of return migration in this particular transnational social field. Then I will delve into the biographical trajectories of three individuals from different age cohorts whose conditions of return were considerably shaped by the fact that the state and other key institutions in the diaspora failed them. This will allow me to move beyond former studies that focus *either* on specific dimensions of involuntary return, such as deportation, or aspects of return migration considered to be voluntary, such as retirement or schooling. After summarising the conditions of each individual return, I will return to my theoretical reflections and concentrate on those aspects that are central to the normative evaluation of return. In the final section, I provide insights into the more-or-less flexible adaptations and adjustments to age-specific roles and duties often present in the background of contingent forms of return.

But before turning to my analysis, some information about my fieldwork techniques and methodology is necessary. In total, I spent twelve months between 2006 and 2010 on Fogo and Brava, two islands located in the southwest of the Cape Verdean archipelago. Initially, I concentrated on how the concept of "family" has evolved historically, what moral expectations and caregiving practices arose from this, and how the ways families act are currently being adapted to the increasing influence of migration policies (Drotbohm 2009, 2018). Although re-migration was not the focus of my work, the ambivalent position of returnees in general and deported migrants in particular was helpful for understanding the importance of an ideal-typical life course and the collective handling of contradictions (Drotbohm 2011). Qualitative methods ranged from participant observation in selected households, ego-centred network-mapping techniques, as well as biographical and semi-structured interviews. During these interviews, I paid special attention to changes in political regimes, for instance, the moment of political independence or important shifts in European or North American migration policies (Drotbohm 2009). Furthermore, the questions I asked during interviews encouraged interviewees to concentrate on events, crises, and biographical ruptures, given that anthropological study of the life course has shown that a rearrangement of social relations can be observed in key biographical events. My proceedings were highly influenced by the methodologies of family histories developed by João de Pina Cabral and Antónia Pedroso de Lima (2005) and Tamara Hareven (1991), all of whom employed life course approaches combined with biographical interviews to study historical and transnational family relations. I subsequently visited selected members of these transnational households in two important sites of the Cape Verdean diaspora – Lisbon (Portugal) and Boston (USA) – to include their interpretations of social norms and practices I already assumed I understood at the time. My own return to the islands again in 2010 revealed the symbolic meaning of return, which, as will be explored in more detail below, is interpreted as an affirmation of social ties and as an expression of loyalty.

Changing Meanings of Return in Cape Verdean Transnational Fields

The historical change in the meaning of migrant return can be observed particularly well on the Cape Verdean islands, located approximately 550 kilometres west of the Senegalese coast: The ecological conditions of these islands must be taken into account in order to understand the specific reasons for migration pressure and the moral assessment of both connectedness and return (Drotbohm 2009, 2011, 2017). After the discovery of the uninhabited and apparently inhospitable archipelago in the sixteenth century, Portuguese sailors used the territory as a trading post for transporting sugar, cotton, and, especially, enslaved persons between the Upper Guinea Coast, Europe, and Brazil in the eighteenth and nineteenth centuries (Meintel 1984; Halter 1993). Over time, a creole society developed out of the encounters between European masters, enslaved Africans, and other immigrant groups who established their lives despite drought, poverty, and political neglect. Over time, migration destinations changed. The global whaling industry led thousands of Cape Verdeans to the United States starting in the 1820s. A century later, many men from the islands abandoned the drought-affected lands and their impoverished lives on the islands for agricultural work in the United States, mainly in southeastern New England, which still hosts the largest Cape Verdean migrant community in the world. Additionally, noteworthy Cape Verdean diaspora communities evolved in Brazil as well as in European countries such as Spain, Italy,

France, the Netherlands, and Luxemburg. After centuries of Cape Verdean migration, the diasporic population now outnumbers the islands' inhabitants (Batalha 2004; Carling and Åkesson 2009), and transnationalism has become the dominant way of living. The relational dynamics between non-migrants and migrants, those living in poverty and those receiving, at least intermittently, remittances from abroad, illuminate social differentiation and reinforce social inequalities.

Regarding the question of how both social cohesion and asymmetries are created in transnational networks, the return of migrants to their country of origin received scholarly attention early on (Brettell 1979; Gmelch 1980; Constable 1999; Carling, Mortensen, and Wu 2011). Initially, migration research made a distinction between diasporic constellations that resulted from experiences of expulsion and exile on the one hand (Cohen 2008), and, on the other hand, the global circulation of merchants or labour migrants whose return was regarded as a constitutive element of the everyday momentum of transnational mobility routines by the middle of the twentieth century (Biao 2013). Spiritual or religious events, especially life-cycle rituals such as baptism, marriage, and funerals offer welcome occasions for migrants to return temporarily to "their islands." By doing so, they reconfirm familial solidarity and reorder social belonging, which has been transformed due to great spatial and temporal distance (Fog Olwig 2002; Gardner and Grillo 2002; Drotbohm 2016). Generally, it is crucial to understand that return usually has positive connotations not only when migrants return for family visits or festivities but also when they return as entrepreneurs to invest in or when they decide to retire as pensioners in their country of origin. To this day, migrant return functions as a hinge within a transnational meritocratic system and is regarded as an opportunity to demonstrate the status and the financial and legal power of successful migrants whose economic standing in their countries of origin is valued as a powerful resource (Tsuda 2009; Saar 2013; Pido 2017).

In addition to these valued forms of return, which are conceived as evidence of success and an expression of superiority, there are, at the same time, more and more involuntary variants of return that carry negative connotations. The increasing global deportation figures are the most striking example. Since the 1990s at the latest, governments around the world have been increasingly using the mechanism of forced return to country of origin as an effective means of dealing with unauthorised immigration and failed asylum petitions (Peutz and De Genova 2010; Drotbohm and Hasselberg 2015). As Jean-Pierre Cassarino correctly notes, "return is euphemistically used as a synonym of readmission or expulsion" (Cassarino 2008: 97). Parallel to these forced returns initiated or carried out by states, there is also an increasing number of self-initiated forms of return migration that can also be seen as deviant, irregular, or even "failures." The reasons for this are not specific to the individual but are structurally diverse. In part, they relate to what sociologist Saskia Sassen calls the "decaying political economy of the twentieth century" (Sassen 2014: 212). According to her, the era of hyper-mobile capital and market deregulation that began in the 1980s reached its peak in the 2000s, produced shrinking economies, austerity politics, environmental decay, and growing indebtedness, which went along with new forms of unemployment and precarity. This diagnosis does not only refer to the lives of transmigrants. On the contrary, the tensions and processes of marginalisation described by Sassen disproportionately affect the poor, Black persons, and precarious workers, especially in the Global North. In these contexts, migrants make up a particularly high proportion of those affected by these economic developments. When mobile subjects are increasingly confronted with more legal restrictions, racism, economic precarity, or the threat of deportation in their country of residence, they may begin to consider the option of returning to their country of origin. This is the case even when their circumstances may not actually correspond to common assumptions and expectations of an ideal return. If "return preparedness" – which, following Cassarino, refers to "the ability, though not always the opportunity, to gather the tangible and intangible resources needed to secure one's own return home" (2008: 101) – we may ask how an ill-prepared return is experienced differently depending on the type of (un-)preparedness, age, or citizenship status.

Three Case Studies

I begin my empirical account with a snapshot of the centre of São Filipe, the main town on the island of Fogo, one of the southernmost Cape Verdean islands, which has approximately 35,000 inhabitants living on 476 square kilometres of land. Here, everyday life usually moves slowly. São Filipe is a cosy municipality, with a town hall, a colonial museum, and a number of shops located on two parallel main streets, as well as several pubs and restaurants. In contrast to mornings, when delivery and pick-up vehicles squeeze their way through the narrow cobblestone streets, islanders run their errands, and the noise of carpenters fills the air, the hot afternoons are usually much quieter. In the early evening, elderly people sit under the trees in the shade, young people go down to the beach, and sometimes you can even hear typical melancholic Cape Verdean notes plucked by someone on his guitar. In view of the long history of transnational Cape Verdean livelihoods, these islands usually see a variety of different return-migrants. In what follows, I will refer to particularly significant and telling variants of involuntary return.

Dona Teresa returns differently

In the first few weeks after Dona Teresa's return, whispers about her arrival could be overheard, one of her neighbours recalled. Although Teresa was barely seen in the streets, everyone knew she was back *para ficar* ('to stay'), as was specified in my conversations with people. In the late afternoons, when it was almost dark, she sometimes walked to the church in her typical conservative clothes, sometimes with her little granddaughter in tow. Teresa was always proper and friendly, but she was also noticeably reserved. Some said that she had not been that reserved before but that this was understandable given all the difficulties she had suffered. Generally, she was spared embarrassment and left alone. And the gossip was relatively minimal.

Originally, Teresa was not from an affluent family. Together with her husband Pino, she had moved to São Filipe, the island's main town at the beginning of the 1960s, where they achieved some modest prosperity with their little grocery store located close to the main street. Several years later, Pino decided to emigrate to the United States with the plan to have his wife and three children join him later. Although he found work quickly, he lived in cramped conditions and delayed his family's reunification. When Teresa finally left in 1966, she took only her young daughter and left her two sons, then six and seven years old, with one of her sisters, who continued to run the family's shop. Teresa assumed and promised she would return within a few months after everything was set up in Boston. However, things turned out to be much more complicated. Overseas, she soon had two more children and the process of legalising her residence was difficult; it took several years until the family was fully reunified. Arrangements of this kind – children temporarily remain in their country of origin with substitute carers while their parents migrate; thus, families are transnationalised for a certain period of time – are widespread globally. Both in the United States and in Europe, family reunification often remains difficult even when migrants succeed in regularising their legal status and finding stable employment (Moskal and Tyrrall 2016; Fresnoza-Flot 2015). On the Cape Verdean islands, such constellations are quite usual. In any case, during the years of her absence, Dona Teresa managed to maintain a good reputation. She always sent regular and reliable remittances and good-quality clothes and consumer items to the two sons she left behind, they attended a "good school," and she provided the family with extra money in case of emergencies. After finally being reunited with her two boys, who were twelve and thirteen years old when they reached Boston, she also stayed in touch with the island community, kept the shop going, and was involved in a small transnational women's club that renovated the church and the central village square. Over the following decades, whenever possible, Teresa travelled to the islands - even if only for shorter visits.

The year prior to Teresa's permanent return, however, had been unusual. From the large number of suitcases and boxes that were carried into their house upon arrival, the neighbourhood realised that this was not a visit but that Teresa had come to stay. I suppose this recognition came with some relief because her return was preceded two years earlier by the return of her eldest son Valdim, then already forty-seven years old, after he had repeatedly been in trouble with US law enforcement for drug possession and was deported after a three-year prison term. In principle, deportees, who are condescendingly referred to as *"deportados,"* never had it easy on the islands – especially if they were deported because of criminal convictions and not purely administrative problems (complications with their immigration status). Kin relationships of deportees usually carry strong social pressure, as involuntary, state-initiated return is usually seen as both a serious misfortune as well as a source of shame for a deportee's relatives who expected much more from the entire migration project (Schuster and Majidi 2015).

As my previous research has shown (Drotbohm 2011), in Cape Verde, it is considered particularly problematic that deported migrants are unable to adequately support their relatives on the islands and that they also absorb remittances that might have been directed towards others. While many deportees suffer from a deportation-related stigma and social exclusion, others have managed to transfer the resources and skills they acquired abroad back to island life (Drotbohm 2017). Valdim, however, did not submit to this moral regime. He resumed his drug use within a short time after his return, and he regularly drank and got into drunken fights, so gainful employment was impossible. The money his parents sent regularly alleviated his situation from an economic point of view, but he had also become involved with a young woman in town. She became pregnant, and after the birth of the child, she pressured him to financially support her and the child.

This information allows us to understand that both Teresa's and Valdim's returns are part of an intergenerational life course in which individual trajectories are linked to specific biographical moments in such a way that the experiences of one inevitably determines the realm of action of the other (Bengtson 2009). To what extent the decision to return has to do with both individual perspectives and specific historical conditions will be discussed below.

Johnny reconsiders "home"

On good days, Johnny, who as a child was called João, was a friendly fellow who was always up for a chat. In the mornings, he usually rushed around the island to do his daily shopping in an open, jeep-like golf cart he had brought back from Boston. In the afternoons, he would often doze off in the shade of a tree that stood in front of his new two-story house in the *achada*, a newly built neighbourhood in São Filipe. From the late afternoon onwards, he was usually in good company: each day Rosita, a pretty, often fashionably dressed woman in her late thirties from the island's interior, brought life into his apartment. She cleaned the kitchen and did the laundry; after work, she liked to make herself comfortable with him under the tree, chatting and giggling, and sometimes she stayed overnight.

In the early 1940s, at the age of four, Johnny had left the islands with his parents and siblings. Growing up in one of the better neighbourhoods of Dorchester, a small town on the outskirts of Boston, he distanced himself from African American or African communities and cultivated his sense of "Americanness" – which was easy, he told me, due to his exceptionally light skin colour and his enrolment in a "white" school. "I actually had nothing to do with Cape Verde. It was written in my passport, but I was American in every way," he explained. After working for his father's company for a few years, he became self-employed as an insurance agent and invested a large part of his money in the then-booming stock market. The situation changed a few years later. Given that he was familiar with the shaky foundation of this particular industry, he should have foreseen the risks of this financial architecture, which collapsed a few years later. He regarded Cape Verde, as he said, as kind of "back door, a real-life exit option."

Johnny's situation is exemplary for a growing number of older migrants who are returning unintentionally to their country of origin for several different reasons. In an interesting comparison between Turkish-German and German retirees, Cagri Kahveci, Elifcan Karacan, and Kira Kosnick (2020) illuminate the challenges of mobile aging, which concerns not only retirement migrants (those who retire to a new place) but also retired labour migrants (those who return to their country of origin in a later phase in life) (see also King et al. 2017). In both cases, low pension incomes and legal insecurities as well as unknown factors associated with potentially declining health play a big role. Other scholars confirm that particular moments of national crisis characterised by increased unemployment and, thus, interrupted pension contributions can have dramatic consequences for the return conditions of aging migrants (Baykara-Krumme 2013; Duci, Dhembo and Vati 2019). Like Johnny, many aging migrants are in precarious situations due to the lack of bilateral agreements on the portability of social security benefits between countries (Horn et al. 2016; Bender et al. 2018). Unlike retirement, lifestyle, or amenity migration (Benson & O'Reilly 20015), this type of re-migration is considered atypical in transnational social fields as it does not signal a successful life and the corresponding economic benefits but rather forces a confrontation with severe, sometimes even existential problems.

In contrast to many transmigrants who keep in touch with their community of origin through visits, remittances, or regular communication, Johnny did not have any family, friends, or property on the island. Comparable to a tourist who only vaguely knows a certain place, much about Cape Verde was alien to him. Although he appreciated the welcoming atmosphere of the islands, he still had strong doubts as to whether he should really stay permanently. The following issues seemed central: he still felt vital, but he was severely obese and suffered from diabetes. Because healthcare in Cape Verde is considered poor and he could not obtain his regular medication there, he was dependent on his access to his American health benefits. This required him to travel to the United States at least once a year and, therefore, produced another worry: he feared that after a certain point in time, he would no longer be able to maintain this type of circular migration. He was also concerned about the future, when he would be less mobile, frailer, and thus also more dependent. In 2007, the year of my fieldwork, there were only a few elderly care homes in Cape Verde, and these were understood as primarily a solution only in emergencies (Drotbohm 2015). Elderly Cape Verdeans usually rely on their female relatives who are expected to help them as they become frailer and as they approach death. It was clear to Johnny that his care expectations, especially in the case of long-term disability, would not be met either in the United States or on the islands. "I certainly have to stay healthy," he pointed out during our conversation.

It took him several months to get in touch with Rosita through a distant cousin. At the time, Rosita was living in precarious circumstances with her four children and her physically disabled mother in the island's hinterlands. Johnny and Rosita's arrangement suited her family, too. While Rosita stayed with Johnny in town, her children, who were between ten and sixteen years old at the time of my research, remained in the village and were looked after by her mother. This economic-social agreement, which goes beyond the employer-domestic employee relationship, is not always approved of by the predominantly Catholic island community, but it is usually tolerated. Johnny pays her a weekly wage and occasionally gives her a little more for her family, which he calls *apoio*, 'support.' Before I explain the peculiarities of his position in the next section, I will turn briefly to Danilsa, a much younger returnee.

Danilsa "goes back culture"

Unlike Johnny's return, Danilsa's cannot be described as voluntary. But at the same time, she was not deported like Teresa's son Valdim. She was the daughter of Cape Verdean high school teachers who migrated to the United States at the beginning of the 1980s and integrated into one of Boston's better neighbourhoods relatively easily. For Danilsa's parents, residence and social networks as well as education were understood as key forms of cultural capital. In a detailed biographical interview, Danilsa described her parents' disappointment when they realised the difficulties she had in school, and that she preferred spending her afternoons laying around and eventually smoking marijuana and shoplifting with friends. She was never a smart or sweet child, Danilsa told me, and her parents had always worried about her future. When she was fourteen years old, she was picked up during a police raid, and her parents made the difficult decision to send her to Cape Verde, where she would live with her maternal grandmother for a while.

Future worries are what cause many first-generation migrants to send their children to their (not the child's) country of origin. These children are actually second-generation immigrants who are both born and socialised abroad. This special form of – more or less involuntary – migration always takes place within the family either by having the children accompany their returning parents (Boehm 2012) or by having children travel on their own and then usually live with relatives who had not migrated. But the motives for sending children "back" vary. In the case of small children, often the lack of time to care for children due to parents' work and high child-care costs are mentioned. Contact with the parents' "culture of origin" and language acquisition is often seen as an opportunity to convey key "cultural values" (Qureshi 2014). In middle-class families especially, it is considered appropriate or even a privilege for parents to send their children to expensive boarding schools in their country of origin, where they are expected to learn a different kind of discipline (Kea 2017). At the same time, sending children "back" can imply a harsh disciplinary measure, especially if the children had previously been involved with gangs or drugs (Bledsoe and Sow 2011; Lee 2016). To date, research makes clear that this type of re-migration can be problematic in many cases, as the children often travel to a country they do not know at all or only barely know (Lee 2016; Hernández-León, Zúñiga and Lakhani 2020). Basically, it is this process that turns these children into migrants, and the term "return" here refers more to a sense of going "back" only from the biographical perspective of their parents, who nostalgically hope that their country of origin will have a positive influence on their children.

However, those who assume that Danilsa would rebel against this distinct form of forced migration would be mistaken. During our interview, she remembered the years in Brockton when she felt unhappy, alone, and neglected by her busy parents. Her everyday life, when she did not do well in school and was responsible for looking after her younger siblings, was *uma bagunca*, i.e. "an overwhelming mess," she said. Of course, she confirmed that her first days on the islands after her return were also stressful, but in a different sense. Through a detailed conversation, it became clear that Danilsa was struggling with her parents' decision, which she saw as a punishment. But at the same time, she confirmed that she had been coping with serious problems in the United States. Her expression, articulated in English language, "I had to go back culture" refers to culture as an adjective, for describing a certain way of return that is focused on "traditional values like family and care," as she said. "Things are better here on the islands. And I'll be able to return to the U.S. and start from scratch." Particularly important to her was her US citizenship, the privileges of which she often emphasised. "I am not a deportee. I can go and come. Soon I will be living in the US again. I'm an American citizen by birth, nobody can take that from me. As soon as I turn eighteen, I mean, after finishing school, I'll buy my ticket and just go." Her hand confidently moved in a way that seemed to echo an airplane's flight route.

Discussion

In the previous section, I brought together three case studies that differ significantly with regard to the age of (re)migrants, their migration trajectories and biographical embedding, as well as their future prospects on the islands following return. However, the three individual cases are comparable because they are interpreted both in their entanglement with family and ethnic networks and with a particular focus on the institutional framings in their former country of residence. Like many other migrants, the three originally had travelled with high hopes for their own educational aspirations or those of their children (Teresa, Valdim, and Danilsa), had invested in their labour biographies, and hoped to be cared for in times of crisis or in old age by the respective state structures (Johnny, Teresa). They had also shared a relatively high level of legal security – at least stable residence status. However, they were unable to capitalise on the conventional and expected promises of transnational livelihoods. Regarding the question of how these life courses are assessed from a Cape Verdean perspective, I will first elaborate on the specific historical conditions of the United States' immigration society and ask how these impacted the family biographies of the individuals above. Based on this foundation, the final section will explain how this plays into the moral evaluation of migrant return.

Emerging legal vulnerabilities beyond the migrant-citizen binary

First, the above examples illuminate collisions between the assumptions of an "ordinary," i.e., ideal-type, life course and structural as well as institutional constraints that are part of international labour regimes. Most importantly, the usual citizen–migrant binarism with which tendencies towards precariousness are often viewed does not apply here. To understand the specifics of an individual's condition of return, an understanding of the "immigrant generation" must be brought together with the specific historical context and the resulting migration regime that contributes significantly to the individual's position. For instance, Dona Teresa belongs to a first immigrant generation that was aware of possible restrictions or losses, above all regarding economic status. Her biographical trajectory is reminiscent of the experiences of the first generation of Cape Verdean labour migrants who went to Massachusetts in the 1950s and 1960s (Halter 1993). While most of them tolerated the challenges caused by their often-limited knowledge of English and the difficulty of transferring their professional skills to the US labour market, they had high expectations for their children's careers. The constellation in Teresa's family is typical insofar as it refers to the fact that the trajectories of succeeding generations can also defy all plans. A significant peculiarity of families that plan out the reunification of children in individual steps is the fact that the residence status of their offspring often differs from their own depending on the child's age and the temporal particularities of the immigration regime under which family reunification was organised.

In a lengthy conversation, Valdim remembered the long years he spent waiting for reunification and his difficult adjustment in the United States, when he had to start school right away. He explained how much he envied his younger US-born siblings, who benefited from being, in his words: "complete Americans." In contrast to them, he and his younger brother only held permanent residency (a "green card") and belonged to a very specific generation of immigrants that are neither first nor second generation, often called "1.5" (Coe 2014). The specifics of the late 1990s also played a role in Valdim's misfortune as border controls and deportations in the United States were restrictively applied (Drotbohm 2011). Like many other "legal residents," his assumption that this legal status or the generally good reputation of his family would offer him a kind of protection was a fallacy. These historical and generation-specific conditions are important for understanding the logic behind Dona Teresa's decision to later accompany her son in his forced return to their country of origin. Given that labour migration is often a family-based investment, past expectations, disappointments, and errors are intertwined. In retrospect, Valdim's parents must have regretted their decision to organise their son's reunification so late, which put him –and ultimately them – at a legal and structural disadvantage.

With Johnny, the pensioner, the situation was quite different. In a biographical interview, he focused primarily on the fact that the Cape Verde Islands at the time of his departure in the late 1940s were still part of the Portuguese colonial empire. He was travelling, as he liked to say, "on the Portuguese ticket." Acquiring US citizenship was still comparatively easy at that time. Later it was not an issue of citizenship but the collapse of the stock market, his unemployment, and the problems associated with health care that called into question his stay in the United States. He was forced to acknowledge that his US citizenship did not protect him from poverty and that he risked receiving only the bare minimum elderly care in the future. Because of this dilemma, his connection to his former homeland, although he hardly remembered the islands, emerged as an alternative opportunity.

Lastly, I turn to Danilsa, who was sent (back) by her parents. Although she was born in the United States and acquired American citizenship at birth, she was still confronted with the pitfalls of social inequalities in American (US) society, particularly regarding the structural intersection of her parents' time-consuming jobs, the lack of adequate childcare and educational options, and high crime rates in some city areas, which are sometimes associated with the inevitability of gang violence, especially for young Blacks. Although these constellations only partially applied to Danilsa's family, her parents, who perceived themselves as more vulnerable to state control, were unable to weather their daughter's rebellious period of adolescence. Danilsa's parents feared that sooner or later, she would end up in prison, and so her mother's brother, who had no children himself, stepped in and offered the dependability and the moral support Danilsa needed.

In summary, the three examples show that power asymmetries that went along with the intersection of global migration and labour regimes, had a profound effect on the life courses of these family members, who were equipped with different resources. Contrary to the expectations of – or myths about – cross-border family lives, these do not have a meritocratic character. Indeed, neither access to citizenship nor a legally regulated residence status decided whether these individuals experienced a life course deemed appropriate, or, as Johnny would say, one that he or she deserved. On the bumpy path of re-migration, involuntariness or even coercion can occur because of state-directed practices like deportation, as in the case of Valdim, as well as due to the lack of an adequate social safety net and weak welfare institutions, as in the cases of Johnny and Danilsa. Interestingly however, these vulnerabilities, which only emerge and harden over the life course, can be evaluated mildly from a moral point of view. As will be shown in the following section, it is not the migrants who fail. Rather, at least according to some perspectives, it is the destination country that is unable to offer its migrant citizens the appropriate backing.

Backing the moral assessment of contingent life courses

Although return migration can be understood as some kind of exit strategy in moments of heightened vulnerability, it is still – and this was elaborated in the second section – subject to collective moral assessment. Those who return irregularly, prematurely, and empty-handed must balance feelings of shame and social stigma (Schuster and Majidi 2015). One form of moral backing refers to the position of returnees within their family networks. For instance, when confronted retrospectively with the problematic outcome of their migration decision, Teresa decided to leave her husband, children, and grandchildren behind and accompany her deported son back to their country of origin. One might almost say that she decided to share in Valdim's legal condemnation. Additionally, she also accepted a high degree of responsibility by taking care of her granddaughter, thereby managing to reconcile Valdim's girlfriend's expectations and compensate for her own (presumably self-imposed) feelings of guilt. Although "being backed" (Yngevesson and Coutin 2006) by her son's deportation, Teresa was still able to rely on the good reputation she had built up during the decades of her absence. In the eyes of the islanders, she demonstrated her commitment not only as a mother and grandmother, but also as a responsible member of the island community by accepting these responsibilities. This acceptance likely facilitated not only her own re-integration after return but eventually also her son's status on the island as he was no longer seen as a collective burden.

With Johnny, the pensioner, the situation was different but still comparable. Unlike many people who age within/surrounded by their families, Johnny was frustrated by the loss of autonomy and his newly emerging dependency, which, as he said, did not comply with his former investments and his social status. He liked to curse the United States, which, according to him, did not keep its promises. In Cape Verde, he emphasised several times, he at least received a minimum pension.[1] However, he accepted that he had to improve his social networks to stabilise his future prospects. His arrangement with Rosita was crucial in this regard. As an *emigrante*, Johnny was perceived as having a moral duty to provide not only for those who cared for him directly but also for his caregivers' networks of depend-

---

[1] In 2007, the time of my fieldwork, every Cape Verdean pensioner received 6,000 escudos per month, the equivalent of 50 €, regardless of whether s/he had paid into the pension fund.

ents. What the islanders called *cuida* 'care,' signalling their approval, can be called "provider love" in other contexts (Ferguson 2015). At the same time, Johnny also received something from this arrangement: Rosita did not only perform "a job"; she rather took care of him in a broader socio-emotional sense. Again, following Ferguson, Rosita also pressed her distributive claims, and Johnny had to prove his eligibility for this type of care. As an outsider who was not able to rely on established reciprocal liabilities from the past, he took the conditionalities of these newly created bonds seriously and was also aware that his "willingness to perform" was evaluated critically in his neighbourhood. "Sometimes they test me, they call me 'cheap,' even the kids on the street call me 'cheap' if I refuse to buy them sweets." On the island of Fogo, the English term "cheap" was introduced into Cape Verdean Creole to indicate the "under-performance" of migrant returnees or, what Ferguson would call, their insufficient contributions to the local "transfer of resources" (Ferguson 2015).

The collective evaluation of return migration becomes even more obvious in the case of Danilsa, as her relatively young age protects her from moral condemnation. While she herself struggled with the idea that her return was viewed suspiciously as "failed" or "senseless," she tried above all to differentiate herself from other similarly young but officially deported migrants, whose legal status on the islands differed from her own. "It may sound strange," Danilsa said at a certain point, "but I feel free here. I can concentrate more on myself here. I also try to avoid getting in trouble." This statement confirms one interpretation of her return conditions. Although her parents had used coerced return as a disciplinary measure, Danilsa accepted that they had managed to protect her from deportation, something that US-American institutions had failed to do. To fully understand the process of her social integration into the village community, however, her self-classification was probably less relevant than the position of her mother's brother Pedro, a businessman, who often travelled back and forth between the islands and the United States. Her uncle Pedro decided to take her under his wing. He financed Danilsa's private school and made sure that she worked regularly in Rosita's little grocery store. In a way, her uncle confirmed Danilsa's social embeddedness and compensated for the contingency of her return when he tried to "straighten" her life course, which was considered important to his entire family.

In summary, it becomes clear that the institutional frameworks of these migrant life paths were weak, but their family and ethnic resources were comparatively solid as these unexpectedly difficult modes of individual return were met with understanding and the necessary forms of material and organisational support.

Conclusion

In times of tightened border control, fragmented welfare protection, and highly volatile labour markets, the conditions of migrants' return are just as contingent and diverse as the reasons and conditions of migration in general. At the same time, the cases compiled here show that returnees who return involuntarily or under insecure conditions are not left to their own devices. On the contrary, we understand that return can serve as a central cultural technique to compensate individuals for the risks they undertook, providing them with an opportunity to adjust to globalised institutional weaknesses and life's contingencies. Return also provides alternative pathways beyond the confines of typical life course regimes.

These various ways of re-migration also show that return became established as a social institution in the course of the centuries-old history of entanglement of the Cape Verde islands and other regions of the world. The myth of the successful worker who returns satisfied to his home country after completing his job in order to enjoy his retirement has been replaced by numerous stabilising social practices that simultaneously intersect with economic, political, and legal frameworks. While the destination country, in this case the United States, does not contribute to solving the problems that arose within its territory, migrants and their families use return as a reorienting and compensating alternative.

Interpreted this way, return has assumed new transformative powers. It generates new trans-local subjectivities that connect the process of self-making in the pursuit of a successful future to several different possible places. Simultaneously, it is also part of the collective moral evaluation of the life course's contingencies and, in ideal cases, facilitates the individual's access to alternative forms of care and social embedding.

References

Batalha, Luís. 2004. *The Cape Verdean Diaspora in Portugal: Colonial Subjects in a Postcolonial World*. Lanham, MD: Lexington Books.

Baykara-Krumme, Helen. 2013. "Returning, Staying, or Both? Mobility Patterns Among Elderly Turkish Migrants After Retirement." *Transnational Social Review* 3: 11–29.

Bengtson, Vern, Glen H. Elder Jr., and Norella M. Putney. 2009. "The Lifecourse Perspective on Ageing: Linked Lives, Timing, and History." *The Cambridge Handbook of Age and Ageing*, edited by Malcolm L. Johnson, 493–501. Cambridge: Cambridge University Press.

Bender, Désirée, Tina Hollstein, and Cornelia Schweppe. 2018. "International retirement migration revisited: From amenity seeking to precarity migration?" *Transnational Social Review* 8, no. 1: 98–102.

Benson, Michaela, and Karen O'Reilly. 2015. "From lifestyle migration to lifestyle in migration: Categories, concepts and ways of thinking." *Migration Studies* 4 no 1: 20–37.

Biao, Xiang. 2013. "Introduction. Return and the Reordering of Transnational Mobility in Asia." In *Return. Nationalizing Transnational Mobility in Asia*, edited by Xiang Biao, Brenda S. A. Yeoh, and Mika Toyota, 1–20. Durham, NC: Duke University Press.

Blendsoe, Caroline H., and Papa Sow. 2011. "Back to Africa: Second Chances for the Children of West African Immigrants." *Journal of Marriage and Family* 73: 747–762.

Boehm, Deborah. 2012. *Intimate Migrations. Gender, Family, and Illegality among Transnational Mexicans*. New York: New York University Press.

Brettell, Caroline. 1979. "Emigrar Para Voltar: A Portuguese Ideology of Return Migration." *Papers in Anthropology* 20 no. 1: 1–20.

Bryceson, Deborah, and Ulla Vuorela. 2002. "Transnational Families in the Twenty-first Century." In *The Transnational Family. New European Frontiers and Global Networks*, edited by Deborah Bryceson and Ulla Vuorela, 3–30. Oxford: Berg.

Bryceson, Deborah Fahy. 2019. "Transnational Families Negotiating Migration and Care Life Cycles across Nation-state Borders." *Journal of Ethnic and Migration Studies* 45: 3042–3064.

Carling, Jørgen, and Lisa Åkesson. 2009. "Mobility at the Heart of a Nation: Patterns and Meanings of Cape Verdean Migration." *International Migration* 47, no. 3: 123–155.

Carling, Jørgen, Elin Mortensen, and Jennifer Wu. 2011. *A Systematic Bibliography on Return Migration*. Peace Research Institute Oslo (PRIO).

Cassarino, Jean-Pierre. 2008. *Return Migrants to the Maghreb Countries: Reintegration and Development Challenges*. Florence: MIREM Project, Robert Schuman Centre for Advanced Studies, European University Institute.

Ciobanu, Ruxandra Oana, Tineke Fokkema, and Mihaela Nedelcu. 2016. "Ageing as a Migrant: Vulnerabilities, Agency and Policy Implications." *Journal of Ethnic and Migration* Studies 43, no. 2: 164–181.

Coe, Kati. 2014. *The Scattered Family. Parenting, African Migrants, and Global Inequality*. Chicago and London: The University of Chicago Press.

Cohen, Robin. 2008. *Global Diasporas. An Introduction*. London: Routledge.

Constable, Nicole. 1999. "At Home but Not at Home: Filipina Narratives of Ambivalent Returns." *Cultural Anthropology* 14, no. 2: 203–228.

De Pina Cabral, João, and Antonia Pedroso de Lima. 2005. "Como fazer uma história de família: Um exercício de contextualizacao social." *Etnográfica* 9, no. 2: 355–388.

Duci, Veronika, Elona Dhembo, and Zana Vathi. 2019. "Precarious Retirement for Ageing Albanian (Return) Migrants." *Südosteuropa* 67, no. 2: 211–233.

Drotbohm, Heike. 2009. "Horizons of Long-distance Intimacies. Reciprocity, Contribution and Disjuncture in Cape Verde." *The History of the Family. An International Quarterly* (Special Issue: Families, Foreignness, Migration, Now and Then) 14, no. 2: 132–149.

Drotbohm, Heike. 2011. "On the Durability and the Decomposition of Citizenship: The Social Logics of Forced Return Migration in Cape Verde." *Citizenship Studies* (Special issue: Subjects of Citizenship) 15, nos. 3/4: 381–396.

Drotbohm, Heike. 2015. "Shifting Care among Families, Social Networks and State Institutions in Times of Crisis: A Transnational Cape Verdean Perspective." In *Anthropological Perspectives on Care. Works, Kinship, and the Life Course*, edited by Erdmute Alber and Heike Drotbohm, 93–116. Basingstoke: Palgrave Macmillan.

Drotbohm, Heike. 2016. "Celebrating Asymmetries. Creole Stratification and the Regrounding of Home in Cape Verdean Migrant Return Visits." In The *Upper Guinea Coast in Global Perspective*, edited by Jacqueline Knörr and Christoph Kohl, 135–156. London: Berghahn.

Drotbohm, Heike. 2017. "Frozen Cosmopolitanism: Coping with Radical Deceleration in Cape Verdean Contexts of Forced Return Migration." In *Identity in an Overheated World*, edited by Thomas Hylland Eriksen and Elisabeth Schober, 42–58. London: Pluto Press.

Drotbohm, Heike. 2018. "Care and Reunification in a Cape Verdean Family: Changing Articulations of Family and Legal Ties." *Ethnography* 21, no. 1: 48–70.

Drotbohm, Heike, and Ines Hasselberg. 2015. "Deportation, Anxiety, Justice: New Ethnographic Perspectives." *Journal of Ethnic and Migration Studies* 41, no. 4: 551–562.

Elder, Glen H. Jr., Monica Kirkpatrick Johnson, and Robert Crosnoe. 2003. "The Emergence and Development of Life Course Theory." *In Handbook of the Life Course*, edited by Jeylan Mortimer and Michael J. Shanahan, 3–22. New York: Kluwer Academic Publishers.

Ferguson, James. 2015. *Give a Man a Fish: Reflections on the New Politics of Distribution*. Durham, NC: Duke University Press: 15–18.

Fog Olwig, Karen. 2002. "A Wedding in the Family: Home Making in a Global Kin Network." *Global Networks* 2, no. 3: 205–218.

Fresnoza-Flot, Asuncion. 2015. "The Bumpy Landscape of Family Reunification: Experiences of First- and 1.5-generation Filipinos in France." *Journal of Ethnic and Migration Studies* 41, no. 7: 1152–1171.

Gardner, Katy, and Ralph Grillo. 2002. "Transnational Households and Ritual." *Global Networks* 2, no. 3: 179–290.

Fouron, Georges, and Nina Glick Schiller. 2001. "All in the Family: Gender, Transnational Migration, and the Nation-State." *Identities: Global Studies in Culture and Power* 7, no. 4: 539–582.

Gmelch, Georges. 1980. "Return Migration." *Annual Review of Anthropology* 9: 135–159.

Halter, Marilyn. 1993. *Between Race and Ethnicity: Cape Verdean American Immigrants, 1860–1965*. Chicago: University of Illinois Press.

Hareven, Tamara. 1991. "Synchronizing Individual Time, Family Time and Historical Time." In *Chronotypes. The Construction of Time*, edited by John B. Bender and David E. Wellbery, 1671–1682. Stanford, CA: Stanford University Press.

Heinz, Walter R., Johannes Huinink, and Ansgar Weymann, eds. 2009. *The Life Course Reader: Individuals and Societies across Time*. Frankfurt am Main: Campus Verl.

Hernández-León, Rubén, Víctor Zúñiga, and Sarah M. Lakhani. 2020. "An Imperfect Realignment: The Movement of Children of Immigrants and Their Families from the United States to Mexico." *Ethnic and Racial Studies* 43, no. 1: 80–98.

Horn, Vincent, Cornelia Schweppe, and Désirée Bender. 2016. "Moving (for) Elder Care Abroad: The Fragile Promises of Old-age Care Facilities for Elderly Germans in Thailand." In *Transnational Aging: Current Insights and Future Challenges*, edited by Vincent Horn and Cornelia Schweppe, 163–177. London and New York: Routledge.

Kahveci, Cagri, Elifcan Karacan, and Kira Kosnick. 2020. "Tactical Mobility: Navigating Mobile Ageing and Transnational Retirement between Turkey and Germany. A Comparison between Turkish-German and German Retirees." *Journal of Ethnic and Migration Studies* 46, no. 15: 3157–3173.

Kea, Pamela. 2017. "Challenging Global Geographies of Power: Sending Children Back to Nigeria from the United Kingdom for Education." *Comparative Studies in Society and History* 59, no. 4: 818–845.

King, Russell, Aija Lulle, Dora Sampaio, and Julie Vullnetari. 2017. "Unpacking the Ageing–migration Nexus and Challenging the Vulnerability Trope." *Journal of Ethnic and Migration Studies* 43, no. 2: 182–198.

Lee, Helen. 2016. "'I Was Forced Here': Perceptions of Agency in Second Generation 'Return' Migration to Tonga." *Journal of Ethnic and Migration Studies* 42: 2573–2588.

Meintel, Deirdre. 1984. *Race, Culture, and Portuguese Colonialism in Cabo Verde.* Syracuse, NY: Maxwell School of Citizenship and Public Affairs.

Moskal, Marta, and Naomi Tyrrell. 2016. "Family Migration Decision-making, Step-migration and Separation: Children's Experiences in European Migrant Worker Families." *Children's Geographies* 14, no. 4: 453–467.

Peutz, Nathalie, and Nicholas De Genova. 2010. "Introduction." In *The Deportation Regime. Sovereignty, Space, and the Freedom of Movement,* edited by Nicholas De Genova and Nathalie Peutz, 1–32. Durham, NC: Duke University Press.

Pido, Eric J. 2017. *Migrant Returns. Manila, Development, and Transnational Connectivity.* Durham, NC: Duke University Press.

Qureshi, Kaveri. 2014. "Sending Children to School Back Home: Multiple Moralities of Punjabi Sikh Parents in Britain." *Journal of Moral Education* 43, no. 2: 213–222.

Saar, Maarja. 2017. "To Return or Not to Return? The Importance of Identity Negotiations for Return Migration." *Social Identities* 24, no. 1: 120–133.

Sassen, Saskia. 2014. *Expulsions. Brutality and Complexity in the Global Economy.* Cambridge, MA: The Belknap Press of Harvard University Press.

Schuster, Liza, and Nassim Majidi. 2015. "Deportation Stigma and Re-migration." *Journal of Ethnic and Migration Studies* 41, no. 4: 635–652.

Tsuda, Takeyuki. 2009. *Diasporic Homecomings. Ethnic Return Migration in Comparative Perspective.* Stanford, CA: Stanford University Press.

Chitra Joshi

Life and Labour on the Road: Mail Runners and Palanquin Bearers in Nineteenth-Century India

The Tale of Hansuli Turn, a novel by Tarashankar Bandopadhyay published in 1951, chronicles the lives of Kahars, many of whom were traditionally employed as palanquin bearers and water carriers in northern India (Russell 1916: 292). The story about a village in the Birbhum region of Bengal in the early twentieth century focuses on the afterlives of those who carried palanquins and worked on indigo plantations owned by European planters in the nineteenth century. The Kahars in Bandopadhyay's novel are landless labourers and sharecroppers caught in an endless cycle of debt. Yet, traces of many of the practices from their days as palanquin carriers remained. Bandopadhyay recounts:

> The Bansbadi Kahars have never at any time needed anything more than a decent footpath. They move on foot, they're foot soldiers on account of that, but in those days they were something else besides foot soldiers; they were professional carriers. With a palanquin on their shoulders they bore Saheb and his Lady, bore brides and grooms . . . Nowadays this profession of theirs has become petty. They're never called for such work except at weddings. Yet carrying work remains, carrying loads up those palanquin-bearing shoulders. Twenty miles with two hundred pounds on their backs. Forty miles, too, but a night's rest is needed on the way. (Bandopadhyay, trans. Baer 2011: 78)

Operating within a tradition of social realism, Bandopadhyay drew on his familiarity with the region and his own personal observations to paint a picture of Kahar lives. Kahars, we are told, came to the region around the turn of the eighteenth century, when European planters cleared jungle lands to plant indigo. They provided the "musclemen" who helped British planters forcibly seize land from local landlords. Kahar labourers performed a variety of functions on the plantations and also served as servants and palanquin bearers. The novel traces the transformation of the palanquin bearers of the nineteenth century into landless labourers and sharecroppers working for the landed gentry in Bengal in the twentieth century. This change, captured in Bandopadhyay's narrative, is important for the insights it gives into the ritual and social world of Kahars.

This essay focuses on the past to which Bandopadhyay refers, a time when runners and palanquin bearers provided the backbone of transport networks in

India, carrying mail and people.[1] How did mobile labour impact the life courses of these labouring groups in the nineteenth century? How did their lives as runners and bearers shape rural life, and conversely, how did the transformation of rural life in colonial India, influence their work and life on the road? How were skills and knowledge transmitted across generations? Since endurance was so crucial to the activity of runners, what did aging mean for them? And finally, how did the spread of new mechanised networks of transport and communications shape the meaning of their life experiences?

Kahar Pasts

In the early nineteenth century, both runners and palanquin bearers in North India were referred to as Kahars. No group, however, was engaged in only one occupation. Kahars were not just carriers. Usually, one male member in a family worked as a palanquin bearer while others – men and women – were involved in a range of other activities, some of which were seasonal. They could be seen carrying water, fishing, making reed baskets and nets, and sinking wells. During the peak seasons of the agricultural calendar when labour was in high demand, most members of Kahar families worked in the fields, digging, ploughing, and transporting the harvest; during the fishing season, they were near water bodies, catching fish with nets they made themselves. Though one family member specialised in the job of running or carrying the palanquin, fluidity marked the work life of others, but they too turned to palanquin carrying whenever they could. In official descriptions, this multiplicity of work forms, distinct but connected, is recognised, but in colonial classificatory discourse, the plurality of this labour is denied. The discourse of caste saw each caste as specialising in one single occupation, and other activities were seen as supplementary.

The evidence recorded with the Law Commission in 1841 categorises Kahars in most districts of Bengal as slaves. Witnesses before the commission noted how Kahars had originally been sold as slaves during famine and other times of distress but remained in a relationship of bondage over generations. A witness from Bihar stated: "a free kahar does not exist, though many may have left their masters and are practically free."[2] Such forms of servitude were more common in some regions of India than in others, for example in South Bihar rather than the north (Prakash

---

1 In a fifty-mile stretch of road between Kanpur and Lucknow, there were annually around 2,700 palanquin bearers carrying mail and passengers in 1860 (Varady 1981: 91).
2 "Slavery in India: Report from the Indian Law Commissioners relating to Slavery in the East Indies" (1841: 204).

1990). Coercive forms of labour and the sexual exploitation of women by landowning castes were characteristic features of this kind of agrestic servitude. Here, inheritance was debt; the tie between generations was debt bondage, and the link to different stages in an individual's life cycle was mediated by the reality of indebtedness.

At times, some Kahars became sharecroppers. The position of Bonwari, a sharecropper in Bandopadhyay's novel, is different from that of ordinary landless labourers. He works on the landlord's fields with his own plough and bullocks and is entitled to a share of the crop in return. In the nineteenth century, rich farmers with capital brought large tracts of "jungle" and "wastelands" under cultivation by using the services of tribal peoples and landless labourers who were given fixed-term leases to clear stretches of land. Most of them were ultimately reduced to the position of sharecroppers with no rights to land (Bose 1994: 93–95). Even as sharecroppers, the Kahars portrayed in Bandopadhyay's novel are trapped in a cycle of servitude. Bondage connected generations.

With the consolidation of colonial rule, the experiences of Kahars changed in many ways. First, the expanding network of commerce and communications made increasing demands on the services of carriers to transport mail and travellers. Work as runners and bearers meant new rhythms of work and new forms of subjugation and control by the contractors who engaged them.[3] Second, this also led to certain slow changes in their status and identity. Ethnographic accounts tell us that travel and work on the road transformed norms of purity and pollution practiced in relation to Kahar carriers (Risley 1982: 370). Within the caste society of the time, all Kahars were usually regarded as belonging to lower castes whose touch was polluting and, thus, a threat to the identity of upper castes. However, merchants and upper-caste elites making long palanquin journeys through spaces away from settled habitations had to reluctantly accept food and water from the bearers who carried them.

Third, this hesitant relaxation of "normal" social codes during travel had deeper implications for the way Kahars were perceived and the spaces within which they could now move. Kahars who were earlier excluded from the interiors of homes were increasingly employed as indoor servants in the nineteenth century. Along with the shift from outdoor to indoor labour, the relaxation of taboos against touch in relation to Kahars was symbolic of the slightly "higher" ritual status they

---

3 Postal runners working for the East India Company were not "employees" of the Company in any formal sense. They were employed through middlemen who were on contract to carry mail for a particular stretch of road. Often there were layers of intermediaries, many of whom had close connections with Company traders and officials and with rural agents who could mobilise labour. See also Joshi (2012: 173–180).

now enjoyed (Risley 1892: 373). Those who entered domestic service and those who began to be employed by planters and the East India Company to carry mail and palanquins saw a distinct transformation in their life as compared to that of their parents and ancestors. It was a generational change that was experienced in conflicting ways.

These changes were manifest in the clothes the bearers wore, in their walk, their sense of self, and their relationship to those in power and with the colonial state. But there was no dramatic transformation for all Kahars. Changes created new structures of difference and hierarchy within the society and the family, fashioning the life course of different members of the Kahar community in distinct ways. A statement by a palanquin bearer recorded in a travel account from the nineteenth century elaborates: "*Palkee* [palanquin] employment is considered creditable and always gladly embraced by the stout sons, who see that *hamals* [bearers] eat well and can dress and live respectably" (Cary 1857: 136). The "weakly" (*sic*) had to do other kinds of labour, carrying loads as porters or doing agricultural work (Cary 1857: 136). Not all had equal access to new notions of respectability and dignity in whatever muted form they were experienced in the lives of bearers. The life courses of the "weak" and the "strong" were dramatically different.

The terms of reference commonly used to describe those in the service of the East India Company symbolise a shift in the way they were perceived. The epithet *"Kumpani ka nokur"*[4] ('servant of the Company') in reference to runners and bearers working for the Company had a double meaning: being a servant of the Company was a sign of servile status, but in popular usage, it also connoted an improved position and sense of respectability. Trying to project liberal ideas of rule in the early nineteenth century, colonial officials in India saw statements like this as an affirmation of colonial governance and its vision of a just order. Service with the company, they wrote, was valued by *dak*[5] runners because, "it ensures them certain sustenance and protection against the grinding tyranny of the zamindars."[6] The fact of the generational shift amongst the Kahars was read as a sign of progress, as a move from bondage to freedom. Official inquiries and com-

---

4 Kittoe to Prinsep, August 9, 1838, F/4/1810, no. 74558, Boards Collection, India Office Records (British Library).

5 The term *"dak"* (also dawk) has its origins in the term "post," referring to the stages at which couriers or other transporters were stationed. *Dak* also came to be used for "mail" and, thus, mail runner.

6 Kittoe on the Midnapore Road, Home Public Proceedings (Progs.), January 6, 1841, no. 25, National Archives India (NAI). A zamindar was a landowner who typically rented out land to tenant farmers.

missions mapped this move between generations: from slavery to liberty, from medieval exploitation to service under company raj – a shift associated also with certain notions of respectability.

Generational time did not unfold in this unproblematic linear time of progress. New structures of oppression and domination, new relations of power and conflict, were inevitably part of the colonial modern that Kahars experienced.

Learning the Skills

In fiction and folklore, men from Kahar families who carried palanquins were known for their 'strong' (*kosh*) shoulders. Bonwari, one of the lead characters in Bandopadhyay's novel, for instance, had ancestors who carried a palanquin continuously on one shoulder for a two-mile road. That is why, says Bandopadhyay, "their home is called 'Kosh shoulder' house" (Bandopadhyay 2011: 19).

Travel accounts and other descriptions from the nineteenth century often view the physical abilities of Kahar bearers and runners in terms of ethnic stereotypes and as attributes that were inherited and passed down from generation to generation within particular castes. Many descriptions point to several generations of palanquin carriers within Kahar families. John Harvey, a British official in Punjab in the 1870s, recorded the statement of Maghi Ram, a Kahar *doolie* (palanquin) bearer affirming, "my (Maghi Ram's) grandfather was a famous long distance kahar, and my father, an old man now, still carries his *banghy* all day."[7] Maghi Ram traced his descent from a long line of Kahar bearers. He was the son of Tika Ram and the grandson of Lalu Ram, both of whom had been palanquin bearers (Hammett 1910: 39).

Running through narratives like these are two contradictory arguments, the first, which saw occupational skills as inherited and natural to individuals of certain castes, and second, one that placed emphasis on training and practice through which expertise was acquired. Statements that foreground the inherited nature of skills tend to misrecognise the learning process, the active agency involved in the transmission of knowledge across generations. Evidence recorded from different regions points towards the long years of walking and carrying through which bearers learned their skills. The statement of a *hamal* (bearer) from western India recorded by a traveller went thus: "We begin to learn about seventeen; an old hand is placed in front, and young one behind, under a pole, with heavy stones at each

---

7 Banghy – a shoulder yoke for carrying loads. Banghy bearers usually carried boxes with a traveller's luggage and mail on either side of the yoke.

end, slung with rope to give the weight of a palanquin, and so the step is learnt" (Cary 1857:135).[8] In these descriptions, the art of carrying is passed down from one generation to the next, with younger members learning to carry a palanquin just as they entered adulthood.

Changing positions and shifting the pole from one shoulder to the other without jolting the traveller were skills learned through repetition and practice over time. Among the set of four bearers carrying a palanquin, the one leading the way had to be adept and alert: "if not steady, able and quick, they may throw down the rest" (Cary 1857: 136). Experienced bearers familiar with routes they travelled could thus anticipate rough stretches and avoid sudden jolts and bumps.[9] The experienced doolie bearer, a traveller described, "never allows his *dhoolie* (palanquin) to be set on the ground, whereby he avoids exasperating detentions at the stages the bearers are changed" (Compton 1904: 188). The skills of a runner or a palanquin carrier, then, were not simply inherited. They were constituted through training and discipline, through practices normalised within caste communities. Rules about treading carefully were incorporated into the verses and songs of palanquin bearers (Opler and Shukla 1968: 216–234). The theme of a song popular in the western Himalayas was about the roughness of the track; it told bearers how to manoeuvre the palanquin around obstacles. Through rhymes full of humour and innuendo, the bearers leading the way called out to those at the rear to tread carefully, warning them about stones and ditches, slush, and other dangers on the road.[10] Songs like this, rendered in the form of rhythmic exchanges between sets of bearers, marked the pace of walking and created shared bonds between them.

Skilled runners combined knowledge of the landscape with agility and speed acquired through a learning process in much the same way as palanquin bearers. Descriptions of travellers in the sixteenth century point towards the significance of training in the making of a good runner. Monserrate, a Jesuit missionary at the court of the sixteenth-century Mughal emperor Akbar, described how professional runners: "practice running in shoes made of lead, or train themselves by repeatedly lifting their feet and moving their legs (whilst remaining standing in one place) till their heels touch their buttocks" (Monserrate 1922: 212). Muscle strength was important not only for endurance but speed. Such descriptions tend to mythi-

---

8 Amelia Cary (also known as Viscountess Falkland) travelled to India in 1848 as wife of the Governor of Bombay. She kept a travel journal *Chow-Chow* in which she recorded notes about her travels in India, Egypt and Syria.

9 Crossing treacherous passes, especially during the rains, was a delicate operation. See, for instance, "Traveling by Dak," *Asiatic Journal* XI, N.S., May–Aug 1813: 184.

10 See, for instance, "A Gossiping Letter from Calcutta," *Irish Monthly* 4 (1876): 52.

cise the king's runners, but nevertheless, they give a sense of the rigorous physical regimen specialist couriers had to follow.

Training occurred at an early age, with young boys walking and running with older family members when they were just about seven or eight years old. But professional work as mail carriers began usually after young men turned seventeen or eighteen. Writing about mail runners in Persia, Jean-Baptiste Tavernier, a seventeenth century French traveller, gives us a vivid picture of the many stages of a runner's learning process:

From six to seven years of age, they only set themselves to walk slowly. The next year they run a league at a time upon a handsome trot, the next year after they run two or three leagues, and so proportionately for the rest. At eighteen years of age they are allow'd a Scrip (sic) of flowr[11] (sic), with a flat piece of copper to bake their Bread upon and Bottle of water, all of which they carry about them when they run. For these people when they are sent out never take the *Caravan*-road, but the shortest cuts through the Deserts, and must therefore accustom themselves to carry their Provision. (Tavernier 1678: 150–151)

We have here a picture of the slow initiation into the more complex all-round training that took place from the age of seven to adulthood. It was necessary to prepare men for difficult terrain and to teach them how to provision themselves adequately for a lonely journey through uninhabited landscapes. In eastern India, there were no deserts as in Persia, but large parts of the region in the early nineteenth century were still densely forested.

Training in Endurance

The extraordinary endurance of runners and palanquin bearers is one of the skills celebrated in nineteenth-century writings. East India Company officials like William Duffin, the resident surgeon in Madras who made inquiries into the health of traditional carriers in South India in the course of his research on indigenous medicine in the late eighteenth century, was struck by the exceptional endurance of *pattamars* (runners). [12] They could, as Duffin pointed out, "perform journeys, almost incredible, in the time allotted" and subsist on only a small quantity of food during the journey. On average, they walked fifty to sixty miles a day, making

---

11 "Scrip of flowr" refers here to small portion of flour.
12 *Pattamar*, a term used for runners or couriers in South India, has Portuguese origins. See Yule and Burnell, *Hobson Jobson* (London 1886), 687.

the journey from Madras to Bombay in around eighteen days, and from Surat to Bombay in three and a half days (Bart 1807: 107–108).

Discussions around questions of endurance and physical exercise in nineteenth-century India were influenced by wider debates on fitness and health in the Anglo-American world during this period (Martschukat 2016: 409–440). In opposition to commonly held ideas that placed emphasis on the natural bodily limits of physical exercise, many scientific theorists now asserted that fatigue was not a physiological fact but a "psychological event" (Scheffler 2015: 392). Arguments that drew causal connections between continuous physical exertion and "bodily depletion" were now questioned. There was a growing body of opinion in favour of the view that exercise and regular activity could create a fit body with enhanced levels of stamina and endurance. Discussions about the endurance of Kahar palanquin bearers fed into this discourse and were shaped by it.

A popular science magazine in 1910 carried a piece on long distance runners, using evidence on Kahar palanquin bearers and *dak* runners in India to assess the impact of prolonged physical exertion on the body. Drawing on evidence gathered by British officials in the nineteenth century, Chas E. Hammett,[13] with expertise in physical education, argued that Kahars who were trained from childhood, "were not only able to stand the strain of running great distances under a heavy load, but thrived under it." Even those born into the profession had to run regularly to remain in good physical form. In a conversation with the British official Harvey, the voice of Maghi Ram, the Kahar interlocutor, is heard saying: "it (palanquin carrying) is much more trying if undergone only occasionally, though we kahars are in a manner born to work" (Hammett 1910: 40).

In Kahar bearers' self-representations, endurance was reflected also in their capacity to bear pain. In their accounts, pain and bodily injury from work appear routinised as part of bearers' everyday worlds. One bearer describes the pain as follows: "At first the pole gives pain to the shoulders, but the flesh gets thickened after a time and at last (we become) quite callous. We sometimes get swollen veins in the legs, but they get well, at least for a time after bleeding them" (Cary 1857: 140).[14] Learning to deal with pain and physical injury was a resource acquired over time through shared experience. Seasoned bearers devised ways of managing pain and helping each other during their journeys. A bearer from Western India was recorded saying: "When very tired, we walk up and down each other's

---

13 Hammett was a Professor of Physical Education and Director, Athletics at the Jacob Tome School, Maryland, USA and was a member of the American Physical Education Association.
14 The practice of bleeding, or "bloodletting" as it was called, involved drawing blood from the veins of a person who was sick. This was common in medieval Europe and in Asia and continued right up to the nineteenth century. See, for instance, Siraisi (1990: 136–141); and Risse (1979: 3–22).

backs after which we feel greatly refreshed" (Cary: 139). In Bengal, bearers some-times used "spongy sheaths" made from the banana plant as shoulder pads and as a protective layer around the palanquin pole to relieve pressure on their clavicles (Hooker 1855: 90). These were practices that came from accumulated (local) knowl-edge passed down through generations. In thinking about skill and training, the line between the acquired and inherited is often thin.

With the expansion of mechanised transport, the lives of runners and palan-quin bearers changed radically. Many found it difficult to withstand the competi-tion from road and rail transport. By the end of the nineteenth century, official ethnographers reported that mail runners and palanquin bearers were gradually forgetting their skills. The new generation within these families neither inherited nor acquired the skills of their ancestors. Russell, an ethnographer of central India, wrote at the turn of the century: "Most of the Kahars and Dhimars have forgotten how to carry a litter, and proceed very slowly with frequent stops to change shoulders or substitute other bearers" (Russell 1916: 292–293). Skills that are ac-quired may also be lost; what is constituted through practice fades without it.

Insecure Lives: Aging and Death

The strong (*kosha*) shoulders of mature bearers, powerfully represented in visual images from the nineteenth century, are symbolic of an ideal notion of a mascu-linist self capable of enduring pain and carrying heavy loads. But what did the long years of strenuous work mean in the life of bearers and runners? Hammett almost romanticises the ability of the Kahars to bear pain and survive into old age with their endurance undiminished. Kahars, he declared, "lived to be old men" (Hammett 1910: 40). But other travellers often told a different story, of tired legs and weary bodies collapsing with fatigue. Occasionally for long journeys, the serv-ices of alternative bearers had to be arranged at great cost and delay when those en route were too "knocked" out to proceed. On the *pattamar* – mail runners of South India – Duffin wrote: "By the end of their journeys, their legs are frequently much swelled and as soon as they have delivered their packets they retire to rest, taking care to have their feet raised higher than their head and body" (Bart 1807: 107). He was convinced that the runners who worked under such gruelling condi-tions could not live long. Their bodies, in fact, were scarred by the burden of years, by the weight of carrying. The lead character in the *Tale of Hansuli Turn* Bonwari, we are told, had a left shoulder that was higher than the right due to the days he carried a palanquin on a slant. "He also moves on a slant. The right foot comes down with great force" (Bandopadhyay 2011: 135). Even as an aging Kahar, Bonwari was known for his exceptional physical strength, but his walk, his body movements bore the marks of the load his shoulders carried in his youth.

Anxieties about physical incapacity and the inability to do strenuous work with advancing age were articulated in statements of bearers and runners in the early nineteenth century. A petition from a *dak* runner in 1839 makes a plea for a "superannuation pension," emphasising that "he is advanced in age and debility and cannot perform the heavy duty which he holds." The petitioner makes a strong case for his request by stressing that "he had served as *harkarah*[15] (courier) for over 30 years – faithfully and diligently."[16] The petition reminded the state of its obligation towards honest labour and its duty to reward the loyal and industrious runner, underlining the responsibility of the state to protect not just the working life, but the entire living life of a runner. They deserved wages for labour not only when they were actively running but also an old-age pension for when they could no longer run.

The petition came at a time when the expansion of shipping and overseas trade created an increased demand for experienced and efficient runners. Mail had to be carried swiftly to steamers departing from Bombay with the "overland mail" to Europe via Egypt (Joshi 2012: 174). Assurances to runners guaranteeing them long-term security became important in this context. In some regions, senior government officials themselves proposed that, "runners should be pensioned when they are disabled from old age and length of service."[17]

How long did runners work? The petition of Ragow Munneram from 1839 referred to above was from a runner who had worked for over thirty years. Assuming that he began work when he was around eighteen years old, he would have been close to fifty when he requested a pension. But Munneram's life course was rather atypical. Ten years before he wished to retire, he had been promoted to the position of an "overseer" runner responsible for looking after the entire route between Nagothana and Mahabaleshwar. He received twelve rupees a month for his supervisory role. His earnings – almost three times that of any ordinary runner (Joshi 2012: 179) – made it possible for him to consider retiring from active work earlier than others with fewer resources.

Runners' lives could be cut short abruptly long before they entered middle age. In dense forest tracts, there was a constant fear of tiger attacks. These anxieties intensified in the early decades of the nineteenth century, when news circulated

---

15 Harkara, also hurcara, etymology *har* = every, *kar* = business. See Yule and Burnell, *Hobson Jobson* (London 1886), 327.

16 Petition from Ragow Munneram, runner of General Post Office, September 11, 1839, Home Public Progs. October 23, 1839, no. 16 & KW (NAI).

17 From Kittoe, June 1840, Home Public Progs., January 6, 1841, no. 26 (NAI).

about numerous fatal attacks on runners on duty. On some routes, runners threatened to stop carrying mail. Postal officials were worried about the continuity of a system so dependent on the services of *dak* runners.

The death of Budhee, a *dak* runner, in 1821, set off a series of exchanges between *dak* contractors in the field, postal officials, and the Board of Revenue, which eventually reached the Governor-General, the highest authority of the East India Company in India. In January 1821, Budhee was attacked by a tiger near Kutkumsandi in the densely forested region of Hazaribagh. The memorial submitted by the *uddadar* ('contractor'/'middleman') Palwan Singh to the Postmaster highlighted the financial distress of the family: "they have no means of support since the death of Budhee."

The appeal provides details – rarely available – about the *dak* runner's household. Budhee, we are told, was survived by his wife Buchnee and three children: the oldest, a son, seven years of age, and two daughters who were younger. Budhee's mother lived in the same house with them.[18] Buchnee, the petition stated, was thirty years old, a disclosure which suggests that her deceased husband was likely to be past his mid-thirties. Unlike Munneram, who had many years of service behind him, Budhee had worked for the Company for only four years before he was killed. The claim that no one else in the family was an earner is not entirely correct. It was a typical male representation and was framed by a discourse that ignored the value of certain types of work. The "unwaged" work of women in the social reproduction of labour – in foraging and collecting and housework – remains invisible not just in this petition but in most official descriptions available to us. We are told that Buchnee, the widow of the deceased runner, was a Ghatwareen. The tribal community of Ghatwals to which she belonged traditionally guarded the mountain passes in the region. Women in the forest tracts of Hazaribagh where she lived were known for their knowledge of the jungle and of varieties of plants and medicinal herbs. Their work of collecting firewood and edibles for everyday consumption was critical for sustaining the family (Damodaran 1995: 129–158).

In response to the petition of Budhee's family, the Governor-General agreed to a pension of three rupees a month. The letter from the Governor General stressed that the Postmaster must give the widow a "proper certificate" so she could be identified in person by the district official making the payment. The fear of

---

18 Playfair, Deputy Post Master to P. Reves, Post Master General, February 21, 1821, Home Public Progs., April 6, 1821, no. 11 (NAI).

fraud was to be overcome through the new instrument of an identification certif-icate.[19]

The discussion around the above petition also shows how the life course of runners was shaped by the conditions of their work. The dangers in the jungle and the possibility of sudden death altered the life course of runners' families. The precariousness of their lives was intensified by the family's dependence on the runner's wage. These concerns lay behind the refusal of runners to work on routes where attacks were frequent. They were worried about their safety. The Postmaster at Kedgeree reported: "dak runners have given me to understand that they will not travel by night between the Talputty and Huldie rivers, until such time as the tigers are either destroyed or drove (sic) away from their present locality."[20] Underlying their threats to stop running was the genuine fear of death. The pressures of new time schedules and the need to run uninterruptedly accord-ing to the demands of imperial *dak* created a greater sense of vulnerability (Joshi 2012: 174). In many regions, the movement of runners at night and the early hours of the morning disturbed the pace of life in the forests. The expanding commercial and military networks of the East India Company and the new demands of time and speed of delivery often violated the codes by which *dak* runners navigated their everyday lives. For jungle runners, the pressures of running for the Company made life seem more perilous. Stories of attacks on runners, of deaths in the forest, disrupted their imagined notions of a normal life.

Dak runners were from communities – Kahar, Gonds, Bhils – familiar with jungle terrain and with the rhythms of predatory animals that inhabited those spaces. Like other forest dwellers, their relationship with tigers and other beasts was marked by awe and fear bound together with a sense of respect (Rangarajan 2012: 95–142; Sivaramakrishnan 1997: 75–112). Rituals propitiating forest deities formed part of the everyday practices through which they negotiated the dangers in the forests (Joshi 2012: 184). Fearing the wrath of the goddess who was said to protect them against danger, they were reluctant to disturb the norms of forest life.

The plea for a pension and protection against risk expressed in the memorial on behalf of Budhee is a response to such anxieties among runners. Postal officials argued: "that as an encouragement to the other runners, the Family of the de-ceased runner should receive some remuneration for the loss they have sus-tained."[21] The official sanction for a pension was an attempt to assuage runners'

---

19 Gov.-General to Board of Revenue, April 6, 1821, Home Public Progs., April 6, 1821, no. 12 (NAI).
20 L. L. Rousseau, Post Master Kedgeree to W. Moore, Deputy Post Master, August 25, 1839, Home Public Progs., August 28, 1839, no. 43 (NAI).
21 Babington to G. Stockwell, Post Mast General, March 26, 1828, Home Public Progs., April 17, 1828, no. 27 (NAI).

fears and a way of ensuring that mail services, dependent so crucially on the labour of *dak* runners, were not disrupted.[22] Pensions also had symbolic value, sustaining the image of the East India Company as an employer who guaranteed security of life.

This discussion around pensions drew on ideas of welfare and old-age security that political activists in Britain and Europe had advocated for since the late eighteenth century. However, pensions, like other social security schemes, became formally part of British public policy only in the late nineteenth century (Jones 2005; Joyce 2013). In India, measures to provide "extraordinary" pensions[23] to those wounded in the performance of public duty were adopted sporadically in the nineteenth century, although regulations providing for social security schemes for industrial workers were not introduced until the post-independence (post-1947) period. Even today, these provisions provide a modicum of security only to a very small segment of "formal" workers[24] and do not cover "informal" or contract workers (Ahuja 2019: 1–42). So, the idea of pension and compensation to runners in the mid-nineteenth century has profound significance.

Some Reflections

This essay examines the life course of palanquin bearers and runners – workers employed in transport and communication who carried mail and travellers in nineteenth century India – focusing on their labour practices. I discuss how skill in carrying and running was acquired during early adulthood through practices that were shared among certain communities. Skill and training not only sustained their labour; it connected the way the older generation related to the young. Knowledge was transmitted down through the generations and preserved within the community.

The services of specialised couriers and palanquin bearers date back to pre-colonial times. However, the expansion and consolidation of the East India Company's power in nineteenth-century India marked a shift in the scale at which communication networks were organised. A larger number of foot runners and palanquin bearers were now mobilised. Many runners worked throughout the year and were dependent largely on their earnings as postal couriers. In difficult "jungle" tracts, communication links were provided by the runner's footfalls. The runners

---

22 See, for instance, Lushington to Board of Revenue, Home Public Progs., Feb. 17, 1825, no. 12 (NAI).
23 On "extraordinary" pensions, see Rajaram (2018). I am grateful to Poorva Rajaram for allowing me to read her dissertation chapter.
24 See footnote 3 above.

were virtually the roads that sustained the flow of information and goods through the harsh terrain. This often gave mail runners who worked in these regions greater leverage (Joshi 2012). On routes running through densely forested areas, new entrants found it difficult to displace the virtual monopoly of established runners, even when the latter demanded almost double the prevailing wage.[25] A postal official grappling with threats of strikes by "jungle" runners admitted: "I have no power to punish the men and if I dismiss them it will be utterly impossible to replace them; of the latter circumstance they are well aware."[26] The figure of the "jungle runner" who the state saw as intractable and impossible to subdue was produced against this background. The forest tracts bordering Bengal and the Central Provinces region, for instance, were areas where experienced runners remained almost indispensable to the Imperial Post even after the mid-nineteenth century, when alternative modes of communication – carts and railways – were expanding their reach.[27]

In other regions, however, in areas well connected to urban centres, the work of runners and palanquin carriers came to a slow end by the late nineteenth century, affecting their life- course dramatically. With the coming of railways, the expansion of road networks, and the use of alternative modes of transportation, runners and bearers were increasingly marginalised in many regions. Maghi Ram, a palanquin bearer, noted wistfully, "kahars (the community of doolie bearers) are no longer in (good) condition since the railways came in." Some, like his twenty-year-old son Gangu, could still travel with a palanquin for over a hundred miles without food or water, but, he explained, they needed to be on the road more regularly to remain in good form (Hammett 1910: 38). The shift in modes of transport inevitably forced them to adapt to the changing context. Many moved in search of new work, labouring in the fields and performing other types of daily labour. The traditional skills of running and carrying were no longer passed on to the young, nor could an older generation ensure that their training and knowledge would sustain their families through life.[28]

---

25 See, for instance, Babington, Post Master Sambulpore to Oldfield, Post Master General, August 19, 1840, Home Public Progs., B, 23 September, 1840, no. 3 (NAI).

26 Post Master Sambulpore to W. Moore, Deputy Post Master, October 3, 1842, Home Public Progs., October 12, 1842, no. 15 (NAI).

27 On other modes, see *Postal Communications* (1852: 85); see also Varady (1981); Sinha (2012: 155–180, 203–232).

28 During the First World War, however, a large number of Kahars were mobilised as stretcher bearers by the British Imperial army. See, Radhika Singha (2020: 43–93).

Postscript

Decline did not follow a unilinear process: the course of transformation differed for *dak* runners in many regions. Where the reach of road networks was limited, foot runners have remained vital to local communication networks. In Purulia in Bengal, traditions of running have continued in the families of *dak* runners up to the present day. Kalipada Mura, who became a runner after the death of his father Khepu Mura (a runner during the colonial period), was still working as a runner at the age of sixty-five. In contemporary descriptions, those like Kalipada Mura carry traces of the runners of old, an image that endures in the literary imagination (Mitra 2010). Frail and elderly runners like Kalipada hold on to a job that still provides them with daily wages for their families. But their work is now sustained in hybrid forms: stretches of walking alternate with riding on other forms of transport. Kalipada sits pillion on his son's bicycle when he is tired.[29] Yountan Gyatso, a runner in present-day Ladakh now well past his mid-fifties, still walks over thirty-five kilometres a day carrying mail to remote villages.[30] But he can no longer carry mail over the frozen river trail – the only route open in the winter months. Even the trained body of a runner comes up against the barriers of age and ecology.

---

29 Kalipada Mura's life is also documented in a film by Anirban Dutta, dir. *The Last Run*, streamed online Docu-Forum online Goethe Institut, Kolkata, November 18, 2020.
30 Yountan Gyatso, in conversation with author, Padum, Ladakh, July 26, 2018. On runners in Ladakh, see documentary by Tyler Wilkinson-Ray, *The Last Runner*, accessed October 20, 2020, https://vimeo.com/274933065.

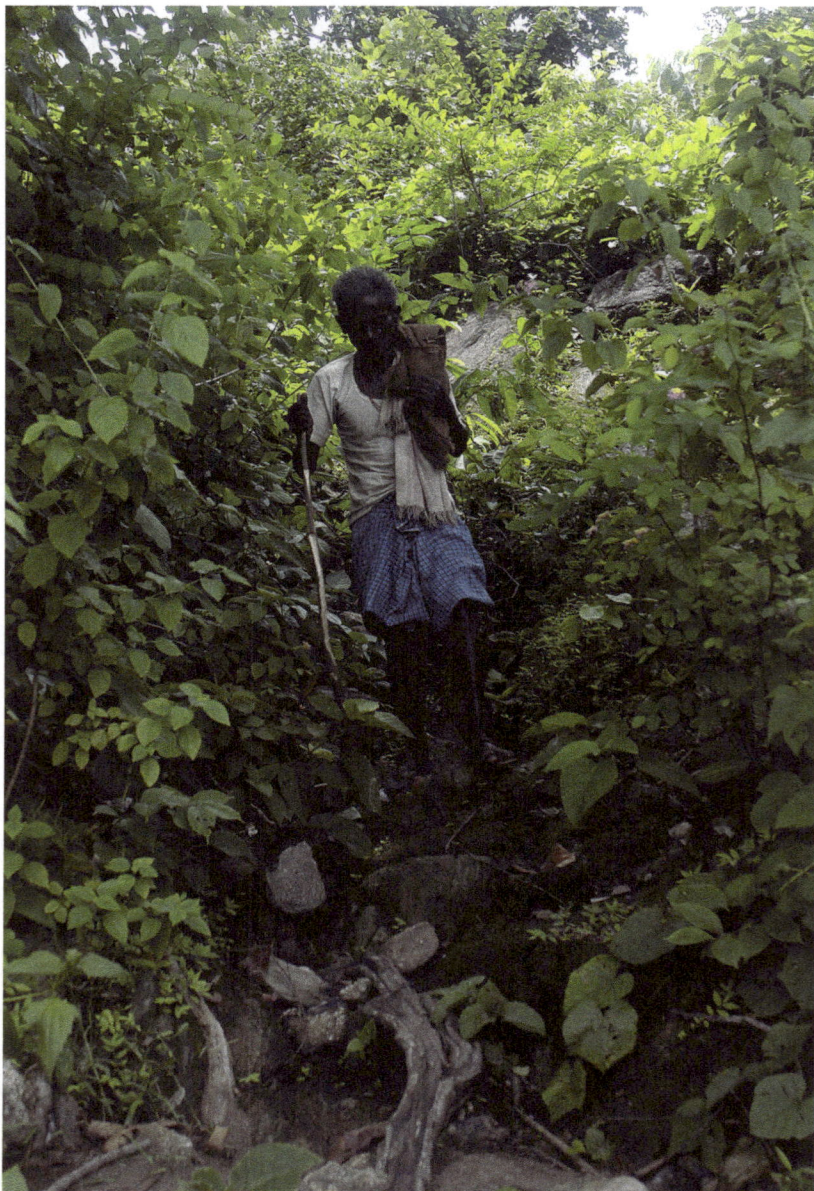

Figure 1: Kalipada Mura: Treading through the forests.
In the early twenty-first century, postal runners still have to negotiate thick forests to deliver mail to remote locations.
Source and photo credit: Sandipan Chatterjee, *Outlook India Magazine*, August 30, 2010.

Figure 2: Moving through watery tracts.
In many regions, postal runners have to cross marshy streams and rivers with their mail bags.
Source and photo credit: Sandipan Chatterjee, *Outlook India Magazine*, August 30, 2010.

References

Bandopadhyaya, Tarashankar. 2001. *The Tale of Hansuli Turn.* Translated by Ben Conisbee Bear. New York: Columbia University Press.

Bart, John Sinclair. 1807. *Code of Health and Longevity or Concise View of the Principles Calculated for the Preservation of Health and the Attainment of Long Life etc.* Vol. 2. Edinburgh: Printed for Arch. Constable and Co. Accessed October 25, 2002. https://www.hathitrust.org/.

Bayly, C. A. 1999. *Empire & Information: Intelligence Gathering and Social Communication in India, 1780–1870.* New Delhi: Cambridge University Press.

Bose, Sugata. 1994. *Peasant Labour and Colonial Capital: Rural Bengal Since 1770.* Cambridge: Cambridge University Press.

Cary, Amelia F. G. 1857. *Chow-Chow: Being Selections from a Journal volume 1.* London: Hurst and Blackett.

Compton, Herbert. 1904. *Indian Life in Town and Country.* London: G.P. Putnam's Sons.

Damodaran, Vinita. 1995. "Famine in a Forest Tract: Ecological Change and the Causes of the 1897 Famine in Chotanagpur, Northern India." *Environment and History* 1, no. 2: 129–158.

Dasgupta, Sangeeta. 2018. "Adivasi Studies from a Historian's Perspective." *History Compass* 16, no. 10: 1–11. Accessed October 22, 2020. https://doi.org/10.1111/hic3.12486.

Dutta, Anirban, dir. 2018. *The Last Run.* Streamed online Docu-Forum online Goethe –Institut, Kolkata. Accessed November 18, 2020.

Hammett, Chas E. 1910. "Middle and Distance Running." *Popular Science Monthly* 77: 28–41. Accessed October 20, 2020. https://archive.org/details/popularsciencemo77newy.

Hooker, Joseph Dalton. 1855. *Himalayan Journals or Notes of a Naturalist in Bengal, the Sikkim and Nepal Himalayas, The Khasia Mountains.* Vol. I. London: John Murray.

Irfan, Habib. 1985. "Postal Communications in Mughal India." *Proceedings of the Indian History Congress* 46: 236–252.

Joshi, Chitra. 2012. "Dak Roads, Dak Runners and the Reordering of Communication Networks." *International Review of Social History* 57, no. 2: 169–189.

Joyce, Patrick. 2013. *The State of Freedom: A Social History of the British State since 1800.* Cambridge: Cambridge University Press.

Martschukat, Jürgen. 2011. "'The Necessity for Better Bodies to Perpetuate Our Institutions, Insure a Higher Development of the Individual and Advance the Conditions of the Race.' Physical Culture and the Formation of the Self in the Late Nineteenth and Early Twentieth Century USA." *Journal of Historical Sociology* 24, no. 4: 472–493.

Mitra, Dola. 2010. "Past the Last Post." Outlook *Magazine*, August 30, 2010. Accessed November 5, 2020. https://magazine.outlookindia.com/story/past-the-last-post/266779.

Monserrate, Antonio. 1922. *The Commentary of Father Monserrate, SJ: On His Journey to the Court of Akbar.* Translated by J. S. Hoyland. Calcutta: Oxford University Press.

Opler, Morris E., and Shaligram Shukla. 1968. "Palanquin Symbolism: The Special Vocabulary of Palanquin- Bearing Castes of North Central India." *The Journal of American Folklore* 81, no. 321: 216–234.

Postal Communication, & c. (India), Return to an Order of the Honourable, the House of Commons, dated 14 December 1852. 1852. British Parliamentary Papers.

Prakash, Gyan. 1990. *Bonded Histories: Genealogies of Labor Servitude in India.* Cambridge: Cambridge University Press.

Rajaram, Poorva. 2021. "'Normal Prospects of Life': Pensions and Insurance in Colonial India c 1813–1947." Ph.D. dissertation, Jawaharlal Nehru University.

Rangarajan, Mahesh. 2012. "The Raj and the Natural World: The Campaign against "Dangerous Beasts" in Colonial India, 1875–1925." In *India's Environmental History: Colonialism, Modernity and the Nation: A Reader,* edited by Mahesh Rangarajan and K. Sivaramakrishnan, 95–142. New Delhi: Permanent Black.

Ray, Rajat Kanta. 1987. "The Kahar Chronicle." *Modern Asian Studies* 21, no. 4: 711–749.

Risley, H. H. 1892. *The Tribes and Castes of Bengal: Ethnographic Glossary Volume I.* Calcutta: Bengal Secretariat Press.

Risse, Guenter B. 1979. "The Renaissance of Bloodletting: A Chapter in Modern Therapeutics." *Journal of the History of Medicine and Allied Sciences* 34, no. 1: 3–22.

Russell, R. V., and Hira Lal. 1916. *Tribes and Castes of the Central Provinces of India Volume III.* London: Macmillan. Reprinted by Asian Educational Society (New Delhi), 1993. Citations refer to the Delhi edition).

Singha, Radhika. 2020. *The Coolie's Great War: Indian Labour in a Global Conflict 1914–1921.* Noida: Harper Collins Publishers India.

Sinha, Nitin. 2012. *Communication and Colonialism in Eastern India.* London: Anthem.

Siraisi, Nancy G. 1990. *Medieval and Early Renaissance Medicine: An Introduction to Knowledge and Practice.* Chicago: Chicago University Press.

Sivaramakrishnan, Kalyanakrishnan. 1997. "A Limited Forest Conservancy in Bengal 1864–1912." *Journal of Asian Studies* 56, no. 1: 75–112.

Slavery: East Indies: Report from the Indian Law Commissioners. 1841. Accessed October 15, 2020. https://www.hathitrust.org/.

Sood, Gagan D. S. 2009. "The Informational Fabric of Eighteenth-Century India and the Middle East: Couriers, Intermediaries and Postal Communication." *Modern Asian Studies* 43, no. 5: 1085–1116.

Wilkinson-Ray, Tyler. 2018. *The Last Runner.* Richmond. https://vimeo.com/274933065 accessed October 20, 2020.

Josef Ehmer
Wage Labour as a Life Phase: Life-Cycle Service and Petty Commodity Production in Early Modern Europe

Introduction

In European history from the Middle Ages up to the early twentieth century, there is hardly any other phenomenon in which the work and life course were as inseparable than the "life-cycle servant." This concept was coined by Peter Laslett in the 1970s (Laslett 1977: 34) and has been prominent in social history and historical demography. It denotes those children, adolescents, or young adults who left their homes and families to work and live in the households of their employers. In contrast to the current definition of the term, life-cycle servants were "productive" rather than "domestic" servants (on terminological issues, see below), working for wages as live-in male and female farmhands, apprentices, and journeymen in crafts and trades or in the transitional zone between the household, workshop, and farmstead. They held their positions only for a certain period, usually entering into such a labour relation for the first time during childhood and exiting it permanently during their twenties or thirties. In many – though not all – European regions and rural and urban communities, the majority, and sometimes the overwhelming majority, of young people shared the experience of life-cycle servitude. Life-cycle service met the labour demands of various forms of pre-capitalist modes of production, and it also experienced a late boom during the transition to industrial capitalism. Across approximately five centuries of European history, it represented a hegemonic life course regime. Only very slowly and with strong regional variations did it disappear from the world of work throughout the late nineteenth and early twentieth centuries.

Life-cycle service is, therefore, important in several respects: From a life course perspective, it overlaps with a formative period of development and mental, bodily, and social maturation. From a work-related perspective, it represents a period of learning and training and the accumulation of individual skills, experiences, and labour capacity. From a labour-related perspective, life-cycle service embodied a complex and highly peculiar labour relation that combined elements of free wage labour, indentured service, and family labour, thus transcending the usual dichotomies of free and unfree labour, productive and reproductive work, and wage labour and unpaid work in the family and household. But in addition to their multifaceted form, life-cycle servants were most likely the largest group of wage earners in early modern Europe. While most forms of wage labour were done seasonally or casually and combined with precarious self-employment as a cottager or a semi-legal urban artisan, servants were consistently employed all year round for about ten to twenty years of their lives (although, of course, not by the same employer). Even when being a wage labourer was not yet a life-long status, it had become a "normal part of the life cycle of a very large part of the population" (De Moor and van Zanden 2010: 13). From a global perspective, since its "discovery" (Laslett 1972: 151) by historians in the 1970s, life-cycle service has been regarded as a unique European institution and, thus, as a major piece of evidence supporting the claim of Europe's "special path" into modernity (Mitterauer 2010).

Nevertheless, life-cycle service is still underappreciated in the history of work and labour as well as in economic history (Whittle 2017b: 18). "Productive servants" in agricultural and artisanal family economies are usually mentioned but seldom systematically integrated into conceptual frameworks. There are, of course, exceptions to this general trend. Alessandro Stanziani (2014), for instance, places emphasis on "intermediate forms between chattel slavery and wage earners, that is serfs, servants, indentured immigrants, and rural laborers." And, he adds, "these actors were not marginal, but rather they were central in the global economic and social dynamics between the seventeenth and mid nineteenth centuries" (Stanziani 2014: 7).[1] Another exception is the historiography of labour laws in Britain, with its emphasis on master-servant relations, including surprising legal continuities in this relationship from the sixteenth to the late nineteenth century and their enormous global influence: "For more than 500 years, the law of master and servant fixed the boundaries of 'free labor' in Britain and throughout the British Empire. Compounded of statutory enactments, judicial doctrine, and social practice, it defined and controlled employment relations for almost a quarter of the world's population in more than 100 colonial and postcolonial jurisdictions" (Hay and Craven 2004: 1; see also Deakin and Wilkinson 2005).

The aim of this chapter is twofold: first, to integrate the life-cycle servant into the history of wage labour and, by doing so, strengthening life course perspectives in labour history. Second, I want to propose an explanatory model for the enormous significance of life-cycle service in early modern Europe that focuses on a specific mode of production. In this respect, my approach differs from other at-

---

1 See also his remarks on the long historical persistence of the institution of service ("The Persistent Servant") in chapter 6 of his book (Stanziani 2014). However, Stanziani attaches no importance to the life-cycle character of service.

tempts to "revisit" the usual narrative of life-cycle service.[2] This chapter is neither about servants in general nor about the whole life course; rather it is about the triangular relationship between life-cycle service as a life course regime, wage labour, and "petty commodity production" (on definitions see below). I look at both the agricultural and urban artisanal worlds of work in early modern Europe and during the transition to industrial capitalism. My evidence and my conclusions are based on a wide range of scholarly literature but also on my own previous and ongoing research and that of colleagues at the University of Vienna.[3]

The Ambiguous Servant, or: Conceptual Problems in Recent Historiography

In modern historiography, it was the "Cambridge Group for the History of Population and Social structure" that first drew attention to the prevalence of non-relatives in the family economy. When in 1972 Peter Laslett summarised the first results of the group's huge research project on household and family in England from 1574 to 1821, he concluded "that the substantial proportion of persons who turn out to be living in the households other than those into which they were born, looks to us like something of a sociological discovery" (Laslett 1972: 151). Non-related children, adolescents, and young adults formed a significant part of early modern households, and Laslett subsumed them under the term "servant" (Laslett 1983: 526, 534). However, he was already aware of a possible misunderstanding of this term in 1972, and he warned that these servants "were not simply domestics, in our sense of the word, the Victorian sense" (Laslett 1972: 152). In early modern England, in contrast, the term "servant" denoted all those who worked for a master, lived in his house, and received a wage, mainly calling forth "the image of a host of ploughmen, carters, dairymaids, and apprentices. Servants were youths hired into the families of their employers" (Kussmaul 1981: 3). This "discovery" led to a shift of the research focus from the family to the household and from the kin group to the work group; it also considerably strengthened life course perspectives.

The size of this group, as revealed by Laslett and his colleagues, was indeed impressive. In their sample of one hundred English communities between 1574 and 1821, servants were present in one-third of all households, in 57 percent of

---

2 See, for instance, Simonton 2011.

3 Most important are the numerous pioneering studies by Michael Mitterauer. Due to size constraints, I can only refer to a small number of secondary sources.

farmers' households, and in 36 percent of the households of craftsmen and trades-men. They constituted about 14 percent of the overall population and "around 60 percent of the population aged fifteen to twenty-four" (Kussmaul 1981: 3, 173). Sim-ilar research based on nominal population listings from the sixteenth to nine-teenth centuries from various regions of continental Europe revealed even higher figures as will be discussed below. In early modern and early industrial England as well as in many other European regions, the majority of the population thus gained experience during their life course through the particular labour relation or "institution" of service.

In the "new social history" from the 1970s onwards, servants became a re-search topic in various contexts. Servants have been an important theme in quan-titative family history; for example, in addition to the "Cambridge Group," the "Vi-ennese school" established by Michael Mitterauer placed emphasis on relations between "family structures and the organization of work and labour" (*Familien-struktur und Arbeitsorganisation*) (e. g., Mitterauer 1973; Ehmer 1980; Ehmer and Mitterauer 1986; Mitterauer 1992b). Servants of all kinds became integrated into histories of childhood and child labour (e. g., Hanawalt 1993; Humphries 2010) and youth (e. g., Mitterauer 1990 and 1992a). Live-in farmhands have been ad-dressed in histories of agriculture and agrarian labour (e. g., Kussmaul 1981; Snell 1985; Woodward 2000; Whittle 2017a; Lambrecht 2017). Live-in apprentices and journeymen gained attention in renewed and refined approaches to the histo-ry of crafts, trades, and guilds (e. g., De Munck 2007; Wallis 2008; Ogilvie 2019). All these approaches have helped produce a corpus of broad empirical evidence about the spread, the rise and decline, and the social and economic functions of life-cycle service, and also about the experiences of servants. However, these various re-search fields are more or less isolated from each other and were neither sufficient-ly interrelated nor integrated.[4]

But why are servants still largely absent from general histories of work and labour? I think the main reason for this is a terminological and conceptual prob-lem. Due to the live-in status of these young workmen and -women, they have often been labelled as "domestic" or "menial servants" (from *intra moenia*, "within the walls").[5] However, already in the sixteenth century's *Domestic Conduct Books*, a distinction was made between servants who worked in their masters' or mistress-es' fields, farm, or workshop and "idle servants" who served his or her personal well-being (Kussmaul 1981: 5). Adam Smith in his *Wealth of Nations* (1776) followed

---

4 Even with respect to rural history, Jane Whittle concludes: "To date, there is only one monograph on rural servants, Ann Kussmaul's *Servants in Husbandry in Early Modern England* (1981), and no book-length study that compares rural service in different European countries" (Whittle 2017b: 2).
5 With reference to William Blackstone Simonton 2011: 209 f.

this distinction. He conceptualised it as contrast between "productive" and "unproductive labour," narrowed the original broad meaning of "domestic" or "menial" to that of "idle," and considered "menial servants" as "barren and unproductive" (Smith 1776; here cited from Fauve-Chamoux 2017: 67–69; see also Deakin and Wilkinson 2005: 45). Similar desires for such a distinction were expressed in other European societies and languages by scholars, politicians, lawmakers, and census takers throughout the eighteenth and the nineteenth centuries (Sarti 2006).[6]

The distinction between "productive" and "domestic" service has two sides: on the one hand, it is misleading because "productive" servants were also partially responsible for the "domestic" tasks of housework and care work – females and children more often than males and adolescents.[7] But on the other hand, the distinction is indispensable for understanding the key role played by servants in the pre-industrial economy and their large numbers. I want to stress that point because it seems to me that it is not taken seriously enough in some fields of recent historiography. In the approaches mentioned above, servants were mainly of interest to researchers because of their "productive" and not of their "domestic" chores and tasks – if they had any. I would think that one of the reasons labour history has not really been interested in this type of wage labourer so far is due to a persistent lack of interest in housework and care work, accompanied by a spontaneous, unconscious equation of "servant" with "domestic servant" in its contemporary, narrow connotation. At the same time, some recent revisionist approaches that have put house- and care work on labour history's agenda contribute to that conceptual confusion by subsuming all live-in agricultural or artisanal workers into a narrowly defined label of "domestic" or by constructing a historical line of development from early modern servants to contemporary domestic workers.[8]

---

6 Prussian agricultural statistics 1819–1861, for instance, differentiate between "servants for the comfort of their masters" (*Gesinde zur Bequemlichkeit der Herrschaft*) and "servants for agricultural and other businesses" (*Gesinde zum Betrieb der Landwirtschaft und anderer Gewerbe*). In 1819, the second category was roughly twenty times larger than the first (Tenfelde 1979: 209).

7 For examples of the division of labour among servants in husbandry by gender and age, see – among many others – Lindström et al. 2017: 237; Lundh 2004: 77 f.

8 The huge – and quite productive – research network "Domestic Service Past and Present and the Formation of European Identity: The Servant Project," for example, includes almost all imaginable live-in occupations from the early modern period to the present, but it avoids any conceptual clarification as the presentation of the project results shows. See Fauve-Chamoux 2004 and Pasleau and Schopp 2006. For another example, see the special issue of *The History of the Family* on "Domestic servants in Comparative Perspective" (Fauve-Chamoux and Wall 2005). As a recent example from gender history, see the bibliography at the open access website of Cambridge University Press that accompanies Wiesner-Hanks 2019. One paragraph in the recommendations "For Further Reading" for chapter 3, "Women's Economic Role," starts with the phrase: "A large percentage of women

In European history, the crux of the matter is, in my view, a consideration of the long-term trend towards separation within the institution of service between "productive labour" in the household economy on the one hand and, on the other, "reproductive work" in the form of housework and care work in the family's private sphere. In the early modern family economy, these two sets of activities had been both interwoven in daily work routines and divided by gender and age. Their complete separation began in the early modern period among the nobility and in urban bourgeois groups. It accelerated with the rise of industrial capitalism and the redefinition of family, gender, and privacy in the bourgeois age. In the long run, the "productive servant" gradually – though not linearly – disappeared, and only the "domestic servant" remained, although to a much lesser extent and with diminished socio-economic importance.[9] My point is that these two types of servants are different not only with respect to their work but even more so with respect to their entirely different historical and socio-economic context. They simply belong to different modes of production.

Life-Cycle Servants as an Element of "Simple Commodity Production"

Households were the basic units of the early modern and early industrial European economy in both agriculture and in the crafts and trades. They produced not only for a family's subsistence but also for feudal rents and/or state taxes and for markets in varying degrees. Therefore, the Marxian notion of "simple" or "petty commodity production" seems to offer a useful conceptual tool. Marx speaks – in the first volume of *Capital* – about a *"Produktionsweise unabhängiger Bauern oder selbständiger Handwerker"* ("the mode of production of isolated peasants and artisans"), and he refers several times to "peasant agriculture on a small scale, and the carrying on of independent handicrafts, which together form the basis of the

---

who worked for wages in the early modern economy were servants." The following commented bibliography is entirely devoted to domestic service (in its current narrow meaning) in towns and cities. Also, recent "global" histories of service contribute to the problem by restricting themselves to *"household* work such as cooking, washing, cleaning as well as *care* work such as taking care of children, elderly and sick persons" (van Nederveen Meerkerk, Neunsinger, and Hoerder 2015: 2). See also Nederveen Meerkerk 2017; Haskins and Lowrie 2018; Sinha and Varma 2019.
9 However, from a global perspective, domestic service might have gained social, cultural, and numerical significance in the context of colonisation. See Haskins and Lowrie 2018.

feudal mode of production, and after the dissolution of that system, continue side by side with the capitalist mode."[10]

The concept of "simple commodity production" becomes particularly fruitful when related to actual developments in the early modern European economy. From the thirteenth century onwards, a fundamental transformation of agrarian structures took place. The manorial system gradually disintegrated in most parts of Western Europe and gave way to a new form of feudal domination through which landlords only marginally claimed labour services from their peasant subjects but continued to collect rent payments in kind and increasingly in cash. In turn, peasants were granted relative freedom and independence to manage the daily work routines performed in their family and household economies. These changes were closely connected to the growth and political independence of cities and, more generally, to the spread of markets and the money economy. Only on this basis does it make sense to speak of "independent" or "autonomous" peasants and artisans. Moreover, socio-economic changes were accompanied by cultural and political ones, namely the intensification of patriarchal power relations in the family and society, which strengthened the authority of the household head *within* both the family and household over all those who lived under his roof, including the non-kin workforce (Ehmer 2021).

The complex composition of households also has conceptual consequences. Recent definitions of "simple" or "petty commodity production," for instance in Gordon Marshall's *Dictionary of Sociology*, state that "the producer does not systematically hire wage workers, but may use unpaid family labour."[11] The historical

---

10 Marx and Engels 1962: 351, 354n24; online English translation: 232; 236n21; ("isolated" is not an accurate translation of either "unabhängig" or "selbständig," JE). Subsequently, Friedrich Engels, in his supplement to the third volume of *Capital*, coined the term "simple commodity production," and he speaks about a "whole period of simple commodity production" (Marx and Engels 1964, online English translation: 640). For a full discussion of the origins of the concept, see Arthur 2005.
11 Scott and Marshall 2015 (online edition). A similar understanding of petty commodity production dominated early theories about "proto-industrialisation," which excluded, by definition, servants and wage workers from the "proto-industrial family economy" (Kriedte, Medick, and Schlumbohm 1981: 54, 98 ff.). Later empirical research, however, integrated servants into proto-industry in two ways: poor proto-industrial producers might send their children into life-cycle service; others might employ servants, particularly when they combined artisanal work with large- and small-scale farming (Schlumbohm 1994: 69, 197 ff., 213 ff., 337 ff.; Ogilvie 1997: 265, 296–301). In the proto-industrial community of Belm (Lower Saxony) in 1858, for instance, live-in servants made up about 40 percent of the age group 15–24 years old (Schlumbohm 1994: 338). I am also wondering whether Marx and Engels explicitly excluded wage labour from their concept of simple commodity production as long as the units of production and the number of workers were small and accumulation was not the primary goal. Interestingly, the first English translation of *Capital*, vol. 1 in 1887

reality, however, was different: Even if the core of a household's labour force consisted of family members, peasants or craftsmen not only used unpaid family labour but did *systematically* hire wage workers. This is particularly true for those large parts of Europe that had been dominated by nuclear family structures since the medieval period (Ehmer 2021; see also Dribe and Lundh 2005: 55). An additional workforce beyond the family was indispensable for two reasons: First, to compensate for the demographic vulnerability of families, expressed in high and unforeseeable mortality and in low fertility, particularly where the "European Marriage Pattern" predominated. Second, a flexible workforce made it easier for producers to increase or to reduce production according to market opportunities or pressures by feudal or state tax authorities. In the long run, this second factor gained additional importance in the context of commercialisation and the transition towards capitalism. The most important (though not the only) share of these wage workers was "servants," i.e., all those young, non-kin workers who belonged to the household of their master and employer, lived and worked there for a longer period of time, and were subordinated to the household head's patriarchal authority.

Hiring life-cycle servants was facilitated and promoted by a further consequence of commercialisation and monetisation in early modern Europe, namely the growing social differentiation of rural societies: from large and affluent farmers to small peasants and cottagers, most of whom were casual wage labourers, all the way down to landless labourers and the rural poor (Kriedte 1984; for an impressive local example, see Schlumbohm 1994: 55). Families and households remained the basic units of production, but different classes of rural populations faced contradictory problems: smallholders had little demand for the labour capacity of their children but had great difficulty feeding them. In England, already in "the late thirteenth century, between 40 and 70 per cent of holdings were too small to absorb the labour of those families resident upon them" (Smith 1984: 23). In contrast, larger holdings had to complement the family's labour force, be it during certain phases of the family life cycle or as a reaction to demographic constraints or because the amount of labour required consistently exceeded the labour capacity of the family. The hiring of a non-family labour force strongly correlated with farm size and the impact of commercialisation (Mitterauer 1986: 193; Lambrecht 2015: 64). In particular, this socio-economic constellation constituted a type of simple commodity production that shared a porous border with agrarian

---

(edited by Engels) translates Marx' non-capitalist independent *Kleinmeister* (Marx and Engels 1962: 354) as "small employer" (English online translation: 233).

capitalism. And simple commodity production was closely intertwined with a specific life course regime embodied in the social figure of the life-cycle servant.

Even if the concept of "simple commodity production" has been only vaguely elaborated so far, it is attractive for several reasons: it avoids simplifying kin-based notions of domestic production by integrating wage labour systematically into the "family economy"; it offers a coherent framework that brings together peasants' and artisans' household economies; it refers to a "whole period" of pre-capitalist production, integrating family and household production into the historical development of the market economy; and it is open to or aware of its persistence *in* and its potential symbiotic relations *with* early phases of industrial capitalism.

Life-Cycle Service in Agriculture

Until the nineteenth century, most life-cycle servants worked as farmhands and maids in agriculture. The commonalities of their living and working conditions across time and space as well as significant temporal and geographical variations are displayed in quite a number of richly detailed regional studies based on various early modern sources.[12] Even if there is no monographic summary yet, these studies leave no doubt whatsoever that life-cycle service in husbandry was the dominant form of wage labour in early modern Europe both in terms of the numbers of servants and labourers and/or the number of days worked.[13] In the following paragraphs, I concentrate on those aspects from this rich corpus of evidence that are most relevant from a life course perspective.

The historical origins of the institution of service are still largely unexplored, but presumably it had emerged already in the high Middle Ages (see Kussmaul 1981: 168–169, 203–204; Mitterauer 2010: 28, 59, 64). In the course of the late Middle Ages and even more so during the early modern period, an increasing number of potential agricultural labourers were available to fill the gaps in labour capacity, and indeed, they were hired by peasants when needed. But this was mainly casual employment undertaken especially during seasonal workload peaks, even if it might have been embedded in long-term patron-client-relations.[14] Meeting the con-

---

12 The best recent overview is Whittle 2017a, and her synthetic introduction (Whittle 2017b) to the collective volume *Servants in Rural Europe, 1400–1900.*

13 On days worked, see, for example, Whittle 2017b: 1; or Stanziani 2014: 160.

14 An important expression of patron-client relations was to rent farm cottages (or simply a chamber) to labourers who then had to be available when needed. In early modern sources, they are often called inmates (*Inwohner*). For the numerical superiority of servants over inmates in seventeenth to nineteenth-century Austria, see Mitterauer 1992c, table 1. For a full account of the eco-

stant demand for labour with live-in servants of both genders and different ages remained the preferred solution. There are two sets of reasons for this: first, those that concern the employment relation of life-cycle service in general, and second, those related to a specific type of agriculture, mainly animal husbandry.

A general advantage of live-in servants for farmers was the permanent availability of farmhands and maids. As English eighteenth-century jurist and politician William Blackstone put it, "labour services meant that you owned a certain person's time" and that you "had the right to benefit from all the time and capacities" of your servant (Stanziani 2014: 151; see also Humphries 2010: 220; Paping 2017: 208). This was particularly important in agriculture, with very long daily hours during the growing season and irregular work rhythms due to weather conditions. The availability and subservience of live-in servants was much greater than that of labourers as the former were subordinated to the patriarchal power of their employer as household head, while labourers usually had their own families and enjoyed some autonomy after working hours and when out of work. A further advantage of live-in servants from the perspective of farmers was servants' contracts – in many European territories enforced by law – which bound them to a farm for a longer period, usually at least a year. This gave farmers long-term control over their labour force as well as flexibility since servants could be dismissed or replaced at the end of the contract.

The subservience of servants was strengthened – and legitimised or naturalised – by age hierarchy. Hiring servants allowed farmers to balance their households' labour force by age and sex. Adolescents or young adults with fully developed physical strength were certainly indispensable for certain tasks, but small children were also useful in many respects. The process of maturation from early childhood to adulthood was accompanied by continuous change and adaptation to and participation in the family economy and in service.[15] The history of life-cycle service is, therefore, to some extent a history of child labour (Beattie 2010). Time and again, children aged five to nine are explicitly labelled as "servants" in early modern sources – even if the very young ones are also called "boy" or

---

nomic, social, and cultural dimensions of patron-client relations among farmers, labourers, and servants – with a focus on the twentieth century – see Ortmayr 1986. With respect to earlier periods, see Schlumbohm 1994: 615–620; Lambrecht 2015: 73.

15 An ideal-typical model of adequate work activities of rural children and adolescents from age four to twenty-one is presented in a German pedagogical treatise from 1789: "Über die Kindheit des Lippischen Landmanns. Stufenfolge der Arbeiten vom Kleinkind bis zum männlichen Alter" (Schlumbohm 1983: 81–87).

"maid."[16] Jane Humphries' analysis of many hundreds of British working-class autobiographies shows that from 1791 to 1850 – the highpoint of child labour in British history – 40 to 50 percent of boys had already begun working for pay before or at nine years old, a considerable part of them as agricultural labourers or (indoor) farm servants. The mean age for starting waged work during this period was about ten in Humphries' sample (Humphries 2010: 177–178, 212; see also Kussmaul 1981: 72).

This was a rather low average compared with early modern data from the continent. A sample of population listings from rural communities in the Archbishopric Salzburg in the seventeenth and eighteenth centuries provides statistically reliable evidence. In some parishes, no children below age ten were registered as servants in the households of their employers, in most of them hardly more than one or two appeared in the listings (Eder 1990: 207–213). The number of live-in servants increased among those between the ages of eleven and fourteen, even if their economic utility at this age was still disputed, for example in conflicts over remuneration. The economic utility of young servants depended both on their individual maturation and on the work tasks they were expected to perform. Such tasks usually included herding geese or goats, looking for sheep, haying, caring for babies and children younger than themselves, spinning, running errands, cooking, cleaning up, fetching water, caring for firewood, and the like, but sometimes even sowing seeds (Thomas 1976: 215). Maids who were a little bit older also cared for elderly peasants when necessary, for example retired fathers or mothers of the head of household. Such activities of children are mentioned over and over again in various early modern sources. On the basis of broad evidence, Seilagh Ogilive concludes that, by and large, "from the age of 11–14 both girls and boys were regarded as productive enough to cover their consumption costs, apparently irrespective of prior education and training, and adults became willing to pay some of them as servants" (Ogilvie 2003, 99–102, here 102).

All these children's tasks may not seem very important, but they were indispensable for the family economy. Anything children could do freed up the capacity of adolescents and adults (Beattie 2010: 56). Children were a particularly flexible labour force, switching constantly from household and care chores to the fields, pastures, and stables. They were – as nineteenth- and twentieth-century autobiographical writers called themselves – "maids-" or "boys-of-all-work."[17] Moreover,

---

16 German sources differentiate, for instance, between *Knecht* and *Jung*, *Magd* and *Mädchen*. See Plaul 1986: 423.

17 See, for instance, Buttinger 1979: 50. Joseph Buttinger describes his entry into agricultural service in Austria in 1917 as a sequence similar to what often appears in early modern sources: He started paid work for a nearby farmer at age eleven during school holydays, herding four cows,

child servants were much more at the mercy of their employers than were adolescents, and they constituted a very cheap labour force. Young children usually received no wage at all beyond bed and board, either in cash or in kind (Kussmaul 1980: 37). Later on, they might perhaps receive some clothing or shoes, and when they started to receive cash wages, these wages were still very low. A Dutch sample from 1754–1831, for example, shows that boys "aged fourteen earned a wage which was 26 per cent of the wage of adult farmhands" (Paping 2017: 219; see also Kussmaul 1981: 145). Live-in child servants were a particularly cheap, submissive, and flexible workforce even if it was one still in the making. The position of boys and girls in this labour relationship improved only with increasing age, physical strength, and self-confidence.[18]

The emergence and spread of a class of land-poor or landless cottagers or labourers during the early modern period had a fundamental effect on the social origins and the status of life-cycle servants. Up to the early nineteenth century, there were still daughters and sons of peasant families who went into service, but they represented a declining minority. Children from large and – to a lesser extent – small farms used to stay with their parents, working in the parental family economy. Jürgen Schlumbohm's findings for Belm, a small German village near Osnabrück, seems to be fairly typical: "78 percent of landless people's children appear to have been in service in 1812, but only 40 percent of smallholders' and 18 percent of land-rich peasants' offspring" (Schlumbohm 1996: 85).[19] The impact of class also determined the age of entry into service. A micro analysis of an Upper Austrian village in the first half of the nineteenth century shows that very few sons of peasants became servants below the age ten, but 16 percent of the sons of day labourers and 22 percent of the sons of inmates did (Mitterauer 1986: 298). Service in husbandry had become a life course phase mainly for the children of the lower rural classes.

An even earlier age for de-facto entering service was the norm for foster children (*Ziehkinder* or *Aufzögling* in German sources). Foster children might have been orphans and they might have been the offspring of relatives of peasants, but increasingly they were the illegitimate progeny of female servants who were neither allowed to marry nor keep their children when working in service. Foster children were usually welcomed by peasant households as a potential supplement to the farm's labour force. Moreover, and in contrast to regular servants, they were

---

sleeping at home, but getting rich meals in the farmhouse. At age 13 he became a constant live-in servant for the very same farmer (ibid., 36–37, 45).

18 For the division of servants' work by age and gender, see, for instance, Lundh 2004: 77 ff.
19 For similar figures in a Dutch region, see Paping 2017: 216. For a cautious account of early modern England, see Kussmaul 1981: 77–78.

not entitled to any wage, and they were subordinated to their foster father or mother in every respect and without temporal limitation. In regions with a high number of agricultural servants, the number of foster children might reach remarkable dimensions.[20]

Service in husbandry was particularly important for livestock farming. Cattle were an almost indispensable element of many forms of the early modern peasant economy, not only as supplier of milk and meat but also as a source of manure/fertilizer and as draught animals. Dairy cattle required continuous supervision, and a long-term personal relationship between animals and carers was highly advantageous. Supervision efforts increased with the spread of "livestock housing," i. e., raising livestock indoors in stables throughout the year, a practice that became common in the Netherlands starting in the sixteenth and in Central Europe in the eighteenth century: "Feeding, milking, caring, and cleaning the animals and the stables" had to be done daily, summer and winter, occasionally even at night, and "a sound knowledge of the peculiarities of each animal is very important" (Mitterauer 1992c: 149 f.). Caring for cattle was more often the task of maids than male farmhands.[21]

Regional specialisation in dairy and animal husbandry emerged due to ecological conditions or specific market opportunities. The highest incidence of live-in farm servants in eighteenth- and nineteenth-century Austria occurred in those Alpine regions that specialised in cattle raising. In some villages in these regions, more than 40 percent of the total population consisted of farmhands and maids; labourers played a minor role. There were fewer servants and a higher share of labourers where a mixed economy or a specialisation in grain production prevailed, and there were very few servants in areas of commercial wine production (Mitterauer 1992c: 144–147). In regions dominated by animal husbandry, life-cycle service also declined much later and more slowly. Figures comparable to those of eighteenth and nineteenth-century Alpine regions are evident in Austrian agricultural statistics from around 1900 and – only slightly lower – from 1930 (Ortmayr 1992: 358–361). In the Austrian provinces of Upper Austria, Salzburg, Carinthia,

---

20 The soul revisions of a manorial estate in the Baltic province of Courland in 1797 registered 12 percent of the entire population as foster children; the Austrian census of 1934 still counted about 160,000 foster children, which is more than 2 percent of the country's entire population, most of them living in the agrarian Alpine districts (Plakans 1975: 11; Sandgruber 2002: 271–271).
21 On the gendered division of servant's labour for sixteenth to nineteenth century Austria, see, for example, Mitterauer 1986: 200–213. For late seventeenth and early eighteenth-century Sweden, see Prytz 2017: 111. Female servants also operated local forms of transhumance, such as Alpine summer meadows (*Almwirtschaft*) or distant Swedish "summer farms" in the forests. On the latter, see Uppenberg 2017: 172.

and Styria in 1890, between 70 and 80 percent of hired agricultural labour consisted of live-in servants; in contrast, in Moravia, which was dominated by large estates and grain production, the share of servants was only about 25 percent.[22] England shows a similar pattern: around 1700, between 50 and 70 percent of all
agricultural labourers were live-in servants, while the census of 1851 shows that
– on average, nationally – agricultural labourers now clearly outnumbered servants in husbandry. However, there was a clear contrast between the northwest
and the southeast. Servants still dominated agriculture in parts of the north and
in Cornwall, while the large farms and estates south of the "Exe-Wash-line" mainly
employed labourers. In 1851, the share of servants in the agricultural labour force
ranged from 3 percent in Bedfordshire to 45 percent in Westmoreland (Snell 1985:
96; Ehmer 1991: 97).

The high incidence and persistence of life-cycle service in husbandry cannot
be explained solely by the advantages it gave to farmers. Two other factors must
be mentioned. First, there were various forms of compulsory service for children
from poorer social groups. This system was most elaborated in England, as will be
discussed in the following paragraph on apprentices in crafts and trades. But continental countries such as Sweden established labour laws that forced non-proper-
tied parents to enter their children into service.[23] Second, for parents, children, or
adolescents who did have a choice, service made sense. Children of the lower rural
classes were of much less use and much more a burden to their families. For poor
families, sending children into service meant that they had one less mouth to feed
and that their children might have access to better and more regular food in the
household of a farmer. Contracts binding children in service for a year protected
them from unemployment, which was a problem in rural societies, particularly
in winter. Living in one's employer's household also protected servants from fluctuations in food prices. In some regions, parents of servants would even receive
some farm products as a "gift" (Lambrecht 2015). Older servants who received
cash wages but did not have to support a family or have any other unavoidable expenses might save enough money over the years to marry and purchase or rent a
cottage, or in some regions perhaps even a small farm, which might secure their
livelihood, at least before the enclosure of common lands and in combination with
casual work as a labourer (Kussmaul 1981: 80–82). In addition, young men and
women who spent many years in service from childhood to adulthood acquired
wide and varied experience with most aspects of farming and rural life. Training

---

22 Calculated on basis of Ehmer 1991: 295, excluding unpaid family members from the category of
"worker" (*Arbeiter*).
23 For Sweden, see Lundh 2004; Uppenberg 2017; and Prytz 2017: 97. For Norway, see Osthus 2017:
119.

by imitating and doing was inherent in their work. Finally, economic rationality was fuelled by the popular belief that "wise parents" would send away their children to prevent their offspring from becoming spoiled if they remained at home (Thomas 1976: 263).

Some factors mitigated the subservience imposed by living in one's master's household. First, in the case of young servants, often their parents negotiated contracts and ensured their enforcement (Lambrecht 2015: 71). Second, most important was the temporal limitation of employment contracts, which gave servants the right to leave, usually after a year. Various sources show that labour turnover was high, and mobility after a contracted number of years more often served the interests of servants rather than those of peasants (Dribe and Lundh 2005). Third, life-cycle service was still a transitional social position that fostered hopes and dreams of social advancement beyond the lowest labouring class, while the exit from service, marriage, and household formation usually marked the definitive end of social mobility.[24] Most of those former servants who did not migrate to cities became agricultural labourers, inmates, cottagers, or – at best – smallholders. These were livelihoods that required the combination of working one's own small or tiny plot with part-time respectively casual wage labour or domestic industry. They lost some of the social security they had as an annually hired servant, but they gained the chance to marry, and as married men and women with a household and a family of their own, they achieved independence and autonomy, even if it was precarious (Schlumbohm 1994: 616). Yet, there seems to be some agreement among contemporary observers and historians that in material terms, single young servants in husbandry were better off than married labourers with children (Lambrecht 2015: 63–71).[25]

Urban Parallels: Life-Cycle Service in Crafts and Trades

One of the major shortcomings in previous research on life-cycle service is that rural and agricultural conditions have been separated from the urban worlds of work, and the focus on service in towns and cities has been the small segment

---

24 In my view, this was a main motive for the postponement of the exit from service and thus of marriage, which characterised the "European Marriage Pattern"; for details, see Ehmer 1991.
25 This paragraph concentrates on Western and Central Europe. For the high incidence of life-cycle service in those early modern Eastern and East Central European regions where agriculture was embedded in feudal manorial systems, see Szoltysek 2015.

of "domestics" (in its narrowest sense) only and not the entire urban economy. Often overlooked or neglected is the fact that the working and living conditions of artisanal apprentices, and to some degree even journeymen, shared a fundamental characteristic with those of male and female servants in husbandry: wage labour was most common in the early life course stages and implied living in the employer's household and under his patriarchal authority. Additionally, individual life courses transcended the borders between villages and towns due to manifold and frequent migrations.

Commonalities between service in husbandry and in crafts and trades are mirrored in early modern and early industrial labour laws and poor laws, particularly in England (and her colonies) (Deakin and Wilkinson 2005). The Statute of Artificers (1563), which remained in force until 1814, concerned "apprentices, servants, and labourers, as well in husbandry as in diverse other arts, mysteries, and occupations." Apprentices should be forced, if required, "to serve in husbandry or in any other kind of art, mystery, or science" (Lane 1996: 2).

There were structural differences as well. First, urban economies experienced a dynamic process of division of labour throughout the late medieval and early modern period, which led to the emergence and institutionalisation of occupations or "callings" that differed greatly with respect to capital and skill requirements as well as in social status and prestige. Specialisation, professionalisation, and formalised notions of "skill" and the completion of training channelled life course trajectories and occupational careers much more intensely than in agriculture.

Second, there was an important difference in the gendered division of labour. Strict vocational boundaries in the long-term process of specialisation and professionalisation implied discrimination against girls and women. Over time, women were less and less accepted as apprentices or masters in the vast majority of guilds. Nevertheless, women remained part and parcel of the artisanal world of work, but in a subordinate role: they participated, for instance, in preparatory work, marketing, and often enough in the production process, even when they were not formally permitted to do so. Moreover, the larger the workshop and number of live-in apprentices and journeymen, the greater the need for female servants who supplied the lodging and board for the male workforce. But once more in contrast to most (although not all) agricultural regions, life-cycle service in urban crafts and trades was numerically dominated by males (Ehmer 1980: 138–140). For this reason, the following reflections focus on male apprentices and on journeymen.

Third, where simple commodity production was controlled by guilds, vocational careers were embedded in dense systems of norms and rules set out in writing and confirmed by the respective political authorities. The tripartite sequence of apprentice-journeyman-master constitutes an institutionalised life course regime and is usually seen as an ideal-typical life course trajectory of male artisans in the guild system. This view is justified to some degree from an *ex post* perspective, as the position of a master required a preceding apprenticeship and, in continental Europe, usually an additional phase as journeyman. Recent research shows, however, that this view is misleading from an *ex ante* perspective. Young boys who entered apprenticeship by no means automatically followed a predefined path but often moved in different directions. Apprenticeship in early modern Europe was a highly flexible system, albeit one with a stable foundation; the vast majority of apprentices lived in the households of their masters and can be characterised, therefore, as life-cycle servants (Reith 1989: 10 ff; De Munck 2007: 207).[26]

Entry into service as an apprentice usually began later than work in agriculture. Apprenticeships commonly began somewhere between the ages of twelve and eighteen, with a peak around fourteen and fifteen and many exceptions in both directions. Sheilagh Ogilvie's guild database, which covers large parts of Europe and spans the thirteenth to nineteenth centuries, reveals that a majority of guilds required a minimum age of fourteen, and the actually observed average age for starting apprenticeship was about sixteen (Ogilvie 2019: 379–380).[27] There were also local customs; for instance, in sixteenth-century London, apprentices started their positions at 18.5 on average and became free at about twenty-six, living-in as single men in their master's household despite this more advanced age (Rappaport 1989: 236). However, in the centuries that followed, the median age at entry into apprenticeship decreased continuously in London and was 14.7 years in 1810 (Wallis, Webb, and Minns 2010: 377).

An English peculiarity with much lower entry ages were so-called "parish apprentices." The Poor Law of 1601 allowed overseers of the poor to apprentice poor children, orphans, or illegitimate children to farmers or artisans at very young ages, sometimes even at four years old, but more often from the age of seven onwards. By law, such "parish apprentices" were bound until the age of twenty-one for women and twenty-four for men (Lane 1996: 12; Wallis 2008).

Not only the entry age but also the duration of apprenticeship terms was highly variable, differing between and within regions and occupations and changing over time in both directions, but with a slight trend towards shorter terms. Ogilvie's analysis of minimum terms imposed by guilds yields a mean length of 4.5 years in the medieval period and 3.5 years in the early modern period, with a

---

26 Construction and building trades are a principal exception. For more discussion on this, see the end of this paragraph.

27 However, this rather high average level is induced to some degree by occupations that required physical strength and where living-in was not mandatory, such as construction. On the age structure of apprentices in Malmö (Sweden) in 1820, excluding carpenters and bricklayers, see Edgren 1986: 370.

range of about two to seven years. Actual individual indentures, however, were even shorter or longer (Ogilvie 2019: 374–378). From a legal perspective, England was an exception, as the Statute of Artificers of 1563 stipulated a general nation-wide minimum indenture of seven years. However, here too, a rich variety of terms existed in practice. In sixteenth-century London, about 40 percent of all apprentices dropped out or ran away (Rappaport 1989: 313–314). A detailed micro-analysis of London and Bristol apprentices in the 1680s and 1690 reveals a surprisingly flexible interpretation of statutory indenture terms (Minns and Wallis 2012). Some apprentices might reside with their master before the official start of their indenture, perhaps as a kind of "trial period" (Minns and Wallis 2012: 562). Others signed their indenture but only arrived in their master's household several months later. Up to half of apprentices disappeared during the years of their indenture, but even more surprisingly, some of them returned in the sixth or seventh year, most likely to gain a legally recognised completion of apprenticeship. In sum, "most apprentices' actual period of service was substantially shorter than the statutory minimum" (Minns and Wallis 2012: 563). The broader historical trend moved in the same direction. For the whole of England, Keith Snell estimates an erosion of actual indentures from six or seven years in the early eighteenth century to four years in 1814 (Snell 1985: 314).

High drop-out rates of apprentices existed not only in England. In seventeenth- and eighteenth-century Antwerp, the proportion of runaways was about 20 percent (De Munck 2007: 190). In various eighteenth- and nineteenth-century Viennese crafts, the drop-out rate of apprentices varied between 20 and almost 60 percent, and most frequently stood at between 25 and 35 percent (Steidl 2003: 253). Occupational trajectories of young artisans were less stable than guild regulations and indenture contracts suggest.

But why did apprenticeships last for several years? An answer to this question requires the combination of two perspectives which are discussed separately and weighted differently in the scholarship: the demand of masters for cheap but nevertheless at least partly skilled labour, and the special requirements of artisanal training and the accumulation of skills and experiences. Which of these two aspects prevailed was influenced by age and – relatedly – by the actual tasks apprentices were expected to perform. In addition to training in a craft or trade, live-in apprentices were also occupied with domestic chores, younger ones more intensively than those who were older. A survey of Braunschweig's master artisans in 1760 reveals a rich variety of tasks: apprentices were regularly responsible for chopping wood, fetching water, cleaning shoes, caring for their masters' babies, or they were sent out for beer and tobacco for the journeymen or sent on errands (Reith 1989: 15). Apprentices often had longer daily hours than journeymen because they had to clean up the workshop after work or fire the oven in early morning. In an early eighteenth-century Parisian printing workshop, the apprentices "had to stagger out of bed at four or five in the morning to open the gate for the earliest arrivals among the journeymen" (Darnton 1984: 76). Such activities were reported in numerous sources, and they were generally regarded as self-evident. However, they were also the subject of disputes. Household chores were the source of continuous conflicts about domestic subordination. Sometimes parents or guardians of apprentices insisted on the primacy of training. Throughout the early modern period, journeymen tried to draw a strict line of demarcation between themselves and (mostly female) domestic servants, which then brought into question the housework done by male apprentices as future journeymen (De Munck 2007: 220).

But there was also a tension between training and labour in the workshop. There is general agreement among scholars of early modern crafts and trades that training was mainly observation and emulation and learning by doing. Processes of trial and error, however, had their limits due to the value of raw materials, which could not be wasted; whatever apprentices produced should be saleable (De Munck 2007: 53 f.). Participation in production was a very gradual process that expanded with increased age and experience, and there was always a tendency to use apprentices for auxiliary, preparatory, or repetitive tasks (Reith 1999: 312). This tendency was bolstered in places where artisanal workshops were integrated into mass production for merchant capitalists.

A brief glance at wages provides further insight into the position of apprentices in their master's household and workshop. As with farmhands, the main component of apprentices' wages consisted of lodging and board. Additionally, apprentices might receive payments in kind such as a pair of shoes and a shirt per year or even a moderate sum of money. The amount of such wages varied according to age, experience, and actual duties. Often apprentices did not earn anything during their first year or years, when they were expected to spend a lot of time on housework. When they were bound to their masters for long terms, they might earn some money in their fifth or sixth year, and they usually received a money wage when they took part in piecework production. For Germany, Reinhold Reith assumes that money wages were more common in the sixteenth century than in the eighteenth and that money wages (as distinct from non-monetary wages) became ascendant again only in the second half of the nineteenth century (1999: 334).

Wages, the duration of contracts, and actual chores were also affected by an additional factor: contrary to customs in agriculture, guilds and masters might ask apprentices to pay enrolment fees to guilds and/or premiums to the master. Such payments were legitimised as compensation for bed, board, and training, but they were also a barrier for entry into a trade, particularly for the sons of poor families (Minns and Wallis 2012). Parents might regard this as an investment in the future career of their sons, paving their child's way towards a mastership or at least to the position of a journeyman or a skilled workman who could expect a salary 50 to 60 percent higher on average – or even higher – than that of an unskilled craftsman (Pfister 2019: 227–230). As with many other matters related to early modern crafts and trades, premium customs constituted a colourful patchwork that differed depending on time, towns, and crafts. Often these premiums did not exist at all, elsewhere they might exceed the value of room and board and constitute a heavy financial burden for parents or guardians (Ogilvie 2019: 118–121). Apprentices who had not paid a premium were usually bound for longer terms and frequently received significantly less payment, be it in money or in kind (Reith 1989: 5).

After having completed their term as apprentices, young artisans – now in their late teens or early twenties – reached the next stage of their occupational careers. They received the freedom to work as journeymen in their respective crafts. Not all of them followed that path; some left their trade and looked for work in other segments of the labour market. Those who remained were confronted yet again with a set of artisanal rules and customs, guild regulations, and labour laws that restricted their working and living conditions and future career prospects. Two aspects are particularly relevant for this chapter: first, in continental Europe, most trades requested journeymen "to be on tramp" for several years before they became eligible to hold the position of master.[28] They travelled from one town to the next or from village to village. When they found work, they stayed as long as their labour was needed or as long as they liked – perhaps a couple of days, weeks, or (rarely) months, and then they moved on. Being on tramp meant a life course phase defined by more-or-less permanent mobility. "Tramping journeymen" constituted a highly flexible, supra-regional workforce that served as an indispensable complement to the relatively stable and fixed labour potential of guild masters. The artisanal life course regime enabled urban crafts and trades to maintain supply-side restrictions in the labour market in the interest of a guaranteed livelihood for resident masters and, at the same time, to respond flexibly to short- and long-term changes in demand (Ehmer 1997).

Second, when journeymen took up employment, they usually boarded with their master and were subject to his paternal authority just like other members of his household. Living in a master's household during such short-term employment was often required by guilds, but in many Central European cities until

---

28 Journeymen on tramp also existed in England, but they were much less associated with the institution of service and with petty commodity production. Here, tramping was practiced also by married skilled workmen to cope with unemployment, and it was less rooted in a long-lasting artisanal tradition. For England in comparative perspective, see Hobsbawm 1979.

the mid-nineteenth century, it was prescribed by law as a means to control a highly fluid and seemingly unruly labour force. However, it was also a comfortable situation for tramping journeymen, even if it might include quarrels concerning the quality of food or the freedom to go out after work – to name just two potential areas of conflict among many others. In the city of Konstanz in southern Germany, for instance, in 1774, more than 90 percent of journeymen lived in their master's households; in most trades, all of them did (Ehmer 1991: 297). Living-in was certainly a hegemonic pattern in most parts of the European continent deep into the nineteenth century. In the Swedish town of Malmö in 1753, all journeymen lived-in (excluding carpenters and bricklayers); in 1820, 83 percent lived-in, and in 1845, 76 percent still roomed in their master's household (Edgren 1986). Like servants in husbandry and apprentices, they were not allowed to marry or to establish a household of their own. Contrary to apprentices, journeymen received higher monetary wages in addition to room and board, and the duration of their employment was much more flexible and sometimes very short depending on local labour market needs. Moreover, in German speaking areas as well as in France and other European regions, there existed journeymen's brotherhoods that strengthened their members' position vis-à-vis their masters.

From this perspective, journeymen, too, were "productive life-cycle servants," albeit a very specific type. Michael Sonenscher's characterisation of the social profile of eighteenth-century French journeymen applies to large parts of continental Europe and for most of the nineteenth century as well: "The workforce of the great majority of urban trades consisted overwhelmingly of young single men . . . It is clear, that work for wages was a temporary condition for the great majority of journeymen . . . By the age of 35 most of them had either become master artisans or abandoned the trades altogether. The relationship between journeymen and their masters was a relationship between young men and older men . . ." (Sonenscher 1989: 100, 193, 197) – men, I might add, who lived under the same roof. Those who did not manage to become a master might also settle down permanently, marry, and work in their profession illegally as "garret-masters," or they found employment in those segments of the labour market that were not restricted to a life course phase.

Finally, life-cycle service by both apprentices and journeyman was surprisingly persistent during the initial phases of industrialisation, although with increasing differentiation in regional and occupational terms. In England, its decline began already in the eighteenth century. Both the duration of the life phase of service (see above in respect to indentures) and its general importance diminished. The 1851 Census of Great Britain shows that live-in apprentices and journeyman had become an insignificant segment of the population. In some parts of the continent, and particularly in the German-speaking world, the situation was different. In Germany, for instance, almost two-thirds of all apprentices still held room and board in their master's household in 1904: in villages and small towns, more than 80 percent of apprentices lived-in, while in larger cities, less than 40 percent did (Reith 1989: 12). Journeymen show a similar pattern. In the cities of the Habsburg Empire and Switzerland, a clear majority of journeymen still boarded with their masters in the 1850s (Ehmer 1994: 73–80). The decline of living-in did not accelerate before the 1860s, and, again, there was occupational differentiation: in 1867, more than two-thirds of Berlin's bakers and butchers still lived with their masters (Ehmer 1991: 298). Moreover, even when living-in declined, the most important alternative was still not the foundation of one's own family and household but lodging as a single man, mainly in working-class families that rented out a chamber or bed.[29]

How can the long-term persistence of life-cycle service in crafts and trades be explained? Based on my own research on the social and economic transformation of the nineteenth century, I offer three hypotheses: First, the growth of petty commodity production in the context of urbanisation and the rising consumer needs of a rapidly growing urban population led to continuously increasing demand for young people trained in a certain trade or willing to learn it. This demand motivated millions of young people to try their luck in large cities, where they looked for work as well as accommodation and board. Second, a core element of the early modern artisanal life course regime continued in large parts of continental Europe well into the latter decades of the nineteenth century, namely the connection between marriage and economic independence as an employer or through self-employment. Even in the late nineteenth century, economic independence was not an unrealistic goal in German-speaking Central Europe. Journeyman postponed marriage until they reached the position of master, or until they became convinced that they would never manage to do so and would remain in a journeymen position for life, or until they abandoned their trade and switched to one of the new occupations in industry (Ehmer 1988). Third was the transformation of many artisanal branches into outwork. The influence of merchant capital opened world markets to artisanal workshops, for example, those specialising in shoemaking and garment manufacture. This outwork economy relied on a skilled but cheap and highly mobile workforce to manage the syncopated rhythms of production between the busy and dead seasons. In London, New York, and other Western metropolitan areas, the foundational unit of this economy was the family of a skilled journeymen who employed his wife and children. In Vienna and other Central European cities, this economy led to a late blossoming or even a revival of the much

---

29 This is particularly true of older journeymen from their mid-twenties onwards; see Ehmer 1994: 61–82.

older social tradition of master artisans' households with live-in apprentices and journeymen (Ehmer 1991: chapter 15). Global capitalism made use of the long-lasting social traditions of petty commodity production and its corresponding life course regime.

Life-cycle service was a basic element of the early modern artisanal world of work and a formative feature of the entire urban economy. Nevertheless, there existed different labour relations and life course patterns as well. The most general examples are the construction trades, such as carpenters, masons, and bricklayers. Labourers in these fields usually belonged to the guild system, and their life course conformed to the ideal-typical career trajectory of apprentice-journeyman-master. But they differed principally from the pattern of life-cycle servants described above as the masters' households were separated from the workplaces of the labourers, which were often large construction sites such as churches or palaces. Large businesses employed large numbers of skilled artisans and their unskilled helpers, including women. Apprentices and journeymen usually did not live in the households of their masters (Edgren 1986; Ehmer 1994: 77, 80). As most labour activities required physical strength, entry into apprenticeships came later than for most other crafts. Due to heavy capital requirements, journeymen had only a small chance to become masters themselves; in fact, most remained in a wage-labour position throughout their entire working life, but they did so as married men with their own household and family (Ehmer 1991: 197–199, 212). This was a segment of the urban economy beyond petty commodity production and life-cycle service that represented a kind of pure wage labour system since the medieval period.

Conclusions

The socio-economic structures of early modern Western, Northern, and Central European societies were shaped by a close relationship between the development of wage labour and a specific life course regime embodied in the social figure of the life-cycle servant. This relationship, in turn, was embedded in a particular mode of production, namely petty commodity production. The aim of the present chapter has been to strengthen awareness among historians of this triangular relationship and its three pillars: petty commodity production, life course regime, and wage labour.

Petty commodity production

In the very centre of this triangular relationship stood the households of independent peasants and artisans in need of an additional labour force to make up for the demographic limitations of their own families. Such households involved a wide range of work activities, housework, and care work, as well as production for subsistence, feudal rents or taxes, and for markets. A live-in workforce that varied in age, gender, skills, and physical strength was perfectly suited for myriad combinations of productive and reproductive labour. Households, however, were not only sites of production and reproduction but were also foundational elements of the social and political order, with the head of household (or the principal married couple) on top of a hierarchical structure. Working in households was a labour relation, but it also entailed a worker's submission to the authority of the head of the household. Petty commodity production was the backbone of the early modern economy and society, and it persisted well into the early phases of industrialising capitalism.

Life course regime

A substantial part of households' non-familial labour force consisted of young, unmarried persons of both genders. Their integration into the world of work implied both learning and training as well as fulfilling labour tasks that were crucial to the household economy. Socialisation of this kind might happen in the parental home, but the basic element of the early modern life course regime was the expectation that boys and girls left home at a certain age – at least for a while – to learn, work for wages, live in their employers' households, and gain a livelihood (Thomas 1976: 215–217). Life-cycle service might last for shorter or longer periods of the life course; it might begin in childhood, and later on, it represented a kind of prolonged childhood and/or adolescence. Servants were certainly not regarded as adults. The common understanding was that marriage and the formation of one's own independent household were the central markers of full personal maturity, and these two events also denoted the definitive end of life-cycle service. This life course regime was not mandatory for all young people, but it was the norm and an institution. Over the course of the early modern period, it became de facto – and in some places even de jure – compulsory for children of the lower classes.

Wage labour

Wage labour took many forms in early modern Europe. Some of them, such as work in construction, mining, or in large enterprises like state-run shipyards, might have been practiced permanently throughout large parts of individuals' working lives if they were not interrupted by unemployment. However, continuous wage labour in large enterprises of this kind was exceptional. Prevailing forms of wage labour were casual wage labour in agriculture in combination with small or tiny holdings (and the use of the commons) and life-cycle service in husbandry and in crafts and trades. Service was only a phase in the entire working lives of individual men and women, but it was practiced continuously by large parts of the young population for many years. Therefore, it can be reasonably assumed that life-cycle service was the numerically predominant form of wage labour in early modern Europe, both with respect to the number of workers and hours of labour performed.

In conclusion, for a very long historical period, life-cycle service was a multifunctional institution that served the needs of different actors. It allowed peasants and artisans to exploit the labour power of children, adolescents, and young, unmarried adults; it offered a livelihood for parentless children and for the offspring of the poor; and it provided a framework for the occupational qualification and cultural socialisation of young people. Most important, perhaps, is that it guaranteed both economic flexibility and the stability of the social order. In a society whose economy, social hierarchy, and cultural values were dominated by independent producers in husbandry as well as in crafts and trades, life-cycle service created a space for gainful employment and, at the same time, for the reproduction of the inferior status of wage labour. Wage labour was the task of the young, and it implied subordination under the employer in all spheres of life: "the young were to serve and the old were to rule" (Thomas 1976: 207). But because employment was based on temporary contracts, servants could change their employers. Moreover, since young and unmarried persons had no family responsibilities, they were not bound to a specific place but could respond flexibly to short-term fluctuations in supply and demand on local, regional, and trans-regional labour markets. Thus, life-cycle servants also formed a particular dynamic element of the early modern and early industrial European economy. During the "long nineteenth century," however, life-cycle service and the corresponding life course regime gradually lost their significance, early in England and rather late in Northern and Central Europe. With the final breakthrough of industrial capitalism and the displacement of petty commodity production to the margins, wage labour ceased to be a life course affair and became hegemonic as norm and practice during all phases of the working life.

References

Arthur, Christopher J. 2005. "The Myth of 'Simple Commodity Production'." Accessed August 18, 2021. https://www.marxists.org/subject/marxmyths/chris-arthur/article2.htm.

Beattie, Cordelia. 2010. "Economy." In *A Cultural History of Childhood and Family*, edited by Sandro Cavallo and Sylvia Evangelisti, 49–67. Oxford/New York: Berg.

Brass, Tom, and Marcel van der Linden, eds. 1997. *Free and Unfree Labour. The Debate Continues.* Bern: Peter Lang.

Buttinger, Joseph. 1979. *Ortswechsel. Die Geschichte meiner Jugend.* Frankfurt am Main: Verlag Neue Kritik.

Darnton, Robert. 1984. *The Great Cat Massacre and Other Episodes in French Cultural History.* New York: Basic Books.

De Moor, Tine, and Jan Luiten van Zanden. 2010. "Girl Power: The European Marriage Pattern and Labour Markets in the North Sea Region in the Late Medieval Early Modern Period." *Economic History Review* 63, no. 1: 1–33.

De Munck, Bert. 2007. *Technologies of Learning. Apprenticeship in Antwerp Guilds from the 15th Century to the End of the Ancien Régime.* Turnhout: Brepols.

Deakin, Simon, and Frank Wilkinson. 2005. *The Law of the Labour Market: Industrialization, Employment, and Legal Evolution.* Oxford: Oxford University Press.

Derks, Hans. 1996. "Über die Faszination des 'Ganzen Hauses'." *Geschichte und Gesellschaft* 22: 221–242.

Dribe, Martin, and Christer Lundh. 2005. "People on the Move: Determinants of Servant Migration in Nineteenth-century Sweden." *Continuity and Change* 20, no. 1: 53–91.

Eder, Franz. 1990. *Geschlechterproportion und Arbeitsorganisation im Land Salzburg 17.–19. Jahrhundert.* Vienna: Verlag für Geschichte u. Politik/Oldenbourg Verlag.

Edgren, Lars. 1986. "Crafts in Transformation?: Masters, Journeymen, and Apprentices in a Swedish Town, 1800–1850." *Continuity and Change* 1, no. 3: 363–383.

Ehmer, Josef. 1980. *Familienstruktur und Arbeitsorganisation im frühindustriellen Wien.* Vienna: Verlag für Geschichte und Politik.

Ehmer, Josef. 1988. "Lohnarbeit und Lebenszyklus im Kaiserreich." *Geschichte und Gesellschaft* 14, no. 4: 448–471.

Ehmer, Josef. 1991. *Heiratsverhalten, Sozialstruktur, ökonomischer Wandel. England und Mitteleuropa in der Formationsperiode des Kapitalismus.* Göttingen: Vandenhoeck & Ruprecht.

Ehmer, Josef. 1994. *Soziale Traditionen in Zeiten des Wandels. Arbeiter und Handwerker im 19. Jahrhundert.* Frankfurt/New York: Campus Verlag.

Ehmer, Josef. 1996. "The 'Life Stairs'. Aging, Generational Relations and Small Commodity Production in Central Europe." In *Aging and Generational Relations Over the Life Course. A Historical and Cross-Cultural Perspective*, edited by Tamara K. Hareven, 53–74. Berlin: Walter de Gruyter.

Ehmer, Josef. 1997. "Worlds of Mobility: Migration Patterns of Viennese Artisans in the 18th Century." In *The Artisan and the European Town*, edited by Geoff Crossick, 172–199. Aldershot: Scolar Press.

Ehmer, Josef. 2021. "A Historical Perspective on Family Change in Europe." In *Research Handbook on the Sociology of the Family*, edited by Norbert F. Schneider and Michaela Kreyenfeld, 143–161. Cheltenham: Edward Elgar Publishing.

Ehmer, Josef, and Michael Mitterauer, eds. 1986. *Familienstruktur und Arbeitsorganisation in ländlichen Gesellschaften.* Wien: Böhlau.

Fauve-Chamoux, Antionette, ed. 2004. *Domestic Service and the Formation of European Identity. Understanding the Globalization of Domestic Work, 16th–21st Centuries*. Bern: Peter Lang.

Fauve-Chamoux, Antoinette, and Richard Wall. 2005. "Domestic Servants in Comparative Perspective: Introduction." *History of the Family* 10, no. 4: 345–354.

Fauve-Chamoux, Antoinette. 2017. "Revisiting Domestic Service as a Pre-marital Labour for Women and Men in Past Europe." *Romanian Journal of Population Studies* 11, no. 2: 57–91.

Goody, Jack, ed. 1971. *The Developmental Cycle in Domestic Groups*. Cambridge: Cambridge University Press.

Goody, Jack. 1996. "Comparing Family Systems in Europe and Asia: Are There Different Sets of Rules?" *Population and Development Review* 22, no. 1: 1–20.

Hanawalt, Barbara. 1993. *Growing up in Medieval London: The Experience of Childhood in History*. Oxford: Oxford University Press.

Haskins, Victoria K., and Claire Lowrie, eds. 2018. *Colonization and Domestic Service. Historical and Contemporary Perspectives*. Abingdon: Routledge.

Hay, Douglas, and Paul Craven, eds. 2004. *Masters, Servants, and Magistrates in Britain and the Empire, 1562–1955*. Chapel Hill: North Carolina University Press.

Hobsbawm, E. J. 1979. *Labouring Men. Studies in the History of Labour*. 6th ed. London: Weidenfeld and Nicolson.

Hoerder, Dirk, Elise van Nederveen Meerkerk, and Silke Neunsinger, eds. 2015. *Towards a Global History of Domestic and Caregiving Worker*. Leiden: Brill.

Humphries, Jane. 2010. *Childhood and Child Labour in the British Industrial Revolution*. Cambridge: Cambridge University Press.

Kriedte, Peter. 1984. *Peasants, Landlords and Merchant Capitalists: Europe and the World Economy 1500–1800*. Cambridge: Cambridge University Press.

Kriedte, Peter, Hans Medick, and Jürgen Schlumbohm. 1981. *Industrialization before Industrialization. Rural Industry in the Genesis of Capitalism*. Cambridge: Cambridge University Press.

Kussmaul, Ann. 1981. *Servants in Husbandry in Early Modern England*. Cambridge: Cambridge University Press.

Lambrecht, Thijs. 2015. "Unmarried Adolescents and Filial Assistance in Eighteenth-Century Rural Flanders." In *Social Networks, Political Institutions, and Rural Societies*, edited by Georg Fertig, 63–87. Turnhout: Brepols.

Lambrecht, Thiis. 2017. "The Institution of Service in Rural Flanders in the Sixteenth Century: A Regional Perspective." In *Servants in Rural Europe, 1400–1900*, edited by Jane Whittle, 37–56. Woodbridge: The Boydell Press.

Lane, Joan. 1996. *Apprenticeship in England, 1600–1914*. London: UCL Press.

Laslett, Peter. 1972. "Mean Household Size in England since the Sixteenth Century." In *Household and Family in Past Time*, edited by Peter Laslett and Richard Wall, 125–158. Cambridge: Cambridge University Press.

Laslett, Peter. 1977. *Family Life and Illicit Love in Earlier Generations: Essays in Historical Sociology*. Cambridge: Cambridge University Press.

Laslett, Peter. 1983. "Family and Household as Work Group and Kin Group: Areas of Traditional Europe Compared." In *Family Forms in Historic Europe*, edited by Richard Wall, Jean Robin, and Peter Laslett, 513–564. Cambridge: Cambridge University Press.

Laslett, Peter. 1988. "The Institution of Service." *Local Population Studies* 40: 55–60.

Lentz, Carola. 2020. *Familie, Arbeit und soziale Mobilität. Ghanaische Perspektiven*. Berlin: De Gruyter.

Lindström, Jonas, Karin Hassan Jansson, Rosemarie Fiebranz, Benny Jacobsson, and Maria Ågren. 2017. "Mistress or Maid: The Structure of Women's Work in Sweden, 1550–1800." *Continuity and Change* 32, no. 2: 225–252.

Lundh, Christer. 2004. "Life Cycle Servants in Nineteenth Century Sweden – Norms and Practice." In *Domestic Service and the Formation of European Identity. Understanding the Globalization of Domestic Work, 16th–21st Centuries*, edited by Antoinette Fauve-Chamoux, 71–86. Bern: Peter Lang.

Marx, Karl, and Friedrich Engels. 1962. *Das Kapital*. Vol.1. Werke Bd. 23, Berlin: Dietz Verlag. English translation by Samuel Moore and Edward Aveling. Accessed August 18, 2021. https://www.marxists.org/archive/marx/works/download/pdf/Capital-Volume-I.pdf.

Marx, Karl, and Friedrich Engels. 1964. *Das Kapital*. Vol.3. Werke Bd. 25, Berlin: Dietz Verlag. English translation by Samuel Moore and Edward Aveling. Accessed August 18, 2021. https://www.marxists.org/archive/marx/works/download/pdf/Capital-Volume-III.pdf.

Minns, Chris, and Wallis, Patrick. 2012. "Rules and Reality: Quantifying the Practice of Apprenticeship in Early Modern England." *Economic History Review* 65, no. 2: 556–597.

Mitterauer, Michael. 1973. "Zur Familienstruktur in ländlichen Gebieten Österreichs im 17. Jahrhundert." In *Beiträge zur Bevölkerungs- und Sozialgeschichte Österreichs*, edited by H. G. Helczmaovszki, 167–222. Wien: Verlag für Geschichte und Politik.

Mitterauer, Michael. 1986. "Formen ländlicher Familienwirtschaft. Historische Ökotypen und familiale Arbeitsorganisation im österreichischen Raum." In *Familienstruktur und Arbeitsorganisation in ländlichen Gesellschaften*, edited by Josef Ehmer and Michael Mitterauer, 185–325. Wien: Böhlau.

Mitterauer, Michael. 1990. "Servants and Youth." *Continuity and Change* 5, no. 1: 11–38.

Mitterauer, Michael. 1992a. *A History of Youth*. Cambridge, MA: Blackwell.

Mitterauer, Michael. 1992b. *Familie und Arbeitsteilung. Historisch vergleichende Studien*. Wien: Böhlau.

Mitterauer, Michael. 1992c. "Peasant and Non-Peasant Family Forms in Relation to the Physical Environment and the Local Economy." *Journal of Family History* 17, no. 1: 139–159.

Mitterauer, M. 2010. *Why Europe? The Medieval Origins of its Special Path*. Chicago, IL: Chicago University Press.

Ogilvie, Sheilagh. 1997. *State Corporatism and Proto-Industry. The Württemberg Black Forest, 1580–1797*. Cambridge: Cambridge University Press.

Ogilvie, Sheilagh. 2003. *A Bitter Living: Women, Markets, and Social Capital in Early Modern Germany*. Oxford: Oxford University Press.

Ogilvie, Sheilagh. 2019. *The European Guilds. An Economic Analysis*. Princeton, NJ: Princeton University Press.

Ortmayr, Norbert. 1986. "Ländliches Gesinde in Oberösterreich." In *Familienstruktur und Arbeitsorganisation in ländlichen Gesellschaften*, edited by Josef Ehmer and Michael Mitterauer, 325–415. Wien: Böhlau.

Ortmayr, Norbert. 1992. "Sozialhistorische Skizze zur Geschichte des ländlichen Gesindes in Österreich." In *Knechte. Autobiographische Dokumente und sozialhistorische Skizzen*, 297–376. Wien: Böhlau.

Osthus, Hanne. 2017. "Servants in Rural Norway c.1650–1800." In *Servants in Rural Europe, 1400–1900*, edited by Jane Whittle, 113–130. Woodbridge: The Boydell Press.

Paping, Richard. 2017. "Dutch Live-In Farm Servants in the Long Nineteenth Century: The Decline of the Life-Cycle Service System for the Rural Lower Classes." In *Servants in Rural Europe, 1400–1900*, edited by Jane Whittle, 203–226. Woodbridge: The Boydell Press.

Pasleau, Suzy, Isabelle Schopp, and Raffaella Sarti, eds. 2006. *Proceedings of the Servant Project.* Vol. 5. Liège: Éditions de l'Université de Liège.

Pfister, Ulrich. 2019. "The Inequality of Pay in Pre-modern Germany, Late 15th Century to 1889." *Jahrbuch für Wirtschaftsgeschichte/Economic History Yearbook* 60, no. 1: 209–243.

Plakans, Andrejs. 1975. "Peasant Farmsteads and Households in the Baltic Littoral, 1797." *Comparative Studies in Society and History* 17, no. 1: 2–35.

Plaul, Hainer. 1986. "Die Struktur der bäuerlichen Familiengemeinschaft im Gebiet der Magdeburger Börde unter den Bedingungen des agrarischen Fortschritts in der zweiten Hälfte des 18. Jahrhunderts." In *Familienstruktur und Arbeitsorganisation in ländlichen Gesellschaften*, edited by Josef Ehmer and Michael Mitterauer, 417–447. Wien: Böhlau.

Prytz, Christina. 2017. "Life-Cycle Servant and Servant for Life: Work and Prospects in Rural Sweden c.1670–1730." In *Servants in Rural Europe, 1400–1900*, edited by Jane Whittle, 95–112. Woodbridge: The Boydell Press.

Rappaport, Steve. 1989. *Worlds within Worlds. Structure of Life in Sixteenth-Century London.* Cambridge: Cambridge University Press.

Reith, Reinhold. 1989. "Berufliche Sozialisation im Handwerk vom 18. bis ins frühe 20. Jahrhundert. Umrisse einer Sozialgeschichte der deutschen Lehrlinge." *Vierteljahrschrift für Sozial- und Wirtschaftsgeschichte* 76, no. 1: 1–27.

Reith, Reinhold. 1999. *Lohn und Leistung. Lohnformen im Gewerbe.* Stuttgart: Franz Steiner Verlag.

Sandgruber, Roman. 2002. "Die Landwirtschaft in der Wirtschaft. Menschen, Maschinen, Märkte." In *Geschichte der österreichischen Land- und Forstwirtschaft im 20. Jahrhundert*, edited by Ernst Bruckmüller, 191–408. Wien: Verlag Carl Ueberreuter.

Sarti, Raffaela. 2006. "Who Are Servants? Defining Domestic Service in Western Europe (16th–21st Centuries)." In *Proceedings of the "Servant Project,"* vol. 2, edited by Suzy Pasleau, Isabelle Schopp, and Raffaela Sarti, 3–59. Liege: Éditions de l'Université de Liege.

Schlumbohm, Jürgen, ed. 1983. *Kinderstuben. Wie Kinder zu Bauern, Bürgern, Aristokraten wurden, 1700–1850.* München: Deutscher Taschenbuch Verlag.

Schlumbohm, Jürgen. 1994. *Lebensläufe, Familien, Höfe. Die Bauern und Heuerleute des Osnabrückischen Kirchspiels Belm in proto-industrieller Zeit.* Göttingen: Vandenhoeck & Ruprecht.

Schlumbohm, Jürgen. 1996. "Micro-History and the Macro-Models of the European Demograph System: Life Course Patterns in the Parish of Belm, Germany – Seventeenth to the Nineteenth Centuries." *The History of the Family* 1, no. 1: 81–95.

Scott, John, and Gordon Marshall, eds. 2015. *A Dictionary of Sociology.* Oxford: Oxford University Press. Quoted from the online version. Accessed August 18, 2021. https://www.encyclopedia.com/social-sciences-and-law/sociology-and-social-reform/sociology-general-terms-and-concepts/petty-0#1O88pettycommodityproduction; https://www.encyclopedia.com/social-sciences-and-law/sociology-and-social-reform/sociology-general-terms-and-concepts/simple.

Simonton, Deborah. 2011. "'Birds of Passage' or 'Career' Women? Thoughts on the Life Cycle of the Eighteenth-Century European Servant." *Women's History Review* 20, no. 2: 207–235.

Sinha, Nitin, Nitin Varma, and Pankaj Jha, eds. 2019. *Servants' Pasts: Sixteenth to Late-Eighteenth Century, South Asia.* Vol. 1. Hyderabad: Orient BlackSwan.

Sinha, Nitin, and Nitin Varma, eds. 2019. *Servants' Pasts: Late-Eighteenth to Twentieth-Century, South Asia.* Vol. 2. Hyderabad: Orient BlackSwan.

Smith Adam. 1776. *An Inquiry into the Nature and Causes of the Wealth of Nations.* Vol. 2. London: W. Strahan and T. Cadell.

Smith, Richard M. 1984. "Some Issues Concerning Families and Their Property in Rural England 1250–1800." In *Land, Kinship and Life-Cycle*, edited by Richard M. Smith, 1–86. Cambridge: Cambridge University Press.

Snell, Keith. 1985. *Annals of the Labouring Poor. Social Change and Agrarian England, 1660–1900.* Cambridge: Cambridge University Press.

Sonenscher, Michael. 1989. *Work and Wages: Natural Law, Politics and the Eighteenth-Century French Trades.* Cambridge: Cambridge University Press.

Stanziani, Alessandro. 2014. *Bondage, Labor and Rights in Eurasia from the Sixteenth to the Early Twentieth Centuries.* London: Berghahn Books.

Steidl, Annemarie. 2003. *Auf nach Wien! Die Mobilität des mitteleuropäischen Handwerks im 18. und 19. Jahrhundert am Beispiel der Haupt- und Residenzstadt.* Munich: Oldenbourg.

Szoltysek, Mikolaj. 2015. *Rethinking East-Central Europe: Family Systems and Co-residence in the Polish-Lithuanian Commonwealth.* Vol. 1. Bern: Peter Lang.

Tenfelde, Klaus. 1979. "Ländliches Gesinde in Preußen. Gesinderecht und Gesindestatistik 1810–1861." *Archiv für Sozialgeschichte* 19: 189–229.

Thomas, Keith. 1976. "Age and Authority in Early Modern England." *Proceedings of the British Academy* LXII: 205–248.

Uppenberg, Carolina. 2017. "The Servant Institution during the Swedish Agrarian Revolution: The Political Economy of Subservience." In *Servants in Rural Europe, 1400–1900*, edited by Jane Whittle, 167–182. Woodbridge: The Boydell Press.

Van Nederveen Meerkerk, Elise. 2017. "Temporary Service? A Global Perspective on Domestic Work and the Life Cycle from Pre-Industrial Times to the Present." *Geschichte und Gesellschaft* 43: 217–239.

Van Nederveen Meerkerk, Elise, Silke Neunsinger, and Dirk Hoerder. 2015. "Domestic Workers of the World: Histories of Domestic Work as Global Labor History." *Towards a Global History of Domestic and Caregiving Worker*, edited by Dirk Hoerder, Elise van Nederveen Meerkerk, and Silke Neunsinger. Leiden: Brill.

Wallis, Patrick. 2008. "Apprenticeship and Training in Premodern England." *The Journal of Economic History* 68, no. 3: 832–861.

Wallis, Patrick, Cliff Webb, and Chris Minns. 2010. "Leaving Home and Entering Service: The Age of Apprenticeship in Early Modern London." *Continuity and Change* 23, no. 3: 377–404.

Weber, Therese, ed. 1985. *Mägde. Lebenserinnerungen an die Dienstbotenzeit bei Bauern.* Wien: Böhlau.

Welskopp, Thomas. 2017. "Kapitalismus und Konzepte von Arbeit. Wie systematisch zentral ist 'freie Lohnarbeit' für den Kapitalismus?" *Geschichte und Gesellschaft* 43: 97–216.

Whittle, Jane, ed. 2017a. *Servants in Rural Europe, 1400–1900.* Woodbridge: The Boydell Press.

Whittle, Jane. 2017b. "Introduction: Servants in the Economy and Society of Rural Europe." In *Servants in Rural Europe, 1400–1900*, edited by Jane Whittle, 1–18. Woodbridge: The Boydell Press.

Wiesner-Hanks, Merry E. 2019. *Women and Gender in Early Modern Europe.* 4th edition. Cambridge: Cambridge University Press.

Woodward, Donald. 2000. "Early Modern Servants in Husbandry Revisited." *Agricultural History Review* 48, no. 2: 141–150.

Notes on Contributors

Erdmute Alber holds the chair of Social Anthropology at the University of Bayreuth. She investigates processes of social change with regard to the interdependencies and mutual entanglements of politics and kinship, primarily in West Africa. Her research is based on historically informed field research and empirical fieldwork. Her current research topics are generational relations, ageing, kinship, the emergence and dynamics of new middle classes, and the global production of illiteracy. Recent publications include *Kinship and Politics: A Reader* (Routledge, 2022) (with Tatjana Thelen) and *Transfers of Belonging: Child Fostering in West Africa in the 20th Century* (Brill, 2018).

Rolf Becker, studied sociology, social psychology, political science, and contemporary history at the University of Mannheim and holds a Ph.D. from the Free University of Berlin. He received his habilitation in 1999 at the Dresden University of Technology. Since 2004, he holds a chair of Sociology of Education and is the director of the Department of Sociology of Education at the University of Bern (Switzerland). He is also the head of the DAB panel study, co-head of the TREE panel study, and a member of the board of the Interfaculty Centre of Educational Research. His current research interests include the sociology of education, social stratification and mobility, survey methodology, and life course research.

Neda Deneva holds a PhD in sociology and social anthropology from Central European University. Her work is situated at the intersection of transnational migration, labour regimes, social citizenship, and social reproduction in Eastern Europe. She has held post-doctoral fellowships at Humboldt University of Berlin; Babeș-Bolyai University, Cluj; the Institut für die Wissenschaften vom Menschen, Vienna; and New Europe College, Bulgaria. Her most recent research at Babeș-Bolyai University focuses on reindustrialisation processes and the precarious labour and housing of Romanian Roma.

Heike Drotbohm is Professor of Social and Cultural Anthropology at Mainz University. Her expertise is on transnational and migration studies, spiritual practice, kinship and care, as well as humanitarianism and pro-migrant activism. She has conducted research among the Haitian diaspora on Cape Verde and with Cape Verdean migrants in Portugal and the United States. She has conducted research in the Haitian diaspora, in Cape Verde and with Cape Verdean migrants in Portugal and in the United States. Most recently, she expanded her research field to include Brazil. For some recent publications, see *Anthropological Perspectives on Care: Work, Kinship, and the Life Course* (with E. Alber, Palgrave, 2015); *Deportation, Anxiety, Justice* (with I. Hasselberg, Routledge, 2017), and *Care beyond Repair* (Oxford Research Encyclopedia of Anthropology, 2022).

Josef Ehmer (1948–2023) was Professor Emeritus of Economic and Social History at the University of Vienna. He was Professor of Modern History at the University of Salzburg (1993–2005), an Associate Fellow at re:work (2010–2021), and a long-term visiting scholar at various international universities and research institutions, including the (former) Max Planck Institute for History in Göttingen, the Cambridge Group for the History of Population and Social Structure, and the European University Institute in Florence. His primary field of research was comparative European social history from the early modern period to the present, with a focus on family and the life course, age and ageing, work and labour, artisans and workers, migrations, and historical demography.

Anette Eva Fasang is Professor of Sociology at Humboldt University of Berlin. Fasang is the Director of the Berlin Graduate School of Social Sciences (BGSS), a Principal Investigator in the Graduate Training Programme "The Dynamics of Demographic Change, Democratic Processes and Public Policy" (DYNAMICS), as well as the Excellence Cluster "Contestations of the Liberal Script" (SCRIPTS). Her research interests include social demography, comparative stratification research, life course sociology, and quantitative methods for longitudinal data analysis. Current research focuses on welfare state effects on work-family life courses and young adult life courses in the Global South.

Therese Garstenauer is Senior Research Fellow (Elise Richter Programme, Austrian Science Fund) at the Department of Economic and Social History at the University of Vienna. She is currently pursuing her habilitation project on the proper conduct of life of government employees in interwar Austria. In spring 2022, she was Visiting Professor at the University of Hradec Králové. She is president of the International Conference of Labour and Social History (ITH). In 2021, she edited a special issue of the *Austrian Journal of Historical Studies* entitled "Historicizing Bureaucratic Encounters."

Chitra Joshi taught for several decades at Delhi University and had teaching assignments and fellowships in institutions in India and beyond. Her publications include *Lost Worlds: Indian Labour and its Forgotten Histories* (Permanent Black, 2003; Anthem, 2005) and book chapters and essays in international journals. She is one of the founding members of the Association of Indian Labour Historians (AILH). She is currently working on a manuscript of a book on labour regimes beyond the factory.

Lamia Karim is a Professor of Anthropology at the University of Oregon and is a cultural anthropologist working in Bangladesh. She has over twenty-five years of research experience and has conducted multiple research projects on women and development. Her latest book *Castoffs of Capital: Work and Love among Garment Workers in Bangladesh* (University of Minnesota Press, 2022) was made possible with a Wenner-Gren Foundation post-doctoral grant and a faculty fellowship at the Institute for Labor Studies at re:work at Humbolt University of Berlin.

Carola Lentz is Senior Research Professor at the Department of Anthropology and African Studies, Mainz University. Her research focusses on West Africa, and she is particularly interested in land rights, ethnicity and nationalism, colonialism, the politics of memory, and the emergence of a middle class. Her book *Land, Mobility and Belonging in West Africa* (Indiana University Press, 2013) received the Melville Herskovits Prize of the African Studies Association. Together with David Lowe, she published *Remembering Independence* (Routledge, 2018), and, together with Isidore Lobnibe, *Imagining Futures: Memory and Belonging in an African Family* (Indiana University Press, 2022). She is a member of the Berlin-Brandenburg Academy of Sciences and Humanities and the National Academy of Sciences Leopoldina. Since 2020, she serves as president of the Goethe-Institut.

Ju Li is an independent scholar. Among her recent publications is *Enduring Change. The Labor and Social History of One Third-front Industrial Complex in China from the 1960s to the Present* (De Gruyter, 2019).

Karl Ulrich Mayer is Director Emeritus of the Max Planck Institute for Human Development and Stanley B. Resor Emeritus Professor of Sociology, Yale University. He received his PhD in sociology at the University of Konstanz in 1973, and his habilitation at the University of Mannheim in 1977. He has held academic positions at Goethe University Frankfurt am Main, the University of Mannheim, the Zentrum für Umfragen, Methoden und Analysen (ZUMA) in Mannheim, the Max-Planck-Institut für Bildungsforschung, Yale University, and New York University at Abu Dhabi. He was also the President of the Leibniz Association (2010–2014), Principal Investigator of the German Life History Study (1979–2005), and Co-Principal Investigator of the Berlin Ageing Study (1988–2003). His research interests include social stratification and mobility, ageing and the life course, and survey methodology.

Mary Jo Maynes is a Professor of History at the University of Minnesota. Her work explores the history of the family in the context of gender, generational, and class relations. Her books include: *Children and Youth as Subjects, Objects, Agents* (New York: Palgrave Macmillan, 2021, with Deborah Levison and Fran Vavrus); *The Family: A World History* (New York: Oxford University Press, 2012, with Ann Waltner); *Telling Stories: The Use of Personal Narratives in the Social Sciences and History* (Ithaca: Cornell University Press, 2008, with Jennifer Pierce and Barbara Laslett); and *Secret Gardens, Satanic Mills: Placing Girls in European History* (Bloomington: Indiana University Press, 2004, with Birgitte Søland and Christina Benninghaus).

Lutz Raphael is Professor of Contemporary History at the University of Trier. His research focuses on the contemporary history of historiography in the era of globalisations and the social history of de-industrialisation in Western Europe since the 1970s. His recent publications include *Jenseits von Kohle und Stahl. Eine Gesellschaftsgeschichte Westeuropas nach dem Boom* (Suhrkamp, 2019) english edition: *Beyond Coal and Steel* A Social History of Western Europe after the Boom. (Polity Press 2023), *Ordnungsmuster und Deutungskämpfe. Wissenspraktiken im Europa des 20. Jahrhunderts* (Vandenhoek & Ruprecht, 2018); (as editor and co-author): *Poverty and Welfare in Modern German History* (Berghahn, 2017); and together with Anselm Doering-Manteuffel and Thomas Schlemmer (eds.), *Vorgeschichte der Gegenwart* (Vandenhoek & Ruprecht, 2016).

Yoko Tanaka is Professor of economic history and labour studies at the University of Tsukuba, Japan. She received her PhD. from the Department of Economics at the University of Tokyo with a dissertation on the labour history of Friedrich Krupp Co. Her research focuses on the long-term structural transformation of industry, business, and work from a historical and comparative perspective, particularly in Germany and Japan. Tanaka is the president of the Japan Association for Social Policy Studies and editor-in-chief of the *Journal of German Studies*, and was the editor of the *Journal of International Japanese Studies* (2012–2014). She was a Research Fellow at re:work at Humboldt University of Berlin (2015–2016) and a Visiting Scholar at Harvard Yenching Institute in the United States (2017–2018).

Ann Waltner is Professor of History at the University of Minnesota. She has written on gender, kinship, and religion in early modern China. She and Mary Jo Maynes wrote *Family: A World History* (Oxford University Press, 2012). Her most recent publication is an e-book on the eighteenth-century Chinese novel, *Dream of the Red Chamber* (https://open.lib.umn.edu/redchamber/). She has edited the *Journal of Asian Studies* (2000–2005), directed the Institute for Advanced Study at the University of Minnesota (2005–2014), and chaired the Department of History at the University of Minnesota (2019–2022).

Susan Zimmermann is Professor at the Central European University in Vienna, Austria. She is a historian of labour, gender, welfare, and women's organisations in East Central Europe and internationally. As principal investigator of the ERC project "Women's Labour Activism in Eastern Europe and Transnationally: From the Age of Empires to the Late 20th Century" she studies trade union politics of women's work in state-socialist Hungary and internationally. Her most recent monograph is *Women's Politics and Men's Trade Unionism: International Gender Politics, Female IFTU-Trade Unionists and the Labuor and Women's Movements of the Interwar Period* (Löcker, 2021).

Index

70/40 problem, of Ice Age Generation   125

abandonment *see* marital abandonment
abortion, debate in state-socialist Hungary
    246, 248
achievement, public employment law based
    on   159
advancement *see* promotion; social advance-
    ment
Africa *see* Benin; Cameroon; Cape Verde islands;
    Ghana; Tanzania
age
    70/40 problem   125
    of apprentices   375
    of child servants   369
    division of labour   28–29
    of industrial workers in France   75
    of public employees in Austria   161
    of Toyota workers   107
age discrimination   32–33
age groups *see* cohorts; generations
agency, vs. structure in life courses   133
agricultural societies
    socioeconomic transformation   275–276
    see also rural population
agricultural workers *see* peasants
agriculture
    life-cycle servants   368–373
    wage workers   367
    see also livestock farming; peasant economy
Amoskeag Manufacturing Company, employ-
    ment of married women   31
anger, of retired Nanfang Steel workers   148–
    149
animal attacks *see* tiger attacks
animal husbandry *see* livestock farming
annual income
    from regular vs. non-regular employment in
        Japan   119, 120
    of Toyota workers   106, 107
Anschluss see Nazi-annexed Austria
Anselmy (Yob family member)   268
antagonism *see* East-West antagonism

anti-Semitism, in Nazi-annexed Austria   169–
    170
apparel industry *see* textile production
apprentices (pre-industrial Europe)   374, 375,
    376–378
apprenticeship (pre-industrial Europe)
    duration   375–376
    see also skills
arranged marriages
    concern about Beninese rural girl's   289–
        290, 293
    vs. love marriages in Bangladesh   217–218
artisans (pre-industrial Europe)
    households   382
    see also apprentices; journeymen
Asia *see* Bangladesh; China; India; Japan; Persia
assessment *see* moral assessment
attacks *see* tiger attacks
Austria
    life-cycle servants   371–372
    see also Nazi-annexed Austria; public employ-
        ment (Austria); Salzburg (Archbishopric)
automobile industry *see* Peugeot; Renault; Toyo-
    ta
autonomy *see* semi-autonomy

babies *see* infants
Bandopadhyay, Tarashankar   339
Bangladesh
    about   204
    divorces   218
    empowerment of women   204
    extended families   206, 216
    family life of rural population   216
    housework roles   216–217
    nuclearisation of family in urban households
        216
    raising children   206
    rural women   204–205
    women workers   208–209
Bangladeshi garment factory workers (female)
    about   24–25, 203
    chapter overview   10–11, 205

confidence   215, 218–219
differences to Western workers   206
education   220
health issues   221
housework roles   217
individuals see Hena; Shikha
inter-religious marriages   219
life goals   212, 222
love vs. arranged marriages   217–218
marital abandonment of   213, 219
older vs. younger   220
religious affiliation   208
research methods   207–208
retirement   222
semi-autonomy   215
summary of life stories   206–207, 211–213, 219–223
wages   214, 220
working conditions   210–211, 213–214
Bangladeshi garment industry
growth   210–211
research on   209
Barth (Yob family member)   273
bearers see palanquin bearers
Beck, Ulrich   44
Becker, Rolf   55–56
Benin
chapter overview   284
family conflicts over foster children   283–284
family conflicts over rural girls   14, 282, 283, 289–293
foster fathers (individuals) see Gunu; Kora; Woru
foster parents of rural woman   281
rural girls as foster children   284
rural girls in urban households   13–14, 281n2
rural girls (individuals) see Gloria; Salimatou
social mobility   282–283
societal change and young women   282
Beti, young middle-class women   286–287
Bielefeld School   264–265
biography, concept   5
birth incentives, in state-socialist Hungary   247
birth rate, in state-socialist Hungary   244
Blossfeld, Hans-Peter   44–45, 55–56
Boston, Cape Verdean migration to   324–325, 326, 327–328, 329

"Brazilianization"   44
Britain
career paths of industrial workers   7–8, 73–74, 79–81
child labour   369
de-industrialisation   78–79
employment of married women   29–30
master-servant relations   360
miners   79–80
unemployment   79
see also England
British India see mail runners; palanquin bearers
"Bubble economy", collapse in Japan   96
Buchnee (widow)   349
Budhee (mail runner)   349
Bulgaria
education   309
migration rates of Roma   312
poverty of Roma   306
ratio of Roma   306n4
return migration of Roma migrants' children to   310
see also Shumen

Cameroon, young middle-class Beti women   286–287
Cape Verde islands
diaspora communities   321–322
history   321
migration to Boston   324–325, 326, 327–328, 329
migration to Massachusetts   330
see also return migration (to Cape Verde islands); São Filipe
capitalism, and subsistence production   264–265
car companies see Peugeot; Renault; Toyota
care work
importance   303
as perceived women's responsibility   11
unpaid vs. paid work   303–304
see also childcare
career paths (working lives)
aspects   48–49
in Britain   7–8, 73–74, 79–81
changes, debate on   41, 42–46, 63–65
de-industrialisation impact on   91–92

in France   7–8, 74–78
in Ghana   268, 272–273
of industrial workers   7–8, 73–87, 91
in Japan   98
of public employees in Austria   153–154,
   157–158, 159–160, 165
of public employees in Europe   154
of Toyota workers   106, 110–111
in West Germany   6–8, 46–58, 60–65, 82–88
of women workers in West Germany   87–88
see also employer changes; employment mobility; employment stability; employment status; promotion
carriers see palanquin bearers
castes see Kahars
catechist, working as   268
Catherine (Yob family member)   269
changes
   career path debate   41, 42–46, 63–65
   dimensions   2
   see also economic transformation; employer
      changes; enforced job change; social trans-
      formation; societal change; turning points;
      vital conjunctures
Chen Qiyuan (entrepreneur)   195
child labour   368–369
childcare
   creche system   249
   and factory work   231
   by Roma extended families   313
   by Roma grandparents   14–15, 297–298,
      302–303, 309
   of Tanzanian teenage mothers   287
childcare leave
   debate on   248–251
   in Europe   251–252
   ILO key actors   252
childcare leave (state-socialist Hungary)
   chapter overview   11–12, 226–227
   introduction of   225–226, 243–244
   key actors   252
   preparations for   230, 233–235, 243, 245
   results and effects   246–247, 253
children
   education of Roma migrants'   297–298, 307–
      308, 310

of impoverished families during Great Depression   285
as life-cycle servants   368–371, 372
"in mobility"   301–302
of public employees in Austria   162–163
raising in Bangladesh   206
return migration   310, 328–329, 331
reunification   330–331
transition into work   19
see also foster children; girls; infants
China
   Great Divergence   180
   marriage   181–182
   textile production   10, 28, 179–180, 186–189,
      193–197
   unmarried women   182
   youth as workers   182
   see also People's Republic of China; Shanghai
Chinese state-owned enterprises
   restructuring   144–145, 146
   see also Nanfang Steel factory
chores see housework
chronology, rural women's perception of   205
civil service see public employment
clerical personnel, in Austria   160
co-habitation, of Ice Age Generation with parents   121, 123, 125
cohorts
   annual income in Japan   120
   concept   5
   employment mobility in West Germany   50–
      51, 54
   employment stability in West Germany   47–
      48, 49, 62–63
   employment status in West Germany   56
   employment status of Toyota workers   112–
      117
   married men and women in Japan   124
   specific see children; older migrants; older
      workers; parents; retired workers; teenage
      mothers; young women; younger workers;
      youth
   unmarried individuals in Japan   122
   women workers in Europe   229
   see also age; generations
collaboration
   ILO and WFTU   235–236

see also mutual support

colonial India see mail runners; palanquin bearers

communication, in Yob family   274–275

communist countries see Hungary (state-socialist); People's Republic of China; Soviet Union

companies
  automobiles see Peugeot; Renault; Toyota
  job shifts in West German   52
  job transfers from Toyota to affiliated   106, 107
  SOEs see Chinese state-owned enterprises
  steel see Nanfang Steel factory
  textile see Amoskeag Manufacturing Company; Hungarian Cloth Factory
  trade see East India Company
  see also employers

company loyalty
  of industrial workers in Western Europe   76, 80
  "lifetime commitment" (Japan)   100
  of Toyota workers   119, 120

company-sponsored activities, for Toyota workers   107

conferences see International Trade Union Conference (1964)

confidence, of Bangladeshi garment women workers   215, 218–219

conflicts see family conflicts

construction workers   381

continuity see company loyalty

corporate culture, at Toyota   104–105, 107

cotton production
  in China   187–188, 193–194
  in Europe   184

countryside see rural ...

couples see married men; married women

couriers see mail runners

Covid pandemic   45–46

crafts and trades
  life-cycle servants   374–381
  see also apprentices; artisans; journeymen

creche system   249

crises see economic crises

Cultural Revolution   138–139, 140

Dagara
  about   260
  family conflicts   270
  new professions for   267
  see also Yob family (Ghana)

dangerous animals see tiger attacks

Danilsa (return migrant)   327–328, 331, 333

databases, of industrial workers' career paths   82–83

de-industrialisation
  in Britain   78–79
  in France   75
  impact on career paths   91–92
  in West Germany   81–82
  in Western Europe   71, 89

de-standardisation, of life courses   22–25, 99

death see sudden death

decision making, in Yob family   272–273

dedication, of Nanfang Steel employee   142–143

demographics
  debate in state-socialist Hungary   245–246
  see also socio-demographics

dependence
  of child servants   370
  of Roma grandparents   311, 312–313
  of Toyota workers   107

deported migrants   325, 330–331

Déri, Erzsébet   230

desperation see hopelessness

diaspora communities, of Cape Verde islands   321–322

Dienstpragmatik (public employment law)   157–160

disciplinary measures, for Bangladeshi garment women workers   214

discrimination see age discrimination

diseases see health issues

dismissals see enforced retirement; removal

division of labour
  by age   28–29
  by gender   26–27
  in urban economies   374

divorces, in Bangladesh   218

domestic labour see housework

domestic servitude, in China   182

Doppelverdienerverordnung (public employment law)   166
drop-out rates, of apprentices   376
Du Zhang (SOE employee)   138–139, 143, 146–147
Duffin, William   345–346

early retirement
  of industrial workers   84–85, 89, 91
  of Nanfang Steel employees   145
  in various employment types   21–22
  see also enforced retirement
East India Company, Kahars in service of   342
East-West antagonism, on women workers' rights   240–241
Eastern European state-socialist countries
  childcare leave   251, 252
  demand for workers   227
  employment guarantees for working mothers   240
  women workers   226
  see also Hungary; Soviet Union
economic boom *see* post-war "boom" period
economic crises
  "Bubble economy" collapse in Japan   96
  impact on public employment   163, 166–167
  see also Great Depression; hyperinflation (post-WWI)
economic reforms
  in PRC   134, 141, 144
  in state-socialist Hungary   244
economic success
  in Japan   95
  see also post-war "boom" period
economic transformation
  to outwork economy   380
  see also de-industrialisation
economies *see* "Bubble economy"; outwork economy; peasant economy; urban economies
"educated urban youth going to the country-side" (movement)   138
education
  of Bangladeshi garment women workers   220
  in Bulgaria   309
  in Ghana   267, 269–270, 271
  higher   20–21

as hope for advancement   20
  importance   309–310
  vs. mobility   298–299, 313
  of Roma migrants' children   297–298, 307–308, 310
  transition into work   20
  work and school-based   19–20
  see also apprenticeship; schools
Elder, Glen   4, 26, 284–285, 286
elderly people *see* older migrants; older workers
emotions *see* anger; hopelessness
employees *see* workers and workforce
employer changes
  in West Germany   52
  see also enforced job change
employers
  "lifetime commitment" in Japan under same   100
  see also companies
employment
  careers *see* career paths (working lives)
  of German women   35, 64
  Ice Age Generation's failure to secure regular   112, 113
  job aspects *see* job …
  of married women   29–30, 31, 32, 34
  recruitment *see* job openings; labour recruitment
  regular vs. non-regular in Japan   8, 117–119, 120
  states of   57–58
  types in Japan   102
  see also lifetime employment; precarious employment; public employment; wage labour; work
employment complexity, in Europe   58–59
employment guarantees, for working mothers   240
employment mobility, in West Germany   50–51, 53–54, 55–56, 61
employment stability, in West Germany   47–48, 49, 62–63, 65
employment status
  of Ice Age Generation vs. regular workers   112, 114–117
  of married men in Japan   123
  of Toyota workers   112–117

in West Germany   53, 56–57
of women in Japan   113, 114, 116–117
employment system, in Japan   95
empowerment, of women in Bangladesh   204
encyclopaedias see *Qinding Gujin tushu jicheng*
endurance, of mail runners in British India
    345–346
enforced job change
    of unskilled workers in France   76
    of younger workers in Britain   80
enforced retirement   170, 171, 213
    see also early retirement
England
    apprentices   375
    duration of apprenticeship   376
    life-cycle servants   372
    servants   361–362
enrolment fees, of apprentices   377–378
enterprises see companies
entrepreneurs see Chen Qiyuan
ethnic groups see Beti; Dagara
Europe
    career paths of public employees   154
    division of labour by gender   27
    employment complexity   58–59
    Great Divergence   180
    marriage   180–181
    servants see life-cycle servants (Europe)
    textile production   10, 28, 179–180, 183–186,
        189–193, 197
    unmarried women   182
    women workers   228, 229
    youth as workers   181
    see also Austria; Britain; Bulgaria; Eastern Eu-
        ropean state-socialist countries; France; Ger-
        many; Hungary; Ireland; Western Europe
European Union
    institutional deficiencies for mobile citizens
        308
    Roma migration within   298, 306–307
evaluation see moral assessment
expectations see hope
experience see qualification; skills
extended childcare leave see childcare leave
    (state-socialist Hungary)
extended families
    in Bangladesh   206, 216

childcare by Roma   313
    conflicts   273–274
    external factors   274
    in Ghana   13, 260, 261, 266
    networks   275
    see also Yob family (Ghana)

factories see Chinese state-owned enterprises;
    Peugeot factory; Renault factory; textile facto-
    ries; Toyota Motor Corporation
factory work
    of Bangladeshi garment women workers
        213–214, 221
    and childcare   231
    of European textile women workers   189–
        190
factory workers see industrial workers
failure, of Ice Age Generation to secure regular
    employment   112, 113
families
    children of impoverished (Great Depression)
        285
    nuclearisation in urban households in Bangla-
        desh   216
    research   262–265
    role in socioeconomic transformation   261
    types   261n5
    see also extended families; multi-generational
        families; nuclear families
family conflicts
    of Dagara   270
    in extended families   273–274
    over foster children in Benin   283–284
    girl vs. father in PRC   137
    over girl's education in Ghana   269
    over rural girls in Benin   14, 282, 283, 289–
        293
    as turning points   292–293
    as vital conjunctures   294
family duties, neglect by married men   249–
    250
family gathering, of Yob family   259
family life
    of rural population in Bangladesh   216
    of Toyota workers   108
family life cycle, concept   25–26
farmers see peasants

farming *see* agriculture
Fasang, Anette   57, 58–59
fathers
  conflict with daughter in PRC   137
  as victim of Cultural Revolution   139–140
  see also foster fathers
feelings *see* anger; hopelessness
fees *see* enrolment fees
females *see* girls; women
feudal power, over peasants   365
filatures
  in China   194–195, 196
  see also spinning
fitness, 19th-century debate on   346
flexible work, vs. long-time work   42–43
Fogo *see* São Filipe
forests
  mail runner in   354 fig.
  see also jungle areas
foster children
  in Benin   283–284
  as life-cycle servants   370–371
foster fathers
  individuals *see* Gunu; Kora; Woru
  reasons for hosting rural girl   290–291
  social pressure on   289–290, 293
foster parents, of rural woman in Benin   281
foster son, waiting for marriage   289–290, 293
France
  automobile industry *see* Peugeot factory; Renault factory
  career paths of industrial workers   7–8, 74–78
  de-industrialisation   75
  journeymen   379
  public employment   166
  silk production   184, 185–186, 192–193
  unemployment   75
"freeters" (Japan)   97–98

garment industry *see* textile production
gatherings *see* family gathering
gender aspects
  apprentices   374
  division of labour   26–27
  housework roles in Bangladesh   216–217
  life courses   25–29

male breadwinner model   30, 33–34
men *see* fathers; married men; Muslim men
  ratio of public employees in Austria   161–162
  see also women
generations
  concept   5
  see also cohorts; "lost generation" (Japan); multi-generational families
Germany
  changes of career paths   63–65
  employment of women   35, 64
  see also West Germany; Wildberg
Ghana
  career paths   268, 272–273
  education   267, 269–270, 271
  ethnic groups *see* Dagara
  extended families   13, 260, 261, 266
  family conflicts   273–274
  social mobility   261–262
  socioeconomic transformation   260–261
Giesecke, Johannes   51–52
girls
  conflict with father in PRC   137
  family conflict over education in Ghana   269
  humiliation of father in Cultural Revolution   139–140
  motherhood of Beti   286–287
  spinning in China   188
  see also rural girls; teenage mothers
globalisation   44–45
Gloria (rural girl)   289–292
goals *see* life goals
Gong Yapin (SOE employee)   139–140, 143–144, 148–149
Goode, William   265
government employment *see* public employment
graduates
  in Japan   117–118
  at Toyota   103, 106, 109, 111
grandparents
  childcare by Roma   14–15, 297–298, 302–303, 309
  dependence of Roma   311, 312–313
  individuals *see* Kalina; Maria; Violeta
Great Depression, children of impoverished families   285
Great Divergence   180

Greipl, Luise   156
Grunow, Daniela   49–51
guarantees *see* employment guarantees
guilds   374–375
Gunu (foster father)   290–291
gyes see childcare leave (state-socialist Hungary)

habitation *see* co-habitation
Hammett, Chas E.   346
Hareven, Tamara K.   4, 31, 203–204
health issues
  of Bangladeshi garment women workers   221
  Covid pandemic   45–46
  of Johnny (return migrant)   327
  of mail runners in British India   347
  of palanquin bearers in British India   347–348
  silkworm disease   192
Heisig, Jan Paul   51–52
Hena (garment worker)   220–222
hierarchies *see* power relations; ranks
higher education   20–21
Hillmert, Steffen   53, 54–55
Hindu women, inter-religious marriages with Muslim men   219
Hinterweger, Josef (public employee)   153
hiring *see* labour recruitment
historical events   285
home ownership, of Toyota workers   108
hope, for advancement by education   20
hopelessness
  of Ice Age individual   125–126
  of "NEET" (Japan)   98
households
  of Budhee (mail runner)   349
  male breadwinner model   30, 33–34
  of peasants and artisans   382
  "standard" (Japan)   101
  see also rural households; urban households
housework
  as perceived women's responsibility   11
  roles in Bangladesh   216–217
  by rural girls in urban households of Benin   281n2

humiliation
  of Bangladeshi garment women workers   214
  in Cultural Revolution   139–140
Hungarian Cloth Factory, women workers with infants   230–232
Hungary (state-socialist)
  abortion debate   246, 248
  birth incentives   247
  birth rate   244
  childcare leave debate   249
  demographic debate   245–246
  economic reform   244
  women workers   228–229
  see also childcare leave (state-socialist Hungary)
husbandry *see* agriculture
husbands *see* married men
hyperinflation (post-WWI), impact on public employees in Austria   163

Ice Age Generation (Japan)
  70/40 problem   125
  about   96
  annual income from non-regular employment   119, 120
  co-habitation with parents   121, 123, 125
  failure to secure regular employment   112, 113
  hopeless individual   125–126
  impact on society   127–128
  as new class   125
  non-regular employment   117
  vs. regular workers' employment status   112, 114–117
  unemployment   97
ILO *see* International Labour Organization
incentives *see* birth incentives
income *see* annual income; wages and salaries
indenture *see* apprenticeship
India
  British India *see* mail runners; palanquin bearers
  castes *see* Kahars
  mail runners   353, 354 fig., 355 fig.
  pensions   351
industrial production, restructuring   88–89

industrial work *see* factory work
industrial workers
  age   75
  in Britain   7–8, 73–74, 79–81
  career paths   7–8, 73–87, 91
  chapter overview   71
  company loyalty   76, 80
  early retirement   84–85, 89, 91
  in France   7–8, 74–78
  older   83–84
  in PRC   8–9, 133–134, 136
  qualification   74–75
  research methods   72
  social mobility   75
  unemployment   75, 79
  in West Germany   7–8, 82–87
  younger vs. older   76–77
  see also Bangladeshi garment factory workers
    (female); miners; Nanfang Steel employees;
    Toyota workforce
industrialisation *see* Second Industrial Revolution
infants, women workers with   230–232, 239–
  240
injury, Kahars' dealing with   346–347
institutionalisation, of life course   18–22
insurances *see* social insurance
inter-religious marriages, Muslim man and
  Hindu woman   219
International Labour Organization (ILO)
  on childcare leave   250–251
  collaboration with WTFU   235–236
  key actors of childcare leave   252
  Recommendation 123 (1965)   253
  reports on women workers with infants
    239–240
  suggestions for women workers   232–233,
    235, 236–237, 238–239, 241–243
International Trade Union Conference (1964),
  charter on women workers   237–238
involuntary return migration   322, 325, 328–
  329, 330, 331–332
Ireland, linen production   190–191

Japan
  annual income from regular vs. non-regular
    employment   119, 120
  automobile industry *see* Toyota
  "Bubble economy" collapse   96
  career patterns   98
  chapter overview   99
  economic and social success   95
  employment status of women   113, 114, 116–
    117
  employment system   95
  employment types   102
  job openings   97
  married men   120–121, 123, 124
  married women   101, 124
  pensions   101
  recruitment system   100
  regular vs. non-regular employment   8, 117–
    119, 120
  social insurance   101
  "standard household"   101
  "standard worker"   100–101, 126–127
  unemployment   97
  unmarried individuals   120, 121, 122–123
  women's standard life   114
  see also "lost generation"
Jelidi, Abdallah (worker)   77–78
Jews
  as public employees in Austria   169
  see also anti-Semitism
job changes *see* employer changes; enforced job
  change
job cuts *see* enforced retirement
job openings
  in Japan   97
  see also labour recruitment
job shifts, in West German companies   52
job transfers, from Toyota to affiliated companies   106, 107
jobs *see* employment
Johnny (return migrant)   325–326, 327, 331,
  332–333
Johnson-Hanks, Jennifer   286–287, 288
Johnstone, Elizabeth   236
journeymen   378–379, 380
jungle areas, mail runners in   350, 351–352

Kádár, János   245
Kahars
  about   339
  in East India Company   342

pain and injury, dealing with   346–347
as sharecroppers   341
skills learning   343–344
status   340–343
types of activities by   340
Kalina (grandmother)   312–313
Kalleberg, Arne L.   43
kinship, analysis of   294
Kneußl, Erich (public employee)   154–155, 159, 165, 170
Kohli, Martin   18
Kora (foster father)   289–290, 293

La Farelle, François-Félix de   186
labour *see* work
labour markets
"Brazilianization"   44
West German   61
labour recruitment
Japanese system   100
of life-cycle servants   365–366
of Nanfang Steel employees   139
of Toyota workforce   103–104, 109
of women workers for filatures   195
see also job openings
labourers *see* workers and workforce
land, as fundamental resource in peasant economy   266
Laslett, Peter   361
laws *see* legal aspects
layoffs *see* enforced retirement
learning
of skills by Kahars   343–344
see also apprenticeship; education
Leckie, George   56–57
legal aspects
achievement in public employment   159
Dienstpragmatik   157–160
Doppelverdienerverordnung   166
restrictions in public employment   167–168, 169–173
Lersch, Philipp M.   56–57
life course regime, concept   5
life courses
concept   3–4, 304
de-standardisation   22–25, 99
Elder's themes   286

gender aspects   25–29
institutionalisation   18–22
interdisciplinary approach   36
multidimensional perspectives on   17
navigating through   17
paradigm contributions   203–204
points of transition   304
principles   4
research on   2–3, 88
structure vs. agency   133
thematic clusters of this volume   6, 12, 15
time as component of   4
and work   1, 4, 36
see also career paths (working lives); linked lives; turning points; vital conjunctures
life-cycle servants (pre-industrial Europe)
about   359, 382, 383
in agriculture   368–373
in Austria   371–372
chapter overview   16–17, 360–361
children   368–371, 372
in crafts and trades   374–381
decline   379–380
in England   372
as live-in servants   368
master-servant relations   360
perspectives   359
research on   360, 373–374
as wage workers   360, 365–366
see also apprentices; journeymen
life goals
of Bangladeshi garment women workers   212, 222
of Bangladeshi rural women   205
life stages   287
"lifetime commitment" (Japan), under same employer   100
lifetime employment, of Toyota workers   109
linen production, in Ireland   190–191
linked lives   5, 26, 284–285, 288, 304–305
linked vital conjunctures   288–289
live-in journeymen   378–379
live-in servants   368
livestock farming, life-cycle servants for   371
long-distance runners *see* mail runners
long-time work, vs. flexible work   42–43

"lost generation" (Japan)   96–97, 98
  see also "freeters"; Ice Age Generation; "NEET"
love marriages, vs. arranged marriages in Bangladesh   217–218
low-paid workers, in Britain   80–81
lower rural class   370
loyalty see company loyalty

Ma Ruixing (SOE employee)   137–138, 145–146
mail runners (British India)
  chapter overview   15–16, 339–340, 351
  end of era   347, 352
  endurance   345–346
  health issues   347
  household   349
  individuals see Budhee; Munneram
  in jungle areas   350, 351–352
  pensions   348, 349–350, 351
  tiger attacks on   348–349
  training   344–345
mail runners (21st-century India)   353, 354 fig., 355 fig.
mail runners (Persia)   345
male breadwinner model   30, 33–34
  see also "standard worker" (Japan)
MamMam (foster son)   289–290, 293
Manchester, NH see Amoskeag Manufacturing Company
Mannlicher, Egbert (public employee)   153–154
Maria (grandmother)   311
marital abandonment, of Bangladeshi garment women workers   213, 219
marital break-ups see divorces
marriage
  in China   181–182
  in Europe   180–181
  of public employees in Austria   159
  see also arranged marriages; inter-religious marriages; love marriages
married men
  of Hena (garment worker)   221–222
  housework roles in Bangladesh   216–217
  in Japan   120–121, 123, 124
  marital abandonment by   213
  neglect of family duties   249–250
married public employees, in Austria   161–162

married women
  employment   29–30, 31, 32, 34
  in Japan   101, 124
  of Toyota workers   108
  work   27–28
married workers, at Toyota   111
Marx, Karl   364–365
Massachusetts
  Cape Verdean migration to   330
  see also Boston
master-servant relations, in Britain   360
maternity see motherhood
Mayer, Karl Ulrich   49–51, 99
men see fathers; married men; Muslim men
MFA (Multi-Fiber Arrangement)   210
middle class
  and extended families in Ghana   261
  young Beti women   286–287
migrant workers
  at Renault factory   77–78
  Turkish in West Germany   84, 86
  unskilled and semi-skilled in Western Europe   90
migration
  Cape Verde to Boston   324–325, 326, 327–328, 329
  Cape Verde to Massachusetts   330
  "children in mobility"   301–302
  deportees   325, 330–331
  research on   322
  reunification of children   330–331
  see also diaspora communities; return migration; Roma migration
miners, in Britain   79–80
mobile citizens, institutional deficiencies in EU for   308
mobility
  "children in"   301–302
  vs. education   298–299, 313
  tramping journeymen   378
  see also employment mobility; migration; social mobility
modernisation   61, 262–263
moonlighting, of Nanfang Steel employee   141
moral assessment, of return migration   332–333
Morse, David A.   235

motherhood 286–288
see also childcare
mothers
employment guarantees for working 240
see also teenage mothers
Multi-Fiber Arrangement (MFA) 210
multi-generational families
independent members 312
vs. nuclear families 262
research methods 304
of Roma migrants 299, 301, 305, 311, 314
Munneram, Ragow (mail runner) 348
Mura, Kalipada (mail runners) 353, 354 fig.
Muslim men, inter-religious marriages with
Hindu women 219
mutual support
of return migrant and caregiver 332–333
in Yob family 273

Nanfang Steel employees
arrival at factory 135–136, 137–138, 139, 140
dedication 142–143
early retirement 145
individuals *see* Du Zhang; Gong Yapin; Ma
Ruixing; Zhang Guirong
moonlighting 141
promotion 142, 143–144
protest of retired 148–149
recruitment 139
reform era impact on 134
summary of life stories 8–9, 150–151
turning points 134–135, 139, 140, 141, 142,
143–144
Nanfang Steel factory
about 134
refusal of industrial workers to join 136
school 143, 146
as TFC project 135
National Federation of Trade Unions (SZOT)
230, 248
Nawiasky, Hans 158
Nazi-annexed Austria 168–173
"NEET" (hopeless Japanese) 98
NEM (New Economic Mechanism) 244
neoliberal period, in PRC 144–145, 146, 149–
150
networks, in extended families 275

New Economic Mechanism (NEM) 244
New Hampshire *see* Amoskeag Manufacturing
Company
Nitsche, Natalie 49–51
non-standard work 43–44
non-work activities, and work 4–5
Notermans, Catrien 287–288
novels *see* Tale of Hansuli Turn
NS (Chinese SOE) *see* Nanfang Steel factory
nuclear families
family life cycle 25–26
male breadwinner model 30, 33–34
vs. multi-generational families 262
"standard household" (Japan) 101
nuclearisation, of family in urban households in
Bangladesh 216

occupational aspects *see* employment; work
Ogilvie, Sheilagh 375–376
older migrants, return migration 326, 327
older workers
age discrimination 32–33
company loyalty in Britain 80
early retirement 89
in West Germany 83–84
vs. younger Bangladeshi women workers
220
vs. younger workers in France 76–77
see also Bangladeshi garment factory workers
(female)
on-the-job training, at Toyota 104
organisations *see* International Labour Organization; unions
outwork economy 380
ownership *see* home ownership

pain, Kahars' dealing with 346–347
palanquin bearers (British India)
chapter overview 15–16, 339–340, 351
end of era 347, 352
health issues 347–348
songs 344
training 343–344
see also Kahars
pandemics *see* Covid pandemic

parents
  co-habitation of Ice Age Generation with
    121, 123, 125
  see also foster parents; grandparents
part-time work   35, 65
payment *see* annual income; wages and salaries
peasant economy, fundamental resources   266
peasants (pre-industrial Europe)
  feudal power over   365
  households   382
  live-in servants for   368
  types   366
pensioners *see* retired workers
pensions
  in India   351
  in Japan   101
  for mail runners in British India   348, 349–
    350, 351
  of Toyota workers   110
People's Republic of China (PRC)
  Cultural Revolution   138–139, 140
  industrial workers   8–9, 133–134, 136
  neoliberal period   144–145, 146, 149–150
  reform era   134, 141, 144
  shifting state policies   134, 144–145
  Third Front Construction era   134, 135, 139
  unpredictable state policies   136
  see also Chinese state-owned enterprises
Persia, mail runners   345
personal training, at Toyota   104
petitions, for pensions of mail runners in British
  India   348
petty commodity production   364–365, 366–
  367, 382
Peugeot factory, younger vs. older workers   77
physical abilities, of Kahars   343
physical exercise, 19th-century debate on   346
political restrictions, in public employment in
  Austria   167–168, 169–170
population *see* rural population
post-war "boom" period, career paths of industrial workers   73–74
postal runners *see* mail runners
poverty
  of children during Great Depression   285
  of Roma in Bulgaria   306
power *see* feudal power

power relations, master-servant in Britain   360
PRC *see* People's Republic of China
precarious employment
  of Bangladeshi garment women workers
    210
  in West Germany   59–60
  see also "freeters" (Japan); low-paid workers;
    unpaid work
predatory animals *see* tiger attacks
pressure *see* social pressure; time pressure
prestige *see* employment status
production *see* industrial production; simple
  commodity production; subsistence production; textile production
professions, new for Dagara   267
promotion
  of Nanfang Steel employees   142, 143–144
  at Toyota   105–106, 107
property *see* home ownership
protest, of retired Nanfang Steel workers
  148–149
public employment (Austria)
  achievement, law based on   159
  career paths   153–154, 157–158, 159–160, 165
  chapter overview   9–10, 155–156, 173–174
  clerical personnel   160
  Dienstpragmatik   157–160
  Doppelverdienerverordnung   166
  duration   159–160
  history   156–157
  impact of economic crises on   163, 166–167
  individuals *see* Hinterweger; Kneußl; Mannlich-
    er
  Jews   169
  male breadwinner model   33
  marriage   159
  railway workers   164–165
  ranks   158–159
  reduction   163–164, 166
  restrictions   167–168, 169–173
  salaries   158
  socio-demographics   160–163
  women   156, 165
public employment (Europe)   154
public employment (France)   166

Qinding Gujin tushu jicheng (encyclopaedia)
187
qualification
of industrial workers in France   74–75
see also graduates; skills

railway workers, in Austria   164–165
ranks, of public employees in Austria   158–159
recruitment *see* labour recruitment
Red Guards   138
reforms *see* economic reforms
refusal, of industrial workers to join Nanfang
Steel factory   136
relationships *see* power relations; sibling relationships
religious affiliation
of Bangladeshi garment women workers
208
see also catechist; Hindu women; Jews; Muslim
men
remigration *see* return migration
removal, of public employees in Nazi-annexed
Austria   168, 170, 172
Renault factory, migrant worker at   77–78
research
on Bangladeshi garment industry   209
on families   262–265
on life courses   2–3, 88
on life-cycle servants   360, 373–374
on migration   322
on servants   361–363, 365n11
on women factory workers   209
research methods (applied to)
Bangladeshi garment factory workers   207–
208
industrial workers   72, 82–83
multi-generational families   304
return migration to Cape Verde islands
320–321
Roma migration   299–300
resentment *see* anger
resistance *see* protest; refusal
restrictions, in public employment in Austria
167–168, 169–173
retired workers, protest at Nanfang Steel factory
148–149

retirement
of Bangladeshi garment women workers
222
enforced   170, 171, 213
as financially protected life phase   21
transition from work into   21–22
working after   22
see also early retirement; pensions
return migration (general)   320
return migration (to Bulgaria), of Roma migrants' children   310
return migration (to Cape Verde islands)
chapter overview   15, 319, 320
of children   328–329, 331
individuals *see* Danilsa; Johnny; Teresa; Valdim
involuntary   322, 325, 328–329, 330, 331–332
moral assessment   332–333
of older migrants   326, 327
as option   334
research methods   320–321
self-initiated   323, 326, 331, 332
temporary   322
reunification, of children   330–331
Ringstedt, Mette Line   287–288
Roma
childcare by extended families   313
childcare by grandparents   14–15, 297–298,
302–303, 309
dependence of grandparents   311, 312–313
individuals *see* Kalina; Maria; Violeta
poverty in Bulgaria   306
ratio in Bulgaria   306n4
Roma migration
chapter overview   14–15, 300, 314
education of children   297–298, 307–308,
310
in EU   298, 306–307
multi-generational families   299, 301, 305,
311, 314
rates   312
research methods   299–300
return migration of children to Bulgaria   310
Rosita (caregiver)   327, 332–333
runners *see* mail runners
rural areas, "educated urban youth going to the
countryside" (movement)   138

rural girls
  family conflicts over Beninese   14, 282, 283,
    289–293
  as foster children in Benin   284
  individuals *see* Gloria; Salimatou
  in urban households of Benin   13–14, 281n2,
    291
rural households, family conflicts over rural girls
  in Benin   14, 282, 283, 289–293
rural population
  family life in Bangladesh   216
  lower class   370
  see also agricultural societies; Dagara; peas-
    ants
rural ties, of Bangladeshi garment women workers   206
rural women
  in Bangladesh   204–205
  foster parents of Beninese   281
Russia *see* Soviet Union

salaries *see* wages and salaries
Salimatou (rural girl)   281, 283
Salzburg (Archbishopric), child servants   369
São Filipe   323
Sargeant, Terry (miner)   79–80
Sassen, Saskia   322–323
schools
  incompatibility for mobile citizens   308
  of Nanfang Steel factory   143, 146
  see also education
Schulz, Wiebke   56–57
Scott, Joan W.   30–31
Second Industrial Revolution   30
Segalen, Martine   263
self-initiated return migration   323, 326, 331,
  332
semi-autonomy, of Bangladeshi garment women
  workers   215
semi-skilled workers, migrants in Western Europe   90
Sennett, Richard   42–43
servants
  in England   361–362
  master-servant relations in Britain   360
  research on   361–363, 365n11
  terminological distinction   361, 362–364

  see also life-cycle servants
servitude
  of Kahars   340–341
  see also domestic servitude
Shanghai
  filatures   196
  textile factories   194
sharecroppers, Kahars as   341
Shikha (garment worker)   219
Shumen
  about   305–306
  childcare by Roma grandmother   297–298
sibling relationships   271–272
Sichuan *see* Nanfang Steel factory
silk production
  in China   188–189, 194–195
  in France   184, 185–186, 192–193
silkworm disease   192
simple commodity production   364–365, 366–
  367, 382
skilled workers
  career paths in West Germany   85–86
  company loyalty of French   76
  see also semi-skilled workers
skills
  Kahars' learning   343–344
  mail runners and palanquin bearers' declining
    347
  see also endurance
social activities, at Toyota   105
social advancement, education as hope for   20
social benefits *see* childcare leave; pensions
social classes
  Ice Age Generation as new   125
  see also lower rural class; middle class
social insurance, in Japan   101
social mobility
  in Benin   282–283
  in Ghana   261–262
  of industrial workers in France   75
social pressure, on foster father   289–290, 293
social success, in Japan   95
social transformation, in Western Europe   71–
  72
socialist countries *see* Hungary (state-socialist);
  People's Republic of China; Soviet Union

societal change, and young women in Benin 282

society

impact of Ice Age Generation on 127–128

see also agricultural societies

socio-demographics, public employees in Austria 160–163

Socio-Economic Panel (SOEP) 82

socioeconomic transformation

of agricultural societies 275–276

in Ghana 260–261

SOEP (Socio-Economic Panel) 82

SOEs *see* Chinese state-owned enterprises

Sonenscher, Michael 379

songs, of palanquin bearers 344

sons *see* foster son

Soviet Union, unions' responsibility for women workers 239

spinning

in China 28, 188

in Europe 28, 185–186

see also filatures

spouses *see* married men; married women

stability *see* employment stability

"standard household" (Japan) 101

"standard worker" (Japan) 100–101, 126–127

Stanziani, Alessandro 360

state-owned enterprises *see* Chinese state-owned enterprises

state-socialist countries *see* Eastern European state-socialist countries; People's Republic of China; Soviet Union

status

of Beninese rural girl in urban household 291

see also employment status

Stawarz, Nico 53, 54

steel factories *see* Nanfang Steel factory

steel workers *see* Nanfang Steel employees

structure, vs. agency in life courses 133

subsistence production, and capitalism 264–265

success *see* economic success; promotion; social success

sudden death, of mail runners in British India 349

support *see* mutual support

SZOT *see* National Federation of Trade Unions

Tale of Hansuli Turn (novel) 339

Tanzania, childcare of teenage mothers 287

Tavernier, Jean-Baptiste 345

teenage mothers, childcare in Tanzania 287

temporary return migration 322

temporary workers, recruitment at Toyota 103

Teodorescu, Elena 235

Teresa (return migrant) 324–325, 332

textile factories

in Shanghai 194

women workers in 189–190, 194

see also Amoskeag Manufacturing Company; Hungarian Cloth Factory

textile production

in China 10, 28, 179–180, 186–189, 193–197

in Europe 10, 28, 179–180, 183–186, 189–193, 197

MFA-regulated 210

see also Bangladeshi garment industry; cotton production; linen production; silk production; spinning; weaving

Third Front Construction (TFC) era 134, 135, 139

tiger attacks, on mail runners 348–349

Tilly, Louise A. 30–31

Timár, János 233–234, 250

time

as component of life courses 4

see also chronology

time pressure, of Bangladeshi garment women workers 214

"timing of lives" 285

Toyota Motor Corporation

corporate culture 104–105, 107

job transfers to affiliated companies 106, 107

working conditions 105

Toyota workforce

annual income 106, 107

average life 108

career paths 106, 110–111

company loyalty 119, 120

company-sponsored activities 107

dependence on company 107

employment status   112–117
family life   108
home ownership   108
in-house associations for   104
lifetime employment   109
pensions   110
promotion   105–106, 107
recruitment   103–104, 109
social activities   105
training   104
trade unions *see* unions
trades *see* crafts and trades
training
   of apprentices   377
   of mail runners   344–345
   of palanquin bearers   343–344
   at Toyota   104
tramping journeymen   378
transformation *see* changes
Turgonyi, Júlia   249–250
Turkish migrant workers, in West Germany
   84, 86
turning points
   family conflicts as   292–293
   of Nanfang Steel employees   134–135, 139,
   140, 141, 142, 143–144
   see also vital conjunctures

unemployment
   of industrial workers in Western Europe   75,
   79
   in Japan   97
   of youth in Britain   79
   see also "NEET" (Japan)
unions
   responsibility for women workers in Soviet
      Union   239
   see also International Trade Union Conference;
      National Federation of Trade Unions; World
      Federation of Trade Unions
United Kingdom *see* Britain
United States
   children of impoverished families during Great
      Depression   285
   reunification of children   330–331
   textile factories *see* Amoskeag Manufacturing
      Company

   see also Massachusetts
unmarried individuals, in Japan   120, 121, 122–
   123
unmarried public employees, in Austria   161–
   162
unmarried women
   in Europe vs. China   182
   in textile factories   189–190
unpaid work
   care work vs. paid work   303–304
   by rural girls in urban households of Benin
      281n2
unskilled workers
   in France   76
   migrants in Western Europe   90
   in West Germany   86–87
urban economies, division of labour   374
urban households
   family conflicts over rural girls in Benin   14,
      282, 283, 289–293
   as foster parents of rural woman in Benin
      281
   nuclearisation of family in Bangladesh   216
   rural girls in Beninese   13–14, 281n2, 291
USA *see* United States
USSR *see* Soviet Union

Valdim (deported migrant)   325, 330–331
Van Winkle, Zachary   57, 58–59
victim, of Cultural Revolution   139–140
village community, work outside of   266–267
Violeta (grandmother)   297–298, 305
vital conjunctures
   about   288
   family conflicts as   294
   see also turning points

wage labour, types   383
wage workers
   in agriculture   367
   life-cycle servants as   360, 365–366
   see also industrial workers
wages and salaries
   of apprentices   377
   of Bangladeshi garment women workers
      214, 220
   of public employees in Austria   158

Watanabe Hirofumi (Ice Age hopeless individual) 125–126
watery tracts, mail runner in   355 fig.
weaving
  in China   188
  in Europe   185
  in France   192–193
  in Ireland   191
West Germany
  career paths   6–8, 46–58, 60–65, 82–88
  de-industrialisation   81–82
  industrial workers   7–8, 82–87
  labour market and modernisation   61
  precarious work   59–60
West vs. East see East-West antagonism
Western Europe
  childcare leave   251–252
  de-industrialisation   71, 89
  demand for workers   227–228
  social transformation   71–72
  women workers   90–91
  see also Austria; Britain; France; Germany
Western workers, differences to Bangladeshi garment factory workers   206
WFTU see World Federation of Trade Unions
widows see Buchnee
Wildberg, spinning   186
wives see married women
women
  abortion debate in state-socialist Hungary 246, 248
  as apprentices   374
  as domestic servants   182
  employment in Germany   35
  employment mobility in West Germany   51, 54
  employment status in Japan   113, 114, 116–117
  empowerment in Bangladesh   204
  part-time work   35
  perceived domestic responsibilities   11
  as public employees in Austria   156, 165
  standard life in Japan   114
  see also girls; Hindu women; married women; mothers; rural women; unmarried women; young women

women workers
  annual income from regular vs. non-regular employment in Japan   120
  in Bangladesh   208–209
  career paths in West Germany   87–88
  in Eastern Europe   226
  Eastern vs. Western views on rights of   240–241
  in Europe   228, 229
  in filatures in China   196
  ILO reports on   239–240
  ILO suggestions for   232–233, 235, 236–237, 238–239, 241–243
  with infants   230–232, 239–240
  International Trade Union Conference charter 237–238
  job shifts and employer changes in West Germany   52
  non-regular employment in Japan   118
  recruitment at Toyota   103–104
  recruitment for filatures   195
  research on   209
  spinning   186
  in state-socialist Hungary   228–229
  in textile factories   189–190, 194
  in textile production   10
  unions' responsibility in Soviet Union   239
  weaving   191
  in Western Europe   90–91
  see also Bangladeshi garment factory workers (female); childcare leave
woods see forests
work
  of apprentices   376–377
  as catechist   268
  and changes   2
  of child servants   369
  children's transition into   19
  division see division of labour
  after enforced retirement   213
  flexible vs. long-time   42–43
  jobs see employment
  and life courses   1, 4, 36
  of married women   27–28
  non-standard   43–44
  and non-work activities   4–5
  outside of village community   266–267

recruitment *see* labour recruitment
after retirement   22
and school-based education   19–20
transition from education into   20
transition into retirement   21–22
see also care work; child labour; factory work;
  housework; part-time work; unpaid work;
  wage labour
work lives *see* career paths (working lives)
workers and workforce
  colonial *see* mail runners; palanquin bearers
  demand in Europe   227–228
  pre-industrial Europe *see* artisans; life-cycle
  servants; peasants
  regular vs. Ice Age Generation's employment
  status   112, 114–117
  "standard" (Japan)   100–101, 126–127
  Western vs. Bangladeshi   206
  youth in Europe vs. China   181–182
  see also clerical personnel; construction workers; industrial workers; low-paid workers;
  married workers; migrant workers; older
  workers; railway workers; retired workers;
  skilled workers; temporary workers; unskilled
  workers; wage workers; women workers;
  younger workers
working conditions
  of Bangladeshi garment women workers
  210–211, 213–214
  at Toyota   105
working lives *see* career paths (working lives)
World Federation of Trade Unions (WFTU), collaboration with ILO   235–236
Woru (foster father)   281, 282
Württemberg *see* Wildberg

yearly income *see* annual income

Yob family (Ghana)
  about   259
  chapter overview   263
  communication   274–275
  conflict over girl's education   269
  decision making   272–273
  fundamental resources   266
  individuals *see* Anselmy; Barth; Catherine
  mutual support   273
  networks   275
  new opportunities   267–269
  sibling relationships   271–272
  status of members   273
  work outside of village community   266–267
young women
  in filatures in China   195
  foster parents of Beninese   281
  inter-religious marriage in Bangladesh   219
  middle-class Beti   286–287
  and societal change in Benin   282
  in textile factories   190
  see also girls
younger workers
  career paths in West Germany   85–86
  enforced job change in Britain   80
  vs. older Bangladeshi women workers   220
  vs. older workers in France   76–77
youth
  "educated urban youth going to the countryside" (movement)   138
  as life-cycle servants   382
  unemployment in Britain   79
  as workers in Europe vs. China   181–182
  see also "lost generation" (Japan)

Zhang Guirong (SOE employee)   136, 141–142,
  147–148